Mastering the Art and Craft

2nd edition

baking
& pastry

2nd edition

Mastering the Art and Craft

baking
& pastry

THE CULINARY INSTITUTE OF AMERICA®

WILEY

JOHN WILEY & SONS, INC.

Photography © 2009 by Ben Fink
Cover marble background photo © 2009 by Spencer Jones/Getty Images, Inc.

THE CULINARY INSTITUTE OF AMERICA

PRESIDENT	Dr. Tim Ryan '77
VICE-PRESIDENT, CONTINUING EDUCATION	Mark Erickson '77
DIRECTOR OF INTELLECTUAL PROPERTY	Nathalie Fischer
EDITORIAL PROJECT MANAGER	Lisa Lahey '00
RECIPE TESTING DATABASE MANAGER	Margaret Wheeler '00

Published by John Wiley & Sons, Inc., Hoboken, New Jersey
Published simultaneously in Canada

For general information on our other products and services or for technical support, please contact our Customer Care Department within the United States at (800) 762-2974, outside the United States at (317) 572-3993 or fax (317) 572-4002.

Wiley also publishes its books in a variety of electronic formats. Some content that appears in print may not be available in electronic books. For more information about Wiley products, visit our web site at www.wiley.com.

Design by Vertigo Design NYC

LIBRARY OF CONGRESS CATALOGING-IN-PUBLICATION DATA

Baking and pastry : mastering the art and craft / the Culinary Institute of America. — 2nd ed.
   p. cm.
 Includes index.
 ISBN 978-0-470-05591-5 (cloth : alk. paper)
 1. Baking. 2. Pastry. 3. Desserts. I. Culinary Institute of America.
 TX763.B3234 2009
 641.8'15—dc22

           2008009576

Printed in the United States of America

10 9 8 7 6 5 4 3

acknowledgments

The Culinary Institute of America would like to thank the following people for their support and dedication to excellence—without their guidance and vision the completion of this edition would not have been possible: Kate Cavotti, Alain Dubernard, Stephen Eglinski, Peter Greweling, Marc Haymon, George Higgins, Eric Kastel, Todd Knaster, Alison McLoughlin, Francisco Migoya, Dieter Schorner, Juergen Temme, Thomas Vaccaro, Stéphane Weber, Hans Welker.

Our gratitude must also be extended to Ben Fink, for without his photographs the lessons and the craft would not be so clearly and beautifully presented; to our partners at John Wiley & Sons, Inc., for their tireless attention to detail; and to Alison Lew at Vertigo Design NYC for her creativity and insight that assembled a beautiful book.

contents

Preface

The audience for which *Baking and Pastry: Mastering the Art and Craft* is written includes pastry professionals and serious home bakers who want to continue their education or refer to a complete guide of baking and pastry techniques, formulas, and presentations. In addition, our students at The Culinary Institute of America will use this book as an important part of their education.

In developing the structure of this book we reflected on the structure of the education students receive at The Culinary Institute of America and used the same philosophy. The first six chapters set the stage for understanding the baking and pastry profession and using the specialized equipment and products that are common in the bakeshop. In these chapters we explain "baking science," or how different ingredients act and react to help the reader gain a deeper understanding of baking formulas specifically and in general. We introduce the fundamental methods of baking and basic calculations that are essential for any baker.

In Chapter 7 we explore the basic methods and principles for making yeast-raised breads and rolls. And in Chapter 8 we further explore yeasted breads made by more complex methods of fermentation.

In Chapters 9 through 14 the reader is exposed to the building blocks of baking, a wide range of formulas and production techniques that make up the foundation for a top-quality bakeshop. Pastry doughs and batters, quick breads and cakes, cookies, creams and custards, and glazes and sauces are the basis for many baking and pastry presentations.

Chapters 15 through 23 turn the reader's attention to assembling and finishing techniques, employing the use of the formulas set forth in the previous chapters. These chapters cover both sweet and savory baked goods, from the simple (pies and breakfast Danish) to the complex (plated desserts and wedding cakes).

Filled and assembled cakes are the focus of Chapter 16. Here, proper assembly techniques are stressed along with combining different flavors and textures. We separate the chapter into two parts, making a distinction between classic and contemporary cakes.

The later chapters draw upon lessons and formulas learned or presented earlier in the book to make more complex presentations. Formulas for making breakfast pastries (viennoiserie), individual pastries, savory baking, and plated desserts are presented in Chapters 17, 18, 19, and 20, respectively. The addition of savory baking to this edition offers the pastry chef, baker, and café owner techniques and formulas that will help develop an hors d'oeuvre menu or simply complement an already existing menu for a café or smaller operation.

The principles and techniques used for creating chocolates and confections can be complex and challenging. The fundamentals of this craft are presented in Chapter 21, which then lead readers to formulas of the kind to create dramatic confections of their own.

Chapter 22 addresses some of the principles, techniques, and materials used in décor. Piping, lettering, marzipan, gum paste, sugar, and chocolate work are just some of the techniques and materials presented. The chapter also focuses on hand tools, equipment, and proper storage and handling of the materials.

Chapter 23, the final chapter, concentrates on wedding and special-occasion cakes. This chapter is a synthesis of many of the techniques and applications presented in earlier chapters. However, we also introduce some new decorating techniques and specialized equipment and materials.

Working on this book has led us to an even richer appreciation not only for the process, but also for the art and craft of baking and pastry. We are confident the reader will not only enjoy this book, but also gain a renewed respect for the field. This book will prove to be the perfect bakeshop companion.

part one

The professional baker and pastry chef

The dessert station on a busy night in a full-service restaurant

chapter one

Career opportunities for baking and pastry professionals

*b*aking originated thousands of years ago and it is integral to human history and still is the source of the most basic foodstuffs. Bread's importance can be seen in the way governments regulated its production, quality, weight, and price. Bakers established the first trade guilds in Rome in 150 b.c.e.

The pastry chef, as the position exists today, evolved through the brigade system. Instituted by Escoffier, it served to streamline work with workstation and specific responsibilities. Pastries were made by the pâtissier (pastry chef). Later, this position separated from the brigade and developed its own organization largely attributed to Marie-Antoine Carême (1784–1833), a Parisian chef and pastry chef whose books on the pastry arts are influential to this day.

Career opportunities for baking and pastry professionals

Bakers and pastry chefs can pursue many options. You might own your own company or work for someone else. It can be a commissary setting, restaurant, or shop specializing in wedding cakes or handcrafted breads. To get a foundation you may work in a cross section of bakeries and kitchens—then specialize in a discipline.

Bakers often follow one of two paths, working in large commercial bakeries that do volume production or smaller shops that produce less volume but higher-quality goods.

Wholesale bakeshops focus on large-scale production, selling finished or unbaked and items, and batters, to supermarkets, cafés, gourmet shops, restaurants, caterers, cafeterias, and the like. Individually owned shops provide a range of services, from a full-service bakeshop to one that specializes in chocolates and confections or wedding cakes. Large hotels rely upon the skills of the pastry chef and baker who are often responsible for breakfast pastries, elaborate pastry displays, wedding cakes, and the like, including the many food outlets and banquet rooms.

The restaurant pastry chef needs a range of baking and pastry skills to create a variety of items—ice cream and cakes, chocolates to serve as *mignardises* and petits fours, even pizza dough. Private clubs and executive dining rooms as well as schools, hospitals, and colleges rely upon executive pastry chefs and master bakers to handle high-volume, high-quality fare. Food producers operate research and development kitchens to test products and formulas and fine-tune them. These large businesses also offer benefits and career advancement within the corporation.

Pastry chefs and bakers often hire caterers, who meet the desires of a special client for a particular event, whether a trade convention, wedding, birthday party, cocktail reception, or gallery opening. Grocery stores hire baking and pastry professionals to develop carryout desserts and signature breads, as well as assisting with research, focus groups, packaging, pricing, and marketing strategies. Consultants in the baking and pastry arts work with clients to develop menus, staffing strategies, marketing plans, packaging, and the like.

Working in the "front of the house" as a salesperson is also an important function. Such professionals understand the needs of today's bakeries and pastry shops, promoting new ways to use familiar products and equipment. Teachers in the baking and pastry arts are vital to degree- and certificate-granting programs. Baking and pastry professionals who teach bring a special awareness of how things work in the real world. Food writers and critics have come with education and experience in the baking and pastry arts. This allows them to write truly informed reviews, articles, columns, books, and content for multimedia and online presentations.

Formal education

All employers look for experience and education—even entry-level positions can require a degree. The increasing emphasis on a formal education has brought about more programs dedicated exclusively to baking and pastry. Employers rely on the craft taught by these schools to establish a common ground of ability.

Both employers and schools recognize that formal education on its own is not enough to ensure excellence. Baking and pastry are practical arts. To master them, you need to work and make job choices that invest in your future.

A special pulled sugar centerpiece

Continuing education

Just as formal education has become important in launching a career, certification and continuing education keep advancing you as a baking arts professional. Because the industry is constantly evolving, continuing education, attending workshops, seminars, and trade shows hone skills while keeping up with new methods, ingredients, techniques, products, and business skills.

Throughout your career, you should evaluate your achievements and goals; take the appropriate steps to keep on top of the latest information geared to both culinary professionals and the world at large. Enter contests and competitions. Educate yourself, learn to use the important tools of your business from budgets to inventory control systems.

Certification

The Retailer's Bakery Association (RBA) and the American Culinary Federation (ACF) have established standards for certifying bakers and pastry chefs. The RBA's certification levels begin with Certified Journey Baker (CJB). The RBA's next level includes three designations: Certified Baker (CB), Certified Decorator (CD), and Certified Bread Baker (CBB). Each level requires that your work history meet certain criteria for you to be eligible to take the exams, which have a written and practical component.

The ACF certifies pastry culinarians, giving Working Pastry Chef (WPC), entry-level certification based on a written test. Individuals working at this level are typically responsible for a shift or a section within a food-service operation. The next level is Executive Pastry Chef (CEPC), which is for department heads who report to a corporate executive or management team. Researchers and others in specialized areas also take the CEPC test. Certified Master Baker (CMB) is the highest certification given by the RBA. The ACF grants the Certified Master Pastry Chef (CMPC) certification, a ten-day exam that combines a written and practical test of classical and contemporary applications. Finally, the RBA and the ACF have specific minimum criteria that must be met before you can apply for certification.

Networking

Developing a professional network can be formal or informal. You begin simply by introducing yourself to others in your field. Then its having business cards at trade shows and other professional encounters. Join culinary arts organizations. Many maintain Web sites—and many culinary artists maintain blogs—that enable you to communicate with other professionals, get ideas, express ideas, and make new contacts. When you first make a good contact, follow up with an e-mail, phone call, or a note. The communication that you develop with your peers will keep your own work fresh and contemporary, and an established network will also make it much easier for you to find your next job—or your next employee.

The business of baking and pastry

As your career evolves, you will move into those positions where your skills as an executive, administrator, and manager are in demand. This does not mean that your ability to make breads and pastries are less important. Plating, presentation, and pricing are daily concerns for any executive pastry chef or baker—and you may still be creating new menu items and products while keeping costs under control and improving profits. Managing a bakery or pastry shop requires the ability to handle four areas effectively: physical assets, information, people (human resources), and time. The greater your management skills in these areas, the greater your potential for success. Many management systems today emphasize the use of "excellence" as a yardstick. Every area of your operation can be used to improve the quality of service you provide to your customers.

Managing physical assets

Physical assets are the equipment and supplies needed to do business: everything from industrial-size mixers to flour to cash registers. In short, anything that affects your ability to do business well. These require control systems that will keep your organization operating at maximum efficiency.

For any baking and pastry operation, the material costs—whatever you use to create, present, sell, and serve your goods—is the biggest expense. For this reason, being a baking and pastry professional entails being your own purchasing agent—or knowing how to work with one—to maintain inventories to produce and market your products and services.

Managing information

Given the sheer volume of information generated each day, the ability to tap into the information resources you need has never been more important. You must not only keep yourself informed of the latest trends, but also develop the ability to look beyond what is current to predict future trends. This will help to keep your business thriving. Restaurants, menus, dining room design, and more change dramatically with societal trends, on-the-go lifestyles, and the interest in world cuisines. Current tastes affect what people eat and where and how they want to eat it. The Internet is a powerful influence as well.

Managing human resources

Every shop relies on the work and dedication of people, whether they are the executive pastry chef, bakers, or wait staff to name a few. No matter how large or small your staff may be, a team effort is one of the major factors in determining whether you succeed. One of the hall-marks of the true professional is being a team member—and this team can simply be you, your clients, and suppliers. Being part of a team requires as much practice and concentration as any baking or pastry technique. The best teams are made of talented individuals who bring not only technical skills to the mix, but passion for excellence. You can immediately recognize a strong team approach in a successful bakeshop or pastry kitchen. Everyone knows what work must be done beyond just their *job description*.

The management of human resources entails legal responsibilities. Everyone has the right to work in an environment that is free from physical hazards and with properly main-tained equipment. Liability insurance must be kept up to date and adequate. Taxes on the earnings have to be paid to federal, state, and local agencies. Employment packages have to be managed, including life insurance, medical insurance, assistance with dependent care, and even adult literacy training and substance abuse programs. In an increasingly tight labor market, benefits can make a difference in the caliber of employees you work with or manage.

Managing time

The days are not long enough. Learning new skills so that you can make the best possible use of time should be an ongoing part of your career. If you look at your operation carefully, you will discover how time is wasted. In most, the top five time wasters are lack of clear priorities for tasks, poor staff training, poor communication, poor organization, and inadequate or non-existent tools for accomplishing tasks. Invest time in these strategies:

REVIEW DAILY OPERATIONS. Until you are clear about what needs to be done and in what order, you cannot begin the process of saving time. Consider the way you, your coworkers, and your staff spend the day. Does everyone have a basic understanding of which tasks are most important? Do they know when to begin a particular task in order to finish it on time? It can be an eye-opening experience to take a hard look at where everyone's workday goes.

TRAIN OTHERS. If you expect someone to do a job properly, take enough time to explain the task carefully. Walk yourself and your staff through the jobs that must be done, and be sure that everyone understands how to do the work, where to find needed items, how far individual responsibility extends, and what to do in case a question—or emergency—comes up. Give your staff the yardsticks they need to evaluate their time and jobs, otherwise you may find yourself squandering precious hours picking up the slack.

LEARN TO COMMUNICATE CLEARLY. Whether you are training a new employee, introduc-ing a new menu item, or ordering a piece of equipment, clear communication is essential. Be specific and be brief without leaving out necessary information.

CREATE AN ORDERLY WORK ENVIRONMENT. If you have to dig through five shelves to find the lid to a storage container for buttercream, you are not using your time wisely. Organize work areas carefully, so that tools, ingredients, and equipment are readily available. Sched-ule—and write out—like activities so they are performed at the same time and in the same way by different people.

PURCHASE, REPLACE, AND MAINTAIN ALL TOOLS AS NECESSARY. A well-equipped kitchen has all the tools necessary to prepare every item on the menu. If you are missing something as basic as a sieve, your *crème anglaise* will not be perfectly smooth. Learn to operate equipment safely and teach others to do the same.

The profession

A professional makes a living from the practice of a craft. Rather than viewing work as simply a means to an end, true professionals have a passion for their craft and a drive for excellence. Some professionals may tell you that they baked for their families or worked in a bakeshop when they were young. Others come to the baking and pastry field after establishing themselves in other areas in the food-service industry. Still others make a switch to the baking and pastry profession as a second or third career.

All professionals must learn the foundations of the profession—handling ingredients and equipment, and standard or basic formulas. At the next level, they apply those foundations, adapting and modifying formulas or finding ways to improve quality and efficiency in their own work. At the highest level, they draw on all they know and use their knowledge, skills, and creativity to produce something—as specific as a new pastry or as intangible as a successful career—that was not there before.

Every member of a profession is responsible for its image. Those who have made the greatest impression know that the cardinal virtues of the baking and pastry profession are an open and inquiring mind, an appreciation of and dedication to quality, and a sense of responsibility—cultivated throughout a career.

COMMITMENT TO SERVICE. The food-service industry is predicated on service, and professionals must never lose sight of that. Good service includes (but is not limited to) providing quality items that are properly and safely prepared, appropriately flavored, and attractively presented—in short, what makes the customer happy.

RESPONSIBILITY. A professional's responsibility is fourfold: to him- or herself, to coworkers, to the business, and to the customer. Waste, disregard for others, misuse of any commodity are unacceptable. Abusive language and profanity, harassment, insensitivity to gender, sexuality, and race do not have a place in the professional bakeshop and pastry kitchen. Self-esteem and attitude toward the establishment need to be positive.

GOOD JUDGMENT. Although not easy to learn, good judgment is a prerequisite for a professional. Good judgment is never completely mastered; rather, it is a goal toward which one can continually strive.

chapter two

Ingredient identification

hoosing ingredients with care, based upon quality, seasonality, and other considerations, including cost, is a prerequisite for high-quality baked goods. Each ingredient has its own set of characteristics, and it is the pastry chef or baker's job to know how to handle all ingredients properly from the time they are received throughout each phase of storage, handling, and preparation.

Flours, grains, and meals

This broad category encompasses both whole grains such as rice and barley and milled or otherwise refined products such as cornmeal and pastry flour. The fruits and seeds of cereal grasses and grains are versatile, universal foods, part of every cuisine and culture. For the most part, they are inexpensive and widely available, providing a valuable and concentrated source of nutrients and fiber.

WHOLE GRAINS are grains that have not been milled. They usually have a shorter shelf life than milled grains.

MILLED GRAINS are polished to remove the germ, bran, and hull. They may have a longer shelf life than whole grains, but some of their nutritive value is lost during processing.

Milled grains that are broken into coarse particles may be referred to as *cracked*. If the milling process continues, *meals* and *cereals* (cornmeal, farina, rye meal) are the result. With further processing, the grain may be ground into a fine powder, known as *flour*, whether wheat, rice, or another type.

Various methods are used for milling: crushing the grains between metal rollers, grinding them between stones, or cutting them with steel blades. Stone-ground grains are preferable in some cases, because they are subjected to less heat during milling than with other methods and so retain more of their nutritive value.

Wheat flour

Each flour has its own characteristics, but wheat flour is the most common type used in the bakeshop. It is the only flour that contains enough gluten-forming proteins to provide the structure essential to baked goods. (For more about gluten in flour, and gluten development, see "Proteins in Flour," page 57.) Flours made from other grains such as rye, rice, corn, millet, barley, oats, and spelt add distinctive flavors and textures to baked goods.

The Wheat Kernel

Before the baker can understand the different varieties of wheat flour, he or she must understand what makes up wheat. The wheat kernel is made up of the following components:

BRAN constitutes 14.5 percent of total kernel weight. The bran is the dark outer coating of the wheat kernel and contains large amounts of insoluble dietary fiber.

ENDOSPERM comprises 83 percent of total kernel weight. The endosperm is the internal portion of the wheat kernel and contains the largest amount of protein and starch. White flour is produced from the endosperm.

GERM is 2.5 percent of total kernel weight. The germ is the embryo of the wheat kernel and contains fats, vitamins, minerals, and some protein.

Wheat is classified by season and color, as follows: *hard red winter wheat, hard white winter wheat, hard red spring wheat, soft red winter wheat,* and *soft white winter wheat.* (*Durum wheat* is a particular type of hard wheat.) Winter wheat is planted in the winter and harvested the following summer; spring wheat is planted in the spring and harvested that summer. Generally, spring wheat produces the hardest flours and winter wheat the softest.

Milling

Milling is the process that separates the wheat kernel into its three parts: bran, germ, and endosperm. Once the bran and germ have been removed, the endosperm is sifted to reduce the particle size to the correct quantity for flour.

Extraction Rate

The extraction rate is the percentage of flour obtained after a grain has been milled. The extraction rate will vary with flour refinement. For example, flour with an 80 percent extraction rate indicates that 80 lb/36.29 kg of flour was obtained from 100 lb/45.36 kg of grain. Whole wheat flour, which has nothing removed, has a 100 percent extraction rate.

Ash

The ash content is a milling standard that determines the mineral (inorganic) material remaining in the flour after milling. Ash content is determined by burning a measured amount of milled flour and weighing the mineral material that remains after incineration. Ash content is related to flour color and type. This information can be found for any flour by checking individual specifications.

Flour Treatments

AGING and **BLEACHING.** Newly milled flour is not ready for the bakeshop. Bakers refer to freshly milled flour as *green flour.* Due to the immature proteins found in the flour, dough made using green flour tends to absorb more water and is not elastic. In addition to having weak proteins, freshly milled flour is yellow in color. When flour is allowed to age naturally for two to three months, oxygen in the air will whiten the flour and develop the proteins.

Chemicals are sometimes used to synthetically replicate the aging and whitening process. Benzoyl peroxide and chlorine dioxide are two of the products used to chemically age and bleach flour. Flour that has been chemically aged and bleached will bear a "bleached flour" label.

OXIDIZING. Potassium bromate, an inorganic compound, is an oxidizing agent added to flour to improve bread volume. When potassium bromate is present in flour, product volume increases by 10 to 15 percent.

ENRICHMENT. Enriched flour has nutrients replaced that were lost during milling. Nutrients added include thiamine, niacin, riboflavin, iron, and calcium. Flour that has been enriched will bear an "enriched flour" label. Enrichment has no effect on baking performance.

Types of Flour

ALL-PURPOSE FLOUR is a blend of hard and soft wheat flours milled from the endosperm of the wheat kernel; the specific blend varies from region to region. Southern all-purpose flour generally has more soft wheat than all-purpose flours in other parts of the county. The protein content in all-purpose flour can range from 8 to 12 percent.

BREAD FLOUR, also known as *patent flour,* is a hard wheat flour made from the endosperm and is used for breads and soft rolls. Its protein content ranges from 11 to 13 percent.

CAKE FLOUR is a soft wheat flour with a protein content ranging from 6 to 9 percent. It is used for cakes and cookies.

CLEAR FLOUR, a hard wheat flour made from the endosperm, has a darker color than bread or high-gluten flour and is typically used in rye breads. The protein content of clear flour ranges from 13 to 15 percent.

DURUM FLOUR, milled from the endosperm of the durum wheat kernel, is a hard wheat flour used in bread making. Its protein content ranges from 12 to 14 percent.

HIGH-GLUTEN FLOUR is milled from the entire endosperm; it is used for bagels and hard rolls. Its protein content is typically 13 to 14 percent.

PASTRY FLOUR has a protein content ranging from 8 to 10 percent. It is used for pie crust dough, muffins, and some biscuits, as well as pastries.

SEMOLINA is a more coarsely ground durum wheat flour, used most typically in pasta making.

WHOLE WHEAT FLOUR is a hard wheat flour milled from the entire wheat kernel, including the bran and germ; because the germ is high in lipids (fats), whole wheat flour can quickly become rancid. Its protein content ranges from 14 to 16 percent.

Other Wheat Products

CRACKED WHEAT is coarsely cracked or cut wheat kernels, and includes the bran and germ. It lends texture and flavor to breads.

VITAL WHEAT GLUTEN is produced from the insoluble gluten protein extracted from flour during the milling process. The protein is dried and ground into a powder. It is used to fortify dough.

Rye

RYE FLOUR behaves quite differently from wheat flour in baking, although rye kernels are milled in a manner similar to that used for wheat kernels. *White rye flour* is the mildest-flavored and lightest-colored rye flour, with a protein content of 8 to 10 percent. *Medium rye flour* has a slightly higher protein content, 9 to 11 percent, and is somewhat darker. *Dark rye flour,* which is milled from the outer portion of the endosperm, has a protein content of 14 to 17 percent. *Pumpernickel flour* (or *rye meal*) is a coarse grind made from the entire rye kernel, with an intense flavor and a dark color.

Other grains and cereals

OATS are cleaned, toasted, and hulled before use. Cleaned whole oats are referred to as *oat groats*.

OAT FLOUR is made from oat groats ground into a fine powder; it contains no gluten.

STEEL-CUT OATS (also called *Scotch, Scottish,* or *Irish oats*) are milled by cracking oat groats into smaller pieces.

ROLLED OATS, sometimes called *old-fashioned oats,* are made by steaming and flattening oat groats.

INSTANT OATS are cracked oat groats that are precooked, dried, and rolled.

BUCKWHEAT is not a type of wheat, but a cereal grain that has a distinctive strong, nutty whole-grain flavor and a relatively high fat content. Buckwheat may be roasted or unroasted. *Roasted buckwheat groats,* sold as kasha, have an intense flavor. *Unroasted groats* have a slightly milder flavor. Both are also milled into meal or flour.

SPELT is a cereal grain that contains less gluten and more protein than wheat. It is used in a variety of baked goods. It is available for use as a whole grain or a white or whole-grain flour.

MILLET is a gluten-free seed with a mild flavor. It is available whole, cracked, or ground into flour.

CORNMEAL is made by grinding dried corn kernels. Its color is determined by the color of the corn kernels used. Cornmeal is available in varying consistencies, from finely to coarsely ground.

Rice

During processing, rice is polished to remove some or all of the bran. White rice has had all the bran removed, while brown rice is only partially polished, leaving behind some of the bran. Rice is categorized generally by the length of the grain: short, medium, or long.

RICE FLOUR is made by grinding white, brown, or sweet rice. It has a mild flavor and is commonly used to make gluten-free baked goods.

Sugars, syrups, and other sweeteners

GRANULATED SUGAR is pure refined sucrose derived from either sugarcane or from sugar beets. Granulated sugar has small, evenly sized crystals, and it is the most commonly used sugar in the bakeshop.

SUPERFINE SUGAR has very small crystals and dissolves quickly. It is sometimes used in cake batters and meringues.

SANDING SUGAR has large crystals and is used primarily to decorate baked goods.

TOP ROW:
Confectioners'
sugar, granulated
sugar, superfine
sugar
MIDDLE ROW:
Isomalt, light
brown sugar, dark
brown sugar,
turbinado sugar
BOTTOM ROW:
Sanding sugar

PEARL or **DECORATING SUGAR** has large pearl-shaped crystals and is also used as a decoration.

BROWN SUGAR is granulated sugar with added molasses. *Light brown sugar* has a mild molasses flavor; *dark brown sugar,* which contains more molasses, has a more pronounced flavor. Store brown sugar in an airtight container to prevent loss of moisture.

TURBINADO SUGAR is a coarse-grained partially refined sugar with a light brown color and a very mild molasses taste.

CONFECTIONERS' SUGAR, also called *powdered sugar* or *icing sugar,* is granulated sugar ground to a powder with cornstarch added (up to 3 percent by weight) to keep it from caking. Confectioners' sugar is available in different grades of fineness (the number in the name reflects the mesh size of the screen used to sift the powdered sugar); 10X sugar is finer than 6X sugar.

ISOMALT is a white crystalline "sugar-free" sweetener made from sucrose and used in diabetic baking. Because it does not break down when heated and absorbs very little water, some pastry chefs like to use isomalt for pulled sugar work.

CORN SYRUP is produced from cornstarch. It contains 15 to 20 percent dextrose (glucose), other sugars, water, and often flavorings. *Light corn syrup* has been clarified to give it its light color; *dark corn syrup* includes refiner's syrup and caramel color and flavor, giving it a darker color and a molasses flavor. Corn syrup resists crystallization, making it suitable for some confectionery work.

GLUCOSE SYRUP is 42 DE corn syrup (see "Benefits of Glucose Syrup," page 64) used in icings, confections, and pulled sugar work.

MOLASSES is a thick, dark brown liquid by-product of sugar refining; it contains sucrose and invert sugars. Molasses has a rich flavor but it is less sweet than sugar. Molasses is available as light, dark, or blackstrap. These are rendered, respectively, from the first, second, and third boiling of the sugar syrup in the refining process, and range from light in color and flavor (*light molasses*) to very dark and intensely flavored (*blackstrap molasses*). Molasses may also be labeled "sulfured" or "unsulfured," depending on whether or not sulfur was used during processing. Sulfured molasses has a stronger flavor than lighter, more delicate unsulfured molasses.

MALT SYRUP, made from sprouted barley and corn, is used in some yeast breads. *Diastatic malt syrup* contains enzymes that break down the flour's starch into sugars. *Nondiastatic malt syrup,* which contains no diastase enzymes, is used to flavor doughs and enhance their color.

GOLDEN SYRUP (or *light treacle syrup*) is processed from sugarcane juice. It can be used in place of corn syrup in confections and baked goods.

HONEY, a naturally inverted sugar (see "Invert Sugar," page 64), is a sweet syrup produced by bees from flower nectar. The flowers, not the bees, determine honey's flavor and color. Honey can range in color and flavor from pale yellow and mild to dark amber and robust, depending on the source of the nectar.

MAPLE SYRUP is a liquefied sugar made from the concentrated sap of the sugar maple tree. Maple syrup is available in several different grades, ranging from Grade AA, which is thin and mild in flavor, to Grade C, which is thick and strongly flavored.

INVERTED SYRUP is derived from sucrose that has been broken down into equal parts of glucose and fructose. Inverted sugar is manufactured by adding an acid, or invertase, to sucrose.

Thickeners

A thickener is any ingredient that is capable of gelling, stabilizing, or thickening. The list of thickeners used in the bakeshop includes gelatin, pectin, plant gums such as agar-agar, and starches. (For an explanation of how starches, gelatin, pectin, and gums thicken liquids, see "Thickeners" in Chapter 4, page 65.)

Gelling agents

GELATIN is a protein processed from the bones, skin, and connective tissue of animals. It may be used as a gelling agent, thickener, stabilizer, emulsifier, or foaming agent. It is available in granulated or sheet form. Sheet gelatin is sold in different bloom strengths, or gauges, but as there is no universal standard of identification, the strengths of different gauge numbers may vary depending on manufacturer.

PECTIN is a gelling agent that occurs naturally in many fruits. It is produced commercially by extraction from citrus or apple skins. Pectin is the gelling agent commonly used in jams, jellies, and preserves. It is also used to make the centers of high-quality jelly beans.

AGAR-AGAR is a gum derived from sea vegetables. It is available powdered, in flakes or blocks, or as brittle strands. It has very strong gelling properties (stronger than those of gelatin), but its higher melting and gelling points make it unsuitable for some uses. Agar-agar is used in some vegetarian products and confections.

Gelatin sheets, granulated gelatin

Starches

PROCESSED and **REFINED STARCHES** are used to thicken and stabilize liquid mixtures. They result in a range of textures and consistencies once they set into a gel. *Arrowroot,* which is sometimes known as arrowroot flour, is derived from the arrowroot plant, a tropical tuber. It is often used for thickening sauces because of the transparent and high-gloss finish it yields. *Potato starch* comes from potatoes that are cooked, dried, and then ground into a fine powder; it may also be called potato flour. *Cornstarch,* ground from corn kernels, is used primarily as a thickener, but it is also sometimes used in conjunction with wheat flour to yield softer results in baked goods. *Tapioca* is derived from the root of the tropical cassava plant, also called manioc. It is available as flakes, granules, and, most commonly, small balls or pellets (called pearl tapioca), and flour; the flour or starch is sometimes called cassava or manioc flour or starch.

MODIFIED (or **CONVERTED**) **STARCHES** are modified through a process involving an acid and hydrolysis. The starches produced in this manner function more efficiently as thickeners for frozen items that will be thawed, as they resist separation.

Dairy products

Milk, cream, and butter are among the dairy products used daily in most bakeshops and pastry kitchens. Customarily, containers and packages are dated to indicate how long the contents will remain fresh.

When storing dairy products, flavor transfer is a particular concern. Store milk, cream, and butter away from foods with strong odors. Wrap cheeses carefully, both to maintain their texture and to prevent their aromas from permeating other foods.

Milk and cream

The milk sold today is typically forced through an ultrafine mesh at high pressure to break up the fat globules, dispersing them evenly throughout the milk in the process known as homogenization. Unless milk is homogenized, it will separate, allowing the cream to rise to the top as the milk sits. Milk is also pasteurized to kill bacteria and other harmful organisms by heating it to a specific temperature for a specific period of time (140°F/60°C for 30 minutes, or 161°F/72°C for 15 seconds). Ultrapasteurized milk and cream are heated to at least 280°F/138°C for at least 2 seconds, increasing their shelf life for 60 to 90 days.

MILK is labeled according to its milk fat content. *Whole milk* contains at least 3 percent milk fat. *Reduced-fat milk* contains 2 percent milk fat, *low-fat milk* contains 1 percent, and *fat-free milk* contains less than 0.1 percent.

CREAM *Heavy* or *whipping cream* must contain at least 35 percent milk fat, and is used for whipping. *Light cream* has between 16 and 32 percent milk fat, and it does not whip easily. It is sometimes used instead of milk to add a richer flavor and creamier texture.

EVAPORATED MILK is whole or fat-free milk that is heated in a vacuum to remove 60 percent of its water content.

SWEETENED CONDENSED MILK is evaporated milk that has been sweetened. It is sold in cans of varying sizes.

NONFAT DRY MILK (powdered milk) is made by removing the water from de-fatted milk. Sold in boxes, it does not contain any milk fat and can be stored at room temperature.

Fermented and cultured milk products

Buttermilk, crème fraîche, sour cream, and yogurt are all produced by inoculating milk or cream with a bacterial strain under precisely controlled conditions. The reaction of the culture with the milk product thickens the milk or cream and gives it a pleasant tangy flavor.

BUTTERMILK was traditionally the by-product of churning milk into butter. Most buttermilk sold today is nonfat milk to which a bacterial strain has been added and, despite its name, contains only a very small amount of butterfat. Buttermilk has a thick texture and a slightly sour flavor.

SOUR CREAM is cultured cream with 16 to 22 percent fat. Low-fat and nonfat versions of sour cream are also available.

YOGURT is a cultured milk product made from whole, low-fat, or nonfat milk; it may be plain or flavored.

CRÈME FRAÎCHE is made by adding an acid to cream that has 30 percent milk fat. The acid thickens the cream but does not cause it to ferment, so crème fraîche has a sweet flavor. Its high fat content gives it a velvety texture.

Cheeses

Cheeses may be categorized in many ways. Included here are only a few cheeses that are well suited and commonly used in baking.

Soft cheeses usually have a high moisture content and are relatively perishable.

FARMER and **BAKER'S CHEESES** are cow's milk cheeses with a mild, tart flavor and soft, grainy texture.

RICOTTA CHEESE is a cow's milk cheese with a very mild, delicate flavor; it can be drained to produce a drier, grainy cheese. *Ricotta impastata* is a smooth, spoonable, dry cheese used when regular ricotta would add too much moisture to a formula, such as cannoli filling.

CREAM CHEESE has a mild, slightly tangy taste and a soft, spreadable texture. The *reduced-fat cream cheese* sometimes called Neufchâtel (not to be confused with French Neufchâtel, a soft unripened cheese) has less fat than regular cream cheese, but it also has more moisture. This Neufchâtel may often be used interchangeably with regular cream cheese without requiring changes to the formula to compensate for the lower fat and higher moisture. Other types of cream cheese include low-fat, nonfat, whipped, and flavored; cream cheese is sold in large blocks, tubs, or smaller packages.

MOZZARELLA CHEESE, made from either cow's or water buffalo's milk, has a mild, slightly tangy flavor and a soft, creamy, slightly elastic texture. Mozzarella is sold fresh or aged, in balls or blocks; it is also available grated.

CHEDDAR CHEESE is a dry semifirm cheese made from cow's milk. During manufacture it undergoes a cheddaring process where the curds are piled and pressed, which causes the expulsion of whey and allows for the development of characteristic Cheddar texture. Cheddar cheese originated in England, but is now commonly made in America and elsewhere.

PARMESAN CHEESE (Parmigiano-Reggiano) is a very hard, crumbly grating cheese. It gets its special flavor and texture from an extended aging period, during which it dries and develops an intense pungency.

Butter

The best-quality butter has a sweet flavor, similar to fresh heavy cream; if salt has been added, it should be barely detectable. The color of butter will vary depending upon the breed of cow, the diet of the cow, and the time of year, but is typically a pale yellow.

Both salted and unsalted butter are available. The designation "sweet butter" indicates only that the butter is made from sweet cream (as opposed to sour). If unsalted butter is desired, be sure that the word "unsalted" appears on the package.

Old butter takes on a very faintly cheesy flavor and aroma, especially when heated. As it continues to deteriorate, the flavor and aroma can become quite pronounced and unpleasant, much like sour or curdled milk.

Grade AA butter has the best flavor, color, aroma, and texture. Grade A butter also is of excellent quality. All grades of butter must contain a minimum of 80 percent milk fat. Grade B may have a slightly acidic taste, as it can be made from soured cream.

Eggs

Eggs are graded by the USDA based on appearance and freshness. The top grade, AA, indicates a very fresh egg (if they have been properly stored and recently purchased) with a white that will not spread unduly once the egg is broken and a yolk that rides high on the white's surface.

Eggs come in a number of sizes: jumbo, extra-large, large, medium, small, and peewee. Large or extra-large eggs are used in most baking formulas.

Rotate stock as necessary to ensure that only fresh eggs are used. Upon delivery, look for shells that are clean and free of cracks. Discard any eggs with broken shells; they are at a high risk for contamination.

Dried eggs are available in various forms: whole eggs, yolks, or whites. *Pasteurized eggs* are sold as whole eggs (which may be fortified), yolks, or whites. They can be purchased in refrigerated or frozen liquid form, as well as dried and powdered. Once thawed, frozen pasteurized eggs are perishable and must be stored and handled like fresh eggs.

Egg substitutes may be entirely egg-free or may be made with egg whites, with dairy or vegetable products substituted for the yolks. Egg substitutes are used for specific types of dietary baking and cooking.

Oils, shortenings, and other fats

Fats and oils provide many functions in baked goods. They tenderize, add flavor, have leavening strength, add moisture, and can create a flaky texture, among many other things.

Oils and shortenings

Vegetable and other similar oils are produced by pressing a high-oil-content food, such as olives, nuts, corn, avocados, or soybeans. The oil may then be filtered, clarified, or hydrogenated, depending on its intended use. All oils and shortenings should be stored in a dry place away from light and extremes of heat.

VEGETABLE OILS are often neutral in flavor and color and have relatively high smoking points. If the label does not specify a source, the oil is usually a blend of oils. *Canola oil* (or *rapeseed oil*) is a light, golden-colored oil extracted from rapeseeds; it is low in saturated fat. *Corn oil* is a mild-flavored refined oil, medium yellow in color, inexpensive, and versatile. *Soybean oil* has a pronounced flavor and aroma; it is found primarily in blended vegetable oils and margarines.

OLIVE OILS vary in heaviness and may be pale yellow to deep green, depending on the particular fruit and the processing method. Cold-pressed olive oil is superior in flavor to thermally refined oil. The finest olive oil available is *extra-virgin olive oil,* with a naturally low level of acid, typically less than 1 percent. *Virgin olive oil,* also known as *pure olive oil,* is the next best grade. Both extra-virgin and virgin olive oils are prized for their flavor. For this reason they are often used in preparations where the oil is not cooked, and in or on products after they have been cooked or baked, to preserve and take advantage of their flavor. A blend of *refined olive oil* (virgin oil that has been thermally treated to remove its undesirable characteristics) and virgin olive oil is commonly used for baking and cooking.

NUT OILS have rich aromas. They are usually more perishable than vegetable or olive oils. Store them under refrigeration to keep them fresh, and use them within a few weeks of opening for the best flavor. Most *peanut oils* are a pale yellow refined oil, with a very subtle scent and flavor, but some less-refined types are darker and have a more pronounced peanut flavor.

OIL SPRAYS are vegetable oils (usually blended) packaged in pump or aerosol spray containers. They are used for lightly coating pans and griddles.

HYDROGENATED SHORTENINGS are produced from liquid fats that have been chemically altered under pressure with purified hydrogen to make them solid at room temperature. Shortening may contain some animal fats unless specifically labeled as vegetable shortening.

EMULSIFYING SHORTENING or **HIGH-RATIO SHORTENING** is a hydrogenated shortening that contains monoglycerides and other agents so that it better absorbs and retains moisture in baked goods. Emulsifying shortening is used in recipes where the amount of sugar and liquids is proportionally greater than the flour.

Other fats

MARGARINE is a solid fat made with hydrogenated vegetable oils and milk, either liquid or milk solids. Regular margarines contain 80 percent fat. Margarine may also contain salt, artificial flavorings, and preservatives. A wide variety of margarines is available, from regular to whipped to reduced-fat and cholesterol-lowering blends, in sticks, blocks, or tubs.

LARD is made from rendered pork fat. It is processed and hydrogenated to make it solid. It may also be treated to neutralize its flavor.

Chocolate

The extraction and processing of chocolate from cacao beans is a lengthy and complex process. The first stage involves crushing the kernels into a paste; at this point it is completely unsweetened and is called *chocolate liquor*. The liquor is then further ground to give it a smoother, finer texture, and sweeteners and other ingredients may be added. The liquor may also be pressed to force out most of the *cocoa butter*. The solids that are left are ground into cocoa powder. Cocoa butter is combined with chocolate liquor to make baking and eating chocolates, or it may simply be flavored and sweetened to make white chocolate. Cocoa butter also has numerous pharmaceutical and cosmetic uses.

Chocolate keeps for several months if wrapped and stored in a cool, dry, ventilated area away from sunlight. Ordinarily it should not be refrigerated, since this could cause moisture to condense on the surface of the chocolate. Under particularly hot and humid kitchen conditions, however, it may be preferable to refrigerate or freeze chocolate to prevent loss of flavor. Sometimes stored chocolate develops a white "bloom." Bloom merely indicates that some of the cocoa butter has melted and then recrystallized on the surface, and chocolate with a bloom can still be safely used. Cocoa powder should be stored in tightly sealed containers in a dry place. It will keep almost indefinitely.

Types of chocolate

COCOA POWDER is a powdered chocolate product with a cocoa butter content ranging from 10 to 25 percent. Dutch-process cocoa powder, which is 22 to 24 percent cocoa butter, has been treated with an alkali to reduce its acidity. Dutch-process cocoa powder is darker in color than natural cocoa powder.

UNSWEETENED CHOCOLATE (also known as *bitter* or *baking chocolate*) contains no sugar. It is approximately 95 percent chocolate liquor and 5 percent cocoa butter.

BITTERSWEET CHOCOLATE typically contains at least 50 percent chocolate liquor, 15 percent cocoa butter, and 35 to 50 percent sugar.

SEMISWEET CHOCOLATE usually contains at least 35 percent chocolate liquor, 15 percent cocoa butter, and 40 percent sugar. This chocolate may be used interchangeably with bittersweet in most recipes.

COUVERTURE CHOCOLATE contains 15 percent chocolate liquor, 35 percent cocoa butter, and 50 percent sugar. Its high fat content makes it ideal for coating candy, pastries, and cakes.

MILK CHOCOLATE is 10 percent chocolate liquor, 20 percent cocoa butter, 50 percent sugar, and 15 percent milk solids.

SWEET CHOCOLATE is 15 percent chocolate liquor, 15 percent cocoa butter, and 70 percent sugar. Both milk and sweet chocolates often contain other added ingredients and flavors.

WHITE CHOCOLATE is made from cocoa butter, sugar, flavorings, and milk. Since 2004, "white chocolate" has had its own standards set by the Food and Drug Administration.

CONFECTIONERY COATING is a chocolate product containing no cocoa butter. Confectionery coating is made with vegetable fats and requires no tempering prior to use. It is also referred to as *summer coating* or *compound chocolate*. Confectionery coating is available in a range of flavors such as milk chocolate and bittersweet chocolate.

TOP ROW:
Milk chocolate,
Dutch-process
cocoa powder,
couverture,
white chocolate,
milk chocolate

BOTTOM ROW:
Cocoa powder,
semisweet
chocolate,
bittersweet
chocolate,
unsweetened
chocolate

Leaveners

There are many different ways in which a baked product may be leavened. Some are leavened through the use of a technique or method, others by the addition of an ingredient, and others still by a combination of the two. (For more information on leavening, see Chapter 4, "Leaveners," pages 59–62.) Ingredients that are added to provide leavening fall into one of two categories, biological (yeast) or chemical (baking soda or baking powder).

Yeast

ACTIVE DRY YEAST is dehydrated, dormant yeast granules. It requires a warm liquid to activate it. Active dry yeast should be stored in an airtight container in the refrigerator or freezer.

RAPID RISE YEAST is a type of dehydrated yeast formulated to provide a quick rise. It is extremely active once rehydrated and dies quickly. Rapid rise yeast should be stored in an airtight container in the refrigerator or freezer.

INSTANT DRY YEAST is derived from cultures that can ferment using both beet sugar and malt sugar, guaranteeing fermentation activity through all phases of the dough. It can be used without rehydration. When working with instant dry yeast, very cold or ice water should be used in the mixing process.

COMPRESSED FRESH YEAST is a highly perishable yeast product. It should have a moist, firm texture and show no discoloration or dry, crumbly spots. Store it under refrigeration.

Chemical leaveners

BAKING POWDER is a mixture of bicarbonate of soda and an acid (the leavening agents) and a starch. It may be double- or single-acting. (For more information on baking powder, see "Chemical Leaveners" in Chapter 4, page 60.)

BAKING SODA is sodium bicarbonate. It requires both an acid and moisture in order to leaven a product. (For more information on baking soda, see "Chemical Leaveners" in Chapter 4, page 60.)

Salt

TABLE SALT may be *iodized*, meaning it contains added iodine, a preventive against goiter, or *noniodized*. Its small, dense, grains adhere poorly to food, dissolve slowly in solution, and are difficult to blend.

KOSHER SALT is a coarse salt that weighs less by volume than table salt. It dissolves more readily and adheres better to food.

SEA SALT is collected through the evaporation of natural saltwater. The salt's thin, flaky layers adhere well to food and dissolve quickly. Sea salt also contains various trace minerals that occur naturally in the waters from which they are collected. As a result, sea salts from different areas of the world taste different. All are generally more complex in flavor than table and kosher salt. Sea salt can be purchased in fine-grain and coarser crystal forms.

ROCK SALT, also known as *bay salt,* is a very coarse salt used in crank ice cream makers. It may have a gray tint from the impurities it contains. Rock salt is generally not manufactured for consumption.

Herbs, spices, and flavorings

Herbs may be used either fresh or dried; note that dried herbs have increased potency. Spices may be used whole or ground. They maintain freshness better if they are stored whole. Extracts are commonly derived from herbs, spices, and nuts. They are prepared in an alcohol-based solution. Extracts can lose their potency with prolonged exposure to air, heat, or light.

Herbs

Fresh herbs should appear fresh and firm, with no evidence of wilting or bruising. Store them under refrigeration, loosely wrapped in dampened paper towels and then plastic. Some herbs such as basil and mint, whose leaves are easily bruised, are best stored as if they were bouquets of flowers, with the stems in cool water, if space permits.

BASIL belongs to the mint family. It has green pointed leaves and a pungent licorice flavor. It may be used fresh or dried.

CHIVE belongs to the onion family and has a mild onion flavor. It has long, slender light green stems and lavender-colored flowers, both of which are edible and used commonly in culinary applications. It is available fresh or dried but is most commonly used as a fresh herb.

CLOCKWISE FROM TOP LEFT: Rosemary, chives, oregano, thyme, mint, flat-leaf parsley, curly parsley, cilantro, basil (center)

21

DILL has blue-green thread-like foliage and yellow feathery flowers that produce small brown seeds, all of which are edible; the seeds have the most pungent flavor.

MINT comes in many varieties. *Peppermint* has a strong flavor. It is available fresh, dried, or as an extract. *Spearmint* has gray-green leaves and a milder flavor than peppermint.

OREGANO belongs to the mint family. It has small oval leaves. Oregano and marjoram are similar in flavor, but oregano is stronger. Both may be used fresh or dried.

PARSLEY has a mild, peppery flavor. Its leaves may be curly or flat (also called *Italian parsley*), depending on the variety. It is available fresh or dried, but is primarily used as a fresh herb.

ROSEMARY is another member of the mint family, with leaves shaped like pine needles. It has a resin-like aroma and flavor and is available fresh, dried, or ground.

Spices

ALLSPICE is the dried berry of the pimiento tree. Its flavor is reminiscent of cinnamon, nutmeg, and cloves. It is available whole or ground.

ANISE and **CARAWAY SEEDS** are both derived from herbs in the parsley family. Anise seeds have a distinct licorice flavor. Anise is available as whole seeds, ground, or as an extract. Caraway seeds are sometimes labeled "kimmel." They are available whole or ground.

CARDAMOM is a plant in the ginger family. Each of its pods contains fifteen to twenty small seeds. Cardamom has a pungent aroma and a sweet and spicy flavor. It is available as whole pods or ground.

CINNAMON is the stripped dried bark of an evergreen in the laurel family. It is sold whole (in sticks) or ground.

CLOVES are the dried unopened buds of a tropical evergreen tree. They have a strong flavor. Cloves are available whole or ground.

MACE is the lacy membrane covering the nutmeg seed. It has a pungent nutmeg flavor and is available ground or whole.

NUTMEG is the seed of the nutmeg tree. It has a sweet and spicy flavor and is available either whole or ground.

PEPPERCORNS may be black, white, green, or pink. *Black peppercorns* are picked when not quite ripe and then dried; the Tellicherry peppercorn is one of the most prized black peppercorns. *White peppercorns* are allowed to ripen before they are picked, then the husks are removed and they are dried. Black and white pepper is available as whole berries, cracked, or ground. *Mignonette*, or *shot pepper*, is a combination of coarsely ground or crushed black and white peppercorns. *Green peppercorns* are picked when underripe, then packed in vinegar or brine or freeze-dried. Drain and rinse brine-packed peppercorns before using; reconstitute freeze-dried peppercorns in water before use. *Pink peppercorns* are the dried berries of the baies rose plant, not a true peppercorn. They are usually available freeze-dried.

Flavorings

VANILLA BEANS are the pods of a delicate orchid flower. Vanilla has a distinct aromatic flavor. Vanilla is available as whole beans and as an extract. Vanilla is also available commercially in powder and paste forms.

GARLIC is the bulb of the garlic plant; each bulb is made up of seven to twelve cloves. It is available fresh, powdered, or granulated.

GINGER is the rhizome of the ginger plant. It has a pungent, hot flavor. It is available fresh, in dried pieces, ground, or crystallized.

Nuts

Nuts have a number of uses, adding flavor and texture to many dishes. Nuts that have not been roasted or shelled will keep longer than those that have. Shelled nuts can be stored in the freezer or refrigerator, if space allows. In any case, they should be stored in a cool, dry, well-ventilated area and checked periodically to be sure they are still fresh.

ALMONDS are teardrop-shaped nuts, part of a fruit that resembles an apricot. They have a pale tan, woody shell. *Sweet almonds* are sold whole, in the shell or shelled, blanched or unblanched, roasted, sliced, or slivered, and as almond paste and other products. The sale of *bitter almonds* is illegal in the United States; however, once processed, they are used to flavor extracts and liquors that are readily available.

BRAZIL NUTS are among the largest nuts. They grow in segmented clusters; each segment contains a hard, wrinkled, three-sided brown seed. Brazil nuts are sold whole, in the shell or shelled.

CASHEWS are kidney-shaped nuts that grow as the appendage of an apple-like fruit (the fruit is not eaten). The shell of the cashew contains toxic oils, so cashews are always sold shelled, raw or toasted, whole or in pieces, or as a nut butter.

CHESTNUTS have hard glossy brown shells covering the round or teardrop-shaped nuts. Chestnuts are sold whole, in the shell or shelled, canned, packed in syrup or water, candied, frozen, in vacuum-sealed packages, or as purée.

COCONUTS are the fruits of a type of palm tree. The "nut" is composed of a woody brown outer shell covered with hairy fibers surrounding a layer of rich white nutmeat. Coconuts are sold whole, and coconut meat is sold shredded or in flakes (sweetened or unsweetened), frozen, or dried (desiccated). Coconut milk, coconut cream, coconut oil, and other coconut-based products are also available.

HAZELNUTS (also called *filberts*) are small, nearly round nuts, rich and delicately flavored. Their shiny, hard shells have a matte spot where they were attached to the tree. Hazelnuts are sold whole, in the shell or shelled, or chopped.

MACADAMIA NUTS are extremely rich, sweet nuts native to Australia. They are pale in color and nearly round. Macadamia nuts are sold shelled and roasted in coconut oil.

PEANUTS are sold in the shell or shelled, raw (or natural), roasted, or dry-roasted, or as a butter.

PECANS have two lobes and a rich flavor. The shell is medium brown, smooth, and glossy. They are sold in the shell or shelled as halves or pieces.

PISTACHIO NUTS naturally have cream-colored shells; the nutmeat is green, with a distinctive sweet flavor. Pistachios are usually sold whole in the shell, raw or roasted (usually salted), natural or dyed red. Occasionally they are sold shelled, whole or chopped.

WALNUTS are mild, tender, oily nuts. They grow in two segments inside a hard shell and are typically light brown with deep ridges patterning the surface. *White walnuts* (or *butternuts*) and *black walnuts* are two North American varieties. Butternuts are richer, while black walnuts have a stronger flavor. Walnuts are sold whole in the shell, shelled as halves or pieces, or pickled.

Seeds

Some of the seeds used in the kitchen are considered spices (celery or fennel seeds, for example), but others, including sunflower and pumpkin seeds, are treated more like nuts. These seeds, and the pastes made from them, should be stored in the same manner as nuts.

ANISE SEEDS are small gray to gray-green almond-shaped seeds that have an intense licorice flavor. They are used whole or ground.

CARAWAY SEEDS are small, light brown, crescent-shaped seeds with an intense flavor. They are commonly used in rye bread.

POPPY SEEDS are tiny, round, blue-black seeds with a rich, slightly musty flavor. They are sold whole and as a paste.

PUMPKIN SEEDS are flat, oval, cream-colored seeds. They have a semihard hull and a soft, oily interior. They are sold whole in the shell (raw or roasted) and shelled (raw or roasted).

CLOCKWISE FROM TOP LEFT: Sunflower seeds, pumpkin seeds (pepitas), fennel, sesame seeds (hulled), sesame seeds (unhulled), caraway seeds, anise seeds, poppy seeds (center)

SESAME SEEDS are tiny flat oval seeds. They may be black, tan, or ivory. They are somewhat oily, with a rich, nutty flavor. Sesame seeds are sold whole, hulled or unhulled, toasted, and as a paste (also known as *tahini*).

SUNFLOWER SEEDS are flat, teardrop-shaped, light tan, oily seeds with a woody black-and-white shell. Sunflower seeds are sold whole in the shell or shelled.

Selecting and handling fresh produce

Fruits and vegetables should be free of bruises, mold, brown or soft spots, and pest damage. They should be plump, not shriveled. Any attached leaves should be unwilted.

Since it is usually not possible to examine produce until it has been delivered to the restaurant or bakery, one way to ensure quality is to buy according to grade. Grading is based on USDA standards. Lower-grade items, particularly fruits, may be used successfully in preparations such as baked pies and puddings, where appearance is not a factor.

Most produce has a noticeably better quality and flavor the closer it is to its source. Fruits that have been shipped, such as apricots, peaches, and strawberries, for example, may require special handling that can drive up their cost, despite continued efforts to develop strains that combine good shipping qualities with superior flavor.

More and more vegetables are being grown hydroponically; that is, in nutrient-enriched water rather than soil. Hydroponic growing takes place indoors under regulated temperature and lighting conditions, so any growing season may be duplicated. Hydroponically grown lettuces, spinach, herbs, and tomatoes are all readily available. Although they have the advantage of being easy to clean, these products may have less flavor than conventionally grown fruits and vegetables.

With a few exceptions (including bananas, potatoes, tomatoes, and dry onions), ripe fruits and vegetables should be refrigerated. Unless otherwise specified, produce should be kept at a temperature of 40° to 45°F/4° to 7°C, with a relative humidity of 80 to 90 percent.

Keep fresh produce dry; excess moisture can promote spoilage. Likewise, most produce should not be peeled, washed, or trimmed until just before use. The outer leaves of lettuce, for example, should be left intact; carrots should remain unpeeled. The exceptions to this rule are the leafy tops on vegetables such as beets, turnips, carrots, and radishes: They should be removed, and either discarded or used as soon as possible, because even after harvesting, these leaves absorb nutrients from the vegetable and increase moisture loss.

Fruits and vegetables that need further ripening, notably peaches and pears, should be stored at room temperature, 65° to 70°F/18° to 21°C. Once the produce is ripe, refrigerate it to keep it from overripening.

Apples

The most commonly available apple varieties include *Golden* and *Red Delicious, McIntosh, Granny Smith, Rome Beauty, Fuji,* and *Gala.* There are, however, hundreds of other varieties grown in orchards throughout the country.

Multipurpose apple varieties, good as table fruit, in baking, for sauces, and for freezing, include *Red* and *Golden Delicious* (firm, sweet, and aromatic), *Granny Smith* (tart, extremely

crisp, and fine-textured), *McIntosh* (sweet and very juicy, with a crisp texture), *Rome Beauty* (firm flesh with a mild tart-sweet flavor), and *Winesap* (firm, tart-sweet, and aromatic).

Baking varieties include *Greening* (mild, sweet-tart flavor; good for pies and sauces; also freezes well), *Jonathan* (tender, semitart flesh), and *Northern Spy* (crisp, firm-textured, and juicy, with a sweet-tart taste).

Fresh apples can be held in climate-controlled cold storage for many months without significant loss of quality. This makes it possible to get good fresh apples throughout the year.

FROM LEFT TO RIGHT: Red d'Anjou pear, green d'Anjou pear, Bosc pear, Asian pear, Forelle pear, Granny Smith apple, Golden Delicious apple, McIntosh apple, Red Delicious apple, Gala apple

Pears

Pears, like apples, are grown in many varieties, the most common being *Bartlett, Bosc, Comice, d'Anjou,* and *Seckel.* Because the flesh of pears is extremely fragile, they are picked for shipping before they have fully ripened. The fruit continues to soften at room temperature. In addition to being eaten out of hand, pears are often poached whole or used in sorbet and tarts.

ASIAN PEARS are apple-shaped fruit with a smooth skin that ranges in color from green to yellow-brown. The white flesh has a juicy, mildly sweet flavor.

BARTLETT PEARS, also known as *Williams pears,* have green skin that turns yellow as the fruit ripens. Red Bartlett pears have a brilliant scarlet-colored skin.

BOSC PEARS have a long neck and dark, russeted skin that turns brown when the fruit is ripe.

COMICE PEARS are round with a short neck and stem and a greenish-yellow skin, sometimes with a reddish blush. They are very sweet and juicy.

D'ANJOU PEARS have green skin that becomes yellow as they ripen and may have brown scarring.

SECKEL PEARS are small and crisp, with green skin and a red blush. They are usually eaten fresh.

Berries

The season for fresh berries varies from region to region, though many berries are widely available as imports from other regions or countries at virtually any time of the year. But even with improved handling and shipping methods, some specialty berries are still only available fresh in season from local purveyors. A variety of processed forms are also available: frozen (individually quick frozen, or IQF, with or without sugar), purées, concentrates, and dried.

With the exception of cranberries, fresh berries are highly perishable and are susceptible to bruising, mold, and overripening in fairly short order. Juice-stained cartons or juice leaking through the carton is a clear indication that the fruit has been mishandled or is old.

Berries (except for cranberries) can be eaten fresh. All can be used in baked items, syrups, purées and sauces, cordials, jellies, jams, and syrups. Some classic berry preparations include strawberry shortcake, fresh berry cobblers, pies, jams, jellies, and ice creams.

BLACKBERRIES, also known as *bramble berries,* resemble raspberries in form but are deep purple in color. Their peak season is mid- to late summer.

BLUEBERRIES are bluish-purple berries with a dusty silver-blue bloom. Typically, smaller berries have a sweeter, more intense flavor than larger berries.

BOYSENBERRIES are a hybrid of the raspberry, blackberry, and loganberry.

CRANBERRIES are shiny red (some have a white blush), firm, and sour.

CURRANTS are small round berries that may be red, black, or white. The red are generally the sweetest.

ELDERBERRIES are small and purple-black. They are typically used in cooked applications, as they have a very sour flavor.

GOOSEBERRIES have a smooth skin and a papery husk that may still be attached when they are sold. They can be green, golden, red, purple, or white. Some have fuzzy skins.

GRAPES are shiny, smooth skinned, and range in color from green to deep purple and in flavor from very sweet to sour. Dried, they are known as *raisins.* Dried seedless Zante grapes are known as dried currants.

RASPBERRIES are actually clusters of tiny fruits (drupes), each containing a seed; red, black, and yellow (golden) or white varieties are available.

STRAWBERRIES are red, shiny, heart-shaped berries with their tiny seeds on the exterior. They are available year-round, but their peak season is late spring to early summer. Generally speaking, small berries have a sweeter, more intense flavor than the larger berries.

Citrus fruits

Citrus fruits are characterized by their extremely juicy segmented flesh, and skins that contain aromatic oils. Grapefruits, lemons, limes, and oranges are the most common citrus fruits. They range in flavor from very sweet (oranges) to very tart (lemons).

GRAPEFRUITS all have yellow skin, sometimes with a rosy blush where the sun hit them. The skin of *white grapefruits* may have a green blush, and the flesh is pale yellow; seedless varieties are available. *Pink grapefruits* have yellow skin with a pink blush; the flesh is pink. The skin of *red grapefruits* has a red blush, and the flesh is deep red with a mellow sweet-tart flavor. Both the pink and red are juiced or eaten fresh.

KUMQUATS are small, oblong fruits with a golden orange peel. The flesh contains small white seeds. With a sweet-tart peel and tart juicy flesh, kumquats are entirely edible.

LEMONS have yellow-green to deep yellow skin and extremely tart flesh; they always have seeds. *Meyer lemons* are not true lemons; they are a hybrid that was imported from China, most likely a cross between an orange and a lemon. They are about the size of a large lemon, with smooth skin. Their flesh is a light orange-yellow color, and the juice is sweeter than regular lemon juice.

ORANGES come in four basic types; juice, eating, bitter, and mandarin. Juice oranges have smooth skin that is somewhat difficult to peel. They are usually plump and sweet, which makes them ideal for juicing. *Eating oranges* include the *navel,* which is large, seedless, and easy to peel. They may or may not have seeds. *Blood oranges* have orange skin with a blush of red. They are aromatic, with pockets of dark red or maroon flesh, and are used for both juice and eating. *Bitter oranges* are used almost exclusively to make marmalade. *Mandarin oranges,*

FROM LEFT TO RIGHT: Grapefruit, navel orange, Mineola tangelo, Valencia orange, lemon, limes, kumquats

a category that includes mandarins, tangerines, and clementines, have loose, relatively thin skins and peel very easily. Mandarins are seedless. Tangerines are juicy with a sweet-tart flavor and usually have many seeds. Clementines have less acid than most oranges and are as fragrant as they are flavorful. Because of their dainty size, they are often featured as a garnish.

LIMES have dark green, smooth skin, and flesh that is tart and seedless. *Key limes* are very small and have light green skin. Their most famous use is in Key lime pie.

Melons

Melons are fragrant, succulent fruits related to squashes and cucumbers. The four major types of melons are cantaloupes, muskmelons, watermelons, and winter melons (including honeydew, casaba, and Crenshaw).

The ability to determine when a melon is ripe eludes some people. Depending upon the type, you may look for a number of different signs, but aroma and heaviness for size are the best general keys to determining ripeness, regardless of variety.

CANTALOUPES have coarse netting or veining over their surface and a yellow to buff background color; the stem end should have a smooth mark to show that the melon ripened on the vine. Their flesh is smooth, orange, juicy, and fragrant.

MUSKMELONS resemble cantaloupes except that they are deeply ridged.

WATERMELONS are most popular and best known in the large oval variety (15 to 30 lb/6.80 to 13.61 kg), with a light-and-dark-green striped rind and pink flesh. Watermelons, however, come in many different varieties with flesh that may be white, yellow, or pink. All varieties have a thick, hard rind and crisp, granular, juicy (or watery) flesh. They are available in seedless varieties.

WINTER MELONS are a group of melons characterized by their late harvest. *Casaba melons* have a light yellow to yellow-green skin that becomes smooth and velvety as the melons ripen. Casabas have a rich melon aroma when ripe. *Crenshaw melons* have very fragrant, salmon-colored flesh and, when ripe, a slight softening near the stem. *Honeydew melons* are juicy with vivid green flesh; their skin loses any greenish cast and develops a velvety and slightly tacky feel when they are ripe. *Persian melons* have dark green skin with yellow markings and yellow-orange flesh. When ripe, they feel heavy for their size and yield slightly when pressed.

FROM LEFT TO RIGHT: Galia (halved with seeds removed), honeydew (halved with seeds), Carlencas (halved and whole), cantaloupe (wedge and halved), watermelon wedge

Stone fruits

Peaches, nectarines, apricots, plums, and cherries are often referred to as stone fruits because they have one large central pit, or stone. In North America, they typically come into peak season through the late spring and into summer. Stone fruits need to be handled delicately because their flesh has a tendency to bruise easily. In addition to their fresh form, they are commonly available canned, frozen, and dried.

APRICOTS have slightly fuzzy skin, like peaches, but are smaller, with somewhat drier flesh. The skin ranges in color from yellow to golden orange, and some have rosy patches.

CHERRIES come in numerous varieties and many shades of red, from the light crimson *Queen Anne* to the almost black *Bing;* some are yellow or golden, such as *Royal Ann.* They vary in texture from firm and crisp to soft and juicy, and flavors run the gamut from sweet to sour. Cherries can be found fresh throughout their growing season, and they are also sold canned, dried, candied, or frozen, and as prepared fillings for Danish, pies, and other pastries. Cherry syrups and cherry-flavored cordials are also available; kirschwasser, a clear cherry cordial, is often used in bakeshops and kitchens.

NECTARINES are similar in shape, color, and flavor to peaches, but they have smooth skin. Like peaches, they are classified as either clingstone or freestone; some varieties have flesh with a texture similar to that of plums.

PEACHES are sweet and juicy, with a distinctive fuzzy skin. They come in many varieties, but all peaches fall into one of two categories: *clingstone* or *freestone.* Clingstone peaches have

CLOCKWISE FROM TOP RIGHT: Assortment of stone fruits in basket, nectarine, purple plum, red plum, apricots, peach, nectarines

31

flesh that clings to the pit, whereas the flesh of freestone peaches separates easily. Depending on the variety, peach flesh ranges from white to creamy yellow to yellow-orange to red, with a whole host of combinations possible.

PLUMS can be as small as an apricot or as large as a peach. When ripe, they are sweet and juicy, and some have tart skins that contrast nicely with their succulent flesh. *Greengage plums,* with green skin and flesh, are a popular dessert variety. *Santa Rosa plums* are red with light yellow flesh. *Black Friar plums* have dark purple skins with a silvery bloom and deep red to purple flesh. *Damson plums,* the best-known cooking plums, have purple skin with a silver-blue bloom. *Prune plums,* also called *Italian plums,* are small, with purple skin and green flesh that is relatively dry and separates cleanly from the pit; they are eaten fresh and dried as prunes, now sometimes called dried plums.

Exotic or tropical fruits

A wide variety of fruits fall into this category, most of which are grown in tropical regions: figs, guavas, kiwis, mangoes, papayas, pineapples, plantains, pomegranates, passion fruit, and star fruit. An ever-increasing number of exotic fruits are available through regular and specialty outlets.

CLOCKWISE FROM TOP LEFT: Bananas, fingerling bananas, pineapple (whole and cut), mangoes, passion fruit (whole and cut), star fruit (whole and cut), kiwi, papaya (whole and cut)

BANANAS, unlike most fruits, are usually picked green and allowed to ripen en route to the buyer. When ripe, they have a firm yellow skin and a few black spots. The flesh is soft and creamy white.

GUAVAS are round to oblong-shaped fruits with light green to yellow edible skin. The flesh usually ranges in color from white to yellow but may even be salmon or red. It contains tiny edible seeds.

KIWIS, or *kiwifruits,* are small oval fruits with brownish hairy skin. The flesh is bright green or golden, with small edible black seeds and a citrus-like flavor.

LYCHEES are small, round fruits with a thin, bumpy red to brown skin and a single large seed. The flesh is gray-white and translucent, with a grape-like texture and a sweet grape-cherry flavor.

MANGOES are round to oval fruits with red to orange-yellow skin that may be tinged with green. They are very juicy and sweet, with an intense and aromatic aroma. The yellow-orange flesh surrounds a large flat seed.

PAPAYAS are pear-shaped fruits with smooth yellow-orange to green skin. The juicy, yellow-orange flesh, which has a melon-peach flavor, surrounds a cluster of small black seeds in the center of the fruit.

PASSION FRUITS are round or egg-shaped fruits with leathery, purple-brown skin. The pulp has a jelly-like consistency and contains many seeds. The pulp and crunchy edible seeds have a sweet-tart, lemony flavor.

PERSIMMONS commonly come in two types, both about the size of a baseball. The *Fuyu persimmon* has a round, slightly flattened shape, with pale orange to brilliant red-orange skin. Its orange flesh is crisp, with a sweet, mild flavor. The *Hachiya persimmon* is heart-shaped, with brilliant orange-red skin. Its soft, orange flesh has a sweet, spicy flavor. The Hachiya is very astringent when not completely ripe.

POMEGRANATES (sometimes called *Chinese apples*) are round and about the size of a grapefruit. The red skin has a leathery texture. Under the skin, thin white membranes encase edible crimson-colored seeds that have a crisp texture and tangy-sweet flavor.

STAR FRUITS (or *carambola*) are egg-shaped fruits with deep chevron ridges that result in a star shape when the fruit is sliced crosswise. The skin is yellow, smooth, and edible. The juicy, crisp, pale yellow flesh has a sweet-tart flavor and contains only a few seeds.

Extracts

The pastry chef and baker use a variety of flavoring extracts for cooking and baking. Many different herbs, spices, nuts, and fruits are used to prepare extracts, which are alcohol based. Common extracts include *vanilla, lemon, mint,* and *almond.*

Extracts can lose their potency if exposed to air, heat, or light. To preserve their flavor, store in tightly capped dark glass jars or bottles away from heat or direct light.

Wines, cordials, and liqueurs

A general rule of thumb for selecting wines, cordials, and liqueurs for use in cooking and baking is that if it is not suitable for drinking, it is not suitable for cooking. Brandies (including fruit brandies and cognac), Champagne, dry red and white wines, port, Sauternes, sherry, stout, ale, beer, and sweet and dry vermouth, as well as liquors and liqueurs such as bourbon, crème de cassis, kirschwasser, gin, Kahlúa, rum, and Scotch are all useful in the bakeshop.

Purchase wines and liqueurs that are affordably priced and of good quality. Table wines lose their flavor and become acidic once they are opened, especially if subjected to heat, light, and air. To preserve flavor, keep them in sealed bottles or bottles fitted with pouring spouts, and refrigerate them when not needed. Fortified wines (Madeira, sherry, and port, for example) are more stable than table wines and can be held in dry storage if there is not enough room to refrigerate them.

Coffee and tea

Coffee and tea may be used to infuse flavor in countless pastry and confection preparations. Tea is most often used to infuse its flavor into a warm liquid that will be added to the item, whereas coffee may be used in its many forms to add its flavor. Coffee beans, ground or whole, may be used to infuse their flavor as is done with tea. Powdered or instant coffee is often dissolved in a small amount of water or other liquid to form a paste that is then added directly to the formula.

chapter three

Equipment identification

just as an artist learns to master all the instruments necessary for painting, sculpting, or drawing, bakers and pastry chefs learn to master a variety of small tools and large equipment. These devices are as important as your own fingers—quite literally an extension of your hands. Tools and equipment of all sorts represent one of the biggest investments in the bakeshop or kitchen.

Scaling and measuring tools

In baking, even more so than in cooking, precise measurement of ingredients is vital to the success of the product. Precise measurements are crucial both to keep costs in line and to ensure consistency of quality and quantity. Measurements are taken of weight, volume, temperature, distance or length, and density.

Scales

Scales must be used correctly to be effective. You want the weight of only the ingredient, not the ingredient and the container holding it. Before using any scale, you must take certain steps to account for the weight of containers. This process is known as *setting a scale to tare* or *setting it to zero*.

BEAM BALANCE (or **BAKER'S**) **SCALES** have two platforms attached on either end of a beam. The point where the beam and the base meet is the fulcrum. At the front of the scale, a weight hangs from a bar notched at 1-oz/30-g increments. To tare, set the container on the scale, and reset the scale so that both sides are level, either by manipulating the weight on the front of the scale or by adding a counterweight to the other side of the scale.

To weigh out an ingredient, slide the hanging weight to the correct notch. To find an ingredient's weight, move the hanging weight until the platforms are level. To set the scale to zero, make sure that the two platforms are level. Beam balances can measure quantities far greater than the maximum weight shown on the scale if counterweights (typically available in 1-, 2-, and 4-lb/454-g, 907-g, and 1.81-kg weights) are used. To use a counterweight, set the weight on the right platform, then add enough of the ingredient to the left platform to make the two platforms level.

Scales. Digital (FRONT), beam balance or baker's balance (MIDDLE), and spring scales (REAR) are the three basic types of scales used in bakeshops and pastry kitchens.

SPRING SCALES have a platform set on top of a pedestal that contains a spring mechanism for weighing and a dial indicator on the front. To tare a spring scale, place the container for measuring the ingredients on the scale and turn the dial so that the pointer or arrow is aligned with zero. Spring scales are designed to read in any number of increments. Some are very sensitive and can measure small amounts, while others are made so that they only measure in large increments.

DIGITAL SCALES have a stainless-steel platform set on an electronic base with a digital display. Scales capable of measuring very small amounts typically have a smaller total capacity. Scales capable of weighing large amounts (more than 4 lb/1.81 kg) are less sensitive when measuring small amounts. To tare a digital scale, you press a button to reset the scale to zero. Most digital scales can switch between metric and U.S. standard weight systems.

Volume measures

GRADUATED PITCHERS or **BEAKERS** and **MEASURING CUPS** and **SPOONS** are commonly used in the bakeshop to measure liquids and pourable ingredients (eggs, molasses, or corn syrup, for example). Pitchers and cups are scaled off with lines or markings to show varying measures. Clear pitchers and cups are easy to fill accurately. For the most accurate results, use the smallest measure possible to measure ingredients, place the vessel on a level surface, and bend down to take the reading at eye level.

DRY MEASURING CUPS are commonly used in recipes written for the home baker. In the bakeshop, they are used to measure small amounts of certain dry ingredients, such as salt, spices, and baking soda. To use measuring cups and spoons for dry ingredients, overfill the measure, then use a straightedge to scrape the excess away; the ingredient should fill the measure evenly up to the rim.

Thermometers

Any bakeshop should have thermometers capable of measuring accurately over a wide range of temperatures.

INSTANT-READ THERMOMETERS are available with both dial and digital readouts. Digital thermometers typically measure a wider range of temperatures more accurately than dial-type thermometers can, and they are usually more accurate when measuring shallow liquids.

STEM-TYPE THERMOMETERS are excellent for checking the internal temperature of products such as doughs or custards; they can also be used to check the temperature of liquids. These thermometers consist of a long stem with a digital or dial head that indicates the temperature.

PROBE THERMOMETERS consist of a plastic digital-readout base with a metal probe on the end of a cord; some have an alarm setting to indicate that a specific temperature has been reached.

CANDY (or **SUGAR** or **DEEP-FAT**) **THERMOMETERS** may be calibrated in degrees only; others also indicate the most commonly used temperatures for sugar cooking (such as thread, soft ball, and hard crack). Candy thermometers should register from 100° to 400°F/38° to 205°C and should be able to withstand temperatures up to 500°F/260°C.

To check a thermometer's accuracy, let it stand for 10 minutes in boiling water. It should read 212°F/100°C. If there is any discrepancy, subtract or add the correct number of degrees to make up for the difference when using the thermometer.

Measuring tools. Pitchers in plastic (gallon and half gallon) and metal (half gallon and quart); nested dry measuring cups and spoons; thermometers from left to right: candy, digital instant-read, dial-type instant read and digital probe; metal ruler (lower left); refractometer (above candy thermometer)

Cutting tools

All cutting tools work best when they are properly maintained. A sharp tool not only performs better but is safer to use. Learn to sharpen knives with a stone and a steel so that you can maintain them yourself. Have severely dulled or damaged tools professionally reground to restore the edge.

Some tools cannot be sharpened. Handle them carefully to extend their useful lives, and replace them when they become difficult to use safely.

Knives

Keeping knives clean helps to extend their lives. Clean knives thoroughly immediately after using them with soap and hot water. Sanitize the entire knife, including the handle, bolster, and blade, as necessary, so that it will not cross contaminate food. Dry knives carefully before storing them or using them again.

Keep knives properly stored when not in use. There are a number of safe, practical ways to store knives, including knife kits or rolls for one's personal collection and slots, racks, and magnetized holders in the kitchen. Storage arrangements should be kept just as clean as knives. Cloth or vinyl rolls should be washed and sanitized periodically. (For more information on care and maintenance of knives, see *In the Hands of a Chef* from The Culinary Institute of America.)

Always use an appropriate cutting surface. Wooden or composition cutting boards are best. Cutting on metal, glass, or marble surfaces will dull and eventually damage the blade of a knife.

To pass a knife safely to someone, present it with the handle toward the other person. Whenever you carry a knife from one area of the kitchen to another, hold the blade point down, with the sharpened edge facing you. Ideally, you should sheathe or wrap the knife before walking anywhere with it, or put it in a carrier.

When you lay a knife down on a work surface, be sure that no part of it extends over the edge of the cutting board or worktable. Also, be sure the blade is facing away from the edge of the work surface. Finally, never try to catch a falling knife.

A basic knife collection includes four essential knives—a chef's or French knife, a utility knife, a paring knife, and a slicer. You might also have a number of special knives and cutting tools for specific purposes.

Types of Knives

CHEF'S or **FRENCH KNIVES** are all-purpose knives used for a variety of chopping, slicing, and mincing tasks. The blade is usually 8 to 14 in/20 to 36 cm long with a straight edge. Look for a high-carbon stainless-steel blade, a full tang (the continuation of the blade that extends into the knife's handle), good balance, and a handle that fits your hand comfortably.

UTILITY KNIVES are similar to chef's knives except that they are smaller and lighter, and used for light cutting chores. Their blades are generally 5 to 7 in/13 to 18 cm long.

A **PARING KNIFE** is a short knife used for peeling and trimming vegetables and fruits. The blades are 2 to 4 in/5 to 10 cm long, and they come in a number of shapes: pointed, bird beak, tourné, and sheep's foot.

SLICERS are used to slice breads, cakes, and pastries. Some slicers have offset handles. Their blades are long and thin and can range in length from 8 to 12 in/20 to 30 cm. They also have a variety of edges. *Bread knives* and other serrated slicers are excellent for slicing foods with a relatively spongy texture, such as most breads and some cakes; the "teeth" saw through the crumb without tearing or pulling. *Slicing blades with straight edges* are used to slice delicate pastries and cakes. *Straight-edge slicing knives* (typically 10 to 12 in/25 to 30 cm long) are also useful for icing and decorating.

Other small tools

There are numerous small tools for specialized use in the professional bakery or pastry shop; here we have listed a sampling.

Graters, zesters, and rasps

GRATERS are made of metal perforated with openings that shred away pieces of an ingredient. The openings range in size from very small for grating nutmeg to large for grating moister foods that might otherwise fall apart. Some graters are flat, others have a curved surface. A *box grater* has at least two grating faces and can usually perform a variety of grating and, often, some slicing tasks.

A **CITRUS ZESTER** is a small hand tool consisting of a metal head with a row of small round holes, attached to a handle. As the head is passed over the citrus fruit, the cutting edges remove the outer layer of colored zest but leave behind the bitter white pith. You can also use a swivel-bladed peeler to cut away thin slices from the skin or a grater with small openings instead of a zester.

A **RASP** is a long (approximately 12 in/30 cm) flat piece of stainless steel with perforations, well-suited for zesting as well as finely grating chocolate and hard cheeses. Some rasps have handles, and perforation sizes range from very fine to rather coarse.

Peelers, reamers, and corers

SWIVEL-BLADED PEELERS remove thin layers of skin (or zest) from fruits and vegetables. They are available in a number of different styles.

A **LEMON REAMER** is a conical tool, 6 to 6½ in/15 to 16.5 cm long, with deep ridges and a handle, that is used for extracting the juice from small citrus fruits such as lemons. Reamers are traditionally made of nonporous wood, but they are now also available in metal or plastic.

An **APPLE CORER** may be a hand tool or a mechanical device. A *manual corer* has a stainless-steel cylinder ⅝ in/1.50 cm diameter with a sawtooth end for cutting into the fruit. Corers are usually 6½ in/16.5 cm long. A *mechanical corer* offers greater efficiency and speed. This device has an arm with three prongs that are inserted into the apple, fixing it on a crank handle that drills it into a cylindrical blade that extracts the core. These corers can simultaneously peel the apples with a small sharp blade as they are rotated.

Spoons and tongs

SPOONS for use in the kitchen may be made of metal, wood, or composite materials. Some spoons have deep bowls; others are flat, more like a paddle. *Slotted* or *perforated spoons* are used to lift foods out of liquids.

Wooden spoons and paddles are made of unfinished tight-grained woods. Wood does not conduct or transfer heat well, so there is no threat of burning your fingers or changing critical temperatures of mixtures. Hardwoods are less likely than soft woods to pick up flavors and stains from food; they are also less likely to split or crack.

SPIDERS and **SKIMMERS** operate on a similar principle to spoons, but are very wide and quite flat, and have very long handles.

PADDLES are used in chocolate and confection work. They scrape clean easily, making it easier to work with mixtures that require careful blending and temperature control, such as chocolate.

TONGS act as an extension of your thumb and forefinger to lift, turn, and transfer hot food or other objects. They have two metal arms that are hinged together and spring-loaded. Some versions can be locked closed. Tongs range in size from 8 to 18 in/20 to 46 cm long.

Whips

WHIPS, also called **WHISKS,** are made from a number of thin wires bound together with a handle. In most whips, the wires are bent to make a closed loop. Whips are used to blend or whisk ingredients, to loosen and evenly distribute ingredients, and to make foams such as whipped cream or meringue. Handheld whips may have as few as two wires or as many as twenty. *Balloon whips* are sphere-shaped and have thin wires to incorporate air for making foams. *Flat whips* often have thicker wires. The thickness of the wires on a whip determines its flexibility and function. Whips range from 10 to 16 in/25 to 41 cm in length.

Spatulas and scrapers

RUBBER SPATULAS are used to scrape mixtures from bowls and into baking pans or other containers, to push foods through sieves, to fold ingredients together, and to spread batters and fillings into even layers. These hand tools have a flexible head of synthetic rubber, silicone, or similar material on the end of a handle. The head is shaped for a specific function and may be narrow or broad, with a pointed, angled, or blunt tip.

Spatulas made from high-temperature-resistant synthetic rubber or silicone can be used to stir and blend ingredients over direct heat, up to 600°F/315°C. Spatulas range in length from 10 in/25 cm to slightly longer than 20 in/51 cm.

PLASTIC BOWL SCRAPERS are like the head of a rubber spatula without a handle. They may be rounded on one side, and are efficient for scraping bowls completely clean, leaving no waste. Clean, sanitize, and air-dry rubber spatulas and bowl scrapers, either in a ware-washing machine or by hand.

METAL SPATULAS look something like knives. They have long metal blades, although the edge of the blade is not sharp, and typically have blunt, rounded ends. Baking spatulas have blunt ends and are made of thinner metal than knives. The handles can be made of polypropylene or wood. The length of the spatulas may range from 4 to 14 in/10 to 36 cm and the handle can be straight or offset. The offset handle is angled so that the blade is about ½ in/1 cm below the handle. Metal spatulas are sometimes referred to as *palette knives.*

Scoops and ladles

SCOOPS have bowls of varying sizes attached to handles. Some scoops have a spring-operated mechanism that pushes batters, ice creams, or other preparations cleanly from the bowl, making it easy to scale them consistently during production or service.

MELON BALLERS, also called *Parisian scoops,* may be round or oval, with straight or fluted edges. The scoop is twisted into the food to make a perfect ball or oval. They are most typically used to portion melon or other ingredients, such as ganache, that are soft enough to scoop but firm enough to hold their shape.

LADLES are used for portioning as well as for measuring pourable ingredients or mixtures such as sauces. The bowl of the ladle holds a specific volume, ranging from 1 fl oz/30 mL to 12 fl oz/360 mL. The bowl is attached to a long handle; some ladles are one piece, while the handles of others are a separate piece of metal attached to the bowl. Ladles with a 45-degree angle between the bowl and the handle work best in most instances.

Hand tools for sifting, straining, and puréeing

SIEVES and **STRAINERS** are used to sift and aerate dry ingredients, as well as to remove any large impurities from them. They are also used to drain or purée cooked or raw foods. Sieves and strainers are produced in a range of sizes to accommodate a variety of tasks. Some are small enough to dust a napoleon with confectioners' sugar, while others are large enough to strain several quarts of ice cream base. Strainers should be made of a heat-resistant material so that hot liquids can be strained immediately upon removal from the stovetop.

A *drum sieve* (or *tamis*) consists of a tinned-steel, nylon, or stainless-steel screen stretched over an aluminum or wood frame. Drum sieves are used for sifting or puréeing. A *champignon* (mushroom-shaped pestle) or a rigid plastic scraper is used to push the food through the screen. *Conical sieves* are used for straining and puréeing foods. The openings in the cone can be of varying sizes, from very large to very small, and depending on the size of the openings can be made either of perforated metal or of a mesh screen. A fine-mesh conical sieve is also known as a *bouillon strainer*. A pointed pestle is effective for pushing the ingredient or product through the mesh.

COLANDERS are stainless-steel, aluminum, or plastic bowls pierced with holes, used for straining or draining foods. Colanders are available in a variety of sizes. Some have loop handles and others have single handles; they may have feet or a round base.

A **FOOD MILL** has a curved blade that is rotated over a disk by a hand-operated crank. Most professional models have interchangeable disks with holes of varying fineness. An exception is the Foley food mill, which has a fixed mesh disk. (Note: Many mixing machines can be used as food mills with attachments that allow them to strain and purée foods.)

CHEESECLOTH is a light, fine-mesh cotton gauze frequently used along with or in place of a fine conical sieve to strain very fine sauces and similar items. It is also used for making sachets. Before use, cheesecloth should be rinsed thoroughly in hot and then cold water to remove any loose fibers. Cheesecloth also clings better to the sides of bowls, sieves, and the like when it is wet. Drape the wet cheesecloth in the bowl or colander and pour the liquid through it.

Tools for bread baking

A **LAME** is a thin-arced razor blade clamped into a small stainless-steel, wooden, or plastic handle. This specialized tool is used to score proofed yeast breads and rolls before they are baked. The blade must be very sharp and used in swift angled motions to create clean slices without pulling or tearing the dough.

A **BENCH KNIFE** has a thin, stiff rectangular steel blade set in a wooden or plastic handle to make it easier to grip and use. The blade, which is usually 6 in/15 cm wide, has no sharpened edges, making it useful for scraping, lifting, folding, and cutting dough.

A **COUCHE,** or heavy linen cloth, is used for proofing baguettes. The shaped dough is arranged in the folds of the cloth and left to proof; the folds and the fabric itself help to preserve the shape of the dough and keep it moist.

LOAF PANS, or tins, are oblong or rectangular pans used to bake pound cakes, other loaf cakes, and quick breads, as well as loaves of yeast-raised bread. They are made of glass or metal, with or without a nonstick coating. They are available in a wide range of sizes from large to mini. A *Pullman loaf* pan has a sliding cover and is used to prepare perfectly square finely grained slicing loaves (also known as *pain de mie*). The pans are typically made of tinned steel. A pan for a 1½-lb/680-g loaf is 4¼ in/10.60 cm wide by 13 in/33 cm long by 4 in/10 cm deep, and a pan for a 2-lb/907-g loaf is 4 by 16 by 4 in/10 by 41 by 10 cm.

BANNETONS, or dough-rising baskets (or *brotformen*), are round or oblong straw or willow baskets used for proofing, molding, and shaping bread. Some are lined with linen.

PEELS are large, flat wooden paddles designed for transferring doughs onto the deck of an oven. To use a peel, sprinkle it with cornmeal before loading the dough onto it. Use a quick jerking motion to slide the dough off the peel onto the deck of the oven.

Tools for pastries and cookies

ROLLING PINS are used to flatten and thin doughs such as yeasted bread, pastry, tart, and cookie doughs, puff pastry, and marzipan. They may be made of wood, metal, marble, or synthetic materials. Some pins have a smooth surface; others are textured or engraved to leave an impression of a pattern or picture on the dough. The task at hand will dictate the type of pin best suited for the job.

Clean and dry rolling pins thoroughly immediately after use. Don't soak wooden pins for extended periods. Pins made of porous materials such as wood may absorb the taste of soaps and detergents and transfer them to delicate doughs, so use only warm water and rub with a soft cloth to clean them.

Rod-and-bearing rolling pins consist of a cylinder made of hardwood with a steel rod inserted through the middle, which is fixed with ball bearings and handles at either end. These heavy pins are used to roll large amounts of stiff doughs. They are available in lengths up to 18 in/46 cm. Pins of this style are also available with a cylinder made of stainless steel or marble. These materials remain cool during rolling, which helps to keep pastry doughs at the proper working temperature.

Straight or *French rolling pins* are straight thick dowels. They were traditionally made of hardwood and now are also available in nylon and aluminum. These pins are typically 1¼ in/3.6 cm to 2 in/5 cm in diameter and 18 to 20 in/46 to 51 cm long. Because they don't have handles, they allow the baker or pastry chef to more easily feel the evenness and thickness of the dough while rolling it out.

Tapered or *"French" rolling pins* are thicker in the center, tapering evenly to both ends. They are usually about 2¾ in/7 cm in diameter at the center and 22 in/56 cm long. Their tapered design makes them most useful for rolling circles of dough to line pie and tart pans.

Marzipan and *basket-weave rolling pins* have a patterned surface to create impressions on marzipan used for décor. These pins are made as rod-and-bearing pins or simply as plain cylinders made of nylon or plastic.

Springerle rolling pins are made of wood or plastic resin. They have ornate and intricate pictures or designs in relief that are traditionally used to imprint springerle or gingerbread cookie doughs before baking. Springerle plaques are also available; the plaque is simply pressed into the rolled dough to imprint it before baking.

COOKIE CUTTERS are used to stamp out individual cookies from rolled doughs. They are made of thin sheet metal (tin, stainless steel, or copper) or plastic that has been molded or formed into shapes (circles, squares, hearts, animals, and so on). The cutting edges must be even and sharp enough to slice through the dough cleanly, and the cutters should be easy to grip.

A **DOUGH DOCKER** has a handle attached to a roller studded with 1- to 2-in/3- to 5-cm rounded spikes of metal or plastic. The docker is used to quickly and cleanly pierce airholes in rolled sheets of dough before baking blind (see page 515).

PASTRY BRUSHES may be made of soft, flexible nylon or unbleached hog bristles. The bristles are blunt cut and 2½ in/6 cm long; the brushes come in a variety of widths for various tasks. They should be washed and air-dried after each use.

A **PASTRY WHEEL** has a very sharp round nickel-plated blade, attached to a handle so that it rotates as it is pushed over rolled dough, making long, smooth, continuous cuts. The diameter of the wheel can range from 2 in/5 cm (for cutting thinner doughs) to 5 in/13 cm (for very thick doughs). The wheels may have straight or fluted edges.

Tools for décor work

PASTRY BAGS are available in various sizes. Many bakeshops and pastry kitchens have turned to disposable bags to prevent cross contamination and food-borne illness. Wash reusable bags, which are usually made of nylon or plastic-coated fabric, with plenty of hot water and enough soap to thoroughly degrease them. Rinse them well and air-dry completely before using again or storing.

PIPING TIPS are generally made of nickel-plated metal and are stamped with a numerical identification code. Although there are no industry-wide standards when it comes to numbering conventions for pastry tips, the numbers do have a relationship to the diameter of the tip's opening: the bigger the number, the larger the opening. Tips may have round, oval, star, or other-shaped openings. The differences in shape and diameter permit the pastry chef to apply a wide range of both simple and complex décor to cakes and pastries.

PARCHMENT PAPER CONES may be used for the same type of work as pastry bags and tips. Parchment paper can be purchased ready cut into triangles for rolling into cones, or pastry chefs may cut their own from sheets of parchment. The size of the cone depends on the size of

Sifting, straining, puréeing, and pastry tools.
TOP ROW: Very fine-mesh conical strainer, drum sieve, cheesecloth
MIDDLE ROW: Rod-and-bearing, textured aluminum French-style, springerle, aluminum French-style with a different texture, straight wood, rod-and-bearing, tapered French, and small straight wooden rolling pins
BOTTOM ROW: Mixing bowls, hotel pans, cutting boards

the parchment triangle. Cones may be rolled leaving the desired size of opening for piping, or the opening may be cut with scissors after the cone is tightly rolled. Different sizes and shapes of openings may be cut to yield a wide range of décor.

CAKE AND DECORATING COMBS are used to make designs by creating a pattern of lines in the icing coating a cake or pastry. They have teeth with different shapes and sizes. A *cake comb* is a thin triangle of stainless steel or plastic with different size tooth grooves on each side. *Rubber decorating combs* have stainless-steel frames to which the combs are attached for use.

WIRE COOLING RACKS are grates made of heavy-gauge chrome-plated steel wire. They have feet that raise them above the counter so that moisture does not collect under cooling baked goods. These racks can also be used for glazing and confectionery work, as they allow the excess glaze or chocolate to run off freely rather than pooling around the base of the confection, pastry, or cake.

TURNTABLES for cake decorating consist of a pedestal topped with a round platform 12 in/30 cm in diameter to hold the cake or pastry as you work. The turntable can be rotated around the rod in the center of the pedestal. Some chefs prefer instead to set cakes on cardboard circles (also called cake circles), which they balance on their fingertips and then gently rotate as they work; this method allows you to keep the cake at eye level while you work, but it does require a bit of coordination.

Tools for confectionery and décor work

Confectionery tools

A **HEAVY COPPER POT** with a pour spout is very useful for sugar cooking. These pots are available in 5-in/13-cm (holding 24 fl oz/720 mL), 6¼-in/15.60-cm (holding 50 fl oz/1.5 L), and 8-in/20-cm (holding 3 qt/2.88 L) diameters. Copper is preferred for sugar cooking because it conducts heat evenly.

A **FONDANT FUNNEL** is a metal or plastic funnel with a manually operated valve at the small opening. These funnels generally have a 1- or 2-qt/960-mL or 1.92-L capacity. They are useful for filling chocolates, making candies, and portioning sauces.

CHOCOLATE MOLDS are used for making figures, such as an Easter bunny, and for making filled chocolates. Clear rigid polycarbonate plastic molds are easier to care for and use than vacuum plastic molds or tin chocolate molds. However, vacuum plastic molds are relatively inexpensive. Tin molds may be both more elaborate and durable, but they must be thoroughly cleaned and dried to prevent rusting (see page 772 for more about working with chocolate molds).

DIPPING TOOLS include a variety of hand tools consisting of stainless- or nickel-plated steel prongs or loops fastened into wooden or plastic handles. They are designed for dipping any nut, fruit, or ganache or candy into a chocolate, syrup, or fondant coating.

CHOCOLATE CUTTERS are made of strong tinned steel or a fiberglass and plastic composite. They range from ¼ in/6 mm to 1½ in/4 cm in diameter and up to 1 in/3 cm in height. The cutting edges are very sharp. Cutters are often crafted and include animal, geometric, and floral shapes, and more. They are sold individually or in sets that can include as many as seventy-four pieces.

Confectionery and décor tools.

Chocolate cutters (oval, round, and diamond shapes), cake and decorating combs, caramel bars, chocolate molds, transfer sheet with hearts, more chocolate cutters, PVC rolling pin for gum paste, palette knife for décor work, ball roller for gum paste work, assorted styluses and cutters for gum paste work, chocolate dipping tools; blown sugar pump, silicone leaf molds for sugar work (center)

CARAMEL BARS, also called *confectioners' rulers,* are metal bars used for framing ganache or caramel while it is in "liquid" form so that it sets to a specific thickness and dimensions for cutting into individual pieces. They are made of nickel-plated steel and are available in lengths of 20 or 30 in/51 or 76 cm. The bars weigh 6 lb/2.72 kg each, giving them enough weight to contain the liquid confection, and range in height from ⅜ to ½ in/9 mm to 1 cm.

A **GUITAR** is a stainless-steel cutter that is used to precisely cut multiple squares, rectangles, triangles, or diamonds out of slabs of a variety of different semisoft confections, such as ganache, caramel, and gelées. Each set comes with at least three interchangeable cutting frames. It consists of a stainless-steel square or rectangular platform with linear spaces that adjust to fit different sized, interchangeable cutting frames that are threaded with stainless-steel wire that cuts through the confections.

TRANSFER SHEETS are acetate sheets with designs imprinted on them in plain or colored cocoa butter. They are used to imprint designs on chocolate.

Décor tools

MARZIPAN and **GUM PASTE MODELING TOOLS** are small hand tools with tips made from high-quality plastic or stainless steel, so they maintain their fine detailing. They come in a variety of shapes for crafting decorations and textures. They are sold individually and in sets of up to twelve.

An **AIRBRUSH** is used to spray food colors onto confections and cakes. It enables the decorator to create a wide range of shades and patterns, as well as to blend colors to produce special effects.

ACETATE SHEETS are shiny, flexible nonstick sheets used for chocolate work, as well as for molding various pastries and cakes. They are sold ten sheets to a box, 15⅞ by 24 in/41 by 61 cm each, as well as in rolls of varying lengths and widths.

To keep sugar soft and malleable so that it can be molded, formed, or blown, the pastry chef applies heat using various tools.

A **BLOW DRYER** can also be used to heat sugar and keep it soft for making pulled and blown sugar pieces. The best ones come with a stand so that they can be operated hands-free.

A **HEAT GUN** looks somewhat like a blow dryer, but it doesn't blow the air with as much force or produce as much heat. It can also be used to heat a bowl of chocolate to keep it in temper.

SUGAR LAMPS have a 24-in/61-cm neck on a weighted base, with an infrared heat bulb.

A **BLOWN SUGAR PUMP** is a rubber squeeze ball that fits in the palm of your hand, attached to an aluminum tip. It is squeezed to blow air into sugar to create a "balloon" that may be shaped and molded by hand as it is expanded. Sugar pumps are approximately 10½ in/26 cm long. A double-bulb pump has an extra air chamber in the rubber squeeze tube to better control the flow of air into the sugar.

Bakeware

Baking pans

HOTEL PANS are stainless-steel pans that come in a number of standard sizes. These pans have a lip that allows them to hang on storage shelves or steam tables made specifically to the same measurements. They are deeper than sheet pans, making them well suited for use as a hot water bath for baking custards and other preparations that require one.

SHEET PANS are flat, rimmed baking pans ranging in size from 17¾ by 25¾ in/45 by 66 cm (full-size sheet pan) to 12⅞ by 17¾ in/33 by 45 cm (half-size sheet pan) to 9½ by 13 in/24 by 33 cm (quarter-size sheet pan), with sides of 1 in/2.5 cm. Sheet pans are made of aluminum, with or without a nonstick coating. In the pastry kitchen or bakery, they are used for baking cookies and sheet cakes, among other things.

CAKE PANS are made in various materials, including glass, silicone, tinned steel, and aluminum (with or without a nonstick coating). They are available in diameters ranging from 2 to 24 in/5 to 61 cm and depths ranging from ¾ to 4 in/2 to 10 cm. Aluminum conducts heat and thus bakes the most evenly, making it the most common material for cake pans.

Bakeware, rings, and molds.
TOP SHELF: Assorted cake pans, parchment paper, madeleine molds, rolled silicone baking mats, tube pan, paisley-shaped ejection molds with a cutter; half sheet pans
MIDDLE SHELF: Copper sugar cooking pot, flexible mold in a pyramid shape, banetton, linen couche, tart and tartlet pans in aluminum pie pans
BOTTOM SHELF: Sauce pots and sauté pans, loaf pans, cake rings, hotel pans, cooling or glazing racks, full sheet pans

SPRINGFORM PANS are available in diameters from 6 to 12 in/15 to 30 cm, with depths ranging from 2½ to 3 in/6 to 8 cm. The ring of a springform pan is joined with a clip closure that creates tension when closed and holds the removable bottom in place. These pans are used for baking cakes that have a delicate structure, making it difficult to unmold them from a traditional rigid cake pan without damaging them. Most springform pans are aluminum.

TUBE PANS have a center tube, so they conduct heat through the center of the batter as well as from the sides and bottom. They are useful for evenly baking heavy batters without overbrowning the outside of the cake. Tube pans also work well for batters that need to bake quickly, such as angel food cake. They are usually made of thin aluminum, with or without a nonstick coating. They come in a range of sizes and may have fluted, molded, or straight sides.

PIE PANS are round pans with sloping sides, commonly made from glass, earthenware, or metal (with or without nonstick coating). They range from 8 to 10 in/20 to 25 cm in diameter and from 1½ to 3 in/4 to 8 cm deep.

TART PANS have fluted sides and removable bottoms. They may be round, square, or rectangular. They are made of tinned steel, with or without a nonstick coating. Round pans range from 4 to 13 in/10 to 33 cm in diameter and ¾ to 2¼ in/2 to 5 cm deep. Square pans are usually 9 in/23 cm across and 1 in/3 cm deep. Rectangular tart pans are 8 by 11 in/20 by 28 cm or 4½ by 14¾ in/11 by 38 cm and 1 in/3 cm deep.

TARTLET PANS are most commonly made of tinned steel, with or without a nonstick coating. They come in various shapes and may have removable or fixed bottoms. They range from 1⅛ to 4 in/3 to 10 cm in size (measured across the base). The sides, which may be plain or fluted, are from ½ to ⅝ in/1 to 1.50 cm high.

Rings and molds

CAKE RINGS are stainless-steel rings available in diameters ranging from 2¾ to 12 in/7 to 30 cm and heights from 1⅓ to 3 in/3.40 to 8 cm. They are used for molding cakes and individual pastries.

FLAN RINGS are straight-sided stainless-steel rings with rounded edges. They are used for baking and molding tarts and European-style flans. They are available in diameters ranging from 2½ to 11 in/6 to 28 cm and are ¾ in/2 cm high.

A **MADELEINE MOLD** is a tinned steel or aluminum sheet with scalloped impressions used for molding the small cakes called madeleines. They are available with or without a nonstick coating and have from twelve to forty cavities per mold. The impressions are available in two sizes—large and small.

FLEXIBLE SILICONE MOLDS are made of silicone-coated fiberglass. They come in many different sizes and shapes for making individual or multiserve desserts and pastries. They can be used for molding chocolate or frozen desserts, as well as for baking pastries and cakes.

MODULAR EJECTION MOLDS are acrylic molds available in different shapes and sizes; each mold comes with an extractor of matching shape and size. They are used to mold frozen, cold, or warm individual pastries that are made with ice creams, or stabilized mousses and creams.

Silicone mats and parchment paper

FLEXIBLE SILICONE BAKING MATS are able to withstand oven temperatures up to 500°F/260°C. They are used for lining sheet pans to give them a nonstick baking surface. They also provide a nonstick heat-resistant surface in candy making. The mats are about ⅛ in/3 mm thick and come in full sheet pan and half sheet pan sizes. They should be stored flat to prevent them from splitting.

PARCHMENT PAPER is grease-resistant, nonstick, heatproof, quick-release coated paper. It has endless uses in the bakeshop and pastry shop, such as lining baking pans and making piping cones for décor work. The paper can be reused until it becomes dark and brittle. It comes in large (full sheet pan size) sheets, in rolls, or precut for special uses such as piping cones or cake pan liners.

Stovetop pots and pans

SAUTÉ PANS (sometimes referred to as skillets) are shallow pans, wider than they are tall. The sides may be sloping (*sauteuse*) or straight (*sautoir*). The different materials used for these pans determine how a particular pan behaves over direct heat. Cast iron heats slowly but maintains an even heat. Stainless steel conducts heat quickly, making it more responsive to temperature changes. Sauté pans are made in a wide range of sizes, with or without nonstick surfaces.

CRÊPE and **OMELET PANS** are similar in construction to each other, though they have a smaller diameter (usually 7 or 8 in/18 or 20 cm in diameter) than sauté pans.

SAUCE POTS are deeper than they are wide, and may have straight or flared sides. They come in a number of standard sizes and are versatile pots, used for preparing anything from a reduction to a sauce or filling.

Large equipment

When working with large equipment such as mixers and sheeters, safety precautions must always be observed. Proper maintenance and cleaning should also be performed consistently in order to keep the equipment in good working order and to prevent injury.

If a machine is unfamiliar to you, ask for instruction in operating it safely; ask for help if you need it, and, if possible, run it while someone familiar with the machine can supervise you.

Many large machines have built-in safety features—always use them. Make sure that the machine is stable, lids are secure, and hand guards are used.

Mixing, chopping, and puréeing equipment

Mixing, chopping, and puréeing equipment has the potential to be extremely dangerous. The importance of observing all the necessary safety precautions cannot be overemphasized.

A **BLENDER** consists of a base that houses the motor, and a removable lidded jar with a propeller-like blade set in the bottom. The speed settings for the motor, of which there may be as many as eighteen or as few as two, are in the base. Jars are made of stainless steel, plastic, or glass, and come in several sizes. Blenders are excellent for puréeing, liquefying, and emulsifying foods because the tall narrow shape of the jar keeps the food circulating and in close contact with the blade.

An **IMMERSION BLENDER** (also known as a *hand blender, stick blender,* or *burr mixer*) is a long, slender one-piece machine that works like an inverted countertop blender. The top part of the machine houses the motor, which generally runs at just one speed, and a plastic handhold with an on/off button extends above the motor. On professional/commercial models, a stainless-steel driveshaft, which varies in length depending on the model, extends from the motor and is attached to the blade, which is immersed in the food being puréed. An immersion blender serves the same functions as a regular blender, but the advantage of an immersion blender is that even large batches of food can be puréed directly in the cooking

Large equipment.
LEFT TO RIGHT:
Immersion (or stick or burr) mixer, 20-qt/19.20- L planetary mixer, food processor

vessel. Some immersion blenders have magnetic bottoms, which allow you to stand them up in the pot and let them run unattended.

VERTICAL CHOPPING MACHINES (VCMs) operate on the same principle as a blender. A motor at the base is permanently attached to a bowl with integral blades. As a safety precaution, the hinged lid must be locked in place before the unit will operate. A VCM is used to grind, whip, emulsify, blend, or crush foods.

A **FOOD CHOPPER** (also called a *buffalo chopper*) is a piece of equipment in which the food is placed in a bowl that rotates when the machine is turned on; the food passes under a hood while blades rotate vertically to chop the food. Some units have hoppers or feed tubes and interchangeable disks for slicing and grating. Food choppers are available in floor and tabletop models. They are generally made of aluminum, with stainless-steel bowls.

A **FOOD PROCESSOR** houses the motor in its base. The work bowl is fitted over a stem and locked into place, along with the appropriate blade or disk. Foods are placed in the bowl or feed tube, the lid is placed on top and locked, and the motor turns the stem and the blade rapidly to grind, purée, blend, emulsify, crush, or knead, or, with special disks, slice, julienne, or shred foods.

Mixers

PLANETARY MIXERS are also known as *vertical mixers*. They get their name from the motion of the mixing attachment, which moves in a path like that of a planet rotating on its axis while revolving around the sun inside the stationary mixing bowl. These mixers come with three standard attachments—a paddle, a whip, and a dough hook—and have multiple uses.

SPIRAL MIXERS are stationary mixers, meaning that the bowl, rather than the mixing attachment, rotates. These mixers have bowls that tilt and only one attachment, a spiral-shaped hook. They are used exclusively for mixing bread doughs. They work the dough quickly but gently enough to control the amount of friction.

OBLIQUE MIXERS, also known as *fork mixers,* are similar in construction to spiral mixers except that their attachment is a fork rather than a spiral. They are also used exclusively for bread doughs and work the dough gently to minimize the amount of friction, as do spiral mixers.

Ovens

CONVENTIONAL OVENS can be located below a range top. Food (in or on pans) is placed on wire racks that may be set at different heights within the oven. The heat source (either gas or electric) is located at the bottom, underneath the floor of the oven, and heat is conducted through the floor.

DECK OVENS normally consist of two to four wide, flat decks stacked one above another, though single-deck models are available. Food is placed directly on the floor of a deck oven rather than on a wire rack as is done in a conventional oven. Some deck ovens have ceramic or firebrick bases; these are used for breads and pastries that require direct intense bottom heat to develop the crust. Deck ovens usually are gas or electric, although charcoal- and wood-burning units are also available. Like conventional ovens, the heat source for deck ovens is located underneath the deck, and heat is conducted through the deck.

STEAM-INJECTION OVENS vent steam into the oven as breads and rolls bake. The steam helps to develop the crust and ensures that yeast-raised breads stay moist long enough to expand properly during baking.

CONVECTION OVENS are available in gas or electric models in a range of sizes. In a convection oven, fans force hot air to circulate around the food, cooking it evenly and quickly.

COMBI OVENS, either gas or electric, combine the advantages of steaming and convection ovens. They can be used in steam mode, hot-air convection mode, or heat/steam (combi) mode. Combi ovens are available in a number of different configurations.

A **MICROWAVE OVEN** uses electricity to generate microwave radiation, which cooks or reheats foods very quickly. Microwave ovens are available in a variety of sizes and power ratings. Some models can double as convection ovens.

Proofers

For professional bread bakers in a high-volume operation, a proofer is an essential piece of equipment. Proofers maintain the most desirable environment for yeast growth. In this way, they help to maintain production schedules and ensure that items are of uniform quality. Some proofers have refrigeration capabilities, making them able to retard yeast growth. Proofers like this are known as proofer/retarders. Retarders also help with production in the same ways as a proofer, by maintaining production schedules and quality standards. They are available as stationary walk-ins or as mobile boxes.

Refrigeration equipment

A **WALK-IN** is the largest type. It usually has shelves arranged around the walls, and some walk-ins are large enough to accommodate rolling carts for additional storage. Some units have pass-through or reach-in doors to facilitate access to frequently required items. It is possible to zone a walk-in to maintain different temperature and humidity levels for storing various foods. Walk-ins may be situated in the kitchen or outside the facility. If space allows, walk-ins located outside the kitchen can prove advantageous, because deliveries can be made at any time without disrupting service.

A **REACH-IN REFRIGERATOR** may be a single unit or part of a bank of units. Reach-ins are available in many sizes. Units with pass-through doors are especially helpful for the pantry area, so that salads, desserts, and other cold items can be retrieved by the wait staff as needed.

ON-SITE REFRIGERATION UNITS include refrigerated drawers or undercounter reach-ins, which hold foods on the line at the proper temperature. They eliminate unnecessary travel, which can create a hazard during peak production periods.

PORTABLE REFRIGERATION is provided by refrigerated carts that can be stationed as needed in the kitchen.

DISPLAY REFRIGERATION CASES are generally used to showcase dessert items or pastries in a restaurant dining room, or cakes and pastries for sale in a shop.

Ice cream machines

Simple **HAND-CRANKED** or **ELECTRIC ICE CREAM MACHINES** have a motor that either turns the paddle within the cooling chamber or rotates the chamber around the paddle. The bowl is usually removable and must be frozen for at least 12 hours before use. Bowls range from 6 to 9 in/15 to 23 cm in diameter and up to 6½ in/16 cm tall. These machines can produce up to a quart of ice cream per batch.

COMMERCIAL ICE CREAM MAKERS have built-in refrigeration units to make large-scale production of ice cream and other frozen confections possible. There are two basic types: continuous and batch. With a *continuous ice cream freezer,* the ice cream base is fed continuously into the machine at a high rate of speed. This type of machine allows for control of overrun, viscosity, and temperature of the finished product. *Batch ice cream freezers* churn a specific amount of ice cream base at one time. Batch ice cream freezers are available in two basic configurations: *horizontal* and *vertical.* Horizontal machines have a cylinder that lies horizontally within the unit. They incorporate a considerable amount of air into the product. Vertical machines have a vertical cylinder within the unit for churning and freezing the base. They incorporate the least amount of air into the product as the mix is scraped and blended.

Professionals and their tools

Most equipment is manufactured by a number of different companies. There will be differences in quality, the number of additional features, shape, size, and cost. Good-quality tools are often more expensive, but they last longer and perform better than poorly made tools. Over time, you will want to accumulate both the basic and more specialized tools of your trade for your own kit or, perhaps, to outfit a shop or kitchen of your own. You can read about tools of all sorts in a variety of industry publications and learn about them at trade shows. Consult Appendix D (page 908) for a list of recommended readings on equipment.

Some of the tools and equipment used in professional kitchens and bakeshops today are the same as those used centuries ago. Others are recent innovations and rely on advanced technology such as computer chips or infrared. The ability to select, use, and safely maintain all equipment is fundamental to the smooth and efficient operation of a kitchen or bakeshop. As new pieces of equipment are developed and introduced, it is your responsibility to learn how they might benefit your operation and your development as a baking and pastry arts professional.

chapter four

Advanced baking principles

*t*here are dozens of scientific principles at work in baking. As an introduction to the topic of food science, this section provides an overview of the most basic of these principles.

Baking science

Food science is an exacting study, dedicated to discovering and clarifying the complex reactions involved in food preparation. A general knowledge of how basic ingredients can be changed through the effects of temperature, agitation, and acids or alkalis gives the baker or pastry chef the freedom to develop new items. It also aids the chef in problem solving, such as changing a formula's original cooking method, finding a suitable shortcut for a long or complex recipe, or substituting one ingredient for another. These challenges may be inspired by a need to liven up or update a menu, cut costs, streamline production, or introduce a new technique or ingredient.

Books and articles on these topics should be part of every baker's or pastry chef's professional reading (see Appendix D, "Readings and Resources," page 908).

Basic baking ingredients

Flour, eggs, water, fat, and usually sugar are necessary in all baking and pastry goods. The ways in which these ingredients interact with one another and other ingredients during mixing and baking dictate the qualities of the end product. For the purposes of understanding how these ingredients influence a finished product, they can be divided into two categories: *stabilizers* and *liquefiers*.

Stabilizers

A stabilizer is any ingredient that helps to develop the solid structure, or "framework," of a finished product. Of the five basic baking ingredients, flour and eggs act as stabilizers. Flour and eggs both lend structure (and nutritional value) to a finished product, but the way each of these ingredients acts is different.

Flour represents the bulk of most of the formulas made in any bakeshop. It acts as a binding and absorbing agent, and it may be thought of as the "backbone" of the majority of bakeshop formulas. It is the gluten (the protein component in flour) that builds structure and strength in baked goods. Different types of flours have different gluten-to-starch ratios, which will create vastly different results in the texture, appearance, and flavor of the final product if used in the same formula. A flour with a higher gluten content will result in a tougher crumb, whereas a flour with a lower gluten content will result in a more tender crumb.

Eggs lend additional stability during baking. They influence the texture and crumb as well; by facilitating the incorporation and distribution of air, they promote an even-grained and fine texture. Eggs also have leavening power. As eggs—whole, yolks, or whites—are whipped, they trap air, which will expand when heated, resulting in a larger and lighter product.

In addition, eggs help to develop flavor and aroma in a product, mostly from the fat and nutrients contained in the yolk. Egg yolks also contribute to a drier finished product, and egg whites add volume and moisture.

Liquefiers

The remaining three of the five basic baking ingredients—water (along with milk and other liquids), fats, and sugar—act as liquefiers. That is, they help to loosen or liquefy a dough or bat-

proteins in flour

Gluten is formed by the proteins present in wheat flour (wheat is the only grain that forms measurable amounts of gluten, making it an indispensable grain in the kitchen or bakeshop). Flour gives strength to a batter or dough and acts to absorb the bulk of the moisture in most baked goods. As the flour takes up water, gluten strands begin to form. To further develop these strands, making them more cohesive and elastic, the mixture is agitated (mixed). Gluten development is essential for certain baked goods such as breads, in which a somewhat chewy texture is desirable; in other baked goods such as cakes, which should be tender and moist, excessive gluten development is a flaw. The differences among desired outcomes for the textures of different types of baked goods led to the development of flours with varying gluten levels.

While the gluten level of the flour has a very significant role in the final texture of a product, the amount of mixing a dough or batter undergoes, particularly if the flour has a moderate to high percentage of gluten, will also have a marked impact.

Gluten is composed of two distinct proteins: *glutenin* and *gliadin*. When flour is mixed with water, the glutenin and gliadin begin to join together (with the water intermingled) to form strands or sheets of gluten. The glutenin provides the elasticity; the gliadin, the extensibility. The formation of these strands provides the structure for many baked goods. If a flour with too little (or no) gluten is used in bread making, the bread will not rise. Yeast is the catalyst for risen bread, but it is also necessary to have well-developed gluten to trap the gases produced by the fermenting yeast for bread to rise.

ter. Some liquefiers such as sugar may actually tighten or bind a dough when first added, but their interaction with other ingredients ultimately tenderizes or loosens the dough or batter.

Water acts to dilute or liquefy water-soluble ingredients such as sugar and salt. It also facilitates the even distribution of sugar, salt, and yeast in a dough if these ingredients are mixed thoroughly with the water before introducing the remaining ingredients in the formula. In bread making, water is typically the primary liquefier. A bread formula with a higher percentage of water results in a more open-grained and softer crumb. In addition, water helps to develop the proteins in flour, necessary for proper leavening. Water also acts as a leavener as it changes to steam and expands.

hydration of a dough or batter

In the baking process, liquid provides the moisture necessary for hydration of the ingredients. The moisture aids in the development of the gluten in the flour, in gelatinization of starches, and in dissolving other ingredients to achieve even distribution and consistency. Typically, the liquid used in baking and pastry formulas is water or milk, or a combination of the two.

Products made with water are less expensive and have a longer shelf life. Those made with milk contain more nutrients and are more flavorful. The sugars present in milk also help these products develop a golden brown color in the oven.

Milk performs many of the same functions as water, but because of its additional components (fat, sugar, minerals, and protein), it serves a number of other functions and adds flavor as well. As the sugar (lactose) in milk caramelizes, it gives a rich color to the product's surface, and can also aid in development of a firm crust. The lactic acid in milk has a tightening effect on the proteins in flour, which serves to increase stability, resulting in a product with a fine grain and texture.

Fats also fall into the category of liquefiers. If the total amount of fat added to a dough or batter equals no more than 3 percent of the weight of the finished dough or product, it acts to increase the elasticity of the proteins in the flour, thereby helping the bread or other product

shortening agents

BUTTER

Butter is made from cow's milk. It is approximately 80 percent fat, 10 to 15 percent water, and 5 percent milk solids. The advantages of using butter in baking are its flavor and lower melting point.

LARD

Lard is rendered pork fat. It is most often used in conjunction with other fats.

OILS

Oil is seldom used in baked goods. Solid fat is more typically a requirement for baking formulas that are made using the creaming method (see page 62); it is necessary for aeration, which lends leavening power and structure to the finished baked item.

SHORTENINGS

Solid shortenings are hydrogenated vegetable fats created for baking. They are made by injecting hydrogen gas into purified oil as it is heated. Hydrogenated fats will have varied melting temperatures depending on the purpose for which they were manufactured. Most are designed to cream well, and thus have a higher melting point.

To create emulsified shortening, mono- and diglycerides are added to shortening, resulting in increased absorption and retention of moisture. Recipes using emulsified shortening have higher ratios of milk, sugar, fat, and eggs to flour, resulting in richer cakes that are less prone to drying out. Emulsified shortening is typically used when the quantity of sugar in a recipe is equal to or greater than the amount of flour.

additional functions of fats and oils in baking

- IMPROVE EATING QUALITIES. Products are more tender and less chewy; in addition, some fats or oils add flavor.

- IMPROVE APPEARANCE. Shortening agents do not dissolve in doughs or batters, but instead become evenly dispersed and incorporate air, resulting in a soft crumb in breads and flakiness in pastries, which make them more appealing to the eye.

- IMPROVE KEEPING QUALITY. Fats delay the retrogradation, or breakdown, of starches, which helps to delay staling.

- ADD FOOD VALUE. Fats constitute a concentrated source of energy.

- ADD VOLUME. Used in conjunction with the creaming method, fats can facilitate the incorporation of air, which expands during baking, into a batter, contributing to leavening.

58

additional functions of sugar in baking

- **AIDS IN THE CREAMING PROCESS.** The crystalline structure of granulated sugar makes it an effective agent for the incorporation of air into batters mixed by the creaming method. The incorporated air is then held by the shortening agent, the other main ingredient in any creaming-method formula.

- **RETAINS MOISTURE AND PROLONGS FRESHNESS.** Sugar absorbs moisture from other ingredients as well as from the atmosphere, thereby helping to keep finished products moist and delay drying out or staling.

- **IMPARTS COLOR TO CRUSTS.** Through caramelization and the Maillard reaction (for more information on browning reactions, see page 63), sugar aids in the development of deep golden crust color during baking, which also adds flavor.

- **CONTRIBUTES FOOD VALUE.** Sugar in moderate amounts can supply some of the carbohydrate requirements of a normal diet.

to expand during baking. In baking, fats and oils are also classified as *shortening agents,* a term derived from their ability to split the long, elastic gluten strands that can toughen doughs and batters. This tenderizing effect renders the strands more susceptible to breaking, or shortening, resulting in a more tender and less dense crumb.

Although sugar has a tendency to tighten up a mixture when it is first incorporated, by its nature it attracts moisture, a characteristic that causes it to ultimately loosen or liquefy a batter or dough. For the gluten in flour to develop, it needs moisture; because sugar attracts moisture, it acts to inhibit gluten development in the batter or dough, preventing it from becoming too tough or elastic. Furthermore, when used in the correct proportion, sugar can help to maintain the elasticity of the gluten strands present in a dough or batter. With maximum elasticity, the gluten can expand more easily so the item is more efficiently leavened, allowing for the proper development of volume and the creation of a moist and tender crumb. During baking, sugar also interacts with the starch component of flour to delay its gelatinization, enabling batters and doughs to stay softer longer, allowing greater spread and rise before setting.

Leaveners

To leaven is to raise, or to make lighter. There are several ways to accomplish this in baking: with yeasts (also known as *organic leaveners*), with *chemical agents* such as baking powder or baking soda, or with steam (*mechanical leavening*). Each method is best suited for specific applications and produces very different results. The different leavening methods may be used alone or in conjunction with one another (as in croissants, for example) to yield different effects.

Yeast

Yeast is a living organism that needs suitable conditions to thrive. Commercially sold baker's yeast is of the strain *Saccharomyces cerevisiae,* which has been determined to be the best suited for bread baking.

Yeast needs warmth, moisture, and food (carbohydrates) to begin fermenting. By definition, fermentation is the anaerobic respiration of microorganisms. The process converts carbohydrates into alcohol and carbon dioxide. The carbon dioxide acts to leaven a dough or batter as the gas is trapped in the web of protein (gluten) strands that developed during the mixing process. The alcohol acts to tenderize the gluten strands, improving the overall texture of the product; it cooks out during baking, leaving no undesirable flavor.

The fermentation process is important in building the internal structure and flavor of the dough. Given the proper environment, yeast cells will continue to ferment until they run out of food, or until the by-products of fermentation begin to poison them and they die. For these reasons, as well as the necessity of maintaining production schedules, it is easy to see why time is an important element in making quality yeast-raised products. Consequently, it is important to understand how the fermentation of yeast can be controlled.

Yeast cells are sensitive to the temperature of the environment. The ideal temperature for fermentation is between 80° and 90°F/27° and 32°C. Lower temperatures will retard or arrest yeast development. Temperatures at or above 105°F/41°C will also slow fermentation. Yeast dies at 138°F/58°C.

While sugar provides an immediate food source for yeast to begin fermentation, too much sugar can act to slow the fermentation process. High concentrations of sugar can have the same dehydrating effect as salt, causing yeast cells to die.

Salt plays many roles in baking, but its contributions are most evident in bread baking. It helps to slow yeast growth and, when used in the correct proportions, will help to control the rate of fermentation. However, too much salt can damage or kill the yeast by dehydrating the cells, resulting in a heavier, denser product. For this reason, salt should never come in direct contact with yeast.

Chemical leaveners

Baking soda and baking powder are the primary chemical leaveners. With these leaveners, an alkaline ingredient—the baking soda or baking powder (which also contains an acid and a starch)—interacts with an acid. The alkali and acid, when combined with a liquid, react to produce carbon dioxide, which expands during baking, leavening the dough or batter.

other functions of salt in bread baking

- STRENGTHENS THE GLUTEN STRANDS.

- CONTRIBUTES TO ELASTICITY, which in turn acts to improve the texture of the final product.

- IS AN IMPORTANT FLAVOR COMPONENT IN BREADS. It enhances both the subtle flavors in the other ingredients and those that result from the fermentation process. Without salt, bread tastes flat.

acid, base, and pH

The pH of a solution is the measure of its acidity or alkalinity. A pH of 7 denotes a neutral solution, which indicates a balance between the negative and positive ions within the solution. If a solution has a pH higher than 7, it is alkaline or base and has a positive charge. If a solution has a pH lower than 7, it is acidic and has a negative charge. Compounds that are charged are unstable, meaning that they have a natural affinity to become neutral. They may break down on their own when heat is applied, or they may break down in reaction to the presence of a compound or element that has the opposite charge.

Baking soda, or sodium bicarbonate, is a common leavening agent for cakes, quick breads, and cookies. Sodium bicarbonate is an alkali and is, therefore, positively charged and seeks to be in a neutral state. (For more information on alkalis, see "Acid, Base, and pH," above.) As sodium bicarbonate reacts with an acid, it breaks down and releases carbon dioxide, which is captured in the dough or batter and causes it to rise (leaven) as it is baked. To break down and be relieved of its charge, sodium bicarbonate requires the presence of an acidic ingredient, such as chocolate, vinegar, a cultured dairy product, fruit juice, or molasses.

Baking powder is a mixture of sodium bicarbonate, an acid, and cornstarch. The sodium bicarbonate (soda) will react with the acid to create carbon dioxide when combined with a liquid, and the carbon dioxide acts to leaven the product. The cornstarch in baking powder absorbs moisture and keeps the acid and alkaline components from reacting with each other before they are mixed into a dough or batter.

There are two types of baking powder: *single-acting* and *double-acting.* Single-acting baking powder contains sodium bicarbonate and cream of tartar (called a *dry acid*). Because cream of tartar is easily dissolved, this type of baking powder needs only to be combined with a liquid for the two substances to react and release the carbon dioxide that will leaven the dough or batter. Double-acting baking powder combines sodium bicarbonate with dry acids that have different solubility rates. One of the acids is easily soluble and will begin to react with the sodium bicarbonate when wet. The other needs heat for it to completely dissolve, delaying its reaction until the product is in the oven.

Mechanical leavening

Mechanical leavening occurs when air or moisture, trapped during the mixing process, expands as it is heated during baking in pockets created by cooking proteins, causing "balloonlike" expansion that aids in the leavening process. This method of leavening occurs when one of three distinct methods is used: foaming, creaming, or lamination.

The foaming mixing method requires that eggs, eggs yolks, or egg whites be beaten to incorporate air until they form a foam. This foam is then added to the batter, folded in so as to disrupt as few of the air bubbles as possible and maintain the volume of the foam. The air trapped in these bubbles then expands during baking and causes the product to rise.

The creaming method of mixing blends fat and sugar together to incorporate air. The creamed mixture is then combined with the remaining ingredients, and as the product bakes, the air trapped during the creaming process expands and leavens it.

In lamination, alternating layers of fat and dough are created through different folding and rolling techniques (for more information on lamination techniques, see "Laminated Doughs" in Chapter 9, page 217). When the dough is baked, the fat melts, releasing water in the form of steam, which acts to leaven the dough. The steam fills the pockets left by the melting fat and expands, causing the product to rise; the fat then "fries" the dough so that the spaces are retained.

Sweeteners

Sweeteners come in many forms, and are an integral part of most baked goods and pastries. They serve a number of important functions including flavor, moisture, leavening, extended shelf life, and color.

Monosaccharides and oligosaccharides

A monosaccharide, or single sugar, is the basic building block of all sugars and starches. Fructose and dextrose are both monosaccharides. These are the simplest sugars. When fructose and dextrose are bonded together, they form a disaccharide, or double sugar, called sucrose—that is, table sugar. Many monosaccharides linked together in long chains are called polysaccharides. Starches such as cornstarch are made up of such chains, thousands of saccharides long. Although starches are also made up of sugar molecules, they do not taste sweet, and they do not dissolve in water when they are in long chains.

Oligosaccharides lie somewhere in between table sugar and the starches present in cornstarch and flour that we are so familiar with. They are chains of sugar molecules—not so long as those in starches, but longer than those in sugars. Like starches, they do not taste sweet; unlike starches, they dissolve in water. All of these terms are vital to understanding corn syrup and glucose, because they are the ingredients in our humble bucket of glucose syrup.

Crystallization of sugar

Crystallization is a process that occurs when sugar is deposited from a solution. This type of deposition allows the sugar molecules to assume their characteristic geometric form. Sugar crystallization is influenced by many things: saturation levels, agitation, temperature, cooling, seeding, invert sugar, and acid. Through manipulation of these factors, the process of crystallization may be controlled to create the typical crystalline and noncrystalline structures used in the bakeshop or pastry kitchen, such as fondant, rock candy, hard candies, and caramel.

In order for sugars to crystallize out of solution, the solution must be sufficiently saturated for precipitation to occur. Typically, in a bakeshop or pastry kitchen, sugar will be dissolved in water through the introduction of heat, which facilitates the dissolving and incorporation of more sugar. The solution may then be heated to a specific temperature, thereby evaporating water and serving to further increase the density, or saturation, of the solution. The more saturated, or "densely packed," a solution, the more likely and more easily it will begin to crystallize. Crystallization occurs as the particles in solution collide with one another; hence agitation is a key contributor to the process. If agitation is initiated while the solution is still hot, large crystals will form as molecules become attached at a slower rate. As the mixture cools, crystals form more readily, promoting rapid growth of many tiny crystals when stirred or otherwise agitated. If the mixture is allowed to cool without agitation and is then stirred, it will crystallize rapidly but will form small crystals rather than large ones.

The introduction of a "seed" will cause crystallization. A seed is anything, from whole sugar crystals to air bubbles to a skewer (as when making rock candy), that will act as a surface for the sugar crystals to adhere to and grow on.

Controlling or delaying crystallization allows the sugar solution to be manipulated or pulled without graining. It allows the confectioner to make chewy caramels that will not crystallize.

Certain ingredients may be introduced into a sugar solution to inhibit crystallization. A small amount of glucose syrup or another invert sugar is often added to the solution. The molecular structure of glucose and other invert sugars is different from that of sucrose. This difference means the invert sugar will inhibit crystallization by getting in the way of the sucrose molecules that start to attach to each other as they begin to crystallize out of the solution. A second way to inhibit crystallization is to introduce a small amount of an acid into the solution. When sucrose (table sugar) is boiled with dilute acids, the acids will cause the inversion of some of the sucrose molecules. The resultant invert sugars will interfere with the crystallization process just as glucose syrup does.

Hygroscopic properties of sugar and salt

Sugar and salt are both hygroscopic, meaning they will readily take up water under certain conditions of humidity. In baked products, they act to retain moisture, extending shelf life. In items such as hard candies, however, this attraction of moisture acts to begin to break down the structure of the candy or other item, causing it to become soft and sticky.

Browning reactions

There are two types of processes that create browning in food: caramelization and the Maillard reaction. Browning occurring from either of these processes results in a rich color and enhances both the flavor and aroma of the food. *Caramelization* occurs when sucrose is present, and only at high temperatures. As sugar is heated, it melts and then begins to break down. As the temperature continues to increase, different compounds will form and then break down, creating different flavors and colors throughout the cooking process. The *Maillard reaction* (for example, the browning of bread crust in the oven) occurs between the reducing sugars and proteins; it can occur at low temperatures more slowly, and at high temperatures over short periods of time. It is a complex browning reaction that results in the particular flavor and color of foods that do not contain much sugar.

saturated and supersaturated sugar solutions

Saturation and supersaturation are vital concepts for the confectioner, as they are directly linked with the process of crystallization. At a given temperature, a specific quantity of water can dissolve only a finite quantity of sugar. The warmer the water, the more sugar it can dissolve. When no more sugar can be dissolved in a certain amount of water at a certain temperature, the solution is said to be *saturated*. When a saturated solution is then heated to evaporate some of the water, the solution becomes *supersaturated*. Supersaturated solutions contain a higher concentration of sugar than could have been initially dissolved in the same amount of water. Supersaturated solutions are delicate systems. Sugar molecules are attracted to each other, and with so many of them in such a small amount of liquid, they are quite likely to join together. This action results in the formation of crystals.

invert sugar

The term *invert sugar* refers to a sugar (sucrose or table sugar) whose optical or refractory properties have been altered. This altering occurs when it is boiled together with a dilute acid, such as cream of tartar (in solution), lemon juice, vinegar, and so on. In the presence of the acid, the sucrose breaks down into its two components, dextrose and fructose.

There are also naturally occurring invert sugars, such as honey. However, many, if not most, of these natural invert sugars contain other components, or impurities, which make them ill-suited for use in the sugar-cooking and candy-making processes, as the impurities typically burn at a much lower temperature than is required to cook the sugar.

benefits of glucose syrup

- MAKES COOKED CONFECTIONS SOFTER AND EASIER TO WORK WITH. Added to cooked sugar in the proper amount, it will increase its elasticity.

- IS A HUMECTANT. That is, when it is added to baked goods, it helps to retain moisture, resulting in a moister product and a longer shelf life.

- IS USUALLY LESS SWEET THAN SUGAR. For example, 42 DE corn syrup is only about 60 percent as sweet as cane sugar. By substituting this syrup for a percentage of the sugar in a formula, the sweetness of baked goods or frozen desserts can be decreased without sacrificing the textural advantages afforded by sugar.

Thickeners

Sauces, puddings, fillings, mousses, and creams can be thickened or stabilized by many ingredients, including gelatin, eggs, and starches such as flour, cornstarch, tapioca, and arrowroot. These thickeners may be used to lightly thicken a mixture, such as a sauce, or to produce something set to a sliceable consistency, like Bavarian cream.

The quantity and type of thickener, as well as how it is stirred or otherwise manipulated, will determine the properties of the finished product. For example, if a custard is cooked over direct heat and stirred constantly, the result will be a sauce that pours easily. Baked in a water bath with no stirring at all, the same custard base will set into firm custard.

Gelatinization of Starches

A Gel Has Not Formed   A Gel Has Formed

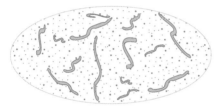
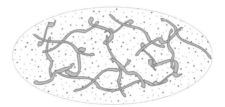

Unbound hydrocolloids in a continuous phase of water

A gel is formed when hydrocolloids bind to form a three-dimensional network that traps water, preventing motion.

When starch granules suspended in water are heated, they begin to absorb liquid and swell, causing an increase in the viscosity of the mixture. This reaction, known as *gelatinization,* allows starches to be used as thickening agents.

Polysaccharides

Polysaccharides are starches that are commonly used as thickening agents in preparations such as sauces and fillings. They are complex carbohydrates composed of two types of starch molecules, both of which are made of long chains of dextrose. One type, known as *amylose,* exists in long linear chains, and the other, *amylopectin,* in dendritic (branched) patterns. The ratio in which the two types of starch molecules occurs in a starch will dictate its use. The higher the percentage of amylose, the more prone the starch is to gel. The more amylopectin present, the more the starch will act to increase viscosity or thicken without causing a gel to form. Starches high in amylose are derived from grain sources such as wheat and corn, while starches with a high percentage of amylopectin are derived from roots and tubers, such as tapioca.

It is only after a starch in liquid is heated that the granules can absorb the liquid and begin to thicken it. As the starch is heated, the molecules within each granule begin to move faster and their bonds begin to loosen, allowing liquid to work its way into the normally tightly bound granules. As the granules absorb the liquid, they swell, making it easier for more liquid to be absorbed. All starches have different temperatures at which they begin to thicken.

Retrogradation

Starches high in amylose that have been gelatinized and then undergo freezing, refrigeration, or aging may begin to *retrograde,* or revert to their insoluble form. This reaction causes changes in food texture and appearance (staling in breads and similar products; cloudiness or graininess in sauces, puddings, and creams). But not all starches have the same tendency toward retrogradation. It is important to choose the correct starch for the application. For example, when making pies to be frozen, it is best to use modified food starch to thicken the filling, rather than cornstarch.

GELLING AND THICKENING AGENTS AND THEIR USES

STARCH	SOURCE	CHARACTERISTICS	USES
Modified food starches	Various	Flavorless; freezes well	Fruit fillings
Cornstarch	Grain	Prone to retrogradation; must be heated to a boil to remove flavor	Sauces, puddings, and fruit fillings
Flour	Grain	Prone to retrogradation; must be heated to a boil to remove flavor	Puddings and fruit fillings
Arrowroot	Tuber	Flavorless; makes a translucent paste that will set to a gel; if over-agitated, overcooked, or used in too large a quantity, may make the product stringy and gooey	Soups and sauces
Tapioca/Cassava	Root	Doesn't set to a gel; doesn't retrograde	Puddings and fruit fillings
Potato	Tuber	If overagitated, overcooked, or used in too large a quantity, may make the product stringy and gooey	Kosher baking
Agar-agar	Sea vegetable	Strong thickening properties; sets to a firm gel; has a very high melting point	Gelées and vegetarian desserts
Pectin	Citrus skins, apples, and other high-pectin fruits	Requires a low pH and high sugar content to form a gel	Jellies, jams, preserves, and gelées
Gelatin	Animal	Melts below body temperature; boiling may reduce its strength; enzymatic reactions with certain fruits will prevent setting	Mousses, aspics, and gelées
Eggs	Animal	If not used in conjunction with a starch, will curdle when over-cooked; yolks create a soft velvety set, whites create a resilient set	Custards, custard sauces, and puddings

enzymes and gelatin

When working with gelatin, it is important to remember that there are a few fruits that contain proteases—enzymes that will break down the collagen in gelatin and not allow it to set (gel). Among these fruits are kiwi, pineapple, papaya, honeydew melon, and banana. To use these fruits in any gelatin-based application, you must first allow the fruit or fruit purée to simmer for 2 to 3 minutes or use and ultra-pasturized purée, to destroy all of the protease enzymes, before adding the gelatin.

Pectin

Pectin is a carbohydrate derived from the cell walls of certain fruits. Some common sources of pectin are apples, cranberries, currants, quince, and the skins of citrus fruits, all of which are high in pectin. Pectin may be used as a gelling agent or as a thickener. To gel, it requires the correct balance of sugar and an acid. Pectin molecules have a natural attraction to water molecules; when pectin is put in solution alone, the molecules will become surrounded by water molecules and will not gel the solution. The addition of an acid interrupts this attraction, and sugar further acts to draw the water away from the pectin molecules, allowing them to connect together and form a three-dimensional network.

Gelatin

Gelatin is typically used to produce light, delicate foams (such as Bavarian creams, mousses, and stabilized whipped cream) that set so they may be molded or sliced. Available in both granulated and sheet form, gelatin must first be rehydrated, or bloomed, in a cool liquid. Once it has absorbed the liquid, it is then gently heated to melt the crystals, either by adding the softened gelatin to a hot mixture, such as a custard sauce, or by gently heating it over simmering water.

Gelatin, a protein derived from the bones and connective tissue of animals, is composed of molecules that attract water. When they first come in contact with water, they swell; then, as they are heated, they completely dissolve. As the mixture cools, the proteins join together to form a three-dimensional web (much as in coagulation) that holds in the moisture. This system is called a gel. When used in making a mousse or Bavarian, the gelatin solution is beaten into a mixture containing many air pockets. The proteins found in the gelatin are thus stretched to hold the air as well as the moisture, creating a stabilized product. Gelatin is also used commercially in the production of ice cream, as it interferes with formation of ice crystals.

Eggs as thickeners

Whole eggs, egg yolks, or whites may be used, alone or in conjunction with other thickeners, to thicken a food. Eggs act to thicken through the coagulation of proteins. As their proteins begin to coagulate, liquid is trapped in the network of set proteins, resulting in a smooth, rather thick texture. This is known as a *partial coagulation,* in which the proteins hold moisture; if the mixture were cooked or baked further, the proteins would fully coagulate and expel water, causing the product to curdle.

Uncoiling and denaturing proteins

At the molecular level, natural proteins are shaped like coils or springs. When natural proteins are exposed to heat, salt, or acid, they denature—that is, their coils unwind. When proteins denature, they tend to bond together, or coagulate, and form solid clumps. An example of this is a cooked egg white, which changes from a transparent fluid to an opaque solid. As proteins coagulate, they lose some of their capacity to hold water, which is why protein-rich foods give off moisture as they cook, even if steamed or poached. Denatured proteins are easier to digest than natural proteins.

Most commonly, proteins are denatured through the application of an acid, agitation, or heat. The addition of one or more of these elements will act to alter the structure of the protein by disrupting the bonds that shape its molecules. This change in structure permits the protein to behave in a different manner. For example, the proteins will extend in length, so that they are more likely to come in contact with one another and bond, forming a web (or coagulating). In this way proteins become useful as a thickening agent that can be used in many applications where starches may not, such as in frozen desserts.

Emulsions

An emulsion is a system of two immiscible liquids (liquids that are unable to be mixed together to form a true solution) that appears to be a completely homogenous mixture but is in fact what is known as a two-phase system, having a dispersed phase and a continuous phase. When mixed to combine, one of the liquids breaks up into minute droplets (dispersed phase) and the other remains as a matrix for the droplets to be dispersed in (continuous phase). There are two types of emulsions, temporary and permanent.

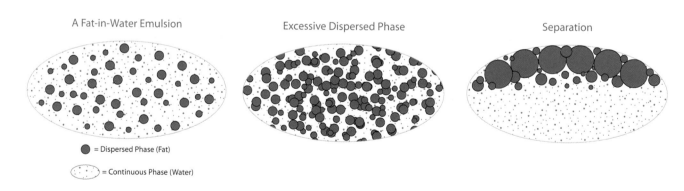

A Fat-in-Water Emulsion   Excessive Dispersed Phase   Separation

● = Dispersed Phase (Fat)

⬭ = Continuous Phase (Water)

LEFT: An emulsion is a suspension of the dispersed phase in the continuous phase.

MIDDLE: An excess of the dispersed phase forces the droplets together.

RIGHT: The result is separation; the droplets are no longer discrete, but coalesce into large drops that do not remain in suspension.

A *temporary emulsion* is one that will separate into two distinct layers in a short period of time. In a *permanent emulsion,* the two liquids do not separate as easily because of the presence of a third element, known as an *emulsifier.* Emulsifiers are naturally occurring substances that are attracted to both fat and water and thus facilitate maintaining a stable emulsion between two immiscible liquids.

Tempering chocolate

Tempered chocolate has a glossy finish, snap, and creamy texture. Cocoa butter, the fat found in chocolate, may set into one of four types of crystals: beta, gamma, alpha, or beta prime. Only the beta crystals are stable and yield the gloss, snap, and proper texture. To temper chocolate, all of the crystals must first be fully melted. For the chocolate to maintain gloss and snap, as it is cooling it must form stable beta crystals. They can be caused to form by gradually reducing the temperature of the melted chocolate until it is at 80°F/27°C, while applying constant agitation. To encourage the formation of the beta crystals, some additional, already tempered chocolate (known as a *seed*) may be added to the mixture.

All chocolate you buy is in temper, if it has been properly stored since its time of manufacture. But if you are going to dip centers, mold it, or use it for other confectionery or décor work, you will need to melt it and temper it again. See Chapter 21, Chocolates and Confections, for more discussion of tempering.

Healthy baking

Today's consumer is increasingly concerned about high-calorie, high-fat foods. Pastry chefs must be aware of this concern and look for ways to curb the fat and calorie content of their pastries and desserts when the market calls for it.

One method pastry chefs are using to cut back on calories is substituting fruit purées (such as apples, dates, and prunes) for pure sugar in their products. This will increase the sugar and moisture content of the product, but it may also change the baking methods. Yogurt is another product pastry chefs are using in their baked goods. Replacing oil or butter with yogurt in a recipe will change the acid, protein, and moisture content of the item, while adding a leavening agent and affecting taste and color. (Strain the yogurt through a cheesecloth overnight to get rid of any lumps or impurities.)

Methods to decrease fat are also quite common and easy for pastry chefs. For example, instead of using whole milk, substitute buttermilk, skim milk, evaporated milk, or even water. A cheesecake can lose fat if it is made with reduced-fat cream cheese rather than regular cream cheese. Fat-free sour cream is available to substitute for regular sour cream. Replacing some eggs with egg whites is another way to cut back on fat; in many instances two egg whites can be used in place of one whole egg.

There are challenges when making substitutions in healthy baking. The moisture content of your dough or batter might change. Baking time and temperature may also have to be adjusted. But the old adage that products with less calories and fat do not taste as good as the original is no longer true.

Gluten-free baking

Celiac disease is an autoimmune disorder of the small intestine that affects one in 133 people in the United States. It is caused by a reaction to a gluten protein found in wheat, rye, and barley and anything derived from these grains. Oats also make this list because they often contain gluten as a result of cross contamination from packaging. In the most extreme cases, these grains could be deadly for a celiac. The only effective treatment is a gluten-free diet.

As celiac disease has become more common, pastry chefs have worked to develop baked goods without the use of wheat, rye, barley, or oats. When making gluten-free products, it is important to make sure to use clean tools and surfaces, have separate cooking utensils, and, if possible, work in a room where wheat, barley, rye, or oats have not been present. It is imperative that no contamination occur when making gluten-free products.

Since wheat flour is not used in gluten-free baking, chefs must use different stabilizers as substitutes. Some of the possibilities include rice flour, potato starch, tapioca starch, whey powder, bean flours, guar gum, and xanthan gum. Other ingredients that are safe to use are distilled alcohols and extracts, rather than fermented ones.

The strides made to allow celiac disease sufferers to enjoy breads and cakes and cookies are an important milestone in how far baking has come in the past decades.

Baking for vegans

A *vegan* is a person who consumes only products of the plant kingdom, excluding eggs, dairy, and any other animal products (including honey).

Baking for vegans may seem nearly impossible, but many products have been developed that are vegan-friendly. Products that can be used for vegan baking include soy milk, soy margarine, vegetable oil, soy yogurt, tofu, flaxseed paste, arrowroot starch, whole wheat flour, oats, mashed sweet and regular potatoes, tahini and nut butters, and agar-agar.

chapter five

Food and kitchen safety

the importance of storing and preparing food properly cannot be overemphasized. In addition to the precautions necessary to guard against food-borne illness, care must also be taken to avoid accidents involving staff or guests. Practicing and monitoring safe procedures will keep both your employees and customers safe from food-borne illness and injury.

Food-borne illness

Foods can serve as carriers for many different illnesses. Food-borne illnesses are caused by *adulterated foods* (foods unfit for human consumption). The source of contamination can be chemical, physical, or biological.

Food contaminants

Food can serve as a carrier of many different illnesses. The most common symptoms of food-borne illnesses include abdominal cramps, nausea, vomiting, and diarrhea, possibly accompanied by fever. The symptoms may appear within a matter of hours after consumption of the affected food, but in some cases several days may elapse before onset. In order for food-borne illness to be officially declared an outbreak, it must involve two or more people who have eaten the same food, and it must be confirmed by health officials.

Food-borne illnesses are caused by adulterated foods (foods unfit for human consumption). The severity of the illness depends on the amount of adulterated food ingested and, to a great extent, the individual's susceptibility. Children, the elderly, and anyone whose immune system is already under siege will generally have much more difficulty than a healthy adult in combating a food-borne illness.

The source of the contamination affecting the food can be chemical, physical, or biological. Insecticides and cleaning compounds are examples of *chemical contaminants* that may accidentally find their way into foods. *Physical contaminants* include such things as bits of glass, rodent hairs, and paint chips, which might cause injury as well as illness. Careless food handling can mean that a plastic bandage or an earring could fall into the food and result in illness or injury.

Biological contaminants account for the majority of food-borne illnesses. These include naturally occurring poisons, known as *toxins,* found in certain wild mushrooms, rhubarb leaves, and green potatoes, among other plants. The predominant biological agents, however, are disease-causing microorganisms known as *pathogens,* which are responsible for up to 95 percent of all food-borne illnesses. Microorganisms of many kinds are present virtually everywhere, and most are helpful—even essential—or harmless; only about 1 percent of microorganisms are actually pathogenic.

Food-borne illnesses caused by biological contaminants fall into two subcategories: intoxication and infection. *Intoxication* occurs when a person consumes food containing toxins from bacteria, molds, or certain plants and animals. Once in the body, these toxins act as poison. Botulism is an example of an intoxication. In the case of an *infection,* the food eaten by an individual contains large numbers of living pathogens. These pathogens multiply in the body and usually attack the gastrointestinal lining. Salmonellosis is an example of an infection. Some food-borne illnesses have characteristics of both an intoxication and an infection. *E. coli* 0157:H7 is an agent that causes such an illness.

The specific types of pathogens responsible for food-borne illnesses are fungi, viruses, parasites, and bacteria.

FUNGI, which include molds and yeast, are more adaptable than other microorganisms and have a high tolerance for acidic conditions. They are more often responsible for food spoilage than for food-borne illness. Fungi are important to the food industry in the production of cheese, bread, and wine and beer.

VIRUSES do not actually multiply in food, but if through poor sanitation practice a virus contaminates food, consumption of that food may result in illness. Infectious hepatitis, caused by eating shellfish harvested from polluted waters (an illegal practice) or by poor hand-washing practices after using the bathroom, is an example. Once in the body, viruses invade a cell (called the *host cell*) and essentially reprogram it to produce more copies of the virus. The copies leave the dead host cells behind and invade still more cells. The best defenses against food-borne viruses are purchasing shellfish only from certified waters and maintaining good personal hygiene.

PARASITES are pathogens that feed on and take shelter in another organism, also called a host. The host receives no benefit from the parasite, and in fact suffers harm, or even death, as a result. Amoebas and various worms, such as *Trichinella spiralis,* which is associated with pork, are among the parasites that contaminate foods. Different parasites reproduce in different ways. An example is the parasitic worm that exists in the larval stage in muscle meats. Even after it is consumed by a human being or another animal, its life cycle, and reproductive cycle, continue. When larvae reach adult stage, the fertilized female releases more eggs, which hatch and travel to the muscle tissue of the host, and the cycle continues.

BACTERIA are responsible for a significant percentage of biologically caused food-borne illnesses. In order to better protect food during storage, preparation, and service, it is important to understand the classifications and patterns of bacterial growth. Bacteria are classified by their requirement for oxygen, by the temperatures at which they grow best, and by their spore-forming abilities. *Aerobic bacteria* require the presence of oxygen. *Anaerobic bacteria* do not require oxygen and may even die when exposed to it. *Facultative bacteria* are able to function with or without oxygen. In terms of sensitivity to temperature, bacteria fall into the following categories:

1. **MESOPHILIC** bacteria grow best between 60° and 100°F/16° and 38°C. Because the temperature of the human body as well as of commercial kitchens falls within that range, mesophilic bacteria tend to be the most abundant and the most dangerous.

2. **THERMOPHILIC** bacteria grow most rapidly between 110° and 171°F/43° and 77°C.

3. **PSYCHROPHILIC** bacteria prefer cooler temperatures, between 32° and 60°F/0° and 16°C.

Bacterial growth and hazardous foods

Many bacteria reproduce by means of fission: One bacterium grows and then splits into two bacteria of equal size. These bacteria divide to form four, the four form eight, and so on. Under ideal circumstances, bacteria will reproduce every twenty minutes or so. In about twelve hours, one bacterium can multiply into sixty-eight billion bacteria, more than enough to cause illness.

Certain bacteria reproduce via sporulation: They are able to form endospores, which protect them against adverse circumstances such as high temperatures or dehydration. Endospores allow an individual bacterium to resume its life cycle if favorable conditions should recur.

Bacteria require three basic conditions for growth and reproduction: a protein source, readily available moisture, and a moderate pH level. The higher the amount of protein in a food, the greater its potential as a carrier of a food-borne illness. The amount of moisture available in a food is measured on the water activity (Aw) scale; this scale runs from 0 to 1, with 1 representing the Aw of water. Foods with a water activity above 0.85 can support bacterial growth.

A food's relative acidity or alkalinity is measured on the scale known as pH. A moderate pH—a value between 4.6 and 10 on the scale, which ranges from 1 to 14—is best for bacterial growth, and most foods fall within that range. Adding a highly acidic ingredient, such as vinegar or citrus juice, to a food can lower its pH and extend its shelf life, making it less susceptible to bacterial growth.

Many foods meet the three conditions necessary for bacterial growth and are therefore considered to be potentially hazardous. Meats, poultry, seafood, tofu, and dairy products (with the exception of some hard cheeses) are all categorized as potentially hazardous foods. Foods do not have to be animal-based to contain protein, and cooked rice, beans, pasta, and potatoes are also potentially hazardous, as are sliced melons, sprouts, and garlic-and-oil mixtures.

Food that contains pathogens in great enough numbers to cause illness may still look and smell normal. Disease-causing microorganisms are too small to be seen with the naked eye, so it is usually impossible to visually ascertain that food is adulterated. And because the microorganisms—particularly the bacteria—that cause food to spoil are different from the ones that cause food-borne illness, food may be adulterated and still have no "off" odor.

Although cooking will destroy many of the harmful microorganisms that may be present, careless food handling after cooking can reintroduce pathogens that will grow even more quickly, without competition for food and space from the microorganisms that cause spoilage. Although shortcuts and carelessness do not always result in food-borne illness, inattention to detail increases the risk of an outbreak that may cause serious illness or even death. The expenses a restaurant can incur as the result of an outbreak of food-borne illness can be staggering. In addition, negative publicity and loss of prestige are blows from which many restaurants can simply never recover.

Avoid cross contamination

Many food-borne illnesses are a result of unsanitary handling procedures in the kitchen. Cross contamination occurs when disease-causing elements or harmful substances are transferred from a contaminated surface to a heretofore uncontaminated one. To avoid cross contamination, adhere to the following practices.

Good personal hygiene is one of the best defenses against cross contamination. The employee who reports for work when he or she has a contagious illness or an infected cut on his or her hand puts every customer and other employees at risk. Any time your hands come in contact with a possible source of contamination, especially your face, hair, eyes, and mouth, they should be thoroughly washed before you continue work.

Food is at greatest risk of cross contamination during the preparation stage. Ideally, separate work areas and cutting boards should be used for raw and cooked foods. Equipment and cutting boards should always be cleaned and thoroughly sanitized between uses. For example, before cutting a piece of pork on the same surface you used to cut chicken, it is important to clean and sanitize not only the cutting surface, but also your hands, the knife, and the sharpening steel. Wiping cloths for this purpose should be held in a double-strength sanitizing solution and placed near each workstation to encourage use.

All food must be stored carefully to prevent contact between raw and cooked items. (See "Receive and Store Foods Safely," page 75.) Do not handle ready-to-eat foods with bare hands. Instead, use a suitable utensil (deli tissue, spatula, tongs, or the like) or single-use food-handling gloves (intended to be used only for a single task and replaced before beginning a new task).

proper hand washing

To cut down on cross contamination and avoid spreading illness, wash your hands as often as you need to, and wash them correctly. The 1999 Food and Drug Administration (FDA) Model Food Code states that hands and forearms should be washed using soap and 110°F/43°C water for twenty seconds. Wash your hands at the beginning of each shift and each new task, after handling raw foods, after going to the bathroom, and after handling money or other nonfood items, to mention just a few points in the workday.

First wet your hands, then apply soap. Use enough soap to work up a good lather. Use a nail brush to clean under your nails and around the cuticles if necessary, and scrub well. (It takes about ten seconds to sing "Happy Birthday"; in order to be sure you have lathered for twenty seconds, try singing this song to yourself twice while washing your hands.) Rinse your hands thoroughly in warm water, and dry them completely using paper towels.

Keep foods out of the danger zone

An important weapon against pathogens is the observance of strict time and temperature controls. Generally, the disease-causing microorganisms found in foods need to be present in significant quantities in order to make someone ill. (There are exceptions, however, *E. coli* 0157:H7 being one.) Once pathogens have established themselves in a food source, they will either thrive or be destroyed, depending upon how long foods are in the danger zone of 41° to 140°F/5° to 60°C.

There are pathogens that can live at all temperature ranges. For most of those capable of causing food-borne illness, the friendliest environment is one with temperatures from 41° to 140°F/5° to 60°C—the danger zone. Most pathogens are either destroyed or will not reproduce at temperatures above 140°F/60°C. Storing food at temperatures below 41°F/5°C will slow or interrupt the cycle of reproduction. (It should be noted that intoxicating pathogens may be destroyed during cooking, but any toxins they have already produced are still there.)

When conditions are favorable, pathogens can reproduce at an astonishing rate. Therefore, controlling the time during which foods remain in the danger zone is critical to the prevention of food-borne illness. Foods left in the danger zone for longer than four hours are considered adulterated. Additionally, one should be fully aware that the four-hour period does not have to be continuous, but is in fact cumulative—which means that the meter starts running again each time the food enters the danger zone. Once the four-hour period has been exceeded, foods cannot be recovered by heating, cooling, or any other method.

Receive and store foods safely

It is not unheard of for foods to be delivered to a food-service operation already contaminated. To prevent this from happening to you, inspect all goods to be sure they arrive in sanitary conditions. Make a habit of checking delivery trucks for signs of unsanitary conditions such as dirt or pests. If the truck is a refrigerated or freezer unit, check the ambient temperature inside to see that it is adequate. Use a thermometer to check the temperature of the product as well. Check expiration dates, and verify that foods have the required government inspection and certification stamps or tags. Randomly sample bulk items, as well as individual packages within cases. Reject any goods that do not meet your standards.

Once you have accepted a delivery, move the items immediately into proper storage conditions. Break down and discard cardboard boxes as soon as possible, because they provide nesting areas for insects, especially cockroaches.

Refrigeration and freezing units should be cleaned regularly. They should be equipped with thermometers to make sure that the temperature remains within a safe range. Although in most cases chilling will not actually kill pathogens, it does drastically slow down their reproduction. In general, refrigerators should be kept at between 36° and 40°F/2° and 4°C, but quality is better served if certain foods can be stored at specific temperatures:

Meat and poultry	32° to 36°F/0° to 2°C
Fish and shellfish	30° to 34°F/−1° to 1°C
Eggs	38° to 40°F/3° to 4°C
Dairy products	36° to 40°F/2° to 4°C
Produce	40° to 45°F/4° to 7°C

Using separate refrigerators for each of these categories is ideal, but if necessary, a single unit can be divided into sections. The front of the box will be the warmest area, the back the coldest.

Reach-in and walk-in refrigerators should be put in order at the end of every shift. Before it is put in the refrigerator, food should be properly cooled, stored in clean containers, wrapped, and labeled clearly with the contents and date. Place drip pans beneath raw foods to catch drips and prevent splashing, and store raw products below and away from cooked foods to prevent cross contamination by dripping. Because air circulation is essential for effective cooling, avoid overcrowding the box, and make sure the fan is not blocked.

Do not stack trays directly on top of food: This will reduce the amount of air that can circulate and may also result in cross contamination. Use the principle of "first in, first out" (FIFO) when arranging food, so that older items are in the front.

Dry storage is used for foods such as canned goods, spices, condiments, cereals, and staples such as flour and sugar, as well as for some fruits and vegetables that do not require refrigeration and have low perishability. As with all storage, the area must be clean, with proper ventilation and air circulation. Foods should not be stored directly on the floor or against the walls, and there must be adequate shelving to prevent overcrowding. The FIFO system should be practiced here as well, and all containers should be labeled with a date. Cleaning supplies should be stored in a separate place from foods.

Hold cooked and ready-to-serve foods safely

Keep hot foods hot and cold foods cold. Use hot-holding equipment (steam tables, double boilers, bain-maries, heated cabinets or drawers, chafing dishes, and so on) to keep hot foods at or above 140°F/60°C. (Do not use hot-holding equipment for cooking or reheating; it cannot be counted on to raise the temperature of the food through the danger zone quickly enough.)

Use cold-holding equipment (ice or refrigeration) to keep cold foods at or below 41°F/5°C. If using ice, the foods should be in a container of some sort, not directly on the ice. Use a perforated insert and drip pan to allow melting ice to drain away from foods.

Cool foods safely

One of the leading causes of food-borne illness is improperly cooled foods. Cooked foods that are to be stored need to be cooled down to below 41°F/5°C as quickly as possible. Cooling to below 41°F/5°C should be completed within four hours or less, unless you use the two-stage cooling method endorsed by the FDA in its 1999 Model Food Code. In the first stage of this method, foods should be cooled down to 70°F/21°C within two hours; in the second stage, foods should reach 41°/5°C or below within an additional four hours, for a total cooling time of six hours.

The proper way to cool hot liquids is to transfer them to a metal container (plastic containers insulate rather than conduct heat), then place the container in an ice water bath that reaches the same level as the liquid inside the container. Bricks or a rack set under the container will allow the cold water to circulate better. Stir the liquid in the container frequently so that the warmer liquid at the center mixes with the cooler liquid at the edges of the container, bringing the overall temperature down more rapidly. Stirring also discourages potentially dangerous anaerobic bacteria from multiplying at the center of the mixture.

Semisolid and solid foods should be refrigerated in single layers in shallow containers, to allow greater surface exposure to the cold air and thus quicker chilling. For the same reason, cut large cuts of meat or other foods into smaller portions, cool to room temperature, and wrap before refrigerating.

Reheat foods safely

Improperly reheated foods are another frequent cause of food-borne illness. When foods are prepared ahead and then reheated before serving, they should move through the danger zone as rapidly as possible and be reheated to at least 165°F/74°C for at least fifteen seconds. As long as proper cooling and reheating procedures are followed each time, foods may be cooled and reheated more than once.

Food handlers must use the proper methods and equipment for reheating potentially hazardous foods, which should be brought to the proper temperature over direct heat (burner, flattop, grill, or conventional oven) or in a microwave oven. A steam table will adequately hold reheated foods above 140°F/60°C, but it will not bring foods through the danger zone quickly enough to be used for reheating them.

Always use an instant-read thermometer to check temperatures; carefully clean and sanitize the thermometer after each use.

Thaw frozen foods safely

Frozen foods can be safely thawed in several ways. Once thawed, they should be used as soon as possible, and for optimal quality and flavor should not be refrozen. The best—though slowest—method is to allow the food to thaw under refrigeration. The food, still wrapped, should be placed in a shallow container on a bottom shelf to prevent any drips from contaminating other items stored nearby or below.

If there isn't time to thaw foods in the refrigerator, covered or wrapped food can be placed in a container under running water that is approximately 70°F/21°C or below. Use a stream of water strong enough to wash loose particles of ice off the food, and do not allow the water to splash onto other food or surfaces. Be sure to clean and sanitize the sink both before and after thawing.

Individual portions that are to be cooked immediately can be thawed in a microwave oven. Liquids, small items, or individual portions can be cooked without thawing, but larger pieces of solid or semisolid foods that are cooked while still frozen become overcooked on the outside before they are thoroughly done throughout.

Do not thaw food at room temperature; it is an invitation to pathogens.

Serve foods safely

The potential for transmitting food-borne illness does not end when the food leaves the kitchen. Restaurant servers should also be instructed in good hygiene and safe food-handling practices. They should wash their hands properly after using the bathroom, eating, smoking, touching their face or hair, and handling money, dirty dishes, or soiled table linens (particularly napkins). Ideally, some servers should be designated to serve foods and others should be responsible for clearing used dishes and linens.

Servers should touch only the edges and bottoms of plates as they transport them from kitchen to dining room. When setting tables, they should never touch the parts of flatware that will come in contact with food, and they should handle glassware by the stems or bases only. Servers should clean side stands, trays, and tray stands before the start of each shift and as necessary during service. They should always fold napkins on a clean surface and handle used napkins as little as possible; table linens should only be used once. And they should serve all foods using the proper utensils; ice and rolls should be handled with tongs, never with fingers.

Hazard analysis critical control points (HACCP)

HACCP is an acronym that is fast becoming commonly used in food service and food safety. It stands for Hazard Analysis Critical Control Points, which is a scientific state-of-the-art food safety program originally developed for astronauts. HACCP takes a systematic approach to the conditions that are responsible for most food-borne illnesses. It is preventive in nature: It attempts to anticipate how food safety problems are most likely to occur and takes steps to prevent them from occurring.

The HACCP system has been adopted by both food processors and restaurants, as well as by the FDA and USDA. At this time, there is no mandate that HACCP must be used by food-service establishments. However, instituting such a plan may prove to be advantageous on a variety of levels.

If you decide to begin instituting HACCP procedures in your restaurant or bakeshop, you should know that an initial investment of time and human resources is required. It is becoming obvious, however, that this system can ultimately save money and time, as well as improve the quality of food you are able to provide your customers.

The heart of HACCP lies in the following seven principles:

1. **ASSESS THE HAZARDS.** The first step in an HACCP program is a hazard analysis of each menu item or recipe. It requires a close look at the process of putting that menu item together, beginning with the delivery of the starting ingredients. Every step in the process must be looked at by designing a flowchart that covers the period from "dock to dish." In addition, it is best to have all persons involved in the flow of the food present when setting up an HACCP program, for the person receiving the food on the loading dock may have an important bit of information that can help set up the program and identify the true flow of food.

The types of hazards you should be concerned with are the biological, chemical, or physical conditions that could cause a food to be unsafe for consumption. The biological hazards are typically microbiological, though the possibility of toxicity (such as from poisonous mushrooms) should not be ignored. Microbiological hazards include bacteria, viruses, and parasites.

2. **IDENTIFY THE CRITICAL CONTROL POINTS.** After you have established a flow diagram and identified the potential hazards, the next step is to identify the critical control points (CCPs). From the moment food is received at your food-service establishment, and throughout production, you have the ability to control what happens to that food (including not accepting it from your vendor if it does not meet your specifications). You must decide which of the different control points (steps) are critical ones. One of the most difficult aspects of putting together an HACCP program is making sure not to overidentify these critical control points, because that could lead to a cumbersome amount of paperwork. In addition, a profusion of CCPs could obscure the real control issues. A critical control point is the place in the utilization of the food in a restaurant or bakeshop where you have the ability to eliminate or reduce an existing hazard or to prevent or minimize the likelihood that a hazard will occur. According to the 1999 FDA Food Code, a critical control point is "a point or procedure in a specific food system where loss of control may result in an unacceptable health risk."

The cooking step, as a rule, is a critical control point. Other critical control points are usually associated with time-temperature relationships (thawing, hot-holding, cold-holding, cooling, and reheating). Some other considerations that should be addressed in identifying a critical control point are as follows: At this step, can food be contaminated? Can the contaminants increase or survive? Can this hazard be prevented through some kind of intervention (commonly referred to as "corrective action")? Can hazards be prevented, eliminated, or reduced by steps taken earlier or later in the flow? And, can you monitor, measure, and document the CCP?

3. **ESTABLISH CRITICAL LIMITS AND CONTROL MEASURES.** Critical limits are generally standards for control measures at each critical control point. Many will have already been established by local health departments, but you may want to establish new critical limits for your food operation that exceed the regulatory standard, or establish a new standard that meets with health department approval. (The 1999 FDA Food Code refers to these possibilities as "variances.")

By way of example, an established critical limit for the cooking step in preparing a chicken dish is a 165°F/74°C final internal temperature. This critical limit prevents the possibility of a patron contracting salmonellosis. If you were to hold this chicken on the line before actual service, it would have to be kept at 140°F/60°C to prevent any proliferation of pathogenic microbes. Holding would be a step in the process that would be considered critical.

Control measures are what you can do ahead of time to facilitate the achievement of your critical limit. For example, when preparing to cook chicken to 165°F/74°C, you should make sure your equipment is working well. Before you roast chicken, you should preheat the oven. If you are going to monitor the temperature of the chicken with a thermometer, you should make sure it is accurately calibrated. You also have to know how to cook and how to take internal temperatures. Therefore, training is often a control measure too.

4. **ESTABLISH PROCEDURES FOR MONITORING CCPS.** The critical limits for each critical control point must identify what is to be monitored. You must also establish how the CCP will be monitored and who will do it. For example, one employee may be designated to monitor the temperature of the roasting chicken. For each batch, the employee should be instructed to check the internal temperature of the largest chicken and the one in the middle of the pan.

   Monitoring helps improve the system by allowing for the identification of problems or faults at any particular point in the process. This allows for more control or improvement in the system because it provides an opportunity to take corrective action if a critical limit was not met. Monitoring lets you know if the desired results were achieved. In the example of the chicken, was it indeed cooked to an acceptable temperature?

5. **ESTABLISH CORRECTIVE ACTION PLANS.** If a deviation or substandard level occurs for any step in the process, a plan of action must be identified. For example, if the roasted chicken was held at an incorrect temperature (120°F/49°C) for too long in a steam table, the corrective action would be to discard it. If frozen fish arrives from the purveyor with a buildup of ice, indicating that it has been defrosted and refrozen again, the fish should be rejected. Specific corrective actions must be developed for each CCP, because the handling of each food item and its preparation can vary greatly from one kitchen to the next.

6. **SET UP A RECORD-KEEPING SYSTEM.** Keep documentation on hand to demonstrate whether or not the system is working. Recording events at CCPs ensures that critical limits are met and preventive monitoring is occurring. Documentation typically consists of time-temperature logs, checklists, and forms.

   It is important to keep the forms readily accessible and easy to fill out. Keeping a temperature log on a clipboard at a grill station and recording internal temperatures of one out of every ten orders that go out to customers would be a realistic responsibility for a line cook. Having reliable and accurately calibrated thermometers on hand is also necessary. Do not make the logs or forms too complicated or cumbersome: This could encourage "dry lab," that is, the falsifying of records.

7. **DEVELOP A VERIFICATION SYSTEM.** This step is essentially establishing procedures to ensure that the HACCP plan is working correctly. Have a supervisor, executive chef, or outside party verify that the plan is working. If procedures are not being followed, try to find out what modifications you can make so the plan works better. The most difficult part of putting an HACCP program plan together is going through it the first time. After the initial paperwork, it essentially involves monitoring and recording. As your employees become accustomed to filling out the forms correctly, they will be establishing positive behaviors that promote food safety. These new behaviors will naturally spill over into the preparation of other recipes, making the development of an HACCP program plan for each new dish easier.

The way in which an individual operation may apply these principles will vary. Adapt the system as necessary to fit your establishment's style. Chain restaurants, for example, receive and process foods differently from à la carte restaurants.

Clean and sanitize

Cleaning refers to the removal of soil or food particles, whereas *sanitizing* involves using moist heat or chemical agents to kill pathogenic microorganisms. For equipment that cannot be immersed in a sink, and for equipment such as knives and cutting boards during food preparation, use a wiping cloth, soaked in a double-strength sanitizing solution and then wrung out, to clean and sanitize the equipment between uses. Iodine, chlorine, or quaternary ammonium compounds are common sanitizing agents. Check the manufacturer's instructions for procedures for use.

Small equipment, tools, pots, and tableware should be run through a ware-washing machine or washed manually in a three-compartment sink. The many kinds of ware-washing machines all use some sanitation method, such as very hot water (usually 180° to 195°F/82° to 91°C) or chemical agents.

Hard water, which contains high levels of iron, calcium, or magnesium, may interfere with the effectiveness of detergents and sanitizing agents and may also cause deposits that can clog machinery. Water-softening additives can prevent these problems.

After sanitizing, equipment and tableware should be allowed to air-dry completely; using paper or cloth toweling could result in cross contamination.

Keep out pests

Careful sanitation procedures, proper handling of foods, and a well-maintained facility all work together to prevent a pest infestation. Besides being destructive and unpleasant, rats, mice, roaches, and flies may harbor various pathogens. Take the following steps to prevent infestation:

- Clean all areas and surfaces thoroughly.
- Wipe up spills immediately and sweep up crumbs.
- Cover garbage, and remove it every four hours.
- Elevate garbage containers on concrete blocks.
- Keep food covered or refrigerated.
- Check all incoming boxes for pests and remove boxes as soon as items are unpacked.
- Store food away from walls and floors, and maintain cool temperatures and good ventilation.
- Prevent pests from entering the facility by installing screened windows and screened self-closing doors.
- Fill in all crevices and cracks, repair weak masonry, and screen off any openings to buildings, including vents, basement windows, and drains.
- If necessary, consult a professional exterminator.

Kitchen safety

The following safety measures should be practiced.

Health and hygiene

Maintain good general health; have regular physical and dental checkups. Do not handle food when ill. Cover your face with a tissue when coughing or sneezing, and wash your hands afterward. Attend to cuts or burns immediately. Keep any burn or break in your skin covered with a clean waterproof bandage, and change it as necessary.

Observe the fundamentals of good personal hygiene. Keep hair clean and neat, and contain it if necessary. Keep fingernails short and well maintained, without polish. Keep your hands away from your hair and face when working with food. Do not smoke or chew gum when working with food.

Begin each shift in a clean, neat uniform. Do not wear your uniform to or from work or school. Store the uniform and all clothing in a clean locker. Do not wear jewelry other than a watch and a plain ring, to reduce risk of personal injury and cross contamination.

Work safely

In addition to the precautions necessary to guard against food-borne illness, care must be taken to avoid accidents to staff and guests.

- Clean up grease and other spills as they occur. Use salt or cornmeal to absorb grease, then clean the area.

- Warn coworkers when you are coming up behind them with something hot or sharp.

- Alert the pot washer when pots, pans, and handles are especially hot.

- Beware of grill fires. If one occurs, do not attempt to put it out with water. Removing excess fat and letting any marinades drain completely from foods to be grilled will help prevent flare-ups.

- Keep fire extinguishers in proper working order and place them in areas of the kitchen where they are most likely to be needed.

- Remove lids from pots in such a manner that the steam vents away from your face, to avoid steam burns.

- Bend at the knees, not the waist, to lift heavy objects.

- Pick up anything on the floor that might trip someone.

- Learn about first aid, CPR, and mouth-to-mouth resuscitation. Have well-stocked first-aid kits on hand (see "First-Aid Supplies," page 83).

- Make sure that all dining room and kitchen staff know how to perform the Heimlich maneuver on a choking person. Post instructions in readily visible areas of the kitchen and dining room.

- Handle equipment carefully, especially knives, mandolines, slicers, grinders, band saws, and other equipment with sharp edges.

- Observe care and caution when operating mixers. Always keep your hands away from an operating mixer.

- Use separate cutting boards for cooked and raw foods, and sanitize after using.
- Wash hands thoroughly after working with raw foods.
- Use tasting spoons, and use them only once—do not "double-dip." Do not use your fingers or kitchen utensils when tasting food.
- Store any toxic chemicals (cleaning compounds and pesticides, for example) away from food to avoid cross contamination.
- Use only dry side towels for handling hot items.
- Use instant-read thermometers (and sanitize them after use) to ensure that adequate temperatures are reached.
- Post emergency phone numbers near every phone.

Practice fire safety

It takes only a few seconds for a simple flare-up on the grill or in a pan to turn into a full-scale fire. Grease fires, electrical fires, or even a waste container full of paper going up when a match is carelessly tossed into it are easy to imagine happening in any busy kitchen. A comprehensive fire safety plan should be in place and a standard part of all employee training.

The first step in avoiding fires is to make sure that the entire staff, both kitchen and dining room, is fully aware of the potential dangers of fire everywhere in a restaurant. If you see someone handling a situation improperly, first get the situation under control, then take the time to explain what your concern is and how to avoid the situation in the future.

Next, be sure that all equipment is up to code. Frayed or exposed wires and faulty plugs can all too easily be the cause of a fire. Overburdened outlets are another common culprit. Any equipment that has a heating element or coil must also be maintained carefully, both to be sure that workers are not likely to be burned and to prevent fires.

Thorough training is another key element in any good fire safety program. Everyone should know what to do in case of a fire. Having frequent fire drills is a good idea. Instruct your kitchen staff in the correct way to handle a grill fire and grease fire.

There should also be fire extinguishers in easily accessible areas. Check each extinguisher to see what type of fire it is meant to control, and make sure you and your staff understand when and how to operate each type.

Proper maintenance of extinguishers and timely inspections by your local fire department are vital. Fire control systems, such as an Ansul system, also need to be serviced and monitored so that they will perform correctly if you need them. Above all, make sure you never try to put out a grease, chemical, or electrical fire by throwing water on the flames.

Everyone should know where the fire department number is posted and who is responsible for calling the department if necessary.

first-aid supplies

Adhesive strips in assorted sizes

Bandage compresses

Sterile gauze dressings, individually wrapped

Rolled gauze bandages

First-aid adhesive tape

Cotton swabs (for applying antiseptic or removing particles from eyes)

Tourniquet

Tongue depressors (for small splints)

Scissors

Tweezers

Needles (for removing splinters)

Rubbing alcohol (for sterilizing instruments such as tweezers and needles)

Mild antiseptic (for wounds)

Antibiotic cream

Syrup of ipecac (to induce vomiting)

Petroleum jelly

The exits from any area of the building should be easy to find, clear of any obstructions, and fully operational. Your guests may have to rely on you and other staff to get them safely out of the building. Identify one spot outside the building, at a safe distance, where everyone should assemble after they've exited safely. Then you will be able to tell immediately who may still be inside the building and need to be rescued by firefighters.

The main rule for fire is to be prepared for all possibilities. You cannot assume it won't happen to you.

Dress for safety

More than simply completing the look of the chef, the parts of the typical chef's uniform play important roles in keeping workers safe as they operate in a potentially dangerous environment. The chef's jacket is double-breasted, which creates a two-layer cloth barrier against steam burns, splashes, and spills. The design also means that the jacket can easily be rebuttoned on the opposite side to cover up spills. The jacket sleeves are long, to protect against burns and scalding splashes, and they should not be rolled up.

The same is true of pants. Shorts, while they may seem like a good idea for a hot environment, are inappropriate because they offer no protection. Pants should be worn without cuffs, which can trap hot liquids and debris. Ideally, pants should have a snap fly and be worn without a belt; if hot grease is spilled on the legs, this allows for fast removal of the pants, which could lessen the severity of the burn.

Be it a tall white toque or a favorite baseball cap, chefs wear hats to contain their hair, preventing it from falling into the food. Hats also help absorb sweat. Neckerchiefs serve a similar sweat-absorbing role. The apron protects the jacket and pants from excessive staining.

Most chefs use side towels to protect their hands when working with hot pans, dishes, or other equipment. They are not meant to be used as wiping cloths—side towels used to lift hot items must be dry in order to provide protection; once they become even slightly damp, they can no longer insulate properly.

While athletic shoes are very comfortable, they are not ideal for working in a kitchen. If a knife should fall from a work surface, most athletic shoes would offer very little protection. Hard leather shoes with slip-resistant soles are recommended, because of both the protection they offer and the support they give your feet.

Jackets, pants, side towels, aprons, and shoes can harbor bacteria, molds, parasites, and even viruses. Because these pathogens can be transmitted with ease from your uniform to foods, a sanitary uniform is important. Wear your uniform at work only, not when traveling to and from the job, where you can pick up pathogens along the way.

Proper laundering can sanitize your uniform to make it safe and clean. If your establishment doesn't use a laundry or uniform service, use hot water, a good detergent, and a sanitizer such as borax or chlorine bleach to remove bacteria and grime. Automatic dish-washing soap (used in household machines) contains an enzyme to help break up stuck-on food. These same enzymes can help to release food stains on uniforms. Add a half cup of dry household dishwasher detergent to the wash water.

Regulations, inspection, and certification

Federal, state, and local government regulations attempt to ensure the wholesomeness of food that reaches the public. Any new food-service business should contact the local health department well in advance of opening to ascertain the necessary legal requirements. A professional chef moving to a new area to work should contact local authorities for ordinances specific to that area. Some states and local jurisdictions offer sanitation certification programs. Certification is often available through certain academic institutions.

The Occupational Safety and Health Administration (OSHA)

OSHA is a federal organization, instituted in 1970, that falls under the purview of the Health and Human Services Administration. Its goal is helping employers and workers to establish and maintain a safe, healthy work environment.

Among OSHA's regulations is the mandate that all places of employment have an adequate and easily accessible first-aid kit on the premises. In addition, any organization that has more than ten employees must keep records of all accidents and injuries to employees that require medical treatment. Any employee requests for improvements in the safety of the workplace, including repair or maintenance of the physical plant and equipment necessary to perform one's job, must be attended to by the organization.

As money for many health and human service organizations has dwindled, OSHA's ability to make on-site inspections has also been reduced. It now concentrates its efforts on providing services where the risk to worker safety is greatest. This does not mean that small businesses can operate with impunity, for any employee can call OSHA's offices and report violations.

Americans with Disabilities Act of 1990

This act is intended to make public places accessible and safe for those with a variety of disabilities. Any new construction or remodeling done to a restaurant must meet ADA standards. They include, for example, providing telephones located so that they can be reached by a person in a wheelchair, and toilets with handrails. Most contractors will have the necessary information, but if you are unsure, contact a local agency.

A special note about smokers

Many restaurants have banned smoking, whether voluntarily as a result of public pressure or because of legislative mandates. While this may improve the air quality within the restaurant itself and provide a more pleasant dining experience for nonsmoking guests, there is one thing that should be kept in mind: Simply banning smoking in the dining room and the bar may not ban smoking from the entire premises. Common sense will tell you that smokers will very likely smoke cigarettes up to the moment they walk in the door, and light up as soon as they step back outside. One carelessly flung match or a single smoldering cigarette butt can spell ruin.

Place sand-filled buckets or urns near the areas where you expect or prefer to have smokers take their cigarette breaks. If you do allow smoking in your restaurant, make sure that bartenders, bus people, and wait staff have a safe way to dispose of the contents of ashtrays.

Of course, smoking should never be allowed in the kitchen area.

Drugs and alcohol in the workplace

One final topic that is of great importance in the workplace is the right of all workers to be free from the hazards imposed by a coworker who comes to work under the influence of drugs or alcohol. The abuse of any substance that can alter or impair one's ability to perform his or her job is a serious concern. Reaction times may be slowed, and the ability to concentrate and to comprehend instructions reduced. Inhibitions are often lowered, and judgment is generally impaired. As a result, people's safety or even their lives can be at stake. A poorly judged effort when emptying the hot oil from the deep fryer could result in permanent disability. A playful attempt at passing a knife could put out an eye. Forgetting to take the time to properly store and reheat foods could lead to an outbreak of food-borne illness that could kill someone.

The responsibilities of a professional working in any kitchen are too great to allow someone suffering from a substance abuse problem to diminish the respect and trust you have built with your customers and staff.

chapter six

Baking formulas and bakers' percentages

a baker or pastry chef needs to perform a number of key calculations in order to have consistently successful results and work efficiently. This chapter provides a brief overview of some of the basic mathematical formulas and calculations used in the bakeshop and pastry kitchen to create standardized production formulas, increase or decrease a formula's yield (a technique known as scaling), and adjust to different production needs.

Baking formulas

Always read through any formula completely before you start. The formula may require a special piece of equipment or a component made separately. Or perhaps the formula makes only ten servings and you need to make fifty. In that case, you will have to scale the formula (see "Formula Calculations," page 90). In increasing or decreasing a formula, you may discover that you need to make equipment modifications as well.

Once you have read through and evaluated or modified the formula, assemble your equipment and ingredients—the baker's *mise en place*. In many formulas, the ingredients list will indicate how the ingredient should be prepared (for example, sifted, melted, or cut into pieces of a certain size) before the actual mixing or assembling begins.

Scaling with precision

Ingredients are purchased and used following one of three measuring conventions: count, volume, or weight. They may be purchased according to one system but measured in another for use in a formula.

Count is a measurement of whole items. The terms *each, bunch,* and *dozen* all indicate units of count measure. If an individual item has been processed, graded, or packaged according to established standards, count can be a useful, accurate way to measure that ingredient. It is less accurate for ingredients requiring some preparation before they are added to the formula or for those without any established standards for purchasing. Apples illustrate the point well. If a formula calls for ten apples, then the yield, flavor, and consistency of the item will change depending upon whether the apples you use are large or small.

Accurate scaling is vital for the best and most consistent results.

Volume is a measurement of the space occupied by a solid, liquid, or gas. The terms *teaspoon (tsp), tablespoon (tbsp), fluid ounce (fl oz), cup, pint (pt), quart (qt), gallon (gal), milliliter (mL),* and *liter (L)* all indicate units of volume measure. Graduated containers (measuring cups) and utensils with a precise volume (such as a 2-ounce ladle or a teaspoon) are used to measure volume. Volume measurements are best suited to liquids, though they are also used for dry ingredients, such as spices, in small amounts. Keep in mind that tools used for measuring volume are not always as precise as they should be. Volume measuring tools need not conform to any regulated standards, so the amount of an ingredient measured with one set of spoons, cups, or pitchers could be quite different from the amount measured with another set. (To learn more about converting volume measures to weight measures, see the table "Converting to a Common Unit of Measure," page 91.)

Weight is a measurement of the mass or heaviness of a solid, liquid, or gas. The terms *ounce (oz), pound (lb), gram (g),* and *kilogram (kg)* all indicate units of weight measure. Scales are used to measure weight, and they must meet specific standards for accuracy regulated by the U.S. National Institute of Standards and Technology's Office of Weights and Measures. (See "Scales" in Chapter 3, page 36, for more about using scales.) In professional kitchens, weight is usually the preferred type of measurement because it is easier to be accurate with weight than with volume measurements.

Standardized formulas

The formulas used in a professional baking and pastry setting must be standardized. Unlike published formulas meant to work in a variety of settings for a wide audience, standardized formulas suit the specific needs of an individual pastry kitchen or bakeshop. Preparing well-written and accurate standardized formulas is a big part of the professional pastry chef's or baker's work, as these are records that include much more than just ingredient names and preparation steps. Standardized formulas establish overall yields, serving sizes, holding and serving practices, and plating information. They set standards for equipment as well as temperatures and times for cooking or baking. These standards help to ensure consistent quality and quantity, and they permit pastry chefs and bakers to gauge the efficiency of their work and reduce costs by eliminating waste as appropriate.

In addition, the wait staff must be familiar enough with an item or plated dessert to be able to answer any questions a customer might have. For example, the type of nuts used in an item may matter very much to an individual who has a nut allergy.

Standardized formulas can be handwritten or stored on a computer, using a formula management program or other such database or program. The formulas should be written in a consistent, clear, easy-to-follow format and be readily accessible to the entire staff. The pastry chef or baker should instruct pastry kitchen or bakeshop staff to follow standardized formulas to the letter unless otherwise instructed, as well as encourage service staff to refer to standardized formulas when a question arises about ingredients or preparation methods.

As you prepare a standardized formula, be as precise and consistent as possible. Include as many of the following elements as necessary:

NAME or **TITLE** of the food item or dish

YIELD for the formula, expressed as one or more of the following: total weight, total volume, or total number of servings

PORTION INFORMATION for each serving, expressed as one or more of the following: number of items (count), volume, or weight

INGREDIENT NAMES, expressed in appropriate detail (specifying variety or brand as necessary)

INGREDIENT MEASURES, expressed as one or more of the following: count, volume, or weight

INGREDIENT PREPARATION INSTRUCTIONS, sometimes included in the ingredient name, sometimes included in the method as a separate step

A variety of volume measuring tools are useful when adapting formulas originally written in common household measures.

EQUIPMENT INFORMATION for preparation, cooking, storing, holding, and serving

PREPARATION STEPS detailing mise en place, mixing, cooking or baking, and temperatures for safe food handling (see also "Hazard Analysis Critical Control Points [HACCP]," page 78)

SERVICE INFORMATION, including how to finish and plate the dessert; sauces and garnishes, if any; and proper service temperatures

HOLDING AND REHEATING PROCEDURES, including equipment, times, temperatures, and safe storage

CRITICAL CONTROL POINTS (CCPS) at appropriate stages in the formula, to indicate temperatures and times for safe food-handling procedures during storage, preparation, holding, and reheating (to learn more about CCPs, see "Identify the Critical Control Points," page 79)

Formula calculations

Often you will need to modify a formula. Sometimes the yield must be increased or decreased. You may be adapting a formula from another source to a standardized format, or you may be adjusting a standardized formula for a special event, such as a banquet or a reception. You may need to convert from volume measures to weight, or from metric measurements to the U.S. system. Or you may want to determine how much the ingredients in a particular formula cost.

The formula conversion factor (FCF)

To increase or decrease the yield of a formula, you need to determine the *formula conversion factor*. Once you know that factor, you then multiply all the ingredient amounts by it and convert the new measurements into appropriate formula units for your pastry kitchen or bakeshop. This may require converting items listed by count into weight or volume measurements, or rounding measurements to reasonable quantities. And in some cases you will have to make a judgment call about those ingredients that do not scale up or down exactly, such as spices, salt, thickeners, and leaveners.

$$\frac{\text{Desired yield}}{\text{Original yield}} = \text{Formula conversion factor (FCF)}$$

The desired yield and the original yield must be expressed in the same way before you can use the formula; that is, both must be in the same unit of measure. For example, if the original formula gives the yield in ounces and you want to make 2 quarts of the sauce, you will need to convert quarts into fluid ounces. Or, if your original formula says that it makes five servings and does not list the size of each serving, you may need to test the formula to determine serving size.

Converting to a common unit of measure

To convert measurements to a common unit (by weight or volume), use the following chart. This information can be used both to convert scaled measurements into practical and easy-to-use formula measures and to determine costs.

For some ingredients, straightforward multiplication or division is all that is needed. To increase a formula for poached pears from five servings to fifty, for example, you would simply multiply five pears by ten; no further adjustments are necessary. But once you have converted them, some other ingredient amounts may need some fine-tuning. You may need to round off a result or convert it to the most logical unit of measure. And measures for ingredients such as thickeners, spices, seasonings, and leavenings, for example, should not always be simply multiplied or divided. If a formula that makes six 6-in/15-cm cakes requires ½ oz/14 g of baking powder, it is not necessarily true that you will need 3 oz/84 g of baking powder to leaven six times the amount of the same batter if you are mixing it all in one batch. In such cases, the only way to be sure is to test the new formula and adjust it until you are satisfied with the result.

Other considerations when converting formula yields include the equipment you have, the production issues you face, and the skill level of your staff. Rewrite steps as necessary to suit the realities of your establishment at this point. It is important to do this now, so you can discover any further changes to the ingredients or methods that the new yield might cause. For instance, to mix enough bread dough to make ten 1-lb/454-g loaves of bread requires a large mixer, but if you only want to make two 1-lb/454-g loaves, you need a much smaller mixing bowl. The smaller batch of dough would fit in the large mixing bowl, but there would not be enough dough for the mixer to be able to mix and develop the structure for the bread properly.

FORMULA MEASURE	COMMON CONVERSION TO VOLUME	COMMON UNIT (U.S.)	COMMON UNIT (METRIC)
1 pound (lb)	N/A*	16 ounces (oz)	454 grams (g)
1 tablespoon (tbsp)	3 teaspoons (tsp)	½ fluid ounce (fl oz)	30 milliliters (mL)
1 cup	16 tablespoons (tbsp)	8 fluid ounces (fl oz)	240 milliliters (mL)
1 pint (pt)	2 cups	16 fluid ounces (fl oz)	480 milliliters (mL)
1 quart (qt)	2 pints (pt)	32 fluid ounces (fl oz)	960 milliliters (mL)
1 gallon (gal)	4 quarts (qt)	128 fluid ounces (fl oz)	3.75 liters (L)

* Most liquids convert uniformly from weight to volume; different solids and semisolids convert differently from weight to volume.

Converting for a different number of servings

Sometimes you need to modify the total yield of a formula to obtain a different number of servings.

Number of servings × Serving size = Total yield

For instance, you may have a sauce formula that makes four servings of 2 fl oz/60 mL each, but you want to make forty servings of 2 fl oz/60 mL each. To make the conversion:

First determine the total original yield of the formula and the total desired yield.

4 × 2 fl oz = 8 fl oz (total original yield)

40 × 2 fl oz = 80 fl oz (total desired yield)

Then determine the formula conversion factor.

$$\frac{80 \text{ fl oz}}{8 \text{ fl oz}} = 10 \text{ (the formula conversion factor or FCF)}$$

Modify the formula as described above by multiplying formula measures by 10.

Converting for a different serving size

Sometimes you need to modify the total yield of a formula to obtain a different number of servings of a different size.

For instance, you may have a sauce formula that makes four servings of 2 fl oz/60 mL each, but you want to make twenty 3-fl oz/90-mL servings. To make the conversion:

First determine the total original yield of the formula and the total desired yield.

4 × 2 fl oz = 8 fl oz (total original yield)

20 × 3 fl oz = 60 fl oz (total desired yield)

Then determine the formula conversion factor.

$$\frac{60}{8} = 7.5 \text{ (the formula conversion factor or FCF)}$$

Modify the formula as described above by multiplying formula measures by 7.5.

Volume versus weight measure

In the professional bakery or pastry shop, most ingredients are measured by weight. When creating standardized formulas for common use, consistency of quality and flavor is the most important objective. Weight is more accurate, leaving less room for error. If a formula is found or developed in volume measurements it should be converted to weight for professional use.

Converting volume measures to weight

Confusion often arises between weight and volume measures when ounces are the unit of measure. It is important to remember that weight is measured in ounces (oz) and volume is measured in *fluid* ounces (fl oz). A standard volume measuring cup is equal to 8 fl oz, but the contents of the cup may not always weigh 8 oz/227 g. One cup (8 fl oz/240 mL) of shredded fresh coconut weighs just under 3 oz/84 g, but 1 cup (8 fl oz/240 mL) of peanut butter weighs 9 oz/255 g. Since measuring dry ingredients by weight is much more accurate, it is the preferred and most common method used for measuring dry ingredients in professional kitchens and bakeshops.

Water is the only substance for which it can be safely assumed that 1 fl oz/30 mL (a volume measure) equals 1 oz/28 g by weight. But you can convert the volume measure of another ingredient into a weight if you know how much a cup of the ingredient (prepared as required by the formula) weighs. This information is available in a number of charts or ingredients databases. You can also calculate and record the information yourself:

- Record a description of the ingredient, and the way it is received (whole, frozen, chopped, canned, etc.).

- Prepare the ingredient as directed by the formula (sift flour, roast nuts, chop or melt chocolate, drain items packed in syrup, and so on). Record this advance preparation, too.

- Measure the ingredient carefully according to the formula, using nested measures for dry ingredients or liquid cups or pitchers for liquid ingredients (see "Volume Measures" in Chapter 3, page 37, for measuring techniques).

- Set up your scale and set it to tare (see "Scales" in Chapter 3, page 36).

- Weigh the ingredient.

- Finally, record the weight of the ingredient, noting all the advance preparation steps involved (sifting, melting, chopping, and so forth).

Converting between U.S. and metric measurement systems

The metric system used throughout the rest of the world is a decimal system, meaning that it is based on multiples of ten. The gram is the basic unit of weight, the liter the basic unit of volume, and the meter the basic unit of length. Prefixes added to the basic units indicate larger or smaller units.

The U.S. system uses ounces and pounds to measure weight, and teaspoons, tablespoons, fluid ounces, cups, pints, quarts, and gallons to measure volume. Unlike the metric system, the U.S. system is not based on multiples of a particular number, so it is not as simple to increase or decrease quantities. Rather, the equivalencies of the different units of measure must be memorized or derived from a chart.

Most modern measuring equipment is capable of measuring in both U.S. and metric units. If, however, a formula is written in a system of measurement for which you do not have the proper measuring equipment, you will need to convert to the other system.

TO CONVERT OUNCES AND POUNDS TO GRAMS: Multiply ounces by 28.35 to determine grams; divide pounds by 2.2 to determine kilograms.

TO CONVERT GRAMS TO OUNCES OR POUNDS: Divide grams by 28.35 to determine ounces; divide grams by 454 to determine pounds.

TO CONVERT FLUID OUNCES TO MILLILITERS: Multiply fluid ounces by 30 to determine milliliters.

TO CONVERT MILLILITERS TO FLUID OUNCES: Divide milliliters by 30 to determine fluid ounces.

Metric Prefixes

kilo (k) = 1,000; 1 kg = 1,000 g

hecto = 100

deka = 10

deci = $\frac{1}{10}$ or 0.1

centi = $\frac{1}{100}$ or 0.01

milli = $\frac{1}{1000}$ or 0.001

TO CONVERT CELSIUS TO FAHRENHEIT: Multiply the degrees Celsius by 9, divide the result by 5, and add 32 to get the Fahrenheit equivalent:

$$\frac{°C \times 9}{5} + 32 = °F$$

To convert Fahrenheit to Celsius: Subtract 32 from the degrees Fahrenheit, multiply the result by 5, and divide the result by 9 to get the Celsius equivalent:

$$\frac{(°F - 32) \times 5}{9} = °C$$

Calculating as-purchased cost per unit (APC)

Most food items purchased from suppliers are packed and priced by wholesale bulk sizes (crate, case, bag, carton, and so on). In kitchen production, the packed amount is generally broken down and often used for several different items. Therefore, in order to assign the correct prices to the formula being prepared, it is necessary to convert purchase pack prices to unit prices, expressed as price per pound, per single unit, per dozen, per quart, and the like.

To find the cost of a unit in a pack with multiple units, divide the as-purchased cost of the pack by the number of units in the pack.

$$\frac{\text{Total cost}}{\text{Number of units}} = \text{Cost per unit (APC)}$$

Number of units × Cost per unit = Total Cost

Calculating yield percentage of fresh fruits and vegetables

For many food items, trimming is required before the items are used. In order to determine an accurate cost for such items, trim loss must be taken into account. The yield percentage is important in determining the quantity to order.

$$\frac{\text{Edible-portion quantity}}{\text{As-purchased quantity}} = \text{Yield percentage}$$

First, record the as-purchased quantity (APQ).

APQ = 5 lb lemons = 80 oz

Trim the item(s), saving unusable trim loss and edible-portion quantity (EPQ) in separate containers. Weigh each separately and record their weights.

EPQ = 36.5 oz lemon juice

Trim loss = 43.5 oz

Divide the EPQ by the APQ to determine the yield percentage.

$$\frac{36.5}{80} = 0.456 \times 100 = 45.6\%$$

Yield percentage = 45.6%

This calculation can also be used to determine the yield percentage of meat, fish, poultry, and other types of ingredients that might be used trimmed.

Calculating as-purchased quantity (APQ) from formula measure

Because many formulas assume the ingredients listed are ready to cook, it is necessary to consider trim loss when purchasing items. In such cases, the edible-portion quantity must be converted to the as-purchased quantity that will yield the desired formula measure.

$$\frac{EPQ}{\text{Yield percentage}} = APQ$$

EXAMPLE

A formula requires 20 lb peeled and diced potatoes. The yield percentage for potatoes is 78 percent (0.78). Therefore, 20 lb divided by 78 percent will equal the amount to purchase.

$$\frac{20 \text{ lb}}{0.78} = 25.65 \text{ lb APQ}$$

Generally, the as-purchased quantity obtained by this method is rounded up (in this example, to 26 lb), since the yield percentage is, by its nature, an estimate.

It should be kept in mind that not all foods, of course, have trim loss. Many pastry and bakeshop ingredients, such as sugar, flour, and spices, are processed or refined foods that have 100 percent yield. Other foods have a yield percentage that depends on how they are to be served. If, for example, the ingredient is to be served by the piece (1 poached pear), or if a formula calls for it by count (15 strawberries), there is no need to consider the yield percentage; the correct number of items is simply purchased to create the desired number of servings. However, if you are making fruit tartlets and the formula calls for 2 oz sliced pineapple and 1 oz sliced strawberries per serving, you must consider the yield percentage when ordering.

Calculating edible-portion quantity (EPQ)

Sometimes it is necessary to determine how many servings can be obtained from raw product, which is known as edible-portion quantity (EPQ). For example, if you have a case of fresh kiwis that weighs 10 lb and you want to know how many 4-oz servings the case will yield, you first need to determine the yield percentage, either by referring to a list of yield percentages or by performing a yield test. (See "Calculating Yield Percentage of Fresh Fruits and Vegetables," page 94.)

$$APQ \times \text{Yield percentage} = EPQ$$

Once you know the yield percentage, you can compute the weight of the kiwis after trimming.

$$10 \text{ lb} \times 0.85 = 8.5 \text{ lb}$$

The second step is to compute how many 4-oz servings the edible-portion quantity, 8.5 lb, will yield.

$$\frac{EPQ}{\text{Serving size}} = \text{Number of servings}$$

$$4 \text{ oz} = ¼ \text{ lb} = 0.25\text{-lb}/113\text{-g serving size}$$

$$\frac{8.5 \text{ lb}}{0.25 \text{ lb}} = 34 \quad \text{or} \quad \frac{3859 \text{ g}}{113 \text{ g}} = 24 \text{ kiwis}$$

NOTE If you do not get a whole number as your result from a similar calculation, you should round down the number of servings, since it would not be possible to serve a partial serving.

Calculating edible-portion cost (EPC)

As discussed earlier, formulas often assume that ingredients are ready to cook. When it comes to costing a formula, the edible-portion cost (EPC) per unit can be calculated from the as-purchased cost (APC) per unit.

$$\frac{APC}{\text{Yield percentage}} = EPC$$

EPC can then be used to calculate the total cost of an ingredient in a formula, as long as EPQ and EPC are expressed for the same unit of measure.

$$EPQ \times EPC = \text{Total cost}$$

Bakers' percentages

Bakers' percentages have two basic functions. First, when a formula is expressed in bakers' percentages, it is easy to see and evaluate the relationships among the different ingredients. An understanding of the relationships between ingredients will help the baker or pastry chef to recognize a faulty formula, and to prepare basic products without the aid of written formulas, if necessary.

The second function of bakers' percentages is to make it easy to use a formula in the bakeshop or pastry kitchen. When a formula is expressed in bakers' percentages, it is easy to scale it up or down.

A percentage is a part of a whole (100 percent). In bakers' percentages, the whole is always the flour; *that is, the flour is always 100 percent.* If there are two or more types of flour, their sum must equal 100 percent. The percentages for all other ingredients are derived from the flour. Because the whole is the flour, and not the sum total of all the ingredients, the sum of all the ingredients will always exceed 100 percent. Occasionally the percentage of another ingredient may exceed 100 percent, if it is required in a greater amount than the flour.

Calculating the percentage value for an ingredient

To determine the percentage value for each ingredient in a formula, simply divide the weight of the ingredient by the weight of the flour and then multiply the result by 100.

$$\frac{\text{Total weight of ingredient}}{\text{Total weight of flour}} = \text{Decimal value} \times 100 = \text{Percent value of ingredient}$$

EXAMPLE

A bread formula calls for 5 lb of flour and 3 lb of diced potato. To calculate the percentage value for the diced potato, divide its weight by the weight of the flour (which is always 100 percent) and then multiply the result by 100.

$$\frac{3 \text{ lb diced potato}}{5 \text{ lb flour}} = 0.60 \times 100 = 60$$

The resulting percentage value is 60 percent.

NOTE Remember that when making any calculations, numerical values must be expressed in the same unit of measure (e.g., pounds, ounces, grams, kilograms); if necessary, convert any values before beginning the calculation.

Calculating the weight of an ingredient when the weight of flour is known

Divide the percentage value of the ingredient by 100 to get its decimal version, then multiply by the weight of the flour.

Decimal value of ingredient × Total weight of flour = Total weight of ingredient

EXAMPLE

A bread formula lists the ingredient values only in percentages. You want to make a batch of dough using 5 lb flour. You need to calculate the weight for the potatoes, which are valued at 60 percent, so you can prep them for making the dough the next day.

$$\frac{60}{100} = 0.6 \text{ decimal value}$$

0.6 × 5 lb flour = 3 lb potatoes

Desired dough temperature

The desired dough temperature (DDT) is the ideal average temperature of a dough while you are working with it. For lean doughs, this temperature is typically 75° to 80°F/24° to 27°C. Working with a lean dough at this temperature will help to keep the gluten strands relaxed. The ideal DDT for enriched doughs is slightly higher, as it is important to keep the fats that have been added to the dough soft while it is being worked. (To learn more about DDT, see "Desired Dough Temperature and British Thermal Units" in Chapter 7, page 106.)

Calculating water temperature from DDT

The DDT, the total temperature factor (TTF), and the sum of the other known temperatures that will influence the DDT are used to calculate the temperature the water should be when it is added to the ingredients so that after mixing the dough will be at or very near the DDT.

To make this calculation, first calculate the TTF. To find the TTF, multiply the DDT by the number of temperature factors to be considered. For a straight mix dough, there are three factors to be considered. For a sourdough or a dough that uses a pre-ferment, there are four or sometimes five factors, depending on the number of elements that are going to be added. These elements include the temperature of the flour, soaker pre-ferment, butter, eggs, really any ingredient that is over 20 percent. Also to be factored in are the ambient temperature and friction created by the mixer.

The flour's temperature is one of the known elements in calculating desired dough temperature (DDT).

After you have found the TTF, subtract the sum of the known temperatures from it to give the ideal temperature for the water. The known temperatures are the temperature of the flour and the room. You also need to know the amount of friction the dough will undergo in the mixer.

EXAMPLE

You are making an enriched straight mix dough. The flour temperature is 65°F, the room temperature is 75°F, and the dough will be mixed for a total of 12 minutes.

First, calculate the TTF.

DDT × TTF factor = TTF
80 × 3 = 240

Then find the value for the mixer friction. In this example, the number 2 is used for the friction factor, but this number may be higher or lower depending on batch size, speed, and type of mixer.

Number of minutes mixing × Friction factor = Mixer friction
$12 \times 2 = 24$

Then find the sum of all the known temperature factors.

Flour temperature + Room temperature + Mixer friction = Sum of known temperature factors
$65 + 75 + 24 = 164$

Finally, find the water temperature.

TTF – Sum of the known temperature factors = Water temperature
$240 - 164 = 76°F$

In warmer climates, it may be advisable to have a colder DDT. If necessary, ice can be used to lower the temperature of the water.

For example, if the calculated water temperature for 40 lb of water is 45°F, but the temperature of the water is 60°F, ice can be used to lower the temperature of the water. To calculate how much ice to use, an "ice Btu factor" (the amount of British thermal units it takes to melt 1 pound of ice) must be determined, using the following equation:

$$\frac{(\text{Total weight of water}) \times (\text{Water temperature} - \text{Desired water temperature})}{144} = \text{Weight of ice}$$

First subtract the actual water temperature from the desired water temperature to find the "degree difference."

$60°F - 45°F = 15°F$

Next, multiply the total weight of water by the "degree difference."

$40 \text{ lb} \times 15°F = 600$

Finally, divide the result by 144, the Btu factor.

$$\frac{600}{144} = 4.16 \text{ lb}$$

The result is the number of pounds of ice needed to achieve the desired water temperature and, ultimately, the DDT. Subtract the number of pounds of ice needed from the total weight of water needed to see how much water you need when adding ice to the formula.

$40 \text{ lb} - 4.16 \text{ lb} = 35.9 \text{ lb}$

In this formula, you will need to reduce the water to 35.9 lb to compensate for the 4.16 lb of ice. If you round the numbers so they can be measured easily, you will need 36 lb of water and 4 lb of ice.

part two

Yeast-raised breads and rolls

CLOCKWISE FROM TOP LEFT: Craquelin (page 187),
Brioche Loaf (page 186), Chocolate and Pecan Babka
(page 189), Brioche Loaf slices, Brioche à Tête (page 138)

chapter seven

Beginner yeast breads and rolls

*W*hen flour, water, yeast, and salt are worked together in the correct proportions for the appropriate amount of time and at the proper temperature, proper gluten structure develops. The bread baker knows that the ingredients play a key role in the quality of the dough, as do the mixing and fermentation methods. The techniques in this chapter take the bread-baking process up through a finished dough.

Direct fermentation

The simplest and fastest method for producing a lean dough is *direct fermentation:* Commercially produced yeast is combined with flour, water, and salt and mixed until the dough is supple and elastic, with well-developed gluten.

Flour, as a main component, provides the structure and crumb in breads through the action of the proteins and starches it contains. The amount of water or other liquids also has an impact on the finished loaf. As the amount of liquid in a dough increases, the bread's structure changes as it promotes the formation of an open crumb.

Some breads are meant to have a more delicate texture, with a softer crust and crumb. In these formulas, sugars and fats, in the form of butter, oil, eggs, or syrups, control or affect how well the gluten develops, how long and elastic the gluten strands become, how the yeast behaves, and how open or closed the crumb is after baking.

Yeast is directly related not only to the texture of the bread but also to its flavor. The direct fermentation method of bread making requires fewer steps and less advance preparation than indirect fermentation methods; however, the lack of a pre-ferment limits the quality of the finished product by limiting fermentation time. (See Chapter 8, page 148, for pre-ferments and indirect fermentation methods.) The processes occurring during fermentation further develop the structure and flavor of the dough—the more time allotted for fermentation, the better the development of the internal structure and flavor of the dough. (For more about gluten development, starch gelatinization, and fermentation, see Chapter 4, pages 57, 65, and 60.)

The stages after mixing and bulk fermentation (i.e., shaping and baking as well as handling, cooling, and storage) also have a great deal to do with the quality of yeast-raised breads, rolls, and cakes. Bread doughs can be given a variety of shapes, ranging from simple boules and round rolls to intricately braided loaves. Proofing the dough after it has been shaped gives it additional time to develop. Simple rustic shapes, such as baguettes and bâtards, are often used for lean doughs. Enriched doughs are soft enough to twist and braid.

The straight mixing method

The straight mixing method is most often used with formulas that rely on direct fermentation. For this mixing method, the ingredients are added in a different order depending on the type of yeast used. If instant dry yeast is used, the yeast should first be blended with the flour, then all the remaining ingredients should be added to the flour-yeast mixture. If active dry or compressed fresh yeast is used, the yeast should first be blended with the water and allowed to fully dissolve. Next the flour should be added and all remaining ingredients should be placed on top of the flour.

After all the ingredients are in the mixing bowl, they should be blended together on low speed until just combined. Then turn the mixer to medium speed and blend the dough to full development.

Stages of Gluten Development

One way to know when to check for gluten development is to understand the changes that occur while mixing. There are four separate mixing stages, no matter what mixing method you use. Each stage shows a clear difference in how far along the dough has developed in gluten structure. You will know when to end the mixing process because the recipe you are using will tell you the level of development you need.

Dough that has reached short development will become a homogenous mass but will fall apart when worked with your hands.

If you are making a lean dough that requires partial or improved gluten development, for example, you should continue mixing, then check the gluten window again periodically. You will know you have reached improved development if the dough holds together more, but tears as you work it.

Dough that has reached the improved gluten development stage holds together, but tears when you check for the gluten window.

Some doughs require intense development, meaning that you need to keep mixing the dough beyond the partial development stage until it is fully developed. If, as you check the gluten window, the dough doesn't tear and holds a thin membrane you can see through, then the gluten is properly developed in this case.

The gluten window is transparent enough to see light through it. This means a dough has reached intense gluten development.

Checking the gluten window is important, and the stakes get higher when you are making an intensely developed bread. If you overmix the dough, the gluten

The gluten window. The ability to stretch dough to a thin membrane indicates full gluten development.

will break down. The dough will go from being smooth and elastic to wet and sticky. Your bread will fail, meaning that it won't rise properly or bake well. On the other hand, if you don't mix the dough enough or mix it improperly, you will also wind up with low volume and poor internal structure. Poorly mixed dough may mean that the flour will not absorb the liquids properly and that the dough turns out irregular. It will have a poor gluten structure, lack elasticity, and the dough will remain wet and sticky.

Stages of mixing bread dough

In bread making, as with any baked item, the proper execution of mixing is crucial to the quality of the end product. When mixing bread dough, there are four identifiable stages that signal a change in structure and the stage of development of the dough.

Stage 1: pickup period

During the pickup period the ingredients are blended on low speed, until just combined. The dough is a wet, sticky, rough mass at this point.

Stage 2: cleanup period or preliminary development

The cleanup period is the preliminary development of the dough. At this point the dough is mixing at a moderate speed and will appear somewhat rough.

Stage 3: initial development period

During the initial development period, the elasticity of the gluten begins to develop and the dough starts to pull away from the sides of the mixing bowl. At this point the mixer should be running at medium speed; a high speed would work the dough too roughly, breaking the structure of the gluten rather than promoting its development.

Stage 4: final development period

At this point the gluten is fully developed. The dough is smooth and elastic and leaves the sides of the bowl completely clean as the mixer is running. To test for full gluten development, remove a piece of dough from the mixer, dip it in flour, and stretch it from underneath. If the dough stretches to form a thin membrane, allowing light to filter through, then the gluten has been properly and sufficiently developed.

When dough is overmixed it will be very sticky and wet and will have little or no elasticity. This occurs because the gluten strands have been broken down; the resulting product will not rise or bake properly.

Advantages of proper mixing

Optimum absorption

Proper gluten development

Slightly shorter fermentation time

TOP LEFT: Stage 1. The pickup stage of dough development

BOTTOM LEFT: Stage 3. Initial dough development

TOP RIGHT: Stage 2. The cleanup stage

BOTTOM RIGHT: Stage 4. Final dough development

substituting one yeast for another

Each of the formulas in this chapter was developed using instant dry yeast. In the past, fresh compressed yeast was the standard variety used by commercial bakers. However, today it is becoming more common for bakeshops to use dry varieties of yeast because they produce excellent results, are easier to store, and have a much longer shelf life. Generally, it is best to follow the manufacturer's instructions for use, as all dry yeast products are not alike.

The most common ratio of yeast to flour is approximately ½ oz/14 g fresh yeast to 18 oz/510 g flour, although this ratio can vary according to the type of bread, the techniques used in production, the retarding, and the ingredients in the formula. Too little yeast will not raise dough sufficiently, while too much will give the bread an overly strong yeast flavor. The bakers' percentages included in the formulas in this chapter indicate the ratios for that dough and can be used as a guide for modification of these and other formulas.

Use the accompanying table to convert from one type of yeast to another.

Active dry yeast should be reactivated in twice its volume amount of water at 105°F/41°C for 3 to 5 minutes before blending with the remaining ingredients in the formula. Combine fresh yeast with some of the milk or water in the formula to blend evenly before adding the remaining ingredients. Instant dry yeast does not have to be activated, but it should not come in direct contact with ice-cold liquids or ice. When converting a formula from fresh yeast to instant or active dry, most manufacturers suggest that the difference in weight be made up with additional water. This additional water will maintain the yield and hydration level of the dough.

TYPE OF YEAST	PERCENTAGE	EXAMPLE
Fresh yeast	100%	10 oz/284 g
Active dry yeast	40%	4 oz/113 g
Instant dry yeast	33%	3⅓ oz/94 g

Desired dough temperature and British thermal units

Dough temperature is important because it directly affects fermentation. Suggested temperatures for certain ingredients are based upon the desired dough temperature (DDT; the DDT is included in each formula). The colder the final temperature of a dough, the longer the fermentation time will be; the warmer the final dough temperature, the more quickly a dough will ferment. The fermentation time directly affects the quality and consistency of the finished product, and impacts production schedules as well, making the desired dough temperature a very important factor in bread baking.

The temperature of a directly fermented dough immediately after mixing is influenced by three factors: the temperature of the ingredients when added, the ambient (room) temperature, and the friction created by the mixer during mixing. (For a dough produced using the indirect fermentation method, all of these factors apply, along with the temperature of all pre-ferments added to the dough.) The sum of all the factors affecting the temperature of a dough is known as the total temperature factor (TTF).

The typical desired dough temperature for most yeast doughs is 75°F/24°C; however, an acceptable temperature for a finished dough may be from 65° to 85°F/18° to 29°C.

To produce a dough within this temperature range, the temperature of the water is critical because it is the easiest factor to control with precision. It is common to use ice water when it is necessary to cool a dough. Cooling a dough by this method is useful, for example, when a long mixing time is predicted, when fermentation needs to be slowed, or when the ambient temperature is high and cannot be controlled. To calculate the quantity of ice, British thermal units or Btu's are used. If a pre-ferment is added that has been stored under refrigeration, it may be necessary to use slightly warm water. See "Desired Dough Temperature" in Chapter 6, page 97, for instructions on calculating the DDT, TTF, and ice Btu factor.

Bulk fermentation

The first fermentation period, known as *bulk fermentation*, develops the flavor of the bread. Bulk fermentation is especially important when using the direct fermentation method; without the addition of pre-ferments, this is the only time to develop flavor through fermentation. Regulating the temperature may extend the time or rate of fermentation during this period. Keeping the dough at cooler temperatures will result in a longer fermentation period and thus more flavor development.

The alcohol produced during fermentation tenderizes the gluten strands, making them more elastic so they expand, allowing the bread to rise properly. More tender gluten strands produce a loaf with a tender and chewy crumb. Gluten is also further developed during this time through the process of folding.

The properly mixed dough is transferred to a lightly oiled bowl or tub (stiff or firm doughs can be placed on a lightly floured tabletop). Cover the dough with a moist cloth or plastic wrap to prevent a skin from forming on the surface and let it rest at the appropriate temperature until it has doubled in size. The times suggested in our formulas are based on fermentation at room temperature (75°F/24°C).

Retarding dough

Retarding dough means to purposely cool the dough, typically at temperatures of around 40°F/4°C, in order to slow the fermentation process. Retarding permits bakers to organize their work to meet production and employee schedules. It also allows the gluten to relax further, since the fermentation is prolonged. This results in dough that is easier to shape. A prolonged fermentation also gives dough time to develop a more pronounced sour flavor, so retarding dough can effectively enhance the quality of doughs made using direct fermentation.

The extended time at lower temperatures during bulk fermentation also means that you can properly ferment dough with a smaller amount of yeast. In fact, adding the full amount of yeast called for in a formula, usually allowed to ferment at around 75°F/24°C, would cause the dough to overferment if it were retarded and would produce a flatter loaf with a coarse grain and crumb.

Folding over the dough

Dough is folded over to redistribute the available food supply for the yeast, equalize the temperature of the dough, expel the built-up fermentation gas (carbon dioxide) and ethyl alcohol, and further develop the gluten in the dough. This may be done during bulk fermentation, bench rest, or final fermentation.

Doughs that have a typical hydration of around 67 percent or less should be treated gently during the folding process. It is more difficult for the gases resulting from the fermentation process to leaven the bread because of its density and the tightness of the gluten. For these reasons, it is important to fold carefully to preserve the already developed structure. A slack (wet) dough, such as that for ciabatta, requires more aggressive treatment when folding over. It is more difficult to develop the gluten in slack doughs; they require more gluten development to hold their shape and retain their inner structure.

In wet doughs, gluten is further developed during folding.

Fiber-enriched doughs

Whole wheat flour and flour made from grains such as rye, barley, buckwheat, rice, oats, millet, corn, and soy all contribute distinctive tastes and textures, as well as nutrition, to breads. They also make them heavier and denser. Typically, some measure of bread flour is included in formulas calling for whole wheat or nonwheat flours in order to develop a light, open crumb.

The bran in whole-grain flours interferes with the development of gluten. Bran cuts the strands of gluten, inhibiting their development and reducing their ability to trap the carbon dioxide produced by the yeast. The higher the percentage of whole wheat or nonwheat flour in a formula, the more pronounced its effect will be on the characteristics of the finished loaf.

One of the ways bread bakers aid the development of gluten in formulas containing these flours is known as *autolyse*. The flour and water are briefly combined first, just enough for a rough mixture to form. For more information, see "Autolyse" in Chapter 8, page 150.

Scaling and preshaping

Accurate scaling guarantees the correct weight of the dough pieces when dividing. However, scaling should be done quickly, so as not to over-age the dough. Scaling time should not exceed 15 to 20 minutes. Proper scaling will also allow for uniformity in proofing and baking times. Dough is usually divided either entirely by hand using a scale, or first divided into large portions by hand and then divided into smaller pieces with a dough divider.

After scaling, the dough is given a gentle first shaping or "preshaping." Always lay the shaped pieces on the bench in the order they are shaped, in regular rows, so that you can start with the first piece when giving the dough the final shaping. The objective of preshaping is to get a smooth, tight skin that will help to trap the gases that develop during fermentation.

During scaling and preshaping, two things happen to the dough: First, because it is cut, the carbon dioxide trapped inside begins to escape, which causes the structure of the dough to begin to collapse; and second, the gluten strands are worked, which causes them to contract, making the dough tighter and tougher to work with.

For large rounds (from 6 oz to 4½ lb/170 g to 2.04 kg)

1. Position the dough so one long edge is parallel to the edge of the work surface.

2. Fold the top edge of the dough down to the bottom edge. Using the heel of your hand, seal the two edges together. Rotate the dough 90 degrees.

3. Fold the top edge of the dough down to the bottom edge. Using the heel of your hand, seal the two edges together. Place seam on bottom.

4. Cup both hands around the dough and pull it toward you, giving it a one-quarter turn; continue until fully tightened.

Accurate scaling guarantees the correct weight of the dough pieces when dividing.

For small rounds (from 2 to 6 oz/57 to 170 g)

1. Position the dough so one long edge is parallel to the edge of the work surface.

2. Fold the top edge of the dough down to the bottom edge. Using the heel of your hand, seal the two edges together. Rotate the dough 90 degrees.

3. Fold the top edge of the dough down to the bottom edge. Using the heel of your hand, seal the two edges together.

4. Place your hand over the ball of dough and curl your fingers so that the first knuckles of your fingers are touching the table. Your fingertips should almost be touching the palm of your hand, and your thumb should be out to the side and touching the table; the heel of your hand should also be touching the table. The dough should be sitting near the top of your palm, near your thumb, forefinger, and middle finger.

5. Using your palm, push the dough away from you in an arc to the right. Using your fingertips, pull the dough toward you in an arc to the left. Repeat this circular motion, applying gentle pressure while rounding the dough, to create a tight, smooth ball.

For large oblongs (from 12 oz to 1¾ lb/340 to 794 g)

1. Position the dough so one long edge is parallel to the edge of the work surface.

2. Stretch the dough into a rectangle 10 in/25 cm long. Fold the left and right edges of the rectangle into the center of the dough, pressing the dough lightly with your fingertips.

3. Fold the top edge of the dough down to the center of the dough, pressing lightly with your fingertips. Fold the top of the dough down to the bottom edge. Seal the two edges together, using the heel of your hand.

4. Roll the dough into an even cylinder 6 in/15 cm long.

For small oblongs (from 3 to 6 oz/85 to 170 g)

1. Turn the dough so one long edge is parallel to the edge of the work surface.

2. Stretch the dough into a rectangle 3 in/8 cm long. Fold the left and right edges of the rectangle into the center of the dough, pressing the dough lightly with your fingertips.

3. Fold the top edge of the dough down to the center of the dough, pressing lightly with your fingertips. Fold the top of the dough down to the bottom edge. Seal the two edges together, using the heel of your hand.

4. Roll the dough into an even cylinder 3 in/8 cm long.

Resting or intermediate fermentation

After bulk fermentation, dividing, and preshaping, the dough is allowed to ferment again. This period has various names: *bench rest, table rest,* or *secondary or intermediate fermentation.* This stage allows the dough to relax and recover from the dividing and preshaping process in preparation for final shaping: It allows the gluten to relax, so the dough will become somewhat slack and easier to manipulate into its final shape, and it allows the yeast cells to recover, rebuilding carbon dioxide and therefore the internal structure of the dough. Normally, this stage lasts from 10 to 20 minutes. It is important to keep the loaves covered with plastic wrap or a moist linen cloth to prevent the formation of a skin or dry crust.

Final shaping

After the secondary fermentation, the dough is given its final shape. Following are two of the most basic and common shaping techniques: a boule and a bâtard. Throughout this and the advanced breads and rolls chapter, various formulas will utilize and illustrate common shapes used for lean and enriched yeast doughs. Brush the dough with egg wash or water, if using, after it is shaped so that the dough can be evenly coated without affecting it after its final rise (see also "Washes," page 113). Any simple garnishes such as seeds or coarse salt can be applied once the surface is brushed with egg wash or water; the wash will hold them in place.

Shaping a boule

FROM LEFT TO RIGHT: Preshape the dough into a round and allow to rest uncovered until relaxed, 15 to 20 minutes.

Cup both hands around the dough. Using your thumbs, push the dough away from you in an arc to the right.

Using the edges of your palms as a guide, pull the dough toward you in an arc to the left.

Shaping a bâtard

FROM LEFT TO RIGHT: Gently flatten the preshaped oblong.

Fold the top of the dough to the center.

Press the seam with your fingertips to tighten the dough.

Roll the ends of the cylinder with the palms of your hands to taper.

French regional shapes

Final fermentation (proofing)

After shaping, the dough undergoes one more fermentation. Some doughs, such as the lean dough used to prepare boules, can simply be placed on a worktable or a board that has been dusted with flour or cornmeal. Other doughs or shapes may be placed on a linen cloth (couche), on sheet pans, in loaf pans, or in baskets (bannetons), wooden molds, or other molds. During this final rise, it is again important to ensure that a skin does not form on the surface of the dough. If you are not using a proof box for this final proof, the dough should be covered. Using the temperature and humidity controls in a proof box will prevent a skin from forming without the dough being covered.

A temperature- and humidity-controlled proof box can provide the necessary relative humidity of approximately 80 percent, so the surface of the dough does not dry out. (Conversely, if the humidity is too high, the loaves will become too sticky for proper crust formation.) The ambient temperature for the final proof should be between 80° and 90°F/27° and 32°C for maximum yeast activity; the ideal temperature is 85°F/29°C. If the temperature during this final proof is too high, insufficient yeast activity will result in poor grain and loss of flavor, and the shelf life of the bread will be shorter. A temperature that is too low will result in a longer proofing time.

Small items such as rolls must be allowed to fully ferment during final proofing because they bake quickly, leaving less time for fermentation in the oven. Large items such as loaves should be proofed to a slightly less developed state than small items, as they require longer baking times and will continue to ferment (or proof) for a longer time in the oven.

Finishing techniques

Scoring and washes, when used, enhance the overall beauty of the finished loaf or roll. Scoring allows for full expansion, as well as controlling the final expansion, so the loaf does not become misshapen. Washes control the crust development during baking.

Scoring

Many breads are scored with a razor, sharp knife, or scissors before they are loaded into the oven. Scoring helps develop a good-quality loaf with an even appearance and crumb. It allows the bread to release steam and continue to expand until the structure is set. By scoring the dough, the baker can control the final shape of the bread by determining where the product expands during baking. Baking an unscored bread results in an unevenly shaped loaf. The structure forms too early to permit full expansion and, consequently, the full development of the internal structure of the loaf.

Some breads, such as baguettes, are scored with traditional patterns that are used as a way to label the breads, making it easy for both clients and staff to identify them.

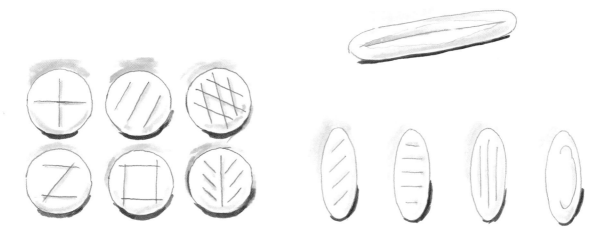

FROM LEFT TO RIGHT: **Scoring patterns for round loaves:** Patterns are evenly distributed over the entire surface. **Scoring patterns for oblong loaves:** Notice they are at the highest points on the loaf.

Washes

Water is often brushed or sprayed on shaped breads before baking to ensure a crisp crust and to promote the gelatinization of the starch on the surface of the bread. Beaten eggs as a wash create a glossy, shiny crust and seal in the moisture in the bread. Typically, whole eggs are used. A wash of only yolks would burn more quickly, especially at the higher temperatures required for baking most breads.

Milk or cream is often used for breads baked at lower temperatures. Because the lactose in milk (or cream) caramelizes at 170°F/77°C, it gives breads a darker crust than water. In addition, the bread will bake a little faster because the milk fat acts to conduct heat.

Baking

After it is placed in the oven, the dough continues to rise for a brief period. This is known as *oven spring*, and it continues during the first few minutes of baking, until the dough reaches an internal temperature of 140°F/60°C, at which point the yeast dies.

Most breads, except those that have been brushed with egg wash, are steamed at the outset of the baking process. The steam gives a final boost of volume, allows for maximum expansion of the dough, and adds sheen and color to the crust. Steam is typically used in baking lean doughs. It helps develop texture and keeps the surface of the dough soft so that it can expand during the beginning stages of baking. It also acts to gelatinize the starches on the surface of the dough to facilitate structure formation.

After the steam evaporates or is vented from the oven, the browning of the crust takes place. The moisture from the steam still remaining on the dough conducts heat rapidly and the surface of the bread sets quickly, thus ending the expansion of the loaf and beginning the development of a crisp, brown crust.

The length of time bread bakes is determined by a number of factors, including the type of bread, the weight of the loaf, the type of oven (hearth, rotating, convection, etc.), oven temperature, and oven humidity.

Lean doughs should be baked in a hot oven (440° to 500°F/227° to 260°C) with steam; enriched doughs should be baked at a slightly lower temperature (350° to 400°F/177° to 204°C). Beyond this, other factors that may affect the specific baking temperature are the type of oven, the size and shape of the product, and the desired crust and color development.

During baking, carbon dioxide and steam are released in the bread and expand to further leaven the bread. The gluten strands (and eggs, if used) stretch and coagulate to develop the internal structure of the bread. The starches gelatinize to form the crust, and flavor and color develop as sugar caramelizes.

Once the loaves are baked, it is important that they be cooled properly in order to preserve the crust and structure of the bread, as well as to allow for final development of flavor. All breads, but especially those made with lean doughs, should be cooled on wire racks to maintain air circulation around the entire loaf. This will prevent moisture from collecting on the bread as it cools.

Enriched doughs

The term *enriching* indicates that ingredients containing fat or sugar are added to the dough. Many different ingredients, such as milk, oil, or butter, may be used to enrich a dough. Often, enriched breads also contain a measure of sugar that as been introduced through either the addition of ingredients that contain some type of sugar (e.g., lactose, through the use of milk), or simply by the addition of a granulated or syrup form of sugar.

The addition of fat or sugar dramatically affects the finished product. The additional fat acts to shorten the gluten strands and increase the elasticity of the gluten in a dough. This will have a tenderizing effect on the finished product, yielding a more tender crumb and the development of a soft crust. Additional sugars promote quick fermentation and browning of the crust during baking.

Lean dough

MAKES 8 LB 7¾ OZ/3.85 KG DOUGH. DDT: 78°F/26°C

Bread flour	100%	5 lb	2.27 kg
Instant dry yeast	0.83%	⅔ oz	19 g
Water	66.9%	53½ fl oz	1.61 L
Salt	2.2%	1¾ oz	50 g

1   Combine the flour and yeast. Add the water and salt to the mixer and then add the flour and the yeast. Mix on low speed with the dough hook attachment for 2 minutes and mix on medium speed for 3 minutes. The dough should be smooth and elastic. Mix to the improved stage of gluten development.

2   Bulk ferment the dough until nearly doubled, about 30 minutes. Fold gently. Ferment for another 30 minutes and fold again. Ferment for another 15 minutes.

3   Divide the dough into pieces 1 lb/454 g each. Preshape the dough into large rounds (for preshaping instructions, see page 109). Let the dough rest, covered, until relaxed, 15 to 20 minutes. (Reminder: When making multiple loaves, work sequentially, starting with the first piece of dough you divided and rounded.)

4   To shape as a boule: Cup both hands around the dough. Using your thumbs, push the dough away from you in an arc to the right, keeping a small piece of dough between the table and the edges of your palms. Using the edges of your palms as a guide, pull the dough toward you in an arc to the left. There should still be a small piece of dough that is squeezed between the table and the edges of your palms. Repeat this circular motion two or three more times, applying gentle pressure while rounding the dough, to create a tight, smooth outer skin. Place the boule seam side up in a lightly floured round basket or seam side down on a board dusted with cornmeal.

5   Proof until the dough springs back slowly to the touch, 1 to 1½ hours. Flip the dough seam side down onto a peel. Score the boule with an arc.

6   Presteam a 460°F/238°C deck oven. Load the bread into the oven and steam for 3 seconds. Bake until the crust is golden brown and the bread sounds hollow when thumped on the bottom, 25 to 30 minutes. Vent during the final 10 minutes. Cool completely on racks.

Bagels

High-gluten flour	100%	5 lb	2.27 kg
Instant dry yeast	0.4%	⅓ oz	9 g
Water	57.5%	46 fl oz	1.38 L
Salt	2.1%	1¾ oz	50 g
Diastatic malt syrup	0.94%	¾ oz	21 g
Malt syrup (per 5 gal/18.75 L water), for boiling		5 oz	142 g
Garnishes such as sesame seeds, poppy seeds, salt		as needed	as needed

1   Combine the flour and yeast. Add the water, salt, and diastatic malt syrup to the mixer and then add the flour and yeast. Mix on low speed with the dough hook attachment for 4 minutes and on medium speed for 5 minutes. The dough should be stiff, dry, and elastic and have strong gluten development.

2   Divide the dough into 5-oz/142-g pieces.

3   Preshape each piece of dough into a small 5-in/13-cm oblong (for preshaping instructions, see page 110). Let the dough rest, covered, for 10 minutes.

4   Start with the first piece of dough that you shaped and work sequentially. Roll each piece of dough under your palms into a cylinder 10 in/25 cm long; begin rolling with your palms near the center of the dough and use even pressure from the center to the ends. Taper the ends very slightly.

5   Shape each cylinder into a ring, overlapping the ends by 1 in/3 cm; make sure the seams are aligned with the rest of the ring. Place two or three of your fingers in the center of the bagel and roll the overlapped ends gently against the worktable until they are the same diameter as the rest of the bagel. (As you work, it may become necessary to moisten your hands or the table to prevent sticking.) After rolling, the bagels should be 4 in/10 cm wide with a hole 2 in/5 cm in diameter.

6   Place the bagels seam side down on cornmeal-dusted sheet pans. Cover the bagels and proof under refrigeration (retard) for 8 hours or overnight.

7   Let the proofed bagels rest at room temperature, covered, for 15 minutes. Meanwhile, bring 5 gal/18.75 L of water to a boil and add the malt syrup.

8   Line sheet pans with silicon-coated parchment paper. Add a few bagels at a time to the water, stir once or twice to keep them from sticking together, and simmer until they rise to the top, about 20 seconds. Place the bagels on a screen to remove excess water. Add garnish as desired.

9   Transfer the bagels to a peel and load them into a 500°F/260°C deck oven. Bake until golden brown but still soft and slightly springy to the touch, 10 to 15 minutes. Cool completely on racks.

bagels

To make bagels successfully, it's important to keep a few guidelines in mind. It is important to use high-gluten flour and malt syrup in the dough. The high-gluten flour helps to develop the characteristic chewiness of a bagel. And the malt syrup contains enzymes that help break down the carbohydrates in the flour into sugars, further developing the texture and flavor of the bagels.

Bagel dough is very tight and dry. The dough should be mixed until it is very smooth. This extensive mixing will make the dough slightly tacky even though it contains little water. Unlike most other breads, bagels should be shaped immediately after the dough is mixed. Then the bagels should be retarded overnight to develop flavor and relax the gluten. Following retarding, they are poached in a mixture of water and malt. The poaching activates the yeast, and the water that remains on the bagels results in the sheen on the surface of the bagels; but most important, since the starches are gelatinized before going into the oven, they seal in moisture, creating a chewy bagel. The bagels must first dry slightly before they are put directly on the deck, or they will stick.

LEFT: Bagel dough has a consistency referred to as *bucky* because of its very stiff consistency.

MIDDLE: Roll the bagel under the palm of your hand to seal the seam and even out its diameter.

RIGHT: Poach the bagels in a malt water bath just until they float to the surface.

Whole wheat lean dough

MAKES 8 LB 10½ OZ/3.93 KG DOUGH. DDT: 78°F/26°C

Bread flour	60%	3 lb	1.36 kg
Whole wheat flour	40%	2 lb	907 g
Instant dry yeast	0.75%	⅔ oz	19 g
Water	70%	56 fl oz	1.68 L
Salt	2.2%	1¾ oz	50 g

1   Combine the flours and yeast. Add the water and salt to the mixer and then add the flour and yeast. Mix on low speed with the dough hook attachment for 3 minutes and on medium speed for 3 minutes. The dough should be soft but with sufficient gluten development. Mix to the improved stage of gluten development.

2   Bulk ferment the dough until nearly doubled, about 30 minutes. Fold gently and ferment for another 30 minutes. Fold again. Ferment for another 15 minutes.

3   Divide the dough into pieces 1 lb/454 g each. Preshape the dough into large oblongs (for preshaping instructions, see page 109). Let the dough rest, covered, until relaxed, 15 to 20 minutes. (Reminder: When making multiple loaves, work sequentially, starting with the first piece of dough you divided and rounded.)

4   To shape as a bâtard: Position the dough lengthwise, parallel to the edge of the work surface with the seam side up, and press lightly with your fingertips. Fold the top edge of the dough down to the center of the dough, pressing lightly with your fingertips to tighten.

5   Fold the dough lengthwise in half and use the heel of your hand to seal the two edges, keeping the seam straight. Roll the dough under your palms into a cylinder 8 in/20 cm long, moving your hands outward from the center of the cylinder toward the ends and slightly increasing the pressure as you move outward, until both ends have an even, gentle taper. Then increase the pressure at the ends of the loaf to seal.

6   Proof, covered, in a couche, until the dough springs back slowly to the touch but does not collapse, 45 minutes.

7   Score the bâtard straight down the center.

8   Presteam a 460°F/238°C deck oven. Load the bread into the oven and steam for 3 seconds. Bake until the crust is golden brown and the bread sounds hollow when thumped on the bottom, 25 to 30 minutes. Vent during the final 10 minutes. Cool completely on racks.

Durum rosemary dough

MAKES 15 LB 9 OZ/7.06 KG DOUGH. DDT: 78°F/26°C

Durum flour	74.1%	6 lb 10 oz	3.01 kg
Bread flour	25.9%	2 lb 5 oz	1.05 kg
Instant dry yeast	0.45%	¾ oz	21 g
Water	70%	100 fl oz	3 L
Salt	2.1%	3 oz	85 g
Rosemary, coarsely chopped	0.7%	1 oz	28 g

1   Combine the flours and yeast. Add the water, salt, and rosemary to the mixer and then add the flour and yeast. Mix on low speed with the dough hook attachment for 3 minutes and on medium speed for 3 minutes. The dough should be slightly stiff with sufficient gluten development. Mix to the improved stage of gluten development.

2   Bulk ferment the dough until nearly doubled, about 40 minutes. Fold gently. Ferment for another 40 minutes.

3   Divide the dough into pieces 1 lb/ 454 g each. Preshape the dough into large rounds (for preshaping instructions, see page 109). Let the dough rest, covered, until relaxed, 15 to 20 minutes. (Reminder: When making multiple loaves, work sequentially, starting with the first piece of dough you divided and rounded.)

4   To shape as a boule: Cup both hands around the dough. Using your thumbs, push the dough away from you in an arc to the right, keeping a small piece of dough between the table and the edges of your palms. Using the edges of your palms as a guide, pull the dough toward you in an arc to the left. There should still be a small piece of dough that is squeezed between the table and the edges of your palms. Repeat this circular motion two or three more times, applying gentle pressure while rounding the dough, to create a tight, smooth outer skin. Place the boule seam side up in a round basket or seam side down on a board dusted with cornmeal.

5   Proof until the dough springs back slowly to the touch, 1 to 1½ hours. Flip the dough seam side down onto a peel. Score the boule with an arc.

6   Presteam a 460°F/238°C deck oven. Load the bread into the oven and steam for 3 seconds. Bake until the crust is golden brown and the bread sounds hollow when thumped on the bottom, 25 to 30 minutes. Vent during the final 10 minutes of baking. Cool completely on racks.

Knot rolls using soft roll dough

MAKES 9 LB 4 OZ/4.20 KG DOUGH. DDT: 78°F/26°C

Bread flour	100%	5 lb	2.27 kg
Instant dry yeast	1.66%	1¼ oz	35 g
Milk, room temperature	50%	40 fl oz	1.20 L
Butter, soft	10%	8 oz	227 g
Eggs (55°F/13°C)	10%	8 oz	227 g
Sugar	10%	8 oz	227 g
Salt	2.5%	2 oz	57 g
Egg wash (page 892)		as needed	as needed

1   Combine the flour and yeast. Add the milk, butter, eggs, sugar, and salt to the mixer and then add the flour and yeast. Mix on low speed for 4 minutes with the dough hook attachment and on medium speed for 3 minutes. The dough should be firm but elastic. Mix to the improved stage of gluten development.

2   Bulk ferment the dough until nearly doubled, about 1 hour. Fold gently.

3   Divide the dough into pieces 4 lb/ 1.8 kg each. Preshape the dough into large rounds (for preshaping instructions, see page 109). Line sheet pans with parchment paper. Let the dough rest, covered, until relaxed, 15 to 20 minutes.

4   Divide the dough into 36 pieces (1¾ oz/50 g each) by hand or using a dough divider. Starting with the first piece of dough that you shaped and working sequentially, flatten a piece of dough slightly with your fingertips. Fold the top edge of the dough down to the center of the dough, pressing lightly with your fingertips to tighten the dough. Fold the dough in half again and use the heel of your hand to seal the two edges together, keeping the seam straight. Roll the dough under your palms into an even rope 6 in/15 cm long.

5   Lay 2 in/5 cm of one end of the rope over your forefinger and middle finger. There should be ½ in/1 cm of dough hanging over your fingers; bring it under your fingers and cross it over the dough sitting on your fingers.

6   Bring the longer piece of dough underneath the dough sitting on your fingers. This will be the base of the knot; there should be ½ in/1 cm of dough to the left of the knot and 2 in/5 cm of dough to the right of it. There should be one side of the roll where the knot is formed and one side of the roll that is smooth. Bring the longer piece of dough around the smooth side of the dough, and pinch the ends of the dough together. Turn the roll so that the pinched ends are on the bottom.

7   Arrange the rolls in rows on the lined sheet pans, spacing them 4 in/10 cm apart. Brush the rolls with egg wash. Proof, covered, until the dough springs back slowly to the touch but does not collapse, 30 to 50 minutes.

8   Lightly brush the rolls again with egg wash. Bake in a 375°F/191°C convection oven until the rolls are golden brown and shiny, about 15 minutes. Cool completely on the pans.

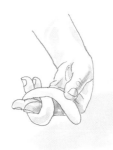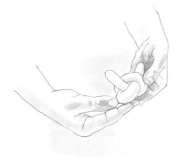

FROM LEFT TO RIGHT: Cross the dough over your hand.

Bring the longer piece of dough underneath the piece of dough sitting on your fingers.

Continue the knot.

Pinch the two ends together.

Parker House rolls

MAKES 3 DOZEN ROLLS (1¾ OZ/50 G EACH). DDT: 75°F/24°C

Soft roll dough (opposite)	4 lb	1.81 kg
Clarified butter, for brushing	as needed	as needed

1   Follow the method for Knot Rolls (opposite) through step 2. Preshape the dough into a round (for preshaping instructions, see page 109). Line sheet pans with parchment paper. Let the dough rest, covered, until relaxed, 15 to 20 minutes.

2   Divide the dough into 36 pieces (1¾ oz/50 g each) by hand or using a dough divider.

3   Reround each piece and let them rest, covered, for 10 minutes.

4   Roll each piece of dough into an oval 5 in/13 cm long and 2½ in/6 cm wide; the dough will be about ⅛ in/3 mm thick. Brush any excess flour off the dough as you work. Fold each oval in half so that they are now 2½ in/6 cm wide, 2½ in/6 cm long, and ¼ in/6 mm thick. Turn the dough so that the folded edge is facing toward you. Roll the bottom 2 in/5 cm of the dough until it is ⅛ in/3 mm thick. The remaining ½ in/1 cm of dough at the top should still be ¼ in/6 mm thick.

5   Arrange the rolls in rows on the lined sheet pans, spacing them 4 in/10 cm apart. Brush with clarified butter. Proof until the dough springs back slowly to the touch, 30 to 40 minutes.

6   Bake in a 375°F/191°C convection oven until the rolls are golden brown and shiny, about 20 minutes. Brush the rolls with clarified butter as soon as they are removed from the oven. Cool completely on the pans.

Shaping Parker House rolls

Grissini (opposite) and Lavash (page 142)

Grissini

MAKES 8 LB 8 OZ/3.86 KG DOUGH. DDT: 78°F/26°C

High-gluten flour	100%	5 lb	2.27 kg
Instant dry yeast	1.66%	1¼ oz	35 g
Milk, room temperature	45%	36 fl oz	1.08 L
Butter, soft	15%	12 oz	340 g
Olive oil	3.75%	3 oz	85 g
Salt	2.5%	2 oz	57 g
Malt syrup	1.9%	1½ oz	43 g
Olive oil, for brushing		as needed	as needed
Optional garnishes: coarse salt, poppy seeds, sesame seeds		as needed	as needed

1   Combine the flour and yeast. Add the milk, butter, olive oil, salt, and malt to the mixer and then add the flour and yeast. Mix on low speed with the dough hook attachment for 4 minutes and on medium speed for 3 minutes. The dough should be very stiff. Let the dough rest for 15 minutes.

2   Bulk ferment the dough until nearly doubled, about 30 minutes.

3   Line sheet pans with parchment paper.

4   Using a rolling pin, roll the dough into rectangles 12 in/30 cm long and the width of the rollers on a pasta machine.

5   Starting with the rollers at the widest opening and resetting them to the next setting after each complete pass, roll the dough through the pasta machine until it is the desired thickness, about ¼ in/6 mm or setting number 5 on most pasta machines. Trim one short edge to even it; this is the edge that should be fed into the pasta machine.

6   Using the fettuccine cutter attachment or by hand, cut the dough lengthwise into strips ¼ in/6 mm wide. Lay the strips crosswise on the parchment-lined sheet pans, making sure they do not touch. Brush the strips lightly with olive oil.

7   Proof, covered, until the dough rises slightly, about 30 minutes. Brush the grissini lightly with olive oil and scatter with salt and any optional garnishes.

8   Bake in a 360°F/182°C convection oven until the grissini are golden brown, 8 to 12 minutes. Cool completely on racks.

NOTE   In step 1, just after mixing you may add inclusions such as cheese, sun-dried tomatoes, herbs, or roasted garlic. Just make sure any inclusions are finely chopped.

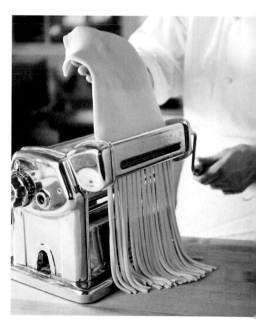

Feeding grissini through a pasta machine

Pain de mie

MAKES 37 LB 13 OZ/17.15 KG DOUGH. DDT: 78°F/26°C

Bread flour	100%	20 lb 15 oz	9.50 kg
Instant dry yeast	0.9%	3 oz	85 g
Salt	2.3%	8 oz	227 g
Sugar	4.1%	13¾ oz	390 g
Olive oil	8.8%	1 lb 13 oz	822 g
Water	64.9%	13 lb 10 oz	6.18 kg

1 Combine the flour and yeast. Add the salt, sugar, oil, and water to the mixer and then add the flour and yeast. Mix on low speed with the dough hook attachment for 4 minutes and on medium speed for 4 minutes. The dough should be a little sticky, but with fairly good gluten development. Mix to the intense stage of gluten development.

2 Bulk ferment the dough until nearly doubled, about 45 minutes.

3 Divide the dough into pieces 2 lb 8 oz/1.13 kg each.

4 Preshape the dough into large oblongs 10 in/25 cm long (for preshaping instructions, see page 109). Let the dough rest, covered, until relaxed, 15 to 20 minutes. (Reminder: When making multiple loaves, work sequentially, starting with the first piece of dough you divided and rounded.)

5 Position the dough lengthwise, parallel to the edge of the work surface with the seam side up, and press lightly with your fingertips. Fold the top edge of the dough down to the center of the dough, pressing lightly with your fingertips to tighten.

6 Fold the dough lengthwise in half and use the heel of your hand to seal the two edges, keeping the seam straight. Roll the dough under your palms into a cylinder 8 in/20 cm long, moving your hands outward from the center of the cylinder toward the ends and slightly increasing the pressure as you move outward, until both ends have an even, gentle taper. Then increase the pressure at the ends of the loaf to seal. Place in oiled Pullman pans.

7 Proof, uncovered, until the pans are three-quarters full and the dough springs back slowly to the touch but does not collapse, 45 to 60 minutes.

8 Place the oiled lids on the pans and bake in a 375°F/191°C oven for 40 minutes, or to an internal temperature of 205°F/96°C. Remove from the pans immediately and cool on racks.

Wheat Pullman loaves

MAKES 14 LB 14 OZ/6.75 KG DOUGH. DDT: 78°F/26°C

Bread flour	60%	4 lb 14¾ oz	2.23 kg
Whole wheat flour	40%	3 lb 4½ oz	1. 49 kg
Instant dry yeast	0.7%	1 oz	28 g
Salt	2.2%	3 oz	85 g
Sugar	4%	5¼ oz	149 g
Canola oil	6.7%	9 oz	255 g
Milk, room temperature	69.3%	5 lb 11 oz	2.58 kg

1   Combine the flours and yeast. Add the salt, sugar, oil, and milk to the mixer and then add the flour and yeast. Mix on low speed with the dough hook attachment for 4 minutes and on medium speed for 4 minutes. The dough should be a little sticky, but with fairly good gluten development. Mix to the intense stage of gluten development.

2   Bulk ferment the dough until nearly doubled, about 45 minutes.

3   Divide the dough into pieces 2 lb 8 oz/1.13 kg each.

4   Preshape the dough into 10-in/25-cm large oblongs (for preshaping instructions, see page 109). Let the dough rest, covered, until relaxed, 15 to 20 minutes. (Reminder: When making multiple loaves, work sequentially, starting with the first piece of dough you divided and rounded.)

5   Position the dough lengthwise, parallel to the edge of the work surface with the seam side up, and press lightly with your fingertips. Fold the top edge of the dough down to the center of the dough, pressing lightly with your fingertips to tighten.

6   Fold the dough lengthwise in half and use the heel of your hand to seal the two edges, keeping the seam straight. Roll the dough under your palms into a cylinder 8 in/20 cm long, moving your hands outward from the center of the cylinder toward the ends and slightly increasing the pressure as you move outward, until both ends have an even, gentle taper. Then increase the pressure at the ends of the loaf to seal. Place in oiled Pullman pans.

7   Proof, uncovered, until the pans are three-quarters full and the dough springs back slowly to the touch but does not collapse, 45 to 60 minutes.

8   Place the oiled lids on the pans and bake in a 375°F/191°C convection oven for 35 minutes, or to an internal temperature of 205°F/96°C. Remove from the pans immediately and cool on racks.

Rye dough with caraway seeds for Pullman loaves

MAKES 25 LB 11 OZ/11.65 KG DOUGH. DDT: 78°F/26°C

Bread flour	76.25%	11 lb 7 oz	5.19 kg
Medium rye flour	23.75%	3 lb 9 oz	1.62 kg
Instant dry yeast	0.6%	1½ oz	43 g
Water	61.25%	147 fl oz	4.41 L
Sugar	1.9%	4½ oz	128 g
Salt	2.2%	5¼ oz	149 g
Vegetable oil	1.9%	4½ oz	128 g
Molasses, unsulfured	1.9%	4½ oz	128 g
Caraway seeds	1.25%	3 oz	85 g

1   Combine the flours and yeast. Add the water, sugar, salt, oil, and molasses to the mixer and then add the flour and yeast. Mix on low speed with the dough hook attachment for 4 minutes and on medium speed for 3 minutes. The dough should be firm but elastic. Blend in the caraway seeds. Mix to the intense stage of gluten development.

2   Bulk ferment the dough until nearly doubled, about 45 minutes.

3   Grease eight 3-lb/1.36-kg Pullman loaf pans and lids generously. Divide the dough into pieces 2 lb 8 oz/1.34 kg each. Preshape the dough into large rounds (for preshaping instructions, see page 109). Let the dough rest, covered, until relaxed, 15 to 20 minutes. (Reminder: When making multiple loaves, work sequentially, starting with the first piece of dough you divided and rounded.)

4   Place the dough lengthwise with the seam side up. Press lightly with your fingertips to stretch it into a rectangle 8 in/20 cm long, using as little flour as possible. Fold the top edge of the dough down to the center of the dough, pressing lightly with your fingertips to tighten the dough.

5   Fold the dough lengthwise in half and use the heel of your hand to seal the two edges together, keeping the seam straight. Roll the dough under your palms into a cylinder 10 in/25 cm long, keeping the pressure even and holding your hands flat and parallel to the work surface to create a smooth, even loaf.

6   Let the dough rest, covered, until relaxed, 15 to 20 minutes.

7   Turn the dough seam side up and position it so that a long side is parallel to the edge of the work surface. Work the dough lightly with your fingertips to release some of the gas, then gently stretch it into a rectangle 16 in/41 cm long and 2½ in/6 cm wide. Fold 1 in/3 cm of each short end in toward the center of the dough. Fold the long sides into the center, overlapping them slightly, and use the heel of your hand to seal the two edges together, keeping the seam straight. Fold the dough lengthwise in half and use your fingertips to seal the edges together, keeping the seam straight.

8   Roll the dough under your palms into a cylinder 18 in/46 cm long, keeping the pressure even and holding your hands flat and parallel to the work surface to create a smooth, even loaf. Push the ends of the loaf toward the center until the cylinder is 16 in/41 cm long. Place the dough seam side down in the greased loaf pans. The dough will spring back on itself slightly and fit snugly in the pan. Proof uncovered until the pans are three-quarters full and the dough springs back slowly to the touch, about 1 hour.

9   Place the oiled lids on the pans and bake at 400° to 375°F/204° to 191°C for 35 minutes, or to an internal temperature of 205°F/96°C. Remove from the pans immediately and cool on wire racks.

Sunflower seed rolls

MAKES 14 LB 11 OZ/6.66 KG DOUGH. DDT: 79°F/26°C

Wheat bran	11.5%	12 oz	340 g
Milk, room temperature	86.5%	90 fl oz	2.70 L
Bread flour	100%	6 lb 8 oz	2.95 kg
Instant dry yeast	0.65%	⅔ oz	19 g
Honey	7.7%	8 oz	227 g
Sunflower oil	5.75%	6 oz	170 g
Salt	2.4%	2½ oz	71 g
Sunflower seeds, lightly toasted, plus more for garnish	11.5%	12 oz	340 g

1   Soak the wheat bran in the milk overnight. Combine the flour and yeast. Add the bran-milk mixture, the honey, oil, and salt to the mixer and then add the flour and yeast. Mix on low speed with the dough hook attachment for 4 minutes and on medium speed for 4½ minutes. The dough should be slightly soft but with full gluten development. It will tighten up during bulk fermentation. Add the sunflower seeds and mix on low speed for 2 minutes. Mix to the intense stage of gluten development.

2   Bulk ferment the dough until nearly doubled, about 1 hour.

3   Divide the dough into pieces 4 lb/1.81 kg each. Preshape the dough into large rounds (for preshaping instructions, see page 109). Let the dough rest, covered, until relaxed, 15 to 20 minutes.

4   Divide each piece of dough into 36 pieces (1⅓ oz/38 g each) by hand or using a dough divider.

5   Press each piece lightly with your fingertips to flatten. Fold the top edge of the dough down to the center of the dough, pressing lightly with your fingertips to tighten the dough. Rotate the dough 90 degrees, fold the dough in half, and use the heel of your hand to seal the two edges together. Cup the roll in your hand and reround the dough, applying gentle pressure to create a tight, smooth ball. Place on parchment-lined sheet pans and egg wash.

6   Proof, covered, until the dough springs halfway back slowly to the touch but does not collapse, about 40 to 50 minutes.

7   Egg wash and sprinkle with seeds.

8   Presteam a 410°F/210°C convection oven. Bake until the rolls have a golden brown crust and sound hollow when thumped on the bottom, about 15 minutes. Cool completely on racks.

VARIATION   Substitute lightly toasted pumpkin seeds for the sunflower seeds.

CLOCKWISE FROM TOP LEFT: Corn Rolls (page 206), Rye Dough with Caraway Seeds for Pullman Loaves (page 126), Cheddar and Onion Rye Dough (page 133), and Sunflower Seed Rolls (opposite)

Beer bread dough

MAKES 15 LB 10½ OZ/7.10 KG DOUGH. DDT: 75°F/24°C

Bread flour	85.6%	6 lb 9¾ oz	3 kg
Medium rye flour	14.4%	1 lb 1¾ oz	503 g
Instant dry yeast	0.4%	½ oz	14 g
Dark beer	57.1%	70½ fl oz	2.12 L
Pâte fermentée (see page 148)	28.5%	2 lb 3¼ oz	1 kg
Cottage cheese	14.4%	1 lb 1¾ oz	503 g
Salt	2.4%	3 oz	85 g

1   Combine the flours and yeast. Add the beer, pâte fermentée, cottage cheese, and salt to the mixer and then add the flour and yeast. Mix on low speed with the dough hook attachment for 3 minutes and on medium speed for 3 minutes. The dough should be sticky but have sufficient gluten development. Mix to the improved stage of gluten development.

2   Bulk ferment the dough until nearly doubled, about 45 minutes. Fold gently. Ferment for another 15 minutes.

3   Divide into pieces 1 lb/454 g each. Preshape the dough into large rounds (for preshaping instructions, see page 109). Let the dough rest, covered, until relaxed, 15 to 20 minutes.

4   Divide each piece of dough into 36 pieces (1⅓ oz/38 g each) by hand or using a dough divider.

5   Press each piece lightly with your fingertips to flatten. Fold the top edge of the dough down to the center of the dough, pressing lightly with your fingertips to tighten the dough. Fold the dough in half again and use the heel of your hand to seal the two edges together, keeping the seam straight.

6   Roll a piece of dough under your palms into a cylinder 3 in/8 cm long, keeping the pressure even and holding your hands flat and parallel to the work surface to create a smooth, even roll. Using your palms, gently taper the ends of the dough by increasing the pressure as you roll outward to the ends of the dough. Mist the rolls with water.

7   Proof, covered, on parchment-lined sheet pans until the dough springs back slowly to the touch but does not collapse, about 30 minutes.

8   Score the rolls with a straight cut down the center.

9   Presteam a 460°F/238°C deck oven. Load the rolls into the oven and steam for 3 seconds. Bake until the rolls have a golden brown crust and sound hollow when thumped on the bottom, about 15 minutes. Vent the rolls when they start to brown. Cool completely on racks.

Belgian apple cider bread

MAKES 18 LB 15½ OZ/8.60 KG DOUGH. DDT: 75°F/24°C

DOUGH			
Bread flour	66.7%	4 lb 6½ oz	2 kg
Medium rye flour	33.3%	2 lb 3¼ oz	9.99 kg
Instant dry yeast	0.33%	⅓ oz	9 g
Apple cider	66.7%	70½ fl oz	2.12 L
Sour cream	33.3%	2 lb 3¼ oz	9.99 kg
Pâte fermentée (see page 148)	83.5%	5 lb 8¼ oz	2.50 kg
Salt	2.25%	2⅓ oz	66 g
APPLE CIDER PASTE			
Medium rye flour		14 oz	397 g
Instant dry yeast		1 oz	28 g
Apple cider		1 lb 8¾ oz	702 g
Salt		½ oz	14 g
White rye flour, for dusting		as needed	as needed

1   To make the dough, combine the flours and yeast. Add the cider, sour cream, pâte fermentée, and salt to the mixer and then add the flour and yeast. Mix on low speed with the dough hook attachment for 4 minutes and on medium speed for 3 minutes. The dough should be sticky but have sufficient gluten development. Mix to the improved stage of gluten development.

2   Bulk ferment the dough until nearly doubled, about 30 minutes. Fold gently. Ferment for another 30 minutes.

3   Divide into pieces 1 lb 8 oz/680 g each. Preshape the dough into large rounds (for preshaping instructions, see page 109). Let the dough rest, covered, until relaxed, 15 to 20 minutes. (Reminder: When making multiple loaves, work sequentially, starting with the first piece of dough you divided and rounded.)

4   To prepare the apple cider paste, combine the flour and yeast. Blend the apple cider with the salt and then mix into the flour-yeast mixture and combine thoroughly.

5   Dust the work surface and rolling pin with rye flour. Turn the dough seam side down. Work the rolling pin from one edge of the dough outward, creating a flap ¼ in/6 mm thick. Repeat this process to create three evenly spaced flaps around the edges of the dough to form a triangle.

6   Turn the dough seam side up. Fold each flap toward the center of the dough to make a triangle, and flip the dough over again, with the flaps on the bottom. Spread 3¼ oz/92 g apple cider paste over the top of the loaf. Dust the top of the loaf with white rye flour.

7   Proof, uncovered, on parchment-lined sheet pans until the dough springs back slowly to the touch, 45 to 60 minutes.

8   Presteam a 450°F/232°C deck oven. Load the bread into the oven and steam for 3 seconds. Bake until the crust is golden brown and the bread sounds hollow when thumped on the bottom, 35 to 40 minutes. Vent during the final 10 minutes. Cool completely on racks.

Prosciutto and provolone bread

MAKES 18 LB 15½ OZ/8.60 KG DOUGH. DDT: 75°F/24°C

Bread flour	100%	10 lb	4.54 kg
Instant dry yeast	1%	1½ oz	43 g
Salt	2.2%	3½ oz	99 g
Water	58.1%	5lb, 3oz	2.6 kg
Olive oil	10.1%	1 lb	454 g
Butter, soft	2.7%	4¹/₃ oz	122 g
Prosciutto, medium dice	32%	3 lb 4 oz	1.45 kg
Provolone, medium dice	2%	3¼ oz	92 g

1   Combine the flour and yeast. Add the salt, water, olive oil, and butter to the mixer; then add the flour and the yeast. Mix on low speed with the dough hook attachment for 4 minutes and on high speed for 3 minutes. Add the prosciutto and cheese and mix on low speed for 2 minutes. Mix to the improved stage of gluten development.

2   Bulk ferment the dough until nearly doubled, about 45 minutes. Fold gently. Ferment for another 15 minutes.

3   Divide the dough into pieces 1 lb 4 oz/567 g each. Preshape the dough into large rounds (for preshaping instructions, see page 109). Let the dough rest, covered, until relaxed, 10 to 15 minutes. (Reminder: When making multiple loaves, work sequentially, starting with the first piece of dough you divided and rounded.)

4   To shape as a boule: Cup both hands around the dough. Using your thumbs, push the dough away from you in an arc to the right, keeping a small piece of dough between the table and the edges of your palms. Using the edges of your palms as a guide, pull the dough toward you in an arc to the left. There should still be a small piece of dough that is squeezed between the table and the edges of your palms. Repeat this circular motion two or three more times, applying gentle pressure while rounding the dough, to create a tight, smooth outer skin. Place the boule seam side up in a lightly floured round basket or seam side down on a board dusted with cornmeal.

5   Proof until the dough springs back halfway slowly to the touch, 45 minutes. Flip the dough seam side down onto a peel and score with a straight cut down the center.

6   Bake in a 450°F/232°C deck oven until the crust is golden brown and the bread sounds hollow when thumped on the bottom, 25 to 30 minutes. Vent during the final 10 minutes. Cool completely on racks.

Cheddar and onion rye dough

MAKES 11 LB/4.99 KG DOUGH. DDT: 78°F/26°C

Bread flour	76.25%	3 lb 13 oz	1.73 kg
Medium rye flour	23.75%	1 lb 3 oz	539 g
Instant dry yeast	0.63%	½ oz	14 g
Water	71.25%	57 fl oz	1.71 L
Salt	2.5%	2 oz	57 g
Sugar	1.9%	1½ oz	43 g
Molasses, unsulfured	1.9%	1½ oz	43 g
Vegetable oil	1.9%	1½ oz	43 g
Cheddar cheese, grated	20%	1 lb	454 g
Yellow onions, medium dice	20%	1 lb	454 g

1 Combine the flours and yeast. Add the water, salt, sugar, molasses, and oil to the mixer and then add the flour and yeast. Mix on low speed with the dough hook attachment for 4 minutes and on medium speed for 4 minutes. Add the cheese and onions and mix on low speed for an additional 2 minutes. The dough should be tight with strong gluten development. Mix to the intense stage of gluten development.

2 Bulk ferment the dough until nearly doubled, 45 minutes. Fold gently.

3 Divide the dough into pieces 4 lb/1.81 kg each. Preshape the dough into large rounds (for preshaping instructions, see page 109). Let the dough rest, covered, until relaxed, 15 to 20 minutes.

4 Divide each piece of dough into 36 pieces (1¾ oz/50 g each) by hand or using a dough divider.

5 Press each piece lightly with your fingertips to flatten. Fold the top edge of the dough down to the center of the dough, pressing lightly with your fingertips to tighten the dough. Rotate the dough 90 degrees, fold the dough in half, and use the heel of your hand to seal the two edges together. Cup the roll in your hand and reround the dough, applying gentle pressure to create a tight, smooth ball. Place on parchment-lined sheet pans.

6 Proof, covered, until the dough springs back halfway slowly to the touch but does not collapse, about 45 minutes.

7 Score the rolls with a straight cut down the center.

8 Presteam a 425°F/218°C deck oven. Load the rolls into the oven and steam for 3 seconds. Bake until the rolls have a golden brown crust and sound hollow when thumped on the bottom, about 15 minutes. Vent during the last 3 minutes. Cool completely on racks.

Challah (three-braid)

MAKES 9 LB 6½ OZ/4.27 KG DOUGH. DDT: 78°F/26°C

Bread flour	100%	5 lb 4 oz	2.38 kg
Instant dry yeast	1.2%	1 oz	28 g
Water	38%	32 fl oz	960 mL
Egg yolks	19%	1 lb	454 g
Vegetable oil	9.5%	8 oz	227 g
Sugar	9.5%	8 oz	227 g
Salt	1.8%	1½ oz	43 g
White rye (or bread) flour, for dusting		as needed	as needed
Egg wash (page 892), made with yolks only		as needed	as needed

1　Combine the flour and yeast. Add the water, egg yolks, oil, sugar, and salt to the mixer and then add flour and yeast. Mix on low speed with the dough hook attachment for 4 minutes and on medium speed for 4 minutes. The dough should be slightly firm and smooth, not sticky. Mix to the intense stage of gluten development.

2　Bulk ferment the dough until nearly doubled, about 1 hour. Fold gently.

3　Divide the dough into 5½-oz/156-g pieces. Preshape the dough into small oblongs (for pre-shaping instructions, see page 110). Allow the dough to rest, covered, until relaxed, 10 to 15 minutes. Fold the dough over in thirds, then shape.

4　Start with the first piece of dough that you shaped and work sequentially. Starting at the center of the dough, roll each piece outward, applying gentle pressure with your palms. Apply very little pressure at the center of the dough, but increase the pressure as you roll toward the ends of the dough. Roll each piece of dough into an evenly tapered strand 12 in/30 cm long. It is imperative that all of the strands be the same length. If they are not, the finished braid will be uneven.

5　Dust the top of the strands very lightly with white rye flour. (This will keep the dough dry as you braid and help maintain the overall definition of the braid.) Lay three strands of dough vertically parallel to each other. Begin braiding in the center of the strands. Place the left strand over the center strand, then place the right strand over the center strand. Repeat this process until you reach the end of the dough. Pinch the ends together tightly. Turn the braid around and flip it over so that the unbraided strands are facing you. Starting again from the left, repeat the braiding process until you reach the end of the dough. Pinch the ends together tightly. Place on parchment-lined sheet pans.

6　Brush the dough lightly with the egg wash. Allow the dough to proof, covered, until the dough springs back halfway slowly to the touch but does not collapse, about 1 hour. There should be a small indentation left in the dough. Egg wash the dough, very gently, before baking.

7　Bake in a 350°F/177°C convection oven until the braids are dark golden brown and shiny, 18 to 22 minutes. Cool completely on racks.

VARIATION   **CHALLAH (SIX-BRAID)**

1   Work through step 2 of the main method. Divide the dough into 2¾-oz/78-g pieces. Preshape the dough into small oblong pieces (for preshaping instructions, see page 110). Allow the dough to rest, covered, until relaxed, 15 to 20 minutes.

2   Start with the first piece of dough that you shaped and work sequentially. Starting at the center of the dough, roll each piece outward, applying gentle pressure with your palms. Apply very little pressure at the center of the dough, but increase the pressure as you roll toward the ends of the dough. Roll each piece of dough into an evenly tapered strand 12 in/30 cm long. It is imperative that all of the strands be the same length. If they are not, the finished braid will be uneven.

3   Dust the top of the strands very lightly with white rye flour. This will keep the dough dry as you braid and help maintain the overall definition of the braid.

4   Lay six strands of dough, separating them through the center, so they are grouped into three and three.

5   Move the strand of dough on the far left (1) under the center strand on the right (4).

6   Bring strand 6 over to the right side. Bring strand 1 over strand 6 and place next to strand 3.

7   Bring strand 2 over to the left side. Bring strand 6 over strand 2 and place next to strand 4.

8   Continue to bring the outer strands over and under the inner strands in this manner. When finished, pinch the ends together and place on parchment-lined sheet pans.

9   Brush the dough lightly with egg wash made solely from egg yolks. Allow the dough to proof, covered, until the dough springs back slowly to the touch but does not collapse, about 1 hour. There should be a small indentation left in the dough. Make sure that the egg wash is dry before you apply a second coat. Egg wash the dough a third time, very gently, before baking.

10   Bake in a 350°F/177°C convection oven until the braids are dark golden brown and shiny, 20 to 25 minutes. Cool completely on racks.

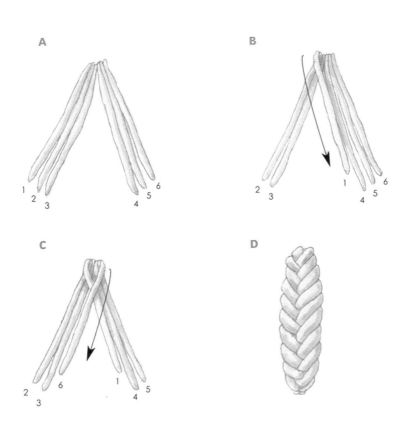

Sweet dough coffee cake

MAKES 12 LB 4½ OZ/5.57 KG DOUGH. DDT: 75°F/24°C

Bread flour	100%	7 lb 8 oz	3.40 kg
Instant dry yeast	1.25%	1½ oz	43 g
Milk	26.6%	32 fl oz	960 mL
Eggs	15%	1 lb 2 oz	510 g
Sugar	10%	12 oz	340 g
Butter, soft	10%	12 oz	340 g
Salt	2%	2½ oz	71 g
Cherry filling (page 521)		3 lb	1.36 kg
Cream cheese filling (page 895)		3 lb	1.36 kg
Egg wash (page 892)		as needed	as needed
Coarse sugar, for garnish		as needed	as needed
Apricot glaze (page 426), warm		1 lb 8 oz	680 g
Fondant (optional)		as needed	as needed

1   Combine the flour and yeast. Add the milk, eggs, sugar, butter, and salt to the mixer and then add the flour and yeast. Mix on low speed with the dough hook attachment for 4 minutes and on medium speed for 4 minutes. The dough should be slightly soft but elastic.

2   Bulk ferment the dough until nearly doubled, about 1 hour.

3   Divide the dough into 1-lb/454-g pieces. Preshape the dough into large oblongs (for pre-shaping instructions, see page 109). Let the dough rest, covered, until relaxed, 15 to 20 minutes. (Reminder: When making multiple cakes, work sequentially, starting with the first piece of dough you divided and rounded.)

4   Position the dough lengthwise, parallel to the edge of the work surface with the seam side up. Roll the dough into a rectangle 10 by 12 in/25 by 30 cm; the dough should be about ¼ in/6 mm thick. Turn the dough so that a short side is facing you.

5   Using a large plain pastry tip, pipe the cherry filling down the center of the dough and then pipe a thinner strip of the cream cheese filling on either side.

6   Make parallel diagonal cuts at a 45-degree angle evenly down both sides of the dough, spacing the cuts about 1 in/3 cm apart. Egg wash. Fold the top left strip diagonally over the filling and press it gently into the dough. Fold the strip on the opposite side over. Continue, alternating sides, for a braided effect. Trim.

7   Transfer to a parchment-lined sheet pan. Brush the dough lightly with egg wash. Proof, covered, until the dough springs back halfway slowly to the touch but does not collapse, 1 to 1½ hours.

8 Brush the dough very lightly again with egg wash. Sprinkle with coarse sugar. Bake in a 350°F/177°C convection oven until dark golden brown and shiny, about 20 to 25 minutes.

9 Brush the warm coffee cake with warm apricot glaze. When cooled, drizzle with fondant icing, if desired. Cool completely on racks.

Raisin dough

MAKES 14 LB 14½ OZ/6.76 KG DOUGH. DDT: 78°F/26°C

Bread flour	100%	6 lb 4 oz	2.84 kg
Instant dry yeast	1.5%	1½ oz	43 g
Milk, room temperature	80%	80 fl oz	2.40 L
Honey	3%	3 oz	85 g
Salt	2%	2 oz	57 g
Raisins	52%	3 lb 4 oz	1.47 kg

1 Combine the flour and yeast. Add the milk, honey, and salt to the mixer and then add the flour and yeast. Mix on low speed with the dough hook attachment for 4 minutes and on medium speed for 4 minutes. The dough should have good gluten development but also be soft and slightly moist. Blend in the raisins. Mix to the intense stage of gluten development.

2 Bulk ferment the dough until nearly doubled, about 1 hour.

3 Divide the dough into pieces 1 lb 4 oz/567 g each. Preshape the dough into large rounds (for preshaping instructions, see page 109). Let the dough rest, covered, until relaxed, 15 to 20 minutes. (Reminder: When making multiple loaves, work sequentially, starting with the first piece of dough you divided and rounded.)

4 To shape as a boule: Cup both hands around the dough. Using your thumbs, push the dough away from you in an arc to the right, keeping a small piece of dough between the table and the edges of your palms. Using the edges of your palms as a guide, pull the dough toward you in an arc to the left. There should still be a small piece of dough that is squeezed between the table and the edges of your palms. Repeat this circular motion two or three more times, applying gentle pressure while rounding the dough, to create a tight, smooth outer skin. Place the boule seam side up in a round basket or seam side down on a board dusted with cornmeal.

5 Proof, covered until the dough springs back slowly to the touch, 1 to 1½ hours. Place the dough seam side down onto a peel. Score the boule with an arc.

6 Presteam a 460°F/238°C deck oven. Load the bread into the oven and steam for 3 seconds. Bake until the crust is golden brown and the bread sounds hollow when thumped on the bottom, 25 to 30 minutes. Vent during the final 10 minutes. Cool completely on racks.

VARIATIONS Substitute currants for the raisins.

Substitute walnuts for half of the raisins.

Brioche à tête

MAKES 11 LB 10¾ OZ/5.29 KG DOUGH. DDT: 75°F/24°C

Bread flour	100%	5 lb	2.27 kg
Instant dry yeast	1.7%	1⅓ oz	38 g
Eggs	40%	2 lb	907 g
Milk, room temperature	20%	16 fl oz	480 mL
Sugar	10%	8 oz	227 g
Salt	2%	1½ oz	43 g
Butter, soft but still pliable	60%	3 lb	1.36 kg
Egg wash (page 892)		as needed	as needed

1   Combine the flour and yeast. Add the eggs, milk, sugar, and salt to the mixer and then add the flour and yeast. Mix on low speed with the dough hook attachment for 4 minutes.

2   Gradually add the butter, with the mixer running on medium speed, scraping down the sides of the bowl as necessary. After the butter has been fully incorporated, mix until the dough begins to pull away from the sides of the bowl.

3   Line a sheet pan with parchment paper and grease the parchment. Place the dough on the prepared sheet pan. Cover tightly with plastic wrap and refrigerate overnight.

Blitzing the butter into the dough while it is mixing

Properly mixed brioche dough after mixing is complete

4   Remove the dough from the refrigerator and divide it into 4 pieces. Divide each by hand into 25 pieces (2 oz/57 g each). Preshape each piece into a round, lightly flouring the work surface as needed. Refrigerate until cool, 20 to 30 minutes.

5   Lightly oil brioche tins.

6   Start with the first piece of dough that you shaped and work sequentially. The remainder of the dough may need to be refrigerated during shaping to keep it cool and workable. Roll each piece of dough into a ball. Lightly coat the side of your hand with flour. Make a head (*tête*) by pinching off one-quarter of the dough ball with the side of your hand and rolling it back and forth on the worktable, making a depression in the dough to pinch but not detach one-quarter of the ball; the larger piece of dough should be about 2¾ in/7 cm long and the tête ¾ in/2 cm long.

7   Flour your fingertips lightly and gently press a hole all the way through the center of the larger portion of dough. Place the tête into the center of the larger piece of dough and push it through the hole. Place each brioche into a greased brioche tin, with the tête on top.

8   Brush the brioches lightly with egg wash, brushing away any excess that accumulates in the crevices. Proof, covered, until the dough springs back slowly to the touch but does not collapse, 1½ to 2 hours.

9   Gently brush the brioches again with egg wash. Bake in a 375°F/191°C deck oven until a rich golden brown, 12 to 15 minutes. Cool for 10 minutes in the tins, then promptly remove and finish cooling on racks.

VARIATION   Substitute Orange Brioche Dough (page 186) for the brioche dough.

LEFT: Making the head on brioche à tête by pinching one-quarter of the dough ball with the side of your hand and rolling back and forth on the work table

MIDDLE: Using your fingertips to make a hole in the center of the larger piece of the dough

RIGHT: Pushing the head of the dough into the hole

Raisin bread with cinnamon swirl

MAKES 16 LB 5¾ OZ/7.42 KG DOUGH DDT: 78°F/26°C

Bread flour	100%	8 lb 1 oz	3.66 kg
Instant dry yeast	0.78%	1 oz	28 g
Milk, room temperature	52.7%	68 fl oz	2.04 L
Butter, soft	9.1%	11¾ oz	333 g
Sugar	9.1%	11¾ oz	333 g
Eggs	9.1%	11¾ oz	333 g
Salt	2.3%	3 oz	85 g
Raisins	18.6%	1 lb 8 oz	680 g
Ground cinnamon	1.2%	1½ oz	43 g
Egg wash (page 892)		as needed	as needed
Cinnamon sugar (page 897), made with brown sugar		12 oz	340 g

1 Combine the flour and yeast. Add the milk, butter, sugar, eggs, and salt to the mixer and then add the flour and yeast. Mix on low speed with the dough hook attachment for 4 minutes and on medium speed for 4 minutes; add the raisins and mix for 2 minutes on low speed, then add the cinnamon, mixing just long enough to create a swirl. The dough should be slightly soft. Mix to the intense stage of gluten development.

2 Bulk ferment the dough until nearly doubled, 45 to 60 minutes.

3 Divide the dough into 1lb 4-oz/567-g pieces. Preshape the dough into large oblongs (for preshaping instructions, see page 109). Lightly grease twelve 2-lb/907-g loaf pans (4½ in/11 cm wide, 8 in/20 cm long, and 3 in/8 cm deep). Let the dough rest, covered, until relaxed, 15 to 20 minutes. (Reminder: When making multiple loaves, work sequentially, starting with the first piece of dough you divided and rounded.)

4 Roll the dough into even rectangles 8 by 12 in/20 by 30 cm. Brush the dough lightly with egg wash and sprinkle 1 oz/28 g cinnamon sugar evenly over the surface. Roll the dough up along the 12-in/30-cm side under your palms into a cylinder 8 in/25 cm long, keeping the pressure even and holding your hands flat and parallel to the work surface to create a smooth, even loaf.

5 Place the dough seam side down in a greased loaf pan. The dough will spring back on itself slightly and fit snugly in the pan. Brush the loaf lightly with egg wash. Proof, covered, until the dough fills the pan and springs back slowly to the touch but does not collapse, 1½ to 2 hours.

6 Gently brush the bread again with egg wash. Score to the first layer of cinnamon. Bake in a 400°F/204°C convection oven for 25 to 30 minutes, or to an internal temperature of 205°F/96°C. Cool completely on racks.

Naan

MAKES 1 LB 11¼ OZ/773 G DOUGH. DDT: 78°F/26°C

All-purpose flour	100%	14 oz	397 g
Instant dry yeast	2.4%	⅓ oz	9 g
Water	42.9%	6 fl oz	180 mL
Clarified butter	14.3%	2 oz	57 g
Plain yogurt	14.3%	2 oz	57 g
Eggs	12.5%	2 oz	57 g
Sugar	7.2%	1 oz	28 g
Salt	1.8%	1½ tsp	7.50 g
Clarified butter, melted		as needed	as needed
Poppy seeds or black onion seeds, for garnish		2 tbsp	12 g

1   Combine the flour and yeast. Add the water, butter, yogurt, eggs, sugar, and salt to the mixer and then add the flour and yeast. Mix on low speed with the dough hook attachment for 4 minutes. The dough should be very elastic but still wet.

2   Bulk ferment the dough until nearly doubled, about 1 hour. Fold gently.

3   Divide the dough into 3-oz/85-g pieces. Preshape the dough into small rounds (for preshaping instructions, see page 109). Let the dough rest, covered, until relaxed, 15 to 20 minutes.

4   Line sheet pans with parchment paper.

5   Work sequentially, starting with the first piece of dough you divided and rounded. Gently stretch each piece of dough into a round 7 in/18 cm in diameter, so that the center is ¼ in/6 mm thick and there is a border ½ in/1 cm wide all around. Pull one edge out to elongate each round slightly, creating a teardrop shape.

6   Place the breads on the sheet pans, brush them with clarified butter, and sprinkle with seeds.

7   Bake in a 425°F/218°C deck oven until golden brown and puffed, about 10 minutes. Cool completely on racks.

Stretching the naan into a teardrop shape

Lavash

MAKES 11 LB 5¼ OZ/5.14 KG DOUGH. DDT: 78°F/26°C

Bread flour	46%	2 lb 14 oz	1.30 kg
Durum flour	20%	1 lb 4 oz	567 g
Cake flour	17%	1 lb 1 oz	482 g
Whole wheat flour	17%	1 lb 1 oz	482 g
Instant dry yeast	0.5%	½ oz	14 g
Milk, room temperature	42.5%	42½ fl oz	1.28 L
Water	29.25%	29¼ fl oz	878 mL
Molasses, unsulfured	3.25%	3¼ oz	92 g
Honey	3.25%	3¼ oz	92 g
Salt	2.5%	2½ oz	71 g
Olive oil		as needed	as needed
Sesame seeds, for garnish		as needed	as needed
Poppy seeds, for garnish		as needed	as needed

1   Combine the flours and yeast. Add the milk, water, molasses, honey, and salt to the mixer and then add the flour and yeast. Mix on low speed with the dough hook attachment for 10 minutes. The dough should pull cleanly away from the sides of the bowl but still be wet and soft. Mix to the intense stage of gluten development.

2   Bulk ferment the dough until nearly doubled, about 30 minutes. Fold gently. Divide the dough into 1-lb/454-g pieces and retard overnight.

3   Preshape the dough into large rounds (for preshaping instructions, see page 109). Lightly brush 11 or 12 sheet pans with olive oil. Refrigerate for 1 hour.

4   Work sequentially, starting with the first piece of dough you divided and rounded. Roll each piece of dough to ¹⁄₁₆ in/1.5 mm thick on a dough sheeter, flouring the dough periodically as you roll it. The dough should be 16½ by 24½ in/42 by 62 cm (see Notes). You may also roll by hand using a rolling pin.

5   Place each sheet of dough on one of the greased sheet pans. If the dough is not big enough to cover the entire pan, have another person help stretch it to fit the sheet pan; use the backs of your hands to gently stretch the dough (see Notes).

6   Brush the top of the dough lightly with water and sprinkle with seeds of your choice.

7   Allow the dough to relax for 15 to 20 minutes.

8   Bake in a 375°F/191°C convection oven until light golden brown, 12 to 15 minutes. Cool completely on racks, then wrap well.

You can also stretch the dough using the backs of your hands, similarly to the way you stretch strudel dough—for information, see "Strudel Dough," page 217, and Apple Strudel, page 550. If you shape the dough by hand, it is important to keep the dough even; if it is stretched unevenly, it will bake unevenly.

You can bake the lavash 70 percent of the way, until it is baked but not yet golden brown, and then reheat before use in a 400°F/204°C oven.

Allowing the dough to rest, covered, under refrigeration overnight (as stated in step 3), rather than for only 15 to 20 minutes, provides for better development of flavor characteristics.

Pita

MAKES 3 LB 5¾ OZ/1.52 KG DOUGH. DDT: 78°F/26°C

Bread flour	50%	1 lb	454 g
Whole wheat flour	50%	1 lb	454 g
Instant dry yeast	0.78%	¼ oz	7 g
Water	62.5%	20 fl oz	600 mL
Olive oil	3.2%	1 oz	28 g
Salt	2.3%	¾ oz	21 g
Sugar	0.4%	¾ tsp	3.75 g

1   Combine the flours and yeast. Add the water, olive oil, salt, and sugar to the mixer and then add the flour and yeast. Mix on low speed with the dough hook attachment for 4 minutes and on medium speed for 3 minutes. The dough should be slightly moist but with strong gluten development. Mix to the intense stage of gluten development.

2   Bulk ferment the dough until nearly doubled, about 60 minutes.

3   Divide the dough into 4½-oz/128-g pieces. Preshape the dough into small rounds (for preshaping instructions, see page 109). Let the dough rest, covered, until relaxed, 15 to 20 minutes.

4   Line sheet pans with parchment paper.

5   Work sequentially, starting with the first piece of dough you divided and rounded. Using a rolling pin, roll each piece of dough into a round 7 in/18 cm in diameter. Transfer the rounds to the sheet pans, cover, and let them relax for 20 minutes.

6   Load the pitas into a 500°F/260°C deck oven and bake until puffed but not browned, 3 to 4 minutes. Stack the pitas five high and wrap each stack in a cloth. Cool before serving.

Durum pizza dough

MAKES 15 LB 11¼ OZ/7.12 KG DOUGH OR 25 9-OZ ROUNDS. DDT: 75°F/24°C

Bread flour	57.8%	5 lb 5 oz	2.41 kg
Durum flour	42.2%	3 lb 14 oz	1.76 kg
Instant dry yeast	0.51%	¾ oz	21 g
Water	63.9%	94 fl oz	2.82 L
Olive oil	3.75%	5½ oz	156 g
Salt	2.7%	4 oz	113 g

1   Combine the flours and yeast. Add the water, olive oil, and salt to the mixer and then add the flour and yeast. Mix on low speed with the dough hook attachment for 4 minutes and on medium speed for 4 minutes. The dough should have good gluten development but still be a little sticky. Mix to the intense stage of gluten development.

2   Bulk ferment the dough until nearly doubled, about 30 minutes. Fold gently.

3   Divide the dough into 9-oz/255-g pieces. Preshape the dough into large rounds (for pre-shaping instructions, see page 109). Let the dough rest, covered, under refrigeration overnight. Remove from the refrigerator 1 hour before use.

4   Using a rolling pin, roll each piece of dough into a 9-in/23-cm round. Transfer the rounds to parchment-lined sheet pans that have been dusted with semolina flour, or place on a peel, also dusted, before topping.

5   Top the dough as desired (see toppings, pages 716 and 717), leaving a 1-in/2.5-cm border to brush with olive oil.

6   Load the pizzas into a 475°F/240°C deck oven and bake until golden brown around the edges, 8 to 12 minutes. Serve at once.

Yeast-raised doughnuts

MAKES 5 LB 5½ OZ/2.42 KG DOUGH. DDT: 80°F/27°C

Bread flour	62.4%	1 lb 10½ oz	751 g
Pastry flour	37.6%	1 lb	454 g
Instant dry yeast	3.2%	1⅓ oz	38 g
Water	50%	21¼ fl oz	638 mL
Eggs	12.4%	5¼ oz	149 g
Sugar	6.5%	2¾ oz	78 g
Nonfat dry milk	6.5%	2¾ oz	78 g
Baking powder	1.75%	¾ oz	21 g
Salt	1.75%	¾ oz	21 g
Ground nutmeg	0.35%	1 tsp	2 g
Emulsified shortening	18.8%	8 oz	227 g
Oil, for frying		as needed	as needed

1 Combine the flours and yeast. Add the water, eggs, sugar, dry milk, baking powder, salt, and nutmeg to the mixer and then add the flour and yeast. Mix on low speed with the dough hook attachment for 2 minutes, or until the ingredients are well incorporated. Add the shortening and mix on medium speed for 8 minutes. Mix to the intense stage of gluten development.

2 Bulk ferment the dough until nearly doubled, about 30 minutes. Fold gently. Ferment for another 30 minutes.

3 Roll the dough to ½ in/1 cm thick. Let the dough rest, covered, until relaxed, 10 minutes.

4 Cut the doughnuts with a doughnut cutter or with two round cutters (use a 3-in/8-cm cutter for the doughnuts and a 1-in/3-cm cutter for the holes; keep the holes centered so the doughnuts fry evenly).

5 Proof covered on parchment-lined sheet pans that have been brushed with oil until the dough springs back slowly to the touch but does not collapse, 15 minutes.

6 Carefully transfer the proofed doughnuts, a few at a time, to a deep fryer at 350°F/177°C and fry until golden brown on the first side, 2 minutes. Turn and fry until the second side is golden and the doughnuts are cooked through, 2 minutes.

7 Lift the doughnuts from the hot oil with a spider or basket, allowing the oil to drain away directly over the fryer. Drain on paper towels before coating or topping as desired.

Berliners

MAKES 4 LB 8 OZ/2.04 KG DOUGH. DDT: 68°F/20°C

Bread flour	100%	2 lb 4 oz	1.02 kg
Instant dry yeast	2.8%	1 oz	28 g
Milk	45.4%	16 fl oz	480 mL
Butter, soft	14.9%	5¼ oz	149 g
Sugar	14.9%	5¼ oz	149 g
Eggs	14.9%	5¼ oz	149 g
Egg yolks	5.7%	2 oz	57 g
Salt	0.7%	1½ tsp	7.50 g
Lemon zest, grated	1.4%	½ oz	14 g
Vanilla extract	1.4%	½ fl oz	15 mL
Oil, for frying		as needed	as needed
Raspberry jam		2 lb 4 oz	1.02 kg
Granulated sugar, for coating		as needed	as needed
Confectioners' sugar, for dusting		as needed	as needed

1   Combine the flour and yeast. Add the milk, butter, sugar, eggs, egg yolks, salt, lemon zest, and vanilla to the mixer and then add the flour and yeast. Mix on low speed with the dough hook attachment for 8 to 12 minutes. The dough should have very strong gluten development and be very tight but smooth. Mix to the intense stage of gluten development.

2   Bulk ferment the dough until nearly doubled, about 30 minutes. Fold gently. Ferment for another 30 minutes.

3   Line a sheet pan with parchment paper and grease the parchment. Divide the dough into 36 pieces (2 oz/57 g each) by hand or with a dough divider. Shape each piece into a tight round and press lightly with the palm of your hand to flatten slightly. Transfer, seam side down, to the sheet.

4   Proof, covered, until the dough springs back slowly to the touch but does not collapse, 45 to 60 minutes.

5   Carefully transfer the proofed Berliners, a few at a time, seam side up, to a deep fryer at 350°F/177°C and fry, covered, until golden brown on the first side, 1 minute. Turn and fry, uncovered, another 1½ minutes. Turn once more and fry until the top is deep golden brown, 20 to 30 seconds. Lift the Berliners from the hot oil with a spider or basket, allowing the oil to drain away over the fryer. Drain on paper towels just until cool enough to handle.

6   Fill a pastry bag fitted with a small plain pastry tip and inject 1 oz/28 g of the raspberry jam into each Berliner. Dip both sides of each one in granulated sugar, place them seam side down on racks, and sift confectioners' sugar over them once they are fully cooled.

chapter eight

Advanced yeast breads and rolls

*t*he way in which yeast is introduced into the dough—by either direct or indirect fermentation—gives the bread baker the range of techniques necessary to create simple lean dough quickly and efficiently and to create hearty breads using such indirect fermentation methods as sponges, poolishes, bigas, and sourdoughs. This chapter examines these more complex methods and presents numerous examples of their use in popular baked goods.

Indirect fermentation and pre-ferments

The longer the yeast in a dough remains active, the better the flavor and texture of the finished bread will be. Indirect fermentation means that some portion of the dough is allowed to ferment on its own before being mixed with the remainder of the formula's ingredients. This portion, often referred to as a *pre-ferment,* typically includes only flour, water (or milk), and some or all of the yeast called for in the final dough.

It is important to plan for pre-ferments in a production schedule. The time requirement for each type of pre-ferment is slightly different, as noted below.

PÂTE FERMENTÉE, or "old dough," is nothing more exotic than a piece of a wheat lean dough reserved from the previous day's production. The dough is covered and refrigerated until needed, then added along with the other ingredients to make a batch of dough, as in the Lean Dough formula on page 153. The yeast in the pâte fermentée has undergone an extended fermentation and has developed an appealing, slightly "sour" flavor.

The **SPONGE** method combines one-third to one-half of the formula's total flour with all the yeast and enough liquid to make a stiff to loose dough. The sponge can be made directly in the mixing bowl, as the fermentation period is typically less than one hour. When the sponge has doubled in size, the remaining ingredients are mixed in to make the final dough.

A **POOLISH** combines equal parts flour and water (by weight) with some yeast (the amount varies according to the expected length of fermentation time, using less for longer, slower fermentations). The poolish is fermented at room temperature long enough to double in volume

LEFT: Sponge just after mixing and after proofing
MIDDLE: Poolish just after mixing and after proofing
RIGHT: Biga just after mixing and after proofing

and start to recede, or decrease, in volume. This may take anywhere from 3 to 15 hours depending on the amount of yeast. The poolish should be mixed in a plastic or other nonreactive container large enough to hold the mixture comfortably as it ferments.

A **BIGA** is the stiffest of the pre-ferments. It contains flour and enough water to equal 50 to 60 percent of the flour's weight, as well as 0.33 to 0.5 percent of the formula's total yeast. After the biga has properly fermented, it must be loosened with a portion of the formula's liquid to make it easier to blend into the dough.

SOURDOUGH is established by capturing wild yeast in a flour and water dough.

Sourdough starters

Sourdough starters add flavor to breads, and in some formulas that may be their primary function. But sourdough is a true leavener. Although it is time-consuming to prepare and maintain a sourdough starter to be used as a primary leavener, breads made with sourdough have a deep, complex flavor and a good texture. A sourdough is acidic enough to enhance the shelf life of breads and rolls. A strong, vigorous sourdough can be maintained indefinitely with proper feedings.

Each sourdough has its own characteristics, depending on both the ingredients selected and the type of wild yeasts in any given environment. Both wheat and rye flours are used in sourdough starters. Wheat flours generate lactic acid; rye develops acetic acid. These acids influence the flavor of the finished bread. Organic flours are easiest to use for starters since they are minimally processed and do not contain the additives found in nonorganic flours.

Establishing a starter

The initial stage of establishing a sourdough calls for mixing flour and water. The dough is then left to rest. As it rests, it attracts the ambient yeasts in the air. Grapes, potatoes, onions, and apples contain a high percentage of the natural yeasts desirable for creating a starter. Adding them to the flour and water mixture will speed the process of creating a starter. When the yeast starts to feed, grow, and reproduce in the mixture, it ferments the dough, making it bubbly and airy and giving it a tangy or sour aroma. The dough will expand to double its original volume, start to fall when the yeast activity peaks, and then begin to decline as the yeast consumes the food source.

Left unattended, the yeast will die. To keep the starter alive, or to maintain or build up an established starter, it should be given additional feedings of flour and water. These feedings should be done on a fairly regular schedule, usually once a day. It is important that the ratio of flour to water used for feeding is the same one used to establish the sour. New starters benefit from at least three and up to five feedings prior to their first use.

Replenishing a starter

Once a starter is established, it should be replenished once or more daily until the desired amount is achieved. After it is built up, it should be replenished to maintain a par level. The starter can be replenished after it has risen and begins to fall. This is the signal that the culture has digested enough nutrients, in turn causing the collapse of the mixture. Replenishing at least three to five times is usually sufficient. The amount of replenishing can vary as long as the temperature and flour-to-water ratio is correct.

When a balanced, vigorous culture is established, it will provide leavening and flavor to bread, and the presence of organic acids from the sourdough and the higher acidity of the bread will give it a better shelf life. Another benefit of a well-balanced and well-maintained culture is that it can be maintained indefinitely.

Sourdough starters that are held under refrigeration and not used frequently must be fed at least every 3 weeks if they are to remain active. To replenish a starter, use the following procedure:

1. Remove the starter from refrigeration and let it rest at 75°F/24°C for 12 to 14 hours.

2. Feed it with a mixture of flour and water; add as much of this mixture as necessary to produce the amount of starter required for your formula. Wheat starters should be fed with a mixture of flour and water that is at 66 percent hydration; for example, for every 1 lb/454 g of flour you add to the starter, add about 10½ oz/315 mL of water. Rye starters should be fed with a mixture that is at 100 percent hydration; add equal amounts of rye flour and water (by weight) to the starter.

3. Feed the starter once more on the following day at the same hydration level and allow it to ferment for 24 hours at 75°F/24°C before using it in a bread formula.

Autolyse

Autolyse mixing may be used in any lean dough, and it is especially useful when making fiber-enriched dough. It means that the flour and water, yeast and pre-ferment are briefly combined, just enough for a rough mixture to form. Then the mixture is left to rest for a period of 10 to 30 minutes, allowing the flour to absorb enough water for gluten development to begin. The gluten relaxes, since mixing is not agitating it. The dough has rested sufficiently when it appears very smooth.

One advantage of the autolyse mixing is that mixing times are shortened, and shorter mixing times produce gluten that has greater extensibility. Another advantage is the development of a sweet aroma and flavor in the baked loaf.

The salt is added to the dough after the autolyse is complete. Added earlier, the salt would tighten the gluten. The dough is mixed until the gluten is properly developed and it is ready for bulk fermentation.

In the initial stage of an autolyse, the dough is very coarse.

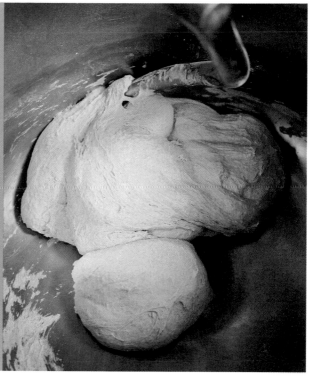

A finished dough made including the autolyse mixing becomes very smooth.

soakers

When adding a significant quantity of smaller grains, or any amount of large, whole grains such as wheat berries, it is best to soak the grains first before incorporating them into the final dough. Whole grains tend to deprive the dough of moisture and will also damage the developing gluten network.

A soaker can be made using one of two methods: hot or cold. A *hot soaker* pregelatinizes the starch of the soaker's grain, which can improve the crust and decrease baking time of some whole-grain breads. Hot soakers work faster, but some chefs feel that there is some loss of flavor and quality. A hot soaker is produced by bringing the liquid to a boil and then incorporating the grains.

Continue to cook the mixture for about 5 minutes over low heat. Set the soaker aside for at least 1 hour or overnight to allow it to cool before adding it to the dough.

A *cold soaker* must be prepared at least a day in advance. For a cold soaker, the grains and liquid are incorporated slightly, covered, and allowed to soak overnight.

Soakers are added to the dough after it has started to develop and are mixed into the dough on medium speed for a few minutes to develop gluten structure, just until they are fully and evenly incorporated.

Dough with a high percentage of rye should have all the grains added at the beginning of mixing.

Multigrain bread

MAKES 13 LB 8 OZ/6.13 KG DOUGH. DDT: 75°F/24°C

SOAKER			
Nine-grain cereal mix	15.6%	1 lb	454 g
Flaxseed	2.2%	2¼ oz	64 g
Sunflower seeds	3.9%	4 oz	113 g
Water	26.6%	1 lb 11 oz	771 g
FINAL DOUGH			
Pâte fermentée (see page 148)	39.1%	2 lb 8 oz	1.13 kg
Bread flour	45.1%	2 lb 14 oz	1.30 kg
Whole wheat flour	33.2%	2 lb 2 oz	964 g
Instant dry yeast	0.6%	⅔ oz	19 g
Salt	2.3%	2½ oz	71 g
Water	43.0%	2 lb 12 oz	1.2 kg
Soaker (above)	48.4%	3 lb 1½ oz	1.40 kg

1   To prepare the soaker, combine the nine-grain cereal mix, flaxseed, sunflower seeds, and water. Cover and soak at room temperature for 18 hours.

2   Let the pâte fermentée ferment at 75°F/24°C for 1 hour. Refrigerate for 16 hours.

3   To prepare the final dough, combine the pâte fermentée, the flours, yeast, salt, and water. Mix on low speed with the dough hook attachment for 4 minutes to incorporate. Increase the speed to medium and mix for 2 minutes. Add half of the soaker and mix on low speed for 2 minutes and on medium speed for 1 minute. Add the remaining half of the soaker and mix on low speed for 2 minutes. Knead for 2 minutes.

4   Bulk ferment the dough until nearly doubled, about 45 minutes. Fold gently. Ferment for another 15 minutes.

5   Divide the dough into pieces 1 lb 4 oz/567 g each. Preshape the dough into large oblongs (for preshaping instructions, see page 109). Let the dough rest, covered, until relaxed, 15 to 20 minutes. (Reminder: When making multiple loaves, work sequentially, starting with the first piece of dough you divided and rounded.)

6   Position the dough lengthwise, parallel to the edge of the work surface with the seam side up, and press lightly with your fingertips. Fold the top edge of the dough down to the center of the dough, pressing lightly with your fingertips to tighten.

7   Fold the dough lengthwise in half and use the heel of your hand to seal the two edges, keeping the seam straight. Roll the dough under your palms into a cylinder 8 in/20 cm long, moving your hands outward from the center of the cylinder toward the ends and slightly increasing the

pressure as you move outward, until both ends have an even, gentle taper. Then increase the pressure at the ends of the loaf to seal. Place on parchment-lined sheet pans.

8   Proof, covered, until the dough springs back slowly to the touch but does not collapse, 45 to 60 minutes.

9   Presteam a 460°F/238°C deck oven. Load the bread into the oven and steam for 3 seconds. Bake until the crust is golden brown and the bread sounds hollow when thumped on the bottom, 20 to 25 minutes. Vent during the final 12 minutes. Cool completely on racks.

Lean dough with pâte fermentée

MAKES 10 LB/4.54 KG DOUGH. DDT: 78°F/26°C

Bread flour	100%	5 lb	2.27 kg
Instant dry yeast	0.63%	½ oz	14 g
Water	67.2%	53¾ fl oz	1.61 L
Pâte fermentée (see page 148)	30%	1 lb 8 oz	680 g
Salt	2.2%	1¾ oz	50 g

1   Combine the flour and yeast. Add the water, pâte fermentée, and salt to the mixer and then add the flour and yeast. Mix on low speed with the dough hook attachment for 4 minutes and on medium speed for 3 minutes. The dough should be slightly soft but very smooth, with sufficient gluten development. Mix to the improved stage of gluten development.

2   Bulk ferment the dough until nearly doubled, about 40 minutes. Fold gently and ferment for another 30 minutes.

3   Divide the dough into 1-lb/454-g pieces. Preshape the dough into large rounds (for preshaping instructions, see page 109). Let the dough rest, covered, until relaxed, 15 to 20 minutes. (Reminder: When making multiple loaves, work sequentially, starting with the first piece of dough you divided and rounded.)

4   Working with the dough seam side down, dust lightly with medium rye flour and use a rolling pin to create a split in the dough 2 in/5 cm wide and 2 in/5 cm deep. Turn the dough, split side down, into a lightly floured banneton or couche.

5   Proof, covered, until the dough springs back slowly to the touch but does not collapse, 1 to 1½ hours. Flip the dough split side up onto a peel.

6   Presteam a 460°F/238°C deck oven. Load the bread into the oven and steam for 3 seconds. Bake until the crust is golden brown and the bread sounds hollow when thumped on the bottom, 25 to 30 minutes. Vent during the final 10 minutes. Cool completely on racks.

VARIATION   **BOULE WITH A CROSS** After the boule has proofed, make two hollows the same size as the one in the split loaf to form a cross in the center of the loaf. The baking instructions are the same.

Baguette

MAKES 8 LB 8 OZ/3.86 KG DOUGH. DDT: 78°F/26°C

POOLISH			
Bread flour	30%	1 lb 8 oz	680 g
Water (55°F/13°C)	30%	24 fl oz	720 mL
Instant dry yeast	0.04%	pinch	pinch
FINAL DOUGH			
Bread flour	70%	3 lb 8 oz	1.59 kg
Instant dry yeast	0.63%	½ oz	14 g
Poolish (above)	60%	3 lb	1.36 kg
Water	37.2%	29¾ fl oz	893 mL
Salt	2.2%	1¾ oz	50 g

1   To prepare the poolish, mix the flour, water, and yeast together by hand until well incorpo-rated. Cover and ferment at 75°F/24°C for 14 to 15 hours, until it has risen and just begun to recede; it will be bubbly and frothy on top.

2   To prepare the final dough, combine the flour and yeast. Add the poolish, water, and salt to the mixer and then add the flour and yeast. Mix on low speed with the dough hook attachment for 4 minutes and on medium speed for 2 minutes. The dough should be soft and smooth, with good gluten development.

3   Bulk ferment the dough until nearly doubled, about 40 minutes. Fold gently and ferment for another 30 minutes. Fold once more. Ferment for another 20 minutes.

4   Divide the dough into 14-oz/397-g pieces. Preshape the dough into large oblongs (for pre-shaping instructions, see page 109). Let the dough rest, covered, until relaxed, 15 to 20 min-utes. (Reminder: When making multiple loaves, work sequentially, starting with the first piece of dough you divided and rounded.)

5   Position the dough lengthwise, parallel to the edge of the work surface with the seam side up. Press lightly with your fingertips to stretch it into a rectangle 10 in/25 cm long, using as little flour as possible. Fold the top edge of the dough down to the center of the dough, pressing lightly with your fingertips to tighten the dough. Fold the dough lengthwise in half and use the heel of your hand to seal the two edges together, keeping the seam straight. Roll the dough under your palms into a cylinder 20 in/51 cm long. Keep the pressure even and hold your hands flat and parallel to the work surface. Move your hands outward from the center of the cylinder toward the ends and slightly increase the pressure as you move outward, until both ends have an even, gentle taper. Then increase the pressure at the ends of the loaf to seal them.

6   Place the loaf seam side down on a linen couche. Proof, covered, until the dough springs back very slowly to the touch, 30 to 45 minutes. (Baguettes should be slightly underproofed when loaded into the oven.)

7 Score the dough with 5 or 7 diagonal lines down the center third of the loaf, overlapping each cut by ½ in/1 cm.

8 Presteam a 475°F/246°C deck oven. Load the bread into the oven and steam for 3 seconds. Bake until the crust is golden brown, the bread sounds hollow when thumped on the bottom, and you hear a crackle when you hold it next to your ear, 20 to 25 minutes. Vent during the final 10 minutes. Cool completely on racks.

TOP ROW: Fold the top edge of the dough, pressing lightly with your fingertips to tighten the dough.

Use the heel of your hand to seal the two edges.

Taper the ends using increased pressure while rolling.

Roll out the dough to even out the center once the ends have been tapered.

BOTTOM ROW: Continue to roll the baguette, gently stretching to the final length.

Place finished baguettes in a couche for the final proof.

Once the baguettes are fully proofed, transfer to the oven peel and score the tops of the finished baguettes.

EPI

1 Follow the main method through step 4.

2 Position the dough lengthwise, parallel to the edge of the work surface with the seam side up. Press lightly with your fingertips to stretch it into a rectangle 10 in/25 cm long, using as little flour as possible. Fold the top edge of the dough down to the center of the dough, pressing lightly with your fingertips to tighten the dough. Fold the dough lengthwise in half and use the heel of your hand to seal the two edges together, keeping the seam straight. Roll the dough under your palms into a cylinder 20 in/51 cm long, keeping the pressure even and holding your hands flat and parallel to the work surface to create a smooth, even loaf. Then taper the final 2 in/5 cm of each end by using increased pressure, tapering the ends evenly.

3 Place the dough seam side down on the linen couche. Proof, covered, until the dough springs back very slowly to the touch, 30 to 45 minutes. (Epi are often slightly underproofed when loaded into the oven.)

4 Transfer the dough to a peel. Using scissors held at a 45-degree angle, starting 2½ in/6 cm from one end of the loaf, make diagonal cuts down the center of the loaf, placing each cut piece to the side as you cut, alternating sides to create the look of a stalk of wheat.

5 Presteam a 475°F/246°C deck oven. Load the bread into the oven and steam for 3 seconds. Bake until the crust is golden brown, the bread sounds hollow when thumped on the bottom, and you hear a crackle when you hold it next to your ear. Vent during the final 5 minutes. Cool completely on racks.

LEFT: Make diagonal cuts down the center of the loaf, placing each cut piece to the side as you cut, alternating sides to create the look of a stalk of wheat.

MIDDLE: Three varieties of epi: single, double, and fougasse

RIGHT: These breads should be baked until crisp and deep golden brown.

Whole wheat dough with poolish

MAKES 15 LB 9¼ OZ/7.07 KG DOUGH. DDT: 79°F/26°C

POOLISH			
Whole wheat flour	100%	3 lb	1.36 kg
Water (55°F/13°C)	100%	48 fl oz	1.44 L
Instant dry yeast	0.08%	pinch	pinch
FINAL DOUGH			
Bread flour	33.3%	3 lb	1.36 kg
Whole wheat flour	33.3%	3 lb	1.36 kg
Instant dry yeast	0.35%	½ oz	14 g
Poolish (above)	66.6%	6 lb	2.72 kg
Water	37.5%	54 fl oz	1.62 L
Salt	2%	2¾ oz	78 g

1   To prepare the poolish, mix the flour, water, and yeast together by hand until well incorporated. Cover and ferment at 75°F/24°C until bubbly, frothy, and just starting to recede, 10 to 15 hours.

2   To prepare the final dough, combine the flours and yeast. Add the poolish, water, and salt to the mixer and then add the flour and yeast. Mix on low speed with the dough hook attachment for 4 minutes and on medium speed for 4 minutes. The dough should be moist, but with strong gluten development. Mix to the improved stage of gluten development.

3   Bulk ferment the dough until nearly doubled, about 30 minutes. Fold gently. Ferment for another 30 minutes.

4   Divide the dough into pieces 1 lb 4 oz/567 g each. Preshape the dough into large oblongs (for preshaping instructions, see page 109). Let the dough rest, covered, until relaxed, 15 to 20 minutes. (Reminder: When making multiple loaves, work sequentially, starting with the first piece of dough you divided and rounded.)

5   Position the dough lengthwise, parallel to the edge of the work surface with the seam side up, and press lightly with your fingertips. Fold the top edge of the dough down to the center of the dough, pressing lightly with your fingertips to tighten.

6   Fold the dough lengthwise in half and use the heel of your hand to seal the two edges, keeping the seam straight. Roll the dough into a cylinder 8 in/20 cm long, moving your hands outward from the center slightly increasing the pressure as you move outward, until both ends have an even, gentle taper. Then increase the pressure at the ends of the loaf to seal.

7   Proof, covered, in a couche until the dough springs back slowly to the touch but does not collapse, 45 minutes. Score the bâtard straight down the center.

8   Presteam a 460°F/238°C deck oven. Load the bread into the oven and steam for 3 seconds. Bake until the crust is golden brown and the bread sounds hollow when thumped on the bottom, 30 to 35 minutes. Vent during the final 10 minutes. Cool completely on racks.

Walnut fig dough

MAKES 7 LB 8 OZ/3.40 KG DOUGH. DDT: 78°F/26°C

Walnuts, toasted and chopped	8.3%	10 oz	284 g
Figs, dried, coarsely chopped	8.3%	10 oz	284 g
Honey	3.3%	4 oz	113 g
Whole wheat dough with poolish (page 157)	80%	6 lb	2.72 kg

1 Combine the walnuts, figs, and honey. Fold the mixture into the dough halfway through bulk fermentation time.

2 Bulk ferment the dough until nearly doubled, about 30 minutes. Fold gently. Ferment for another 30 minutes and fold again. Ferment for another 15 minutes.

3 Divide the dough into 15-oz/425-g pieces. Preshape the dough into large oblongs (for pre-shaping instructions, see page 109). Let the dough rest, covered, until relaxed, 15 to 20 minutes. (Reminder: When making multiple loaves, work sequentially, starting with the first piece of dough you divided and rounded.)

4 Position the dough lengthwise, parallel to the edge of the work surface with the seam side up, and press lightly with your fingertips. Fold the top edge of the dough down to the center of the dough, pressing lightly with your fingertips to tighten.

5 Fold the dough lengthwise in half and use the heel of your hand to seal the two edges, keeping the seam straight. Roll the dough under your palms into a cylinder 8 in/20 cm long, moving your hands outward from the center of the cylinder toward the ends and slightly increasing the pressure as you move outward, until both ends have an even, gentle taper. Then increase the pressure at the ends of the loaf to seal.

6 Proof, covered, in a couche until the dough springs back slowly to the touch but does not collapse, 1 hour 20 minutes.

7 Score the bâtard with two parallel diagonal lines.

8 Presteam a 450°F/232°C deck oven. Load the bread into the oven and steam for 3 seconds. Bake until the crust is golden brown and the bread sounds hollow when thumped on the bottom, 35 to 40 minutes. Vent during the final 10 minutes. Cool completely on racks.

Tomato dough

MAKES 9 LB 9¾ OZ/4.36 KG DOUGH. DDT: 78°F/26°C

POOLISH			
Bread flour	100%	1 lb 1 oz	482 g
Water (55°F/13°C)	100%	18 fl oz	540 mL
Instant dry yeast	0.03%	pinch	pinch
ROASTED TOMATOES			
Tomatoes, cut in half	43.75%	2 lb 6½ oz	1.09 kg
Olive oil		as needed	as needed
Basil, chopped	0.85%	¾ oz	21 g
Garlic, roughly chopped	0.55%	½ oz	14 g
Salt		as needed	as needed
Cracked black pepper		as needed	as needed
FINAL DOUGH			
Bread flour	71.5%	3 lb 15 oz	1.79 kg
Whole wheat flour	9%	8 oz	227 g
Instant dry yeast	0.85%	¾ oz	21 g
Poolish (above)	38.6%	2 lb 2 oz	964 g
Water	1.7%	1½ fl oz	45 mL
Sugar	2.8%	2½ oz	71 g
Butter (75°F/24°C)	2.8%	2½ oz	71 g
Salt	2%	1¾ oz	50 g

1   To prepare the poolish, mix the flour, water, and yeast together by hand until well incorporated. Cover and ferment at 75°F/24°C for 10 to 15 hours, until it has risen and just begun to recede; it will be bubbly and frothy on top.

2   Place the tomatoes on a baking sheet, cut side up. Drizzle with olive oil and scatter with the basil, garlic, salt, and pepper. Roast the tomatoes in a 400°F/204°C oven until slightly dry, about 20 minutes. When the tomatoes are cool enough to handle, remove the skins; reserve the garlic. Drain off excess juice and oil from the tomatoes; roughly chop and reserve to add in the next step.

3   To prepare the final dough, combine the flours and yeast. Add the roasted tomatoes and reserved garlic, the poolish, water, sugar, butter, and salt to the mixer and then add the flour and yeast. Mix on low speed with the dough hook attachment for 3 minutes and on medium speed for 2 minutes. The dough should be soft and smooth, with good gluten development. Mix to the improved stage of gluten development.

4   Bulk ferment the dough until nearly doubled, about 45 minutes. Fold gently. Ferment for another 30 minutes.

5 Divide the dough into pieces 1 lb 4 oz/567 g each. Preshape the dough into large rounds (for preshaping instructions, see page 109). Let the dough rest, covered, until relaxed, 15 to 20 minutes. (Reminder: When making multiple loaves, work sequentially, starting with the first piece of dough you divided and rounded.)

6 Cup both hands around the dough. Using your thumbs, push the dough away from you in an arc to the right, keeping a small piece of dough between the table and the edges of your palms. Using the edges of your palms as a guide, pull the dough toward you in an arc to the left. There should still be a small piece of dough that is squeezed between the table and the edges of your palms. Repeat this circular motion two or three times, applying gentle pressure while rounding the dough, to create a tight, smooth outer skin. Place the boule seam side up in a round basket or seam side down on a board dusted with cornmeal.

7 Proof until the dough springs back slowly to the touch, 1 to 1½ hours. Flip the dough, seam side down, onto a peel. Score the boule with a spiral.

8 Presteam a 460°F/238°C deck oven. Load the bread into the oven and steam for 3 seconds. Bake until the crust is golden brown and the bread sounds hollow when thumped on the bottom, 25 to 30 minutes. Vent during the final 10 minutes. Cool completely on racks.

adding flavorings and garnishes

Fresh herbs, roasted garlic, ground or whole spices, grated cheeses, dried fruits, and nuts are some of the ingredients added to bread doughs for flavor or as garnish. Formulas calling for salty or acidic ingredients may require modification so that these ingredients do not interfere dramatically with yeast activity or the desired flavor of the bread. Finely ground or dry ingredients may be added at the beginning of the mixing time. In other cases, it may be easier to work the garnish into the dough halfway through bulk fermentation. The dough can be put back in the mixer and the garnish mixed in on low speed just until evenly blended, or the garnish may be folded by hand into the dough.

Generally, the folding method is best for hard ingredients, such as nuts, that can damage the gluten strands, or for soft ingredients, such as olives, that you do not want to break.

Spread or flatten the dough on a lightly floured surface. Sprinkle the garnish ingredients evenly over the dough and fold it over gently. Continue to fold until the garnish ingredients are evenly distributed throughout the dough.

Adding garnish to a dough by folding it in

Semolina dough

MAKES 90 LB/40.90 KG DOUGH (90 LOAVES). DDT: 78°F/26°C

BIGA			
Durum flour	16.7%	8 lb 10 oz	3.91 kg
Semolina flour	16.7%	8 lb 10 oz	3.91 kg
Water	18.3%	9 lb 8 oz	4.30 kg
Fresh yeast	0.01%	¼ tsp	1.30 g
FINAL DOUGH			
Durum flour	16.7%	8 lb 10 oz	3.91 kg
Semolina flour	16.7%	8 lb 10 oz	3.91 kg
Bread flour	33.3%	17 lb 4 oz	7.82 kg
Olive oil	4.2%	2 lb 2 oz	964 g
Water	48.9%	25 lb 4 oz	11.50 kg
Instant dry yeast	0.5%	4 oz	113 g
Biga (above)	51.7%	26 lb 11 oz	12.10 kg
Salt	2.2%	1 lb 2 oz	510 g
Sesame seeds, for garnish		as needed	as needed

1   To prepare the biga, combine the flours, water, and yeast and mix on low speed with the paddle attachment for 3 minutes, or until thoroughly combined. Transfer to a container, cover, and ferment at 75°F/24°C for 18 hours.

2   To prepare the final dough, combine the flours, olive oil, water, yeast, and biga and mix on low speed with the dough hook attachment for 3 minutes. Let the dough rest in the mixer for 15 minutes. Add the salt and mix on low speed for an additional 3 minutes.

3   Bulk ferment the dough until nearly doubled, about 45 minutes. Fold gently and ferment for another 15 minutes.

4   Divide the dough into 1-lb/454-g pieces. Preshape the dough into large oblongs 8 in/20 cm long (for preshaping instructions, see page 109). Let the dough rest, covered, until relaxed, 15 to 20 minutes. (Reminder: When making multiple loaves, work sequentially, starting with the first piece of dough you divided and rounded.)

5   Position the dough lengthwise, parallel to the edge of the work surface with the seam side up, and press lightly with your fingertips. Fold the top edge of the dough down to the center of the dough, pressing lightly with your fingertips to tighten. Fold the dough lengthwise in half and use the heel of your hand to seal the two edges, keeping the seam straight. Roll the dough under your palms into a cylinder 14 in/36 cm long, moving your hands outward from the center of the cylinder toward the ends and slightly increasing the pressure as you move outward, until both ends have an even, gentle taper. Then increase the pressure at the ends of the loaf to seal.

6   Dip each oblong into sesame seeds and place seam side up in a couche.

7   Proof, covered, until the dough springs back slowly to the touch but does not collapse, 30 to 40 minutes. Score the loaves with an arc.

8   Presteam a 470°F/243°C deck oven. Load the bread into the oven and steam for 3 seconds. Bake until the crust is golden brown and the bread sounds hollow when thumped on the bottom, 20 minutes. Vent during the final 8 minutes. Cool completely on racks.

Lean dough with biga

MAKES 8 LB 8 OZ/3.86 KG DOUGH. DDT: 78°F/26°C

BIGA			
Bread flour	100%	1 lb 8 oz	680 g
Water (60°F/16°C)	55%	13¼ fl oz	398 mL
Instant dry yeast	0.03%	pinch	pinch
FINAL DOUGH			
Bread flour	70%	3 lb 8 oz	1.59 kg
Instant dry yeast	0.63%	½ oz	14 g
Water	50.6%	40½ fl oz	1.22 L
Biga (above)	46.6%	2 lb 5¼ oz	1.06 kg
Salt	2.2%	1¾ oz	50 g

1   To prepare the biga, combine the flour, water, and yeast and mix on low speed with the dough hook attachment for 3 minutes, or until thoroughly combined. Transfer to a container, cover, and ferment at 75°F/24°C for 18 to 24 hours, until the biga has risen and begun to recede.

2   To prepare the final dough, combine the flour and yeast. Add the water, biga, and salt to the mixer and then add the flour and yeast. Mix on low speed with the dough hook attachment for 4 minutes and on medium speed for 2 minutes. The dough should still be slightly soft but very smooth, with sufficient gluten development. Mix to the improved stage of gluten development.

3   Bulk ferment the dough until nearly doubled, about 40 minutes. Fold gently and ferment for another 30 minutes. Fold again. Ferment for another 20 minutes.

4   Divide the dough into 14-oz/397-g pieces. Preshape the dough into large oblongs (for preshaping instructions, see page 109). Let the dough rest, covered, until relaxed, 15 to 20 minutes. (Reminder: When making multiple loaves, work sequentially, starting with the first piece of dough you divided and rounded.)

5   Position the dough lengthwise, parallel to the edge of the work surface with the seam side up, and press lightly with your fingertips. Fold the top edge of the dough down to the center of the dough, pressing lightly with your fingertips to tighten.

6　Fold the dough lengthwise in half and use the heel of your hand to seal the two edges, keeping the seam straight. Roll the dough under your palms into a cylinder 8 in/20 cm long, moving your hands outward from the center of the cylinder toward the ends and slightly increasing the pressure as you move outward, until both ends have an even, gentle taper. Then increase the pressure at the ends of the loaf to seal.

7　Proof, covered, in a couche until the dough springs back slowly to the touch but does not collapse, 30 to 40 minutes.

8　Score the baguette 5 to 7 times down the center.

9　Presteam a 460°F/238°C deck oven. Load the bread into the oven and steam for 3 seconds. Bake until the crust is golden brown and the bread sounds hollow when thumped on the bottom, 20 to 25 minutes. Vent during the final 6 to 8 minutes. Cool completely on racks.

CLOCKWISE FROM TOP: Semolina Dough (page 161), onion-topped Foccacia (page 168), Multigrain Bread (page 152), Walnut Fig Dough (page 158), Baguette (page 154), Lean Dough with Biga (opposite).

Roasted potato bread

MAKES 11 LB 6 OZ/5.16 KG DOUGH. DDT: 78°F/26°C

WHOLE WHEAT BIGA			
Bread flour	50%	9¼ oz	262 g
Whole wheat flour	50%	9¼ oz	262 g
Water (60°F/16°C)	68%	28½ fl oz	950 mL
Instant dry yeast	0.03%	pinch	pinch
SOAKER			
Cracked wheat	100%	3¼ oz	92 g
Water (90°F/32°C)	100%	3¼ fl oz	98 mL
ROASTED POTATOES			
Yukon gold potatoes, washed and peeled	50%	2 lb 8¼ oz	1.14 kg
Olive oil		as needed	as needed
Salt		as needed	as needed
Ground black pepper		as needed	as needed
FINAL DOUGH			
Bread flour	70.5%	3 lb 8½ oz	1.60 kg
Whole wheat flour	2.5%	2 oz	57 g
Medium rye flour	4%	3¼ oz	92 g
Instant dry yeast	0.3%	¼ oz	7 g
Water	50%	24¼ fl oz	728 mL
Whole wheat biga (above)	38.6%	1 lb 15 oz	879 g
Soaker (above)	8%	6½ oz	184 g
Salt	2.5%	2 oz	57 g
Potatoes, peeled, thinly sliced, and reserved in cold water		4 oz	113 g
Olive oil		as needed	as needed

1   To prepare the biga, combine the flours, water, and yeast and mix on low speed with the dough hook attachment for 3 minutes, or until thoroughly combined. Transfer to a container, cover, and ferment at 75°F/24°C for 18 to 24 hours, until the biga has risen and begun to recede.

2   To prepare the soaker, combine the cracked wheat and water in a plastic tub. Cover and soak at room temperature for at least 8 and up to 15 hours.

3 To prepare the roasted potatoes, cut them into quarters and toss them with olive oil to coat lightly. Season with salt and pepper. Roast in a 400°F/204°C convection oven until soft in the center, about 25 minutes. Cool the potatoes completely.

4 To prepare the final dough, combine the flours and yeast. Add the water, biga, soaker, and salt to the mixer and then add the flour and yeast. Mix on low speed with the dough hook attachment for 4 minutes. Add the roasted potatoes and mix on medium speed for 2 minutes. The dough should be slightly stiff and the potatoes evenly distributed. Mix to the improved stage of gluten development.

5 Bulk ferment the dough until nearly doubled, about 30 minutes. Fold gently and ferment for another 30 minutes. Fold again. Ferment for another 15 minutes.

6 Divide the dough into pieces 1 lb 2 oz/510 g each. Preshape the dough into large oblongs (for preshaping instructions, see page 109). Let the dough rest, covered, until relaxed, 15 to 20 minutes. (Reminder: When making multiple loaves, work sequentially, starting with the first piece of dough you divided and rounded.)

7 Dust the work surface with rye flour. Position the dough lengthwise, parallel to the edge of the work surface with the seam side up. Fold the dough lengthwise in half and seal the two edges together by pressing firmly with the heel of your hand, keeping the seam straight. Roll the dough under your palms into an even cylinder 12 in/30 cm long with tapered ends.

8 Dust a small rolling pin and use it to make a depression 3 in/8 cm wide down the center of the dough; the dough at the bottom of the hollow should be only ¼ in/6 mm thick.

9 Roll the two long edges of the dough toward each other until they meet in the middle. Place the dough seam side up in a couronne basket, forming a horseshoe shape.

10 Proof, covered, until the dough springs back slowly to the touch, 45 to 60 minutes. Flip the dough seam side down onto a peel. Score it with one long slash from end to end and place a potato slice in the center of the dough at the top of the horseshoe. Brush lightly with olive oil.

11 Presteam a 435°F/224°C deck oven. Load the bread into the oven and steam for 3 seconds. Bake until the crust is golden brown and the bread sounds hollow when thumped on the bottom, 45 to 60 minutes. Vent the bread once it starts to brown. Cool completely on racks.

Rosemary bread

MAKES 10 LB 3¼ OZ/4.63 KG DOUGH. DDT: 78°F/26°C

BIGA			
Bread flour	100%	1 lb	454 g
Water (60°F/16°C)	55%	8½ fl oz	255 mL
Instant dry yeast	0.08%	pinch	pinch
FINAL DOUGH			
Bread flour	83.3%	5 lb	2.27 kg
Instant dry yeast	0.25%	¼ oz	7 g
Water	50%	48 fl oz	1.44 L
Biga (above)	25%	1 lb 8 oz	680 g
Milk	6.75%	6½ fl oz	195 mL
Olive oil	2.6%	2½ oz	71 g
Salt	1.6%	1½ oz	43 g
Rosemary, coarsely chopped	0.5%	½ oz	14 g

1   To prepare the biga, combine the flour, water, and yeast and mix on low speed with the dough hook attachment for 3 minutes, or until thoroughly combined. Transfer to a container, cover, and ferment at 75°F/24°C for 18 to 24 hours, until the biga has risen and begun to recede; it should still be bubbly and airy.

2   To prepare the final dough, combine the flour and yeast. Add the water, biga, milk, olive oil, salt, and rosemary in the mixer and then add the flour and yeast. Mix on low speed with the dough hook attachment for 4 minutes and on medium speed for 3 minutes. The dough should still be slightly soft, with good gluten development. Mix to the improved stage of gluten development.

3   Bulk ferment the dough until nearly doubled, about 30 minutes. Fold gently, and ferment for another 30 minutes.

4   Divide the dough into pieces 1 lb 4 oz/567 g each. Preshape the dough into large oblongs (for preshaping instructions, see page 109). Let the dough rest, covered, until relaxed, 15 to 20 minutes. (Reminder: When making multiple loaves, work sequentially, starting with the first piece of dough you divided and rounded.)

5   Using the backs of your hands, stretch the dough gently and evenly into a rough rectangle 6 by 8 in/15 by 20 cm. It is very important to keep the thickness of the dough even. Place on parchment-lined sheet pans. Proof, covered, until the dough springs back slowly to the touch but does not collapse, 30 to 40 minutes.

6   Starting at one corner of the dough, score the dough three times, scoring from the same corner to each of the three other corners. Then score the dough two more times in between the first three slashes, radiating out from the same corner to the corresponding side.

7   Presteam a 450°F/232°C deck oven. Load the bread into the oven and steam for 3 seconds. Bake until the crust is golden brown and the bread sounds hollow when thumped on the bottom, 25 to 30 minutes. Vent during the final 10 minutes. Cool completely on racks.

Ciabatta

MAKES 9 LB/4.08 KG DOUGH. DDT: 78°F/26°C

BIGA			
Bread flour	100%	1 lb 10 oz	737 g
Water (60°F/16°C)	50%	13¼ fl oz	398 mL
Instant dry yeast	0.03%	pinch	pinch
FINAL DOUGH			
Bread flour	67.1%	3 lb 5¾ oz	1.52 kg
Instant dry yeast	0.3%	¼ oz	7 g
Water	56.6%	45¼ fl oz	1.36 L
Biga (above)	50%	2 lb 7¼ oz	1.11 kg
Salt	2.3%	2 oz	57 g

1   To prepare the biga, combine the flour, water, and yeast and mix on low speed with the dough hook attachment for 3 minutes, or until thoroughly combined. Transfer to a container, cover, and ferment at 75°F/24°C for 18 to 24 hours, until the biga has risen and begun to recede; it should still be bubbly and airy.

2   To prepare the final dough, combine the flour and yeast. Add the water, biga, and salt in the mixer and then add the flour and yeast. Mix on low speed with the dough hook attachment for 4 minutes and on medium speed for 1 minute. The dough should be blended but not too elastic (ciabatta dough is a wet, slack dough).

3   Bulk ferment the dough in a tub or bowl until nearly doubled, about 30 minutes. Fold gently in half four times (the dough should feel like jelly). Ferment for another 30 minutes. Fold in half again, gently, two times. Allow the dough to ferment for another 15 minutes.

4   Place the dough on the table and dust the top of it with flour. (Reminder: Keep the work surface well floured when working with ciabatta dough.) Using the palms of your hands, gently stretch the dough into a rectangle 16 in/41 cm long and 1½ in/4 cm thick. Be careful to avoid tearing or puncturing the dough with your fingertips. Using a floured bench scraper, divide the dough into two rectangles 4½ by 10 in/11 by 25 cm.

5   Flip the dough over onto floured linen couches. Gently stretch each piece into a rough rectangle.

Stretch the dough slightly to place it onto a couche.

6   Proof, covered, until the dough springs back slowly to the touch but does not collapse, 30 to 45 minutes.

7   Lightly flour the top of the dough. Flip each ciabatta over onto a small floured board, and then slide each one onto a floured peel.

8   Presteam a 460°F/238°C deck oven. Load the ciabatta into the oven and steam for 3 seconds. Bake until the crust is golden brown and the ciabatta sounds hollow when thumped on the bottom, 25 to 30 minutes. Vent during the final 10 minutes. Cool completely on racks.

Focaccia

MAKES 11 LB 6¼ OZ/5.17 KG DOUGH. DDT: 78°F/26°C

BIGA			
Bread flour	100%	1 lb 8 oz	680 g
Water (60°F/16°C)	55.2%	13¼ fl oz	398 mL
Instant dry yeast	0.03%	pinch	pinch
FINAL DOUGH			
Bread flour	76.9%	5 lb	2.27 kg
Instant dry yeast	0.5%	½ oz	14 g
Water	53.8%	56 fl oz	1.68 L
Biga (above)	35.8%	2 lb 5¼ oz	1.06 kg
Olive oil	6.25%	6½ oz	184 g
Salt	1.9%	2 oz	57 g
Olive oil		as needed	as needed
GARNISHES (OPTIONAL)			
Fresh herbs		as needed	as needed
Garlic, sliced and sautéed		as needed	as needed
Roasted tomato slices		as needed	as needed
Onions, sliced and sautéed		as needed	as needed
Coarse salt		as needed	as needed

1   To prepare the biga, combine the flour, water, and yeast and mix on low speed with the dough hook attachment for 3 minutes, or until thoroughly combined. Transfer to a container, cover, and ferment at 75°F/24°C for about 8 hours, until the biga has risen and begun to recede; it should still be slightly bubbly and airy.

2 To prepare the final dough, combine the flour and yeast. Add the water, biga, olive oil, and salt to the mixer and then add the flour and yeast. Mix on low speed with the dough hook attachment for 4 minutes. The dough should be very loose.

3 Bulk ferment the dough until nearly doubled, about 45 minutes. Fold gently. Ferment for another 45 minutes.

4 Divide the dough into 1-lb/454-g pieces. Preshape the dough lightly into large rounds (for preshaping instructions, see page 109). (Reminder: When making multiple loaves, work sequentially, starting with the first piece of dough you divided and rounded.)

5 Brush the dough lightly with olive oil. Using only your fingertips, gently press the dough down, and then stretch it into a circle 10 in/25 cm in diameter, keeping the thickness of the dough even. Place on parchment-lined sheet pans.

6 Proof, covered, until the dough springs back slowly to the touch but does not collapse, 30 to 45 minutes.

7 Brush the dough lightly with olive oil again. Gently stipple the dough, creating random indentations with your fingertips. Scatter with any optional toppings, if desired.

8 Presteam a 460°F/238°C deck oven. Load the focaccia into the oven and steam for 3 seconds. Bake until the crust is golden brown and the focaccia sounds hollow when thumped on the bottom, 25 to 30 minutes. Vent during the final 10 minutes. Brush lightly with olive oil and sprinkle with salt if desired. Cool completely on racks.

Dimple the proofed focaccia with your fingertips.

Wheat sourdough starter

MAKES 1 LB 8 OZ/680 G STARTER

INITIAL SOUR (DAYS 1 AND 2)			
Water (85°F/29°C)	100%	4 fl oz	120 mL
Organic wheat or durum flour	100%	4 oz	113 g
FIRST FEEDING (DAY 3)			
Initial sour (above)	100%	4 oz	113 g
Water (85°F/29°C)	100%	4 fl oz	120 mL
Organic wheat or durum flour	100%	4 oz	113 g
SECOND FEEDING (DAY 4)			
Sour after first feeding (above)	200%	8 oz	227 g
Water (85°F/29°C)	100%	4 fl oz	120 mL
Organic wheat or durum flour	100%	4 oz	113 g
THIRD FEEDING (DAY 5)			
Sour after second feeding (above)	33%	4 oz	113 g
Water (60°F/16°C)	66%	8 fl oz	240 mL
Organic wheat flour	100%	12 oz	340 g

1   Mix the ingredients for the initial sour. Cover and let rest at 75°F/24°C for 24 hours. The flour and water tend to separate overnight; recombine on the second day. Let rest for another 24 hours at 75°F/24°C.

2   On the third day, combine 4 oz/113 g of the initial sour mixture with the water for the first feeding and blend to fully combine; discard excess sour. Blend in the flour for the first feeding. Cover and let rest at 75°F/24°C for 24 hours.

3   On the fourth day, combine 8 oz/227 g of the sour mixture from step 2 with the water for the second feeding and blend to fully combine; discard excess sour. Blend in the flour for the second feeding. Cover and let rest at 75°F/24°C for 24 hours.

4   On the final day, combine 4 oz/113 g of the sour from step 3 with the water for the third feeding and blend to fully combine; discard excess sour. Blend in the flour for the third feeding. Let the starter rest covered at 75°F/24°C for 24 hours before using in a bread formula. Repeat step 4 two or three more times before using.

Rye sourdough starter

MAKES 19½ OZ/553 G STARTER

INITIAL SOUR (DAYS 1 AND 2)			
Water (80°F/27°C)	100%	4 fl oz	120 mL
Organic rye flour	100%	4 oz	113 g
FIRST FEEDING (DAY 3)			
Initial sour (above)	100%	4 oz	113 g
Water (80°F/27°C)	100%	4 fl oz	120 mL
Organic rye flour	100%	4 oz	113 g
SECOND FEEDING (DAY 4)			
Sour after first feeding (above)	200%	8 oz	227 g
Water (80°F/27°C)	100%	4 fl oz	120 mL
Organic rye flour	100%	4 oz	113 g
THIRD FEEDING (DAY 5)			
Sour after second feeding (above)	33%	4 oz	113 g
Water (60°F/16°C)	66%	8 fl oz	240 mL
Organic rye flour	100%	8 oz	227 g
Salt		¼ oz	7 g

Follow the method used for Wheat Sourdough Starter on page 170. Note the different hydration level for the Rye Sourdough Starter. Repeat the third feeding 2 or 3 more times before using.

Whole wheat sourdough

MAKES 16 LB 5¼ OZ/7.41 KG DOUGH. DDT: 76°F/24°C

Bread flour	50%	3 lb 12 oz	1.70 kg
Whole wheat flour	50%	3 lb 12 oz	1.70 kg
Water	75%	90 fl oz	2.70 L
Wheat sourdough starter (page 170)	40%	3 lb	1.36 kg
Salt	2.7%	3¼ oz	92 g

1   Combine the flours, water, and sourdough and mix on low speed with the dough hook attachment for 4 minutes. Let the dough rest for 15 minutes. Add the salt and mix 1 minute on low speed and 2 minutes on medium speed. The dough should be slightly soft but elastic. Mix to the improved stage of gluten development.

2   Bulk ferment the dough until nearly doubled in volume, about 1 hour. Fold gently and ferment for another hour. Fold again. Ferment for another 20 minutes.

3   Divide the dough into pieces 1 lb 8 oz/680 g each. Preshape the dough into large oblongs (for preshaping instructions, see page 109). Let the dough rest, covered, until relaxed, 15 to 20 minutes. (Reminder: When making multiple loaves, work sequentially, starting with the first piece of dough you divided and rounded.)

4   Position the dough lengthwise, parallel to the edge of the work surface with the seam side up, and press lightly with your fingertips. Fold the top edge of the dough down to the center of the dough, pressing lightly with your fingertips to tighten.

5   Fold the dough lengthwise in half and use the heel of your hand to seal the two edges, keeping the seam straight. Roll the dough under your palms into a cylinder 8 in/20 cm long, moving your hands outward from the center of the cylinder toward the ends and slightly increasing the pressure as you move outward, until both ends have an even, gentle taper. Then increase the pressure at the ends of the loaf to seal.

6   Proof, covered, until the dough springs back slowly to the touch but does not collapse, 45 minutes.

7   Score the bâtard with an arc.

8   Presteam a 470°F/243°C deck oven. Load the bread into the oven and steam for 3 seconds. Bake until the crust is golden brown and the bread sounds hollow when thumped on the bottom, 35 to 40 minutes. Vent during the final 15 minutes. Cool completely on racks.

White wheat sourdough

MAKES 15 LB 4 OZ/6.92 KG DOUGH. DDT: 79°F/26°C

Bread flour	92.8%	6 lb 10½ oz	3.02 kg
Water	68%	78 fl oz	2.34 L
Wheat sourdough starter (page 170)	41.8%	3 lb	1.36 kg
Whole wheat flour	7.2%	8¼ oz	234 g
Salt	2.8%	3¼ oz	92 g

1   Combine the flour, water, and sourdough and mix on low speed with the dough hook attachment for 4 minutes. Let the dough rest for 15 minutes. Add the salt and mix 1 minute on low and 2 minutes on medium speed. The dough should be slightly soft but elastic. Mix to the improved stage of gluten development.

2   Bulk ferment the dough until nearly doubled in volume, about 1 hour. Fold gently and ferment for another hour. Fold again. Ferment for another 20 minutes.

3   Divide the dough into pieces 1 lb 8 oz/680 g each. Preshape the dough into large oblongs (for preshaping instructions, see page 109). Let the dough rest, covered, until relaxed, 15 to 20 minutes. (Reminder: When making multiple loaves, work sequentially, starting with the first piece of dough you divided and rounded.)

4   Position the dough lengthwise, parallel to the edge of the work surface with the seam side up, and press lightly with your fingertips. Fold the top edge of the dough down to the center of the dough, pressing lightly with your fingertips to tighten.

5   Fold the dough lengthwise in half and use the heel of your hand to seal the two edges, keeping the seam straight. Roll the dough under your palms into a cylinder 8 in/20 cm long, moving your hands outward from the center of the cylinder toward the ends and slightly increasing the pressure as you move outward, until both ends have an even, gentle taper. Then increase the pressure at the ends of the loaf to seal.

6   Proof, covered, until the dough springs back slowly to the touch but does not collapse, 45 minutes.

7   Score the bâtard with an arc.

8   Presteam a 470°F/243°C deck oven. Load the bread into the oven and steam for 3 seconds. Bake until the crust is golden brown and the bread sounds hollow when thumped on the bottom, 35 to 40 minutes. Vent during the final 15 minutes. Cool completely on racks.

Apple and walnut sourdough

MAKES 15 LB 13¾ OZ/7.19 KG DOUGH. DDT: 77°F/25°C

Bread flour	83.1%	6 lb 5 oz	2.86 kg
Whole wheat flour	16.9%	14 oz	397 g
Water	84.3%	70 fl oz	2.10 L
Wheat sourdough starter (page 170)	49.4%	2 lb 9 oz	1.16 kg
Salt	3.3%	2¾ oz	78 g
Granny Smith apples, coarsely chopped	14.5%	12 oz	340 g
Walnuts, lightly toasted and coarsely chopped	14.5%	12 oz	340 g
Ground cinnamon	1.2%	1 oz	28 g

1   Combine the flours, water, and sourdough and mix on low speed with the dough hook attachment for 4 minutes. Let the dough rest for 15 minutes. Add the salt and mix for 1 minute on low speed and 3 minutes on medium speed. The dough should be slightly soft but elastic.

2   Bulk ferment the dough until nearly doubled, about 1 hour. Fold gently and ferment for another hour. Fold again. Ferment for another 20 minutes. Toss together the apples, walnuts, and cinnamon and fold into the dough (see "Adding Flavorings and Garnishes," page 160).

3   Divide the dough into pieces 1 lb 4 oz/567 g each. Preshape the dough into large oblongs (for preshaping instructions, see page 109). Let the dough rest, covered, until relaxed, 15 to 20 minutes. (Reminder: When making multiple loaves, work sequentially, starting with the first piece of dough you divided and rounded.)

4   Position the dough lengthwise, parallel to the edge of the work surface with the seam side up, and press lightly with your fingertips. Fold the top edge of the dough down to the center of the dough, pressing lightly with your fingertips to tighten.

5   Fold the dough lengthwise in half and use the heel of your hand to seal the two edges, keeping the seam straight. Roll the dough under your palms into a cylinder 8 in/20 cm long, moving your hands outward from the center of the cylinder toward the ends and slightly increasing the pressure as you move outward, until both ends have an even, gentle taper. Then increase the pressure at the ends of the loaf to seal.

6   Proof, covered, in a couche until the dough springs back slowly to the touch but does not collapse, 30 minutes.

7   Score the bâtard with a slash down the center.

8   Presteam a 470°F/243°C deck oven. Load the bread into the oven and steam for 3 seconds. Bake until the crust is golden brown and the bread sounds hollow when thumped on the bottom, 35 minutes. Vent during the final 10 minutes. Cool completely on racks.

Sourdough with rye flour

MAKES 15 LB 9¾ OZ/7.08 KG DOUGH. DDT: 76°F/24°C

Bread flour	60%	4 lb 8 oz	2.04 kg
Medium rye flour	40%	3 lb	1.36 kg
Water	65%	78½ fl oz	2.36 L
Wheat sourdough starter (page 170)	40%	3 lb	1.36 kg
Salt	2.7%	3¼ oz	92 g

1 Combine the flours, water, and sourdough and mix on low speed with the dough hook attachment for 3 minutes. Let the dough rest for 15 minutes. Add the salt and mix on medium speed for 3 minutes, or until the dough is slightly soft but elastic.

2 Bulk ferment the dough until nearly doubled, about 1 hour. Fold gently and ferment for another hour. Fold again. Ferment for another 20 minutes.

3 Divide the dough into pieces 1 lb 8 oz/680 g each. Preshape the dough into large oblongs (for preshaping instructions, see page 109). Let the dough rest, covered, until relaxed, 15 to 20 minutes. (Reminder: When making multiple loaves, work sequentially, starting with the first piece of dough you divided and rounded.)

4 Position the dough lengthwise, parallel to the edge of the work surface with the seam side up, and press lightly with your fingertips. Fold the top edge of the dough down to the center of the dough, pressing lightly with your fingertips to tighten.

5 Fold the dough lengthwise in half and use the heel of your hand to seal the two edges, keeping the seam straight. Roll the dough under your palms into a cylinder 8 in/20 cm long, moving your hands outward from the center of the cylinder toward the ends and slightly increasing the pressure as you move outward, until both ends have an even, gentle taper. Then increase the pressure at the ends of the loaf to seal.

6 Proof, covered, in a couche until the dough springs back slowly to the touch but does not collapse, 30 minutes.

7 Score the bâtard with an arc in the center.

8 Presteam a 475°F/246°C deck oven. Load the bread into the oven and steam for 3 seconds. Bake until the crust is golden brown and the bread sounds hollow when thumped on the bottom, 25 to 30 minutes. Vent during the final 10 minutes. Cool completely on racks.

Multigrain sourdough

MAKES 12 LB 5 OZ/5.58 KG DOUGH. DDT: 78°F/26°C

SOAKER			
Nine-grain cereal mix	30.33%	1 lb	454 g
Sunflower seeds	12.32%	6½ oz	184 g
Oats	12.32%	6½ oz	184 g
Water	60.66%	32 fl oz	960 mL
FINAL DOUGH			
Bread flour	100%	3 lb 5 oz	1.50 kg
Instant dry yeast	1.23%	¼ oz	7 g
Water	45.5%	24 fl oz	720 mL
Pâte fermentée (see page 148)	75.83%	2 lb 8 oz	1.13 kg
Wheat sourdough starter (page 170)	30.33%	1 lb	454 g
Molasses, unsulfured	2.37%	1¼ oz	35 g
Soaker (above)	115%	3 lb 13 oz	1.73 kg
Salt	2.84%	1½ oz	43 g

1 To prepare the soaker, combine the nine-grain cereal mix, sunflower seeds, and oats with the water in a plastic tub and cover. Soak at room temperature until the soaker has absorbed the water and is slightly dry, 8 to 12 hours.

2 To prepare the final dough, combine the flour and yeast. Add the water, pâte fermentée, sourdough, molasses, soaker, and salt to the mixer and then add the flour and yeast. Mix on low speed with the dough hook attachment for 4 minutes. Let the dough rest for 15 minutes. Mix on medium speed for 3 minutes, or until the dough is slightly stiff. Mix to the improved stage of gluten development.

3 Bulk ferment the dough until nearly doubled, about 30 minutes. Fold gently and ferment for another 30 minutes. Fold again. Ferment for another 30 minutes.

4 Divide the dough into 1-lb/454-g pieces. Preshape the dough into large oblongs (for pre-shaping instructions, see page 109). Let the dough rest, covered, until relaxed, 15 to 20 minutes. (Reminder: When making multiple loaves, work sequentially, starting with the first piece of dough you divided and rounded.)

5 Position the dough lengthwise, parallel to the edge of the work surface with the seam side up, and press lightly with your fingertips. Fold the top edge of the dough down to the center of the dough, pressing lightly with your fingertips to tighten.

6 Fold the dough lengthwise in half and use the heel of your hand to seal the two edges, keeping the seam straight. Roll the dough under your palms into a cylinder 8 in/20 cm long, moving your hands outward from the center of the cylinder toward the ends and slightly increasing the

pressure as you move outward, until both ends have an even, gentle taper. Then increase the pressure at the ends of the loaf to seal.

7   Proof, covered, in a couche until the dough springs back slowly to the touch but does not collapse, 45 minutes.

8   Score the bâtard with three parallel diagonal lines.

9   Presteam a 470°F/243°C deck oven. Load the bread into the oven and steam for 3 seconds. Bake until the crust is golden brown and the bread sounds hollow when thumped on the bottom, 25 to 30 minutes. Vent during the final 10 minutes. Cool completely on racks.

Chocolate cherry sourdough

MAKES 19 LB 6½ OZ/8.80 KG DOUGH. DDT: 78°F/26°C

Espresso beans, ground	5.3%	4¼ oz	120 g
Water	81.25%	65 fl oz	1.95 L
Wheat sourdough starter (page 170)	63.2%	3 lb 2½ oz	1.43 kg
Pâte fermentée (see page 148)	40%	2 lb	907 g
Bread flour	100%	5 lb	2.27 kg
Cocoa powder	10.6%	8½ oz	241 g
Instant dry yeast	0.95%	¾ oz	21 g
Salt	3.2%	2½ oz	71 g
Chocolate chunks	41.9%	2 lb 1½ oz	950 g
Dried cherries	41.9%	2 lb 1½ oz	950 g

1   Line a fine-mesh strainer with cheesecloth and place the ground espresso in it. Pour 26½ fl oz/795 mL boiling water over the coffee. Cool to room temperature.

2   Combine the cooled espresso, the remaining water, the sourdough, and pâte fermentée and mix on low speed just until blended, about 1 minute. Add the flour, cocoa powder, yeast, and salt and mix on low speed for 4 minutes and then on medium speed for 4 minutes. Add the chocolate chunks and dried cherries and mix on low speed until well combined, about 1 minute. The dough should be slightly loose. Mix to the improved stage of gluten development.

3   Bulk ferment the dough until nearly doubled, about 45 minutes. Fold gently. Let the dough ferment for another 45 minutes.

4   Divide the dough into pieces 1 lb 8 oz/680 g each.

5   To shape as a boule: Cup both hands around the dough. Using your thumbs, push the dough away from you in an arc to the right, keeping a small piece of dough between the table

and the edges of your palms. Using the edges of your palms as a guide, pull the dough toward you in an arc to the left. There should still be a small piece of dough that is squeezed between the table and the edges of your palms. Repeat this circular motion two or three more times, applying gentle pressure while rounding the dough, to create a tight, smooth outer skin. Place the boule seam side up in a round basket or seam side down on a board dusted with cornmeal.

6   Proof until the dough springs back slowly to the touch, 45 minutes. Flip the dough seam side down onto a peel. Score the boule with three parallel horizontal lines.

7   Presteam in a 425°F/218°C deck oven. Load the bread into the oven and steam for 3 seconds. Bake until the crust is golden brown and the bread sounds hollow when thumped on the bottom, 25 to 30 minutes. Vent during the final 5 minutes. Cool completely on racks.

Durum sourdough

MAKES 22 LB ½ OZ/9.99 KG DOUGH. DDT: 75°F/24°C

Durum flour	50%	5 lb	2.27 kg
Bread flour	50%	5 lb	2.27 kg
Instant dry yeast	0.32%	½ oz	14 g
Water	82.5%	132 fl oz	3.96 L
Wheat sourdough starter (see page 170)	35%	3 lb 8 oz	1.59 kg
Salt	2.5%	4 oz	113 g

1   Combine the flours and yeast. Add the water and sourdough to the mixer and then add the flour and yeast. Mix on low speed with the dough hook attachment for 4 minutes. Allow the dough to rest for 15 minutes. Add the salt and mix on low speed with the dough hook attachment for 4 minutes. The dough should be fairly loose.

2   Bulk ferment the dough until nearly doubled, about 2 hours, folding the dough gently every 30 minutes, for a total of three folds.

3   Divide the dough into pieces 2 lb 6 oz/1.08 kg each. Preshape the dough into large rounds (for preshaping instructions, see page 109). Let the dough rest, covered, until relaxed, 15 to 20 minutes. (Reminder: When making multiple loaves, work sequentially, starting with the first piece of dough you divided and rounded.)

4   To shape as a boule: Cup both hands around the dough. Using your thumbs, push the dough away from you in an arc to the right, keeping a small piece of dough between the table and the edges of your palms. Using the edges of your palms as a guide, pull the dough toward you in an arc to the left. There should still be a small piece of dough that is squeezed between the table and the edges of your palms. Repeat this circular motion two or three more times, applying gentle pressure while rounding the dough, to create a tight, smooth outer skin. Place the boule seam side up in a round basket or seam side down on a board dusted with cornmeal.

5 Proof, covered, until the dough springs back slowly to the touch, 1 to 1½ hours. Flip the dough seam side down onto a peel. Score the boule with an arc.

6 Presteam in a 450°F/232°C deck oven. Load the bread into the oven and steam for 3 seconds. Bake until the crust is golden brown and the bread sounds hollow when thumped on the bottom, 40 to 50 minutes. Vent during the final 15 minutes. Cool completely on racks.

100 percent rye sourdough

MAKES 10 LB 14 OZ/4.93 KG DOUGH. DDT: 80°F/27°C

Medium rye flour	100%	3 lb 13¾ oz	1.75 kg
Instant dry yeast	0.8%	½ oz	14 g
Rye sourdough starter (page 171)	92.7%	3 lb 9¼ oz	1.62 kg
Water	85.4%	52¾ fl oz	1.58 L
Salt	2.8%	1¾ oz	50 g

1 Combine the flour and yeast. Add the sourdough, water, and salt to the mixer and then add the flour and yeast. Mix on low speed with the dough hook attachment for 5 to 6 minutes. The dough should be loose and clay-like, with no elasticity or gluten development.

2 Bulk ferment the dough until nearly doubled, 30 minutes.

3 Divide the dough into 2-lb/907-g pieces. Preshape the dough into large oblongs (for pre-shaping instructions, see page 109). Lightly grease five 2-lb/907-g loaf pans (4½ in/11 cm wide, 8 in/20 cm long, and 3 in/8 cm deep). Let the dough rest, covered, until relaxed, 15 to 20 minutes. (Reminder: When making multiple loaves, work sequentially, starting with the first piece of dough you divided and rounded.)

4 Place the dough lengthwise parallel to the edge of the worktable with the seam side up. Press lightly with your fingertips to stretch it into a rectangle 8 in/20 cm long, using as little flour as possible. Fold the top edge of the dough down to the center of the dough, pressing lightly with your fingertips to tighten the dough.

5 Fold the dough lengthwise in half and use the heel of your hand to seal the two edges together, keeping the seam straight. Roll the dough under your palms into a cylinder 10 in/25 cm long, keeping the pressure even and holding your hands flat and parallel to the work surface to create a smooth, even loaf.

6 Place the dough seam side down in a greased loaf pan. Proof, covered, until the dough fills the pan and starts to crack at the surface, 30 to 40 minutes.

7 Presteam a 450°F/232°C deck oven. Load the bread into the oven and steam for 5 seconds. Bake until the crust is a deep golden brown and the sides of the bread spring back when pressed, about 1 hour. Vent during the final 20 minutes. Remove the bread from the pan and cool completely on racks.

Multigrain rye sourdough

MAKES 15 LB/6.80 KG DOUGH. DDT: 79°F/26°C

SOAKER			
Nine-grain cereal mix	21.5%	18¾ fl oz	563 mL
Flaxseed	13.8%	12 oz	340 g
Sunflower seeds	7.8%	7 oz	198 g
Water (90°F/32°C)	56.9%	49½ fl oz	1.49 L
FINAL DOUGH			
Bread flour	61.6%	3 lb 2½ oz	1.43 kg
Medium rye flour	38.4%	1 lb 15½ oz	893 g
Instant dry yeast	1.2%	1 oz	28 g
Rye sourdough starter (page 171)	42.5%	2 lb 5 oz	1.05 kg
Water	36.9%	30¼ fl oz	908 mL
Soaker (above)	106%	5 lb 7 oz	2.47 kg
Salt	3.4%	2¾ oz	78 g

1 To prepare the soaker, combine the nine-grain cereal mix, flaxseed, and sunflower seeds with the water in a plastic tub. Soak at 75°F/24°C until the soaker has absorbed the water and is slightly dry, 8 to 12 hours.

2 To prepare the final dough, combine the flours and yeast. Add the sourdough, water, soaker, and salt to the mixer and then add the flour and yeast. Mix on low speed with the dough hook attachment for 4 minutes and on medium speed for 3 minutes. Mix to the improved stage of gluten development.

3 Bulk ferment the dough until nearly doubled, about 30 minutes.

4 Divide the dough into pieces 1 lb 8 oz/680 g each. Preshape the dough into large oblongs (for preshaping instructions, see page 109). Let the dough rest, covered, until relaxed, 5 minutes.

5 Position the dough lengthwise, parallel to the edge of the work surface with the seam side up, and press lightly with your fingertips. Fold the top edge of the dough down to the center of the dough, pressing lightly with your fingertips to tighten.

6 Fold the dough lengthwise in half and use the heel of your hand to seal the two edges, keeping the seam straight. Roll the dough under your palms into a cylinder 8 in/20 cm long, moving your hands outward from the center of the cylinder toward the ends and slightly increasing the pressure as you move outward, until both ends have an even, gentle taper. Then increase the pressure at the ends of the loaf to seal.

7 Proof, covered, in a couche until the dough springs back slowly to the touch but does not collapse, 35 minutes.

8 Score the bâtard straight down the center.

9   Presteam in a 470°F/243°C deck oven. Load the bread into the oven and steam for 3 seconds. Bake until the crust is golden brown and the bread sounds hollow when thumped on the bottom, 35 to 40 minutes. Vent during the final 10 minutes. Cool completely on racks.

Rustic rye sourdough

MAKES 12 LB 4 OZ/5.556 KG DOUGH. DDT: 78°F/26°C

Medium rye flour	56.25%	2 lb 13 oz	1.28 kg
Bread flour	43.75%	2 lb 3 oz	992 g
Instant dry yeast	0.63%	½ oz	14 g
Water	75%	60 fl oz	1.80 L
Rye sourdough starter (page 171)	41.9%	2 lb 1½ oz	950 g
Salt	2.5%	2 oz	57 g
Sunflower seeds, lightly toasted	25%	1 lb 4 oz	567 g

1   Combine the flours and yeast. Add the water, sourdough, and salt to the mixer and then add the flour and yeast. Mix on low speed with the dough hook attachment for 4 minutes. Allow the dough to rest for 15 minutes. Add the sunflower seeds and mix on medium speed for 3 minutes. The dough should be slightly wet but elastic. Mix to the improved stage of gluten development.

2   Bulk ferment the dough until nearly doubled, about 30 minutes.

3   Divide the dough into pieces 1 lb 8 oz/680 g each. Preshape the dough into oblongs (for preshaping instructions, see page 109). Let the dough rest, covered, until relaxed, 5 minutes.

4   Position the dough lengthwise, parallel to the edge of the work surface with the seam side up, and press lightly with your fingertips. Fold the top edge of the dough down to the center of the dough, pressing lightly with your fingertips to tighten.

5   Fold the dough lengthwise in half and use the heel of your hand to seal the two edges, keeping the seam straight. Roll the dough under your palms into a cylinder 8 in/20 cm long, moving your hands outward from the center of the cylinder toward the ends and slightly increasing the pressure as you move outward, until both ends have an even, gentle taper. Then increase the pressure at the ends of the loaf to seal.

6   Proof, covered, in a couche until the dough springs back slowly to the touch but does not collapse, 30 minutes.

7   Score the bâtard straight down the center.

8   Presteam in a 470°F/243°C deck oven. Load the bread into the oven and steam for 3 seconds. Bake until the crust is golden brown and the bread sounds hollow when thumped on the bottom, 30 to 40 minutes. Vent during the final 10 minutes. Cool completely on racks.

Whole-grain carrot dough

MAKES 13 LB 13¾ OZ/6.29 KG DOUGH. DDT: 80°F/27°C

SOAKER			
Nine-grain cereal mix	46.3%	2 lb 12 oz	1.25 kg
Rolled oats	7.4%	9 oz	255 g
Water	46.3%	44 fl oz	1.32 L
FINAL DOUGH			
High-gluten flour	52.6%	2 lb 3¼ oz	999 g
Medium rye flour	47.4%	1 lb 15¾ oz	900 g
Instant dry yeast	1.5%	1 oz	28 g
Rye sourdough starter (page 171)	63%	2 lb 10¼ oz	1.20 kg
Water	47.7%	32 fl oz	960 mL
Soaker (above)	144.7%	6 lb 1 oz	2.75 kg
Pumpkin seeds, lightly toasted	10.5%	7 oz	198 g
Carrots, grated	6.7%	4½ oz	128 g
Salt	3%	2 oz	57 g
Malt syrup	1.5%	1 oz	28 g
Rolled oats, for sprinkling		as needed	as needed

1   To prepare the soaker, combine the nine-grain cereal mix and rolled oats with the water in a plastic tub. Soak at room temperature until the soaker has absorbed the water and is slightly dry, 8 to 12 hours.

2   To prepare the final dough, combine the flours and yeast. Add the sourdough and water to the mixer and then add the flour and yeast. Mix on low speed with the dough hook attachment for 4 minutes. Allow the dough to rest for 15 minutes. Add the soaker, pumpkin seeds, carrots, salt, and malt syrup and mix on medium speed for 3 minutes. The dough should be slightly sticky but have sufficient gluten development. Mix to the improved stage of gluten development.

3   Bulk ferment the dough until nearly doubled, about 30 minutes.

4   Divide the dough into 1-lb/454-g pieces. Preshape the dough into large oblongs (for pre-shaping instructions, see page 109). Let the dough rest, covered, until relaxed, 5 minutes. (Reminder: When making multiple loaves, work sequentially, starting with the first piece of dough you divided and rounded.)

5   Position the dough lengthwise, parallel to the edge of the work surface with the seam side up, and press lightly with your fingertips. Fold the top edge of the dough down to the center of the dough, pressing lightly with your fingertips to tighten.

6   Fold the dough lengthwise in half and use the heel of your hand to seal the two edges, keeping the seam straight. Roll the dough under your palms into a cylinder 8 in/20 cm long, moving your hands outward from the center of the cylinder toward the ends and slightly increasing the pressure as you move outward, until both ends have an even, gentle taper. Then increase the pressure at the ends of the loaf to seal. Place on parchment-lined sheet pans that have been lightly dusted with cornmeal.

7   Proof, covered, until the dough springs back slowly to the touch but does not collapse, 30 minutes.

8   Sprinkle the top of each loaf with rolled oats.

9   Presteam in a 450°F/232°C deck oven. Load the bread into the oven and steam for 3 seconds. Bake until the crust is golden brown and the bread sounds hollow when thumped on the bottom, 25 to 30 minutes. Vent during the final 10 minutes. Cool completely on racks.

Vollkornbrot European pumpernickel

MAKES 19 LB 8 OZ/8.85 KG DOUGH. DDT: 80°F/27°C

CRACKED RYE SOURDOUGH STARTER			
Rye sourdough starter (page 171)	10%	6½ oz	184 g
Steel-cut cracked rye	100%	3 lb 13¾ oz	1.75 kg
Water	100%	61¾ fl oz	1.85 L
SOAKER			
Steel-cut cracked rye	52.75%	1 lb 10½ oz	751 g
Water, boiling	47.25%	23¾ fl oz	713 mL
FINAL DOUGH			
Cracked rye sourdough starter (above)	162.2%	8 lb 1¾ oz	3.68 kg
Instant dry yeast	1.25%	1 oz	28 g
Steel-cut cracked rye	100%	5 lb	2.27 kg
Soaker (above)	62.8%	3 lb 2¼ oz	1.42 kg
Water	60%	48 fl oz	1.44 L
Salt	3.75%	3 oz	85 g

1   To prepare the cracked rye sourdough starter, mix the rye sourdough starter, cracked rye, and water in a plastic tub. Cover and ferment for 18 to 20 hours at 75°F/24°C. The starter should be bubbly and have a light alcohol aroma.

2   To prepare the soaker, combine the cracked rye with the water in a plastic tub. Soak at 75°F/24°C until the rye has absorbed the water and is slightly dry, 8 to 12 hours.

3   To prepare the final dough, combine the cracked rye sourdough starter, yeast, cracked rye, soaker, water, and salt and mix on low speed with the dough hook attachment for 8 minutes and on medium speed for 5 minutes. The dough should be very loose and very sticky.

4   Bulk ferment the dough in the mixing bowl until nearly doubled, 30 minutes.

5   After the dough has fermented, mix on low speed for 15 seconds to expel the carbon dioxide that has built up.

6   Grease nine or ten 3-lb/1.36-kg Pullman loaf pans and lids generously. Divide the dough into pieces 2 lb/907 g each. Preshape the dough into large rounds (for preshaping instructions, see page 109). Let the dough rest, covered, until relaxed, 15 to 20 minutes. (Reminder: When making multiple loaves, work sequentially, starting with the first piece of dough you divided and rounded.)

7   Place the dough lengthwise with the seam side up. Press lightly with your fingertips to stretch it into a rectangle 8 in/20 cm long, using as little flour as possible. Fold the top edge of the dough down to the center of the dough, pressing lightly with your fingertips to tighten the dough.

8 Fold the dough lengthwise in half and use the heel of your hand to seal the two edges together, keeping the seam straight. Roll the dough under your palms into a cylinder 10 in/25 cm long, keeping the pressure even and holding your hands flat and parallel to the work surface to create a smooth, even loaf.

9 Let the dough rest, covered, until relaxed, 15 to 20 minutes.

10 Turn the dough seam side up and position it so that a long side is parallel to the edge of the work surface. Work the dough lightly with your fingertips to release some of the gas, then gently stretch it into a rectangle 2½ in/6 cm wide and 16 in/41 cm long. Fold 1 in/3 cm of each short end in toward the center of the dough. Fold the long sides into the center, overlapping them slightly, and use the heel of your hand to seal the two edges together, keeping the seam straight. Fold the dough lengthwise in half and use your fingertips to seal the edges together, keeping the seam straight.

11 Roll the dough under your palms into a cylinder 18 in/46 cm long, keeping the pressure even and holding your hands flat and parallel to the work surface to create a smooth, even loaf. Push the ends of the loaf toward the center until the cylinder is 16 in/41 cm long. Place the dough seam side down in the greased loaf pan. The dough will spring back on itself slightly and fit snugly in the pan. Proof, uncovered, until the pan is three-quarters full and the dough springs back slowly to the touch, about 1 hour. Lightly spray with water.

12 Place the lids on the pans and let the dough to proof for an additional 15 minutes.

13 Bake in a 425°F/218°C deck oven for 1 hour and 15 minutes. Cool completely on racks.

CLOCKWISE FROM TOP CENTER:

Six-Braid Challah (page 135), Brioche Loaf round (page 186), Gugelhopf (page 192) Christmas Stollen (page 194), Day of the Dead Bread (page 207), Hot Cross Buns (page 201), Panettone (page 190)

Brioche loaf

MAKES 11 LB 10¾ OZ/5.29 KG DOUGH. DDT: 75°F/24°C

Bread flour	100%	5 lb	2.27 kg
Instant dry yeast	1.7%	1⅓ oz	38 g
Eggs	40%	2 lb	907 g
Milk, room temperature	20%	16 fl oz	480 mL
Sugar	10%	8 oz	227 g
Salt	2%	1½ oz	43 g
Butter, soft but still pliable	60%	3 lb	1.36 kg
Egg wash (page 892)		as needed	as needed

1   Combine the flour and yeast. Add the eggs, milk, sugar, and salt to the mixer and then add the flour and yeast. Mix on low speed with the dough hook attachment for 4 minutes.

2   Gradually add the butter with the mixer running on medium speed, scraping down the sides of the bowl as necessary. After the butter has been fully incorporated, mix on medium speed for 15 minutes or until the dough begins to pull away from the sides of the bowl.

3   Line a sheet pan with parchment paper and grease the paper. Place the dough on the sheet pan. Cover tightly with plastic wrap and refrigerate overnight.

4   Lightly grease ten to twelve 2-lb/907-g loaf pans (4½ in/11 cm wide, 8 in/20 cm long, and 3 in/8 cm deep).

5   Remove the dough from the refrigerator and divide it by hand into 2-oz/57-g pieces. Pre-shape each piece into a round, lightly flouring the work surface as needed. (Reminder: Refrigerate the dough as necessary during shaping to keep it cool and workable.) Refrigerate the rolls until cool, about 15 minutes.

6   Place the pieces of dough in the loaf pan in two rows of four. Brush lightly with egg wash, brushing away any excess that accumulates in the crevices. Proof, covered, until the dough is almost double in size and springs back slowly to the touch but does not collapse, 1 to 2 hours.

7   Gently brush the dough again with egg wash. Bake in a 375°F/191°C deck oven until the crust is a rich golden brown and the sides of the bread spring back fully when pressed, 30 to 35 minutes. Remove from the pans and cool completely on racks.

VARIATIONS   **CRAQUELIN DOUGH** Add 3 lb/1.36 kg sugar cubes to orange brioche dough after step 3. Cut up the dough into small chunks. Place half the dough into the mixer. Add the sugar cubes and then the other half of the dough (see Craquelin, at right).

ORANGE BRIOCHE DOUGH Add 1 oz/28 g finely grated orange zest to the brioche dough with the butter in step 2.

Craquelin

MAKES 1 LOAF. DDT: 82°F/28°C

Craquelin dough (at left)	12 oz	340 g
Orange brioche dough (at left)	3 oz	85 g
Crystal sugar, for sprinkling	as needed	as needed

1   Coat a panettone wrapper (5 in/13 cm in diameter and 6 in/15 cm high) with a light film of fat. Preshape the craquelin into a large round (for preshaping instructions, see page 109). Let the craquelin dough rest, covered, until relaxed, about 45 minutes. Meanwhile, preshape the brioche dough into a round and let it rest, covered and under refrigeration, until relaxed, about 30 minutes.

2   Roll the orange brioche dough into a 6-in/15-cm circle. Egg wash and wrap it around the craquelin dough to enclose it completely, and gather the edges together at the bottom to form a boule. Place the loaf seam side down in the prepared paper wrapper. Egg wash.

3   Proof, covered, until the dough springs back slowly to the touch but does not collapse, 2 to 3 hours.

4   Egg wash and sprinkle crystal sugar. Score the loaf with an X in the center or snip the entire surface with scissors.

5   Presteam a 375°F/191°C convection oven. Load the bread into the oven and steam for 5 seconds. Bake until the crust is golden brown and the sides of the bread spring back fully when pressed through the wrapper, 25 to 30 minutes. Cool completely on a rack.

VARIATION   To make small craquelin, divide the craquelin dough into 2½-oz/71-g pieces and the orange brioche dough into 1-oz/28-g pieces. Follow the method above but when preshaping, use the method for small rounds on page 109.

Form a thin sheet of brioche dough around the craquelin.

Honey challah

MAKES 1 LOAF. DDT: 78°F/26°C

SPONGE			
Bread flour	11.4%	3⅓ oz	95 g
Instant dry yeast	1.4%	½ oz	14 g
Water	11.6%	3⅓ oz	95 g
FINAL DOUGH			
Bread flour	88.6%	1 lb 9½ oz	723 g
Water	11.6%	3⅓ oz	95 g
Eggs	22.4%	6½ oz	184 g
Egg yolks	5.7%	1½ oz	43 g
Vegetable oil	9.2%	2¾ oz	78 g
Sugar	10%	2¾ oz	78 g
Honey	5.7%	1⅔ oz	47 g
Salt	2.1%	⅔ oz	19 g
Sponge (above)	24.3%	7 oz	198 g
White rye flour, for dusting		as needed	as needed
Egg wash (page 892), made with yolks only		as needed	as needed

1　To prepare the sponge, combine the flour, yeast, and water and mix on low speed with the dough hook attachment for 3 minutes. Ferment at 75°F/24°C for 20 minutes.

2　To prepare the final dough, combine the flour, water, eggs, egg yolks, oil, sugar, honey, salt, and sponge and mix on low speed with the dough hook attachment for 6 minutes. Scrape down the bowl and mix on high speed for 6 minutes for full gluten development.

3　Bulk ferment the dough until nearly doubled, about 35 minutes.

4　Divide the dough into 2⅔-oz/76-g pieces. Preshape the dough into small oblongs (for pre-shaping instructions, see page 110). Let the dough to rest, covered, for 15 to 20 minutes.

5　Start with the first piece of dough that you shaped and work sequentially. Starting at the center of the dough, roll each piece outward, applying gentle pressure with your palms. Apply very little pressure at the center of the dough, but increase the pressure as you roll toward the ends of the dough. Roll each piece of dough into an evenly tapered strand 12 in/30 cm long. It is imperative that all of the strands be the same length. If they are not, the finished braid will be uneven.

6　Dust the top of the strands very lightly with white rye flour. (This will keep the dough dry as you braid and help maintain the overall definition of the braid.)

7　Lay three strands of dough vertically parallel to each other. Begin braiding in the center of the strands. Place the left strand over the center strand, then place the right strand over the center strand. Repeat this process until you reach the end of the dough. Pinch the ends together tightly.

8 Turn the braid around and flip it over so that the unbraided strands are facing you. Starting again from the left, repeat the braiding process until you reach the end of the dough. Pinch the ends together tightly. Place on parchment-lined sheet pans.

9 Brush the dough lightly with egg wash made solely from egg yolks. Allow the dough to proof, covered, until the dough springs back lightly to the touch but does not collapse, about 1 hour. There should be a small indentation left in the dough. Make sure that the egg wash is dry before you apply a second coat. Brush very gently with egg wash a third time before baking.

10 Bake in a 375°F/204°C oven until the braids are dark golden brown and shiny, about 20 minutes, or until the internal temperature is 195°F/91°C. Cool completely on a rack.

Chocolate and pecan babka

MAKES 4 LOAVES (1 LB 5 OZ/595 G EACH) DDT: 75°F/24°C

Brioche Loaf dough (page 186)	100%	3 lb 5 oz	1.5 kg
Chocolate filling (page 895)	34%	1 lb 2 oz	510 kg
Pecans, toasted and coarsely chopped	26.4%	14 fl oz	397 g

1 Scale the brioche dough into two 1 lb 10½ oz/750 g pieces and roll each into a 10 by 12-inch/25 by 30-cm rectangle. Place on a parchment-lined sheet pan, cover, and refrigerate overnight.

2 Allow the brioche dough and chocolate filling to stand at room temperature for 30 minutes.

3 Start with one piece of dough and work sequentially. Place on a floured work surface and roll to an 18-inch/46-cm square. Spread half of the filling on the dough, leaving a ½-inch/1-cm border at the top and bottom. If the filling is too stiff to spread, warm slightly in the microwave. Sprinkle half the pecans evenly over the filling.

4 Fold the top edge of the dough down to the bottom, pressing lightly with your fingertips to tighten. Repeat folding the top onto the bottom until there is no more dough to fold over. Press on the seam to seal it.

5 Place the dough seam side down on a work surface and lightly flour the dough. Cut the dough in half crosswise and place each half with the cut end facing you. Lightly press on the dough with your fingertips to flatten it and create more surface area. Cut the dough into three strands, keeping the strands connected at the top with an uncut portion.

6 To braid the three strands together, place the left strand over the center strand, then place the right strand over the center strand. Repeat this process until you reach the end of the dough. Pinch the ends together tightly. Repeat with the remaining dough, filling, and nuts.

7   Place in four 2-lb/907-g loaf pans (4½ in/11 com wide, 8 in/20 cm long, and 3 in/8 cm deep) greased loaf pans. Proof covered until the dough is almost double in size and springs back slowly to the touch but does not collapse, 2½ to 3 hours.

8   Bake in a 400°F/204°C oven for 45 to 50 minutes, to an internal temperature of 205°F/96°C.

9   Remove from the oven and let sit in the pans from 5 minutes. Remove from the pans and cool completely on a rack.

Panettone

MAKES 10 LB 4½ OZ/4.66 KG DOUGH. DDT: 78°F/26°C

SPONGE			
Bread flour	100%	1 lb 5 oz	595 g
Milk (80°F/27°C)	66.7%	14 fl oz	420 mL
Instant dry yeast	6%	1¼ oz	35 g
FINAL DOUGH			
Sponge (above)	57%	2 lb 4¼ oz	1.03 kg
Bread flour	67%	2 lb 10½ oz	1.20 kg
Eggs	25.2%	1 lb	454 g
Milk	18.9%	12 fl oz	360 mL
Sugar	14.6%	9¼ oz	262 g
Salt	2.75%	1¾ oz	50 g
Glucose syrup	2%	1¼ oz	35 g
Orange zest, grated	0.75%	½ oz	14 g
Lemon zest, grated	0.75%	½ oz	14 g
Instant dry yeast	0.75%	½ oz	14 g
Butter (55°F/13°C)	18.9%	12 oz	340 g
Candied orange peel	12.75%	8 oz	227 g
Candied lemon peel	12.75%	8 oz	227 g
Raisins	12.6%	8 oz	227 g
Golden raisins	12.6%	8 oz	227 g
Egg wash (page 892)		as needed	as needed
Unsalted butter		as needed	as needed

1 To prepare the sponge, mix the flour, milk, and yeast on low speed with the dough hook attachment until blended, about 2 minutes. Cover and ferment until the sponge has risen and just begun to recede, about 45 minutes at 75°F/24°C.

2 To prepare the final dough, combine the sponge, flour, eggs, milk, sugar, salt, glucose, orange and lemon zests, and yeast. Mix on low speed with the dough hook attachment for 4 minutes and on medium speed for 2 minutes. Gradually add the butter, then mix on medium speed for 10 minutes. The dough should be soft but very elastic. Blend in the orange and lemon peels and raisins.

3 Bulk ferment the dough until nearly doubled, about 1 hour.

4 Divide the dough into pieces 1 lb 4 oz/567 g each. Grease a large paper panettone wrapper. Round the dough to create a tight, smooth boule. Place the dough seam side down in the panettone wrapper. Lightly brush the top of the loaf with egg wash.

5 Proof, covered, until the dough springs back slowly to the touch but does not collapse, about 1 hour 15 minutes.

6 Lightly brush the bread with egg wash again. Score the bread with an X in the center. Insert a small pat of unsalted butter in the center of the cut.

7 Bake in a 385°F/196°C convection oven until the panettone is golden brown and the sides spring back fully when touched through the wrapper, 22 to 25 minutes. Cool completely on racks.

Gugelhopf

MAKES 15 LB 8¼ OZ/7.04 KG DOUGH. DDT: 79°F/26°C

SPONGE			
Bread flour	100%	2 lb 4 oz	1.02 kg
Milk (75°F/24°C)	100%	36 fl oz	1.08 L
Instant dry yeast	7.6%	2¾ oz	78 g
Vanilla beans, split and scraped (seeds only)		4 each	4 each
FINAL DOUGH			
Sugar	20.75%	1 lb 6 oz	624 g
Salt	1.4%	1½ oz	43 g
Butter, soft	20.75%	1 lb 6 oz	624 g
Eggs	13.2%	2 lb	907 g
Bread flour	66%	4 lb 6 oz	1.98 kg
Sponge (above)	70.5%	4 lb 10¾ oz	2.12 kg
Raisins	20.75%	1 lb 6 oz	624 g
Almonds, chopped	3.75%	4 oz	113 g
Egg wash (page 892)		as needed	as needed
Unsalted butter		as needed	as needed

1 To prepare the sponge, mix the flour, milk, yeast, and vanilla bean seeds on low speed with the dough hook attachment until blended, about 2 minutes. Cover and ferment until the sponge has risen and just begun to recede, about 30 minutes at 75°F/24°C.

2 To prepare the final dough, cream the sugar, salt, and butter on medium speed with the dough hook attachment, scraping down the bowl periodically until smooth, fluffy, and lighter in color, about 5 minutes. Gradually add the eggs, scraping down the bowl periodically.

3 Add the bread flour and the sponge. Mix on low speed for 4 minutes and on medium speed for 4 minutes, until the dough is completely smooth.

4 Add the raisins and almonds. Mix on low speed for about 2 minutes. The dough should be moist but have strong gluten development.

5 Bulk ferment the dough until nearly doubled in size, 30 to 40 minutes.

6 Divide the dough into pieces 1 lb 4 oz/567 g each. Preshape the dough into large rounds (for preshaping instructions, see page 109). Let the dough rest, covered, until relaxed, 10 minutes. (Reminder: When making multiple loaves, work sequentially, starting with the first piece of dough you divided and rounded.)

7 Grease a large paper panettone wrapper. Reround the dough to create a tight, smooth boule. Place the dough seam side down in the panettone wrapper. Lightly brush the top of the loaf with egg wash.

8 Proof, covered, until the dough springs back slowly to the touch but does not collapse, about 1 hour 40 minutes.

9 Lightly brush the bread with egg wash again. Score the bread with an X in the center. Insert a small pat of unsalted butter in the center of the cut.

10 Bake in a 385°F/196°C convection oven until the gugelhopf is golden brown and the top springs back when touched, 35 to 40 minutes. Cool completely on a rack.

Christmas stollen

MAKES 9 LB 10¾ OZ/4.39 KG DOUGH. DDT: 80°F/27°C

FRUIT AND NUT MIXTURE			
Golden raisins	53.2%	2 lb 3¼ oz	9.99 kg
Candied lemon peel	15.5%	10½ oz	298 g
Candied orange peel	0.6%	4½ oz	128 g
Dark rum	5.2%	3½ fl oz	105 mL
Almonds, whole, blanched	19.5%	13¼ oz	376 g
SPONGE			
Bread flour	100%	1 lb 6 oz	624 g
Milk (50°F/10°C)	60.3%	13¼ fl oz	398 mL
Instant dry yeast	0.5%	1 oz	28 g
FINAL DOUGH			
Sponge (above)	88%	2 lb 4¼ oz	1.03 kg
Bread flour	50%	1 lb 6 oz	624 g
Butter	54.5%	1 lb 8 oz	680 g
Almond paste	4.5%	2 oz	57 g
Sugar	4.5%	2 oz	57 g
Salt	2.25%	1 oz	28 g
Lemon zest, grated	0.57%	1¼ tsp	6.75 g
Ground cloves	0.15%	pinch	pinch
Ground ginger	0.15%	pinch	pinch
Ground allspice	0.15%	pinch	pinch
Ground cinnamon	0.15%	pinch	pinch
Fruit and nut mixture (above)	154.5%	4 lb 3 oz	1.90 kg
GARNISH			
Clarified butter, melted		as needed	as needed
Vanilla sugar (page 901), for coating		as needed	as needed
Confectioners' sugar, for dusting		as needed	as needed

1   To prepare the fruit and nut mixture, rinse the raisins and lemon and orange peels with warm water and combine them with the rum in a plastic container. Cover and let the mixture soak at 75°F/24°C for at least 8 and up to 24 hours. Reserve the almonds to be added later.

2   To prepare the sponge, mix the flour, milk, and yeast on low speed with the dough hook attachment until blended, about 2 minutes. Cover and ferment at 75°F/24°C until the sponge has risen and just begun to recede, 30 to 40 minutes.

3   To prepare the final dough, mix the sponge, flour, butter, almond paste, sugar, salt, lemon zest, cloves, ginger, allspice, and cinnamon on medium speed with the dough hook attachment for 3 minutes. The dough should be sticky but have sufficient gluten development.

4   Bulk ferment the dough until nearly doubled, about 35 minutes. Add the almonds to the fruit mixture and very carefully fold it into the dough (see "Adding Flavorings and Garnishes," page 160). Bulk ferment the dough until nearly doubled again, about 15 minutes.

5   Divide the dough into 1-lb/454-g pieces. Preshape the dough into large rounds (for pre-shaping instructions, see page 109). Let the dough rest, covered, until relaxed, 15 to 20 minutes. (Reminder: When making multiple loaves, work sequentially, starting with the first piece of dough you divided and rounded.)

6   Gently flatten the dough with your fingertips. Working with the seam side up, fold the dough in half. Seal the two edges by pressing firmly with the heel of your hand, keeping the seam straight. Roll the dough under your palms into a cylinder 8 in/20 cm long, keeping the pressure even and holding your hands flat and parallel to the work surface to create a smooth, even roll.

7   Turn the dough lengthwise, parallel to the edge of the worktable with the seam side down. Roll half of the dough into a flap ¼ in/6 mm thick in the shape of a semicircle. The edges of the flap should be ½ in/1 cm thick.

8   Fold ½ in/1 cm of the left and right sides of the dough toward the center of the dough. Roll the folded left and right edges of the dough so that they are the same thickness as the rest of the flap of dough.

9   Make an indentation lengthwise down the center of the thicker half of the dough with a straight rolling pin. Fold the flap over and insert the thicker edge of the flap into the indentation. Press into place by gently rolling with the rolling pin. Place on parchment-lined sheet pans.

10   Proof, covered, until the dough relaxes slightly, about 30 minutes.

11   Bake in a 350°F/177°C deck oven until the stollen is golden brown and sounds hollow when thumped on the bottom, 30 to 35 minutes. Cool on racks just until the bread can be handled; it should still be warm.

12   While the bread is still hot, remove any burnt fruit or nuts from the outside. Brush the sides, top, and bottom of the bread with clarified butter and roll in vanilla sugar. Cool completely on racks.

13   Dust the stollen with sifted confectioners' sugar just before wrapping or slicing.

Soft pretzels

MAKES 8 LB 13¾ OZ/4.02 KG DOUGH. DDT: 75°F/24°C

Bread flour	100%	5 lb 8 oz	2.49 kg
Instant dry yeast	1.7%	1½ oz	43 g
Water	50%	44 fl oz	1.32 L
Butter, soft, cubed	5.1%	4½ oz	128 g
Malt syrup	2.25%	2 oz	57 g
Salt	2%	1¾ oz	50 g
LYE SOLUTION			
Water (105°F/41°C)		32 fl oz	960 mL
Sodium hydroxide pellets		1¼ oz	35 g
Coarse salt, for garnish		as needed	as needed

1   Combine the flour and yeast. Add the water, butter, malt syrup, and salt to the mixer and then add the flour and yeast. Mix on low speed with the dough hook attachment for 2 minutes and on medium speed for 8 minutes. The dough should be stiff, with strong gluten development.

2   Bulk ferment the dough until nearly doubled, about 50 minutes.

3   Divide the dough into 5½-oz/156-g pieces. Preshape the dough into small oblongs (for pre-shaping instructions, see page 110). Let the dough rest, covered, until relaxed, 5 to 10 minutes.

4   Work sequentially, starting with the first piece of dough you divided and rounded. One at a time, stretch each piece of dough into a rectangle 10 in/25 cm long. Fold the top edge of the dough down to the center of the dough, pressing lightly with your fingertips. Fold the top edge of the dough to the bottom edge. Using the heel of your hand, seal the two edges together.

5   Turn the dough seam side down. Starting with each of your hands 2 in/5 cm from the center of the dough, roll the dough under your palms until it is 30 in/76 cm long, with a thicker portion 4 in/10 cm long in the center.

6   Lay the dough on the table and cross the ends over each other, leaving 3 in/8 cm of dough on each side of the crossing point (the thicker center of the dough should be closest to you). Twist the ends together once. Bring the ends of the dough over and attach them to either side of the thicker center of the dough, pressing gently to seal them. Transfer to a parchment-lined sheet pan.

7   Proof, covered, until the dough gives slightly when touched, about 30 minutes.

8   Relax the dough under refrigeration until it forms a skin, about 25 minutes.

9   To prepare the lye solution, combine the water and sodium hydroxide pellets, stirring until the pellets are completely dissolved. (Reminder: Wear protective gloves and goggles; be careful not to get any of the solution on your skin.)

10 Remove the pretzels from the refrigerator and allow them to stand for 5 to 10 minutes. (Reminder: If you dip the pretzels right away, the water temperature will drop and the sodium hydroxide will be less likely to stay in solution.)

11 Using tongs, dip the pretzels in the lye solution and then place them on screens to drain. Discard the lye solution once you have finished removing the pretzels by pouring it down the drain; it cannot be reused. Sprinkle the pretzels immediately with coarse salt. Make an incision 3 in/8 cm long and ¼ in/6 mm deep in the thickest part of each pretzel.

12 Place the pretzels on sheet pans lined with a silicone mat or lightly oiled parchment paper and bake in a 475°F/246°C deck oven (with the vent open) until deep golden brown, 12 to 15 minutes. Cool completely on racks.

FROM LEFT TO RIGHT:
Place the dough in a U shape on the table and cross the ends.
Twist the ends together once.
Bring the ends back down and gently press to adhere.

Pita with poolish

MAKES 7 LB/3.18 KG DOUGH DDT: 78°F/26°C

POOLISH			
Bread flour	23.1%	15 oz	425 g
Water	23.1%	15 oz	428 g
Instant dry yeast	0.03%	¼ oz	7 g
FINAL DOUGH			
Bread flour	76.9%	3 lb 2½ oz	1.43 kg
Water	46.2%	1 lb 14¼ oz	856 g
Instant dry yeast	0.3%	¼ oz	7 g
Salt	1.5%	1 oz	28 g
Poolish (above)	46.2%	1 lb 14¼ oz	858 g

1   To prepare the poolish, combine the flour, water, and yeast and mix on low speed with the dough hook attachment for 3 minutes. Ferment for 18 hours.

2   To prepare the final dough, combine the flour, water, yeast, salt, and poolish and mix on low speed with the dough hook attachment for 4 minutes and on medium speed for 3 minutes. Mix to the improved stage of gluten development.

3   Bulk ferment the dough until nearly doubled in volume, about 1 hour.

4   Divide the dough into 3-oz/85-g pieces. Preshape the dough into small rounds (for preshaping instructions, see page 109). Let the dough rest, covered, until relaxed, 15 to 20 minutes.

5   Work sequentially, starting with the first piece of dough you divided and rounded. Using a rolling pin, roll each piece of dough into a round 7 in/18 cm in diameter. Transfer to parchment-lined sheet pans, cover, and let the rounds relax for 20 minutes.

6   Bake in a 500°F/260°C deck oven until puffed but not browned, 3 to 4 minutes. Stack the pitas five high and wrap each stack in a cloth. Cool in a cloth to retain moisture before serving.

Naan with biga

MAKES 13 LB 5 OZ/6.04 KG DOUGH. DDT: 74°F/23°C

BIGA			
Bread flour	17.3%	1 lb 3¼ oz	546 g
Instant dry yeast	0.01%	0.02 oz	0.5 g
Water	11.2%	12½ oz	355 g
FINAL DOUGH			
Bread flour	77.7%	5 lb 6½ oz	2.45 g
Whole wheat flour	5%	5⅔ oz	161 g
Water	33.3%	2 lb 5 oz	1.05 kg
Plain yogurt	41.4%	2 lb 14 oz	1.30 kg
Olive oil	3.1%	3½ oz	99 g
Instant dry yeast	0.4%	½ oz	14 g
Salt	1.9%	2 oz	57 g
Biga (above)	28.6%	1 lb 15¾ oz	900 g

1   To prepare the biga, mix together the flour, yeast, and water on low speed with the dough hook attachment for 4 minutes and on medium speed for 2 minutes. Ferment for 18 hours.

2   To make the final dough, combine the flours, water, yogurt, olive oil, yeast, salt, and biga and mix on low speed with the dough hook attachment for 4 minutes. The dough should be very elastic but still wet.

3   Bulk ferment the dough until nearly doubled, about 1 hour. Gently fold. Let the dough ferment for another 30 minutes.

4   Divide the dough into 6 equal portions. Ferment the dough, covered, for 45 minutes.

5   At the oven, cut each portion into 6 pieces and stretch each to 3 in/8 cm wide and 10 in/25 cm long. If desired, gently depress the centers. Spray with water and place garnish such as seeds, if desired, in the center of each bread.

6   Bake in a 500°F/260°C deck oven for 8 to 10 minutes, or until a light golden brown. Cool completely on racks.

Filled flatbread

MAKES 8 FLATBREADS (9 OZ/255 G EACH). DDT: 75°F/24°C

Olive oil	2 oz	57 g
Garlic, minced	1 oz	28 g
Green peppers, minced	11 oz	312 g
Canned plum tomatoes, drained, seeded, and coarsely chopped	1 lb 1½ oz	496 g
Green onions, minced	2 oz	57 g
Salt	1 tsp	5 g
Red pepper flakes	1 tsp	2 g
Ground caraway	¼ tsp	0.50 g
Ground coriander	¼ tsp	0.50 g
Ground cumin	¼ tsp	0.50 g
Flat-leaf parsley, minced	2 oz	57 g
Naan dough (page 199)	3 lb 5½ oz	1.52 kg
Olive oil, for frying	as needed	as needed

1   To prepare the filling, heat the olive oil in a sauteuse. Add the garlic and cook over medium heat until it just begins to lightly brown. Add the peppers and cook for 2 minutes, or until they soften, stirring occasionally. Add the tomatoes and simmer for 15 minutes, or until the mixture thickens, stirring occasionally.

2   Add the green onions, salt, red pepper flakes, caraway, coriander, and cumin and simmer for 1 minute. Stir in the parsley. Transfer the filling to a stainless-steel bowl and allow to cool to room temperature.

3   Divide the dough into sixteen 3¼-oz/92-g pieces. Preshape the dough into small rounds (for preshaping instructions, see page 109). Let the dough rest, covered, until relaxed, 10 to 15 minutes.

4   Work sequentially, starting with the first piece of dough you divided and rounded. Using a rolling pin, roll each piece of dough into a round 6 in/15 cm in diameter. Spread 3 oz/85 g filling in the center of each of 8 rounds, leaving a 1-in/3-cm border all around. Brush the exposed border with water.

5   Place one of the remaining 8 rounds on top of each of the filled pieces of dough. Pinch the edges of each bread together and then stretch the dough gently into a round 9 in/23 cm in diameter.

6   Heat a small amount of olive oil in a sauteuse until it is almost smoking. Add one bread and cook for 1 minute, then flip it over. Fry for another 2 to 2½ minutes, or until there are light brown specks on the bottom. Flip the bread over once again and fry for another minute, or until lightly browned. Fry the remaining breads, adding more oil as necessary.

7   Keep the breads warm by wrapping them in a cotton cloth and shingling them in a basket.

Hot cross buns

MAKES 9 LB 8 OZ/4.31 KG DOUGH. DDT: 75°F/24°C

SPONGE			
Bread flour	39.9%	1 lb 9¾ oz	730 g
Instant dry yeast	2.5%	1½ oz	43 g
Milk	50%	2 lb ⅛ oz	914 g
FINAL DOUGH			
Bread flour	60.1%	2 lb 6¾ oz	1.10 kg
Eggs	15.3%	10 oz	298 g
Lemon zest, puréed	1.5%	1 oz	28 g
Butter	15.3%	10 oz	298 g
Honey	3.2%	2 oz	57 g
Malt syrup	0.5%	⅓ oz	9 g
Sugar	15.3%	10 oz	298 g
Ground cinnamon		pinch	pinch
Ground nutmeg	0.1%	pinch	pinch
Ground allspice	0.05%	pinch	pinch
Salt	2.5%	1½ oz	43 g
Sponge (above)	92.4%	3 lb 11½ oz	1.69 kg
Currants	30%	1 lb 3⅓ oz	548 g
Candied lemon peel	12.1%	7½ oz	205 g
Egg wash (page 892)		as needed	as needed
Hot cross topping (page 202)		as needed	as needed
Danish glaze (page 898)		as needed	as needed

1   To prepare the sponge, combine the flour, yeast, and milk and mix on low speed with the dough hook attachment for 2 minutes and on medium speed for 1 minute. Ferment for 30 minutes.

2   To prepare the final dough, combine the flour, eggs, lemon zest, butter, honey, malt syrup, sugar, cinnamon, nutmeg, allspice, salt, and sponge and mix for 4 minutes on low speed with the dough hook attachment and for 4 minutes on high speed. Mix in currants and candied peel for 1 minute on low speed until smooth.

3   Ferment the dough until nearly doubled, about 45 minutes.

4   Divide the dough into 2-oz/57-g pieces. Shape each piece of dough into a tight round. Ferment for another 15 minutes.

5 Reshape the pieces of dough into tight rounds and place on a sheet tray lined with parchment paper, leaving approximately 3 in/8 cm between each bun. Lightly brush the dough with egg wash. Ferment the dough for another 45 minutes.

6 Brush the tops of the dough pieces with egg wash and let them dry for 5 minutes. Fill a pastry bag fitted with a #2 tip with the topping and pipe across the top of each roll.

7 Bake in a 375°F/191°C deck oven until golden brown, 18 minutes.

8 Heat the glaze. Remove the buns from the oven and brush with the hot glaze. Cool completely on racks.

Hot cross topping

MAKES 3 LB/1.36 KG

Butter, melted	8 oz	227 g
Sugar	8 oz	227 g
Eggs	1½ oz	43 g
Milk	6 oz	168 g
Vanilla extract	½ oz	14 g
Lemon zest, puréed	⅓ oz	9 g
Cake flour	1 lb	454 g

Make the topping the day of baking. In a mixer with the paddle attachment, mix the butter, sugar, eggs, milk, vanilla, and lemon zest, scraping down the bowl occasionally. Add the flour and mix thoroughly, scraping down the bowl. Use immediately.

Bagel dough with sponge

MAKES 20 LB/9 KG DOUGH (ENOUGH FOR 60 BAGELS). DDT: 78°F/26°C

SPONGE			
High-gluten flour	30%	3 lb 11 oz	1.67 kg
Water	30%	3 lb 11⅔ oz	1.69 kg
Instant dry yeast	0.1%	1¼ tsp	5 g
Malt syrup	0.5%	1 oz	28 g
FINAL DOUGH			
High-gluten flour	70%	8 lb 11 oz	3.94 kg
Water	27%	3 lb 5⅔ oz	1.52 kg
Instant dry yeast	0.4%	¾ oz	21 g
Salt	2.3%	4½ oz	128 g
Diastatic malt syrup, for dough	0.9%	1¾ oz	50 g
Sponge (above)	60.6%	7 lb 8⅓ oz	3.41 kg
Malt syrup, for boiling (per 1 gal/3.84 L water)		1 fl oz	30 mL
Garnishes such as sesame seeds, poppy seeds, salt		as needed	as needed

1 Mix the sponge the same day as the final dough. Combine all the sponge ingredients and mix on low speed with the dough hook attachment for 4 minutes. Ferment until doubled in size, about 1½ hours.

2 To prepare the final dough, add the flour, water, yeast, salt, and diastatic malt syrup to the sponge and mix on low speed with the dough hook attachment for 4 minutes. Mix on medium speed for 6 minutes, until smooth. The dough should be stiff, dry, and elastic and have strong gluten development.

3 Divide the dough into 5-oz/142-g pieces. Preshape each piece of dough into a small 5-in/13-cm oblong (for preshaping instructions, see page 110). Cover and ferment for 5 minutes.

4 Shape each piece into a 10-in/25-cm oblong. Moisten 1 in/3 cm of an end with water and overlap with the other end, working the shape until even throughout. Place on a tray sprinkled with semolina, with the seam down.

5 Retard the dough, covered, in the refrigerator or store in the freezer overnight.

6 If the bagels have been frozen, thaw overnight under refrigeration. Cook the bagels by dropping them into boiling water with malt syrup added. After they float, 15 to 20 seconds cooking time, remove and place them on a parchment-lined tray. Garnish, if desired, while still wet. Air-dry slightly. Transfer the bagels to a peel and load them into a 500°F/260°C deck oven. Bake until golden brown but still soft and slightly springy to the touch, 14 minutes. Cool completely on racks.

Bialys

MAKES 18 LB 8 OZ/8.40 KG DOUGH. DDT: 78°F/26°C

SPONGE			
High-gluten flour	30%	3 lb 6 oz	1.53 kg
Instant dry yeast	0.1%	1¼ tsp	5 g
Water	30%	3 lb 6¹⁄₁₆ oz	1.5 kg
FINAL DOUGH			
High-gluten flour	70%	7 lb 14 oz	3.60 kg
Water	31%	3 lb 8 oz	1.59 kg
Instant dry yeast	0.4%	¾ oz	21 g
Salt	2.3%	4 oz	113 g
Malt syrup	0.4%	¾ oz	21 g
Sponge (above)	60%	6 lb 12⅓ oz	3.07 kg
Flour, for dusting		as needed	as needed
TOPPING			
Onions, medium dice		1 lb 4 oz	567 g
Olive oil		1 oz	28 g
Salt		2 tsp	10 g
Poppy seeds		1¾ tsp	3.50 g
Olive oil		as needed	as needed

1   To prepare the sponge, combine the flour, yeast, and water and mix on low speed with the dough hook attachment for 4 minutes. Ferment until nearly doubled in size, about 1½ hours.

2   To prepare the final dough, combine the flour, water, yeast, salt, malt syrup, and sponge and mix on low speed with the dough hook attachment for 4 minutes and on high speed for 6 minutes until smooth.

3   Divide the dough into 4½-oz/128-g pieces. Preshape the dough into small rounds (for pre-shaping instructions, see page 109). Let the dough rest, covered, until relaxed, 15 minutes.

4   Dust both sides of each piece of dough with flour and make a depression in the center with your fingers, or use a round 2-lb/907-g balance beam counterweight wrapped with plastic wrap. This will make a flat center 3 in/8 cm in diameter. Place the pieces of dough on trays sprinkled with semolina. Retard the dough, covered, in the refrigerator or freezer overnight.

5   If the dough is frozen, place it in the refrigerator to thaw overnight. Keep the dough at room temperature for 30 minutes before shaping.

6   To prepare the topping, sauté the onions in the olive oil until translucent. Add the salt and poppy seeds. Allow to cool completely.

7 Shape each piece of bialy dough into an oblong and place 9 bialys on a parchment-lined sheet pan (3 across and 3 down).

8 Brush with olive oil and place the filling on top. Transfer the bialys to a peel.

9 Presteam a 450°F/232°C oven. Load the bialys in the oven and steam for 3 seconds. Bake until golden brown but still soft and slightly springy to the touch, 12 to 14 minutes. Vent during the final 10 minutes. Cool completely on racks.

CLOCKWISE FROM TOP RIGHT: Soft Pretzels (page 196), Bialys with caramelized onions (page 204), Bialys with poppy seeds and onions (page 204), plain Bagel (page 116), sesame seed Bagel (page 116), cinnamon raisin bagel.

Corn rolls

MAKES 25 ROLLS (2 OZ/57 G EACH) DDT: 82°F/28°C

CORN SOAKER			
Milk (1st)	59.3%	14¾ oz	417 g
Cornmeal	21.4%	5¼ oz	150 g
Milk (2nd), room temperature	32.3%	8 oz	227 g
FINAL DOUGH			
Soaker	112.9%	1 lb 12 oz	794 g
Vegetable oil	5.0%	1¼ oz	35 g
Honey	10 %	2¼ oz	62 g
Malt syrup	0.4%	¾ tsp	3 g
Bread flour (1st)	62.5%	15½ oz	439 g
Corn flour	16.1%	4 oz	113 g
Instant dry yeast	0.4%	¾ tsp	3 g
Salt	2.8%	¾ oz	20 g
Corn, whole kernels	16.1%	4 oz	113 g
Bread flour (2nd)	2.4%	⅔ oz	17 g
Egg wash (page 892)		as needed	as needed
Salt, for garnish		as needed	as needed
Cornmeal, for garnish		as needed	as needed

1   To prepare the corn soaker, bring the first milk to a hard boil. Pour over the cornmeal in a mixer bowl. Stir to combine and let sit for 2 minutes. Mix on high speed for 3 minutes using the paddle attachment. Mix in the second milk in three additions. Cover and refrigerate overnight.

2   To prepare the final dough, warm the soaker over a water bath to 85°F/29°C. Add the oil, honey, and malt and mix on medium speed for 1 minute.

3   With the mixer off, add the first bread four, corn flour, and yeast. Toss the corn with the second bread flour and add to the mixer. Add the salt on top.

4   Mix on medium speed for 6 minutes with the dough hook attachment. Mix on high speed for 4 minutes. The dough will have good gluten development but will be tacky. Place in a lightly oiled bowl and cover with plastic wrap.

5   Bulk ferment the dough until nearly doubled, 45 to 60 minutes. Fold gently.

6   Preshape the dough into small rounds (for preshaping instructions, see page 109). Line sheet pans with parchment. Let the dough rest covered until relaxed, 15 to 20 minutes.

7   Divide the dough into 25 pieces (2 oz/57 g each) by hand or using a dough divider. Shape each piece into a round, lightly flouring the work surface as needed.

8   Arrange the rolls in rows on the lined sheet pans, spacing them 4 in/10 cm apart. Proof covered until the dough springs back slowly to the touch but does not collapse, 45 to 60 minutes.

9   Lightly brush the rolls with egg wash and sprinkle with salt and cornmeal.

10   Bake in a 450°F/232°C convection oven until the rolls are golden brown and shiny, 15 to 20 minutes. Cool completely on the pans.

Day of the Dead bread

MAKES 16 LB 10 OZ/7.57 KG DOUGH. DDT: 75°F/24°C

SPONGE			
Bread flour	50%	2 lb 6¼ oz	1.08 kg
Instant dry yeast	1.5%	1¼ oz	35 g
Milk	30.9%	1 lb 7⅔ oz	671 g
FINAL DOUGH			
Sponge (above)	82.4%	3 lb 15 oz	1.79 kg
Eggs	33.8%	1 lb 10 oz	737 g
Bread flour	50%	2 lb 6¼ oz	1.08 kg
Malt syrup	0.5%	⅓ oz	9 g
Salt	2.3%	1¾ oz	50 g
Butter, soft but still pliable	49.5%	2 lb 6 oz	1.08 kg
Sugar	24.8%	1 lb 3 oz	539 g
Lemon zest, puréed	1.5%	1¼ oz	35 g
Orange zest, puréed	4.5%	3½ oz	99 g
Vanilla extract	0.9%	⅔ oz	19 g
Ground cinnamon	0.2%	1½ tsp	3 g
Orange blossom water	0.5%	2 tsp	10 mL
BONES AND FINISHING			
Bread flour		as needed	as needed
Egg wash (page 892)		as needed	as needed
Melted butter		as needed	as needed
Vanilla sugar (page 901), for rolling		as needed	as needed

1 To prepare the sponge, combine the flour, yeast, and milk and mix on low speed with the paddle attachment for 2 minutes. Ferment for 1 hour.

2 To prepare the final dough, combine the sponge, eggs, flour, malt syrup, and salt with one-third of the butter. Mix on low speed with the paddle attachment for 4 minutes, then on high speed for 4 minutes. Add half of the remaining butter, keeping the dough on the hook and scraping the bowl often. Add the sugar, lemon and orange zests, vanilla, cinnamon, and orange blossom water in 2 additions. Add the remainder of the butter and mix until fully incorporated.

3 To make the "bone dough," remove 18 percent of the main dough. Add 30 percent of that dough's weight in bread flour and mix until a homogeneous dough is formed.

4 Ferment the doughs separately for 20 minutes, or until doubled in size. Gently fold over. Ferment for another 20 minutes, or until doubled in size.

5 Divide the main dough into 9-oz/255-g pieces; divide the bone dough into ¾-oz/21-g portions. You will need 3 or 4 bones for each loaf.

6 Shape the main dough pieces into tight rounds and roll the bones out to 3-in/8-cm oblongs. Take each large round and make a hole in the center. Place on parchment-lined sheet pans. For each loaf, roll out 3 of the bone pieces into long ropes that are the diameter of the loaf, spreading your fingers and pressing them into the ropes so that they take on a wavy appearance. Drape the ropes over the loaves at even intervals so that the round is visually divided into sixths, like a sliced pie. Take a final bone piece for each loaf and round it up into a tight ball. Place a ball in the hole in the center of each loaf. Brush the loaf with egg wash. Ferment the dough for another 45 to 60 minutes, or until doubled in size.

7 Lightly brush the dough with egg wash.

8 Bake in a 365°F/185°C convection oven until golden brown, 20 to 25 minutes. Remove from the oven, brush with melted butter, and roll in vanilla sugar. Cool completely on racks.

part three

Baking building blocks

chapter nine

Pastry doughs and batters

Pastry doughs are the foundation for a wide range of preparations. Pie dough, short dough, and puff pastry are only a few examples. All are made of the same basic ingredients, but different preparation techniques give them vastly different characteristics, making each suitable for different applications. Pastry batters such as crêpe batter or pâte à choux also serve as elemental preparations and are used in countless classical and contemporary desserts.

Rubbed doughs

The characteristic texture of rubbed doughs is developed by rubbing together the fat and the flour, leaving flakes of fat visible.

There are two basic types of rubbed doughs: *flaky* and *mealy*. The larger the flakes of fat are before the liquid is added, the flakier and crisper the baked crust will be. If the flakes of butter or shortening are rubbed into the dough just until they are about the size of peas, the dough will be what is often referred to as "flaky" pie dough. When the liquid is added, the dough is worked just enough to allow the moisture to be absorbed by the flour and just until the ingredients to come together, at which point the dough should be allowed to rest and cool under refrigeration.

Flaky pie dough is best for pies, tarts, and other preparations where the filling is baked in the crust. It is not well suited for preparations where the crust is completely prebaked and allowed to cool and then a liquid filling is added that must set under refrigeration. After baking, the pockets that lend the flaky texture in this type of dough easily allow juices or liquids to leak from the crust.

If the butter or shortening is more thoroughly worked into the dough, until the mixture resembles coarse meal, the result will be what is sometimes referred to as a "mealy" dough. Mealy pie doughs have a finer, more tender texture than do flaky pie doughs. With the fat more evenly interspersed in the flour, its ability to shorten gluten strands present in the dough becomes more apparent, as the resulting dough is very tender. As with flaky pastry dough, mealy dough should be wrapped in plastic wrap and allowed to rest under refrigeration so the butter or other fat will firm and the gluten will relax before the dough is worked and rolled.

Mealy doughs are well suited for all types of pies and tarts, but most particularly for formulas that require a fully baked shell (see "Blind Baking Pie and Tart Shells," page 515) filled with a precooked filling, such as a cream, that will have to set under refrigeration before it can be sliced and served. They are also best for custard pies and for creating decorative tops such as lattice.

The basic steps for making rubbed doughs are:

1. Combine the dry ingredients. Pastry and all-purpose flours are, in general, ideal for the rubbed dough method. Cake flour is too high in starch, so it will not absorb enough water and will produce a dough with a pasty consistency. Bread flour, because of its high protein content, will absorb water quickly and in comparatively great quantities, developing gluten readily and in great amounts. This will make a dough that is tough

A cross section of flaky dough shows layers of fat interspersed throughout the dough.

and elastic. On the other hand, pastry flour and all-purpose flour have the proper balance of starch and protein, with the desired amount of water absorption and gluten development to produce a dough that is both flaky and tender.

2. Flake the firm fat into the flour. Fat contributes to the development of a flaky texture in pastry doughs. The amount of fat and the way it is added to the other ingredients in a formula have a significant impact on the finished baked good. Leaving the fat in pieces or chunks, rather than combining it thoroughly, gives doughs a flaky texture. When a rubbed dough is baked, the pieces of fat melt to create pockets in the interior of the dough. As the fat melts, steam is released from the moisture held in the fat. This steam expands the pockets, which then become set as the dough continues to bake, thus creating a flaky, textured baked good. The larger the flakes of fat left in the dough, the flakier the baked dough will be.

   Butter, lard, hydrogenated shortening, and other fats may be used in the production of rubbed doughs. All of these fats are solid at room temperature, and when cold have a firm consistency that makes it possible to use them for this method. Of all the fats, butter alone will yield the most flavor, but it is difficult to handle because it has a lower melting point than shortening and lard.

3. Add all the liquid at once to the flour-fat mixture and blend the dough quickly but thoroughly. Water is the most common liquid in rubbed dough formulas, but milk or cream may also be used. When substituting milk or cream for water in a rubbed dough formula, decrease the amount of fat to adjust for the fat present in the milk or cream.

   Always keep rubbed doughs cool during mixing for best results to achieve a flaky final texture. When butter or shortening is more thoroughly incorporated into the dough, resulting in a coarse meal rather than large flakes, the resulting baked dough becomes less flaky but more tender, as the even distribution of fat serves to shorten structure-providing gluten strands in the flour as it bakes.

4. Turn out the dough onto a lightly floured work surface.

5. Gather and press it together into a disk or a flat rectangle.

6. Wrap the dough tightly in plastic wrap and chill it under refrigeration until firm enough to work. The period of rest and cooling before working and rolling is vital to ensure that the fat does not become too soft nor the flour overworked.

   Soft fat prevents the separation of the baked dough into layers, and overworked flour can result in a tough, rather than tender, final baked good.

7. Always keep rubbed doughs cool during mixing and when working with them. The ideal working temperature is 60°F/16°C. If the dough becomes too warm, the fat may become too soft and absorb into the dough, destroying the layers in the dough.

TOP LEFT: Combine the fat into the flour by rubbing the chunks between your fingers to make smaller bits.

TOP RIGHT: The combined fat and flour will have a coarse to fine mealy texture, depending on how flaky you want the crust and what type of filling you plan to use.

BOTTOM LEFT: Add the water all at once to the mixture to form a "shaggy mass."

BOTTOM RIGHT: The prepared dough will have a smooth texture and appearance. Wrap it in plastic wrap and refrigerate to firm up and relax the dough before rolling it out.

Short dough

Short dough contains a high percentage of fat, which produces a very tender and crumbly crust. If worked excessively, however, a short dough will become tough. Cake flour is the preferred choice for short doughs because of its ability to absorb moisture. Short doughs include eggs, either whole eggs or yolks, and sometimes sugar, which contribute to the flavor and color of the dough, as well as to its tender texture.

The basic steps for making short doughs are:

1. Combine the sugar and butter and mix only until it forms a smooth paste to ensure even blending. Do not mix vigorously so that air is incorporated.

2. Add the eggs gradually, a few at a time, and blend them in carefully. To prevent the mixture from breaking or curdling, have the eggs and any other liquid ingredients at room temperature, and blend them in carefully.

3. Add the dry ingredients and mix at low speed until just combined. Overmixing will make the dough tough.

4. Turn out the dough onto a lightly floured work surface, shape it into a disk or flat triangle, and wrap tightly in plastic wrap. Refrigerate for at least 1 hour before using. If the dough appears to be somewhat rough or coarse when it is removed from the mixer, work it gently by hand just until it comes together. Refrigerate before using to allow the dough to firm up and the gluten to relax. The butter becomes soft during the mixing process, making short dough difficult to work with immediately after mixing. Allowing the gluten to relax will create a more tender, less tough baked dough.

Crumb crusts

Crumb crusts are simple, flavorful, quick-to-make crusts. They are typically used in two types of preparations: pudding or cream pies and cheesecakes. Graham crackers are most commonly used as the base for crumb crusts, but other types of cookies may be used for different flavors.

The crumbs are sweetened as necessary and blended with butter; sometimes a small amount of egg white is added to help make the crust hold together after baking. The crumb mixture is then pressed into an even layer into the pie or other baking pan and prebaked to evaporate some moisture and make the crust more flavorful and crisp.

Scale the crust into prepared pans and press into an even layer about ¼ in/6 mm thick. Crumb crusts should be baked at 350°F/177°C until set and light golden brown, about 7 minutes. Cool the crust completely before filling.

For pudding and cream pies, the filling is cooked, then poured into the cooled baked crust, and refrigerated until set. For cheesecakes, the batter is poured into the cooled baked crust and then baked until set.

Pâte à choux

Pâte à choux is a cooked batter created through the combination of liquid, butter, flour, and eggs. When finished it is piped into various shapes that, once baked, expand and dry into crisp hollow pastry. The basic steps for making pâte à choux are:

1. Combine the liquid and fat and bring to a rolling boil. Usually either water or milk is used as the liquid in the batter, and the two yield very different results. Milk will cause the pastry to darken more quickly in the oven before it has dried out enough to become crisp; that, along with the solids present in the milk, will produce more tender, flavorful pastry. When water is used, the temperature of the oven can be manipulated, starting with a very high temperature to encourage full expansion, and then a lower temperature to dry out the pastries, creating a fully dried pastry that will be very crisp and light.

2. Add the flour all at once, stirring constantly to prevent lumps from forming, and continue to cook until the mixture pulls away from the sides of the pan. The type of flour is also important. Flours with a higher percentage of protein are able to absorb more liquid and will allow for the addition of a greater amount of eggs, yielding a lighter finished product. Additionally, a flour with a higher protein content will develop more gluten strands, making a more elastic dough, which will also help create a lighter finished product. For these reasons, bread flour, which has a protein content of 12 to 13 percent, is best. All of the flour must be added to the boiling liquid at once and blended in very quickly to ensure the full hydration of the starch granules in the flour and the formation

LEFT: As pâte à choux is stirred and cooked, a film starts to develop on the bottom of the pot.

RIGHT: Properly mixed pâte à choux, after the eggs are fully incorporated

of a smooth paste. The mixture should be stirred quickly and vigorously. The precooking and agitation of the batter allows for greater moisture absorption as well as the development of the gluten in the flour, which creates light, crisp pastry.

3. Transfer the mixture to the bowl of a mixer and, using the paddle attachment, mix for a few moments to cool the batter slightly.

4. Add the eggs gradually, in three or four additions, mixing the dough until it is smooth again each time. Scrape the sides and the bottom of the bowl as necessary. The dough should have a pearl-like sheen and be firm enough to just hold its shape when piped.

Strudel dough

Strudel dough is a slightly enriched soft dough. Bread flour is used for strudel dough because of its higher protein content, which accounts for the development of the elasticity of the dough that allows it to be stretched to make thin layers of pastry. The dough is mixed well to develop the gluten and then allowed to rest in a warm place (cold dough has less elasticity and is therefore more difficult to work with). The dough is then stretched until extremely thin and transparent. Commercially made phyllo dough, another thin flaky dough, is often used in place of strudel dough.

Laminated doughs

Laminated doughs include croissant, puff pastry, and Danish. Proper layering (lamination) is vital, as it is the combination of fat and dough in even layers that causes expansion and creates the ultimate flaky texture characteristic of laminated doughs. When the dough is baked, the fat melts, creating pockets where released steam from the moisture in the dought acts to leaven the dough. As the steam leaves the pockets in between the dough layers, causing the product to expand and rise, the remaining fat "fries" the dough so that the air spaces are retained.

Creating the proper number of fat and dough layers is critical to the success of laminated doughs. With too few layers, the steam will escape and the pastry will not rise. Folding the dough too many times can be a problem because the layers of fat and dough merge together as the fat begins to become incorporated into the dough, rather than remaining as separate layers, thus preventing the dough from rising.

Folding may be the most important factor in making a laminated dough, as the distinct layers of fat and dough must be maintained throughout the process. The dough must be rolled out evenly and the corners kept squared throughout the lock-in (the stage at which the roll-in butter is introduced to the dough) and all subsequent folds to ensure proper layering.

The basic steps for laminated doughs are:

1. A previously prepared dough (the initial dough) is folded and rolled together with a block of fat called a roll-in. To prepare the dough, sift together the flours. Blend in the butter on low speed with a dough hook attachment until pea-size nuggets form.

2. Combine the water and salt; add all at once to the dough, and mix on low speed until smooth. Dough that is to be laminated must be mixed carefully. Overmixing can result in too much gluten formation, making the dough elastic and difficult to roll out.

3. Shape the dough into a rough square or rectangle. Transfer to a sheet pan lined with parchment paper, wrap the dough in plastic wrap, and allow it to relax under refrigeration for 30 to 60 minutes. The dough should be gently rolled into the desired shape for the lock-in before it is refrigerated to reduce the amount of manipulation necessary during lock-in and lamination. While the dough is resting, prepare the roll-in fat.

4. To prepare the roll-in, the butter should be worked, either by hand or carefully using a stand mixer, until it is smooth and malleable but not overly soft. A number of different types of fats may be used in lamination. However, butter lends the best flavor and mouthfeel.

5. Mix the butter and flour (if using) until smooth. A small amount of flour may be added to the butter to make it easier to work with and to absorb excess moisture in the butter. It is important that the fat be completely smooth, as any lumps will tear the dough as it is rolled in, preventing proper layering.

6. Transfer the roll-in to a sheet of parchment paper. Cover with a second sheet and roll into a rectangle. Square off the edges, cover with plastic wrap, and refrigerate until firm but still pliable. Do not allow the roll-in to become cold. The temperature of the roll-in is also very important. It should be the same consistency as the dough when the two are rolled together. The butter must not be allowed to become so soft that it begins to ooze from the dough as it is rolled, nor should it be so firm that it could tear the dough or break into bits during rolling. Before use, the roll-in may be allowed to stand at room temperature for a few minutes if it is too hard, or re-refrigerated if it becomes too soft.

7. To lock the roll-in into the dough, turn out the dough onto a lightly floured work surface and roll it into a square or rectangle, keeping the edges straight and the corners squared. The roll-in fat can be added to the dough using one of several methods: envelope, single-fold, or three-fold. For the *envelope method,* the dough is rolled into a square or a rectangle. The roll-in is rolled into a smaller square or rectangle, and placed diagonally in the center of the dough so that each corner points to the center of a side of the dough. The corners of the dough are then folded over the fat envelope-style so that they meet in the center.

   In the *single-fold method,* the roll-in is rolled into a rectangle that is half the size of the dough square or rectangle, and placed on one half of the dough, then the other half of the dough is folded over it and the edges are sealed to completely encase the roll-in fat.

   In the *three-fold method,* the fat is rolled into a rectangle that covers two-thirds of the dough. The third of the dough not covered with the roll-in fat is folded over to cover half of the roll-in, or the center of the rectangle, and then the remaining side (or third) is folded over that. The edges are then sealed to completely encase the roll-in fat.

8. Administer a four-fold. Cover the dough in plastic wrap and allow it to rest for 30 minutes under refrigeration. For a four-fold or book-fold, divide the sheet of pastry visually into quarters, and fold the outer quarters into the middle so that their edges meet. Then fold the dough over as if closing a book. This type of fold quadruples the number of layers in the dough each time.

9. Turn the dough 90 degrees from its position before it was refrigerated and roll it out into a rectangle, making sure the edges are straight and the corners are squared. Administer a second fold (envelope, single-fold, or three-fold). Cover the dough in plastic wrap

and allow it to rest for 30 minutes under refrigeration. Repeat this process two more times for a total of four folds, turning the dough 90 degrees each time before rolling and allowing the dough to rest, covered in plastic wrap under refrigeration, for 30 minutes between each fold.

After the roll-in is added to the dough, each subsequent fold is usually either a three-fold or a four-fold. Each time, before folding and rolling the dough, brush any excess flour from its surface. When you fold the dough, the corners should squarely meet and the edges should be straight and perfectly aligned. After each fold, refrigerate the dough to allow it to relax and the butter to chill; the length of time the dough will need to rest will depend in large part on the temperature of the kitchen. For each fold, the dough is turned 90 degrees from the previous one to ensure that the gluten is stretched equally in all directions. Too much stress in one direction will make the dough difficult to roll and rise unevenly and misshapen during baking as the gluten contracts.

10. After completing the final fold, wrap the dough in plastic wrap and allow it to rest under refrigeration for 30 minutes before using.

Lock-in

 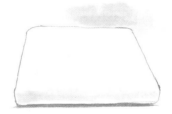

The first step of a lock-in: Place the roll-in on one half of the dough.

The second step of a lock-in: Fold the dough over the roll-in (envelope method).

Single-fold

To administer a single-fold, divide the sheet of dough visually in half, and fold the dough over itself to form two layers. This type of fold doubles the number of layers in the pastry.

Three-fold

For a three-fold, divide the sheet of pastry visually into thirds, and fold one of the outer thirds of the dough over the middle third of the pastry. Fold the remaining outer third of the dough over the folded dough. This fold triples the number of layers in the dough each time.

Roll the dough to the proper dimensions and visualize it in thirds.

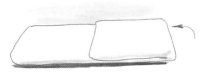

Fold one third of the dough over the center third.

Fold the final third over the center. Refrigerate before rolling and folding again.

Four-fold

For a four-fold or book-fold, divide the sheet of pastry visually into quarters, and fold the outer quarters into the middle so that their edges meet. Then fold the dough over as if closing a book. This type of fold quadruples the number of layers in the dough each time.

Roll the dough to the proper dimensions and visualize it in uneven quarters.

Fold the two ends so they meet off center.

Fold the ends over to meet precisely. Refrigerate before rolling and folding again.

Inverted puff pastry

The same rules apply for inverted puff pastry as for all other laminated doughs. For inverted puff pastry, however, the butter layer, rather than the dough, is the outer layer. The dough is worked less when preparing inverse dough, for a more tender result.

Blitz puff pastry

When rolling out blitz dough, it is more important to maintain the ½-in/1-cm thickness of the dough than to maintain the precise dimensions of the rectangle. It is very important that the dough be rolled thin enough to flatten the butter sufficiently to achieve the "puff" effect when the dough is baked.

LEFT: With the first three-fold, the large butter chunks are very visible.

RIGHT: As the dough is rolled out after the final fold, you can see the smoothness of its final texture.

Because there is no roll-in, blitz puff pastry is easier and faster to make than traditional puff dough. However, the flavor and quality of blitz puff dough should be just as good as that of traditionally made dough, and a well-made blitz dough will have no significant textural differences from the traditional dough. The only time blitz puff pastry should not be substituted for traditionally made puff pastry is in an application such as vol-au-vents, where a very high, even rise is required.

Storage of laminated dough

To prepare puff pastry and other laminated doughs for freezing, and to ease their use when frozen, follow this simple procedure: Roll the dough approximately ¼ in/6 mm thick. If necessary, cut the dough into smaller sheets the size of a sheet pan (17¾ by 25¾ in/45 by 66 cm) or half sheet pan (12⅞ by 17¾ in/33 by 45 cm). Layer the sheets on a sheet pan, placing a sheet of appropriately sized parchment paper between each one. Wrap the pan tightly in plastic wrap and place in the freezer. (Use the same method for refrigerated storage.)

As you cut puff pastry, you may create scraps, or trim. They can be reserved to be rerolled and used in pastries where a dramatic high straight rise is not critical. Recommendations for the use of these scraps are the same as for blitz puff pastry; they should not be used for items that require a high and even rise. Layer the scraps on top of each other, keeping them flat to preserve the layers of fat and dough. Then the dough may be rolled and stored under refrigeration or frozen.

It is easy to see the layers in this chocolate puff pastry.

Basic pie dough

MAKES 6 LB 6 OZ/2.89 KG

All-purpose flour	3 lb	1.36 kg
Salt	1 oz	28 g
Butter, cut into pieces, chilled	2 lb	907 g
Cold water	16 fl oz	480 mL

1   Combine the flour and salt in the mixer. Add the butter and blend on medium speed with the dough hook attachment until pea-size nuggets form, about 3 minutes. Add the water all at once and continue to mix until the dough just comes together.

2   Turn out the dough onto a lightly floured work surface. Scale the dough as desired. Wrap tightly and refrigerate for at least 1 hour before rolling. (The dough can be held under refrigeration or frozen.)

VARIATION   Replace 1 lb/454 g of the butter with an equal amount of shortening.

Pâte brisée

MAKES 4 LB/1.81 KG

Cake flour	2 lb 4 oz	1.02 kg
Salt	¾ oz	21 g
Butter, cubed	1 lb 2 oz	510 g
Water	8 fl oz	240 mL
Eggs	4 oz	113 g

1   Combine the flour and salt in the mixer. Add the butter and blend on medium speed with the dough hook attachment until a paste forms, about 4 minutes.

2   Combine the water and eggs. Add the egg and water mixture gradually to the flour while mixing on low speed, and mix until a shaggy mass forms. Tightly wrap the mixture with plastic wrap and allow it to rest under refrigeration for 1 hour.

3   Turn out the dough onto a lightly floured work surface. Gather and press it together. Scale the dough as desired. Wrap tightly and refrigerate for at least 1 hour before rolling. (The dough can be held under refrigeration or frozen.)

VARIATION   **WHOLE WHEAT PÂTE BRISÉE** Substitute 4 oz/113 g whole wheat flour for 8 oz/227 g of the cake flour.

1-2-3 cookie dough

MAKES 6 LB/2.72 KG

Sugar	1 lb	454 g
Butter, soft	2 lb	907 g
Vanilla extract	1 tbsp	15 mL
Eggs, room temperature	8 oz	227 g
Cake flour, sifted	3 lb	1.36 kg

1   Cream together the sugar and butter with the paddle attachment, starting on low speed and increasing to medium speed, scraping down the bowl periodically, until smooth and light in color, about 5 minutes.

2   Combine the vanilla and eggs and add them gradually, scraping down the bowl and blending until smooth after each addition. Turn off the mixer and add the flour all at once. Mix on low speed until just blended. Do not overmix.

3   Turn out the dough onto a lightly floured work surface. Scale the dough as desired. Wrap tightly and refrigerate for at least 1 hour before rolling. (The dough can be held under refrigeration or frozen.)

VARIATIONS   **LEMON COOKIE DOUGH** Add 1 tbsp/9 g finely grated lemon zest in step 1.

1-2-3 COOKIE DOUGH WITH GRAHAM CRACKER CRUMBS Replace 8 oz/227 g of the cake flour with an equal amount of graham cracker crumbs and add in step 2 with the flour.

Savory short dough

MAKES 4 LB/1.81 KG

Cake flour, sifted	2 lb	907 kg
Butter, soft	1 lb 4 oz	567 g
Salt	¾ oz	21 g
Eggs	10 oz	284 g

1   Combine the cake flour, butter, and salt and mix on medium speed with the paddle attachment until combined, about 5 minutes.

2   Add the eggs gradually, a few at a time, and mix until the dough is fully blended.

3   Turn out the dough onto a lightly floured work surface. Scale the dough as desired. Wrap tightly and refrigerate for at least 1 hour before rolling. (The dough can be held under refrigeration or frozen.)

Rich short dough

MAKES 6 LB 6 OZ/2.89 KG

Confectioners' sugar, sifted	1 lb	454 g
Butter, soft	2 lb	907 g
Vanilla extract	1 tsp	5 mL
Lemon zest, grated	1 tsp	3 g
Egg yolks, room temperature	1 lb	454 g
Cake flour, sifted	3 lb	1.36 kg

1 Cream together the sugar and butter with the paddle attachment, starting on low speed and increasing to medium speed, scraping down the bowl periodically, until smooth and light in color, about 5 minutes.

2 Combine the vanilla extract and lemon zest with the egg yolks and add them gradually, scraping down the bowl and blending until smooth after each addition. Turn off the mixer and add the flour all at once. Mix on low speed until just blended. Do not overmix.

3 Turn out the dough onto a lightly floured work surface. Scale the dough as desired. Wrap tightly and refrigerate for at least 1 hour before rolling. (The dough can be held under refrigeration or frozen.)

Chocolate short dough

MAKES 5 LB/2.27 KG

All-purpose flour	2 lb 3 oz	992 g
Dutch-process cocoa powder	3 oz	85 g
Butter, soft	1 lb 8 oz	680 g
Sugar	12 oz	340 g
Vanilla extract	1 tsp	5 mL
Eggs, room temperature	6 oz	170 g

1 Sift together the flour and cocoa powder.

2 Cream the butter and sugar with the paddle attachment, starting on low speed and increasing to medium speed, scraping down the bowl periodically, until smooth and light in color, about 5 minutes.

3 Combine the vanilla and eggs and add them gradually, scraping down the bowl and blending until smooth after each addition. Turn off the mixer and add the dry ingredients all at once, mixing on low speed until just blended. Do not overmix.

4 Turn out the dough onto a lightly floured work surface. Scale the dough as desired. Wrap tightly and refrigerate for at least 1 hour before rolling. (The dough can be held under refrigeration or frozen.)

Cornmeal short dough

MAKES 8 LB 6 OZ/3.80 KG

All-purpose flour, sifted	2 lb 4 oz	1.02 kg
Cornmeal	1 lb 4 oz	567 g
Salt	1½ tsp	7.5 g
Butter, soft	2 lb	907 g
Sugar	1 lb 4 oz	567 g
Egg yolks, room temperature	12 oz	340 g
Water, room temperature	4 fl oz	120 mL

1 Combine the flour, cornmeal, and salt.

2 Cream together the butter and sugar with the paddle attachment, starting on low speed and increasing to medium speed, scraping down the bowl periodically, until smooth and light in color, about 5 minutes. Add the egg yolks gradually, a few at a time, scraping down the bowl and blending until smooth after each addition. Turn off the mixer and add the dry ingredients all at once and mix on low speed until just blended. Add the water and blend just until incorporated.

3 Turn out the dough onto a lightly floured work surface. Scale the dough as desired. Wrap tightly and refrigerate for at least 1 hour before rolling. (The dough can be held under refrigeration or frozen.)

Almond paste short dough

MAKES 4 LB/1.81 KG

Almond paste, broken into pieces	1 lb 4 oz	567 g
Butter, soft	1 lb	454 g
Eggs, room temperature	6 oz	170 g
Cake flour, sifted	1 lb 4 oz	567 g

1   Cream together the almond paste and butter with the paddle attachment, starting on low speed and increasing to medium speed, scraping down the bowl periodically, until smooth and light in color, about 5 minutes. Add the eggs gradually, a few at a time, scraping down the bowl and blending until smooth after each addition. Turn off the mixer and add the flour all at once. Mix on low speed until just blended.

2   Turn out the dough onto a lightly floured work surface. Scale the dough as desired. Wrap tightly and refrigerate for at least 1 hour before rolling. (The dough can be held under refrigeration or frozen.)

Almond dough

MAKES 5 LB/2.27 KG

Pastry flour	1 lb 6 oz	624 g
Baking powder	½ oz	14 g
Butter, soft	1 lb 2 oz	510 g
Sugar	1 lb 2 oz	510 g
Vanilla extract	1½ tsp	7.50 mL
Eggs, room temperature	6 oz	170 g
Almonds, finely crushed	1 lb 2 oz	510 g

1   Sift together the flour and baking powder.

2   Cream the butter and sugar with the paddle attachment, starting on low speed and increasing to medium speed, scraping down the bowl periodically, until smooth and light in color, about 5 minutes. Combine the vanilla and eggs and add them gradually, scraping down the bowl and blending until smooth after each addition. Turn off the mixer and add the flour mixture and the almonds all at once. Mix on low speed until just blended. Do not overmix.

3   Turn out the dough onto a lightly floured work surface. Scale the dough as desired. Wrap tightly and refrigerate for at least 1 hour before rolling. (The dough can be held under refrigeration or frozen.)

Linzer dough

MAKES 4 TORTES (10 IN/25 CM EACH), OR 275 SMALL COOKIES

Butter	1 lb 8 oz	680 g
Sugar	1 lb 2 oz	510 g
Vanilla extract	½ tsp	2.50 mL
Eggs, room temperature	4½ oz	128 g
Cake flour	1 lb 14 oz	851 g
Ground cinnamon	½ oz	14 g
Fine cake crumbs	4 oz	113 g
Baking powder	½ oz	14 g
Hazelnuts, toasted and ground	12 oz	340 g

1   Cream the butter and sugar with the paddle attachment, starting on low speed and increasing to medium speed, until smooth, about 5 minutes.

2   Combine the vanilla and eggs and add them gradually, scraping down the bowl and blending until smooth after each addition.

3   Sift together the flour, cinnamon, cake crumbs, and baking powder. Turn off the mixer and add the dry ingredients all at once, mixing on low speed until just blended. Do not overmix.

4   Add the hazelnuts and mix until just blended.

5   Turn out the dough onto a lightly floured work surface. Scale the dough as desired. Wrap tightly and refrigerate for at least 1 hour before rolling. (The dough can be held under refrigeration or frozen.)

Graham cracker crust

MAKES 2 LB 2 OZ/964 G

Graham cracker crumbs	1 lb 8 oz	680 g
Light brown sugar	4 oz	113 g
Butter, melted	6 oz	170 g

1   Process the graham cracker crumbs, brown sugar, and butter in a food processor just until crumbly, about 5 minutes.

2   The crust is ready to be pressed into prepared pans and baked.

SCALING NOTE   Use about 3 oz/85 g per 6-in/15-cm pan and 5 oz/142 g per 8-in/20-cm pan.

Pâte à choux

MAKES 3 LB/1.36 KG

Milk	8 fl oz	240 mL
Water	8 fl oz	240 mL
Salt	small pinch	small pinch
Butter, cubed	8 oz	227 g
Bread flour	12 oz	340 g
Eggs	1 lb	454 g

1   Bring the milk, water, salt, and butter to a boil over medium heat, stirring constantly. Once the butter has melted, add the flour all at once and stir vigorously to combine. Continue to stir until the mixture forms a mass and pulls away from the sides of the pan, about 3 minutes.

2   Transfer the mixture to the mixer and beat briefly on medium speed with the paddle attachment. Add the eggs 2 at a time, beating until smooth after each addition and checking the consistency of the dough. Stop adding eggs when the dough slowly slides down the paddle.

3   The pâte à choux is ready to be piped and baked (see "Piped Pastries" in Chapter 18, page 640).

NOTES   For a drier and lighter blond pâte à choux, substitute an equal part of water for the milk.

For a shiny finish, egg wash the pâte à choux prior to baking.

VARIATION   **CHOCOLATE PÂTE À CHOUX** Substitute cocoa powder for 2 oz/57 g of the flour and increase the amount of sugar by 1½ oz/43 g.

Crêpes

MAKES 45 TO 50 CRÊPES

Milk	24 fl oz	720 mL
Heavy cream	12 fl oz	360 mL
Eggs	1 lb 2 oz	510 g
Vegetable oil	1 fl oz	30 mL
Sugar	1½ oz	43 g
Salt	pinch	pinch
Flavorings (optional)	as needed	as needed
Bread flour	1 lb 2 oz	510 g
Butter, for cooking	as needed	as needed

1   Blend the milk, cream, eggs, oil, sugar, and salt in a bowl. Add the flavorings to the milk mixture, if using. Add the flour and whisk until evenly blended.

2   Strain the batter through a fine-mesh sieve. Let the batter rest under refrigeration for at least 30 minutes and up to 8 hours.

3   Melt a small amount of butter in a crêpe pan. Ladle just enough crêpe batter into the pan to cover the surface, rotating the pan to facilitate the spread of the batter over its surface as it is being ladled in.

4   Cook for about 2 minutes on each side, just until light golden brown. Transfer to a plate and layer between waxed paper. Cover the stack of finished crêpes with plastic wrap and refrigerate or freeze for later use.

NOTE   Examples of flavorings are rum, Grand Marnier, vanilla, citrus zests, or mint.

Strudel dough

MAKES 1 LB 11¾ OZ/787 G

Bread flour	1 lb	454 g
Salt	1½ tsp	7.50 g
Water	13 fl oz	390 mL
Vegetable oil	2½ oz	71 g
Vegetable oil, for coating	as needed	as needed

1   Sift together the flour and salt. Transfer to the mixer. Add the water and oil and blend on low speed using a dough hook attachment until just blended. Mix on high speed until the dough is smooth, satiny, and very elastic, about 10 minutes.

2   Turn out the dough onto a work surface and gather it into a ball. Rub it with oil and wrap in plastic wrap. Let the dough rest at room temperature for 1 hour, or refrigerate it overnight before using. Allow the dough to come to room temperature before stretching. (See Apple Strudel, page 550.)

Butter puff pastry dough

MAKES 8 LB 12 OZ/3.97 KG

DOUGH		
Bread flour	2 lb	907 g
Pastry flour	8 oz	227 g
Salt	1 oz	28 g
Butter, soft	8 oz	227 g
Water, cold	18 fl oz	540 mL
ROLL-IN		
Butter, pliable (60°F/16°C)	2 lb 4 oz	1.02 kg
Bread flour	4 oz	113 g

1   To prepare the dough, place the flours, salt, butter, and water in the mixer and blend on low speed with the dough hook attachment until a smooth dough is formed. Shape the dough into a rough rectangle. Line a sheet pan with parchment paper and dust the paper lightly with flour. Transfer the dough to the sheet pan, wrap in plastic wrap, and refrigerate for 30 to 60 minutes.

2   To prepare the roll-in, blend the butter and flour on low speed with the paddle attachment until smooth, about 2 minutes. Transfer to a sheet of parchment paper. Form into a rectangle ½ in/1 cm thick. Cover with plastic wrap. Refrigerate until firm but still pliable. Do not allow the roll-in to become hard.

3   To lock the roll-in into the dough, turn out the dough onto a lightly floured work surface and roll it into a rectangle twice the size of the roll-in, keeping the edges straight and the corners squared. Administer a lock-in (see step 7, page 218).

4   Administer a four-fold (see page 220). Cover the dough with plastic wrap and allow it to rest for 30 to 45 minutes under refrigeration.

5   Turn the dough 90 degrees from its position before it was refrigerated and roll out into a rectangle 16 by 24 in/41 by 61 cm, making sure the edges are straight and the corners are squared. Administer a second four-fold. Cover the dough in plastic wrap and allow it to rest under refrigeration for 30 minutes. Repeat this process two more times for a total of four four-folds, turning the dough 90 degrees each time before rolling and allowing the dough to rest, covered in plastic wrap, under refrigeration for 30 minutes between each fold.

6   After completing the final fold, wrap the dough in plastic wrap and allow it to rest under refrigeration for 30 minutes before using.

VARIATIONS   **CHOCOLATE PUFF PASTRY** Substitute Dutch-process cocoa powder for 2 oz/57 g of the flour for the roll-in.

GARLIC PUFF PASTRY Add to the roll-in when blending the butter with the flour: 1 oz/28 g chopped garlic, 1½ oz/43 g chopped shallot, ¾ oz/21 g chopped parsley, and ½ oz/14 g salt.

Inverse puff pastry

MAKES 11 LB 13 OZ/5.36 KG

WATER DOUGH		
Bread flour	3 lb	1.36 kg
Salt	1½ oz	43 g
Water	28 fl oz	840 mL
Butter, soft	8 oz	227 g
BUTTER DOUGH		
Butter, cold	4 lb 8 oz	2.04 kg
Cake flour	2 lb	907 g

1   To prepare the water dough, combine the flour, salt, water, and butter on medium speed with the dough hook attachment until completely blended, about 8 minutes.

2   Form the dough into a rough rectangle 8 by 24 in/20 by 61 cm and transfer it to a parchment-lined sheet pan. Press the dough into the sheet pan, wrap it tightly in plastic wrap, and let it relax under refrigeration for 30 to 60 minutes.

3   To prepare the butter dough, blend the butter and flour on high speed with the dough hook attachment until smooth, about 2 minutes. Transfer the dough to a sheet of parchment paper. Cover with a second sheet and roll into a rectangle 16 by 24 in/41 by 61 cm. Square off the edges using your hands or the rolling pin, cover with plastic wrap, and refrigerate until firm but still pliable.

4   To lock the water dough into the butter dough, turn the butter dough out onto a lightly floured work surface. Place the water dough on half of the butter dough rectangle and fold the butter dough over to encase the water dough. Press the edges together to seal. Turn the dough 90 degrees and roll out into a rectangle 16 by 24 in/41 by 61 cm, making sure the edges are straight and the corners are squared.

5   Administer a four-fold (see page 220) and roll out to the same dimensions as before.

6   Administer a second four-fold and roll out to the same dimensions as before. Cover the dough in plastic wrap and allow it to rest for 1 hour under refrigeration.

7   Make two more book folds, resting the dough between folds for a total of four four-folds, refrigerating and turning the dough 90 degrees each time before rolling. After completing the final fold, wrap the dough in plastic wrap and allow it to firm under refrigeration for at least 2 hours. (The dough can be held under refrigeration or frozen.)

Blitz puff pastry

MAKES 5 LB/2.27 KG

Cake flour	1 lb	454 g
Bread flour	1 lb	454 g
Butter, 1-in/3-cm cubes, chilled	2 lb	907 g
Salt	¾ oz	21 g
Water, cold	18 fl oz	540 mL

1   Combine the cake and bread flour in the mixer. Add the butter and toss with your fingertips until the butter is coated with flour. Combine the salt and water and add to the flour all at once. Mix on low speed with the dough hook attachment until the dough forms a shaggy mass.

2   Tightly cover the mixture with plastic wrap and let it to rest under refrigeration, until the butter is firm but not brittle, about 20 minutes.

3   Place the shaggy mass on a lightly floured work surface and roll out into a rectangle that is ½ in/1 cm thick and approximately 12 by 30 in/30 by 76 cm.

4   Administer a four-fold (see page 220), roll out the dough to the same dimensions, and administer a second four-fold. Tightly wrap the dough in plastic wrap and allow it to rest under refrigeration for 30 minutes.

5   Repeat this process two more times for a total of four four-folds, refrigerating and turning the dough 90 degrees each time before rolling. After completing the final fold, wrap the dough in plastic wrap and allow it to firm under refrigeration for at least 1 hour. (The dough can be held under refrigeration or frozen.)

Croissant dough

MAKES 5 LB 8 OZ/2.26 KG

DOUGH		
Milk	1.58 lb	171 g
Malt syrup	4 fl oz	120 mL
Bread flour	2 lb 8 oz	1.13 g
Yeast	1 oz	28 g
Sugar	4 oz	113 g
Butter, pliable	5 oz	142 g
ROLL-IN		
Butter, pliable	1 lb 8 oz	680 g

1   To prepare the dough, place the milk, malt syrup, flour, yeast, sugar, and butter in the mixer, making sure the butter is pliable. Mix 4 minutes at low speed with the paddle attachment, scraping the bowl periodically. Mix an additional 2 minutes at high speed.

2   Turn out the dough onto a lightly floured surface. Cover the dough and ferment at 75°F/24°C, about 2 hours.

3   Fold over the dough and spread it into a rectangle 12 by 16 in/30 by 41 cm on a parchment-lined sheet pan. Retard in the refrigerator.

4   Prepare the roll-in butter by pounding it with a rolling pin to make it pliable and working to half the size of the dough; wrap and refrigerate overnight.

5   Remove the roll-in butter and if necessary make it pliable by pounding with a rolling pin.

6   Lock in the butter (see page 218). Make sure the edges are straight and the corners are squared.

7   Immediately administer a four-fold (see page 220). Wrap the dough in plastic wrap and let it rest in the refrigerator for 30 minutes.

8   Administer a three-fold (see page 220). Wrap the dough in plastic wrap and let it rest in the refrigerator for 30 minutes.

9   Administer a final three-fold. Wrap the dough in plastic wrap and place it in the freezer for 2 hours. Refrigerate before shaping and baking.

Danish dough

MAKES 10 LB 8 OZ/4.76 KG

DOUGH		
Bread flour	4 lb	1.81 kg
Sugar	7¼ oz	206 g
Instant dry yeast	1 oz	28 g
Salt	1 oz	28 g
Butter, soft	6 oz	170 g
Eggs	13 oz	369 g
Milk	28 fl oz	840 mL
ROLL-IN		
Butter, cold	3 lb	1.36 kg

1 To prepare the dough, blend the flour, sugar, yeast, salt, butter, eggs, and milk on low speed with the dough hook attachment, about 2 minutes. Increase to medium speed and mix for an additional 4 minutes.

2 Turn out the dough onto a lightly floured surface. Cover the dough and ferment at 75°F/24° C until doubled in volume, about 2 hours.

3 Fold over the dough and spread it into a rectangle 12 by 16 in/30 by 41 cm on a parchment-lined sheet pan. Wrap the dough tightly with plastic wrap and let it rest overnight or for 8 hours under refrigeration to completely relax the gluten.

4 Using a rolling pin, pound out the roll-in butter to make it pliable and lump-free. Shape it into a rectangle 8 by 24 by ½ in/20 by 61 by 1 cm. Chill the butter slightly.

5 To lock the roll-in into the dough, turn out the dough onto a lightly floured work surface and roll it into a rectangle 16 by 24 by ½ in/41 by 61 by 1 cm, keeping the edges straight and the corners squared. Place the roll-in on half of the dough rectangle. Fold the remaining half of the dough over the roll-in. Seal the edges, turn the dough 90 degrees, and roll into a rectangle 16 by 24 by ½ in/41 by 61 by 1 cm, making sure the edges are straight and the corners are squared.

6 Administer a four-fold (see page 220). Cover the dough in plastic wrap and allow it to rest for 30 minutes under refrigeration.

7 Turn the dough 90 degrees from its position before it was refrigerated and roll into a rectangle 16 by 24 by ½ in/41 by 61 by 1 cm thick, making sure the edges are straight and the corners are squared. Administer a three-fold (see page 220). Cover the dough in plastic wrap and let it to rest for 30 minutes under refrigeration. Repeat this process one more time for a total of two three-folds.

8 After completing the final fold, wrap the dough in plastic wrap and allow it to rest under refrigeration for at least another 30 minutes before using. (The dough can be held under refrigeration or frozen.)

Fig Newton dough

MAKES 7 LB 14 OZ/3.57 KG

Dried figs	15 oz	425 g
Golden raisins	15 oz	425 g
Sliced almonds	15 oz	425 g
Cake flour	1 lb 4 oz	567 g
Baking soda	1 tbsp	9 g
Butter	1 lb 8 oz	680 g
Sugar	1 lb	454 g
Salt	1 tsp	5 g
Vanilla extract	1 tbsp	15 mL
Eggs	4 oz	113 g
Milk	2 fl oz	60 mL
Oats	15 oz	425 g

1   Finely chop the figs, raisins, and almonds.

2   Sift together the flour and baking soda.

3   Cream the butter, sugar, salt, and vanilla on medium speed with the paddle attachment, until smooth, about 5 minutes.

4   Add the eggs one at a time, making sure each addition is fully incorporated before adding more. Scrape down the sides of the bowl as needed. Blend in the milk.

5   Add the sifted dry ingredients slowly, mixing on low speed just until combined.

6   Add the fruit-nut mixture and the oats and mix on low speed to combine.

7   Turn out the dough onto a lightly floured work surface. Scale the dough as desired. The dough is ready to roll and fill or may be wrapped tightly and refrigerated for up to 1 week.

chapter ten

Quick breads and cakes

quick breads and cakes are served as breakfast pastries or simple desserts. They are also "foundation preparations" used for assembled cakes and tortes, including wedding and other special-occasion cakes. The pastry chef uses seven basic mixing methods—blending; creaming; two-stage; cold, warm, and separated foaming; and combination—to prepare all of these.

Basic principles of quick breads and cakes

There are certain rules that apply to the preparation of any quick bread or cake regardless of the mixing method used. For all quick breads and cakes, it is important to sift the dry ingredients together both to remove lumps and to blend the dry ingredients evenly, which will in turn help to ensure a fully combined batter with minimal mixing time. A short mixing time is an important factor, as gluten development is undesirable. Another asset of sifting the dry ingredients is that it will evenly distribute the leavener. Chemical leaveners, which are often used in quick breads and cakes, must be evenly distributed to ensure uniform texture and crumb.

All ingredients should be at room temperature before they are combined. Ingredients that are too cold may cause the batter to separate. Usually liquids should be added incrementally to a batter to ensure full hydration and complete incorporation of the dry ingredients.

In nearly all mixing methods used for quick breads and cakes, the development or introduction of air cells into the batter is very important to the process. In creamed batters this is achieved as the fat and sugar are creamed together, while in foamed cakes the air cells are developed as the eggs are beaten and folded into the batter. Regardless of the method of development and incorporation, air cells facilitate the leavening of a product and are important to the proper development of structure and crumb during baking. If air cells are not fully developed, the resulting product will lack leavening and have a dense, coarse crumb.

Pan preparation

Pans are lined with parchment paper to ease the process of removing a baked product from the pan. For creamed or foamed batters that must be spread rather than poured, it is important to apply a thin film of butter or other fat to the pan before placing the parchment in the base of the pan. The fat will keep the paper stationary while the batter is spread. This is particularly important when using large pans. The sides of the pan should also be greased and lightly floured, or greased with pan grease, which already contains a measure of flour. Pans used for sponge cakes should be lined with parchment, but the sides of the pans should remain untreated.

Angel food cakes require no pan preparation. The full rise of this cake partially depends on the batter being able to cling to the side of the pan as it rises during baking. Angel food cakes should also have no treatment to the bottom of the pans, as they are cooled upside down to facilitate removal and to help retain their height and inner structure after cooling.

Pans should be filled approximately three-quarters full with batter, unless otherwise specified in the formula's method. This should allow sufficient room for the product to rise during baking. Pans filled with batters made by the creaming, chiffon, and two-stage mixing methods should be gently tapped on a counter to help remove any large air bubbles that may have developed as the batter was scaled into the pan.

Cooling quick breads and cakes

After removal from the oven, quick breads and cakes should be allowed to cool slightly in the pan before unmolding. To remove a cake or quick bread from the pan, run a small knife or metal spatula between the cake and the pan. Press the tool to the pan so as not to cut or damage the item in any way. Invert the pan onto a wire rack, tap lightly, and lift gently to release. Peel the parchment paper from the bottom of the cake to allow steam to escape. Items must cool completely before they are filled, iced, glazed, or otherwise decorated.

The pans for angel food cakes receive no treatment, which could make the cakes difficult to unmold. However, this type of cake is cooled upside down, allowing steam to build between the pan and the cake, making it easier to release.

Cheesecakes should cool completely in the pan at room temperature and then be wrapped tightly and refrigerated until the custard has completely set, typically overnight (about 8 hours). To unmold a cheesecake, remove the plastic wrap and run a small knife or metal spatula between the pan and the cake. Press the tool to the pan to ensure the item to be unmolded is not cut or damaged in any way. Warm the bottom of the pan gently over an open burner, place a cake round that has been tightly wrapped in plastic on top of the cake, invert, and gently tap to release. Remove the pan and invert the cake to set it right side up.

Storing quick breads and cakes

Quick breads and cakes stale quickly when left exposed to air. Cakes and quick breads may be stored tightly wrapped in plastic wrap and frozen for up to 3 weeks without adverse effects. They may be left to thaw at room temperature before use.

The blending mixing method

The blending method consists of making two mixtures, one with the wet ingredients and one with the dry, then combining the two together.

1. Sift the flour with the other dry ingredients. All-purpose or pastry flour is used for most items made by this method because of its moderate protein content. Special flours such as cornmeal or whole wheat flour may replace some or all of the white wheat flour in a given formula to add flavor and develop a different texture. The flour(s) should be sifted together with the other dry ingredients, such as baking soda, baking powder, sugar, salt, cocoa, or ground spices.

   It is important to sift the dry ingredients, as sifting removes lumps and incorporates all ingredients together. Thoroughly blending the dry ingredients also ensures that the leavening agent will be evenly distributed in the mixture. Sifting will ultimately help to create a fully combined batter needing minimal mixing time.

2. Combine the wet ingredients. Cream, milk, buttermilk, water, and even watery vegetables like zucchini all add moisture to a baking formula. Fats shorten developing gluten strands, which helps to create a tender texture in the baked good. Solid fats like butter or shortening are most often melted for this method so they can be blended with the other liquid ingredients. All ingredients should be at room temperature before being added, as those that are too cold may cause the batter to separate.

LEFT: For the blending method, the combined wet ingredients are added to the combined dry ingredients.
RIGHT: A properly mixed batter should be uniform in color and texture throughout. (Cream Scones, page 251, pictured here.)

3. Add all the wet ingredients to the dry ingredients all at once and blend, using a mixer or by hand, just until the dry ingredients are evenly moistened. Mixing these batters as briefly as possible ensures a light, delicate texture. Overmixed batters may develop too much gluten and the resulting item will not have the desired fine, delicate texture.

4. Scrape the bowl down once or twice to mix the batter evenly.

The creaming mixing method

Muffins, cakes, quick breads, cookies, and other baked goods made with the creaming method develop their light and airy structure through the incorporation of air during mixing and by use of chemical leaveners. For the creaming method, first the fat and sugar are "creamed" or blended until very smooth and light. Then the eggs are added, and finally the sifted dry ingredients are added in two or three additions; if there is any liquid, the dry ingredients and liquid are added alternately, starting and ending with the dry ingredients. It is important that ingredients for a creamed batter or dough are at room temperature and the fat (butter, shortening, nut paste, etc.) is soft before beginning to mix.

1. Cream together the fat and sugar on medium speed with the paddle attachment, scraping down the sides and bottom of the bowl occasionally as you work to ensure all the fat is blended evenly. Cream the fat and sugar until the mixture is pale in color and light and smooth in texture; when the butter and sugar have this appearance, it indicates that a sufficient amount of air has been incorporated into the mixture. If the ingredients are not sufficiently creamed, the final product will be dense and lack the light, tender qualities characteristic of creamed baked goods. There are formulas made by the creaming method, however, such as some cookies, where minimum air incorporation is desirable. In these cases the butter and sugar are blended for a shorter amount of time, just until the mixture is smooth.

2. Once the butter and the sugar are properly creamed, the eggs should be added gradually and in stages, mixing until fully incorporated and scraping down the bowl after each addition. Scraping down the bowl is important to develop a completely smooth batter. Adding the eggs in batches will help to prevent the batter from separating. Blending eggs into the butter-sugar mixture creates an emulsion (for more about emulsions, see page 68). The more eggs added, the more difficult it becomes to sustain the emulsion, and the mixture can begin to separate, developing a curdled or broken appearance. Using eggs at room temperature or warming the eggs slightly (not above 80°F/27°C) when an unusually large amount is to be added will help to emulsify and fully blend the mixture. If the mixture should separate, continue to mix until it becomes smooth again. However, sometimes this curdled appearance is unavoidable because of the ratio of eggs to fat. In these instances, blend in the eggs to create as smooth a mixture as possible, and when the dry ingredients are added make sure to blend to a smooth consistency.

3. The sifted dry ingredients are generally added in one of two ways: all at once, or alternating with the liquid ingredient (milk, juice, etc.). When adding the dry and liquid ingredients alternately, add one-third of the dry ingredients, then about one-half of the liquid ingredients, mixing until smooth and scraping down the bowl after each addition. Repeat this sequence until all of the dry and liquid ingredients have been added. Increase the speed and beat the batter just until it is evenly blended and smooth. Sometimes, but not often, the liquid may be added to the creamed mixture immediately after the eggs. This is done only when the amount of liquid is very small, as it is likely to cause the creamed mixture to begin to separate. It is difficult to get a creamed mixture to accept a large amount of liquid. Regardless of the method of addition, after adding the dry ingredients, mix the dough or batter minimally, or just until incorporated. Excessive mixing would act to develop gluten, which would toughen the dough or batter and, therefore, the final product.

4. Add any remaining flavoring or garnishing ingredients, mixing or folding until they are just incorporated.

Note the difference in texture and color between butter and sugar when they are just brought together (left) and fully creamed (right).

LEFT: The first stage in the two-stage mixing method. Make sure the fat, dry ingredients, and half the liquid are fully combined.

RIGHT: The second stage. Blending the remaining liquid into the batter.

The two-stage mixing method

This mixing method was designed to be used when making high-ratio cakes; containing a higher proportion of sugar and emulsifiers than other cakes, a high-ratio cake is one in which the weight of the sugar is equal to or greater than the weight of the flour, and the weight of the eggs is equal to or greater than the weight of the fat.

1. Combine or sift together all dry ingredients.

2. Combine all the wet ingredients, including the eggs. The high ratio of shortening and eggs acts as an emulsifier. When added to the dry and liquid ingredients, this emulsion helps to create a smooth batter.

3. In the first stage of mixing, combine the dry ingredient mixture with all of the fat and half of the liquid mixture and mix for 4 minutes on medium speed, scraping down the bowl periodically to ensure the batter is mixed evenly.

4. In the second stage, blend the remaining liquid into the batter in three equal parts, mixing for 2 minutes after each addition, for a total of 6 minutes. Scrape the bowl periodically to make certain that the batter is blended evenly. The development of flavor and texture in a product created using the two-stage mixing method can be attributed to the specific and longer mixing times called for in this method as compared to others.

Angel food mixing method

Angel food cake is a light, spongy cake based on beaten egg whites and sugar (a meringue) that is stabilized with flour. All of the leavening in an angel food cake is supplied by the air that is whipped into the meringue. It is drier than sponge or chiffon cakes because it does not contain any fat. These cakes have good structure, but because they contain no fat, they have a unique texture, which makes them less desirable for use in layer cakes or as a component of any layered, sliced dessert or pastry.

1. Assemble all equipment and ingredients and sift the flour before beginning to mix. It is important to assemble all equipment and ingredients prior to beginning mixing, as thorough preparation will ensure the batter goes from the mixer to the oven in the shortest amount of time; reducing the time the batter stands in the mixer will prevent a loss of volume in the batter and thus should result in a cake with maximum volume.

2. Beat the egg whites until they form soft peaks. Continue whipping and add the sugar, streaming it in gradually with the machine running. All of the leavening in an angel food cake is supplied by the air that is whipped into the meringue.

   Eggs lend stability to a product when baking. They also have leavening power; egg whites especially, as they are whipped, trap air, which expands when heated. This ultimately creates a larger and lighter product as demonstrated in this cake's characteristically spongy and airy texture. When sugar is added in the whipping process, the combination of the eggs' moisture along with the mixing agitation causes the sugar to begin dissolving; the sugar in turn coats the air bubbles in the eggs, making them more stable.

3. Once the meringue has medium, glossy peaks, fold in the sifted dry ingredients by hand, working quickly to reduce the deflation of the beaten egg whites.

   Flour acts as perhaps the most common stabilizer in baking; its gluten content (the protein component) builds structure and strength in baked goods. It is important that the flour is sifted, as sifting introduces air into the mixture, as well as preventing an uneven, lumpy texture.

4. Sprinkle the tube pan with a small amount of water before adding the batter to help develop a thin crisp crust on the cake.

dried fruits

Plumping dried fruits by macerating them in a liquid will make them tender and juicy, eliminating any possibility of the undesirable leathery texture they can sometimes have in finished baked goods. Plumping dried fruits also serves to keep the amount of liquid in the formula balanced, as dried fruits can absorb moisture from the dough or batter if they are not first plumped. Furthermore, the liquid used for plumping the fruit can add its own flavor. Fruit can be plumped in liquor such as brandy or rum, or in fruit juices or apple cider. Choose a liquid that complements the other flavors in the formula.

To plump fruit, place it in a bowl, add enough liquid to cover, and allow it to stand until rehydrated and softened. Soaking time will depend on the fruits, their age, and the particular drying process used. However, overnight is usually sufficient.

For quicker maceration, combine the dried fruit and liquid in a saucepan and bring to a simmer over medium heat. Remove from the heat and let the fruit stand in the liquid, covered, until plumped.

When dried fruit is added to a formula, whether plumped or not, it is often first tossed in a small measure of flour, which will help to prevent the fruit from sinking to the bottom of the pan during baking.

Cold and warm foaming methods

A foaming method is any method in which eggs are whipped or beaten to incorporate air before they are mixed into a batter. The air incorporated into the eggs creates a light and airy batter as well and helps to leaven the final baked item. The air trapped in the eggs will form pockets that, during baking, will expand and cause the product to rise.

When using a foaming method, it is important that all ingredients and equipment be assembled and receive any preliminary treatment before beginning to mix the ingredients; this will help to assure that the foaming process proceeds as quickly as possible, thus preventing any loss of volume in the batter.

Flour and any other dry ingredients should be sifted thoroughly to ensure full aeration. Butter should be melted and allowed to cool slightly.

Cold foaming method

1. Place the eggs and sugar in the bowl of a mixer large enough to accommodate the volume of the fully beaten eggs.

2. Using the wire whip attachment, whip the mixture to maximum volume on high speed. Remove the bowl from the mixer. To determine when the eggs have reached maximum volume, watch as they are beaten; when the aerated mixture just begins to recede, maximum volume has been achieved. They will typically expand 4 to 6 times their original volume.

3. Fold the sifted dry ingredients into the beaten eggs gently and gradually, but quickly, to prevent excessive loss of volume. For folding, use a large rubber spatula or other implement with a large, broad, flat surface. This will allow for a larger amount of batter to be lifted with each fold, facilitating the rapid incorporation of ingredients without breaking down the fragile aerated structure.

4. Fold the melted fat into the batter last. You may want to temper in the butter; some chefs feel this eases the fat's full incorporation and lessens any deflating effects on the batter. To do this, first lighten the butter by incorporating a small amount of batter. Then fold this mixture into the remaining batter.

5. Immediately after mixing, scale the batter into each prepared pan and bake.

Warm foaming method

1. Place the eggs and sugar in the bowl of a mixer and place the bowl over a pan of barely simmering water. Stir the mixture with a wire whip until it reaches 110°F/43°C. Heating the eggs with the sugar before beating allows the mixture to achieve maximum volume faster and creates a more stable foam because the sugar has been dissolved and the protein in the eggs has become more elastic.

2. Using the wire whip attachment, whip the mixture to maximum volume on high speed.

3. After the egg mixture has reached maximum volume, reduce the mixer speed to medium and continue to blend for 5 additional minutes. Whipping at high speed creates large air bubbles; continuing to mix at a lower speed divides the bubbles, reducing their size and creating a more stable foam, thereby stabilizing the batter.

TOP LEFT: The eggs and sugar are combined and gently heated in a double boiler.

TOP RIGHT: The eggs are whipped in a mixer until they just begin to recede.

BOTTOM LEFT: The flour is folded into the foamed eggs gently so as to minimize their deflation.

BOTTOM RIGHT: The finished batter is poured into the prepared pans.

4. Fold the sifted dry ingredients into the beaten eggs gently and gradually, but quickly, to prevent excessive loss of volume. For folding, use a large rubber spatula or other implement with a large, broad, flat surface. This will allow for a larger amount of batter to be lifted with each fold, facilitating the rapid incorporation of ingredients without breaking down the fragile aerated structure.

5. Fold the melted fat into the batter last. You may want to temper in the butter; some chefs feel this eases the fat's full incorporation and lessens any deflating effects on the batter. To do this, first lighten the butter by incorporating a small amount of batter. Then fold this mixture into the remaining batter.

6. Immediately after mixing, scale the batter into each prepared pan and bake.

Separated foam mixing method

In this variation on a standard cold foam mixing method, the whole eggs are separated and beaten separately into two foams. These foams are then folded together. The separated foam mixing method is slightly more difficult than the cold foaming method because the egg whites, which are whipped alone, can rapidly lose volume. For this reason it is important when using this mixing method that all ingredients and equipment are assembled and receive any preliminary treatment before you begin to mix the batter (e.g., line pans, sift dry ingredients, melt fat, etc.). Dry ingredients should be sifted for aeration as well as to preventatively smooth any lumps that may require extra mixing as dry ingredients are incorporated into the delicate aerated egg mixture.

1. Separate the egg whites from the egg yolks.

2. Whip the egg yolks with a portion of the sugar to the ribbon stage, or until the mixture has thickened enough to fall in ribbons from the whip and is pale yellow in color. Set this foam aside. Whipped egg yolks are stable and won't lose volume.

3. Whip the whites, using a clean whip, until soft peaks form. Gradually add the remaining sugar with the mixer running on medium speed, and continue whipping on medium or high speed until the whites form medium peaks. The point to which the whites are beaten is important. If the whites are beaten to stiff peaks, the additional agitation they undergo during folding will cause them to become overbeaten. Overbeaten eggs are less elastic, more difficult to incorporate, will break down more easily, will not develop a stable internal structure, and have less leavening power.

4. Immediately after the whites reach their desired peak, gently fold them into the foamed egg yolks. To fully blend these two components, first combine a small measure of the whites with the yolks to lighten them and make their consistency more akin to that of the whites. Fold the remaining whites into the yolk mixture.

    Bringing the consistency of the yolks closer to that of the whites is a step taken to facilitate the quickest incorporation of the whites into the mixture. The more quickly the two egg mixtures are incorporated, the less the amount of volume lost.

5. Fold the sifted dry ingredients into the egg mixture gently and gradually, but quickly, to prevent excessive loss of volume. For folding, use a large rubber spatula or other imple-

LEFT: The egg yolks are beaten with a little sugar to the ribbon stage.

RIGHT: A portion of the beaten whites are folded into the beaten yolks to lighten them and ease their full incorporation while maintaining the lightest possible batter.

ment with a large, broad, flat surface to allow for a larger amount of batter to be lifted with each fold, facilitating the rapid incorporation of ingredients without breaking down the fragile aerated structure.

6. Fold the melted fat into the batter last.

7. Immediately after mixing, scale the batter into each prepared pan and bake. The batter should be scaled into pans and baked immediately to prevent any loss of volume in the batter as it stands.

Combination mixing method

The combination mixing method combines the creaming mixing method with the foaming method. This combination gives the cake qualities of both methods: the rich, moist crumb of a creamed cake as well as some of the lightness of a batter that has the additional leavening power of beaten egg whites.

1. Prepare the pan(s), assemble ingredients, and sift dry ingredients. When making anything using this method, as with other foamed batters, advance preparation (pan preparation, sifting, ingredients assembly, etc.) is critical to successful completion. Advance preparation is necessary to ensure that the mixing process proceeds quickly and smoothly; this will result in a batter able to maintain maximum volume before baking.

2. Cream together the butter and some of the sugar. This step helps to develop air cells, which will facilitate the leavening process during baking. Evenly creamed butter and sugar will have a pale color and a light and smooth texture.

3. Blend the whole eggs and yolks into the creamed mixture.

4. Beat the egg whites until soft peaks form and then stream in the sugar gradually with the mixer running on medium speed. Beat the egg whites until medium peaks form.

Beaten egg whites add significant additional leavening power to the final product. The point to which they are beaten is important; if whites are beaten to stiff rather than medium peaks, the additional agitation they receive during folding will cause them to be overbeaten. Overbeaten egg whites are less elastic and harder to incorporate, will break down more easily, will not develop a stable internal structure, and will have less leavening power.

5. To incorporate the egg whites into the creamed mixture while keeping as much volume as possible, first add about one-third of the beaten egg whites, blending them in gently but thoroughly, to lighten the creamed mixture. After that, the batter will accept the remaining egg whites more easily and with less vigorous mixing, allowing for less loss of volume.

Gentle folding prevents the whites from being overworked and aids in preserving the volume created by the air pockets in both the existing meringue as well as in the creamed mixture.

6. Gently fold in the remaining egg whites just until evenly blended.

7. Fold in the sifted dry ingredients and any garnishes quickly but gently. The dry ingredients are added last because if they were added to the creamed mixture before the meringue, the batter would be much too stiff to accept the light, airy meringue.

8. Immediately after mixing, scale the batter evenly into each prepared pan and bake.

For the combination method, beaten whites are folded into a creamed batter to add structure and leavening.

chiffon mixing method

The chiffon mixing method is simple to execute and produces a beautiful cake with a tender, moist crumb with ample structure and stability, making it a good choice for building tiered cakes. All advance preparation (pan preparation, etc.) is important for chiffon cakes, as it is for other foamed cakes (for more information on advance preparation for foamed cakes, see page 244); however, it is less critical here, as batters made by the chiffon mixing method are more stable than batters in which beaten (foamed) egg whites are used.

To make a chiffon cake, sift together the dry ingredients and mix in a portion of the sugar. Blend all the wet ingredients together except for the egg whites. Next, blend the wet ingredients into the sifted dry ingredients. Beat the egg whites until soft peaks form, then stream in the remaining sugar gradually with the mixer running on medium speed. Continue beating the egg whites until medium peaks form.

Finally, fold the meringue into the batter. To do this, first lighten the batter by incorporating approximately one-third of the egg whites. Then gently fold in the remaining two-thirds of the beaten egg whites.

CLOCKWISE FROM LEFT: Pumpkin Quick Bread (page 253), Morning Glory Muffins (page 617), Cranberry Orange Muffins (page 615), and Raisin Cream Scones (page 251)

Ginger cake

MAKES 35 CAKES (2 OZ/57 G EACH)

Butter	8 oz	227 g
Dark brown sugar	7 oz	198 g
Light corn syrup	10½ oz	298 g
Molasses, unsulfured	10½ oz	298 g
Ginger, finely minced	1 tbsp	15 g
Ground cinnamon	1½ tsp	3 g
Baking soda	1 tbsp	9 g
Milk	13 fl oz	390 mL
Eggs	6 oz	170 g
All-purpose flour, sifted	1 lb	454 g

1 Lightly butter and dust with flour 35 baking pans (3 in/8 cm in diameter, 1½ in/4 cm high).

2 Melt the butter, add the brown sugar, corn syrup, molasses, ginger, and cinnamon, and blend well. Remove from the heat.

3 Blend the baking soda with the milk, add the eggs, and add to the sugar mixture.

4 Add the sifted flour and blend well. Pour 2 oz/57 g of the batter into each prepared pan.

5 Bake at 375°F/191°C for 30 to 40 minutes, or until a skewer inserted in the center of a cake comes out clean. Be careful not to overbake; the cake should be very moist yet baked through.

6 Cool completely in the pans on racks.

Cream scones

MAKES 40 SCONES (APPROXIMATELY 1¾ OZ/50 G EACH)

Pastry flour	1 lb 10 oz	737 g
Salt	2 tsp	2 g
Baking powder	1 oz	28 g
Sugar	3 oz	85 g
Butter, cubed, cold	12 oz	340 g
Eggs	2 oz	57 g
Egg yolks	2 oz	57 g
Heavy cream	15 fl oz	450 mL
Garnish (see Variations; optional)	12 oz	340 g
Egg wash (page 892)	as needed	as needed

1   Line a sheet pan with parchment paper.

2   Sift together the flour, salt, baking powder, and sugar.

3   Add the butter to the dry ingredients, mixing on low speed with the paddle attachment to incorporate.

4   Combine the eggs, yolks, and heavy cream.

5   Add the egg mixture to the sifted dry ingredients and butter all at once, mix to incorporate, then add the garnish, if using. Do not overmix.

6   Place the dough on the prepared sheet pan, and pat or roll it until it is approximately 1 in/3 cm thick. Chill in the refrigerator until firm, at least 1 hour.

7   Cut the dough into the desired shape, brush with egg wash, let rest for 5 minutes, and brush with egg wash again.

8   Bake at 400°F/204°C until golden brown, 15 to 18 minutes.

9   Cool the scones on the sheet pan for a few minutes, then transfer them to racks to cool completely.

VARIATIONS   Garnishes may include currants, raisins, dried cherries or cranberries, chocolate chunks, nuts, and savory items.

Buttermilk biscuits

MAKES 40 BISCUITS (1½ OZ/43 G EACH)

All-purpose flour	3 lb	1.36 g
Sugar	4 oz	113 g
Baking powder	3 oz	85 g
Salt	¾ oz	21 g
Butter, cubed, cold	1 lb	454 g
Eggs	8 oz	227 g
Buttermilk	24 fl oz	720 mL
Egg wash (page 892)	as needed	as needed

1   Line a sheet pan with parchment paper.

2   Sift together the flour, sugar, baking powder, and salt.

3   Add the butter and rub together until the mixture has the appearance of a coarse meal.

4   Combine the eggs and buttermilk. Add to the flour mixture, kneading gently until the ingredients hold together.

5   Roll out the dough on a lightly floured work surface to a thickness of 1 in/3 cm and cut out the biscuits using a 2-in/5-cm cutter.

6   Place the biscuits on the prepared pan and lightly brush with egg wash.

7   Bake at 425°F/218°C until golden brown, about 15 minutes.

8   Transfer the biscuits to racks and cool completely.

Pumpkin quick bread

MAKES 10 LOAVES (1 LB 14 OZ/851 G EACH)

Raisins	2 lb 4 oz	1.02 kg
Water	28 fl oz	840 mL
Bread flour	3 lb	1.36 kg
Pastry flour	8 oz	227 g
Baking powder	1¼ oz	35 g
Pumpkin purée	3 lb 5 oz	1.5 kg
Sugar	4 lb 8 oz	2.04 kg
Eggs	1 lb 8 oz	680 g
Baking soda	¾ oz	21 g
Salt	1 oz	28 g
Ground cloves	¼ tsp	1.25 mL
Ground nutmeg	¼ oz	7 g
Ground cinnamon	¼ oz	7 g
Vegetable oil	1 lb 8 oz	680 g

1   Soak the raisins in the water overnight, or until thoroughly plumped.

2   Coat the loaf pans with a light film of fat.

3   Sift together the flours and baking powder.

4   Combine the pumpkin purée, sugar, eggs, baking soda, salt, and spices and mix on medium speed with the paddle attachment for 8 minutes.

5   Gradually add the oil, scraping the bowl often.

6   Add the sifted dry ingredients all at once, mix to incorporate, and then add the raisins and water.

7   Scale 1 lb 14 oz/851 g dough into each prepared loaf pan.

8   Bake at 350°F/177°C until the bread springs back when pressed and a tester inserted near the center comes out clean, 45 to 60 minutes.

9   Cool the loaves in the pans for a few minutes, then unmold onto racks and cool completely.

NOTE   Muffins made from this batter should be baked at 425° to 450°F/218° to 232°C for best results.

Banana bread

MAKES 6 LOAVES (1 LB 14 OZ/851 G EACH)

All-purpose flour	2 lb 13 oz	1.28 kg
Baking powder	2½ tsp	7.50 g
Baking soda	¾ oz	21 g
Salt	1½ tsp	7.50 g
Bananas, very ripe, unpeeled	4 lb 4 oz	1.93 kg
Lemon juice	1 tbsp	15 mL
Sugar	2 lb 13 oz	1.28 kg
Eggs	12 oz	340 g
Vegetable oil	14 fl oz	420 mL
Pecans, coarsely chopped	8 oz	227 g

1   Coat the loaf pans with a light film of fat.

2   Sift together the flour, baking powder, baking soda, and salt.

3   Peel and purée the bananas with the lemon juice.

4   Combine the banana purée, sugar, eggs, and oil and mix on medium speed with the paddle attachment until blended. Scrape down the bowl as needed.

5   Add the sifted dry ingredients and mix until just combined. Scrape down the bowl as needed. Mix in the pecans.

6   Scale 1 lb 14 oz/851 g batter into each prepared pan. Gently tap the filled pans to burst any large air bubbles.

7   Bake at 350°F/177°C until the bread springs back when pressed and a tester inserted near the center comes out clean, about 55 minutes.

8   Cool the loaves in the pans for a few minutes, then unmold onto racks and cool completely.

Zucchini quick bread

MAKES 9 LOAVES (1 LB 14 OZ/851 G EACH)

Bread flour	3 lb	1.36 kg
Pastry flour	8 oz	227 g
Baking powder	1¼ oz	35 g
Baking soda	¾ oz	21 g
Salt	1 oz	28 g
Ground cloves	¼ oz	7 g
Ground cinnamon	¼ oz	7 g
Sugar	4 lb 8 oz	2.04 kg
Eggs	1 lb 8 oz	680 g
Vegetable oil	1 lb 8 oz	680 g
Zucchini, grated	5 lb	2.27 kg
Pecans, coarsely chopped	1 lb	454 g

1   Coat the loaf pans with a light film of fat.

2   Sift together the flours, baking powder, baking soda, salt, and spices.

3   Combine the sugar, eggs, and oil and mix on medium speed with the paddle attachment until blended. Scrape down the bowl as needed.

4   Add the sifted dry ingredients and mix until just combined.

5   Blend the zucchini and pecans into the batter.

6   Scale 1 lb 14 oz/851 g batter into each prepared loaf pan. Gently tap the filled pans to burst any air bubbles.

7   Bake at 350°F/177°C until the bread springs back when pressed and a tester inserted near the center comes out clean, about 55 minutes.

8   Cool the loaves in the pans for a few minutes, then unmold onto racks and cool completely.

NOTE   Muffins made with this batter should be baked at 400°F/204°C for best results.

Old-fashioned pound cake

MAKES 4 CAKES (1 LB 10 OZ/737 G EACH)

Salt	¼ oz	7 g
Cake flour	1 lb 8 oz	680 g
Cornstarch	5 oz	142 g
Baking powder	¾ oz	21 g
Butter, soft	1 lb 4 oz	567 g
Sugar	1 lb 8 oz	680 g
Lemon zest, grated	1 oz	28 g
Eggs, room temperature	2 lb	907 g

1   Coat the loaf pans with a light film of fat and line with parchment paper.

2   Sift together the salt, cake flour, cornstarch, and baking powder.

3   Cream together the butter and sugar with the whip attachment, starting on low speed and increasing to medium speed, for 5 minutes.

4   Combine the lemon zest with the eggs and add alternately with the flour in 3 stages on low speed.

LEFT: The two batters are gently and only slightly combined to create marbling.
RIGHT: The marbling effect is revealed throughout after baking.

5 Scale 1 lb 10 oz/737 g batter into each pan. Bake in a 375°F/191°C oven until the cake springs back when pressed and a tester inserted near the center comes out clean, 45 to 50 minutes. Cool slightly in the pans. Unmold and cool completely on racks.

VARIATIONS **LEMON POUND CAKE** Add the grated zest and juice of 3 lemons to the butter and sugar before creaming them together. Scale and bake as directed above.

MARBLE POUND CAKE Add 12 oz/340 g melted and cooled bittersweet chocolate: After blending the batter, transfer one-third of the batter to a separate bowl and add the melted chocolate, folding it in thoroughly using a rubber spatula. Gently pour the chocolate batter into the plain batter. Using the handle of a wooden spoon, gently swirl the batters together with 3 or 4 strokes. Do not overblend. Scale and bake as directed above.

Sour cream streusel pound cake

MAKES 8 CAKES (1 LB 9 OZ/709 G EACH)

FILLING		
Dark brown sugar	1 lb 8 oz	680 g
Walnuts, finely chopped	8 oz	227 g
Chocolate chips	8 oz	227 g
Ground cinnamon	¼ oz	7 g
Cocoa powder	¼ oz	7 g
CAKE BATTER		
Salt	½ oz	14 g
Cake flour	3 lb	1.36 kg
Baking powder	¾ oz	21 g
Baking soda	¼ oz	7 g
Butter, soft	2 lb	907 g
Sugar	2 lb	907 g
Eggs, room temperature	2 lb	907 g
Vanilla extract	1 tsp	5 mL
Sour cream	2 lb	907 g

1 Coat the loaf pans with a light film of fat.

2 To prepare the filling, combine all the filling ingredients and mix on medium speed with the whip attachment until smooth, about 5 minutes.

3 To prepare the cake batter, sift together the salt, flour, baking powder, and baking soda.

4 Cream together the butter and sugar with the paddle attachment, starting on low speed and increasing to medium speed, until smooth, about 5 minutes.

5 Combine the eggs, vanilla, and sour cream.

6 Add the egg mixture alternately with the flour mixture in 3 stages on low speed.

7 Scale 11 oz/312 g batter into each prepared pan.

8 Add 2½ oz/71 g of the filling and cover with 11 oz/312 g of batter.

9 Add 2½ oz/71 g of the filling on top. Lightly stir the filling into the pound cake with a knife (as you would do for marble pound cake).

10 Bake at 380°F/193°C until firm to the touch, 40 minutes. Allow to cool slightly in the pans. Unmold and cool completely on racks.

FROM LEFT: **Rum Cake (opposite), Gugelhopf (page 192), and Old-Fashioned Pound Cake (page 256)**

Rum cake

MAKES 6 BUNDT CAKES (9 IN/23 CM EACH)

CAKE		
Cake flour	3 lb	1.36 kg
Baking powder	1½ oz	43 g
Butter, soft	2 lb	907 g
Sugar	3 lb 8 oz	1.59 kg
Salt	1 tbsp	15 g
Eggs	1 lb 6 oz	624 g
Egg yolks	1 lb 6 oz	624 g
Orange zest, grated	⅓ oz	10 g
Lemon zest, grated	⅓ oz	10 g
Milk	24 fl oz	720 mL
RUM SYRUP		
Sugar	3 lb	1.36 kg
Water	24 fl oz	720 mL
Light corn syrup	1 lb	454 g
Dark rum	12 fl oz	360 mL

1 Coat the Bundt pans with a light film of fat.

2 To prepare the cake, sift together the flour, baking powder and salt.

3 Cream together the butter and sugar with the paddle attachment starting on low speed and increasing to medium speed and scraping down the bowl as needed, until the mixture is smooth and light in color, about 5 minutes.

4 Blend the eggs, yolks, and zests and add in 3 additions, mixing until fully incorporated after each addition and scraping down the bowl as needed.

5 Add the sifted dry ingredients alternately with the milk on low speed in 3 additions, mixing until smooth and fully incorporated after each addition.

6 Scale 2 lb/907 g batter into each prepared cake pan.

7 Bake at 350°F/177°C until a skewer inserted near the center of the cake comes out clean, about 30 minutes.

8 To prepare the syrup, combine the sugar, water, and corn syrup and bring to a boil. Remove from the heat and let cool. Stir in the rum.

9 Cool the cakes in the pans for a few minutes, then invert onto racks. Brush the warm cakes with the rum syrup.

Lemon buttermilk cake

MAKES 6 BUNDT CAKES (8 IN/20 CM EACH)

Bread flour	3 lb 13 oz	1.73 kg
Baking soda	2 tsp	11 g
Salt	2 tsp	10 g
Butter, soft	2 lb	907 g
Sugar	3 lb 6 oz	1.53 kg
Eggs	1 lb 8 oz	680 g
Lemon zest, grated	1¼ oz	35 g
Buttermilk	32 fl oz	960 mL
Lemon juice	6 fl oz	180 mL

1   Coat the Bundt pans with a light film of fat.

2   Sift together the flour, baking soda, and salt.

3   Cream the butter and sugar with the paddle attachment, starting on low speed and increasing to medium speed and scraping down the bowl as needed, until the mixture is smooth and light in color, about 5 minutes.

4   Blend the eggs and lemon zest and add in 3 additions, mixing until fully incorporated after each addition and scraping down the bowl as needed.

5   Add the sifted dry ingredients alternately with the buttermilk in 3 additions, mixing on low speed until just incorporated. Add the lemon juice and blend.

6   Scale 2 lb 6 oz/1.08 kg batter into each prepared pan.

7   Bake at 350°F/177°C until the cakes spring back when lightly touched and a skewer inserted near the center comes out clean, about 60 minutes.

8   Cool the cakes in the pans for a few minutes, then unmold onto racks to cool completely.

Polenta cake

MAKES 6 CAKES (8 IN/20 CM EACH)

All-purpose flour	1 lb 5 oz	595 g
Baking powder	1 oz	28 g
Salt	¾ oz	21 g
Butter, soft	2 lb 13 oz	1.28 kg
Sugar	3 lb 3 oz	1.45 kg
Eggs	2 lb 4 oz	1.02 kg
Egg yolks	2 lb 4 oz	1.02 kg
Vanilla extract	1 tbsp	15 mL
Cornmeal	1 lb 5 oz	595 g

1 Coat the pans with a light film of fat and line them with parchment circles.

2 Sift together the flour, baking powder, and salt.

3 Cream together the butter and sugar with the paddle attachment, starting on low speed and increasing to medium speed and scraping down the bowl as needed, until the mixture is smooth and light in color, about 5 minutes.

4 Whisk together the eggs, egg yolks, and vanilla. Gradually add to the butter mixture, mixing on low speed and scraping down the bowl periodically, until evenly blended.

5 Turn off the mixer and add all of the sifted dry ingredients and the cornmeal at once, mixing on low speed until evenly moistened.

6 Scale 1 lb 14 oz/851 g batter into each prepared pan. Gently tap the pans to release any large air bubbles.

7 Bake at 350°F/177°C until a skewer inserted near the center of a cake comes out clean, 50 to 60 minutes.

8 Cool the cakes in the pans for a few minutes, then unmold onto racks to cool completely.

VARIATION **ALMOND POLENTA CAKE** Substitute almond extract for the vanilla extract.

Marjolaine

MAKES 2 FULL SHEET PANS (16 BY 24 IN/41 BY 61 CM EACH)

Egg whites	2 lb	907 g
Sugar	2 lb 4 oz	1.02 kg
Hazelnuts, finely ground	1 lb 6 oz	624 g
Almonds, finely ground	1 lb 6 oz	624 g
All-purpose flour	6 oz	170 g

1   Line sheet pans with parchment paper.

2   Whip the egg whites to soft peaks on medium speed with the whip attachment. Add 12 oz/340 g of sugar gradually to the egg whites and whip on high speed to maximum volume.

3   While mixing, combine the hazelnuts, almonds, flour, and the remaining 1 lb 8 oz/680 g of the sugar.

4   Fold the dry ingredients into the beaten egg whites.

5   Spread the meringue evenly on the parchment-lined sheet pans.

6   Bake at 370°F/188°C until light golden brown, about 20 minutes.

7   Immediately remove the marjolaine from the hot pans by inverting onto racks, to prevent it from drying out. Peel off the parchment and cool completely.

Christmas fruitcake

MAKES 6 LOAVES (3 LB/1.36 KG EACH)

Golden raisins	2 lb 4 oz	1.02 kg
Dark raisins	2 lb 4 oz	1.02 kg
Candied fruit, diced	4 lb 8 oz	2.04 kg
Candied cherries	12 oz	340 g
Honey	12 oz	340 g
Dry sherry	16 fl oz	480 mL
Bread flour	1 lb 8 oz	680 g
Salt	1½ oz	43 g
Ground ginger	1 tbsp	6 g
Ground cloves	2 tsp	4 g
Ground cinnamon	1 tbsp	6 g
Sugar	1 lb 3½ oz	553 g
Butter, soft	1 lb 8 oz	680 g
Eggs	1 lb 8 oz	680 g
Walnuts	12 oz	340 g

1   Combine the golden and dark raisins, candied fruit, candied cherries, honey, and dry sherry and let soak overnight, or until the raisins are fully plumped.

2   Coat the loaf pans with a light film of fat and dust with flour.

3   Sift the flour, salt, and spices together.

4   Cream together the sugar and butter with the paddle attachment, starting on low speed and increasing to medium speed and scraping down the bowl as needed, until the mixture is smooth and light in color, about 5 minutes.

5   Add the eggs gradually, a few at a time, mixing on low speed until fully incorporated and scraping down the bowl as needed.

6   Turn off the mixer and add the sifted dry ingredients all at once to the butter mixture. Mix until smooth. Fold in the walnuts and the fruit mixture.

7   Scale 3 lb/1.36 kg batter into each prepared pan.

8   Bake at 275°F/135°C until a skewer inserted near the center of the cake comes out with a few moist crumbs, 2 to 2½ hours.

9   Cool the cakes in the pans for a few minutes, then unmold onto racks to cool completely.

NOTE   The cakes may be finished with a coating of Apricot Glaze (page 426) or a dusting of confectioners' sugar after it has cooled completely.

High-ratio white cake

MAKES 6 CAKES (8 IN/20 CM EACH)

Sugar	2 lb 10 oz	1.19 kg
Cake flour	2 lb 8 oz	1.13 kg
Baking powder	1½ oz	43 g
Salt	1 oz	28 g
Milk	18 fl oz	540 mL
Eggs	10½ oz	298 g
Egg whites	13½ oz	383 g
Vanilla extract	1½ fl oz	45 mL
Butter, soft	1 lb 8 oz	680 g

1   Coat the pans with a light film of fat and line them with parchment circles.

2   Sift together the sugar, flour, baking powder, and salt.

3   Combine the milk, eggs, egg whites, and vanilla.

4   Blend the butter with the dry ingredients and half of the milk mixture. Mix on medium speed with the paddle attachment, scraping down the bowl periodically, until smooth, 4 minutes.

5   Add the remaining milk mixture in 3 additions, mixing for 2 minutes after each addition.

6   Scale 1 lb 8 oz/680 g batter into each prepared pan.

7   Bake at 350°F/177°C until the cake springs back when lightly touched in the center, about 35 minutes.

8   Cool the cakes in the pans for a few minutes, then unmold onto racks to cool completely.

VARIATION   **HIGH-RATIO YELLOW CAKE** Increase the quantity of whole eggs to 13½ oz/383 g and substitute 10½ oz/298 g egg yolks for the egg whites. Follow the method above.

High-ratio chocolate cake

MAKES 6 CAKES (8 IN/20 CM EACH)

Sugar	2 lb 2½ oz	978 g
Cake flour	13½ oz	383 g
Cocoa powder, sifted	7½ oz	213 g
Baking powder	1½ oz	43 g
Baking soda	1½ oz	43 g
Salt	1½ tsp	7.50 g
Milk	18 fl oz	540 mL
Eggs	1 lb 6½ oz	638 g
Light corn syrup	6 oz	170 g
Vanilla extract	1½ fl oz	45 mL
Butter, soft	1 lb 6½ oz	638 g

1   Coat the pans with a light film of fat and line them with parchment circles.

2   Sift together the sugar, flour, cocoa powder, baking powder, baking soda, and salt.

3   Combine the milk, eggs, corn syrup, and vanilla.

4   Blend the butter with the dry ingredients and half of the milk mixture. Mix with the paddle attachment, starting on low speed and increasing to medium speed and scraping down the bowl periodically, until smooth, 4 minutes.

5   Add the remaining milk mixture in 3 additions, mixing for 2 minutes after each addition.

6   Scale 1 lb 8 oz/680 g batter into each prepared pan.

7   Bake at 350°F/177°C until the cake springs back when lightly touched in the center, about 35 minutes.

8   Cool the cakes in the pans for a few minutes, then unmold onto racks to cool completely.

Devil's food cake

MAKES 6 CAKES (8 IN/20 CM EACH)

Sugar	3 lb 13 oz	1.72 kg
Cake flour	2 lb 5 oz	1.05 kg
Baking soda	1¼ oz	35 g
Baking powder	2½ tsp	7.50 g
Eggs	1 lb 8 oz	680 g
Butter, melted and kept warm	1 lb 9 oz	709 g
Water, warm	50 fl oz	1.50 L
Vanilla extract	1 fl oz	30 mL
Cocoa powder, sifted	15 oz	425 g

1   Coat the pans with a light film of fat and line them with parchment circles.

2   Sift together the sugar, flour, baking soda, and baking powder.

3   Combine the eggs, butter, water, and vanilla and mix with the paddle attachment. Blend in the sifted dry ingredients, scraping down the bowl periodically, until a smooth batter forms. Add the cocoa powder and mix until evenly blended.

4   Scale 2 lb 3 oz/992 g batter into each prepared pan.

5   Bake at 350°F/177°C until a skewer inserted near the center of a cake comes out clean, about 45 minutes.

6   Cool the cakes in the pans for a few minutes, then unmold onto racks to cool completely.

Angel food cake

MAKES 5 TUBE CAKES (8 IN/20 CM EACH)

Sugar	2 lb 8 oz	1.13 kg
Cream of tartar	½ oz	14 g
Cake flour	15½ oz	439 g
Salt	1½ tsp	7.50 g
Egg whites	2 lb 8 oz	1.13 kg
Vanilla extract	1 tbsp	15 mL

1   Sprinkle the insides of the tube pans lightly with water.

2   Combine 1 lb 4 oz/567 g of the sugar with the cream of tartar. Sift together the remaining 1 lb 4 oz/567 g sugar with the flour and salt.

3   Whip the egg whites and vanilla to soft peaks on medium speed wtih the whip attachment.

4   Gradually add the sugar and cream of tartar mixture to the egg whites, whipping on high speed to maximum volume.

5   Gently fold the sifted sugar and flour mixture into the egg whites until just incorporated.

6   Scale 15 oz/425 g batter into each prepared tube pan.

7   Bake at 350°F/177°C oven until the cake springs back when lightly touched, about 35 minutes.

8   Invert each tube pan onto a funnel or long-necked bottle on a rack to cool. Alternatively, for each cake, invert a small ramekin on top of a rack and prop the cake pan upside down and at an angle on the ramekin. Let the cakes cool completely upside down.

9   Carefully run a palette knife around the sides of each pan and around the center tube to release the cake. Shake the pan gently to invert the cake onto the rack.

Vanilla sponge

MAKES 4 CAKES (8 IN/20 CM EACH)

Butter, melted	9 oz	255 g
Vanilla extract	1 fl oz	30 mL
Eggs	1 lb 11 oz	765 g
Egg yolks	9 oz	255 g
Sugar	1 lb 11 oz	765 g
All-purpose flour, sifted	1 lb 11 oz	765 g

1   Coat the cake pans with a light film of fat and line them with parchment circles.

2   Blend the butter with the vanilla.

3   Combine the eggs, egg yolks, and sugar in a mixer bowl. Set over a pan of barely simmering water and whisk constantly until the sugar dissolves and the mixture reaches 110°F/43°C.

4   Transfer to the mixer and whip on high speed with the whip attachment until the foam reaches maximum volume. Reduce the speed of the mixer to medium and mix for 15 minutes to stabilize the mixture.

5   Fold in the flour. Temper the butter mixture with a small portion of the batter and fold into the larger portion of batter.

6   Scale 1 lb/454 g batter into each prepared cake pan, filling the pans two-thirds full.

7   Bake at 350°F/177°C until the tops of the cakes spring back when lightly touched, about 30 minutes.

8   Cool the cakes in the pans for a few minutes, then unmold onto a sheet pan lined with parchment paper that is dusted with confectioners' sugar to cool completely.

VARIATION   **CHOCOLATE SPONGE** Replace 4 oz/113 g of the flour with Dutch-process cocoa powder. Sift the cocoa powder together with the flour. Follow the remaining method as stated above.

Flourless chocolate cake

MAKES 6 CAKES (9 IN/23 CM EACH)

Eggs	3 lb	1.36 kg
Egg yolks	1 lb 2 oz	510 g
Granulated sugar	1 lb 6 oz	624 g
Semisweet chocolate, melted and kept warm	3 lb 12 oz	1.7 kg
Salt	½ oz	14 g
Vanilla extract	1 fl oz	30 mL
Heavy cream, chilled	64 fl oz	1.92 L
Confectioners' sugar	as needed	as needed

1   Lightly butter the cake pans and line them with parchment circles.

2   Combine the eggs, egg yolks, and sugar in a mixer bowl and whisk over a double boiler until the sugar dissolves and the mixture reaches 110°F/43°C.

3   Transfer to the mixer and whip on high speed with the whip attachment until the foam reaches maximum volume. Reduce the speed of the mixer to medium and mix for 15 minutes to stabilize the mixture.

4   Fold the chocolate, salt, and vanilla into the egg mixture and whip with the whip attachment on medium speed until the mixture cools.

5   Meanwhile, in a separate bowl, whip the heavy cream to medium peaks.

6   Using a rubber spatula, fold the whipped cream into the chocolate mixture in 2 additions.

7   Scale 2 lb/907 g batter into each prepared pan.

8   Bake in a water bath at 400°F/204°C until the cakes are firm to the touch in the center and have formed a crust, about 25 minutes.

9   Let the cakes cool completely in the pans. Unmold and dust with confectioners' sugar before serving.

Chocolate XS

MAKES 6 CAKES (8 IN/20 CM EACH)

Butter, soft	as needed	as needed
Water	24 fl oz	720 mL
Sugar	2 lb 11½ oz	1.23 kg
Semisweet chocolate, chopped	1 lb 13 oz	822 g
Bittersweet chocolate, chopped	2 lb 2 oz	964 g
Butter, melted	2 lb 11 oz	1.22 kg
Eggs	3 lb 10 oz	1.64 kg
Vanilla extract	1 fl oz	30 mL

1 Brush the insides of the cake pans with the softened butter and line them with parchment circles.

2 Combine the water and 1 lb 13 oz/822 g of the sugar in a heavy-bottomed saucepan and bring to a boil. Remove from the heat and add the chocolates; stir until the chocolate is melted. Stir in the melted butter. Let cool to room temperature.

3 Whip the eggs with the remaining 14½ oz/411 g sugar and the vanilla on high speed with the whip attachment to maximum volume.

4 Gently fold the melted chocolate mixture into the egg mixture.

5 Scale 2 lb 5 oz/1.05 kg batter into each prepared pan.

6 Bake in a water bath at 350°F/177°C until the tops of the cakes feel firm, about 1 hour.

7 Cool, then wrap in plastic wrap and refrigerate overnight, or until completely chilled in the pans, before unmolding.

Carrot cake

MAKES 6 CAKES (8 IN/20 CM EACH)

Sugar	4 lb 4 oz	1.93 kg
Salt	1¼ oz	35 g
Bread flour	2 lb 2 oz	964 g
Ground cinnamon	1¼ oz	35 g
Baking powder	½ oz	14 g
Baking soda	1¼ tsp	8 g
Eggs	2 lb 6 oz	1.08 kg
Vegetable oil	30 fl oz	900 mL
Carrots, grated	2 lb 8 oz	1.13 kg
Walnuts, chopped	12 oz	340 g

1   Coat the pans with a light film of fat and line them with parchment circles.

2   Combine the sugar and salt. Sift together the flour, cinnamon, baking powder, and baking soda.

3   Whip the eggs on medium speed with the whip attachment until thick, about 8 minutes. Increase the mixer speed to high and continue whipping until the eggs thicken to the ribbon stage, about 8 minutes.

4   Gradually add the oil, whipping on high speed until evenly blended.

5   Gradually add the sugar mixture, whipping at medium speed. Add the sifted flour mixture, mixing on low speed until just incorporated.

6   Fold in the grated carrots and chopped walnuts.

7   Scale 1 lb 3 oz/539 g batter into each prepared pan.

8   Bake at 350°F/177°C until a skewer inserted near the center of the cake comes out clean, about 50 minutes.

9   Cool the cakes in the pans for a few minutes, then unmold onto racks to cool completely.

Pumpkin cake

MAKES 6 CAKES (8 IN/20 CM EACH)

Eggs	12 each	12 each
Sugar	4½ oz	128 g
Vegetable oil	4 oz	113 g
Pumpkin purée	5 oz	142 g
Baking soda	1 oz	28 g
All-purpose flour	8 oz	227 g
Ground allspice	¼ tsp	0.50 g
Ground cinnamon	1 tsp	2 g
Ground nutmeg	¼ tsp	0.50 g

1   Coat the loaf pans with a light film of fat and line them with parchment paper.

2   Combine the eggs and sugar and blend on medium speed with the paddle attachment. Slowly add the oil and mix on until incorporated. Add the pumpkin purée and mix until incorporated.

3   Sift together the baking soda, flour, allspice, cinnamon, and nutmeg. Add to the egg mixture and mix just until combined.

4   Scale 3 lb 12 oz/1.70 kg of batter into each prepared pan.

5   Bake in a 300°F/149°C convection oven until the center springs back when lightly touched and the surface is a light golden brown, 20 to 30 minutes. Cool in the pan for a few minutes, then unmold onto racks to cool completely.

Roulade

MAKES 1 FULL SHEET PAN (17¾ BY 25¾ IN/45 BY 66 CM)

Egg yolks	1 lb	454 g
Sugar	6 oz	170 g
Vanilla extract	1 tbsp	15 mL
Egg whites	8 oz	227 g
Bread flour, sifted	6 oz	170 g

1 Line a sheet pan with parchment paper.

2 Whip together the egg yolks, 2 oz/57 g of the sugar, and the vanilla on high speed with the whip attachment until thick and light in color, about 5 minutes.

3 Whip the egg whites on medium speed with a clean whip attachment until frothy. Gradually add the remaining 4 oz/113 g sugar while continuing to whip, then whip until medium peaks form.

4 Gently blend one-third of the beaten egg whites into the egg yolk mixture to lighten it to a similar consistency as the beaten egg whites. Gently and quickly fold in the remaining egg whites.

5 Gradually fold in the sifted flour.

6 Spread the batter in the prepared sheet pan.

7 Bake at 400°F/204°C until the cake springs back when touched, 7 to 10 minutes.

8 Immediately unmold the cake onto a clean sheet pan. Cool completely.

Spread the batter for a roulade sponge evenly.

Chocolate roulade

MAKES 2 FULL SHEET PANS (17¾ BY 25¾ IN/45 BY 66 CM)

Cake flour	4 oz	113 g
Cocoa powder	4 oz	113 g
Egg yolks	1 lb	454 g
Sugar	8 oz	227 g
Vanilla extract	2 tsp	10 mL
Egg whites	1 lb	454 g
Sugar	8 oz	227 g

1 Line the sheet pans with parchment paper.

2 Sift together the flour and cocoa powder.

3 Whip together the egg yolks, 2½ oz/71 g of the sugar, and the vanilla on high speed with the whip attachment until thick and light in color, about 5 minutes.

4 Whip the egg whites on medium speed with a clean whip attachment until frothy. Gradually add the remaining 5½ oz/156 g sugar while continuing to whip, then whip until medium peaks form.

5 Gently blend one-third of the beaten egg whites into the egg yolk mixture to lighten it to a similar consistency as the beaten egg whites. Gently and quickly fold in the remaining egg whites.

6 Gradually fold in the sifted ingredients.

7 Spread the batter in the prepared sheet pans.

8 Bake at 400°F/204°C until the cake springs back when touched, 7 to 10 minutes.

9 Immediately unmold each cake onto a clean sheet pan. Cool completely.

Chocolate soufflé cake

MAKES 6 CAKES (9 IN/23 CM EACH)

Bittersweet chocolate, finely chopped	5 lb 7 oz	2.47 kg
Butter	2 lb 7 oz	1.11 kg
Vanilla extract	1 fl oz	30 mL
Salt	½ oz	14 g
Egg yolks	3 lb 6 oz	1.53 kg
Eggs	12 oz	340 g
Sugar	1 lb 14 oz	851 g
Grand Marnier	12 fl oz	360 mL
Egg whites	3 lb 6 oz	1.53 kg

1   Line the bottoms of the cake pans with buttered parchment paper. Line the sides of the cake pans with buttered parchment strips that extend 3 in/8 cm above the top of each pan to form a collar.

2   Melt the chocolate and butter together in a double boiler, whisking gently to blend. Cool completely. Stir in the vanilla and salt.

3   Whip the egg yolks, eggs, and 10 oz/284 g of the sugar on high speed with the whip attachment until light, scraping down the bowl as needed, about 5 minutes.

4   Add the Grand Marnier and whip until incorporated.

5   In a separate bowl, whip the egg whites on medium speed with a clean whip attachment until frothy. Gradually add the remaining 20 oz/507 g sugar and continue to whip until medium peaks form.

6   Fold one-third of the beaten egg whites into the yolk mixture to lighten it to a similar consistency as the beaten egg whites. Fold in the chocolate mixture, then fold in the remaining egg whites.

7   Pour the batter into the prepared pans.

8   Bake at 375°F/191°C until set, about 35 minutes.

9   Cool the cakes in the pans completely before unmolding.

Dobos sponge

MAKES 48 LAYERS (8 IN/20 CM EACH)

Egg yolks	2 lb 8 oz	1.13 kg
Sugar	2 lb	907 g
Vanilla extract	1 tbsp	15 mL
Egg whites	3 lb 8 oz	1.59 kg
Cake flour, sifted	2 lb	907 g
Butter, melted	10 oz	284 g

1   Draw forty-eight 8-in/20-cm circles on sheets of parchment, using a cake circle or pan as a guide. Place the parchment with the ink or pencil side down so it does not come in contact with the batter.

2   Beat the egg yolks, 10½ oz/298 g of the sugar, and the vanilla on high speed with the whip attachment until pale and thick, about 5 minutes.

3   Whip the egg whites on medium speed with a clean whip attachment until soft peaks form. Gradually add the remaining 2½ oz/610 g sugar while continuing to whip, then whip until medium peaks form.

4   Fold one-third of the beaten egg whites into the yolk mixture to lighten it to a similar consistency as the beaten egg whites. Gently and quickly fold in the remaining egg whites.

5   Fold in the sifted flour.

6   Fold in the melted butter.

7   Using an offset spatula, spread 3½ oz/99 g batter evenly inside each of the traced circles.

8   Bake at 425°F/218°C until light golden brown, 5 to 7 minutes.

9   Immediately transfer the sponge circles to cooling racks. Cool completely.

Hazelnut sponge cake

MAKES 6 CAKES (8 IN/20 CM EACH)

Cake flour	11 oz	312 g
Bread flour	4 oz	113 g
Ground cinnamon	1 tsp	2 g
Hazelnuts, toasted and finely ground	11 oz	312 g
Egg yolks	1 lb 14 oz	851 g
Confectioners' sugar, sifted	9 oz	255 g
Vanilla extract	2 tsp	10 mL
Lemon zest, grated	1 tbsp	9 g
Salt	½ oz	14 g
Egg whites	1 lb 14 oz	851 g
Granulated sugar	9 oz	255 g

1   Coat the cake pans with a light film of fat and line them with parchment circles.

2   Sift together the cake flour, bread flour, and cinnamon. Combine the hazelnuts with the sifted dry ingredients.

3   Whip together the egg yolks, confectioners' sugar, vanilla, lemon zest, and salt on high speed with the whip attachment until thick and light in color, about 5 minutes.

4   Whip the egg whites on medium speed with a clean whip attachment until soft peaks form. Gradually add the granulated sugar while continuing to whip until medium peaks form.

5   Gently blend one-third of the beaten egg whites into the egg yolk mixture to lighten it to a similar consistency as the beaten egg whites. Gently and quickly fold in the remaining egg whites.

6   Gradually fold in the dry ingredients.

7   Scale 1 lb/454 g batter into each prepared cake pan.

8   Bake at 350°F/177°C until the center of a cake is firm to the touch, 25 to 30 minutes.

9   Cool the cakes in the pans for a few minutes, then unmold onto racks to cool completely.

Pistachio sponge

MAKES 1 FULL SHEET PAN (17¾ BY 25¾ IN/45 BY 66 CM)

Almond paste	8 oz	227 g
Pistachio paste	2 oz	57 g
Confectioners' sugar	9 oz	255 g
Egg yolks	6 oz	170 g
Eggs	3 oz	85 g
Egg whites	10 oz	284 g
Granulated sugar	1 oz	28 g
Cake flour, sifted	7 oz	198 g
Clarified butter, melted	2 oz	57 g

1 Line a sheet pan with parchment paper.

2 Mix together the almond paste, pistachio paste, and confectioners' sugar on medium speed with the paddle attachment until well combined.

3 Whip together the egg yolks, eggs, and the nut paste and confectioners' sugar mixture on high speed with the whip attachment until thick and light in color, about 5 minutes.

4 Whip the egg whites on medium speed with a clean whip attachment until frothy. Gradually add the granulated sugar while continuing to whip, then whip until medium peaks form.

5 Gently blend one-third of the beaten egg whites into the egg yolk mixture to lighten it to a similar consistency as the beaten egg whites. Gently and quickly fold in the remaining egg whites.

6 Gradually fold in the flour.

7 Fold in the clarified butter.

8 Spread the batter in the prepared sheet pan.

9 Bake at 400°F/204°C until the cake springs back when touched, 7 to 10 minutes.

10 Immediately unmold the cake onto a clean sheet pan. Cool completely.

Madeleine sponge

MAKES 2 FULL SHEET PANS (17¾ BY 25¾ IN/45 BY 66 CM)

Butter	1 lb 4 oz	567 g
All-purpose flour	1 lb 8 oz	680 g
Confectioners' sugar	12 oz	354 g
Baking powder	¾ oz	21 g
Salt	¼ oz	7 g
Eggs	1 lb 8 oz	680 g
Milk	5 fl oz	150 mL
Invert sugar	12 oz	354 g
Vanilla extract	½ oz	14 g

1   Line the sheet pans with parchment paper.

2   Melt the butter to 105°F/41°C.

3   Sift together the flour, confectioners' sugar, baking powder, and salt.

4   Mix together the eggs, milk, invert sugar, and vanilla extract on medium speed with the paddle attachment until smooth, about 5 minutes. Add the dry ingredients and mix on low speed until just incorporated. Add the melted butter and mix until incorporated.

5   Spread 3 lb 2 oz/1.42 kg of batter into each of the prepared sheet pans.

6   Bake in a 350°F/177°C convection oven until light golden brown, 10 to 12 minutes. Immediately unmold each cake onto a clean sheet pan. Cool completely.

Havana cake

MAKES 6 CAKES (8 IN/20 CM EACH)

NUT BATTER		
Bread flour	9 oz	255 g
Hazelnuts, toasted and finely ground	1 lb 1 oz	482 g
Almond paste	15 oz	425 g
Sugar	15 oz	425 g
Butter, soft	13 oz	369 g
Salt	½ tsp	2.50 g
Vanilla extract	1 tbsp	15 mL
Eggs	1 lb 3 oz	539 g
CHOCOLATE BATTER		
Cocoa powder	5½ oz	156 g
Ground cinnamon	½ oz	14 g
Hazelnuts, toasted and finely ground	1 lb 7 oz	652 g
Salt	½ tsp	2.50 g
Egg whites	1 lb 12 oz	794 g
Sugar	1 lb 9 oz	709 g
Vanilla extract	1 tbsp	15 mL

1   Lightly butter the cake pans and line them with parchment circles.

2   To prepare the nut batter, sift the flour into a bowl. Blend in the ground hazelnuts.

3   Cream together the almond paste, sugar, butter, salt, and vanilla on medium speed with the paddle attachment, scraping down the bowl as needed, until the mixture is smooth and light in color, about 5 minutes. Blend the eggs and add in 3 additions, mixing until fully incorporated after each addition and scraping down the bowl as needed. Add the dry ingredients, mixing on low speed until just incorporated.

4   To prepare the chocolate batter, sift together the cocoa powder and cinnamon. Blend in the ground hazelnuts. Stir in the salt.

5   Whip the egg whites on medium speed with the whip attachment until soft peaks form. Gradually add the sugar while continuing to whip, then whip until stiff peaks form.

6   Fold the dry ingredients gradually into the whipped egg whites. Fold in the vanilla.

7   Spread 6¾ oz/191 g of the chocolate batter in an even layer at the bottom of each pan. Pipe 14½ oz/411 g of the nut batter through a pastry bag fitted with a large plain tip in a spiral on top of the chocolate batter, and spread into an even layer. Spread another 6¾ oz/191 g of the chocolate batter on top, and smooth the top.

8   Bake at 350°F/177°C until a skewer inserted near the center of the cake comes out clean, about 45 minutes.

9   Cool the cakes in the pans for a few minutes, then unmold onto racks to cool completely.

Flourless sponge

MAKES 3 FULL SHEET PANS (17¾ BY 25¾ IN/45 BY 66 CM)

Egg yolks	3 lb	1.36 kg
Salt	pinch	pinch
Vanilla extract	2 tsp	10 mL
Egg whites	3 lb	1.36 kg
Sugar	3 lb	1.36 kg
Dutch-process cocoa powder, sifted	15 oz	425 g

1   Line the sheet pans with parchment paper.

2   Whip together the egg yolks, salt, and vanilla on high speed with the whip attachment, until thick and light in color, about 5 minutes.

3   Whip the egg whites on medium speed with a clean whip attachment until frothy. Gradually add the sugar while continuing to whip, then whip until stiff peaks form.

4   Gently blend one-third of the beaten egg whites into the egg yolk mixture to lighten it to a similar consistency as the beaten egg whites. Gently and quickly fold in the remaining egg whites.

5   Gradually fold in the cocoa powder.

6   Spread the batter in the prepared sheet pans.

7   Bake at 400°F/204°C until the cake springs back when touched, 7 to 10 minutes.

8   Immediately unmold the cakes onto clean sheet pans. Cool completely.

Spanish vanilla cake

MAKES 6 CAKES (8 IN/20 CM EACH)

Bread flour	1 lb 14 oz	851 g
Almonds, toasted and ground	1 lb 14 oz	851 g
Chocolate shavings (page 831)	12 oz	340 g
Almond paste	2 lb 7 oz	1.11 kg
Lemon zest, grated	1 oz	28 g
Vanilla extract	3 fl oz	90 mL
Salt	1½ tsp	7.50 g
Egg yolks	1 lb 8 oz	680 g
Egg whites	2 lb 10 oz	1.19 kg
Sugar	2 lb 4 oz	1.02 kg
Butter, melted and kept warm	15 oz	425 g

1   Lightly butter the cake pans and line them with parchment circles.

2   Mix together the bread flour, toasted almonds, and chocolate shavings.

3   Cream together the almond paste, lemon zest, vanilla, and salt with the paddle attachment, starting on low speed and increasing to medium speed and scraping down the bowl as needed, until smooth, about 5 minutes.

4   Blend the egg yolks and add in 3 additions, scraping down the bowl as needed.

5   Whip the egg whites on medium speed with the whip attachment until soft peaks form. Gradually add the sugar while continuing to whip, then whip until medium-soft peaks form.

6   Gently blend one-third of the beaten egg whites into the almond paste mixture to lighten it to a similar consistency as the beaten egg whites. Gently fold in the remaining egg whites.

7   Gradually fold in the flour mixture until just incorporated. Fold in the melted butter.

8   Scale 1 lb 15 oz/879 g batter into each prepared cake pan.

9   Bake at 350°F/177°C until the center of the cake springs back when touched, 35 to 40 minutes.

10   Cool the cakes in the pans for a few minutes, then unmold onto racks to cool completely.

Chocolate almond cake

MAKES 6 CAKES (8 IN/20 CM EACH)

Bread flour	10 oz	284 g
Almonds, toasted and finely ground	1 lb 12 oz	794 g
Butter, soft	1 lb 12 oz	794 g
Confectioners' sugar	1 lb 12 oz	794 g
Egg yolks	1 lb 5 oz	595 g
Eggs	13 oz	369 g
Bittersweet chocolate, melted	2 lb 1 oz	936 g
Egg whites	1 lb 12 oz	794 g

1   Coat the cake pans with a light film of fat and line them with parchment circles.

2   Combine the flour and the almonds.

3   Cream together the butter and 1 lb 4 oz/567 g of the confectioners' sugar with the paddle attachment, starting on low speed and increasing to medium speed and scraping down the bowl as needed, until the mixture is smooth and light in color, about 5 minutes.

4   Whisk together the egg yolks and eggs and warm them over a hot water bath, whisking constantly, to 85°F/29°C. Gradually add the warm eggs to the creamed mixture, mixing on low speed and scraping down the bowl as needed, until evenly blended.

5   Add the chocolate all at once and mix, scraping down the bowl periodically, until evenly blended.

6   Whip the egg whites on medium speed with the whip attachment until soft peaks form. Gradually add the remaining 8 oz/227 g confectioners' sugar while continuing to whip, then whip until medium peaks form.

7   Fold the egg whites into the chocolate mixture. Fold in the dry ingredients.

8   Scale 2 lb 8 oz/1.13 kg batter into each prepared cake pan.

9   Bake at 375°F/191°C until the center of the cake is firm to the touch, 45 to 50 minutes.

10 Cool the cakes in the pans for a few minutes, then unmold onto racks to cool completely.

Patterned Joconde sponge

MAKES 2 FULL SHEET PANS (17¾ BY 25¾ IN/45 BY 66 CM)

STENCIL BATTER		
Butter, soft	3½ oz	99 g
Confectioners' sugar, sifted	3½ oz	99 g
Egg whites	4 oz	113 g
Cake flour, sifted	2 oz	57 g
Cocoa powder, sifted	1 oz	28 g
SPONGE BATTER		
Cake flour, sifted	3 oz	85 g
Blanched almond flour	10 oz	284 g
Eggs	12 oz	340 g
Confectioners' sugar	10 oz	284 g
Egg whites	8 oz	227 g
Granulated sugar	1 oz	28 g
Butter, melted and cooled	2 oz	57 g

1   To prepare the stencil batter, cream the butter and confectioners' sugar together in a food processor fitted with a metal chopping blade.

2   Add the egg whites gradually with the food processor running.

3   Blend in the flour and cocoa powder.

4   Place a stencil on a silicone pad or parchment paper. Spread the batter in a thin layer over the stencil, scrape the batter off, and remove the stencil, leaving behind the stenciled batter pattern. Transfer the silicone pad or parchment paper to a flat sheet pan and freeze.

5   To prepare the sponge batter, combine the cake flour with the almond flour.

6   Whip the eggs and confectioners' sugar on high speed with the whip attachment until very light, 5 to 10 minutes.

7   Whip the egg whites on medium speed with a clean whip attachment until frothy. Gradually add the granulated sugar while continuing to whip, then whip until medium peaks form.

8   Fold one-third of the beaten egg whites into the yolk mixture to lighten it to a similar consistency as the beaten egg whites. Gently but thoroughly fold in the remaining beaten egg whites.

9   Gradually fold in the flour mixture.

10   Fold in the cool melted butter. Run a wire whip through the batter several times to deflate it slightly.

11 Divide the batter evenly between the prepared pans, spreading it quickly, before the stencils melt, but gently to avoid losing volume.

12 Bake at 400°F/204°C until the cakes are a light golden brown, 5 to 7 minutes.

13 Cool the cakes in the pans for a few minutes, then unmold onto racks to cool completely.

LEFT: A stencil is used to apply the pattern to the parchment before pouring in the batter.

RIGHT: The pattern remains sharp and distinct after baking.

Coconut Joconde

MAKES 1 FULL SHEET PAN (17¾ BY 25¾ IN/45 BY 66 CM)

Pastry flour	2 oz	57 g
Desiccated coconut, ground	8 oz	227 g
Eggs	10½ oz	298 g
Confectioners' sugar	6 oz	170 g
Egg whites	6 oz	170 g
Granulated sugar	2 oz	57 g
Butter, melted	2 oz	57 g

1   Line a sheet pan with parchment paper.

2   Sift the pastry flour and toss it with the coconut.

3   Whip together the eggs and confectioners' sugar on high speed with the whip attachment until thick and light in color, about 5 minutes.

4   Whip the egg whites on medium speed with a clean whip attachment until frothy. Gradually add the granulated sugar while continuing to whip, then whip until medium-stiff peaks form.

5   Gently blend one-third of the beaten egg whites into the egg yolk mixture to lighten it to a similar consistency as the beaten egg whites. Gently and quickly fold in the remaining egg whites.

6   Gradually fold in the flour and coconut mixture.

7   Stream in the melted butter while folding the batter.

8   Spread the batter evenly in the prepared sheet pan.

9   Bake at 400°F/204°C until the cake springs back when touched, 7 to 10 minutes.

10   Immediately unmold the cake onto a clean sheet pan. Cool completely.

Chiffon sponge

MAKES 8 CAKES (8 IN/20 CM EACH)

Cake flour	3 lb 3 oz	1.45 kg
Baking powder	2¼ oz	64 g
Salt	¾ oz	21 g
Sugar	2 lb 12 oz	1.25 kg
Egg yolks	4 lb	1.81 kg
Vegetable oil	5 oz	142 g
Water, warm	48 fl oz	1.44 L
Vanilla extract	1 oz	28 g
Egg whites	4 lb	1.81 kg
Lemon juice	2 oz	57 g
Cream of tartar	¼ oz	7 g

1   Coat the cake pans with a light film of fat and line them with parchment circles.

2   Sift together the flour, baking powder, and salt. Combine with 14½ oz/411 g of the sugar in the bowl of a mixer.

3   Combine the yolks, oil, water, and vanilla.

4   Add the yolk mixture slowly to the dry ingredients on medium speed while mixing with the whip attachment. After a paste has formed, scrape down the sides of the bowl. Continue adding the yolk mixture until all is incorporated. Beat for an additional 2 minutes on medium speed.

5   Whip the egg whites on medium speed with a clean whip attachment until frothy. Gradually add the remaining 1 lb 13½ oz/838 g sugar, the lemon juice, and the cream of tartar while continuing to whip, then whip until medium peaks form.

6   Fold one-third of the beaten egg whites into the yolk mixture to lighten it to a similar consistency as the beaten egg whites. Gently but thoroughly fold in the remaining beaten egg whites.

7   Fill each pan slightly more than halfway with batter.

8   Bake at 350°F/177°C until the cake springs back when touched, 20 to 30 minutes.

9   Cool in the pans for a few minutes, then unmold onto racks to cool completely.

VARIATIONS   **LEMON CHIFFON SPONGE** Add the grated zest of 2 lemons in step 3 and substitute lemon juice for the water. Follow the remaining method as stated above.

LIME CHIFFON SPONGE Add the grated zest of 3 limes in step 3 and substitute lime juice for the water. Follow the remaining method as stated above.

ORANGE CHIFFON SPONGE Add the grated zest of 1 orange in step 3 and substitute orange juice for the water. Follow the remaining method as stated above.

Chocolate chiffon sponge

MAKES 8 CAKES (8 IN/20 CM EACH)

Cake flour	3 lb 2 oz	1.42 kg
Dutch-process cocoa powder	1 lb 4 oz	567 g
Baking powder	2½ oz	71 g
Baking soda	1¼ oz	35 g
Salt	1 oz	28 g
Sugar	1 lb 2 oz	510 g
Egg yolks	1 lb 14 oz	851 g
Vegetable oil	1 lb 8 oz	680 g
Water, warm	2 lb 12 oz	1.25 kg
Vanilla extract	1 oz	28 g
Bittersweet chocolate, melted and cooled	1 lb 4 oz	567 g
Egg whites	3 lb 2 oz	1.42 kg
Cream of tartar	½ oz	14 g

1   Coat the cake pans with a light film of fat and line them with parchment circles.

2   Sift together the flour, cocoa powder, baking powder, baking soda, and salt. Combine with 6 oz/170 g of the sugar in the mixer.

3   Combine the yolks, oil, water, vanilla, and chocolate.

4   Add the yolk mixture slowly to the dry ingredients while mixing on medium speed with the whip attachment. After a paste has formed, scrape down the sides of the bowl. Continue adding the yolk mixture until all is incorporated. Beat for an additional 2 minutes on medium speed.

5   Whip the egg whites medium speed with a clean whip attachment on until frothy. Gradually add the remaining 12 oz/340 g sugar and the cream of tartar while continuing to whip, then whip until medium peaks form.

6   Fold one-third of the beaten egg whites into the yolk mixture to lighten it to a similar consistency as the beaten egg whites. Gently but thoroughly fold in the remaining beaten egg whites.

7   Fill each pan slightly more than halfway with batter.

8   Bake at 350°F/177°C until the cake springs back when touched, 20 to 30 minutes.

9   Cool in the pan for a few minutes, then unmold onto racks to cool completely.

Lemon cake

MAKES 6 CAKES (8 IN/20 CM EACH)

All-purpose flour	2 lb 13 oz	1.28 kg
Cornstarch	12 oz	340 g
Baking powder	1 oz	28 g
Butter, soft	3 lb 10½ oz	1.66 kg
Confectioners' sugar	2 lb 13 oz	1.28 kg
Lemon zest, grated	4 oz	113 g
Egg yolks	2 lb	907 g
Egg whites	2 lb	907 g
Granulated sugar	12½ oz	354 g
LEMON SYRUP		
Lemon juice	6 fl oz	180 mL
Confectioners' sugar	2 lb	907 g

1   Coat the cake pans with a light film of fat and line them with parchment circles.

2   Sift together the flour, cornstarch, and baking powder.

3   Cream the butter, confectioners' sugar, and lemon zest with the paddle attachment, starting on low speed and increasing to medium speed and scraping down the bowl as needed, until the mixture is smooth and light in color, about 5 minutes.

4   Gradually add the egg yolks a few at a time, mixing on low speed until fully incorporated after each addition and scraping down the bowl as needed.

5   Whip the egg whites on medium speed with the whip attachment until frothy. Gradually add the granulated sugar while continuing to whip, then whip until medium peaks form.

6   Fold one-third of the beaten egg whites into the egg yolk mixture to lighten it to a similar consistency as the beaten egg whites. Gently fold in the remaining egg whites.

7   Gradually fold the sifted dry ingredients into the mixture.

8   Scale 2 lb 4 oz/1.02 kg batter into each prepared cake pan. Gently tap the pans to release any air bubbles.

9   Bake at 350°F/177°C until a skewer inserted near the center of the cake comes out clean, about 1 hour.

10   To prepare the syrup, whisk together the lemon juice and confectioners' sugar in a stainless-steel bowl until smooth.

11   Cool the cakes in the pans for a few minutes, then unmold onto racks.

12   Brush the cakes with the lemon glaze while they are still warm.

Almond apple financiers

MAKES 84 FINANCIERS (1 BY 2 IN/3 BY CM EACH)

POACHED APPLES		
Lemon juice	3 fl oz	90 mL
Water	17¾ fl oz	533 mL
Sugar	4½ oz	128 g
Apples, Golden Delicious	10½ oz	298 g
CAKE		
Almond paste	3½ oz	99 g
Sugar	3½ oz	99 g
Butter	3½ oz	99 g
Eggs, room temperature	4½ oz	128 g
Cake flour, sifted	1½ oz	43 g
Dates, ¼-in/6-mm dice	3½ oz	99 g

1   Place the flexible financier molds on a sheet pan.

2   To poach the apples, combine the lemon juice, water, and sugar in a saucepan, bring to a boil, and boil for 15 seconds or until the sugar is dissolved. Reduce the heat to a simmer.

3   Meanwhile, peel and core the apples. Cut the apples in half, then slice each half into 6 wedges.

4   Place the apples in the syrup and simmer them for 8 minutes. Remove from the heat and let the apples sit in the syrup until cool. The apples should be slightly translucent at the edges but not fully cooked.

5   Refrigerate the apples in their poaching liquid until about 1 hour before use. Strain the apples and discard the syrup. Air-dry the apples on a rack for 1 hour.

6   To make the cake, combine the almond paste and sugar in the mixer and mix on medium speed with the paddle attachment until pea-size particles form, about 5 minutes.

7   Add the butter to the almond paste mixture and cream on medium speed until smooth and light, about 7 minutes. Scrape down the bowl as needed.

8   Add the eggs in 3 additions, mixing until fully incorporated after each addition and scraping down the bowl as needed.

9   Add the sifted flour and mix on low speed until just incorporated. Do not overmix.

10   Place the batter in a pastry bag with a ½-in/1-cm hole cut at the bottom. Pipe into the flexible financier molds so they are three-quarters full.

11 Garnish each filled mold with 2 apple slices arranged in an S shape. Sprinkle diced dates on top.

12 Bake at 375°F/191°C until light golden, 18 to 20 minutes. Let cool for 15 to 20 minutes, wrap in plastic wrap, and freeze before unmolding.

13 Serve at room temperature. Store in an airtight container so the cake does not dry out.

Cheesecake

MAKES 6 CHEESECAKES (8 IN/20 CM EACH)

Graham cracker crust (page 228)	1 lb 14 oz	851 g
Cream cheese	7 lb 8 oz	3.40 kg
Sugar	2 lb 4 oz	1.02 kg
Salt	½ oz	14 g
Eggs	1 lb 14 oz	851 g
Egg yolks	3 oz	85 g
Heavy cream	15 fl oz	450 mL
Vanilla extract	1½ fl oz	45 mL

1 Lightly butter the cake pans and line them with parchment circles.

2 Press 2½ oz/71 g of the crust mixture evenly into the bottom of each pan.

3 Combine the cream cheese, sugar, and salt and mix on medium speed with the paddle attachment, occasionally scraping down the bowl, until the mixture is completely smooth, about 3 minutes.

4 Whisk the eggs and egg yolks together. Add the eggs to the cream cheese mixture in 4 additions, mixing until fully incorporated after each addition and scraping down the bowl as needed.

5 Add the heavy cream and vanilla and mix until fully incorporated.

6 Scale 2 lb 8 oz/1.13 kg batter into each prepared pan. Gently tap the pans to release any air bubbles.

7 Bake in a hot water bath at 325°F/163°C until the centers of the cakes are set, about 1 hour 15 minutes.

8 Cool the cakes completely in the pans on racks. Wrap the cakes, in the pans, in plastic wrap and refrigerate overnight to fully set.

9 To unmold, apply the gentle heat of a low open flame to the bottom and sides of each cake pan. Run a knife around the side of the pan. Place a plastic wrap–covered cake circle on top of the cake, invert, and tap the bottom of the pan to release the cake if necessary. Remove the pan, peel off the paper from the bottom of the cake, and turn onto a cake circle or serving plate.

NOTE Cheesecakes are often served plain as they come out of the oven, chilled and unmolded. However, toppings may be added after the cake is removed from the pan that reflect its flavor profile. A chocolate or marble cheesecake can be glazed with ganache, a thin layer of curd can top a lemon cheesecake, or a pumpkin cheesecake could be lightly dusted with cinnamon or confectioners' sugar. The most common topping for a cheesecake is fresh seasonal fruit.

VARIATIONS **CHOCOLATE CHEESECAKE** To 2 lb 8 oz/1.13 kg batter for each 8-in/20-cm cake, add 2½ oz/71 g sifted cocoa powder and blend well. Proceed as directed from step 6.

LEMON CHEESECAKE To 2 lb 8 oz/1.13 kg batter for each 8-in/20-cm cake, add 2 fl oz/60 mL lemon juice and the grated zest of 1 lemon and blend well. Proceed as directed from step 6.

MARBLE CHEESECAKE To 8 oz/227 g batter for each 8-in/20-cm cake, add 2 oz/57 g melted bitter-sweet chocolate. Pour the chocolate batter into 2 lb/907 g of the plain batter and gently swirl three or four times with the end of a wooden spoon. Do not overmix. Pour the marbleized batter into the prepared pan and proceed as directed from step 6.

PUMPKIN CHEESECAKE To 1 lb 7 oz/652 g batter for each 8-in/20-cm cake, add 10 oz/284 g pumpkin purée and blend well. Proceed as directed from step 6.

WHITE CHOCOLATE CHEESECAKE To 2 lb 8 oz/1.13 kg batter for each 8-in/20-cm cake, add 5 oz/142 g melted white chocolate and blend well. Proceed as directed from step 6.

LEFT: Run a knife around the sides of the cheesecake.

RIGHT: Invert the cake out of the pan onto the cardboard circle that has been tightly wrapped with plastic wrap.

Walnut cheesecake

MAKES 6 CHEESECAKES (8 IN/20 CM EACH)

Graham cracker crust (page 228)	1 lb 14 oz	851 g
Confectioners' sugar, sifted	10½ oz	298 g
Cream cheese	6 lb 10½ oz	3.02 kg
Maple syrup	1 lb 6 oz	624 g
Eggs	1 lb 6 oz	624 g
Sour cream	1 lb	454 g
Walnut praline paste (page 901)	3 lb 5½ oz	1.52 kg
Vanilla extract	1 fl oz	30 mL
White chocolate, melted and cooled	1 lb 6 oz	624 g
Dragée walnuts, roughly chopped	9 oz	255 g

1   Lightly butter the cake pans and line them with parchment circles.

2   Press 2½ oz/71 g of the crust mixture evenly into the bottom of each pan.

3   Cream the sugar, cream cheese, and maple syrup on medium speed with the paddle attachment, scraping down the bowl periodically, until smooth, fluffy, and lighter in color, about 5 minutes.

4   Gradually add the eggs and sour cream, scraping down the bowl periodically. Add the walnut praline paste and vanilla and blend thoroughly.

5   Transfer 2 lb/907 g of the cheesecake batter to another bowl and blend in the white chocolate. Blend the white chocolate mixture into the remaining cheesecake batter.

6   Scale 2 lb 8 oz/1.13 kg batter into each prepared pan. Sprinkle 1½ oz/43 g chopped dragée walnuts over each cheesecake. Gently tap the pans to release any air bubbles.

7   Bake in a hot water bath at 325°F/163°C until the centers of the cakes are set, about 1 hour 15 minutes.

8   Cool the cakes completely in the pans on racks. Wrap the cakes in the pans in plastic wrap and refrigerate overnight to fully set.

9   To unmold, apply the gentle heat of a low open flame to the bottom and sides of each cake pan. Place a plastic wrap–covered cake circle on top of the cake, invert, and tap the bottom of the pan to release the cake if necessary. Remove the pan, peel off the paper from the bottom of the cake, and turn onto a cake circle or serving plate.

Mascarpone cheesecake

MAKES 4 CHEESECAKES (10 IN/25 CM EACH)

Graham cracker crust (page 228)	15 oz	425 g
Cream cheese	3 lb	1.36 kg
Mascarpone	2 lb	907 g
Sugar	1 lb 8 oz	680 g
Eggs	1 lb 4 oz	567 g
Sour cream	1 lb	454 g
Egg yolks	10 oz	284 g
Lemon extract	1 tbsp	15 mL
Vanilla extract	1 tbsp	15 mL

1   Lightly butter the cake pans and line them with parchment circles.

2   Press 2½ oz/71 g of the crust mixture evenly into the bottom of each pan.

3   Cream the cream cheese, mascarpone, and sugar on medium speed with the paddle attachment, scraping down the bowl periodically, until smooth, fluffy, and lighter in color, about 5 minutes.

4   Gradually add the eggs, sour cream, and egg yolks, scraping down the bowl periodically. Add the lemon and vanilla extracts and blend thoroughly, about 5 minutes more.

5   Scale 2 lb 8 oz/1.13 kg batter into each prepared pan. Gently tap the pans to release any air bubbles.

6   Bake in a hot water bath in a 325°F/163°C oven until the centers of the cakes are set, about 1 hour 15 minutes.

7   Cool the cakes completely in the pans on racks. Wrap the cakes in the pans in plastic wrap and refrigerate overnight to fully set.

8   To unmold, apply the gentle heat of a low open flame to the bottom and sides of each cake pan. Place a plastic wrap–covered cake circle on top of the cake, invert, and tap the bottom of the pan to release the cake if necessary. Remove the pan, peel off the paper from the bottom of the cake, and turn onto a cake circle or serving plate.

Dacquoise

MAKES 10 TO 12 FLOWERS (3½ IN/9 CM IN DIAMETER)

Confectioners' sugar	4½ oz	128 g
Bread flour	½ oz	14 g
Almond flour	4½ oz	128 g
Egg whites	5¾ oz	163 g
Granulated sugar	½ oz	14 g
Confectioners' sugar, for dusting	as needed	as needed

1   Line a sheet pan with parchment paper. Trace twelve 3½-in/9-cm rounds on the paper and turn the paper over to avoid contact between the pen or marker and the batter.

2   Sift together the confectioners' sugar, bread flour, and almond flour.

3   Whip the egg whites on medium speed with the whip attachment until frothy. Gradually add the granulated sugar while continuing to whip, then whip until medium-stiff peaks form.

4   Gently and quickly fold the dry ingredients into the beaten egg whites.

5   Fill a pastry bag fitted with a #6 straight tip with the batter. Pipe flower petals within the traced rounds onto the parchment-lined sheet pan, meeting in the center of the circle for the beginning and end of each petal.

6   When finished piping, dust the batter with confectioners' sugar. Wait 10 minutes and dust again with confectioners' sugar.

7   Bake at 350°F/177°C until golden brown, 10 to 15 minutes.

8   Let the flowers cool on the pan for a few minutes, then remove and store in an airtight container until needed.

Coconut dacquoise

MAKES 2 FULL SHEET PANS (17¾ BY 25¾ IN/45 BY 66 CM)

Almond flour	3 oz	85 g
Cake flour	5 oz	142 g
Confectioners' sugar	1 lb 9 oz	709 g
Salt	pinch	pinch
Desiccated coconut	1 lb 4 oz	567 g
Egg whites	1 lb 14 oz	851 g
Granulated sugar	10 oz	284 g

1   Line the sheet pans with parchment paper.

2   Sift together the flours, confectioners' sugar, and salt, and combine with the coconut.

3   Whip the egg whites on medium speed with the whip attachment until frothy. Gradually add the granulated sugar while continuing to whip, then whip until medium peaks form.

4   Gently fold the dry ingredients into the beaten egg whites.

5   Spread 2 lb 13 oz/1.28 kg of batter into each of the prepared sheet pans.

6   Bake in a 350°F/177°C convection oven until the cake springs back when touched, 10 to 12 minutes. Cool completely, then remove from the pans and store in an airtight container until needed.

Almond dacquoise

MAKES 2 FULL SHEET PANS (17¾ BY 25¾ IN/45 BY 66 CM)

Almond flour	1 lb 7 oz	652 g
Cake flour	5 oz	142 g
Confectioners' sugar	1 lb 9 oz	709 g
Salt	pinch	pinch
Egg whites	1 lb 14 oz	851 g
Granulated sugar	10 oz	284 g

1   Line the sheet pans with parchment paper.

2   Sift together the flours, confectioners' sugar, and salt.

3   Whip the egg whites on medium speed with the whip attachment until frothy. Gradually add the granulated sugar while continuing to whip, then whip until medium peaks form.

4   Gently fold the dry ingredients into the beaten egg whites.

5   Spread 2 lb 13 oz/1.28 kg of batter into each of the prepared sheet pans.

6   Bake in a 350°F/177°C convection oven until the cake springs back when touched, 10 to 12 minutes. Cool completely, then remove from the pans and store in an airtight container until needed.

Soft hazelnut dacquoise

MAKES 1 HALF SHEET PAN (12⅞ BY 17¾ IN/33 BY 45 CM)

Confectioners' sugar	7 oz	198 g
Almond flour	3½ oz	99 g
Hazelnut flour	5¼ oz	149 g
Egg whites	10½ oz	298 g
Granulated sugar	2¾ oz	78 g
All-purpose flour	1½ oz	43 g

1   Line a half sheet pan with parchment paper.

2   Sift together the confectioners' sugar, almond flour, and hazelnut flour.

3   Whip the egg whites on medium speed with the whip attachment until frothy. Gradually add the granulated sugar while continuing to whip, then whip until medium-stiff peaks form.

4   Gently fold the dry ingredients into the beaten egg whites.

5   Fill a pastry bag fitted with a #4 tip with the mixture. Pipe lines of meringue the width of the prepared sheet pan.

6   Bake at 360°F/182°C until golden brown, 10 to 12 minutes. Cool completely, then remove from the pan and store in an airtight container until needed.

Dacquoise meringue

Granulated sugar	5½ oz	156 g
Egg whites	5½ oz	156 g
Confectioners' sugar	5½ oz	156 g
Almonds, toasted and ground	4½ oz	128 g
Cake flour	1 oz plus 1 teaspoon	29 g

1   Line a sheet pan with parchment paper. Trace twenty-eight 2½-in/6-cm rounds on the paper and turn the paper over to avoid contact between the pen or marker and the batter.

2   Whip together the granulated sugar and egg whites on high speed with the whip attachment until stiff peaks form, 8 to 10 minutes.

3   Sift together the confectioners' sugar, ground almonds, and cake flour. Gently fold them into the stiff egg whites with a rubber spatula until just combined.

4   Fill a pastry bag fitted with a #2 tip with the mixture. Begin piping in the center of each traced round, and in a circular motion work your way to the outside of the round.

5   Bake the meringue at 300°F/149°C for 12 to 15 minutes, until the meringue hardens. Cool completely, then remove from the pan and store in an airtight container until needed.

Savarin

MAKES 24 CAKES (3 IN/8 CM IN DIAMETER)

Bread flour	4 oz	113 g
Instant dry yeast	1 tsp	6 g
Milk, 90°F/32°C	4¼ fl oz	128 mL
Salt	pinch	pinch
Eggs	7 oz	198 g
Butter, very soft	6 oz	170 g
Cake flour	8 oz	227 g
Vanilla extract (optional)	as needed	as needed

1   Combine the bread flour and yeast on low speed and mix with the paddle attachment until well combined.

2   Add the warmed milk and salt and mix on low speed until it forms a smooth paste. Do not overmix. Cover the mixing bowl with plastic wrap and proof at 80° to 85°F/27° to 29°C for 1 hour, or until the dough has tripled in size.

3   Place the bowl back on the mixer and add the eggs while mixing on low speed until the eggs are fully incorporated.

4   Add 3 oz/85 g of the butter and mix on low speed until smooth. Add 4 oz/113 g of the cake flour and mix until smooth. Add the remaining butter and flour and mix until smooth. Do not overmix.

5   Fill a pastry bag fitted with a #6 straight tip with the batter and pipe into flexible savarin molds, filling them three-quarters full.

6   Proof for about 1 hour 15 minutes at 80° to 85°F/27° to 29°C until the dough has increased 1½ times in size.

7   Bake at 390°F/199°C until evenly golden brown, about 25 minutes.

8   Let the cakes cool in the molds to room temperature and, once cool, wrap in plastic wrap and freeze the molds overnight. Thaw for 1 hour at room temperature before serving.

Biscuit Russe

MAKES 28 BISCUITS (14 CAKES)

Ground almonds	1½ oz	43 g
Ground hazelnuts	1½ oz	43 g
Sugar	5¼ oz	149 g
Egg whites	5¼ oz	149 g
Confectioners' sugar	as needed	as needed

1   Line a sheet pan with parchment paper. Trace twenty-eight 2½-in/6-cm rounds on the paper and turn the paper over to avoid contact between the pen or marker and the batter.

2   Mix the ground almonds and hazelnuts with 1¾ oz/50 g of the sugar.

3   Place the egg whites in a bowl and whisk until frothy. Gradually add the remaining 3½ oz/99 g sugar while continuing to whip, then whip until soft, medium, or stiff peaks form, as desired. Gently fold the ground nut mixture into the beaten egg whites.

4   Fill a pastry bag fitted with a #4 tip with the batter. Begin piping in the center of each traced round, and in a circular motion work your way to the outside of the round.

5   Sprinkle confectioners' sugar over the piped biscuits, wait 10 minutes, and sprinkle them with confectioners' sugar again.

6   Bake in a 340°F/171°C convection oven until the biscuits are hard and golden brown, 10 to 12 minutes. Cool completely, then remove from the pan and store in an airtight container until needed.

chapter eleven

Cookies

the word *cookie* derives from a Dutch word that means "small cake." Using this as the contemporary definition, the term *cookie* can include anything from the classic chocolate chunk to the twice-baked biscotti to glazed and filigreed petits fours. Each type of cookie requires different shaping techniques such as rolling, stamping, and molding. Many are filled, glazed, or otherwise finished after baking.

General pan preparation for cookies

To ensure proper baking and even spread, use only flat pans. Pans should usually be lined with either parchment paper or silicone baking mats. Some cookies, such as tuiles, bake best on silicone baking mats. If these are not available, butter and flour the pans (see page 305 for pan preparation for stenciled tuile cookies). Generally, however, flouring pans for baking cookies is not desirable, as the flour could prevent the full spread of a cookie. Greasing pans for cookies is also not commonly recommended, as the fat may cause excessive spreading and browning of the bottoms.

For cookies with a particularly high fat content that tend to brown easily, it is good practice to use two stacked sheet pans. Double-panning will create an air pocket that insulates the cookies, allowing for gentle heating of the bottoms.

Place cookies in orderly rows on the prepared pans, leaving enough room for them to spread.

General cooling instructions for cookies

Most cookies should be removed from the pan as quickly as possible after baking to prevent further browning. Some cookies, however, are too soft to be removed immediately and should be allowed to cool briefly on the baking pan just until they have set enough to be transferred to a wire cooling rack. Cookies such as tuiles may be molded as soon as they are removed from the oven.

Drop cookies

Drop cookies are those that are made from doughs and batters firm enough to hold shape on a sheet pan.

1. Prepare the dough as instructed using either the creaming method or foaming method. Dough prepared using the creaming method achieves leavening in part through the air that is incorporated as the fat and sugar are creamed together. The foaming method incorporates air that expands and leavens during baking through the beating of eggs, yolks, or whites to create air pocket–rich foam that is gently blended into a batter.

2. To portion drop cookies, fill a scoop of the appropriate size with the dough and level it off, then release it onto the parchment-lined sheet pan. Some recipes may call for the portioned drop of dough to be flattened for a more even final spread. If slicing drop cookie dough to portion the cookies, scale the dough into manageable portions and shape each one into a log. Wrap the dough in parchment paper or plastic wrap, using it to compress the dough into a compact cylinder, and refrigerate or freeze until firm. Slice the dough into uniform slices.

3. Bake. Most drop cookies are golden brown around the edges and on the bottom when properly baked. For many of these cookies, the upper surface should still look moist but not wet.

4. Cool completely before storing in airtight containers at room temperature or freezing.

LEFT: Portion drop cookies onto a sheet tray, leaving enough room to account for the spread during baking.

RIGHT: Cookie dough is easily portioned by slicing after it is fully chilled.

Bar cookies

Bar cookies are baked in large sheets and portioned after baking.

1. Prepare the dough or batter as directed.

2. Spread the dough or batter evenly in the pan to ensure uniform baking. Some bar cookies, such as lemon bars, are made of layers of different components. Each component should be spread carefully and evenly; in some cases, it may be necessary to chill one layer before adding another layer.

3. Bake as directed.

4. If the bars are to be glazed or iced, allow the sheet to cool completely before adding the glaze or icing. To ensure clean, straight cuts, especially when working with a glazed or iced cookie, chill the full sheet before cutting it, and dip the knife in warm water and wipe it clean before each cut.

5. Store. Bar cookies generally have a shorter shelf life than other cookies because the exposed sliced edges stale relatively quickly.

Accuracy of measurement is required to cut uniform cookies. Pecan Diamonds (page 311) shown here.

Traditional rolled and cut-out cookies

1. Prepare the dough as directed. Refrigerate the dough after mixing to allow it to firm up.

2. Prepare the sheet pans before beginning to roll out the dough. Pans are prepared ahead of time so that cookies may be transferred directly to the pan after cutting.

3. Divide the dough into manageable portions. Work with one portion at a time and keep the remainder tightly wrapped and refrigerated.

4. Lightly dust the work surface with flour. All-purpose or bread flour is most often used. Bread flour is used for dusting both because it is lower in starch and because its slightly more granular texture dusts a surface more evenly without clumping. For certain types of cookies you may use confectioners' sugar for dusting. Some doughs are particularly soft and delicate and should instead be rolled between two sheets of parchment paper.

5. Roll out the dough to ¹⁄₁₆ to ⅛ in/1.5 to 3 mm thick. The precise thickness depends on the formula. When rolling, occasionally rotate the dough 90 degrees to ensure that the dough is rolled to an even thickness.

6. Cut the cookies and quickly transfer to the prepared pans so they don't become mis-shapen when transferred. Rolled and cut cookies generally do not spread much, so they can be placed relatively close together on the sheet pans.

7. Bake as directed. When using cutters of varying sizes and shapes, bake cookies of like sizes together to ensure even baking.

8. Cool and store.

LEFT: **Begin rolling the dough, rolling perpendicular to the edge of the table.**

CENTER: **Turn the dough 90 degrees.**

RIGHT: **Lift the dough and dust the table underneath with flour.**

Stenciled cookies

1. Prepare the batter as directed. Stenciled cookies are made using batters that can be spread very thin and baked without losing their detailed shape.

2. Line the pans with silicone baking mats. If baking mats are unavailable, grease and flour inverted sheet pans and freeze them before using; freezing will solidify the fat and flour coating so it will not come off during the stenciling process.

3. Place the stencil on the prepared pan and use a small offset spatula to spread a thin, even layer of batter over it. It is important to spread the batter evenly so the cookies bake uniformly. Carefully lift the stencil and repeat.

4. Bake as directed. Stenciled cookies bake quickly and should be watched almost constantly.

5. Shape the cookies as required. To shape stenciled cookies, drape them over a rolling pin to create the classic tuile shape, twist around a dowel to create a spiral, or drape over a cup or ramekin to make a container, to name only a few variations. The cookies must be warm and pliable enough to mold without cracking; if necessary, return the pan of baked cookies to the oven to rewarm them briefly. For this reason, stenciled cookies should be made in small batches; if the pan must be returned to the oven too many times, the last cookies on the pan may burn.

6. Store. Protect delicate stenciled cookies from breakage. Store molded stenciled cookies in airtight containers so they don't lose their shape due to exposure to humidity.

Press batter through the stencil with spatula. Use a variety of different stencils to create cookie garnishes.

Molded cookies

Molded cookies may be formed by hand, stamped or pressed, or piped into carved or cast molds to create an intricate design.

1. Prepare the cookie dough as directed. If the dough is too soft to hold its shape, refrigerate it after mixing until it is firm enough to work with.

2. Roll out the dough on a lightly floured surface. Flouring prevents the dough from sticking or adhering to a surface.

3. Press the dough with the molds. Molded cookies can be formed by hand, stamped, or pressed, or piped into carved or cast molds to create an intricate design.

4. Bake as directed. Most molded cookies are baked immediately after they are formed. However, springerle must air-dry for several hours to ensure that they retain their intricate patterns; drying allows a crust to form on the top surface of the cookies, which will preserve the impression during baking by preventing the surface from rising or cracking. Because these cookies are leavened, they will expand from the bottom.

5. Cool and store.

LEFT: Tuile cookies are molded while they are still hot from the oven and can be rewarmed for easier shaping.
RIGHT: Press rolled springerle dough firmly with the mold.

Twice-baked cookies

1. Prepare the dough as directed, by either the creaming or the foaming method.

2. Pipe the dough or form it into logs or loaves.

3. Bake until the internal structure is set but the color is not fully developed.

4. Let the logs cool briefly and slice the cookies.

5. The logs are generally allowed to cool briefly but not completely, so that they won't be too brittle when sliced.

6. Slice and arrange on sheet pans. A serrated blade is less likely to chip and fray the edges of the cookies as they are sliced.

7. Bake the cookies again, at a lower temperature. This will dry them fully and develop more flavor and color; any seeds and nuts will toast at this point and the sugars in the dough will caramelize.

8. Cool and store.

Slicing biscotti before it is baked a second time

Piping cookies

1. Prepare the pans, pastry bag, and pastry tip. For piped cookie batters or doughs made with meringue or beaten egg whites, this step is especially important. Preparing materials ahead of time prevents delicate physically aerated batters from losing volume from being left to stand too long.

2. Prepare the batter or dough as directed.

3. Fill the pastry bag. To fill a pastry bag with batter, first place the pastry tip in the bag (if using one). Fold the top of the bag down to make a cuff, and use a rubber spatula to fill the bag. Twist the top of the bag to seal, and squeeze to release any air in the tip of the bag.

4. Pipe the cookies onto prepared pans. Use constant, even pressure. To finish each cookie, release the pressure and lift the tip away; if the tip is lifted away before the pressure is released, the batter or dough will form a "tail" at the top of the cookie, which is likely to become dark or burn during baking.

Chocolate chunk cookies

MAKES 4 DOZEN COOKIES

Pastry flour	1 lb 5 oz	595 g
Salt	⅓ oz	9 g
Baking soda	⅓ oz	9 g
Butter	14 oz	397 g
Granulated sugar	10 oz	284 g
Light brown sugar	6½ oz	184 g
Eggs	6 oz	170 g
Vanilla extract	1 tsp	5 mL
Chocolate chunks	1 lb 5 oz	595 g

1   Line sheet pans with parchment paper.

2   Sift together the flour, salt, and baking soda.

3   Cream the butter and sugars on medium speed with the paddle attachment, scraping down the bowl periodically, until the mixture is smooth and light in color, about 5 minutes.

4   Combine the eggs and vanilla. Add to the butter-sugar mixture in 3 additions, mixing until fully incorporated after each addition and scraping down the bowl as needed.

5   On low speed, mix in the sifted dry ingredients and the chocolate chunks until just incorporated.

6   Divide the dough into 1½-oz/43-g pieces and place on the prepared pans. Alternatively, the dough may be divided into 2-lb/907-g pieces, shaped into logs 16 in/41 cm long, wrapped tightly in parchment paper, and refrigerated until firm enough to slice. Slice each log into 16 pieces and arrange on the prepared sheet pans in even rows.

7   Bake at 375°F/191°C until golden brown around the edges, 12 to 14 minutes. Cool completely on the pans. Store in an airtight container.

VARIATION   **CHOCOLATE CHERRY CHUNK COOKIES** Add 2 lb/907 g chopped dried cherries along with the chocolate in step 5.

Mudslide cookies

MAKES 3 DOZEN COOKIES

Cake flour	2½ oz	71 g
Baking powder	1½ tsp	4.50 g
Salt	pinch	pinch
Unsweetened chocolate	5½ oz	156 g
Bittersweet chocolate	1 lb	454 g
Butter	3 oz	85 g
Eggs	12 oz	340 g
Sugar	1 lb	454 g
Vanilla extract	1 tsp	5 mL
Walnuts, chopped	5½ oz	156 g
Chocolate chips	1 lb 2 oz	510 g

1   Line sheet pans with parchment paper.

2   Sift together the flour, baking powder, and salt.

3   Melt the unsweetened and bittersweet chocolate together with the butter in a bowl over a pot of barely simmering water. Stir to blend.

4   Beat the eggs, sugar, and vanilla on high speed with the whip attachment until light and thick, 6 to 8 minutes. Blend in the chocolate mixture on medium speed. On low speed, mix in the dry ingredients until just blended. Blend in the walnuts and chocolate chips until just incorporated.

5   Divide the dough into 2-oz/57-g pieces and arrange on the prepared sheet pans in even rows. Alternatively, the dough may be divided into 2-lb/907-g pieces, shaped into logs 16 in/41 cm long, wrapped tightly in parchment paper, and refrigerated until firm enough to slice. Slice each log into 16 pieces and arrange on the prepared sheet pans in even rows.

6   Bake at 350°F/177°C until the cookies are cracked on top but still appear slightly moist, about 12 minutes. Cool slightly on the pans. Transfer to racks and cool completely. Store in an airtight container.

NOTES   The middle will still be very soft when this cookie is finished baking. Only the sides will be firm to the touch.

These are also good with the addition of dried cherries or cranberries.

Hermit cookies

MAKES 3 DOZEN COOKIES

Cake flour	1 lb 4 oz	567 g
Baking soda	⅓ oz	9 g
Sugar	12 oz	340 g
Butter	6 oz	170 g
Molasses, unsulfured	3 oz	85 g
Ground allspice	¼ tsp	0.50 g
Ground cinnamon	¼ tsp	0.50 g
Salt	pinch	pinch
Eggs	3 oz	85 g
Water	2½ fl oz	75 mL
Currants, plumped (see page 243)	8 oz	227 g
Fondant	as needed	as needed

1   Line sheet pans with parchment paper.

2   Sift together the flour and baking soda.

3   Cream together the sugar and butter on low speed with the paddle attachment, increasing to medium speed until light and fluffy, about 5 minutes. Blend in the molasses, allspice, cinnamon, and salt, scraping down the bowl periodically, until the mixture is smooth and light in color, about an additional 5 minutes.

4   Whisk together the eggs and water. Add to the butter-sugar mixture in 3 additions, alternating with the sifted dry ingredients, mixing until fully incorporated after each addition and scraping down the bowl as needed. Mix in the currants until just incorporated.

5   Fill a pastry bag with fitted with a #6 piping tip with the batter and pipe 1½-in/4-cm rounds onto the prepared sheet pans.

6   Bake at 375°F/191°C until the rounds are light golden brown, 8 to 10 minutes. Transfer to racks and cool completely.

7   Place the cookie rounds on a wire rack over a sheet pan. Heat the fondant and thin to a glazing consistency (for instructions on working with fondant, see page 410). Glaze a small circle in the center of the rounds with fondant and allow to set completely. Store in an airtight container.

Pecan diamonds

MAKES 1 HALF SHEET PAN, 100 PIECES (1 IN/3 CM)

Rich short dough (page 224)	2 lb	907 g
PECAN FILLING		
Butter, cubed	1 lb	454 g
Light brown sugar	1 lb	454 g
Granulated sugar	4 oz	113 g
Honey	12 oz	340 g
Heavy cream	4 fl oz	120 mL
Pecans, chopped	2 lb	907 g

1   Roll out the short dough on a lightly floured work surface to a rectangle 13 by 18 in/33 by 46 cm and ⅛ in/3 mm thick. Lay it gently in a sheet pan so that it completely lines the bottom and sides. Dock the dough with a pastry docker or the tines of a fork.

2   Bake at 350°F/177°C until light golden brown, about 10 minutes.

3   To make the filling, combine the butter, sugars, honey, and cream in a heavy-bottomed saucepan and cook without stirring over medium-high heat until the mixture reaches 240°F/116°C. Add the nuts and stir until fully incorporated. Immediately pour into the prebaked crust and spread into an even layer.

4   Place the half sheet pan on a full sheet pan to catch any filling if it boils over. Bake at 350°F/177°C until the filling bubbles or foams evenly across the surface and the crust is golden brown, about 45 minutes. Cool completely in the pan.

5   Using a metal spatula, release the sheet from the sides of the pan and invert the slab onto the back of a sheet pan. Transfer to a cutting board, flipping it over so it is right side up. Trim off the edges. Cut into diamonds with 1-in/3-cm sides. Store in an airtight container.

Rugelach

MAKES 48 PIECES

DOUGH		
Bread flour	13½ oz	383 g
Pastry flour	2½ oz	71 g
Salt	pinch	pinch
Butter, softened	1 lb	454 g
Cream cheese	13½ oz	383 g
FILLING		
Jam	7½ oz	213 g
Nuts, chopped	9 oz	255 g
Cinnamon sugar (page 897)	1½ oz plus extra for sprinkling	42 g plus extra for sprinkling
Egg wash (page 892)	as needed	as needed

1   Line sheet pans with parchment paper.

2   Sift together the bread flour, pastry flour, and salt.

3   Mix the butter and cream cheese on medium speed with the paddle attachment until smooth, 5 minutes. On low speed, mix in the sifted dry ingredients until just combined. Scrape down the bowl as necessary to blend evenly.

4   Turn the dough out onto a lightly floured work surface. Roll the dough to an even thickness of ½ in/1 cm in a rectangle approximately 16 by 26 in/41 by 66 cm and give it one three-fold (see page 220). Scale the dough into 1-lb/454-g portions and shape into disks.

5   Wrap the dough in plastic wrap and let it rest under refrigeration until cool enough to roll out.

6   Roll out each disk on a lightly floured work surface to a circle ⅟₁₆ in/1.5 mm thick and 14 in/36 cm in diameter. Spread the dough with 2½ oz/71 g jam and sprinkle with 3 oz/85 g chopped nuts and ½ oz/14 g cinnamon sugar. Cut into 16 wedges. Roll each one into a crescent, beginning at the wide end. Transfer to prepared sheet pans, leaving about 1 in/3 cm between cookies. Lightly brush the cookies with egg wash and sprinkle each with cinnamon sugar.

Rolling with the pizza method

7   Bake at 375°F/191°C until light golden brown, about 10 minutes. Transfer to racks and cool completely. Store in an airtight container.

NOTE   Rugelach dough can be used immediately. You can use all or part of the dough as you wish; freeze the rest for later use.

Working with 8-oz/227-g pieces of dough, roll each piece into a rectangle approximately 8 in/20 cm wide and 1⁄16 in/1.5 mm thick. Spread 5 oz/142 g raspberry jam over the rolled dough and sprinkle with 3½ oz/99 g roughly chopped pecans or walnuts and ½ oz/14 g cinnamon sugar. Roll up the dough from the longer side of the rectangle to form a long log. Lightly brush the top of the log with egg wash and sprinkle with ½ oz/14 g cinnamon sugar. Cut the log into 1-in/3-cm sections, place on parchment-lined sheet pans, and bake as directed above.

Florentine squares

MAKES 1 HALF SHEET PAN, 165 PIECES (1 IN/3 CM)

1-2-3 cookie dough (page 223)	2 lb	907 g
FILLING		
Sugar	13 oz	369 g
Heavy cream	11 fl oz	165 mL
Honey	5½ oz	156 g
Butter	5½ oz	156 g
Almonds, sliced, raw	11 oz	312 g
Dried cranberries	2 oz	57 g
Pistachios, coarsely chopped	2 oz	57 g
Orange zest, grated (optional)	¼ oz	7 g
All-purpose flour	½ oz	14 g

1   Line a half sheet pan with parchment paper.

2   Roll out the dough on a lightly floured work surface to a rectangle 13 by 18 in/33 by 46 cm and 1⁄8 in/3 mm thick. Lay it gently in the half sheet pan so that it completely lines the bottom and sides. Dock the dough with a pastry docker or the tines of a fork.

3   Bake at 375°F/191°C until the dough is light golden brown, about 10 minutes.

4   To make the filling, cook the sugar, cream, honey, and butter in a heavy-bottomed saucepan over medium heat, stirring constantly, until the mixture reaches 240°F/116°C.

5   Remove from the heat and fold in the almonds, dried cranberries, pistachios, orange zest (if using), and flour.

6   Pour onto the prebaked crust and spread into an even layer.

7   Bake at 375°F/191°C until golden brown, 15 to 20 minutes. Cool. (The cookies may be slightly warm when they are cut.)

8   Using a metal spatula, release the sheet from the sides of the pan. Transfer to a cutting board. Trim off the edges. Cut into 1¼-in/3-cm squares. Store in an airtight container.

CLOCKWISE FROM UPPER RIGHT:
Almond Spritz (page 325), Vanilla Kipferl (page 319), star-shaped Sugar Cookies (page 316), Shortbread Cookies (page 335), Oatmeal Raisin Cookies (page 333), moon-shaped Sugar Cookies (page 316)

Brandy snaps

MAKES 12 DOZEN COOKIES

Butter, melted	11 oz	312 g
Light brown sugar	7¾ oz	220 g
Dark corn syrup	14 oz	397 g
Brandy	¾ fl oz	23 mL
Bread flour, sifted	7 oz	198 g
Ground ginger	½ tsp	1 g

1 Line sheet pans with silicone baking mats.

2 Combine the butter, sugar, corn syrup, and brandy. Add the flour and ginger and mix until smooth.

3 Portion the batter with a #100 scoop onto the lined sheet pans, spacing the cookies 4 in/ 10 cm apart.

4 Bake at 350°F/177°C until light golden brown, about 5 minutes. Remove from the oven and cool slightly. Form into desired shapes while warm.

VARIATION **SESAME BRANDY SNAPS** Add 1¼ oz/35 g sesame seeds to the finished batter.

Sugar cookies

MAKES 10 DOZEN COOKIES

All-purpose flour	2 lb	907 g
Salt	1 tsp	5 g
Butter, soft	1 lb	454 g
Sugar	15 oz	425 g
Eggs	4 oz	113 g
Milk, room temperature	3 fl oz	90 mL
Vanilla extract	1 tbsp	15 mL

1 Line sheet pans with parchment paper.

2 Sift together the flour and salt.

3 Cream the butter and sugar with the paddle attachment, starting on low speed and increasing to medium speed, until light and fluffy, about 5 minutes.

4 Combine the eggs, milk, and vanilla. Alternately add the sifted dry ingredients and egg mixture to the butter-sugar mixture in 2 to 3 additions, blending until fully incorporated after each addition.

5 Divide the dough into 4 equal pieces, wrap each tightly in plastic wrap, and refrigerate until firm enough to roll.

6 Working with one piece of dough at a time, roll out the dough on a lightly floured work surface to ⅛ in/3 mm thick. Using a 2½-in/6-cm round cutter, cut out the cookies. Place the cookies in even rows on the prepared sheet pans. Collect the scraps of dough, press together, wrap, and refrigerate until firm enough to reroll.

7 Bake at 375°F/191°C until golden around the edges, about 12 minutes. Transfer to racks and cool completely. Store in an airtight container.

Linzer cookies

MAKES 65 COOKIES

Linzer dough (page 227)	1 lb 8 oz	680 g
Confectioners' sugar, sifted	as needed	as needed
Raspberry jam	as needed	as needed

1 Line sheet pans with parchment paper.

2 Divide the dough into 4 equal pieces, wrap each tightly in plastic wrap, and refrigerate. Working with one piece of the dough at a time, roll out the dough on a lightly floured work surface to ⅛ in/3 mm thick. Using a 1½-in/4-cm fluted cutter, cut out rounds of dough. Using a 1-in/3-cm plain round cutter, cut out a hole from the center of half of the pieces to make rings. Transfer to the prepared sheet pans, placing the rings and circles on separate pans and arranging them in evenly spaced rows. Collect the scraps of dough, press together, wrap, and refrigerate until firm enough to reroll.

3 Bake at 350°F/177°C until light golden brown, 8 to 10 minutes. Transfer to racks and cool completely

4 Sift confectioners' sugar over the rings. Fill a pastry bag fitted with a #4 straight tip with the jam and pipe a small mound of jam onto the center of each circle cookie. Carefully center the sugar-dusted rings onto the jam-filled bottoms and press gently to secure. Store in an airtight container.

Citrus shortbread cookies

MAKES 3 DOZEN COOKIES

Butter, soft	10½ oz	298 g
Confectioners' sugar, sifted	5½ oz	156 g
Egg yolks	1½ oz	43 g
Orange zest, grated	2½ oz	71 g
Lemon zest, grated	2½ oz	71 g
Vanilla bean, seeds only	1 each	1 each
Vanilla extract	1½ tsp	7.50 mL
Cake flour, sifted	15 oz	425 g

1 Line sheet pans with parchment paper.

2 Cream the butter and sugar on medium speed with the paddle attachment until light and smooth, about 5 minutes. Blend together the egg yolks, orange and lemon zests, vanilla seeds, and vanilla extract. Add to the butter mixture in 2 to 3 additions, mixing until fully incorporated after each addition and scraping down the bowl as needed. On low speed, mix in the flour until just blended, scraping down the bowl as needed. Wrap the dough tightly in plastic wrap and chill until firm enough to roll.

3 Roll out the dough on a lightly floured work surface to ¼ in/6 mm thick. Cut into rectangles 2 by 3 in/5 by 8 cm and transfer to the prepared sheet pans. Collect the scraps of dough, press together, wrap, and refrigerate until firm enough to reroll.

4 Bake at 350°F/177°C until the edges are a very light gold, about 20 minutes. Transfer to racks and cool completely. Store in an airtight container.

Citrus white chocolate sablés

MAKES 3 LB/1.36 KG

Butter	1 lb	454 g
Confectioners' sugar	5 oz	142 g
All-purpose flour	1 lb 2 oz	510 g
Cornstarch	3 oz	85 g
Salt	pinch	pinch
Vanilla bean, seeds only	2 each	2 each
Lime zest, grated	1 tbsp	9 g
White chocolate, cut into small chunks	8 oz	227 g

1   Line baking sheets with parchment paper.

2   Cream the butter and sugar on medium speed with the paddle attachment until light and smooth, about 5 minutes.

3   Add the flour, cornstarch, and salt and blend on medium speed until just incorporated. Add the vanilla bean seeds, lime zest, and white chocolate chunks and blend just to incorporate.

4   Divide the dough into 4-oz/113-g pieces. Roll out each piece on a lightly floured work surface to a 6-in/15-cm circle and place on the baking sheets.

5   Bake in a 325°F/163°C convection oven for 5 minutes.

6   Trim the edges with a 6-in/15-cm ring cutter. Return to the oven to bake 5 minutes more or until golden at the edges.

7   Transfer to racks and cool completely. Store in an airtight container.

Vanilla kipferl

MAKES 12 DOZEN COOKIES

Butter, soft	14 oz	397 g
Confectioners' sugar	6 oz	170 g
Ground cinnamon	1 tsp	2 g
Salt	pinch	pinch
Vanilla extract	1½ tsp	7.50 mL
Egg yolks	¾ oz	21 g
Cake flour, sifted	1 lb	454 g
Hazelnuts, toasted and finely ground	4 oz	113 g
Confectioners' sugar or vanilla sugar (page 901)	as needed	as needed

1   Line sheet pans with parchment paper.

2   Cream the butter, confectioners' sugar, cinnamon, and salt with the paddle attachment, starting on low speed and increasing to medium speed, until light and smooth, about 8 minutes. Scrape down the bowl as needed.

3   Combine the vanilla and the egg yolks. Add to the creamed mixture and mix until smooth and evenly blended. Turn off the mixer and add all of the flour and the ground hazelnuts. On low speed, mix until just blended, scraping down the bowl as needed to blend evenly.

4   Wrap the dough tightly in plastic wrap and chill until firm enough to roll.

5   Shape the dough into ropes ½ in/1 cm in diameter. Cut each rope into 2-in/5-cm lengths and gently form into tapered crescent shapes. Place in even rows on the prepared sheet pans.

6   Bake at 350°F/177°C until golden around the edges, 10 to 12 minutes.

7   While the cookies are still warm, toss gently in confectioners' sugar to coat. Cool completely and repeat when cooled. Store in and airtight container.

Madeleines

MAKES 10 DOZEN SMALL MADELEINES (1 IN/3 CM EACH)

All-purpose flour	6⅓ oz	179 g
Baking powder	¼ oz	7 g
Butter	6⅓ oz	179 g
Granulated sugar	6 oz	170 g
Light brown sugar	¾ oz	21 g
Lemon zest, grated	½ tsp	1.50 g
Salt	pinch	pinch
Eggs	7 oz	198 g
Vanilla extract	2 tsp	10 mL

1   Lightly coat madeleine pans with softened butter and dust with flour.

2   Sift together the flour and baking powder.

3   Cream the butter, sugars, and lemon zest with the paddle attachment, starting on low speed and increasing to medium speed, until light and fluffy, about 5 minutes. Scrape down the bowl as needed. Combine the salt, eggs, and vanilla. Add to the butter-sugar mixture in 2 or 3 additions, mixing until fully incorporated after each addition. Turn off the mixer and add the sifted dry ingredients, mixing on low speed and scraping down the bowl as needed during mixing to blend evenly.

4   Fill a pastry bag fitted with a #4 plain tip with the batter and pipe into the prepared madeleine pans, filling the molds three-quarters full.

5   Bake at 400°F/204°C until the edges are a medium golden brown, about 10 minutes.

6   Transfer the pans to racks and cool slightly before unmolding and serving. Store in an airtight container.

Madeleine batter must be piped immediately after mixing.

Chocolate madeleines

MAKES 10 DOZEN SMALL MADELEINES (1 IN/3 CM EACH)

Butter	5 oz	142 g
Semisweet chocolate, finely chopped	3 oz	85 g
Cocoa powder, sifted	2 tbsp	18 g
Sugar	6 oz	170 g
All-purpose flour, sifted	9 oz	255 g
Salt	pinch	pinch
Eggs	6 oz	170 g
Egg yolks	1 oz	28 g
Vanilla extract	1 tsp	5 mL

1   Lightly coat madeleine pans with softened butter and dust with flour.

2   Melt the butter and chocolate in a bowl over a pot of barely simmering water, whisking gently to blend. Remove from the heat.

3   Whisk together the cocoa powder, sugar, flour, and salt. Stir into the melted chocolate mixture. Blend the eggs, egg yolks, and vanilla extract, add to the batter, and stir until just combined.

4   Place the batter over a pot of barely simmering water and heat, stirring constantly, just until warm, about 2 minutes. Remove from the heat.

5   Fill a pastry bag fitted with a #2 plain tip with the batter and pipe into the prepared madeleine pans, filling each mold half full.

6   Bake at 375°F/191°C until firm to the touch and lightly crisp along the edges, about 12 minutes.

7   Turn out onto a parchment-lined sheet pan while still warm. Store in an airtight container.

Springerle

MAKES 6 DOZEN COOKIES

Cake flour	1 lb 4 oz	567 g
Bread flour	1 lb 4 oz	567 g
Baking soda	½ tsp	3 g
Anise seed, ground	½ oz	14 g
Confectioners' sugar	2 lb 8 oz	1.13 kg
Eggs	1 lb	454 g
Salt	pinch	pinch

1   Line sheet pans with parchment paper.

2   Sift together the flours, baking soda, and anise seed into a large bowl and make a well in the center.

3   Whip together the confectioners' sugar, eggs, and salt on high speed with the whip attachment to maximum volume, 3 to 5 minutes. Pour the egg mixture into the well of the dry ingredients and knead into a smooth dough.

4   Roll out the dough on a lightly floured work surface to ½ in/1 cm thick, and then press with springerle molds. Alternatively, roll with a springerle rolling pin and cut into cookies. (The yield above is based on rectangular molds 1 by 2 in/3 by 5 cm.) Place the cookies on the prepared sheet pans.

5   Air-dry the cookies for a minimum of 6 hours, until a slight crust forms.

6   Bake at 300°F/149°C until dry and set but still white with no hint of browning, about 25 minutes. Transfer to racks and cool completely. Store in an airtight container.

Almond anise biscotti

MAKES 32 COOKIES

Bread flour	2 lb	907 g
Baking soda	1 tbsp	17 g
Eggs	1 lb 2 oz	510 g
Sugar	1 lb 3 oz	539 g
Salt	¾ tsp	3.75 g
Anise extract	2 tsp	10 mL
Almonds, whole, lightly toasted	1 lb 4 oz	567 g
Anise seed, chopped slightly	4 oz	113 g

1   Line a sheet pan with parchment paper.

2   Sift together the flour and baking soda.

3   Whip the eggs, sugar, salt, and anise extract on high speed with the whip attachment until thick and light in color, about 5 minutes. On low speed, mix in the dry ingredients until just incorporated. Add the almonds and anise seed by hand and blend until evenly combined.

4   Form the dough into a log 4 in/10 cm wide by 16 in/41 cm long and place on the prepared sheet pan.

5   Bake at 300°F/149°C until light golden brown and firm, about 1 hour. Remove the pans from the oven and cool for 10 minutes. Lower the oven temperature to 275°F/135°C.

6   Using a serrated knife, cut each strip crosswise into slices ½ in/1 cm thick. Place on sheet pans and bake, turning the biscotti once halfway through the baking time, until golden brown and crisp, 20 to 25 minutes. Transfer to racks and cool completely. Store in an airtight container.

Chocolate biscotti

MAKES 48 COOKIES

Bread flour	1 lb 6 oz	624 g
Baking soda	1 tbsp	17 g
Cocoa powder	3½ oz	99 g
Eggs	1 lb 2 oz	510 g
Sugar	1 lb 1 oz	482 g
Vanilla extract	1 tbsp	15 mL
Almond extract	1 tsp	5 mL
Salt	¾ tsp	0.5 g
Almonds, whole, toasted lightly	1 lb 12 oz	794 g
Chocolate chunks, coarsely chopped	15 oz	426 g

1   Line a sheet pan with parchment paper.

2   Sift together the flour, baking soda, and cocoa powder.

3   Whip the eggs, sugar, vanilla and almond extracts, and salt on high speed with the whip attachment until thick and light in color, 6 to 8 minutes. On low speed, mix in the sifted dry ingredients until just incorporated. Using a rubber spatula, fold in the almonds and chocolate.

4   Form the dough into a strip 24 in/61 cm long on the prepared sheet pan.

5   Bake at 300°F/149°C until a skewer inserted in the center of the strip comes out clean, about 1 hour. Remove from the oven and cool for 5 to 10 minutes. Lower the oven temperature to 275°F/135°C.

6   Using a serrated knife, cut the strip into slices ½ in/1 cm thick. Place on prepared sheet pans and bake for 12 minutes. Flip the biscotti over and continue baking until completely dried and crisp, 12 to 15 minutes. Transfer to racks and cool completely. Store in airtight container.

Almond spritz cookies

MAKES 12 DOZEN COOKIES

Almond paste	10 oz	284 g
Egg whites	7 oz	198 g
Butter, soft	1 lb 4 oz	567 g
Sugar	10 oz	284 g
Salt	1½ tsp	7.50 g
Rum	1½ tsp	7.50 mL
Vanilla extract	1 tbsp	15 mL
Cake flour, sifted	1 lb 7 oz	652 g
Raspberry jam	6 oz	170 g

1   Line sheet pans with parchment paper.

2   Blend the almond paste with 1 oz/28 g of the egg whites (about one white) on low speed with the paddle attachment until smooth. Add the butter, sugar, and salt and cream together on medium speed until light and fluffy, 5 minutes. Add the remaining 6 oz/170 g egg whites, the rum, and vanilla extract and mix until completely blended. On low speed, mix in the flour until just blended.

3   Using a pastry bag fitted with a #4 star tip, pipe the dough onto the prepared sheet pans into round 1½ in/4 cm in diameter. Make a small indent in the center of each round using a skewer. Using a parchment cone, pipe a little raspberry jam into each indentation.

4   Bake at 375°F/191°C until light golden brown, about 10 minutes. Transfer to racks and cool completely. Store in airtight container.

NOTE   If desired, dip half of each cookie in tempered chocolate after they have completely cooled.

Piping free-form cookies

Anise cookies

MAKES 5 DOZEN COOKIES

Cake flour	6 oz	170 g
Bread flour	3 oz	85 g
Confectioners' sugar, sifted	8½ oz	241 g
Eggs	4½ oz	128 g
Egg yolks	1 oz	28 g
Anise seed, crushed	1 tbsp	6 g
Anise extract	1 tsp	5 mL

1 Line sheet pans with parchment paper.

2 Sift together the cake and bread flours.

3 Blend the sugar, eggs, and egg yolks in the bowl of the mixer and heat over a pan of barely simmering water, whisking constantly, until the mixture reaches 110°F/43°C. Remove from the heat.

4 Whip on high speed to the ribbon stage with the whip attachment. Fold in the sifted dry ingredients with a rubber spatula. Fold in the anise seed and extract until just incorporated.

5 Using a pastry bag fitted with a #5 plain tip, pipe the batter into drops 1 in/3 cm in diameter on the prepared sheet pans.

6 Bake at 375°F/191°C until light golden brown, about 10 minutes. Transfer to racks and cool completely. Store in an airtight container.

Coconut macaroons

MAKES 100 MACAROONS (1 IN/3 CM DIAMETER)

Egg whites	8 oz	227 g
Sugar	1 lb 1 oz	482 g
Desiccated coconut	1 lb 6 oz	624 g
Vanilla extract	1 tsp	5 mL
Coating chocolate, melted, for dipping (optional)	as needed	as needed

1 Line sheet pans with parchment paper.

2 Combine the egg whites and sugar in a bowl and heat over simmering water until the mixture reaches 140°F/60°C, whipping constantly. Remove from the heat and mix in the coconut and vanilla with a wooden spoon until just incorporated.

3 Using a #100 scoop, portion the batter, pressing each scoop lightly, and place in even rows on the prepared pans. Air-dry until slightly dry, about 1 hour.

4 Bake at 375°F/191°C until the light golden brown, about 12 minutes. Cool completely on the pans.

5 If desired, dip the macaroons in melted chocolate. Allow to harden before storing in an airtight container.

Almond macaroons

Sugar	1 lb 4 oz	567 g
Egg whites	6 oz	170 g
Almond paste	1 lb	454 g
Vanilla extract	2 tsp	10 mL
Almond extract	2 tsp	10 mL

1   Line sheet pans with parchment paper.

2   Combine 1 lb/454 g of the sugar and the egg whites in a bowl and heat over simmering water until the mixture reaches 140°F/60°C, whipping constantly. Remove from the heat and mix in the almond paste, vanilla extract, and almond extract with a wooden spoon until just incorporated.

3   Using a pastry bag fitted with a #6 plain tip, pipe rounds 1 in/3 cm in diameter in even rows on the prepared pans.

4   Before baking, use a folded damp towel to touch the tops of the cookies, just enough to moisten them. Sprinkle with the remaining sugar.

5   Bake at 375°F/191°C until light golden brown, about 12 minutes. Cool completely on the pans. Store in an airtight container.

Coffee macaroons

MAKES 10 MOUNDS (5 IN/13 CM EACH) OR 100 MACAROONS (1 IN/3 CM EACH)

Egg white powder	⅓ oz	9 g
Granulated sugar	2 oz	57 g
Confectioners' sugar	1 lb	454 g
Almond flour	8¾ oz	248 g
Decaffeinated coffee granules	4 packs	4 packs
Egg whites	7 oz	198 g

1   Line sheet pans with parchment paper.

2   Combine the egg white powder and granulated sugar.

3   Sift the confectioners' sugar and combine with the almond flour and coffee granules.

4   Make a soft-peak meringue with the egg whites and granulated sugar mixture. Incorporate the almond flour–coffee mixture into the meringue.

5   Using a pastry bag fitted with a medium-size plain tip, pipe the dough onto the prepared pans using a 5-in /13-cm stencil. Let the dough sit for 30 minutes.

6   Bake in a 275°F/135°C convection oven until golden brown, about 10 minutes. Cool completely on the pans. Store in an airtight container.

Coconut frangipane cake

MAKES 48 OVALS (2 BY 3½ IN/5 BY 9 CM)

Butter	14 oz	411 g
Confectioners' sugar	1 lb 2 oz	510 g
All-purpose flour	7 oz	198 g
Light rum	1¾ fl oz	53 mL
Eggs	10½ oz	298 g
Heavy cream	10½ fl oz	315 mL
Desiccated coconut, dried with little sugar*	10½ oz	298 g
Simple syrup (page 900), for brushing	as needed	as needed
Rum, for brushing	as needed	as needed
Swiss meringue (page 416)	as needed	as needed

*To dry with a little sugar, toss with 2 oz/57 g of sugar and place on a parchment lined sheet pan in a 300°F/149°C oven for 10 minutes or until dry.

1   Cream the butter, sugar, and flour on medium speed with the paddle attachment until smooth, about 2 minutes.

2   Combine the rum, eggs, and heavy cream. Add to the creamed mixture one-quarter at a time, blending until well combined. Add the coconut and blend.

3   Place oval flexible molds on a sheet pan. Fill a pastry bag fitted with a #6 straight tip with the batter and pipe the frangipane halfway up in the molds.

4   Bake at 350°F/177°C until the cakes are golden brown and thoroughly baked, 8 to 12 minutes.

5   With a brush, soak the cakes with simple syrup and rum. Once the cakes have cooled, remove from the molds. Fill a pastry bag fitted with a flat tip (rose petal) with the Swiss meringue. Pipe the meringue on top of the cake with a snake-like motion. Brûlée the cakes with a torch until the tops are golden brown. Freeze until needed.

Frangipane cake

MAKES 1 HALF SHEET PAN, 50 PETITS FOURS (1 IN/3 CM EACH)

Almond paste	7 oz	198 g
Butter, soft	7 oz	198 g
Sugar	7 oz	198 g
Eggs	9 oz	255 g
Cake flour, sifted	3 oz	85 g

1 Line a half sheet pan with parchment paper.

2 Cream the almond paste, butter, and sugar on medium speed with the paddle attachment until light and fluffy, about 10 minutes. Blend the eggs and add in 2 or 3 additions, fully incorporating and scraping down the bowl after each addition. On low speed, mix in the flour until just blended.

3 Spread the batter evenly in the prepared sheet pan.

4 Bake at 375°F/191°C until golden brown, about 20 minutes. Cool completely in the pan.

5 Wrap tightly in plastic wrap while in the pan and refrigerate or freeze until needed, up to 3 weeks. (To assemble petits fours, see page 331.)

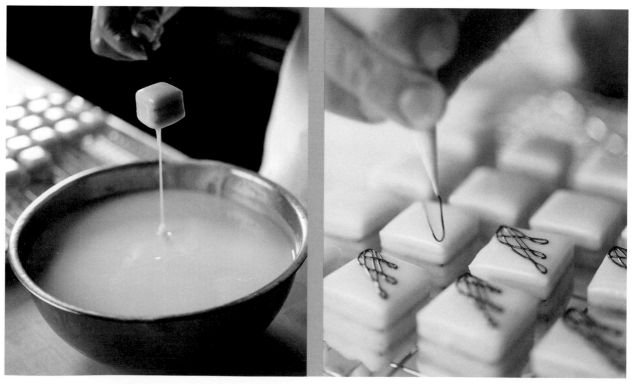

LEFT: Dipping petits fours in warmed fondant

RIGHT: Piping a filigree on petits fours for décor (see Appendix B, page 903, for piping designs)

glazed petits fours

The term *petit four* refers to a small sweet item that can be consumed in one or two bites. This category, also called *mignardises*, includes a wide variety of pastries. Classic glazed petits fours are just one type. Frangipane is the cake of choice for glazed petits fours not only because of its flavor, but because its dense, moist crumb makes it suitable for dipping in fondant without causing the cake to crumble.

The cake must be chilled before unmolding, cutting, or assembling the petits fours. After the cake has cooled, invert it onto a rack and remove the parchment. Cut the cake crosswise into three equal pieces. Spread the top of the first layer with a very thin coating of apricot jam. Top with the second layer of cake, putting the top of the cake down, and spread with jam. Top with the third layer. Spread the last layer with a very thin coating of jam (each finished petit four should be no higher than 1 in/3 cm).

Roll out 8 oz/227 g marzipan to ⅛ in/3 mm thick and cover the top of the frangipane. Trim off any excess marzipan and invert the layered cake onto a parchment-lined sheet pan so the marzipan is on the bottom.

Tightly wrap the layered sheet in plastic wrap and refrigerate or freeze until firm. Cut the petits fours into rectangles, squares, or diamonds with a knife or into a variety of shapes (circles, ovals, flowers, etc.) using different cutters.

To dip and glaze the cut petits fours, heat and thin fondant (see page 410) in a bowl that is deep enough to accommodate the petits fours. One at a time, place a petit four upside down in the fondant and gently press it down until the bottom of the cake is level with the surface of the fondant. Remove the glazed cake using two forks (one at the top and one at the base) and place it on an icing screen to allow the fondant to set completely before adding any décor.

The classical décor for glazed petits fours is piped filigree, but there are other contemporary décor options; see Appendix B, page 903.

Use precise measure or cutters to cut petits fours.

ON CAKE PLATE FROM LEFT: **Coconut Macaroons** (page 327), **Madeleines** (page 320), **Linzer Cookies** (page 316)
IN FRONT: **Rugelach** (page 312)

Oatmeal raisin cookies

MAKES APPROXIMATELY 2 DOZEN COOKIES (2 OZ/57 G EACH)

All-purpose flour	9 oz	255 g
Baking soda	½ tsp	2.5 mL
Ground cinnamon	1 tsp	5 mL
Salt	½ tsp	2.5 mL
Butter	12 oz	340 g
Light brown sugar	14 oz	397 g
Granulated sugar	5 oz	142 g
Eggs	10 oz	284 g
Vanilla extract	2 tsp	10 mL
Rolled oats	14 oz	397 g
Raisins, plumped (see "Dried Fruits," page 243)	6 oz	170 g

1   Line sheet pans with parchment paper.

2   Sift together the flour, baking soda, cinnamon, and salt.

3   Cream the butter and sugars on medium speed with the paddle attachment, scraping down the bowl periodically, until the mixture is light and smooth, about 10 minutes. Blend the eggs and vanilla and add to the butter-sugar mixture in 3 additions, mixing until fully incorporated after each addition and scraping down the bowl as needed.

4   On low speed, mix in the sifted dry ingredients and the oats and raisins until just incorporated.

5   Divide the dough into 2-oz/57-g pieces and place on the prepared sheet pans in even rows. Alternatively, the dough may be divided into 2-lb/907-g pieces, shaped into logs 16 in/41 cm long, wrapped tightly in parchment paper, and refrigerated until firm enough to slice. Slice each log into 16 pieces and arrange on the prepared sheet pans in even rows.

6   Bake at 375°F/191°C until light golden brown, about 12 minutes. Cool slightly on the pans. Transfer to racks and cool completely. Store in an airtight container.

NOTE   The middle will still be very soft when this cookie is finished baking. Only the sides will be firm to the touch.

VARIATION   **OATMEAL FRUIT COOKIES** Omit the raisins. Add 8 oz/227 g chopped dried pears, 8 oz/227 g chopped dried apricots, 8 oz/227 g dried blueberries, 8 oz/227 g chopped dried strawberries, 1 lb/454 g dried cranberries, and 8 oz/227 g toasted sliced almonds along with the oats in step 4.

Cake brownies

MAKES 1 HALF SHEET PAN

Semisweet chocolate, chopped	1 lb 6 oz	624 g
Butter	1 lb 6 oz	624 g
Eggs, room temperature	1 lb 10 oz	737 g
Sugar	2 lb 10 oz	1.19 kg
Vanilla extract	1 tbsp	15 mL
Cake flour	1 lb	454 g
Cocoa powder	5½ oz	156 g
Walnuts, coarsely chopped	1 lb	454 g

1   Line a half sheet pan with parchment.

2   Melt the chocolate and butter in a bowl over barely simmering water, blending gently. Remove the bowl from the heat.

3   Combine the eggs, sugar, and vanilla and whip on high speed with the whip attachment until light and thick in color, about 8 minutes.

4   Blend one-third of the egg mixture into the melted chocolate to temper it, then return it to the remaining egg mixture and blend on medium speed, scraping down the bowl as needed. On low speed, mix in the flour, cocoa powder, and nuts until just blended. The batter will be very wet. Pour the batter into the prepared sheet pan and spread evenly.

5   Bake at 350°F/177°C until a crust forms but the center is still moist, 30 to 40 minutes. Cool completely in the pan.

6   Cut into bars 2 by 3 in/5 by 8 cm. Store in an airtight container.

NOTE   The brownies may be glazed with 2 lb/907 g Hard Ganache (page 421). To glaze the brownies, trim the edges while they are in the pan. Invert the pan of uncut brownies onto the back of another sheet pan and then flip them once more, so they are right side up, onto a wire rack over a sheet pan. Pour the warm ganache over the brownies and spread it evenly. Refrigerate the brownies for about 30 minutes, until the ganache is firm. Slice the brownies into the dimensions given above using a warm sharp knife.

Shortbread cookies

MAKES APPROXIMATELY 2 DOZEN COOKIES (2 OZ/57 G EACH)

Cake flour	8 oz	227 g
Bread flour	8 oz	227 g
Salt	pinch	pinch
Butter	11 oz	312 g
Sugar	12 oz	340 g
Orange zest	½ oz	14 g
Egg yolks	2 oz	57 g
Almonds, sliced, blanched	as needed	as needed
Egg whites, beaten	as needed	as needed
Vanilla sugar (page 901)	as needed	as needed

1   Line sheet pans with parchment paper.

2   Sift together the flours and salt.

3   Cream the butter, sugar, and orange zest with the paddle attachment, starting on low speed and increasing to medium speed, until light and smooth, about 5 minutes. Scrape down the bowl as needed.

4   Blend in the egg yolks on medium speed, scraping down the bowl as needed. On low speed, mix in the dry ingredients until just blended.

5   Add a little water, a few drops at a time, if necessary, to make a workable dough. Scrape down the bowl as needed during mixing to blend evenly. Wrap the dough tightly in plastic wrap and refrigerate until firm enough to roll.

6   Roll out the dough on a lightly floured work surface to ¼ in/6 mm thick. Cut into rectangles 2 by 3 in/5 by 8 cm and transfer to the prepared sheet pans. Chill for 30 minutes. (Collect the scraps of dough, add a small amount of water to make a workable dough, press together, wrap, and refrigerate until firm enough to reroll and cut out additional cookies.)

Shortbread has a dense, almost crumbly texture.

7   Toss the almonds with the beaten egg whites and vanilla sugar and sprinkle evenly on top of the shortbread.

8   Bake at 350°F/177°C until the edges are a very light gold, about 20 minutes. Transfer to racks and cool completely. Store in an airtight container.

Checkerboard cookies

MAKES 10 DOZEN COOKIES

VANILLA DOUGH		
Cake flour	2 lb 4 oz	1.02 kg
Butter, small cubes, cold	1 lb 12 oz	794 g
Confectioners' sugar	13½ oz	383 g
Salt	pinch	pinch
Orange zest, grated	2 tsp	6 g
Egg yolks	8 oz	227 g
Vanilla extract	2 tsp	10 mL
CHOCOLATE DOUGH		
Cake flour	15 oz	425 g
Cocoa powder	3 oz	85 g
Butter, small cubes, cold	14 oz	397 g
Confectioners' sugar	6¾ oz	191 g
Orange zest, grated	1 tsp	3 g
Salt	pinch	pinch
Egg yolks	4 oz	113 g
Vanilla extract	1 tsp	5 mL

1   Line sheet pans with parchment paper.

2   To make the vanilla dough, sift the flour. Cream together the butter, sugar, salt, and orange zest with the paddle attachment, starting on low speed and increasing to medium speed until smooth, about 8 minutes. Gradually add the egg yolks and vanilla, mixing until fully incorporated after each addition and scraping down the bowl as needed. On low speed, mix in the sifted flour just until incorporated.

3   Divide the vanilla dough into 4 pieces. Form each piece into a square 5 by 5 in/13 by 13 cm and ½ in/1 cm thick, wrap in plastic wrap, and refrigerate until firm enough to roll.

4   Meanwhile, make the chocolate dough. Sift together the flour and cocoa powder. Cream together the butter, sugar, orange zest, and salt with a paddle attachment, starting on low speed and increasing to medium speed, until light and smooth, 6 to 8 minutes. Gradually add the egg yolks and vanilla to the butter-sugar mixture, mixing until fully incorporated after each addition and scraping down the bowl as needed. On low speed, mix in the sifted dry ingredients until just incorporated.

5   Divide the chocolate dough in half. Form each piece into a square 5 by 5 in/13 by 13 cm and ½ in/1 cm thick, wrap in plastic wrap, and refrigerate until firm enough to roll.

6   Working on a lightly floured work surface, roll out one piece of the vanilla dough into a square about 6 by 6 in/15 by 15 cm and ¼ in/6 mm thick; set aside. Roll out a piece of the chocolate dough to the same dimensions. Brush the vanilla dough lightly with water and gently press the chocolate dough on top. Roll out another piece of vanilla dough to the same dimensions, brush the chocolate layer lightly with water, and gently press the vanilla dough on top. Roll out the remaining piece of chocolate dough to the same dimensions, brush the vanilla layer lightly with water, and gently press the chocolate dough on top. Wrap the layered dough in plastic wrap and refrigerate or freeze until firm enough to cut.

7   Trim the edges of the layered dough square to even them to 6 by 6 in/15 by 15 cm.

8   Cut the square into twenty-four ¼-in/6-mm strips. Form 6 logs of 4 strips each, stacking them so the chocolate and vanilla doughs alternate to form a checkerboard.

9   Roll out one piece of the vanilla dough on a lightly floured work surface into a strip 6 by 15 in/15 by 38 cm and ⅛ in/3 mm thick; cut this in thirds to form 3 strips, 5 by 6 in/13 by 15 cm. Brush the vanilla dough lightly with water, place one of logs on one strip, and roll up, gently pressing each side on the counter to adhere the vanilla dough "casing." Smooth the overlapping side. Repeat the process with the remaining 2 strips of vanilla dough and checkerboard logs.

10   Repeat the process, rolling out the remaining piece of vanilla and covering the remaining logs.

11 Wrap the logs in plastic wrap and refrigerate until firm enough to cut.

12 Trim one end of each log and cut 20 cookies, each ¼ in/6 mm thick, from each log. Place on the prepared sheet pans.

13 Bake at 350°F/177°C until lightly brown on the edges, 15 minutes. Transfer to racks and cool completely. Store in an airtight container.

VARIATION This recipe can be used to make ribbon and pinwheel cookies.

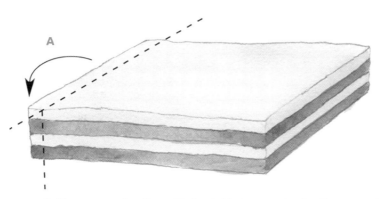

A

Roll two squares of vanilla cookie dough 6 inches by 6 inches by ¼ inch thick. Repeat process with the chocolate dough. Brush a chocolate square of dough with water, place a vanilla layer on top, brush with water, and repeat process with the second chocolate and vanilla dough squares, for a total of 4 layers. Refrigerate until firm. Carefully cut into slices ¼ inch thick.

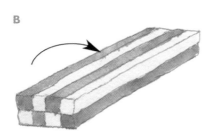

B

Assemble the block by laying 4 slices on top of each other, brushing with water between layers, alternating the colors to form a checkerboard. Refrigerate until firm.

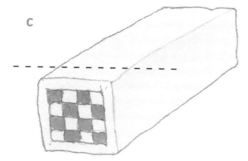

C

D

Roll a piece of vanilla cookie dough ⅛ inch thick, brush with water, and wrap around the checkerboard block. Refrigerate until firm.

Slice the block ¼ inch thick.

Russian tea cookies

MAKES 100 COOKIES (1 OZ/28 G EACH)

Walnuts, chopped	12 oz	340 g
Confectioners' sugar	5 oz	142 g
Butter	1 lb	454 g
Vanilla extract	1½ tsp	7.50 mL
Rum	1½ tsp	7.50 mL
All-purpose flour	1 lb 1 oz	482 g
Confectioners' sugar, for dusting	as needed	as needed

1   Line sheet pans with parchment paper.

2   Grind the walnuts with 1¾ oz/50 g of the sugar in a food processor to a fine meal.

3   Cream the butter, the remaining 3¼ oz/92 g sugar, the vanilla, and rum on medium speed with the paddle attachment until light and smooth, 5 to 6 minutes. Scrape down the bowl as needed. On low speed, mix in the flour and ground nuts until just blended. Scrape down the bowl as needed during mixing to blend evenly.

4   Roll the dough into ¾-in/2-cm balls and flatten slightly, or scoop the dough using a #50 scoop, and place on the prepared sheet pans. Chill for at least 1 hour.

5   Bake at 325°F/163°C until light golden brown, about 20 minutes.

6   While the cookies are still warm, transfer to racks and dust generously with confectioners' sugar. Cool to room temperature. Dust again with confectioners' sugar. Store in an airtight container.

NOTE   These cookies are also known as Mexican wedding cookies.

Ladyfingers

MAKES 170 COOKIES

Egg yolks	10 oz	284 g
Granulated sugar	13 oz	369 g
Egg whites	13 oz	369 g
Cake flour, sifted	12 oz	340 g
Confectioners' sugar	as needed	as needed

1   Line sheet pans with parchment paper.

2   Whip the egg yolks with 9 oz/255 g of the granulated sugar on high speed with the whip attachment until thick and light, about 8 minutes.

3   Whip the egg whites on medium speed with a clean whip attachment until soft peaks form. Add the remaining 4 oz/113 g sugar to the whites in a steady stream, then increase to high speed and whip until medium peaks form.

4   Working quickly but gently, fold the egg whites into the yolks. Fold in the sifted cake flour.

5   Fill a pastry bag fitted with a #4 plain tip with the batter and pipe into 3-in/8-cm lengths on the prepared pans. Dust generously with confectioners' sugar.

6   Bake at 400°F/204°C until the edges turn a light golden brown, about 15 minutes.

7   Transfer to racks and cool completely. Store in an airtight container.

VARIATION   **CHOCOLATE LADYFINGERS** Substitute 2 oz/57 g cocoa powder for 2 oz/57 g of the cake flour and sift it with the flour before proceeding as directed above.

Piping ladyfingers over a stencil ensures they are uniform in size.

Langue du chat sandwiches

MAKES 3 LB 7 OZ/1.56 KG DOUGH, 116 SANDWICH COOKIES

Cake flour, sifted	12 oz	340 g
Bread flour, sifted	4 oz	113 g
Butter	14 oz	397 g
Confectioners' sugar, sifted	14 oz	397 g
Vanilla extract	2 tsp	10 mL
Egg whites	10 oz	284 g
Hard ganache (page 421), nut paste, or jam, for filling	1 lb 13 oz	822 g
Confectioners' sugar, for dusting	as needed	as needed

1   Line sheet pans with parchment paper.

2   Sift together the cake and bread flours.

3   Cream together the butter, sugar, and vanilla with the paddle attachment, starting on low speed and increasing to medium speed and scraping down the bowl often, until smooth and light, about 5 minutes. Blend the egg whites and add in 2 or 3 additions, fully incorporating and scraping down the bowl after each addition.

4   Fill a pastry bag fitted with a #4 plain tip with the batter and pipe into strips 3 in/8 cm long on the prepared sheet pans, leaving a 2-in/5-cm space between cookies.

5   Bake at 375°F/191°C until golden brown around the edges, 12 to 15 minutes. Transfer to racks and cool completely.

6   Sandwich 2 cookies together with 2 tsp/10 mL of ganache or other filling. Dust the tops lightly with confectioners' sugar.

Baklava

MAKES 1 HALF SHEET PAN, APPROXIMATELY 200 PIECES

Butter, melted	14 oz	397 g
Phyllo dough	2 packages	2 packages
Walnuts, coarsely chopped	1 lb	454 g
Cinnamon sugar (page 897)	2 oz	57 g
Sugar	14 oz	397 g
Water	8 fl oz	240 mL
Light corn syrup	9 oz	255 g
Honey	9 oz	255 g

1   Brush the bottom and sides of a half sheet pan with enough melted butter to coat.

2   Lay down one layer of the phyllo dough in the buttered pan and brush with a thin coating of melted butter. Keep layering the phyllo and butter for a total of 7 sheets.

3   Sprinkle a thin layer of walnuts and cinnamon sugar on the sheets and layer 3 more sheets of phyllo and melted butter on top.

4   Repeat step 3 two more times, creating 3 sections of walnuts and cinnamon sugar.

5   Layer 7 phyllo sheets with melted butter to make a top layer. Brush the top layer with butter.

6   Wrap the pan tightly in plastic wrap and place in the refrigerator for approximately 20 minutes to firm up.

7   Using a sharp paring knife, score the baklava three-quarters of the way through, cutting diamond shapes approximately 1 by 1 in/3 by 3 cm.

8   Bake at 375°F/191°C until lightly brown, about 12 minutes.

9   While it is baking, bring the sugar, water, corn syrup, and honey to a boil.

10   Pour the entire amount of syrup over the baked pastry and cool to room temperature.

11   Cut entirely through the pastry before serving. Stor in an airtight container.

Peanut butter cookies

MAKES 3 DOZEN COOKIES

Peanuts, shelled, blanched	10 oz	284 g
All-purpose flour	1 lb 2 oz	510 g
Baking soda	½ oz	14 g
Light brown sugar	1 lb	454 g
Granulated sugar	1 lb	454 g
Butter	1 lb	454 g
Salt	½ oz	14 g
Eggs	8 oz	227 g
Creamy peanut butter	1 lb 8 oz	680 g

1   Line sheet pans with parchment paper.

2   Toast the peanuts in a 350°F/177°C oven for 8 to 12 minutes, until golden brown and aromatic. Allow the peanuts to cool completely.

3   Sift together the flour and baking soda.

4   Cream together the sugars, butter, and salt with the paddle attachment, starting on low speed and increasing to medium speed, until light and fluffy. Scrape down the bowl as needed.

5   Add the eggs in 2 or 3 additions, mixing until fully incorporated after each addition. Scrape down the bowl as needed to blend evenly.

6   Add the peanut butter and blend together.

7   Add the sifted flour and baking soda and the cooled peanuts. Mix on low speed just long enough to combine the ingredients.

8   Use a 2 fl oz/59 mL scoop to divide the dough into 2-oz/57-g portions. Arrange the dough on the prepared pans in even rows.

9   Bake at 350°F/177°C until golden brown, 8 to 10 minutes. Cool completely before removing from the pan. Store in an airtight container.

Lace nut tuiles

MAKES 100 COOKIES

Walnuts, pecans, hazelnuts, or almonds, shelled	10 oz	284 g
Sugar	10 oz	284 g
Butter, soft	8 oz	227 g
Orange zest, grated	1 oz	28 g
Light corn syrup	10 oz	284 g
All-purpose flour, sifted	3 oz	85 g

1   Line sheet pans with silicone baking mats. Have assembled shaping implements such as cups, dowels, or rolling pins, depending on the desired shapes.

2   Grind the nuts to a coarse meal.

3   Cream the sugar, butter, and orange zest on medium speed with the paddle attachment until light and smooth, about 5 minutes. Scrape down the bowl as needed. Gradually add the corn syrup, mixing until smooth and evenly blended. On low speed, mix in the flour. Fold in the nuts by hand, or mix on low speed until just combined. Scrape down the bowl as needed to blend evenly.

4   Roll the dough into 1-in/3-cm balls. Place 4 in/10 cm apart on the prepared pans and flatten slightly.

5   Bake at 350°F/177°C until an even light brown, 5 minutes. Remove from the oven and shape while still warm. Or leave the cookies flat and cool in the pans on racks. Store in an airtight container.

Chocolate tuiles

MAKES 15 OZ/425 G BATTER

Cake flour	2⅓ oz	67 g
Dutch-process cocoa powder	1¼ oz	35 g
Butter	2¼ oz	64 g
Confectioners' sugar	4½ oz	128 g
Egg whites, room temperature	3½ oz	99 g
Vanilla extract	1 tsp	5 mL
Confectioners' sugar, for dusting	as needed	as needed

1   Line sheet pans with silicone baking mats. Have assembled shaping implements such as cups, dowels, or rolling pins, depending on the desired shapes.

2   Sift together the cake flour and cocoa powder.

3   Cream together the butter and sugar with the paddle attachment, starting on low speed and increasing to medium speed until smooth, 5 minutes. Scrape down the bowl as needed.

4   Add the egg whites and vanilla and mix on medium speed until fully incorporated. Scrape down the bowl as needed.

5   Turn off the mixer and add the dry ingredients. Mix on low speed until just incorporated. Do not overmix.

6   Thinly spread the batter over a stencil on the silicone baking mat using a small offset spatula.

7   Bake at 325°F/163°C until golden brown but still soft, 8 to 10 minutes.

8   Using a rolling pin or similar rounded item, shape a curve in the tuile while still hot. Reheat as necessary to shape.

9   Store in an airtight container and dust with confectioners' sugar as needed for assembly.

Banana tuiles

MAKES 15¾ OZ/447 G BATTER

Banana purée	9 oz	255 g
Water	2¼ fl oz	33.75 mL
Cake flour	2¼ oz	64 g
Confectioners' sugar	2¼ oz	64 g
Chocolate tuile batter (page 345)	as needed	as needed

1   Line sheet pans with the silicone baking mats. Have assembled shaping implements such as cups, dowels, or rolling pins, depending on the desired shapes.

2   Combine the banana purée, water, cake flour, and confectioners' sugar in a 1-qt/960 mL bain-marie and pulse with an immersion blender until smooth, 1 minute.

3   Lightly spray cooking spray over the silicone mats.

4   Using an offset spatula, spread a thin layer of the banana tuile batter onto your chosen stencil.

5   With a parchment cone, pipe a little chocolate tuile batter onto the spread banana tuile batter in squiggly lines or the design of your choice.

6   Bake at 275°F/135°C until golden brown, 8 to 9 minutes.

7   Using a rolling pin or similar rounded item, shape the tuile into a curve while still hot. Reheat as necessary to shape.

8   Cool to room temperature and store in airtight container.

Honey tuiles

MAKES 2 LB 12½ OZ/1.26 KG BATTER

All-purpose flour	13 oz	369 g
Confectioners' sugar	10 oz	284 g
Butter, soft	10½ oz	298 g
Honey	6 oz	170 g
Egg whites	5 oz	142 g

1   Line sheet pans with silicone baking mats. Have assembled shaping implements such as cups, dowels, or rolling pins, depending on the desired shapes. Using an offset spatula and the desired stencil, spread the batter onto the prepared sheet pans.

2   Sift together the flour and confectioners' sugar.

3   Cream together the butter and honey on medium speed with the paddle attachment until smooth, about 5 minutes. Add the egg whites, blending until fully incorporated. On low speed, mix in the flour mixture. Scrape down the bowl as needed during creaming and mixing to blend evenly.

4   Transfer the batter to a storage container, cover, and refrigerate until firm enough to spread without running.

5   Bake at 325°F/163°C until golden brown, about 10 minutes. Remove from the oven and shape while still warm. Reheat as necessary to shape. Or leave the cookies flat and cool in pans on racks. Store in an airtight container.

VARIATION   **CHOCOLATE HONEY TUILES** Substitute cocoa powder for 2 oz/57 g of the all-purpose flour and sift the two together with the confectioners' sugar.

Nougatine tuiles

MAKES 1 LB 14 OZ/851 G BATTER

Glucose syrup	8 oz	227 g
Sugar	8 oz	227 g
Almonds, finely ground	8 oz	227 g
Butter	6 oz	170 g

1   Line a half sheet pan with a silicone baking mat.

2   Heat the glucose syrup and sugar in a heavy-bottomed saucepan over medium heat until the sugar dissolves. Add the almonds and butter and bring to a boil. Remove from the heat.

3   Spread onto the prepared sheet pan while it is still warm. As it starts to cool, cover with parchment and roll out to an even thickness.

4   Bake at 325°F/163°C until golden brown, about 15 minutes.

5   Flip the sheet of nougatine onto a sheet of parchment paper and cut into desired shapes, then bend to shape as desired. Reheat as necessary to shape. Store in an airtight container.

Meringue sticks

MAKES 3 LB/1.36 KG MERINGUE

Sugar	2 lb	907 g
Egg whites	1 lb	454 g
Cocoa nibs, crushed	as needed	as needed
Cocoa powder	as needed	as needed

1   Line a sheet pan with parchment paper.

2   Place the sugar and egg whites in the bowl of a double boiler. Gently whisk the mixture until it reaches 140°F/60°C. Whip the mixture on high speed with the whip attachment until stiff peaks form. Continue whipping until cool.

3   Fill a pastry bag fitted with a #2 or #3 plain tip with the meringue and pipe sticks 3 to 4 in/8 to 10 cm long onto the prepared pan. Sprinkle one-third of the sticks with cocoa nibs, sprinkle one-third with cocoa powder, and leave one-third plain.

4   Let dry overnight in the oven with the pilot light only or bake at 180°F/82°C until dry.

5   Store in an airtight container.

Peanut crispy base

MAKES 10 TO 12 DISKS (2½ IN/6 CM IN DIAMETER)

Gianduja (page 807)	2½ oz	71 g
Crisp rice cereal	1 oz	28 g
Peanuts, dry roasted, blanched	1½ oz	43 g

1   Melt the gianduja to about 110°F/43°C in a bowl over barely simmering water.

2   Coarsely grind the rice cereal and peanuts in a food processor. Transfer to a bowl.

3   Pour the melted gianduja over the ground nuts and cereal and stir with a rubber spatula to combine.

4   Spread the chocolate mixture on a sheet of parchment paper, top with a second sheet, and roll out to ¹⁄₁₆ in/1.5 mm thick.

5   Freeze the mixture in the parchment paper until firm. Remove from the freezer and gently remove the top parchment paper. Cut disks with a straightedge cutter 2½ in/6 cm diameter. Reserve frozen until needed.

Coffee crispy base

MAKES 12 OZ/340 G

Dark chocolate, chopped	5 oz	142 g
Vegetable oil	1¼ oz	35 g
Butter	1 oz	28 g
Freeze-dried decaffeinated coffee	One individual packet	One individual packet
Pailleté feuilletine	5 oz	142 g

1 Melt the chocolate with the oil and butter. Blend in the coffee.

2 Fold the mixture into the pailleté feuilletine.

3 Press into prepared pans or molds according to the recipe. Allow to set completely before layering or unmolding.

Décor biscuit

MAKES 2 SHEET PANS

Confectioners' sugar	12 oz	340 g
Almond flour	12 oz	340 g
All-purpose flour	5¾ oz	163 g
Heavy cream	3 fl oz	90 mL
Egg whites	27 oz	765 g
Granulated sugar	13⅓ oz	377 g
Coconut, grated and sweetened, for sprinkling	as needed	as needed

1 Sift together the confectioners' sugar and the flours.

2 Mix the dry ingredients with the cream and 5 oz/142 g of the egg whites with the paddle attachment on medium speed until it forms a smooth paste, about 5 minutes.

3 Prepare a common meringue (see page 415) with the remaining 22 oz/624 g egg whites and the granulated sugar.

4 Fold the meringue into the almond mixture until just incorporated.

5 Spread 35 oz/992 g of batter per sheet pan and then sprinkle with coconut.

6 Bake in a 350°F/177°C convection oven for about 7 minutes, until golden brown. Completely cool in the pan. Store wrapped in plastic wrap.

Phyllo dough décor

MAKES APPROXIMATELY 8 RECTANGLES (2 BY 3½ IN/5 BY 9 CM)

Phyllo dough	1 sheet	1 sheet
Clarified butter, melted	2 oz	57 g
Confectioners' sugar, sifted	as needed	as needed
Almond slices	30 each	30 each

1   Lay 1 sheet of phyllo dough out on a clean wooden surface. Using a pastry brush, brush lightly with the clarified butter. Dust lightly with sifted confectioners' sugar.

2   Fold the phyllo dough in half lengthwise. Brush the top of the dough with another coat of clarified butter.

3   Using a straightedge as a guide, cut the phyllo dough into rectangles 2 by 3½ in/5 by 9 cm each.

4   Garnish each rectangle with 3 almond slices overlapping in the center. Dust with sifted confectioners' sugar.

5   Place the rectangles in between 2 silicone baking mats and bake at 375°F/191°C for 5 minutes or until golden brown.

6   Let the dough cool still sandwiched. Store in an airtight container.

Rustle

MAKES 1 HALF SHEET PAN

Praline paste	8¾ oz	248 g
Milk chocolate, melted	2 oz	57 g
Pailleté feuilletine	4⅓ oz	123 g
Butter, softened	1 oz	28 g
Hazelnuts, roughly chopped	¾ oz	21 g

Line a half sheet pan with a silicone baking mat. Mix the praline paste with the chocolate. Blend in the pailleté feuilletine and butter until just combined. Blend in the hazelnuts. Spread on the silicone mat and freeze wrapped in plastic.

chapter twelve

Custards, creams, mousses, and soufflés

When the pastry chef combines eggs, milk, and sugar and bakes them, the result may be a smooth and creamy crème brûlée or a silky crème caramel. When these same ingredients are stirred together over gentle heat, vanilla sauce, or crème anglaise, is the result. Starches or gelatin can be included to produce textures that range from thick but spoonable to a sliceable cream. Folding in meringue or whipped cream produces mousse, Bavarian cream, diplomat cream, chibouste, or a soufflé.

Baked custards

A simple baked custard calls for blending eggs, a liquid such as milk or cream, and sugar and baking until set. There are two basic methods for making a custard base: cold and warm. For the cold method of mixing a custard base, the ingredients are simply stirred together, then poured into molds and baked. The warm method of creating baked custards is best used when creating large batches or when seeking an optimal finished product quality for batches large and small. It produces a silkier, more even texture in the finished custard than does the cold method, as well as allowing the baker to infuse the milk or cream with flavorings such as coffee, tea, or spice.

1. Heat the milk or cream and some of the sugar, stirring with a wooden spoon until the sugar is completely dissolved. Milk or cream is the most common base for custard; heavy cream lends a richer flavor and mouthfeel than milk. Mascarpone, cream cheese, or another soft fresh cheese may be substituted for part of the cream to yield a richer and firmer result.

   Using a wooden spoon will prevent heat transfer from the mixture to the surface of the tool that you hold. Its lack of ability to conduct heat will also prevent any change in temperature of the heating mixture.

2. Add the flavorings at this point and allow steeping, if necessary, off the heat and covered, long enough for them to impart a rich, full flavor. Vanilla beans, coffee, tea, and spices are commonly used as flavorings in baked custards. Vanilla and coffee beans, whole or ground, as well as tea, may be left to steep in the mixture and then strained out once infused. Powdered or instant coffee may be added and dissolved into a small extraction of the mixture, which is then stirred back into the mixture as a whole.

3. Return the mixture to a boil.

4. Blend the eggs and the remaining sugar to make a liaison. The proportion of eggs also may be varied, as may the choice of whole eggs, yolks only, or a combination. Use extra yolks along with whole eggs for a softer custard. Use only egg yolks for a richer, creamier mouthfeel. Use all whole eggs to give more structure to custard that is to be unmolded.

5. Whisking constantly, slowly add about one-third of the hot milk, a few ladlefuls at a time, to the liaison to temper it. Slowly incorporating the milk into the liaison of egg and sugar is done to control the temperature rise that occurs when adding the hot milk into the cooler mixture. Without tempering, the abrupt addition of the hot milk would begin to cook the egg in the liaison.

6. Once the liaison is tempered, you can add the rest of the hot milk more rapidly without scrambling the egg mixture.

7. Pour the mixture through a fine-mesh strainer. This step ensures that any scrambled egg created during tempering is removed from the final custard mixture.

8. Ladle the custard into molds. The molds can be coated with a light film of softened butter if you intend to unmold the custard. This coating will help the custard to be freed without cracking or damage to the integrity of the custard once it is later removed from the mold.

9. Bake the custard in a hot water bath. Using a hot water bath ensures even baking through gentle heat at a constant temperature. Hot water baths also prevent the formation of a crust on the surface of the custard, as well as any rapid expansion that would result in cracks on the custard's surface.

10. To check the custard for doneness, shake the mold gently. When the ripples on the surface move back and forth, rather than in concentric rings, the custard is properly baked.

11. Romovo the molds from the water bath and wipe the ramekins dry. If not removed from the water bath, the custards will continue to cook. This can result in overdone custards that lack a smooth texture and have a pronounced, "eggy" flavor.

12. Place on a cool sheet pan, allow them to cool, and then store under refrigeration.

Tempering the eggs by adding some of the hot milk

hot water bath

A hot water bath, or bain-marie, ensures gentle heat at a constant temperature, allowing for even baking or cooking. Select a pan with sides at least as high as the sides of the molds. Set the molds in the pan as they are filled, leaving about 1 in/3 cm around each mold so it will be surrounded by hot water. Set the pan securely on the oven deck or rack. Add enough very hot or boiling water to the pan to come to about two-thirds of the height of the molds. Be careful not to splash or pour any water into the custards. After the custards are properly baked and removed from the oven, they should also be removed from the hot water bath.

pan preparation for unmolded baked custards

Generally, pans or ramekins that are to be used for baked custards do not need any preparation. The one exception is a custard that is to be unmolded, such as crème caramel. In this case, some chefs choose to give the baking containers a very light coating of softened butter or other fat.

Unmolding custards

Crème caramel is perhaps the most common baked custard that is served unmolded; for this reason the formula must be balanced with enough eggs (whole or yolks) so that the custard will keep its shape when unmolded. The custard should be unmolded carefully so that the sides remain smooth. The custard will be smooth, glossy, and creamy white except near the top, where some of the caramel will have baked into the custard, imparting some of its rich flavor and golden color.

It is imperative that the custard be left under refrigeration for a minimum of 24 hours in order for the caramel to liquefy and create the characteristic sauce for this dessert.

To unmold a custard that has been baked in a ramekin, run a knife or metal spatula around the rim, pressing against the side of the ramekin rather than the custard so as to avoid cutting or marring it. Invert onto a service plate and tap lightly to release. If the custard was baked in an individual aluminum cup, simply invert the mold onto a service plate and puncture the bottom to release the custard.

LEFT: A hot water bath ensures gentle, even heat, a requirement for beautiful custard.
RIGHT: Run a knife around the edge of the mold and invert onto a plate to unmold.

Stirred creams and puddings

Stirred puddings and creams both contain milk (or a similar dairy base), sugar, and a starch, and both are cooked by stirring over direct heat. Creams and puddings are prepared on the stovetop. They must be cooked, stirring constantly, until they come to a full boil, both so the starch is heated sufficiently to thicken the mixture and to remove any undesirable flavor and mouthfeel that uncooked starch would contribute. The starch in the mixture prevents the coagulation of the egg proteins, allowing these products to be cooked to higher temperatures than those made without a starch. Stirred custards, such as vanilla sauce or zabaglione should never be boiled, as they are thickened with eggs rather than starch.

LEFT: The custard must be stirred as it thickens to prevent it from scorching on the bottom of the pan.

RIGHT: Test for nappé by dragging a finger through the custard sauce on the back of a wooden spoon.

LEFT: Strain the prepared vanilla sauce through a fine-mesh sieve into a bain-marie in an ice bath to ensure it is completely smooth and cools quickly.

RIGHT: Placing parchment or plastic wrap directly on the surface of the custard prevents the formation of a skin as it cools.

bread pudding

Bread pudding is a traditional baked custard that is made with bread and flavorings that are mixed together with a simple custard mixture. Any type of bread can be used, but enriched breads such as brioche and challah impart the best flavor. One of the most important steps in making any bread pudding is allowing the bread sufficient time to absorb some of the custard mixture; if the bread is not allowed to soak in the custard for long enough, the texture of the pudding will suffer.

Pour the mixed custard over the cubed bread and other filling ingredients, just to cover.

Gelatin

Gelatin is used as a stabilizer in many bakeshop preparations. In small amounts, gelatin adds body; in greater amounts, it can set a liquid so firmly that it can be sliced or cut into shapes. Using the precise amount of gelatin is crucial: If too little is used, it will not add enough stabilizing power, while if too much is used, the texture will become rubbery and unpalatable, and the flavor undesirable.

Gelatin is a protein composed of molecules that attract water; gelatin is rehydrated, or bloomed, in order to allow these molecules to swell, absorbing moisture.

Since the product will begin to set immediately after the gelatin is added, always prepare all molds, service containers, and so forth before beginning preparation. Some gelatin-stabilized items are served in their molds; others are unmolded before service. To unmold, dip the mold briefly into very hot water, then invert the mold onto a plate and tap it gently to release the item.

1. Gelatin must be rehydrated, or bloomed, and then melted before use. To bloom, soak it in the amount of liquid specified in the formula, which should be approximately 8 fl oz/240 mL of a water-based liquid for every 1 oz/28 g of granulated gelatin. An alternate method commonly used for blooming sheet gelatin is to soak the sheets in enough cold water to completely submerge them. If this method is used, after blooming gently squeeze and wring the sheets to force the excess water out, so as not to add additional liquid to the formula, which would change the consistency and flavor of the finished product.

2. After it is bloomed, the gelatin must be melted. To melt bloomed gelatin, place it in a pan or bowl over low heat or a hot water bath until liquefied. Then stir the melted gelatin into a warm or room-temperature base mixture. (If the base is cold, the gelatin may set up unevenly.) If the base is quite warm or hot (at least 105°F/41°C), however, you may opt to add the bloomed gelatin directly to the hot base, rather than melting it separately, and allow the base's heat to melt the gelatin. Be sure to stir gelatin added this way until it is completely blended into the base.

   As the bloomed gelatin is heated, the water-attracting molecules dissolve completely. Through cooling, the proteins in the gelatin mixture join together to form a three-dimensional web that holds the absorbed moisture. It is the development of this system in the gelatin that results in what we know of as a gel; when added to other mixtures, or bases, the presence of this protein web is what results in a set, stabilized product.

Bloomed sheet gelatin (left); bloomed granulated gelatin (right)

Steamed puddings

Plum pudding (also known as Christmas pudding) is probably the best-known steamed pudding. Steamed puddings are cake-like. Unlike other puddings in this chapter, they contain very little—if any—dairy products such as milk or cream. The traditional base for steamed puddings is a mixture of bread crumbs and suet. Some steamed puddings are based on cake crumbs and butter.

1. To steam a pudding, place a wire rack in a pot large enough to allow the mold to be surrounded by water.

2. Add enough water to the pot so that approximately half the mold will be immersed.

3. Bring the water to a boil and carefully place the mold in the pot, setting it securely on the wire rack. Molds for steamed puddings are typically ceramic or metal, and sometimes are referred to as *basins*. Pudding molds commonly have a center tube and fluted sides. Some have a lid that clamps in place; however, if a mold is lidless, use buttered parchment paper, plastic wrap, or foil to tightly seal the batter.

4. Cover the pot and bring the water to a gentle boil. Check the pot often and add more boiling water as necessary to ensure that the water level remains constant.

Mousse

The name for this delicate dessert comes from a French word that translates literally as "frothy, foamy, or light." To make a mousse, an aerator such as whipped cream or a meringue is folded into a base such as a fruit purée, vanilla sauce, cream or pudding, curd, sabayon, or pâte à bombe. The base should be light and smooth so the aerator can be incorporated easily. Stabilizers such as gelatin may be used in varying amounts, depending on the desired result. If a mousse is stabilized with gelatin, it will begin to set immediately, so prepare all molds, serving containers, and so forth before beginning preparation.

Folding is the technique used to combine a foamy mixture, such as meringue, whipped cream, or beaten egg whites, into a base mixture. The base is usually denser or firmer than the foam and will inevitably collapse the foam somewhat. Proper folding ensures that the foam loses as little volume as possible.

1. To make an egg-safe mousse, use pasteurized egg whites or a Swiss or Italian meringue. Whip the base until soft peaks form.

2. Cool the base if necessary before adding the foam. Add the foam to the base, rather than the other way around, and if using more than one foam, add the least stable one last. For example, if you are adding both a meringue and whipped cream, add the meringue first and then the cream.

3. Working quickly, add a small amount of the foam to the base to lighten it. Some pastry chefs add the foams in thirds for the greatest possible volume. Fold the foam in with a rubber spatula or other tool with a similar broad, flat surface. Using a circular motion, gently run the spatula over the mixture, down and across the bottom of the bowl, and back up to the top again. Rotate the bowl as you work to mix the foam in evenly. Continue to fold the base and foam together until you have an even color and consistency, with no visible pockets of meringue, whipped cream, or the like.

4. Immediately pipe or ladle into prepared pastries or molds. Refrigerate until completely set.

Fold the cream in gently and quickly to maintain volume.

Portion the mousse immediately after preparation.

Bavarian cream

A Bavarian cream is vanilla sauce stabilized with gelatin and lightened and aerated with an equal proportion (by weight) of whipped cream. Bavarian cream can be used for individual dessert preparations. It can be piped and used in cakes, tortes, and charlottes.

Since the Bavarian cream will begin to set immediately once it is finished, any molds, service containers, and so on should be prepared before beginning preparation.

Folding by hand with a whip

1. Whip the cream and reserve under refrigeration so it is ready to be folded into the vanilla sauce mixture. Reserving the whipped cream under refrigeration prevents the fat in the cream from melting, thus keeping the cream full and aerated.

2. The vanilla sauce should be allowed to cool but should not be cold. Gelatin is likely to set up unevenly when added to a cold base; it is important that the vanilla sauce not be cold so that with the addition of the gelatin, it is able to set up evenly.

3. Blend any flavorings to be added, such as melted chocolate, fruit purée, or liqueur, into the vanilla sauce. The sauce should be intensely flavored, as the whipped cream will dilute its flavor. The addition of the whipped cream serves to lighten and aerate the gelatin-stabilized vanilla sauce.

4. The finished Bavarian can be molded or used as a filling or topping.

Hot soufflés

A hot soufflé is made with a flavored base lightened by folding in whipped egg whites, much like a mousse, but rather than being stabilized and chilled, it is baked to further expand the air bubbles trapped in the egg whites and served directly from the oven. Pastry cream and fruit purées are the most common bases for dessert soufflés. If using a flavored pastry cream, it should have a pronounced flavor, as the meringue will lessen the flavor intensity of the base. Any pastry cream can serve as the base for a soufflé. However, specific formulations of pastry cream can increase the stability of the soufflé by the type and amount of starch used. The formula included here uses flour, but in some cases you may want to combine different starches to achieve specific desired results.

A properly sugared soufflé mold is coated with sugar over the rim of the mold.

1. Before preparing the soufflé mixture, prepare the ramekins. Coat the inside and rim of each ramekin lightly but evenly with softened butter. Dust the molds with granulated or confectioners' sugar. The sugar coating will help the soufflé batter to rise as it bakes. Sugar attracts moisture, which in baking turns to steam, assisting in the rising of the batter. A properly sugared soufflé mold is coated with sugar inside as well as over the greased rim.

2. The base for a soufflé should be as light as possible before folding in the meringue. To lighten a pastry cream that has just been prepared, it should be beaten until cool. One that has been under refrigeration should be beaten until completely smooth.

3. Beat the meringue to soft peaks. Folding the meringue into the flavored base will agitate the meringue, acting to further aerate and bring it to stiffer peaks, and it is important that the foam still have enough elasticity to expand as it bakes. Meringue beaten to stiff peaks will not expand as much during baking, and the soufflé will not rise as high. After the meringue has been folded into the base until evenly mixed, the batter should have a consistency similar to that of a soft peak meringue.

4. Immediately fill the prepared ramekins. Wipe away any drops of batter.

5. Bake the soufflés until they rise about 1 in/3 cm (or more) above the rims of the molds and are lightly set. Baking the soufflés serves to further expand the air bubbles trapped in the egg whites, thus causing the product to rise. A properly raised soufflé should rise tall and straight above the rim of the mold.

6. Serve them immediately, with an appropriately flavored sauce or other garnish. Hot soufflés must be served immediately because shortly after removal from the oven, they will begin to deflate.

Crème brûlée

MAKES 10 SERVINGS (5 FL OZ/150 ML EACH)

Heavy cream	32 fl oz	960 mL
Granulated sugar	6 oz	170 g
Salt	pinch	pinch
Vanilla beans	1 each	1 each
Egg yolks, beaten	5½ oz	156 g
Brûlée sugar blend (page 896)	5 oz	142 g
Confectioners' sugar, for dusting	4½ oz	128g

1   Combine the cream, 3 oz/85 g of the sugar, and the salt in a nonreactive saucepan and bring to a simmer over medium heat, stirring gently with a wooden spoon. Remove from the heat. Split the vanilla bean, scrape the seeds from the pod, add both the pod and seeds to the pan, cover, and steep for 15 minutes.

2   Bring the cream to a boil.

3   Meanwhile, blend the egg yolks with the remaining 3 oz/85 g sugar. Temper by gradually adding about one-third of the hot cream, stirring constantly with a whisk. Add the remaining hot cream. Strain and ladle into ramekins, filling them three-quarters full.

4   Bake in a water bath at 325°F/163°C until just set, 20 to 25 minutes.

5   Remove the custards from the water bath and wipe the ramekins dry. Refrigerate until fully chilled.

6   To finish the crème brûlée, evenly coat each custard's surface with a thin layer (1⁄16 in/1.5 mm) of brûlée sugar. Use a propane torch to melt and caramelize the sugar. Lightly dust the surface with confectioners' sugar and serve.

Caramelize the sugar on top of the crème brûlée with a torch.

NOTE   Vanilla extract can be substituted for the vanilla bean. Blend 1 tbsp/15 mL into the custard just before portioning into the ramekins. Vanilla beans that are used to infuse flavor into preparations such as custards can be rinsed under cold water, dried, and stored for a later use, such as making Vanilla Sugar (page 901).

VARIATIONS   **CINNAMON CRÈME BRÛLÉE** Add 3 cinnamon sticks to the cream mixture in step 1. Strain after steeping and proceed as directed above.

COCONUT CRÈME BRÛLÉE Add 2 oz/57 g toasted coconut to the cream mixture in step 1. Strain after steeping and proceed as directed above.

COFFEE CRÈME BRÛLÉE Add 1 oz/28 g coarsely ground dark roast coffee beans to the cream mixture in step 1. Strain after steeping and proceed as directed above.

Chocolate crème brûlée

MAKES 10 SERVINGS (5 FL OZ/150 ML EACH)

Heavy cream	32 fl oz	960 mL
Sugar	6 oz	170 g
Salt	pinch	pinch
Vanilla beans	1 each	1 each
Egg yolks, beaten	5½ oz	156 g
Bittersweet chocolate, melted	6 oz	170 g
Brûlée sugar blend (page 896)	5 oz	142 g
Confectioners' sugar, for dusting	4½ oz	128 g

1   Combine the cream, 3 oz/85 g of the sugar, and the salt in a nonreactive saucepan and bring to a simmer over medium heat, stirring gently with a wooden spoon. Remove from the heat. Split the vanilla bean, scrape the seeds from the pod, add both the pod and seeds to the pan, cover, and steep for 15 minutes.

2   Bring the cream to a boil.

3   Meanwhile, blend the egg yolks with the remaining 3 oz/85 g sugar. Temper by gradually adding about one-third of the hot cream, stirring constantly with a whisk. Add the remaining hot cream. Gradually add about one-third of the hot custard to the chocolate, whipping constantly, then add the remaining hot custard. Strain and ladle into ramekins, filling them three-quarters full.

4   Bake in a water bath at 325°F/163°C until just set, 20 to 25 minutes.

5   Remove the custards from the water bath and wipe the ramekins dry. Refrigerate until fully chilled.

6   To finish the crème brûlée, evenly coat each custard's surface with a thin layer (1⁄16 in/1.5 mm) of brûlée sugar. Use a propane torch to melt and caramelize the sugar. Lightly dust the surface with confectioners' sugar and serve.

Pumpkin crème brûlée

MAKES 10 SERVINGS (5 FL OZ/150 ML EACH)

Heavy cream	24 fl oz	720 mL
Pumpkin purée	8 oz	227 g
Sugar	6 oz	170 g
Salt	pinch	pinch
Vanilla beans	1 each	1 each
Egg yolks, beaten	5½ oz	156 g
Brûlée sugar blend (page 896)	5 oz	142 g
Confectioners' sugar, for dusting	4½ oz	128 g

1   Combine the cream, pumpkin purée, 3 oz/85 g of the sugar, and the salt in a nonreactive saucepan and bring to a simmer over medium heat, stirring gently with a wooden spoon. Remove from the heat. Split the vanilla bean, scrape the seeds from the pod, add both the pod and seeds to the pan, cover, and steep for 15 minutes.

2   Bring the cream to a boil.

3   Meanwhile, blend the egg yolks with the remaining 3 oz/85 g sugar. Temper by gradually adding about one-third of the hot cream, stirring constantly with a whisk. Add the remaining hot cream. Strain and ladle into ramekins, filling them three-quarters full.

4   Bake in a water bath at 325°F/163°C until just set, 20 to 25 minutes.

5   Remove the custards from the water bath and wipe the ramekins dry. Refrigerate until fully chilled.

6   To finish the crème brûlée, evenly coat each custard's surface with a thin layer (1/16 in/1.5 mm) of brûlée sugar. Use a propane torch to melt and caramelize the sugar. Lightly dust the surface with confectioners' sugar and serve.

Vanilla and rosemary cremeux

MAKES 2 CAKE PANS (6 IN/15 CM EACH)

Gelatin sheets	¼ oz	7 g
Milk	8 fl oz	240 mL
Heavy cream	8 fl oz	240 mL
Sugar	3½ oz	99 g
Salt	pinch	pinch
Vanilla beans	1 each	1 each
Rosemary	¼ oz	7 g
Egg yolks	6 oz	170 g

1   Bloom the gelatin in cold water. Drain and set aside.

2   In a saucepan, combine the milk and cream, 2½ oz/71 g of the sugar, and the salt and bring to a simmer over medium heat, stirring gently with a wooden spoon. Remove from the heat. Split the vanilla bean, scrape the seeds from the pod, add both the pod and seeds and the rosemary to the pan, cover, and steep for 15 minutes.

3   Bring the cream to a boil.

4   Meanwhile, blend the egg yolks with the remaining 1 oz/28 g sugar. Temper by gradually adding about one-third of the hot milk and cream mixture, stirring constantly with a whisk. Add the remaining hot milk and cream.

5   With the pan removed from the heat, add the bloomed gelatin. Strain and cool in an ice water bath until it just starts to thicken.

6   Pour into the cake pans or other desired molds lined with plastic wrap and freeze.

Banana cremeux

MAKES 10 SERVINGS

Bananas, fully ripe, unpeeled	6 oz	170 g
Gelatin sheets	1 each	1 each
Heavy cream	4 fl oz	120 mL
Milk	1 fl oz	30 ml
Vanilla beans, split and scraped	½ each	½ each
Sugar	1¾ oz	50 g
Egg yolks	3 oz	85 g

1   Place the bananas in a half hotel pan and roast the bananas in their skins in a 350°F/177°C oven until they crack, the skin turns black, and they begin to seep, about 15 minutes.

2   Let the bananas cool to room temperature.

3   Bloom the gelatin in cold water. Drain and set aside.

4   Bring 3 fl oz/90 mL of the cream, the milk, the vanilla bean and seeds, and half of the sugar to a boil in a medium sauce pot over medium heat.

5   Meanwhile, combine the yolks, the remaining cream, and the remaining sugar in a bowl and mix together with a whisk until well blended.

6   Temper the yolk mixture by gradually adding about one-third of the hot cream mixture, whisking constantly. Return the tempered egg mixture to the remaining hot cream in the sauce pot and cook, stirring constantly, until the mixture thickens enough to coat the back of a spoon (180°F/82°C).

7   Remove from the heat and let the mixture cool slightly.

8   Peel the skin off the bananas. Remove the pod of the vanilla bean. Combine the cream mixture with the roasted bananas in a blender and blend for 30 seconds, until smooth.

9   Pour the mixture into a bowl and temper 3 oz/85 g of the warm blended mixture with the bloomed gelatin. Return the melted gelatin mixture to the rest of the mixture. Strain through a fine-mesh sieve.

10   Using a confectionery funnel, evenly fill flexible disk molds 1½ in wide by ½ in deep/4 cm wide by 1 cm deep three-quarters full. Wrap with plastic wrap and freeze the molds for at least 12 hours. Keep frozen until needed and carefully unmold while still frozen for assembly.

Basil cremeux

MAKES 1 LB 11½ OZ/780 G

Gelatin sheets	¼ oz	7 g
Milk	8 oz	227 g
Heavy cream	8 oz	227 g
Salt	pinch	pinch
Sugar	3½ oz	100 g
Vanilla beans	1 each	1 each
Egg yolks	6 each	6 each
Basil purée (see Note)	as needed	as needed

1 Bloom the gelatin in cold water. Drain and set aside.

2 Combine the milk and cream with the salt and 2 oz/57 g of the sugar in a nonreactive saucepan and bring to a boil, stirring to dissolve the sugar. Split the vanilla bean, scrape the seeds from the pod, add both the pod and seeds to the pan, cover, and steep for 15 minutes. Strain before use.

3 Meanwhile, blend the egg yolks with the remaining 1½ oz/43 g sugar using a whisk.

4 Temper the egg yolks by gradually adding one-third of the hot milk, whisking constantly. Return the tempered egg mixture to the remaining hot milk in the saucepan and continue cooking until the mixture thickens enough to coat the back of a spoon.

5 Add the basil purée to the vanilla sauce and adjust to taste. Blend, stirring gently. Strain.

6 Add the bloomed gelatin and, stirring constantly, cool over an ice water bath to 70°F/21°C.

7 Pour into molds as desired and freeze.

NOTE   To prepare the basil purée, blanch basil leaves in boiling water for 5 seconds. Shock in cold water. Purée with Simple Syrup (page 900) to a thick, smooth consistency.

Macadamia cremeux

MAKES 3 LB 12 OZ/1.70 KG

Gelatin sheets	⅓ oz	9 g
Heavy cream	2 lb	907 g
Salt	pinch	pinch
Sugar	5 oz	142 g
Vanilla beans	3 each	3 each
Egg yolks	12 each	12 each
Macadamia nut paste (see Note)	8 oz	227 g

1 Bloom the gelatin in cold water. Drain and set aside.

2 Combine the cream with the salt and 3 oz/85 g of the sugar in a nonreactive saucepan and bring to a boil, stirring to dissolve the sugar. Split the vanilla bean, scrape the seeds from the pod, add both the pod and seeds to the pan, cover, and steep for 15 minutes.

3 Meanwhile, blend the egg yolks with the remaining 2 oz/57 g sugar using a whisk.

4 Temper the egg yolks by gradually adding one-third of the hot cream, whipping constantly. Return the tempered egg mixture to the remaining hot cream in the saucepan and continue cooking until the mixture thickens enough to coat the back of a spoon.

5 Add the macadamia nut paste to the vanilla sauce. Blend using an immersion blender.

6 Off the heat, add the bloomed gelatin and, stirring constantly, cool over an ice water bath to 70°F/21°C.

7 Pour into molds as desired and freeze.

NOTE To make macadamia nut paste, toast nuts in a 300°F/149°C oven. Place in the food processor and process until a slightly chunky paste is obtained.

Crème caramel

MAKES 6 SERVINGS (4 OZ/113 G EACH)

CARAMEL		
Sugar	5 oz	142 g
CUSTARD		
Milk	7 fl oz	105 mL
Heavy cream	7 fl oz	30 mL
Sugar	1¾ oz	50 g
Vanilla beans (optional)	1 each	1 each
Eggs	10 oz	284 g

1   To prepare the caramel, add a small amount of the sugar to a medium-hot pan set over medium heat and allow it to melt, then add the remaining sugar in small increments, allowing each addition to fully melt before adding the next. Continue this process until all the sugar has been added to the pan, and cook to the desired color. Carefully divide the liquid among the bottoms of the ramekins.

2   To prepare the custard, warm the milk and cream and half of the sugar and remove from the heat. If using a vanilla bean, split the bean, scrape the seeds from the pod, add both the pod and seeds to the pan, cover, and steep for 15 minutes.

3   Combine the eggs and the remaining sugar.

4   Temper by gradually adding about one-third of the hot milk and cream, stirring constantly with a whisk. Add the remaining hot milk and cream. Do not return to the heat.

5   Strain and divide the custard mixture among the prepared ramekins.

6   Bake in a water bath at 325°F/163°C until just set, 20 to 25 minutes.

7   Remove the custards from the water bath and wipe the ramekins dry. Refrigerate until fully chilled.

VARIATION   **CRÈME CARAMEL WITH GRAND MARNIER** Add 1 fl oz/30 mL of Grand Marnier in step 4 after adding the remaining hot milk and cream.

Pots de crème

MAKES 12 SERVINGS (4 FL OZ/120 ML EACH)

CARAMEL		
Sugar	5 oz	142 g
CUSTARD		
Milk, warm	16 fl oz	480 mL
Heavy cream, warm	16 fl oz	480 mL
Eggs	6 oz	170 g
Egg yolks	2 oz	57 g
Sugar	3 oz	85 g
Semisweet chocolate, melted	4 oz	113 g
Vanilla extract	1 tbsp	15 mL

1   To prepare the caramel, add a small amount of the sugar to a medium-hot pan set over medium heat and allow it to melt, then add the remaining sugar in small increments, allowing each addition to fully melt before adding the next. Continue this process until all the sugar has been added to the pan, and cook to the desired color.

2   To make the custard, carefully add the milk and cream to the caramel over the heat, stirring to incorporate, and bring to a boil.

3   Meanwhile, blend the eggs and egg yolks with the sugar to make the liaison. Temper by adding about one-third of the hot cream mixture, whisking constantly. Add the remaining hot cream mixture. Gradually add about one-third of the hot custard to the chocolate, whisking constantly, then add the remaining hot custard and the vanilla. Strain and ladle into ramekins, filling them three-quarters full.

4   Bake in a water bath at 325°F/163°C until fully set, about 30 minutes.

5   Remove the custards from the water bath and wipe the ramekins dry. Refrigerate until fully chilled.

Pastry cream

MAKES 3 LB/1.36 KG

Milk	32 fl oz	960 mL
Sugar	8 oz	227 g
Butter	3 oz	85 g
Salt	pinch	pinch
Cornstarch	3 oz	85 g
Eggs	12 oz	340 g
Vanilla extract or vanilla beans, seeds only	1 tbsp 1 bean	15 mL 1 bean

1   Combine 24 fl oz/720 mL of the milk, 4 oz/113 g of the sugar, the butter, and salt in a nonreactive saucepan and bring to a boil over medium heat, stirring to dissolve the sugar.

2   Meanwhile, combine the cornstarch with the remaining 4 oz/114 g sugar. Stirring with a whisk, add the remaining 8 oz/240 mL milk. Add the eggs and vanilla extract or vanilla bean seeds, stirring with the whisk until the mixture is completely smooth.

3   Temper the egg mixture by adding about one-third of the hot milk, stirring constantly with the whisk. Return the mixture to the remaining hot milk in the saucepan. Continue cooking, stirring vigorously with the whisk, until the pastry cream comes to a boil and the whisk leaves a trail in it.

4   Pour the pastry cream into a large shallow nonreactive pan or plastic-lined sheet pan. Cover with plastic wrap placed directly on the surface of the cream, and cool over an ice water bath.

5   Store the pastry cream, covered, under refrigeration for up to 3 days.

VARIATIONS   **HONEY PASTRY CREAM** Omit the 4 oz/113 g of sugar added with the milk in step 1. Blend 6 oz/170 g honey and 1 tsp/3 g grated orange zest with 1 lb/454 g of the pastry cream immediately after it is finished cooking.

LIQUEUR-FLAVORED PASTRY CREAM Add 4 fl oz/120 mL liqueur to 1 lb/454 g of the pastry cream immediately after it is finished cooking.

Pistachio cream

MAKES 3 LB 4½ OZ/1.50 KG

Gelatin, granulated	½ oz	14 g
Whole milk	19 fl oz	570 mL
Pistachio paste	4 oz	113 g
Sugar	3 oz	85 g
Egg yolks	6 oz	170 g
Kirsch	2 tbsp	30 mL
Whipped cream	1 lb 3 oz	539 g

1   Bloom the gelatin in 4 fl oz/120 mL cold water.

2   Combine the milk with the pistachio paste and 1½ oz/43 g of the sugar in a nonreactive saucepan and bring to a boil, stirring to dissolve the sugar.

3   Meanwhile, blend the egg yolks with the remaining 1½ oz/42 g sugar using a whisk.

4   Temper the egg yolks by gradually adding one-third of the hot milk, whipping constantly. Return the tempered egg mixture to the remaining hot milk in the saucepan and continue cooking until the mixture thickens enough to coat the back of a spoon.

5   Remove the sauce from the heat and add the bloomed gelatin. Stir to dissolve the gelatin.

6   Strain the sauce through a fine-mesh sieve into a bain-marie and chill in an ice water bath to 72°F/22°C. Once cooled, stir in the kirsch and whipped cream.

7   Store the pistachio cream, covered, under refrigeration.

Vanilla pudding

MAKES 2 LB 10 OZ/1.19 KG, 10 SERVINGS (4 OZ/113 G EACH)

Milk	32 fl oz	960 mL
Sugar	6½ oz	184 g
Salt	pinch	pinch
Cornstarch	1¾ oz	50 g
Egg yolks	2½ oz	71 g
Butter	½ oz	14 g
Vanilla extract	2 tsp	10 mL

1   Combine 24 fl oz/720 mL of the milk, 3½ oz/99 g of the sugar, and the salt in a nonreactive saucepan and bring to a boil, stirring gently with a wooden spoon.

2   Meanwhile, combine the cornstarch with the remaining 3 oz/85 g sugar. Stirring with a whisk, add the remaining 8 fl oz/240 mL milk. Add the egg yolks, stirring with the whisk until the mixture is completely smooth.

3   Temper the egg mixture by adding about one-third of the hot milk, stirring constantly with the whisk. Return the tempered egg mixture to the remaining hot milk in the saucepan. Continue cooking, stirring constantly with the whisk, until the pudding comes to a boil. Remove from the heat and stir in the butter and vanilla extract.

4   Pour into serving dishes, or use as desired. Cover and refrigerate until fully chilled.

VARIATION   **CHOCOLATE PUDDING** Melt 5 oz/142 g bittersweet chocolate with the butter over a pan of barely simmering water; set aside. In step 3, after blending in the vanilla, gradually incorporate one-third of the hot pudding into the chocolate mixture, stirring constantly with the whip. Add the chocolate mixture to the remaining pudding and blend to fully combine. Proceed as directed above.

Rice pudding

MAKES 2 LB 10 OZ/1.19 KG, 10 SERVINGS (4 OZ/113 G EACH)

Milk	32 fl oz	960 mL
Sugar	4 oz	113 g
Cinnamon stick	1 each	1 each
Orange slice	1 each	1 each
Long-grain white rice, rinsed	3 oz	85 g
Cornstarch	¼ oz	7 g
Eggs	3 oz	85 g
Vanilla extract	1 tsp	5 mL

1   Combine the milk, 2 oz/57 g of the sugar, the cinnamon stick, and orange slice in a nonreactive saucepan and bring to a boil. Add the rice and simmer over low heat until tender, about 30 minutes.

2   Meanwhile, just as the rice is finished cooking, combine the cornstarch with the remaining 2 oz/57 g sugar. Add the eggs, stirring with a whisk until the mixture is completely smooth.

3   Remove the orange slice and cinnamon stick from the rice. Temper the egg mixture by adding about one-third of the hot milk-rice mixture, stirring constantly with the whisk. Return the tempered egg mixture to the remaining hot milk in the saucepan. Continue cooking, stirring constantly with the whisk, until the pudding comes to a boil. Remove from the heat and blend in the vanilla extract.

4   Pour into serving dishes, or use as desired. Cover and refrigerate until fully chilled.

Bread and butter pudding

Dark raisins	3 oz	85 g
Rum	4 fl oz	120 mL
Enriched bread	9 oz	255 g
Butter, melted	3 oz	85 g
Milk	32 fl oz	960 mL
Sugar	6 oz	170 g
Eggs, beaten	12 oz	340 g
Egg yolks, beaten	2¼ oz	64 g
Vanilla extract	½ tsp	2.50 mL
Ground cinnamon	½ tsp	1 g
Salt	½ tsp	2.50 g
Butter, soft, for brushing	as needed	as needed

1 Place the raisins in a bowl and add the rum. Set aside to plump for 20 minutes, then drain.

2 Cut the bread into ½-in/1-cm cubes. Place on a sheet pan and drizzle with the melted butter. Toast in a 350°F/177°C oven, stirring once or twice, until golden brown.

3 Combine the milk and 3 oz/85 g of the sugar in a nonreactive saucepan and bring to a boil.

4 Meanwhile, blend the eggs, egg yolks, vanilla, and the remaining 3 oz/85 g sugar to make the liaison. Temper by gradually adding about one-third of the hot milk, whisking constantly. Add the remaining hot milk and strain the custard into a bowl.

5 Add the toasted bread, cinnamon, salt, and the drained raisins to the custard. Soak over an ice water bath for at least 1 hour to allow the bread to absorb the custard. Lightly brush 8 ramekins with softened butter.

6 Ladle the mixture into the prepared ramekins, filling them three-quarters full. Bake in a water bath at 350°F/177°C until just set, 45 to 50 minutes.

7 Remove the custards from the water bath and wipe the ramekins dry. Refrigerate until fully chilled.

NOTE The pudding can also be baked in a large hotel pan and portioned for service.

VARIATIONS **CHOCOLATE BREAD PUDDING** Omit the raisins and rum. Melt 6 oz/170 g bittersweet chocolate and blend into the hot custard before straining. Proceed as directed above.

DRIED CHERRY AND ORANGE BREAD PUDDING Substitute dried cherries for the raisins and brandy for the rum. Add the grated zest of 1 large or 2 small oranges to the milk before heating it, and proceed as directed above.

PUMPKIN BREAD PUDDING Whisk 8 oz/227 g pumpkin purée into the hot custard after straining. Increase the cinnamon to 2½ tsp/5 g and add 1 tsp/2 g grated nutmeg along with it. Proceed as directed above.

CLOCKWISE FROM UPPER LEFT:
Rice Pudding (page 373), Chocolate Mousse (page 380), Panna Cotta (page 376), Pumpkin Crème Brûlée (page 363), Pots de Crème (page 369), Bread and Butter Pudding (opposite)

Panna cotta

Gelatin, granulated	½ oz	14 g
Water	4 fl oz	120 mL
Heavy cream	32 fl oz	960 mL
Sugar	12 oz	340 g
Salt	½ tsp	2.50 g
Buttermilk	30 fl oz	900 mL

1   Bloom the gelatin in the water and melt. Combine the cream, sugar, and salt in a nonreactive saucepan and heat, stirring, over medium heat to dissolve the sugar; make sure the mixture does not simmer. Remove from the heat.

2   Add gelatin to the cream mixture, blending well. Let the mixture cool to 100°F/38°C and stir in the buttermilk.

3   Pour into ramekins. Cover tightly and refrigerate for several hours or until set.

VARIATIONS   **CHAI PANNA COTTA** Add 1 tsp/30 mL Chai Tea to warm cream mixture, cover, and allow to steep for 10 to 15 minutes. Strain the cream before adding the gelatin. Proceed as directed above.

CINNAMON PANNA COTTA Add 3 cinnamon sticks to the warm cream mixture, cover, and allow to steep for 10 to 15 minutes. Remove the cinnamon sticks and reheat the cream before adding the gelatin. Proceed as directed above.

LEMON PANNA COTTA Add 1 tsp/3 g finely grated lemon zest to the cream mixture in step 1. Proceed as directed above.

Fruit curd

MAKES 2 LB 2 OZ/964 G

Gelatin sheets	3 each	3 each
Water	4 fl oz	120 mL
Citrus juice or fruit purée	8 oz	227 g
Sugar	10 oz	284 g
Eggs	8 oz	227 g
Butter, cubed	8 oz	227 g

1   Bloom the gelatin in the water. Drain and set aside. Whisk together the juice, sugar, and eggs. Add the butter and place the mixture in a bowl over barely simmering water.

2   Cook the mixture, stirring it every 3 to 5 minutes, until it is thickened and approximately 165°F/74°C. Remove the pot from the heat and add the soaked gelatin to the mixture, and then strain the mixture through a fine-mesh strainer.

3   Pour the curd into a large shallow nonreactive pan or plastic-lined sheet pan. Cover with plastic wrap placed directly on the surface of the curd, and cool over an ice water bath.

4   Store the curd, covered, under refrigeration.

Lemon curd

MAKES 2 LB 2 OZ/964 G

Butter, cubed	1 lb 5 oz	595 g
Sugar	1 lb 2 oz	510 g
Lemon juice	18 fl oz	540 mL
Lemon zest, grated	1¼ oz	35 g
Egg yolks	1 lb 2 oz	510 g

1   Combine 10½ oz/298 g of the butter, 9 oz/255 g of the sugar, and the lemon juice and zest and bring to a boil over medium heat, stirring gently to dissolve the sugar.

2   Meanwhile, blend the egg yolks with the remaining 9 oz/255 g sugar. Temper by gradually adding about one-third of the lemon juice mixture, stirring constantly with a whisk. Return the tempered egg mixture to the saucepan. Continue cooking, stirring constantly with the whisk, until the mixture comes to a boil.

3   Stir in the remaining butter.

4   Strain the curd into a large shallow container or bowl. Cover with plastic wrap placed directly on the surface of the curd. Cool over an ice water bath.

5   Store the curd, covered, under refrigeration.

VARIATIONS   **GRAPEFRUIT CURD** Replace the lemon juice with grapefruit juice and the lemon zest with grapefruit zest.

LIME CURD Replace the lemon juice with lime juice and the lemon zest with lime zest.

ORANGE CURD Replace the lemon juice with orange juice and the lemon zest with orange zest, and reduce the sugar by 4 oz/113 g.

Plum pudding

MAKES 64 FL OZ/1.92 L

Suet	8 oz	227 g
Bread crumbs, fresh	8 oz	227 g
Dried currants	12 oz	340 g
Dark raisins	12 oz	340 g
Dark brown sugar	8 oz	227 g
Blanched almonds, chopped	4 oz	113 g
Candied orange peel, diced	4 oz	113 g
Candied cherries, quartered	6 oz	170 g
Lemon zest, grated	1 tsp	3 g
Eggs	9 oz	255 g
Whiskey	2 fl oz	60 mL
Hard sauce (pages 460 to 461), for serving	as needed	as needed

1   Line a mold with plastic wrap, leaving enough overhang to cover the pudding.

2   Place the suet and bread crumbs in a food processor and process until smooth. Transfer to the mixer, add the remaining ingredients, and mix on medium speed with the paddle attachment until blended.

3   Fill the prepared mold. Cover the pudding with the excess plastic wrap and then cover with foil.

4   Steam the pudding in a steamer until firm, about 4 hours. The pudding can be wrapped in plastic wrap and refrigerated after reaching room temperature. Steam the pudding until warm before service.

5   Serve warm with hard sauce.

NOTE   The suet should be as clean and white as possible. Be sure to trim off any meat scraps.

Raspberry mousse

MAKES 3 LB 5 OZ/1.50 KG

Gelatin, granulated	1⅓ oz	37 g
Water, cold	10 fl oz	300 mL
Heavy cream	14 fl oz	420 mL
Raspberry purée	1 lb 8 oz	680 g
Egg whites	5 oz	142 g
Sugar	9 oz	255 g

1   Assemble and prepare the desired pastries, containers, or molds that are to be used in the application of the mousse before beginning preparation.

2   Bloom the gelatin in the water and melt.

3   Whip the heavy cream to medium peaks. Cover and reserve under refrigeration.

4   Warm 12 oz/340 g of the raspberry purée in a saucepan. Remove from the heat. Add the melted gelatin to the purée and stir to incorporate. Blend in the remaining 12 oz/340 g purée. Cool the raspberry purée–gelatin mixture to 70°F/21°C.

5   Combine the egg whites and sugar in a mixer bowl. Set over a pot of simmering water and heat, stirring constantly with a whisk, until the mixture reaches 145°F/63°C. Transfer to the mixer and whip on high speed with the whip attachment until stiff peaks form. Continue beating until the meringue has completely cooled.

6   Gently blend one-third of the meringue into the raspberry purée mixture to lighten it. Fold in the remaining meringue, thoroughly incorporating it. Fold in the reserved whipped cream.

7   Immediately pipe or ladle into prepared pastries or molds. Refrigerate until completely set.

VARIATIONS   **COCONUT MOUSSE** Substitute coconut milk or Coco Lopez for the raspberry purée.

MANGO MOUSSE Substitute mango purée for the raspberry purée.

PASSION FRUIT MOUSSE Dilute passion fruit concentrate as directed and substitute it for the raspberry purée.

PEAR MOUSSE Substitute pear purée for the raspberry purée.

STRAWBERRY MOUSSE Substitute strawberry purée for the raspberry purée.

Chocolate mousse

MAKES 3 LB 9 OZ/1.62 KG

Heavy cream	30 fl oz	900 mL
Dark chocolate, 64%, finely chopped	15 oz	425 g
Gelatin sheets	3 each	3 each
Water, cold	10 fl oz	300 mL
Eggs	6 oz	170 g
Egg yolks	3 oz	85 g
Sugar	3 oz	85 g

1   Assemble and prepare the desired pastries, containers, or molds that are to be used in the application of the mousse before beginning preparation.

2   Whip the cream to soft peaks. Cover and reserve under refrigeration.

3   Melt the chocolate in a bowl over barely simmering water (the bottom of the bowl should not touch the water). Bring the chocolate to 120°F/49°C.

4   Meanwhile, submerge the gelatin sheets in the water and allow them to bloom for about 5 minutes.

5   Combine the eggs, egg yolks, and sugar in a bowl over simmering water, whisking constantly until it reaches 135°F/57°C.

6   Pour the egg and sugar mixture in the mixer and whip on high speed with the whip attachment until light in color and foamy.

7   Meanwhile, strain the gelatin well and melt it over a gentle water bath. Add the melted gelatin to the still-warm egg and sugar mixture and continue to whip until it reaches room temperature, 75°F/24°C.

8   Combine the mixture into the melted chocolate, whisking vigorously.

9   Fold in the whipped cream, thoroughly incorporating it.

10 Immediately pipe or spread into prepared pastries or containers. Cover and refrigerate until completely set.

VARIATION   **CHOCOLATE CHAI MOUSSE** Heat the cream and add 1 tbsp/30 mL of Chai tea. Cover and allow to steep for 5 minutes. Refrigerate the cream until fully chilled before whipping to soft peaks. Proceed as directed above.

Dark chocolate mousse

MAKES 1 LB 5½ OZ/610 G

Bittersweet chocolate, chopped	5 oz	142 g
Butter	4 oz	113 g
Egg yolks	3 oz	85 g
Glucose syrup	½ oz	14 g
Egg whites	6 oz	170 g
Sugar	3 oz	85 g

1   Assemble and prepare the desired pastries, containers, or molds that are to be used in the application of the mousse before beginning preparation.

2   Melt the chocolate and butter together in a bowl over simmering water, to 120°F/49°C.

3   Combine the egg yolks and glucose in a mixer bowl and whisk together until thoroughly blended. Place the bowl over a pot of simmering water and heat, whisking constantly, until the mixture is thickened and very foamy and has reached 180°F/82°C.

4   Temper the yolk mixture into the melted chocolate and butter, adding a small amount of the yolk mixture at first, then adding the rest in a thin stream while whisking vigorously.

5   Meanwhile, make an Italian meringue with the egg whites and the sugar (see page 405).

6   Gently fold the meringue into the chocolate mixture, incorporating it.

7   Immediately pipe or spread into prepared pastries or containers. Cover and refrigerate until completely set.

White chocolate mousse pâte à bombe

MAKES 7 LB/3.18 KG

Heavy cream	48 fl oz	1.44 L
Gelatin sheets	8 each	8 each
White chocolate, chopped	2 lb 7 oz	1.1 kg
Milk	11 fl oz	330 mL
Sugar	6½ oz	184 g
Water	4 fl oz	120 mL
Egg yolks	8 oz	227 g

1   Assemble and prepare the desired pastries, containers, or molds that are to be used in the application of the mousse before beginning preparation.

2   Whip the cream to soft peaks. Cover and reserve covered under refrigeration.

3   Bloom the gelatin in cold water.

4   Melt the chocolate in a mixer bowl over barely simmering water. Bring the milk to a boil and gently stir into the melted chocolate.

5   Drain the gelatin, add it to the chocolate-milk mixture, and stir well until the gelatin melts.

6   Combine the sugar and water in a pot and boil to 250°F/121°C.

7   Meanwhile, whip the yolks on high speed with the whip attachment until light in color. Pour the sugar syrup into the yolks as they are whipping and whip until cool to make a pâte à bombe.

8   Fold the pâte à bombe into the chocolate mixture. Gently fold in the reserved whipped cream.

9   Immediately pipe or spread into prepared pasteries or containers. Cover and refrigerate until completely set.

Coffee mousse

MAKES 1 LB 12 OZ/793 G

Heavy cream	9½ oz	269 g
Gelatin sheets	4 each	4 each
Kahlúa	1 fl oz	30 mL
Coffee extract	2 tbsp	30 mL
Egg yolks	7½ oz	213 g
Sugar	6 oz	170 g
Egg whites	2½ oz	71 g

1   Assemble and prepare the desired pastries, containers, or molds that are to be used in the application of the mousse before beginning preparation.

2   Whip the cream to soft peaks. Cover and reserve under refrigeration.

3   Bloom the gelatin by completely submerging it in cold water, then strain and melt it with the Kahlúa and coffee extract in a saucepan over low heat.

4   Combine the egg yolks and 2½ oz/71 g of the sugar in a mixer bowl and whisk until thoroughly blended. Place the bowl over simmering water and heat, whisking constantly, until the mixture is thickened and very foamy and has reached 145°F/63°C.

5   Transfer the yolk and sugar mixture to the mixer and whip on high speed with whip attachment until cool.

6   Measure out 6 oz/170 g of the yolk and sugar mixture and add the melted gelatin.

7   Meanwhile, make an Italian meringue with the egg whites and the remaining 3½ oz/99 g of sugar (see page 405).

8   Measure out 3⅓ oz/94 g of the Italian meringue for the mousse.

9   Fold one-third of the yolk mixture into the meringue, and then fold in remaining yolk mix.

10   Fold in the whipped cream, thoroughly incorporating it.

11   Immediately pipe or spread into prepared pastries or containers. Cover and refrigerate until completely set.

NOTE   Use meringue once it is at medium peak and still slightly warm.

Dark coffee mousse

MAKES 1 LB 6 OZ/624 G

Heavy cream	11½ fl oz	345 mL
Eggs	2 each	2 each
Sugar	1½ oz	43 g
Instant coffee granules	1 oz	28 g
Bittersweet chocolate, finely chopped	6 oz	170 g
Gelatin sheets	2 each	2 each
Coffee extract	⅒ oz	3 g

1 Assemble and prepare the desired pastries, containers, or molds that are to be used in the application of the mousse before beginning preparation.

2 Whip the cream to soft peaks. Cover and reserve under refrigeration.

3 Combine the eggs, sugar, and instant coffee in a mixer bowl and whisk until thoroughly blended. Place the bowl over simmering water and heat, whisking constantly, until the mixture is thickened and very foamy and has reached at least 165°F/74°C.

4 Melt the chocolate in a bowl over barely simmering water. Reserve the chocolate at 110°F/43°C.

5 Bloom and strain the gelatin, and then melt with the coffee extract. Add to the egg-sugar-coffee mixture. Once cool, add 3 oz/85 g of the softly whipped cream to the chocolate and whisk until the mixture is homogeneous.

6 Immediately fold the egg-sugar-coffee mixture into the chocolate before the chocolate starts to set up.

7 Fold in the remaining cream.

8 Immediately pipe or spread into prepared pastries or containers. Cover and refrigerate until completely set.

Caramel mousse

MAKES 2 LB 14 OZ/1.30 KG, ENOUGH FILLING FOR TWO 6-IN/15-CM CAKES

Heavy cream	14½ fl oz	435 mL
Gelatin sheets	4 each	4 each
Water, cold	1 fl oz	30 mL
Soft caramel (see Note)	1 lb 1½ oz	496 g
Egg yolks	4 oz	113 g
Sugar	5¼ oz	148 g
Egg whites	3⅓ oz	94 g
Salt	pinch	pinch

1   Assemble and prepare the desired pastries, containers, or molds that are to be used in the application of the mousse before beginning preparation.

2   Whip the cream to soft peaks. Cover and reserve under refrigeration.

3   Bloom the gelatin by completely submerging it in the water, 5 minutes. Strain the gelatin and melt it with 1 fl oz/30 mL water in a saucepan over low heat until dissolved.

4   Warm the soft caramel to 100°F/38°C and add the melted gelatin to it. Mix until fully incorporated.

5   Combine the egg yolks and 1 oz/28 g of the sugar in the mixer and whip on medium speed with the whip attachment until thoroughly blended. Place the bowl over a pot of simmering water and heat, whisking constantly by hand, until the mixture is thickened, light in color, and very foamy and has reached at least 145°F/63°C.

6   Transfer the bowl to the mixer and whip on medium speed with the whip attachment until cool.

7   Meanwhile, make a Swiss meringue with the egg whites, salt, and the remaining 4¼ oz/120 g sugar (see page 405).

8   Fold the egg yolk—sugar mixture into the soft caramel, followed by the meringue and lastly the whipped cream. Continue to fold until all components are fully incorporated.

9   Immediately pipe or spread into prepared pastries or containers. Cover and refrigerate until completely set.

NOTE   To make the soft caramel, place two 14-oz/397-g cans of sweetened condensed milk in a pot so they are immersed in water. Keep the cans covered and the water at a low boil for 5 hours. For safety, cool slightly before opening.

Chocolate caramel mousse

MAKES 4 LB 2 OZ/1.87 KG

Heavy cream	40½ fl oz	1.22 L
Sugar	4 oz	113 g
Egg yolks	6½ oz	184 g
Gelatin sheets	4 each	4 each
Milk chocolate, melted	15 oz	425 g

1 Assemble and prepare the desired pastries, containers, or molds that are to be used in the application of the mousse before beginning preparation.

2 Whip 32 fl oz/960 mL of the cream to soft peaks. Cover and reserve under refrigeration.

3 Heat the remaining cream in a medium saucepan over low heat. Do not allow to boil.

4 Place the sugar in a heavy-bottomed saucepan and heat over medium heat until it melts and turns a deep amber color, about 350°F/177°C. Carefully stir in the hot cream.

5 Temper the egg yolks with the caramel, adding 2 fl oz/60 mL of egg yolks at a time. Cook this mixture to 160°F/71°C. Transfer to a mixer bowl and whip on high speed with the whip attachment until cool.

6 Bloom the gelatin in cold water, strain, melt, and add to the caramel mixture. Add the caramel mixture quickly to the melted chocolate, stirring with a whisk to combine.

7 Gently fold in the whipped cream and mix until fully incorporated.

8 Immediately pipe or spread into prepared pastries or containers. Cover and refrigerate until completely set.

Lemon mousse lemon filling for sheet cakes

MAKES 2 LB 7 OZ/1.11 KG

Gelatin, granulated	2½ oz	71 g
Water, cold	20 fl oz	600 mL
Heavy cream	24 fl oz	720 mL
Lemon curd (page 377), warm	12 oz	340 g
Sorbet syrup (page 488)	3 fl oz	90 mL
Lemon fruit compound	1 tbsp	7 g

1 Assemble and prepare the desired pastries, containers, or molds that are to be used in the application of the mousse before beginning preparation.

2   Bloom the gelatin in the water and melt.

3   Whip the cream to medium peaks. Cover and reserve under refrigeration.

4   Blend together the lemon curd with the sorbet syrup and lemon fruit compound, stirring with a whisk. Add the melted gelatin. Strain and cool to 70°F/21°C.

5   Gently blend one-third of the reserved whipped cream into the lemon curd mixture. Fold in the remaining whipped cream, thoroughly incorporating it.

6   Immediately pipe or spread into prepared pastries or containers. Cover and refrigerate until completely set.

VARIATION   **GRAPEFRUIT MOUSSE** Replace the lemon curd with Grapefruit Curd (page 377).

Cream cheese mousse

MAKES 1 LB 10 OZ/737 G, ENOUGH TO FILL 50 PAULINA MOLDS

Heavy cream	18 fl oz	540 mL
Cream cheese	1 lb 5 oz	595 g
Sugar	7 oz	198 g
Glucose syrup	⅓ oz	9 g
Water	3½ fl oz	105 mL
Egg yolks	5 each	5 each
Gelatin, granulated	½ oz	14 g
Water	2 fl oz	60 mL

1   Assemble and prepare the desired pastries, containers, or molds that are to be used in the application of the mousse before beginning preparation.

2   Whip the cream to soft peaks. Cover and reserve under refrigeration.

3   Place the cream cheese in the mixer and mix on medium speed with the paddle attachment until soft and creamy.

4   Heat the sugar, glucose syrup, and water to 240°F/116°C in a saucepan over medium heat to make a pâte à bombe. Place the egg yolks in the mixer and add the pâte à bombe while whipping on high speed with the whip attachment. Continue to whip the mixture until it reaches maximum volume.

5   Bloom the gelatin, strain, and melt, then add it to the warm pâte à bombe.

6   Mix in the softened cream cheese and mix on medium speed until smooth, about 5 minutes.

7   Gently blend one-third of the whipped cream into the cream cheese mixture. Fold in the remaining whipped cream, thoroughly incorporating it. Immediately pipe or spread into prepared pastries or containers. Cover and refrigerate until completely set.

Bavarian cheese mousse

MAKES 2 LB 13 OZ/1.278 KG, ENOUGH FOR THREE 6-IN/15-CM CAKES

Gelatin, granulated	⅓ oz	9 g
Water, cold	2½ fl oz	75 mL
Heavy cream	16 fl oz	480 mL
Cream cheese, soft	1 lb 5¼ oz	602 g
Sugar	5¼ oz	149 g
Salt	pinch	pinch
Lemon zest, grated	1 tsp	3 g
Orange zest, grated	1 tsp	3 g
Vanilla extract	2 tsp	10 mL

1   Assemble and prepare the desired pastries, containers, or molds that are to be used in the application of the mousse before beginning preparation.

2   Bloom the gelatin in the water for 15 minutes at room temperature.

3   Whip the cream to soft peaks. Cover and reserve under refrigeration.

4   Cream the cream cheese, sugar, salt, lemon and orange zests, and vanilla on medium speed with the paddle attachment until smooth, about 5 minutes.

5   Place the bloomed gelatin in a saucepan and heat to 130°F/54°C. Temper by gradually adding the heated gelatin to the cream cheese mixture to ensure a smooth and consistent mousse.

6   Gently blend the whipped cream into the cream cheese mixture, thoroughly incorporating it.

7   Immediately pipe or spread into prepared pastries or containers. Cover and refrigerate until completely set.

NOTE   It is important to make sure the cheese is sufficiently warm when making this mousse or it will set too rapidly.

Mascarpone mousse

MAKES 2 LB/907 G

Brandy	1 tbsp	15 mL
Lemon juice	1 tbsp	15 mL
Vanilla extract	1 tbsp	15 mL
Gelatin sheets	4 each	4 each
Heavy cream	15 fl oz	450 mL
Egg yolks	5 oz	142 g
Sugar	6½ oz	184 g
Egg whites	4 oz	113 g
Mascarpone	13½ oz	383 g

1   Assemble and prepare the desired pastries, containers, or molds that are to be used in the application of the mousse before beginning preparation.

2   Combine the brandy, lemon juice, and vanilla in a bowl and add the gelatin sheets to bloom. Place the bloomed gelatin and liquid in a saucepan and heat it to 130°F/54°C or until the gelatin has dissolved. Keep warm.

3   Whip the cream to soft peaks. Cover and reserve under refrigeration.

4   Combine the egg yolks and 2 oz/57 g of the sugar in a mixer bowl and whisk until thoroughly blended. Place the bowl over simmering water and heat, whisking constantly, until the mixture is thickened and very foamy and has reached at least 145°F/63°C.

5   Transfer the bowl to the mixer and whip on high speed with the whip attachment until cool.

6   Meanwhile, make a Swiss meringue with the egg whites and the remaining 4½ oz/127 g of sugar (see page 405).

7   Whip the meringue to medium peaks, stream the melted gelatin into the still-warm meringue, and continue to whip on high speed until stiff.

8   Fold the yolk-sugar mixture into the mascarpone, fold in the meringue, then fold in the whipped cream until just incorporated.

9   Immediately pipe or spread into prepared pastries or containers. Cover and refrigerate until completely set.

Pumpkin cheesecake mousse

MAKES 8 LB 8 OZ/3.86 KG, ENOUGH FOR FOUR 6-IN/15-CM CAKES

Gelatin, granulated	1 oz	28 g
Water, cold	8 fl oz	240 mL
Heavy cream	64 fl oz	1.92 L
Cream cheese, room temperature	2 lb	907 g
Light brown sugar	1 lb	454 g
Ground cinnamon	1 tsp	2 g
Ground nutmeg	1 tsp	2 g
Ground cloves	¼ tsp	0.5 g
Ground ginger	½ tsp	1 g
Salt	¼ tsp	1.25 g
Vanilla extract	2 tbsp	30 mL
Pumpkin purée	1 lb 2 oz	510 g

1   Assemble and prepare the desired pastries, containers, or molds that are to be used in the application of the mousse before beginning preparation.

2   Bloom the gelatin in the water.

3   Whip the cream to soft peaks. Cover and reserve under refrigeration.

4   Combine the cream cheese, sugar, spices, salt, and vanilla and mix on medium speed with the paddle attachment until light and smooth. Add the pumpkin purée and mix just to combine.

5   Melt the gelatin to 120°F/49°C and temper into the cheese mixture slowly by adding warm gelatin to the cheese mixture while stirring constantly with a whisk.

6   Fold in the whipped cream.

7   Divide among the pans, leveling the tops with a spatula. Cover and refrigerate until completely set.

Chocolate sabayon mousse

MAKES 3 LB 6 OZ/1.53 KG

Bittersweet chocolate, chopped	8 oz	227 g
Gelatin, granulated	½ oz	14 g
Water	2 fl oz	60 mL
Brandy	3 fl oz	90 mL
Heavy cream	24 fl oz	720 mL
Vanilla extract	1 tbsp	15 mL
Egg yolks	6¾ oz	191 g
Sugar	4 oz	113 g
Dry sherry	6 fl oz	180 mL

1   Assemble and prepare the desired pastries, containers, or molds that are to be used in the application of the sabayon before beginning preparation.

2   Melt the chocolate over barely simmering water. Turn off the heat and keep the chocolate warm over the hot water.

3   Bloom the gelatin in the water and brandy.

4   Whip the cream with the vanilla to very soft peaks. Cover and reserve under refrigeration.

5   Combine the egg yolks, sugar, and sherry in a stainless-steel bowl and whisk until thoroughly blended. Place the bowl over simmering water and heat, whisking constantly, until the mixture is thick and foamy and has reached at least 165°F/74°C. Remove from the heat.

6   Melt the gelatin and add to the egg yolk mixture. Gradually fold in the chocolate. Cool to 80°F/27°C.

7   Gently blend one-third of the reserved whipped cream into the chocolate mixture. Fold in the remaining whipped cream, thoroughly incorporating it.

8   Immediately pipe or spread into prepared pastries or containers. Cover and refrigerate until completely set.

VARIATION   MOCHA MOUSSE Replace the dry sherry with an equal amount of cold espresso.

Pistachio mousseline

MAKES 1 LB 7 OZ/652 G

Italian buttercream (page 418)	7 oz	198 g
Pistachio paste	2 oz	57 g
Pastry cream (page 370)	14 oz	397 g
Food color (optional)	as needed	as needed

1   Combine the buttercream and pistachio paste in a bowl and mix with a rubber spatula until well combined.

2   Fold in the pastry cream. Do not overmix.

3   Add a very small amount of food color, if you like, and mix using a toothpick.

4   Reserve under refrigeration, with plastic wrap touching the surface of the mousseline, until needed. This will keep for up to 3 days.

Praline mousseline

MAKES 1 LB 7 OZ/652 G

Italian buttercream (page 418)	14 oz	397 g
Praline paste	2 oz	57 g
Pastry cream (page 370)	7 oz	198 g

1   Combine the buttercream and praline paste in a bowl and mix with a rubber spatula until well combined.

2   Gently fold in the pastry cream. Do not overmix.

3   Reserve under refrigeration, with plastic wrap touching the surface of the mousseline, until needed. This will keep for up to 3 days.

Bavarian cream

MAKES 4 LB 8 OZ/2.04 KG

Gelatin, granulated	1 oz	28 g
Water	8 fl oz	240 mL
Heavy cream	32 fl oz	960 mL
Vanilla sauce (page 428), warm	32 fl oz	960 mL

1   Assemble and prepare the desired pastries, containers, or molds that are to be used in the application of the cream before beginning preparation.

2   Bloom the gelatin in the water and melt.

3   Whip the cream to soft peaks. Cover and reserve under refrigeration.

4   Blend the melted gelatin into the vanilla sauce. Strain, then cool in an ice water bath to 75°F/24°C, or until it begins to thicken.

5   Gently blend one-third of the vanilla sauce mixture into the reserved whipped cream. Fold into the remaining vanilla sauce mixture, thoroughly incorporating it.

6   Immediately pour into prepared molds. Cover and refrigerate until completely set.

VARIATIONS   **CHOCOLATE BAVARIAN CREAM** Melt 12 oz/340 g of bittersweet or milk chocolate. Blend approximately one-third of the warm vanilla sauce with the chocolate. Blend the chocolate mixture into the remaining vanilla sauce. Proceed as directed above.

LEMON BAVARIAN CREAM Reduce the vanilla sauce to 4 fl oz/120 mL and add 8 oz/227 g Lemon Curd (page 377). Blend the vanilla sauce and lemon curd together just before the gelatin is added. Proceed as directed above.

LIQUEUR BAVARIAN CREAM Add 6 fl oz/180 mL orange liqueur to the vanilla sauce just before the gelatin is added. Proceed as directed above.

PRALINE BAVARIAN CREAM Add 8 oz/227 g praline paste to the vanilla sauce just before the gelatin is added. Proceed as directed above.

RASPBERRY BAVARIAN CREAM Reduce the vanilla sauce to 16 fl oz/480 mL and blend in 16 fl oz/480 mL raspberry purée and 4 oz/113 g sugar. Proceed as directed above.

WINE BAVARIAN CREAM Reduce the vanilla sauce to 16 fl oz/480 mL and add 16 fl oz/480 mL Chablis. Blend the vanilla sauce and Chablis and proceed as directed above.

Yogurt Bavarian cream

MAKES 4 LB 8 OZ/2.04 KG

Gelatin, granulated	1 oz	28 g
Water	8 fl oz	240 mL
Heavy cream	32 fl oz	960 mL
Plain yogurt, room temperature	24 fl oz	720 mL
Lemon sauce (page 429), warm	4 fl oz	120 mL
Lemon zest, grated	2½ tsp	7.50 g

1   Assemble and prepare the desired pastries, containers, or molds that are to be used in the application of the cream before beginning preparation.

2   Bloom the gelatin in the water and melt.

3   Whip the cream to soft peaks. Cover and reserve under refrigeration.

4   Combine the yogurt with the vanilla sauce. Blend in the melted gelatin. Strain, blend in the lemon zest, and cool over an ice water bath to 75°F/24°C.

5   Gently blend one-third of the vanilla sauce mixture into the reserved whipped cream. Fold in the remaining vanilla sauce mixture into the whipped cream mixture, thoroughly incorporating it.

6   Immediately pour into prepared pastries or molds. Cover and refrigerate until completely set.

Diplomat cream

MAKES 2 LB 2 OZ/964 G

Heavy cream	16 fl oz	480 mL
Gelatin, granulated	1½ tsp	7 g
Water	2 fl oz	60 mL
Pastry cream (page 370), flavored as desired, warm	1 lb	454 g

1   Assemble and prepare the desired pastries, containers, or molds that are to be used in the application of the cream before beginning preparation.

2   Whip the cream to soft peaks. Cover and reserve under refrigeration.

3   Bloom the gelatin in the water and melt. Blend into the pastry cream. Strain, then cool over an ice water bath to 75°F/24°C.

4　Gently blend one-third of the reserved whipped cream into the pastry cream mixture. Fold in the remaining whipped cream, thoroughly incorporating it.

5　Immediately pipe into prepared pastries or containers. Cover and refrigerate until completely set.

VARIATION　**ORANGE DIPLOMAT CREAM** Replace the pastry cream with an equal amount of Orange Curd (page 377).

Strawberry yogurt Bavarian

MAKES 1 LB/454 G

Plain yogurt	14 oz	397 g
Gelatin sheets	2 each	2 each
Heavy cream	4 fl oz	120 mL
Strawberry purée	2½ oz	71 g
Sour cream	2 oz	57 g
Sugar	2 oz	57 g

1　Reserve 4¼ oz/120 g of extra yogurt before draining. Drain the remaining yogurt in a perforated container that has been lined with two layers of cheesecloth. Drain for 1 hour and 30 minutes. Measure the yogurt after it is drained to ensure there is 5½ oz/156 g. Discard the liquid drained from the yogurt. If necessary add some of the reserved yogurt to bring the drained quantity to 5½ oz/156 g.

2　Bloom the gelatin in ice-cold water for 4 minutes. Drain well.

3　Whip the cream by hand over an ice water bath to soft-medium peaks. Reserve the whipped cream under refrigeration.

4　In a bowl, whisk together the yogurt, strawberry purée, sour cream, and sugar until well combined.

5　Place 2 oz/57 g of the yogurt mixture in a sauce pot. Over low heat, mix the yogurt with the gelatin until the gelatin dissolves.

6　Mix the yogurt-gelatin mixture with the rest of the yogurt mixture. Quickly and gently fold in the whipped cream. Let cool to room temperature, then refrigerate until needed.

VARIATION　For the Strawberries Three Ways plated dessert (page 755), pour the yogurt over each of the ten to twelve 2-oz/57-g cups filled with the Strawberry Terrine (page 402) to the top. Freeze until ready to assemble.

Tiramisù cream

MAKES 1 LB 8 OZ/680 G

Heavy cream	8 fl oz	240 mL
Egg yolks	2½ oz	71 g
Sugar	3 oz	85 g
Sweet Marsala	3 fl oz	90 mL
Mascarpone cheese, soft	8 oz	227 g

1   Assemble and prepare the desired pastries, containers, or molds that are to be used in the application of the cream before beginning preparation.

2   Whip the cream to soft peaks. Cover and reserve under refrigeration.

3   Combine the egg yolks, sugar, and Marsala in a stainless-steel bowl and whisk until thoroughly blended. Place the bowl over simmering water and heat, whisking constantly, until the mixture is thick and foamy and has reached at least 165°F/74°C.

4   Remove from the heat and whip on high speed with the whip attachment until cool.

5   Fold the egg yolk mixture into the mascarpone. Gently blend in one-third of the reserved whipped cream. Fold in the remaining whipped cream.

6   Immediately pipe or spread into prepared pastries or containers. Cover and refrigerate until completely set.

NOTE   To stabilize Tiramisù Cream for use in unmolded or sliced presentations, add 1½ tsp/7 g granulated gelatin, bloomed and melted, to the foam in step 3.

VARIATION   **SAUTERNES CRÈME** Substitute Sauternes for the sweet Marsala and stabilize with 1½ tsp/7 g granulated gelatin, bloomed in 2 fl oz/60 mL of water and melted.

Italian cream

MAKES 2 LB/907 G

Heavy cream	16 fl oz	480 mL
Egg whites	6 oz	170 g
Sugar	9 oz	255 g
Gelatin sheets	¼ oz	7 g
Vanilla extract	1 tbsp	15 mL

1   Assemble and prepare the desired pastries, containers, or molds that are to be used in the application of the cream before beginning preparation.

2   Whip the cream to soft peaks. Cover and reserve under refrigeration.

3   Prepare an Italian meringue with the egg whites and sugar (see page 405).

4   Bloom the gelatin in cold water, drain, and melt.

5   Slowly pour the gelatin and vanilla into the meringue when it is still warm and at medium peaks.

6   Gently blend in one-third of the reserved whipped cream. Fold in the remaining whipped cream.

7   Immediately pipe or spread into prepared pastries or containers. Cover and refrigerate until completely set.

Passion fruit chibouste

MAKES 4 LB/1.81 KG

Gelatin, granulated	½ oz	14 g
Water	12 fl oz	360 mL
Passion fruit juice	32 fl oz	960 mL
Sugar	1 lb 8 oz	680 g
Cornstarch	4 oz	113 g
Eggs	8 oz	227 g
Egg yolks	6 oz	170 g
Egg whites	1 lb 4 oz	567 g

1   Assemble and prepare the desired pastries, containers, or molds that are to be used in the application of the chibouste before beginning preparation.

2   Bloom the gelatin in 4 fl oz/120 mL of the water.

3   Combine 27 fl oz/810 mL of the passion fruit juice and 4 oz/113 g of the sugar in a saucepan and heat to melt the sugar.

4   Meanwhile, blend the cornstarch with the remaining 5 fl oz/150 mL passion fruit juice. Blend the cornstarch mixture with the eggs, egg yolks, and 4 oz/113 g of the sugar.

5   Temper the egg mixture by gradually adding one-third of the hot passion fruit juice mixture, stirring constantly with a whisk. Return the tempered egg mixture to the remaining juice in the saucepan and continue cooking until it comes to a boil. Remove from the heat and add the bloomed gelatin. Cover to keep warm.

6   Place the egg whites in a mixer fitted with the whip attachment.

7   Combine the remaining 1 lb/454 g sugar and 8 fl oz/240 mL water and bring to a boil, stirring to dissolve the sugar. Boil without stirring until the mixture reaches 240°F/116°C (soft ball stage).

8   When the sugar syrup reaches 230°F/110°C, begin beating the egg whites on high speed.

9   When the sugar syrup reaches 240°F/116°C, and the egg whites have reached soft peaks, pour the hot syrup into the whipping egg whites and whip to medium peaks.

10   Fold the meringue into the passion fruit base while still warm.

11   Immediately pour into molds.

NOTE   Passion fruit juice generally comes in concentrated form. Make sure to reconstitute according to manufacturer's instructions before use.

VARIATION   **LEMON-LIME CHIBOUSTE** Substitute 12 fl oz/360 mL of lemon juice and 20 fl oz/600 mL of lime juice for the passion fruit juice. Follow the remaining steps as directed above.

Pastry cream for soufflés

MAKES 1 LB 10 OZ/737 G

Milk	16 fl oz	480 mL
Sugar	5 oz	142 g
All-purpose flour	3 oz	85 g
Eggs	2 oz	57 g
Egg yolks	1½ oz	43 g

1   Combine 4 fl oz/120 mL of the milk with 2½ oz/71 g of the sugar in a saucepan and bring to a boil, stirring gently with a wooden spoon.

2   Meanwhile, combine the flour with the remaining 2½ oz/71 g sugar. Stirring with a whisk, add the remaining 12 fl oz/360 mL milk. Add the eggs and egg yolks, stirring with the whisk until the mixture is completely smooth.

3   Temper the egg mixture by adding one-third of the hot milk, stirring constantly with the whisk. Return the mixture to the remaining hot milk in the saucepan. Continue cooking, vigorously stirring with the whisk, until the pastry cream comes to a boil and the whip leaves a trail in it.

4   Pour the pastry cream onto a large shallow container or bowl. Cover with plastic wrap placed directly against the surface of the cream, and cool over an ice water bath.

5   Store the pastry cream, covered, under refrigeration.

Chocolate soufflé

MAKES 5 SOUFFLÉS (4 FL OZ/120 ML EACH)

Butter	1½ oz	43 g
Bittersweet chocolate, chopped	5 oz	142 g
Pastry cream for soufflés (page 399), cooled	1 lb 1 oz	482 g
Egg yolks	1 oz	28 g
Egg whites	6 oz	170 g
Sugar	2½ oz	71 g

1   Coat the inside of the ramekins with a film of softened butter, making sure to coat the rims as well as the insides, and dust with sugar.

2   To prepare the soufflé base, melt the butter and chocolate together in a bowl over barely simmering water, gently stirring to blend. Blend the chocolate mixture into the pastry cream. Blend in the egg yolks and set aside.

3   To prepare the meringue, whip the egg whites on medium speed with the whip attachment until soft peaks form.

4   Gradually sprinkle in the sugar while continuing to whip, then whip the meringue to medium peaks.

5   Gently blend approximately one-third of the meringue into the chocolate base. Fold in the remaining meringue, thoroughly incorporating it.

6   Portion the soufflé mixture into the prepared ramekins.

7   Bake at 350°F/177°C until fully risen, about 20 minutes. Serve immediately, with an appropriately flavored sauce or other garnish.

VARIATIONS   **CINNAMON SOUFFLÉ** When making the pastry cream, infuse the milk with 3 cinnamon sticks. Omit the chocolate, and fold the melted butter into the pastry cream. Follow the remaining method above.

GRAND MARNIER, KAHLÚA, FRANGELICO, OR AMARETTO SOUFFLÉ Substitute 1½ fl oz/45 mL of the chosen liqueur and 2 extra egg yolks for the chocolate. Blend the liqueur and egg yolks into the pastry cream with the melted butter. Follow the remaining method above.

LEMON OR ORANGE SOUFFLÉ When making the pastry cream, infuse the milk with ¼ oz/7 g grated lemon or orange zest. Omit the chocolate, and fold the melted butter into the pastry cream. Follow the remaining method above.

PRALINE OR PISTACHIO SOUFFLÉ Substitute 2 oz/57 g praline or pistachio paste and 2 egg yolks for the chocolate. Blend the nut paste and egg yolks into the pastry cream with the melted butter. Follow the remaining method above.

PUMPKIN SOUFFLÉ Substitute 2 oz/57 g pumpkin purée and 2 egg yolks for the chocolate. Blend the purée and egg yolks into the pastry cream with the melted butter. Follow the remaining method above.

WHITE CHOCOLATE SOUFFLÉ Substitute white chocolate for the bittersweet chocolate.

Raspberry soufflé

MAKES 4 SOUFFLÉS (4 FL OZ/120 ML EACH)

Raspberry purée	7 oz	198 g
Sugar	9 oz	255 g
Egg whites	5 oz	142 g

1   Coat the inside of the ramekins with a film of softened butter, making sure to coat the top rims of the ramekins as well as the insides, and dust with sugar.

2   Combine the purée and sugar in a saucepan and cook over medium heat, stirring to dissolve the sugar, until the mixture reaches 240°F/116°C.

3   Meanwhile, place the egg whites in the bowl of a mixer fitted with the whip attachment. When the sugar-purée mixture reaches 230°F/110°C, begin whipping the egg whites on medium speed.

4   When the sugar-purée mixture reaches 240°F/116°C, and the egg whites have reached soft peaks, increase the mixer speed to high and carefully pour the hot mixture into the egg whites. Whip only to soft peaks.

5   Immediately put the mixture into a pastry bag and fill the prepared ramekins. Bake at 350°F/177°C until fully risen and lightly browned, about 20 minutes.

Strawberry terrine

MAKES 10 TO 12 SERVINGS (2 OZ/57 G EACH)

Gelatin sheets	1½ each	1½ each
Strawberry purée	2¾ oz	78 g
Superpomme	¾ oz	21 g
Sugar	¾ oz	21 g
Strawberries, small dice	4¼ oz	120 g

1   Bloom the gelatin in ice-cold water for 4 minutes. Drain well.

2   Mix the purée, Superpomme, and sugar in a sauce pot and bring to a boil over high heat. Reduce the heat to low and add the diced strawberries to the sauce, cooking for 2 to 3 minutes, until the strawberries are tender.

3   Remove from the heat and add the bloomed gelatin. Stir until the gelatin has dissolved.

4   Place the mixture in an ice water bath and stir occasionally to evenly cool the mixture. Cool to room temperature.

5   Evenly pour the mixture into cups, just under one-third full. Place on a sheet tray and freeze overnight.

chapter thirteen

Icings, glazes, and sauces

*t*he use of an icing, glaze, or sauce can mean the difference between a plain baked item and a more elaborate pastry or dessert. These preparations have a wide range of uses, limited only by the imagination of the pastry chef or baker. The techniques and applications involved in making and using them are important to master, as they act to balance and adjust flavors and textures, making them an integral part of any pastry or dessert with which they are paired.

Meringues

Whipping egg whites and sugar together creates the light yet stable aerated mixture known as a *meringue*. Meringue is commonly used for topping and filling cakes and pastries. It can also be flavored and dried in a low oven to make cookies; containers that can be used to hold fruit, mousse, or sorbet; or layers for cakes. Meringue is also used as an ingredient in mousses and batters to lighten, aerate, and leaven them.

A basic ratio for a meringue is one part egg whites to two parts sugar. As the egg whites are whipped, air is incorporated and the whites break into smaller and smaller globules to form bubbles. When sugar is whipped into the egg whites, the agitation of the mixture and the moisture of the whites begin to dissolve the sugar, which in turn surrounds the air bubbles, coating them and making them more stable.

There are a few basic rules to keep in mind for making a successful meringue. All utensils must be impeccably clean and dry. Make sure that no traces of fat of any kind come in contact with the egg whites, whether in the form of grease on the utensils or other equipment or from traces of egg yolk in the whites themselves. Fat will interfere with the protein strands and will prevent the egg whites from developing into a foam.

A small amount of an acid (cream of tartar, lemon juice, or vinegar) will relax the proteins, helping to stabilize the meringue. You can introduce an acid simply by wiping the bowl clean with lemon juice or vinegar before adding the egg whites or by adding a small amount of cream of tartar to the whites just as they begin to foam. Never use cream of tartar when whipping in a copper bowl, as it will cause a toxic reaction, turning the whites slightly green.

Room-temperature egg whites will whip up more readily. Be careful to use sugar that is free of impurities such as flour or other ingredients. Whip the egg whites on high speed until they are frothy, then gradually add the sugar while continuing to whip to the desired consistency (soft, medium, or stiff peak). Avoid overwhipping egg whites, as they become dry and lumpy, making them difficult to incorporate into other ingredients. Prepare meringue (especially common meringue) just before you intend to use it, because it will begin to collapse if it stands for any length of time.

Soft, medium, and stiff peak meringues

Types of meringues

There are three different types of meringue: *common* (or French), *Swiss*, and *Italian*.

Common (or French) Meringue

Common or French meringue is the simplest to prepare, but the least stable. Unless pasteurized egg whites are used, due to the dangers of salmonella, uncooked or unbaked common meringue should not be eaten. French meringue is most commonly used as a leavening agent in batters, and is also often employed in making meringue shells or bases or layers for cakes, or for piping decorations that are to be baked. This meringue is best prepared right before its intended use, as it will begin to collapse if it stands for any length of time.

1. Place the egg whites, salt, and vanilla extract in a mixing bowl and whip on high speed until they are frothy.

2. Gradually add the sugar while continuing to whip to the desired consistency.

Swiss Meringue

Swiss meringue is one of the more stable meringue varieties. Swiss meringue can be piped or baked and dried in the oven. It may also be used to lighten mousses and creams, to fill cakes, or to add piped borders and other decorative elements to products.

1. Stir egg whites with sugar with a whip over a hot water bath until they reach 165°F/74°C (115°F/46°C for pasteurized whites). Whipping the egg breaks the whites into small globules to form bubbles. This aerates the mixture, giving the final product volume and lightness in texture. The agitation created in stirring, as well as the heat from the water bath, dissolves the sugar, which then surrounds the air bubbles in the whites, making them more stable.

2. Transfer the egg whites to a mixer and whip to the desired peak. A medium peak should be attained if the desired use is to add the meringue to lighten creams, while a stiff peak should be created if the meringue is intended for piping and other décor work.

Italian Meringue

Italian meringue is the most stable of the meringues and is commonly used in various mousses and buttercreams and for décor work.

1. Whip egg whites in a mixer. Egg whites should be whipped with a whip attachment for proper aeration. Whipping the egg breaks the whites into small globules to form bubbles. This aerates the mixture, giving the final product volume and a lightness in texture.

2. Cook sugar to the soft ball stage (240°F/116°C), then add in a thin, steady stream to the whipping egg whites when they have reached the medium peak stage. Whip the whites on medium speed to the desired peak.

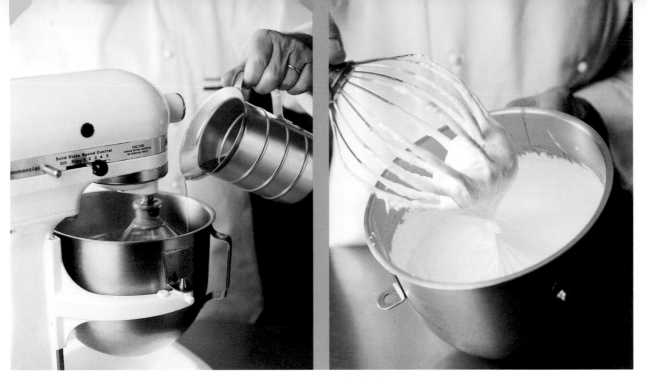

Adding hot syrup to the egg whites   The finished meringue

Stages of meringue: soft, medium, and stiff peaks

Each of the various stages of meringue—soft, medium, and stiff peak—is best suited for specific applications. A soft-peak meringue will cling to the whip when lifted but will not form pointed peaks. Soft-peak meringue is commonly used in soufflés. With medium-peak meringue, peaks will form when the whip is lifted from the meringue but will droop slightly. Medium-peak meringue is used to lighten mixtures such as creams and batters. When the whip is lifted from a stiff-peak meringue, sharp points will form and remain in the meringue. Stiff-peak meringue is the best choice for piping and décor work, as it holds its shape. All meringues should be glossy and smooth. If a stiff-peak meringue appears dry, dull, or lumpy, it has been overwhipped and will be difficult to work with.

Buttercream

Buttercream is an essential preparation in the pastry shop. Made with fresh sweet butter, natural flavorings, and other top-quality ingredients, it is excellent as a filling or icing for many cakes and pastries. There are four types of buttercream: *Italian, German, Swiss,* and *French.* Each of these types of buttercream has different characteristics that make them best suited for different applications.

Layers or coatings of buttercream should be even and thin. It should completely cover the layer or outside of the pastry or cake without being excessively thick. It should add enough moisture, flavor, and texture to complement without overpowering the pastry or cake to which it is applied.

Allow cold buttercream to come to room temperature before using. Then place it in the bowl of a mixer fitted with the paddle attachment and mix until smooth and spreadable.

Italian buttercream

Italian buttercream is made with meringue, butter, and flavorings. A meringue-based buttercream may be made with either an Italian or Swiss meringue. The use of egg whites in Italian buttercream results in a relatively white-colored product that is very light in texture. The light color and texture of a finished Italian buttercream make it a common choice in wedding cakes or for any pastries requiring white frosting.

1. Combine sugar and water in a heavy-bottomed saucepan and bring to a boil over medium-high heat, stirring to dissolve the sugar. Continue cooking, without stirring, until it reaches the soft ball stage (240°F/116°C). A heavy-bottomed saucepan is used, as it conducts heat most evenly.

2. Whip egg whites in a mixer fitted with the whip attachment on medium speed until frothy. Beat the meringue to medium peaks. A whip attachment is used, as it best incorporates air into the product being mixed. It is important not to overwhip the meringue, for a stiff-peaked meringue is resistant to incorporation into other ingredients.

3. When the sugar syrup reaches 240°F/116°C, add it to the meringue in a slow, steady stream while whipping on medium speed. Whip on high speed until the meringue has cooled to room temperature.

Add the soft butter chunks to the meringue while the mixer is running.

4. Add soft butter gradually, mixing until fully incorporated after each addition and scraping down the sides of the bowl as necessary. Scraping down the sides of the bowl ensures a thoroughly mixed, smooth buttercream. When using a mixer that doesn't touch the bottom of the bowl, make sure to additionally scrape the bottom as needed.

5. Blend in vanilla. The buttercream is now ready for use or may be tightly covered and stored under refrigeration.

As butter is added to an Italian buttercream, it may look broken (right), but after continued whipping, it develops a very smooth, even consistency (left).

Swiss meringue buttercream

The egg whites in a Swiss meringue buttercream are aerated through whipping, and stabilized by the dissolving sugar, creating a meringue able to be successfully incorporated with other ingredients. The combination of the fluffy consistency and the paleness of the Swiss meringue buttercream make it ideal for use in wedding cakes and any pastries where a white buttercream is desired.

1. Place sugar and egg whites in a stainless-steel bowl and whisk to combine. Set the bowl over a pan of barely simmering water and heat, whisking constantly, to 165°F/74°C. Whisking the sugar and egg whites over heat creates the Swiss meringue element of the buttercream.

2. Transfer the mixture to a mixer fitted with a whip attachment and whip on high speed until the meringue is cool.

3. Gradually add butter to the meringue while whipping on high speed; the buttercream should be light and creamy. Blend in vanilla. The element of meringue in the buttercream creates a product that is light in texture as well as in color.

4. Cover the buttercream with plastic wrap and store under refrigeration.

German buttercream

German buttercream is a combination of pastry cream, butter, and flavorings. The pastry cream also contributes to the cream's yellow color. Because it is yellow in color, it is unsuitable for some purposes where a white icing is desired. German buttercream has a richer texture than meringue-based buttercreams due to the whole eggs present in the pastry cream.

1. Cream together butter and sugar until light and fluffy. The mixture of butter and sugar becomes fluffy due to the incorporation of air into the mixture through the creaming process.

2. Gradually add pastry cream, mixing until fully incorporated after each addition and scraping down the sides of the bowl as necessary.

3. Store covered under refrigeration until ready to use. German buttercream has a notably short shelf life and is unsuitable for being made in large batches and stored.

French buttercream

French buttercream is made with either whole eggs or egg yolks, butter, cooked sugar syrup, and flavorings. It is similar to meringue-based Italian buttercream in technique, but the egg yolks make it richer and give it a yellow color.

1. Whip eggs in a mixer fitted with a whip attachment on high speed until light and fluffy, about 5 minutes. Using egg yolks in addition to whole eggs will make the final buttercream rich in flavor, as well as give the product a yellow color.

2. Combine sugar and water in a heavy-bottomed saucepan and bring to a boil, stirring to dissolve the sugar. Continue cooking, without stirring, until the mixture reaches 240°F/116°C. A heavy-bottomed saucepan is used, as it conducts heat most evenly.

3. Slowly pour the hot sugar syrup into the eggs while whipping on medium speed. Continue to whip until cool.

4. Gradually add butter, beating until incorporated after each addition and scraping down the sides of the bowl as necessary. Scraping down the sides of the bowl ensures a thoroughly mixed, smooth buttercream. When using a mixer that doesn't touch the bottom of the bowl, make sure to scrape the bottom as needed.

5. Blend in vanilla.

6. Store covered under refrigeration until ready to use.

Flavoring buttercream

Many different flavorings are compatible with buttercream. Of course, depending on the intended use, the amount of flavoring can be reduced or increased. Flavors may also be combined. It is often practical to make a large batch of buttercream and then flavor small portions as desired. Flavorings to be added to buttercream ideally should be at room temperature so they can easily be incorporated.

Whipped cream

There are two important considerations when whipping cream: temperature and fat content. Use cold cream (at approximately 40°F/4°C) and a chilled bowl, and use a cream that contains at least 30 percent fat. The fat present in cream coats the air as it is incorporated to form stable air bubbles. Whipped cream is used to fill, ice, and decorate cakes, tarts, and pastries, and it is served as an accompaniment to endless types of desserts. It is also used to aerate and lighten various creams and mousses.

1. Place cold cream in a chilled bowl of a mixer. Whipping cream in a very warm environment can prove difficult. The cold temperature prevents the fat in the cream from melting, which allows for better incorporation of air. Heat causes the fat in the cream to melt, making it impossible to whip.

2. Whip cream on high speed until it reaches desired peaks. As whipping continues, more bubbles form, which then cling together, causing the cream to stiffen. Whipped cream can be flavored in many ways: with extracts, liqueurs, or fruit purées.

Soft whipped cream peaks   Stiff whipped cream peaks

Fondant

Fondant is the traditional glaze for petits fours, éclairs, and doughnuts, among other pastries. Most kitchens and bakeshops use purchased fondant. For fondant to have its characteristic glossy finish, it must be warmed until it is liquid enough to flow readily (105°F/41°C). Small items are typically dipped into the fondant, using a dipping fork or similar tool. Larger items are set on racks on sheet pans and the fondant is poured, ladled, spooned, or drizzled over them. Assemble all your equipment before beginning and keep the fondant warm as you work. (See page 411 for more about a glazing setup.)

1. Place fondant in a stainless-steel bowl and heat over a hot water bath to heat. Do not let fondant exceed 105°F/41°C. Heating fondant reduces it to the liquid state needed to achieve the product's characteristically glossy finish. Fondant should be warmed until it is able to flow readily.

2. Thin the fondant to the desired consistency with warm water, corn syrup, or another liquid such as liqueur.

3. If desired, color or flavor the fondant. Once it has been melted, plain fondant can be colored and flavored as desired by adding coloring pastes, purées, concentrates, or chocolate. To make chocolate fondant, add about 3 oz/85 g melted unsweetened chocolate to 1 lb/454 g warmed fondant. Gradually add the chocolate to the fondant. The amount of chocolate may be adjusted to suit the desired flavor and color.

Fondant must be thinned to the proper dipping consistency to ensure a thin, even coating of glaze.

glazing with fondant, mirror glazes, or hard ganache

To glaze a pastry means to enrobe it in a thin coating of one of many and varied products, including fondant, ganache, and jam- or gelatin-based (mirror) glazes. Glazing adds visual appeal as well as flavor, and it also helps to increase the shelf life of the finished item by sealing in moisture.

Any glaze should be smooth, fluid, and free of any lumps. A well-applied glaze should always be in a thin, smooth layer.

Coat the item with the glaze quickly and do not disturb it as it sets for a perfect shine.

choosing a sauce

The proper sauce is essential for a successful dessert presentation. Always serve a sauce that will complement or enhance, not overwhelm, the textures and flavors of the dessert. You may want to avoid serving a dessert with a sauce of the same consistency and texture; for example, do not serve creamy vanilla sauce with ice cream. Instead, use a fruit coulis or another sauce that will provide contrast.

The basic types of sauces used in the pastry kitchen include custard (i.e., vanilla sauce or crème anglaise), sabayon, chocolate, fruit (using fresh, frozen, or dried fruit), caramel, and reduction. There are many variations on these basic preparations. By adding or substituting ingredients, you can adapt these sauces to suit any type of dessert item.

Vanilla sauce

Vanilla sauce, also known as *crème anglaise,* is one of the fundamental preparations for all pastry shops. It is actually a stirred custard, made with the same ingredients used to prepare a basic baked custard. Because the mixture is stirred constantly as the eggs thicken over heat, the custard stays loose and pourable instead of setting firmly, as it would if baked. Vanilla sauce is used as a sauce accompaniment to many desserts, and also serves as the base for other classical and contemporary applications, such as Bavarian cream and ice cream.

Before you start the sauce, prepare an ice bath. Have a strainer and a container to hold the finished sauce nearby.

1. Combine milk and heavy cream with salt and half of the sugar in a saucepan and bring to a boil, stirring to dissolve the sugar.

2. Blend egg yolks with the remaining half of the sugar, using a wire whip.

3. Temper the egg yolks by adding hot milk, whipping constantly. Egg yolks should be tempered, as the addition of too much hot liquid too quickly will result in the cooking of the eggs, causing them to scramble.

4. Return the tempered egg mixture to the hot milk in the saucepan and continue cooking carefully over low heat until the mixture thickens enough to coat the back of a spoon. Because the mixture is stirred constantly as the egg is heated, the custard stays loose instead of becoming firmly set.

5. Strain the sauce into a metal container, stir in the vanilla extract, and chill in an ice water bath. After cooking the sauce, immediately pour it through a sieve into the waiting container. Set the container in the ice bath to stop the cooking process, and stir the sauce occasionally as it cools. (If the custard is just slightly overcooked, immediately transfer it to a blender, add a little cold milk or cream, and process until smooth. Blending will rehomogenize the sauce, and the milk or cream will cool it. The rescued sauce will not have quite the same flavor and texture as a properly made sauce, but it should be fine for use as a component in another preparation.)

6. Cover tightly with plastic wrap and store under refrigeration.

Sabayon

Sabayon is a rich, substantial sauce of foamed egg yolks, sugar, and wine (Marsala is traditional in the Italian version, *zabaglione*). This sauce can be made ahead but is usually made to order due to its ease of preparation. Sabayon, however, may also serve as the base for a mousse and may be stabilized with gelatin and used as a cake or torte filling.

As sabayon is a very rich sauce, it is traditionally served with fresh fruit, berries, or other lean or acidic ingredients. It can be flavored as desired. If chocolate is added, the sauce will lose some of its airiness; the melted chocolate should be stirred in at the very end of the cooking process.

1. Combine egg yolks, sugar, and liquor in the bowl of a mixer and whip together until thoroughly blended. Examples of liquor or wine flavorings used in sabayon include Marsala, Champagne, bourbon, framboise, and Calvados.

2. Place the bowl over a pot of simmering water and heat, whisking constantly until the mixture is thickened and very foamy and has reached 180°F/82°C. The yolks are whipped constantly as they cook over simmering water until a dense, thick foam develops. The mixture should be whipped vigorously. Whipping the mixture serves to incorporate air, developing the foam. Heating the mixture as it is whipped serves a dual purpose. It stabilizes

Beat the sabayon to the ribbon stage.

the foam so that the volume is retained and also cooks the eggs sufficiently to make them safe for consumption. A properly thickened sabayon "ribbons" off the whisk.

3. Transfer the bowl to a mixer fitted with a whip attachment and whip until cool.

4. Transfer the sabayon to a container and cover it with plastic wrap placed directly against the surface to prevent a skin from forming. Sabayon may also be served warm or at room temperature.

Chocolate sauce

The success of any chocolate sauce depends primarily on the quality of the chocolate. Use the best-quality chocolate available to ensure a smooth, richly flavored sauce. Dark chocolate sauces can be made from unsweetened or bittersweet chocolate or a combination of the two. To get the most intense flavor, add a measure of cocoa powder, but be sure to adjust the sauce's flavor and sweetness with sugar.

Chocolate sauce

1. Combine sugar, water, and corn syrup in a heavy-bottomed saucepan and bring to a boil over medium-high heat. Remove from the heat.

2. Place cocoa powder in a bowl and add enough of the hot sugar syrup to make a paste, stirring until smooth.

3. Gradually add the remaining syrup and mix until fully incorporated. Adding the syrup slowly ensures that the final mixture is fully hydrated and evenly incorporated.

4. Add melted chocolate and blend until fully incorporated. The chocolate must also be melted carefully to prevent it from scorching or becoming grainy.

5. Strain the sauce through a fine-mesh sieve.

6. Serve warm or chilled.

Fruit sauces

There are two basic categories of fruit sauces: *coulis,* which is a smooth puréed mixture made using fresh or frozen fruits; and *compote,* which is a chunky mixture made using either dried, fresh, or frozen fruits. Either type of sauce may be cooked or uncooked. However, coulis are typically cooked, or heated only slightly to facilitate the full incorporation of sugar. Compotes, on the other hand, may be simmered for a period of time to infuse flavors, soften dried fruits, or reduce liquids.

It is important to remember to select the highest-quality fruit available. Only the ripest, most flavorful fruits will yield a good-quality sauce. Fruit must be tasted to be evaluated for flavor and sugar content so that any formula can be adjusted as necessary to achieve the desired sweetness.

Fruit sauces may be used as a base for flourless soufflés, or to flavor Bavarian cream, buttercream, and other fillings and frostings.

1. For a basic coulis, combine fruit, sugar, and lemon juice in a saucepan and heat over medium heat.

2. Simmer, stirring, until the sugar has dissolved, about 10 minutes.

3. Strain the coulis through a fine-mesh sieve. Straining ensures that the final coulis will be as smooth as possible, free of any seeds or other unwanted fruit product.

4. Add sugar or lemon juice to taste, if necessary.

Caramel sauce

There are two basic types of caramel sauce: *clear* and *enriched*. Clear caramel sauce is made by cooking sugar to a deep, richly flavorful caramel and then adding a liquid. A good standard ratio for making clear caramel sauce is two parts by weight of sugar to one part liquid. The liquid added to the caramel to make the sauce may be anything from water to fruit juices to liqueurs or any combination thereof, depending on the desired flavor profile. Clear caramel sauce does not require that any enrichments be added; however, a small amount of butter is often used to "finish" the sauce by stirring it in after the addition of liquid.

Enriched caramel sauces, like their clear counterparts, start with caramelizing sugar, but always have butter and some type of liquid dairy product, usually heavy cream, added as an enrichment. The fat and emulsifiers present in the butter and cream add body and flavor to the sauce. It is important to remember that the liquid (water, fruit juice, liqueur, cream, etc.) that is to be added to caramel must be warmed first to prevent spattering of hot liquid or sugar.

Flavors can be infused into clear or enriched caramel sauces by adding ingredients such as spices, teas, or coffee beans to the mixture after liquid has been added. These ingredients should be allowed to steep with the sauce for a few minutes to impart their full flavor and then strained from the sauce before serving. Caramel sauce can be used not only as a sauce accompaniment for a plated dessert but also as the filling for a confection, for décor, or as the base or flavoring for a filling.

Adding butter to a caramel sauce

1. In a saucepan, bring cream to a boil over medium heat. Leave over very low heat to keep warm.

2. Prepare an ice water bath.

3. Combine sugar and glucose syrup in a heavy-bottomed saucepan and cook slowly over moderate heat, stirring constantly until all the sugar has dissolved. Stop stirring and continue to cook to a golden caramel. Remove from the heat and shock the saucepan in the ice water bath to stop the cooking.

4. Remove from the ice water bath and stir in the butter. Carefully stir in hot cream, mixing until fully blended. Cool. The fat and emulsifiers present in the butter and cream add body and flavor to the sauce.

Reduction sauces

Reduction sauces have a coating consistency. Reduction sauces are prepared by simmering juices, wines, or other alcoholic beverages over low to moderate heat to thicken and develop their individual characteristic flavors. Reducing liquids to create this type of sauce not only serves to enhance the desired flavor of the ingredient, but may also concentrate undesirable characteristics. For this reason, be careful when selecting ingredients for a reduction sauce, as some do not reduce successfully.

1. Combine juices or wines and other alcoholic beverages and simmer over low to moderate heat. The reduction will create the desired consistency, so monitor the sauce as it is cooking for consistency at the required service temperature.

2. Once the sauce has reduced and thickened, strain through a fine-mesh sieve.

3. Serve warm or cold.

Reduction sauces have a coating consistency.

Common meringue

MAKES 1 LB 8 OZ/680 G

Egg whites	8 oz	227 g
Salt	pinch	pinch
Vanilla extract	1 tsp	5 mL
Sugar	1 lb	454 g

1 Place the egg whites, salt, and vanilla in a bowl and whisk until frothy.

2 Gradually add the sugar while continuing to whisk, then whisk to the desired consistency.

Swiss meringue

MAKES 1 LB 5 OZ/595 G

Egg whites	8 oz	227 g
Vanilla extract	1 tsp	5 mL
Salt	pinch	pinch
Sugar	1 lb	454 g

1   Place the egg whites, vanilla, salt, and sugar in the mixer bowl and stir until thoroughly combined.

2   Place the bowl over barely simmering water and slowly stir the mixture until it reaches between 115° and 165°F/46° and 74°C, depending on use.

3   Transfer the mixture to the mixer and whip on high speed with the whip attachment until the meringue is the desired consistency.

Italian meringue

MAKES 1 LB 8 OZ/680 G

Sugar	1 lb	454 g
Water	4 fl oz	120 mL
Egg whites	8 oz	227 g
Salt	pinch	pinch
Vanilla extract	1 tsp	5 mL

1   Combine 12 oz/340 g of the sugar with the water in a heavy-bottomed saucepan and bring to a boil over medium-high heat, stirring to dissolve the sugar. Continue cooking without stirring until the mixture reaches the soft ball stage (240°F/116°C).

2   Meanwhile, place the egg whites, salt, and vanilla in the mixer bowl fitted with the whip attachment.

3   When the sugar syrup has reached approximately 230°F/110°C, whip the whites on medium speed until frothy. Gradually add the remaining 4 oz/113 g sugar and beat the meringue to soft peaks.

4   When the sugar syrup reaches 240°F/116°C, add it to the meringue in a slow, steady stream while whipping on medium speed. Whip on high speed to stiff peaks. Continue to beat on medium speed until completely cool.

Chocolate meringue

MAKES 1 LB 8¾ OZ/702 G

Egg whites	8 oz	227 g
Granulated sugar	13 oz	369 g
Confectioners' sugar	3 oz	85 g
Cocoa powder	¾ oz	21 g

1   Place the egg whites in a bowl and whisk until frothy.

2   Gradually add the granulated sugar while continuing to whisk, then whisk to the desired consistency.

3   Sift together the confectioners' sugar and cocoa and fold into the meringue.

Swiss meringue buttercream

MAKES 2 LB 12 OZ/1.25 KG

Sugar	1 lb	454 g
Egg whites	8 oz	227 g
Butter, cut into medium chunks, soft	1 lb 4 oz	567 g
Vanilla extract	2 tsp	10 mL

1   Place the sugar and egg whites in a stainless-steel bowl and whisk to combine. Set the bowl over barely simmering water and heat, whisking constantly, to 165°F/74°C.

2   Transfer the mixture to the mixer and whip on high speed with the whip attachment until the meringue is the desired consistency.

3   Gradually add the butter to the meringue while whipping on high speed; the buttercream should be light and creamy. Blend in the vanilla.

4   Cover and store in the refrigerator until ready to use.

Italian buttercream

MAKES 6 LB 9 OZ/2.98 KG

Sugar	2 lb	907 g
Egg whites	1 lb	454 g
Water	8 fl oz	240 mL
Butter, soft	3 lb	1.36 kg
Vanilla extract	1 tbsp	15 mL
Flavoring	as needed	as needed

1 Combine 8 oz/227 g of the sugar with the egg whites in the mixer bowl.

2 Combine the water with the remaining sugar in a saucepan. Cook the mixture until it reaches the soft ball stage (240°F/116°C).

3 When the sugar syrup reaches 230°F/110°C, begin whipping the egg whites on medium speed with the whip attachment. The egg whites should reach soft peaks at the same time the sugar reaches the desired temperature.

4 Stream the hot sugar into the whipping whites. Continue whipping until cooled to room temperature.

5 While the meringue is cooling, cut the butter into 1-in/3-cm cubes.

6 Once the meringue is cool, switch to the paddle attachment and gradually add the butter on medium speed. Cream until smooth and light; flavor as desired.

7 Cover and store under refrigeration until ready to use.

VARIATIONS **CHOCOLATE BUTTERCREAM** Add 3 oz/85 g melted and cooled bittersweet chocolate to 1 lb/454 g prepared buttercream.

COFFEE BUTTERCREAM Add ½ oz/14 g coffee paste, ½ fl oz/15 mL brandy, and 1 tsp/5 mL vanilla extract to 1 lb/454 g prepared buttercream.

HAZELNUT BUTTERCREAM Add 2 oz/57 g praline paste, 1 tbsp/15 mL brandy, and 1 tsp/5 mL vanilla extract to 1 lb/454 g prepared buttercream.

KIRSCH BUTTERCREAM Add 2 oz/57 g melted and cooled white chocolate and 1 fl oz/30 mL kirsch to 1 lb/454 g prepared buttercream.

MILK CHOCOLATE BUTTERCREAM Add 2 oz/57 g melted and cooled milk chocolate to 1 lb/454 g prepared buttercream.

MOCHA BUTTERCREAM Add 3 oz/85 g melted and cooled bittersweet chocolate and 1 Tbsp/30 mL espresso powder to 1 lb/454 g prepared buttercream.

WHITE CHOCOLATE BUTTERCREAM Add 2 oz/57 g melted and cooled white chocolate to 1 lb/454 g prepared buttercream.

French buttercream

MAKES 3 LB/1.36 KG

Whole eggs	8 oz	227 g
Egg yolks	8 oz	227 g
Sugar	1 lb 2 oz	510 g
Water	4 fl oz	120 mL
Butter, cut into medium chunks, soft	1 lb 8 oz	680 g
Vanilla extract	2 tsp	10 mL

1 Whip the eggs and yolks on high speed with the whip attachment until light and fluffy, about 5 minutes.

2 Combine the sugar and water in a heavy-bottomed saucepan and bring to a boil, stirring to dissolve the sugar. Continue cooking without stirring until the mixture reaches 240°F/116°C.

3 Slowly pour the hot sugar syrup into the eggs while whipping on medium speed. Continue to whip until cool.

4 Gradually add the butter, beating until incorporated after each addition and scraping down the sides of the bowl as necessary. Blend in the vanilla.

5 Cover and store under refrigeration until ready to use.

German buttercream

MAKES 2 LB 4 OZ/1.02 KG

Butter, soft	1 lb	454 g
Confectioners' sugar, sifted	4 oz	113 g
Pastry cream (page 370)	1 lb	454 g

1 Cream together the butter and sugar on mediuum speed with the paddle attachment until light and fluffy, about 5 minutes.

2 Gradually add the pastry cream, mixing until fully incorporated after each addition and scraping down the sides of the bowl as necessary.

3 Cove and store under refrigeration until ready to use.

Cream cheese icing

MAKES 2 LB/907 G

Cream cheese	1 lb	454 g
Butter, soft	8 oz	227 g
Confectioners' sugar, sifted	8 oz	227 g
Vanilla extract	1 tbsp	15 mL

1   Blend the cream cheese on low speed with the paddle attachment until smooth.

2   Add the butter in stages, and blend well. Add the confectioners' sugar and blend on low speed until fully incorporated. Beat on high speed until light and fluffy, about 5 minutes. Blend in the vanilla.

3   Cove and store under refrigeration until ready to use.

VARIATION   **LEMON CREAM CHEESE ICING** Add the grated zest of 1 lemon to the icing with the vanilla.

Chantilly cream

MAKES APPROXIMATELY 8 OZ/227 G

Heavy cream	8 fl oz	240 mL
Confectioners' sugar	1 oz	28 g
Vanilla extract	¾ tsp	4 g

1   Whisk the cream by hand over an ice water bath to medium peaks.

2   Add the sugar and vanilla and continue to whisk by hand to stiff peaks.

3   Cove and store under refrigeration until ready to use.

VARIATIONS   **CINNAMON CHANTILLY CREAM** Add ½ tsp/1 g ground cinnamon to the cream before whipping.

COFFEE CHANTILLY CREAM Add 1 oz/28 g coffee concentrate (page 897) to the cream before whipping.

Soft ganache

MAKES 3 LB 6 OZ/1.53 KG

Dark chocolate, finely chopped	1 lb 4 oz	567 g
Heavy cream	32 fl oz	960 mL

1   Place the chocolate in a stainless-steel bowl.

2   Bring the cream to a simmer.

3   Pour the hot cream over the chocolate. Allow to stand for 1 minute, then gently stir to blend. Strain and cool.

4   Cover with plastic wrap and refrigerate overnight before using.

5   Whip the ganache to desired peaks for use.

NOTE   For a lighter-flavored ganache, add an equal amount of cream (by volume) to the chilled ganache before whipping.

VARIATIONS   **MEDIUM GANACHE** Increase the amount of chocolate to 2 lb/908g and follow the method above.

SOFT MILK CHOCOLATE GANACHE Substitute milk chocolate for the dark chocolate.

SOFT WHITE CHOCOLATE GANACHE Substitute white chocolate for the dark chocolate.

Hard ganache

MAKES 5 LB/2.27 KG

Dark chocolate, finely chopped	4 lb	1.81 kg
Heavy cream	32 fl oz	960 mL

1   Place the chocolate in a stainless-steel bowl.

2   Bring the cream just to a simmer. Pour the hot cream over the chocolate, allow to stand for 1 minute, and stir until the chocolate is thoroughly melted.

3   Use the ganache immediately, or cover and store under refrigeration. Rewarm before use.

Cinnamon ganache

MAKES 1 LB/454 G

Heavy cream	3 fl oz	90 mL
Milk	3 fl oz	90 mL
Ground cinnamon	1 tsp	2 g
Cinnamon sticks	1 each	1 each
Light corn syrup	½ oz	14 g
Milk chocolate, finely chopped	10 oz	284 g

1 Combine the cream, milk, cinnamon, and corn syrup and bring to a simmer.

2 Remove the pot from heat, remove the cinnamon stick, and pour over the chopped chocolate. Allow to sit for 1 minute, then stir gently to combine. Allow to rest, covered, for about 20 minutes.

3 Portion and use immediately, or cover and store in the refrigerator for later use. To use, reheat in a double boiler.

Hard ganache is an emulsion of chocolate and cream.

TOP TO BOTTOM: Soft, medium, and hard ganache

Chocolate caramel ganache

MAKES 12 OZ/340 G

Sugar	5¼ oz	149 g
Lemon juice	2 drops	2 drops
Light corn syrup, warm	½ oz	14 g
Bittersweet chocolate, 70%, finely chopped	5¼ oz	149 g
Butter	2 oz	57 g
Dark rum	⅓ fl oz	10 mL
Heavy cream, warm	6 fl oz	180 mL
Salt	pinch	pinch

1   Combine the sugar and lemon juice in a sauce pot and cook, stirring gently, to a rich golden brown. Add the warmed corn syrup to the caramel. Remove the pan from the heat.

2   Pour the caramel over the chopped chocolate and allow to stand for 1 minute. Stir gently to combine.

3   Add the butter, rum, cream, and salt and stir until smooth.

4   Cool overnight in the refrigerator or cool to room temperature.

5   Table the ganache (see page 764 for tabling instructions) prior to spreading or piping.

Milk chocolate glaze

MAKES 4 LB/1.81 KG

Gelatin sheets	¾ oz	21 g
Milk	16 fl oz	480 mL
Glucose syrup	7 oz	198 g
Milk chocolate	1 lb 5 oz	595 g
Pâte à glacier, blond	1 lb 5 oz	595 g

1   Bloom the gelatin in cold water. Bring the milk and glucose syrup to a boil.

2   Squeeze the water out of the gelatin and add it to the hot liquid. Pour over the chocolates, stirring to combine.

3   Use the glaze on frozen desserts at 85°F/29°C.

Ultra-shiny chocolate glaze

MAKES 32 FL OZ/960 ML

Gelatin, granulated	1 oz	28 g
Water, cold	16 fl oz	480 mL
Bittersweet chocolate, chopped	2½ oz	71 g
Water	9½ fl oz	285 mL
Sugar	1 lb 2 oz	510 g
Dutch-process cocoa powder	5½ oz	156 g
Heavy cream	5½ fl oz	165 mL

1   Bloom the gelatin in the cold water and melt. Combine with the chocolate in a stainless-steel bowl.

2   Bring the water, sugar, cocoa powder, and cream to just below a boil over medium heat.

3   Pour the hot mixture over the gelatin and chocolate and let stand for 1 minute. Stir to melt and combine. Strain.

4   Use immediately.

Mirror glaze

MAKES 18 FL OZ/540 ML (SEE NOTES)

Gelatin sheets	4 each	4 each
Liquid, sweetened, flavored	16 fl oz	480 mL

1   Bloom the gelatin in enough cold water to cover it completely. Squeeze the water from the bloomed gelatin sheets.

2   Warm the flavored liquid. Add the gelatin to the warm liquid and stir to dissolve.

3   Cool over an ice water bath to 70°F/21°C before pouring onto mousse cakes in rings.

4   Chill to set before removing the cake ring.

NOTES   Mirror glaze should be cool but still liquid when poured onto delicate mousses.

If the glaze does not stay level when placed in the refrigerator, prop the cakes or pan level before the glaze sets.

This formula yields enough to glaze the tops of three 10-in/25-cm cakes or 1½ full sheet cakes.

Spiced mirror glaze

MAKES 30 FL OZ/900 ML

Water	20 fl oz	600 mL
Sugar	12 oz	340 g
Vanilla beans	1 each	1 each
Allspice berries	3 each	3 each
Cinnamon sticks	2 each	2 each
Cloves	1 each	1 each
Ground nutmeg	¼ tsp	0.50 g
Ground ginger	¼ tsp	0.50 g
Orange zest, grated	1 tbsp	9 g
Lemon juice	4 fl oz	120 mL
Gelatin, granulated	¾ oz	21 g
Rum	1 fl oz	30 mL

1   Combine 15 fl oz/450 mL of the water with the sugar in a saucepan and bring to a boil over medium heat, stirring to dissolve the sugar. Split the vanilla bean, scrape the seeds into the sugar syrup, and add the pod. Add the allspice berries, cinnamon sticks, clove, nutmeg, ginger, orange zest, and lemon juice. Remove from the heat and steep for 15 minutes, then strain.

2   Bloom the gelatin in the rum and the remaining 5 fl oz/150 mL water and melt. Blend the melted gelatin with the spiced mixture.

3   Cool the glaze to 70°F/21°C. Use immediately.

Caramel glaze

MAKES 2 LB/907 G

Gelatin sheets	½ oz	14 g
Sugar	15 oz	425 g
Lemon juice	1 fl oz	30 mL
Water	10 fl oz	300 mL
Heavy cream	12½ fl oz	375 mL
Vanilla beans	1 each	1 each
Salt	pinch	pinch
Cornstarch	1 oz	28 g

1   Bloom the gelatin in cold water.

2   Combine the sugar and lemon juice and cook to medium amber color.

3   Slowly add 7½ fl oz/225 mL of the water, the cream, vanilla bean, and salt.

4   Combine the cornstarch with the remaining water to make a slurry.

5   Whisk in the slurry and bring to a boil. Remove from the heat.

6   Squeeze the water out of the gelatin and add the gelatin to the hot caramel mixture.

7   Strain. It is ready to use now or may be refrigerated and rewarmed for later use.

Apricot glaze

MAKES 24 FL OZ/720 ML

Gelatin, granulated	1¼ oz	35 g
Water	8 fl oz	240 mL
Light corn syrup	12 oz	340 g
Lemon juice	4 fl oz	120 mL
Apricot jam	6 oz	170 g

1   Bloom the gelatin in the water and melt.

2   Combine the corn syrup, lemon juice, and apricot jam in a saucepan and bring to a boil over medium heat. Blend in the melted gelatin.

3   Cool the glaze to 75°F/24°C. Use immediately.

Thread glaze

MAKES 2 LB/907 G

Sugar	1 lb 8 oz	680 g
Water	8 fl oz	240 mL

Combine the sugar and water in a heavy-bottomed saucepan and bring to a boil over medium heat, stirring to dissolve the sugar. Boil, without stirring, until the mixture reaches 234°F/112°C. Use the glaze immediately.

Grapefruit mirror glaze

MAKES 1 LB/454 G

Gelatin, granulated	½ oz	14 g
Grapefruit juice, cold	16 fl oz	480 mL

1   Bloom the gelatin in the grapefruit juice in a stainless-steel bowl. Set the bowl over a pan of simmering water and stir to dissolve the gelatin.

2   Cool the glaze to 70°F/21°C before using.

Mango mirror glaze

MAKES 2 LB 4 OZ/1.02 KG (ENOUGH FOR SIX 8-IN/20-CM CHARLOTTES)

Mango purée	1 lb	454 g
Hero Gel	1 lb	454 g
Water	4 fl oz	120 mL

1   Combine the fruit purée, Hero Gel, and water in a sauce pot. Heat until dissolved.

2   Strain. Cool to 110°F/43°C.

3   Pour over chilled cake and refrigerate for 20 minutes, then unmold.

VARIATION   32 fl oz/960 mL fruit purée or juice combined with 8 sheets of bloomed gelatin may be applied to cakes and pastries as "Mirror Glaze."

Other fruit purées may be substituted for the mango purée.

Chocolate mirror glaze

MAKES 1 LB 4 OZ/567 G (ENOUGH FOR ABOUT 20 DOMES)

Gelatin sheets	5 each	5 each
Sugar	9 oz	255 g
Water	5 fl oz	150 mL
Dutch-process cocoa powder	2¾ oz	78 g
Crème fraîche	3 oz	85 g
Dark chocolate, 64%, finely chopped	2 oz	57 g

1   Bloom the gelatin in cold water until softened, about 5 minutes. Drain.

2   Bring the sugar, water, cocoa powder, and crème fraîche to a boil in a sauce pot, stirring constantly until the sugar dissolves.

3   Pour the boiling mixture over the chocolate. Stir with a wooden spoon until the chocolate is completely melted.

4   Melt the gelatin in a bowl over barely simmering water.

5   Add approximately 1 oz/28 g of the chocolate mixture to the melted gelatin. Temper the chocolate-gelatin mixture into the remaining chocolate mixture.

6   Cool to room temperature and refrigerate until ready to use. Reheat glaze to 120°F/49°C to use.

Vanilla sauce

MAKES 48 FL OZ/1.44 L

Milk	16 fl oz	480 mL
Heavy cream	16 fl oz	480 mL
Salt	1 tsp	5 g
Sugar	8 oz	227 g
Egg yolks	10 oz	284 g
Vanilla extract	1 tbsp	15 mL

1   Combine the milk and cream with the salt and 4 oz/113 g of the sugar in a nonreactive saucepan and bring to a boil, stirring to dissolve the sugar.

2   Meanwhile, blend the egg yolks with the remaining sugar using a whisk.

3   Temper the egg yolks by gradually adding one-third of the hot milk, whipping constantly. Return the tempered egg mixture to the remaining hot milk in the saucepan and continue cooking until the mixture thickens enough to coat the back of a spoon.

4   Strain the sauce into a metal container and chill in an ice water bath. Stir in the vanilla extract.

5   Stir the sauce occasionally to ensure quick and even cooling. Cool to 40°F/4°C.

6   Cover tightly with plastic wrap and store under refrigeration.

VARIATIONS   **CINNAMON SAUCE** Add 1 cinnamon stick to the milk mixture and bring to a boil. Cover and allow to steep for 5 to 10 minutes. Strain into a clean saucepan, bring back to a boil, and proceed as directed above.

COFFEE SAUCE Add ½ oz/14 g coarsely ground coffee beans to the milk mixture and bring to a boil. Cover and allow to steep for 5 to 10 minutes. Strain into a clean saucepan, bring back to a boil, and proceed as directed above.

LEMON SAUCE Add ½ oz/14 g grated lemon zest to the milk mixture and bring to a boil. Cover and allow to steep for 5 to 10 minutes. Strain into a clean saucepan, bring back to a boil, and proceed as directed above.

PEANUT BUTTER SAUCE Add 4 oz/113 g creamy peanut butter to 16 fl oz/480 mL Vanilla Sauce. Blend using an immersion blender, cover, and chill.

Sabayon

MAKES 32 FL OZ/960 ML

Egg yolks	12 oz	340 g
Sugar	12 oz	340 g
White wine	12 fl oz	360 mL

1   Combine the egg yolks, sugar, and wine in the bowl of a mixer and whip together until thoroughly blended. Place the bowl over simmering water and heat, whisking constantly, until the mixture is thickened and very foamy and has reached 180°F/82°C.

2   Transfer the bowl to the mixer and whip on high speed with the whip attachment until cool.

3   Transfer the sabayon to a container and cover it with plastic wrap placed directly against the surface to prevent a skin from forming. Sabayon may be served warm or at room temperature.

NOTE   If desired, whip 24 fl oz/720 mL of heavy cream to medium peaks and fold into the cooled sabayon.

VARIATIONS   **BOURBON SAUCE** Substitute bourbon for the white wine.

CALVADOS SABAYON Substitute Calvados for the white wine.

CHAMPAGNE SABAYON Substitute Champagne for the white wine.

FRAMBOISE SABAYON Substitute framboise for the white wine.

HONEY SABAYON Substitute honey for the sugar.

ZABAGLIONE Substitute Marsala for the white wine.

Raspberry sabayon

MAKES 32 FL OZ/960 ML

Egg yolks	9 oz	255 g
Sugar	9 oz	255 g
Raspberry liqueur	6 fl oz	180 mL
Heavy cream	12 fl oz	360 mL

1   Combine the egg yolks, sugar, and liqueur in the bowl of a mixer and whisk until thoroughly blended. Place the bowl over simmering water and whisk constantly until the mixture is thickened and very foamy and has reached approximately 180°F/82°C.

2   Transfer the bowl to the mixer and whip on high speed with the whip attachment until cool.

3   Whip the cream to soft peaks and gently fold into the sabayon.

4   Serve immediately.

Calvados sabayon sauce

MAKES 32 FL OZ/960 ML

Egg yolks	8 oz	227 g
Sugar	8 oz	227 g
Calvados or other apple brandy	5½ fl oz	165 mL
Heavy cream	8 fl oz	240 mL

1   Combine the egg yolks, sugar, and Calvados in the bowl of a mixer and whisk until thoroughly blended. Place the bowl over simmering water and heat, whisking constantly, until the mixture is thickened and very foamy and has reached approximately 180°F/82°C.

2   Transfer the bowl to the mixer on high speed with the whip attachment and whip until cool.

3   Whip the heavy cream to soft peaks and fold into the sabayon.

4   Serve immediately.

Hot fudge sauce

MAKES 32 FL OZ/960 ML

Bittersweet chocolate, melted	13½ oz	383 g
Cocoa powder	3 oz	85 g
Water	11 fl oz	330 mL
Butter	7 oz	198 g
Sugar	13 oz	369 g
Light corn syrup	4½ oz	128 g
Salt	½ tsp	2.50 g
Vanilla extract	1 tbsp	15 mL

1   Place the melted chocolate, cocoa powder, and water in a saucepan over low heat and stir gently until fully combined. Add the butter, sugar, corn syrup, and salt and simmer over medium heat until thick, about 5 minutes.

2   Remove from the heat and add the vanilla extract.

3   Serve warm.

Chocolate fudge sauce

MAKES 2 LB/907 G

Bittersweet chocolate, finely chopped	6 oz	170 g
Butter	2½ oz	71 g
Water	9 fl oz	270 mL
Sugar	8 oz	227 g
Light corn syrup	5½ oz	156 g
Brandy	4½ tsp	23 mL

1   Melt the chocolate and butter in a stainless-steel bowl over barely simmering water, stirring gently to combine.

2   Stir in the water. Stir in the sugar and corn syrup.

3   Transfer the mixture to a saucepan and simmer over low heat until the sugar has melted and all the ingredients are thoroughly combined, about 5 minutes.

4   Remove from the heat and cool slightly. Stir in the brandy.

5   Serve warm.

Chocolate sauce

MAKES 32 FL OZ/960 ML

Sugar	10 oz	284 g
Water	16 fl oz	480 mL
Light corn syrup	4½ oz	128 g
Cocoa powder, sifted	4 oz	113 g
Bittersweet chocolate, melted	1 lb	454 g

1   Combine the sugar, water, and corn syrup in a heavy-bottomed saucepan and bring to a boil over medium-high heat. Remove from the heat.

2   Place the cocoa powder in a bowl and add enough of the hot sugar syrup to make a paste, stirring until smooth. Gradually add the remaining syrup and mix until fully incorporated.

3   Add the melted chocolate and blend until fully incorporated.

4   Strain through a fine-mesh sieve.

5   Serve warm or chilled.

Raspberry coulis

MAKES 32 FL OZ/960 ML

Raspberries (fresh or frozen)	2 lb	907 g
Sugar	1 lb	454 g
Lemon juice	2 fl oz	60 mL

1   Combine the raspberries, 8 oz/227 g of the sugar, and 1 fl oz/30 mL of the lemon juice in a saucepan over medium heat. Simmer, stirring, until the sugar has dissolved, about 10 minutes.

2   Strain the coulis through a fine-mesh sieve.

3   Adjust the flavor balance with sugar and/or lemon juice, if necessary.

NOTE   If desired, add a slurry made of 2 fl oz/60 mL water and 1 oz/28 g cornstarch per 32 fl oz/960 mL of coulis to the sauce to thicken it. Bring the coulis to a boil, gradually whisk in the slurry, and bring back to a boil. Cool.

VARIATIONS   **KIWI COULIS** Substitute kiwi purée for the raspberries.

MANGO COULIS Substitute chopped mango for the raspberries.

STRAWBERRY COULIS Substitute fresh or frozen strawberries for the raspberries.

Papaya coulis

MAKES 32 FL OZ/960 ML

Papaya, peeled, seeded, and cubed	2 each	2 each
Pineapple, peeled, cored, and cubed	½ each	½ each
Coconut milk	4 fl oz	120 mL
White crème de cacao	2 tbsp	30 mL
Rum	1 tbsp	15 mL
Orange juice	8 fl oz	240 mL
Lemon juice	4 fl oz	120 mL
Lime juice	2 fl oz	60 mL
Lemongrass, chopped	1 stalk	1 stalk
Sugar	3 to 6 oz	85 to 170 g

1   Purée the papaya and pineapple in a food processor.

2   Transfer the purée to a saucepan, add the coconut milk, crème de cacao, rum, the orange, lemon, and lime juices, the lemongrass, and 3 oz/85 g sugar and mix well. Bring to a simmer and remove from the heat.

3   Strain through a fine-mesh sieve.

4   Add more sugar, if necessary.

5   Cover and store in the refrigerator until ready to use. Serve warm or cold.

Pineapple-sage coulis

MAKES 32 FL OZ/960 ML

Pineapple, medium	1 each	1 each
Coconut milk	4 fl oz	120 mL
Papaya, peeled and cubed	4 oz	113 g
Sugar	3 to 5 oz	85 to 142 g
Malibu rum	1 fl oz	30 mL
Sage leaves	6 to 8 each	6 to 8 each
Lime juice	1 fl oz	30 mL
Lemon juice	2 fl oz	60 mL

1   Peel and core the pineapple and cut into pieces. Place the pineapple in a nonreactive saucepan with the coconut milk, papaya, 3 oz/85 g of the sugar, and the rum. Bring to a simmer and add the sage leaves. Cover, remove from the heat, and cool thoroughly.

2   Remove and discard the sage leaves. Transfer the pineapple mixture to a food processor and purée. Strain through a fine-mesh sieve.

3   Stir in the lime and lemon juices, blending thoroughly.

4   Add more sugar, if necessary.

Plum röster

MAKES 32 FL OZ/960 ML

Plums, pitted and sliced	3 lb	1.36 kg
Sugar	5 oz	142 g
Water	6 fl oz	180 mL
Red wine (Burgundy)	6 fl oz	180 mL
Cinnamon sticks	2 each	2 each

1   Combine all the ingredients in a saucepan, bring to a simmer over medium heat, and simmer until the plums are tender, about 30 minutes.

2   Remove the cinnamon sticks. Pass the mixture through a food mill or press through a fine-mesh sieve, working as much of the pulp through the mesh as possible.

3   Return the mixture to the saucepan and simmer to reduce by half.

4   Serve warm.

Raspberry sauce

MAKES 32 FL OZ/960 ML

Raspberry purée	16 fl oz	480 mL
Sugar	8 oz	227 g
Water	9 fl oz	270 mL
Tapioca starch	½ oz	14 g

1   Combine the raspberry purée, sugar, and 8 fl oz/240 mL of the water in a saucepan and bring to a boil.

2   Meanwhile, make a slurry with the tapioca starch and the remaining 1 fl oz/30 mL water.

3   Slowly whisk the slurry into the boiling purée. Return the mixture to a boil, stirring constantly with a whisk until thickened.

4   Strain the sauce through a fine-mesh strainer. Cool over an ice water bath.

5   The sauce is ready to use immediately, or may be covered and stored in the refrigerator until needed.

Passion fruit sauce

MAKES 32 FL OZ/960 ML

Passion fruit purée	1 lb 5 oz	595 g
Sugar	4 to 8 oz	113 to 227 g
Water	1 fl oz	30 mL
Cornstarch	½ oz	14 g
Lemon juice	1 fl oz	30 mL

1   Combine the fruit purée and 4 oz/113 g of the sugar in a saucepan and bring to a boil over medium heat.

2   Meanwhile, make a slurry with the water and cornstarch. Slowly whisk the slurry into the boiling purée and bring back to a boil, whisking until thickened. Remove from the heat.

3   Adjust the flavor with more sugar and the lemon juice as necessary. Cool over an ice water bath. The sauce is ready to use immediately, or may be covered and stored in the refrigerator until needed.

VARIATIONS   **COCONUT SAUCE** Substitute coconut purée for the passion fruit purée.

PAPAYA SAUCE Substitute papaya purée for the passion fruit purée.

RASPBERRY SAUCE Substitute raspberry purée for the passion fruit purée.

Citrus sauce

Orange juice	12 fl oz	360 mL
Vanilla beans, split and scraped	1 each	1 each
Cinnamon sticks	2 each	2 each
Sugar	1½ oz	43 g
Butter	3 oz	85 g
Orange suprêmes	36 each	36 each

1   Combine the orange juice, vanilla bean seeds and pod, cinnamon sticks, and sugar in a sauce pot and bring to a boil until the liquid reduces by half, about 10 minutes. Whisk the liquid constantly during the reduction process.

2   Remove the pot from the heat and strain into a clean pot. Thicken the sauce by vigorously whisking in the butter. Add the orange suprêmes.

3   Reserve the sauce warm or reheat at service so it is served warm.

Hot strawberry syrup

MAKES 32 FL OZ/960 ML

Strawberries (fresh or frozen)	3 lb	1.36 kg
Sugar	1 lb	454 g
Water	12 fl oz	360 mL
Vanilla beans, seeds only	1 each	1 each
Lemon juice	4 fl oz	120 mL

1   If using frozen strawberries, thaw slightly. Slice the strawberries.

2   Combine the strawberries, sugar, and water in a saucepan, bring to a simmer over medium heat, and simmer until the strawberries are soft, about 15 minutes.

3   Strain through a fine-mesh sieve, pressing against the solids with the back of a ladle.

4   Pour the liquid into a saucepan, add the vanilla bean seeds and the lemon juice, and simmer until reduced by half, or to the consistency of a syrup, about 30 minutes.

5   Serve hot or cover and refrigerate until ready to reheat and use.

Savarin syrup

MAKES 5 LB 6 OZ/2.44 KG

Pineapple skins, cleaned*	1 each	1 each
Water	48 fl oz	1.36 kg
Orange juice	16 fl oz	480 mL
Vanilla beans, split and scraped	1 each	1 each
Cinnamon sticks	2 each	2 each
Black peppercorns	10 each	10 each
Sugar	1 lb 2 oz	510 g
Neutral gel**	4 oz	113 g

*Reserve pineapple for roasting the next day.

**Not used in the syrup, but as a glaze after the savarin has been soaked.

1   Clean the pineapple: Cut off the top and bottom. Stand the pineapple straight up and trim the skin top to bottom with a serrated knife. Remove any "eyes." Turn the pineapple on its side and, using a large slicer, round and cut an even cylinder. Reserve the cylinder for roasting; use all the trim for the syrup.

2   Combine the pineapple skin and trim, water, orange juice, vanilla bean seeds and pod, cinnamon sticks, peppercorns, and sugar in a nonreactive saucepan and boil for 10 minutes. Let cool to room temperature. Chill overnight.

3   The next day, strain the syrup through cheesecloth and squeeze out as much flavor as possible from the solids. Store covered in the refrigerator.

4   To use for soaking, bring the syrup to a boil. Dunk thawed savarin in very hot, but not boiling, syrup, until the savarin has absorbed as much liquid as it can without falling apart. (You can dunk up to 5 savarin at a time.)

5   Remove the soaked savarin from the liquid with a slotted spoon. Let drain on a cooling rack over a sheet pan and refrigerate.

6   To use for glazing, combine the neutral gel with just enough of the savarin syrup to loosen the gel. Dunk the savarin in the glaze in an éclair fashion. Keep refrigerated.

Caramel simple syrup

MAKES 1 LB/454 G

Sugar	8 oz	227 g
Lemon juice	3 drops	3 drops
Water, warm	8 fl oz	240 mL

1   Combine the sugar and lemon juice in a medium sauce pot and cook to a deep amber color, stirring gently.

2   Add the warm water slowly while stirring constantly with a whisk. Stir until fully combined. Cover and store in the refrigerator.

Banana syrup

MAKES 10 OZ/284 G

Mineral water	8 fl oz	240 mL
Sugar	2 oz	57 g
Bananas, fully ripe, sliced ½ in/1 cm thick	1 each	1 each

1   Combine all the ingredients in a sauce pot, bring to a boil, and then reduce the heat to low to simmer for 10 minutes.

2   Strain through a fine-mesh sieve and let cool to room temperature. Cover and store in the refrigerator until use.

Blood orange sauce

MAKES 32 FL OZ/960 ML

Blood orange juice	20 fl oz	600 mL
White wine	6 fl oz	180 mL
Sugar	6½ oz	184 g
Arrowroot	1 oz	28 g
Water	1½ fl oz	45 mL
Lemon juice	1 fl oz	30 mL

1   Combine the blood orange juice, wine, and sugar in a heavy-bottomed saucepan. Bring to a boil over medium heat, stirring occasionally to dissolve the sugar. Remove from the heat.

2   Make a slurry with the arrowroot and water. Gradually whisk the slurry into the orange juice mixture and return to a boil, whisking constantly. Immediately remove from the heat.

3   Stir in the lemon juice. Strain through a fine-mesh sieve. Cool and refrigerate until needed.

Strawberry tarragon sauce

MAKES 9 OZ/255 G

Strawberry purée	6 oz	170 g
Sugar	1½ oz	43 g
Modified starch	½ tsp	2.50 mL
Water	2 fl oz	60 mL
Tarragon, chopped	1½ tbsp	4.50 g

1   Place the purée and sugar in a medium sauce pot and bring to a boil over high heat. Meanwhile, make a slurry with the starch and water.

2   Add the slurry to the purée, whisking constantly. Bring the mixture back to a boil for 15 seconds.

3   Strain through a fine-mesh strainer and cool in a water bath.

4   When completely cool, add the tarragon. Refrigerate until needed.

Lime rickey sauce

MAKES 64 FL OZ/1.92 L

Sugar	1 lb 5 oz	595 g
Lime juice	10½ fl oz	315 mL
Light rum	32 fl oz	960 mL

1   Combine all of the ingredients in a saucepan and bring to a boil over medium heat, stirring to dissolve the sugar. Boil without stirring until the sauce reaches 220°F/104°C.

2   Remove from the heat and cool completely. Serve chilled or at room temperature.

Chunky strawberry sauce

MAKES 20 FL OZ/600 ML

Strawberries	12 oz	340 g
Sugar	7 to 10 oz	198 to 284 g
Water	9 fl oz	270 mL
Lemon juice	1 tbsp	15 mL
Cornstarch	¾ oz	21 g
Orange liqueur	2 fl oz	60 mL

1   Chop 12 of the strawberries into ½-in/1-cm cubes. Reserve.

2   Combine the remaining strawberries, the sugar, 8 fl oz/240 mL of the water, and the lemon juice in a nonreactive saucepan and bring to a boil. Simmer for 2 to 3 minutes.

3   Remove from the heat and purée using an immersion blender. Return to the heat and bring back to a boil.

4   Meanwhile, make a slurry with the cornstarch and the remaining 1 fl oz/30 mL water. Gradually whisk the slurry into the sauce and bring back to a boil, whisking until the sauce thickens enough to coat the back of a spoon. Blend in the orange liqueur.

5   Cool the sauce over an ice water bath. Refrigerate until needed.

6   Just before serving, fold in the reserved chopped strawberries.

NOTE   Depending on how ripe the strawberries are, the amount of sugar may need to be adjusted.

White pear and huckleberry sauce

MAKES 12 OZ/340 G

Poire William (brandy)	3½ fl oz	75 mL
Water	1 tbsp	15 mL
Dried huckleberries	1 oz	28 g
Pear purée	6 oz	170 g
Sugar	1½ oz	43 g
Lemon juice	1½ tsp	7.5 mL
Modified starch	1 tsp	5 mL

1   Combine the Poire William and water and soak the huckleberries overnight.

2   Strain through a fine-mesh sieve and reserve the liquid and huckleberries separately.

3   Combine the pear purée, sugar, lemon juice, and all but 1 fl oz/30 mL of the soaking liquid in a sauce pot. Bring to a boil over medium-high heat.

4   Make a slurry with the starch and the reserved liquid. Gradually add to the boiling mixture, stirring constantly.

5   Bring the mixture to a rapid boil again until the mixture thickens, remove from heat, and let cool to room temperature.

6   Strain the sauce and add the reserved huckleberries. Refrigerate until needed.

Coconut ginger sauce

MAKES 32 FL OZ/960 ML

Coconut milk	24 fl oz	720 mL
Papaya, small dice	1 each	1 each
Lemongrass, finely chopped	2 stalks	2 stalks
Ginger, peeled and thinly sliced	2 oz	57 g
Malibu rum	2 fl oz	60 mL
Sugar	3 to 6 oz	85 to 170 g
Lemon juice	1 to 2 fl oz	30 to 60 mL

1   Combine the coconut milk and papaya in a saucepan and simmer over low heat until the papaya is tender, about 15 minutes.

2   Transfer to a food processor and purée. Strain through a fine-mesh sieve and return to the saucepan.

3   Add the lemongrass, ginger, and rum and bring to a simmer. Remove from the heat, cover, and steep overnight under refrigeration.

4   Strain the sauce. Add the sugar and lemon juice as needed and stir with a whisk to combine. Refrigerate until needed.

Lemon verbena sauce

MAKES 24 FL OZ/720 ML

Large lemon verbena leaves	12 each	12 each
Water	14 fl oz	420 mL
Lemon juice	6 fl oz	180 mL
Glucose syrup	1 oz	28 g
Sugar	2 oz	57 g
Lemongrass, chopped	1 stalk	1 stalk
Cornstarch	½ oz	14 g
White wine	1 fl oz	30 mL

1   Reserve 4 of the lemon verbena leaves. Combine the remaining 8 leaves, the water, lemon juice, glucose, sugar, and lemongrass in a saucepan and bring to a simmer. Remove from the heat, cover, and steep for 10 minutes.

2   Cool, cover, and refrigerate overnight.

3   Strain through a fine-mesh strainer into a saucepan and bring to a boil.

4   Make a slurry with the cornstarch and white wine. Gradually whisk the slurry into the sauce and bring back to a boil, whisking until the sauce thickens enough to coat the back of a spoon.

5   Allow the sauce to cool to room temperature.

6   Just before serving, mince the reserved minced leaves and add to the sauce.

Burnt orange sauce

MAKES 48 FL OZ/1.44 ML

Oranges	1½ each	1½ each
Milk	32 fl oz or more	960 mL or more
Sugar	8 oz	227 g
Egg yolks	6 oz	170 g
Vanilla extract	¼ tsp	1.25 mL

1   Place the oranges on a sheet pan and roast in a 375°F/191°C oven until golden brown. Cut the oranges into quarters.

2   Bring the milk to a boil and add the roasted oranges. Chill over an ice water bath, cover, and refrigerate for 24 hours.

3 Strain the milk and add enough fresh milk to bring it back to 32 fl oz/960 mL.

4 Combine the milk with 4 oz/113 g of the sugar in a saucepan and bring to a boil, stirring to dissolve the sugar.

5 Whisk together the egg yolks and the remaining sugar.

6 Temper the egg yolks by gradually adding one-third of the hot milk, whisking constantly. Return the tempered egg mixture to the remaining hot milk in the saucepan and continue cooking until the mixture thickens enough to coat the back of a spoon.

7 Strain the sauce into a metal container, stir in the vanilla, and chill in an ice water bath.

8 Cover with plastic wrap and store under refrigeration.

Fruit salsa

MAKES 1 LB 14 OZ/851 G

Papaya, small dice	5 oz	142 g
Mango, small dice	5 oz	142 g
Honeydew melon, small dice	5 oz	142 g
Strawberries, small dice	5 oz	142 g
Passion fruit juice	1 fl oz	30 mL
Mint, finely chopped	1 tbsp	3 g
Amaretto liqueur	3 fl oz	90 mL
Orange juice	8 fl oz	240 mL
Sugar	3 oz	85 g

1 Combine the fruits, passion fruit juice, and mint. Set aside to macerate.

2 Combine the Amaretto, orange juice, and sugar and bring to a boil. Boil until reduced to 7 fl oz/210 mL. Cool to room temperature.

3 Gently blend the reduced liquid into the fruit.

4 Refrigerate until needed.

Orange marinade

MAKES 14 FL OZ/420 ML

Orange juice	4 fl oz	120 mL
Honey	8 oz	227 g
Orange liqueur	4 fl oz	120 mL

1 Combine the orange juice and honey in a saucepan and bring to a simmer.

2 Remove from the heat and stir in the orange liqueur. Cool to room temperature.

3 Store, tightly covered, in the refrigerator.

Fruit soaker

MAKES 48 FL OZ/1.44 L

Port, tawny	8 fl oz	240 mL
Orange liqueur	4 fl oz	120 mL
Raspberry liqueur	4 fl oz	120 mL
Sugar	1 oz	28 g
Seasonal fruit, assorted	2 lb 8 oz	1.13 kg

1 Combine the port, orange and raspberry liqueurs, and sugar in a saucepan and bring to a boil over medium heat, stirring to dissolve the sugar.

2 Cool to room temperature. Clean, peel, and slice the fruit as needed.

3 Pour the port mixture over the fruit, cover, and allow to macerate overnight, tightly covered, under refrigeration.

Raisin sauce

MAKES 24 FL OZ/720 ML

Raisins or currants	12 oz	340 g
Apple cider	64 fl oz	1.92 L
Light brown sugar	4 oz	113 g
Ground cinnamon	½ tsp	1 g
Ground nutmeg	¼ tsp	0.5 g
Vanilla beans, seeds only	2 each	2 each
Apple brandy	4 fl oz	120 mL

1   Combine the raisins and 8 fl oz/240 mL of the cider in a saucepan and bring to a simmer over low heat. Remove from the heat and allow the raisins to plump for at least 30 minutes.

2   Combine the remaining 56 fl oz/68 L apple cider, the sugar, cinnamon, nutmeg, and vanilla bean seeds in a saucepan. Bring to a simmer and reduce by two-thirds, about 30 minutes.

3   Drain the raisins.

4   Remove the pan from the heat and stir in the apple brandy and raisins.

5   Serve warm or chilled.

Dried cherry sauce

MAKES 1 LB 10 OZ/737 G

Sugar	3 oz	85 g
Red wine	13 fl oz	390 mL
Water	6 fl oz	180 mL
Orange juice	1 fl oz	30 mL
Lemon juice	1 fl oz	30 mL
Vanilla beans	1 each	1 each
Dried cherries	4 oz	113 g
Cornstarch	½ oz	14 g

1   Combine the sugar, 12 oz/360 mL of the red wine, the water, and orange and lemon juices in a saucepan. Split the vanilla bean, scrape the seeds into the pan, add the pod, and bring the mixture to a boil. Remove from the heat and add the cherries.

2   Refrigerate covered overnight.

3 Strain, reserving the cherries. Pour the sauce into a saucepan and bring to a boil.

4 Make a slurry with the cornstarch and the remaining 1 fl oz/30 mL red wine. Gradually whisk the slurry into the sauce and bring back to a boil, whisking until the sauce thickens enough to coat the back of a spoon.

5 Cool to room temperature.

6 Add the reserved cherries and serve at once.

Candied cranberry compote

MAKES 32 FL OZ/960 ML

Sugar	1 lb 12 oz	794 g
Water	24 fl oz	720 mL
Cranberries (fresh or frozen)	1 lb 14 oz	851 g
Orange juice	4 fl oz	120 mL
Cinnamon sticks	1 each	1 each

1 To prepare the candied cranberries, combine 1 lb 8 oz/680 g of the sugar and 12 fl oz/360 mL of the water in a heavy-bottomed saucepan and bring to a simmer over medium-high heat, stirring until the sugar has dissolved.

2 Add the cranberries and poach until tender; do not allow the syrup to come to a boil. Remove from the heat and allow the cranberries to cool completely in the sugar syrup.

3 Drain the cranberries and spread them on a parchment-lined sheet pan. Dry in a 200°F/93°C oven until they are just slightly sticky, about 1½ hours. Reserve.

4 To prepare the sauce, combine 6 oz/170 g of the cranberries with the remaining 12 fl oz/360 mL water, the orange juice, the remaining 4 oz/113 g sugar, and the cinnamon stick in a saucepan and simmer over medium heat until the cranberries burst and are very soft, about 20 minutes.

5 Remove the cinnamon stick and purée the mixture in a food processor. Transfer to a bowl and gently stir in the remaining candied cranberries. Add more sugar, if necessary.

6 Store, tightly covered, in the refrigerator.

Fig compote

MAKES 2 LB 8 OZ/1.13 KG

Dried figs	1 lb 3 oz	539 g
Raisins	9 oz	255 g
Vanilla beans, split and scraped	1 each	1 each
Lemon juice	1 fl oz	30 mL
Orange zest, grated	1 each	1 each
Honey	8½ oz	241 g
Ground cinnamon	1 tsp	2 g
Almonds, lightly toasted and finely chopped	4 oz	113 g
Port, tawny	3 fl oz	90 mL

1   Chop the figs and raisins in a food processor until the fruits are approximately small dice.

2   Combine with the remaining ingredients.

3   Use immediately or cover and store covered in the refrigerator for later use.

Poached apple compote

MAKES 1 LB 10 OZ/737 G

Honey Crisp apples	8 oz	227 g
Apple cider	12 fl oz	360 mL
Cinnamon sticks	1 each	1 each
Sugar	6 oz	170 g
Lemon	½ each	½ each
Gelatin sheets	⅓ oz	9 g

1   Cut the apples into small dice, place in a pot, and cover with the apple cider. Add the cinnamon stick, sugar, and lemon. Keep just below a simmer and poach until the apples are just tender, about 10 minutes.

2   Drain and reserve the apples. Reduce the poaching liquid to 8 fl oz/240 mL.

3   Bloom the gelatin in cool water, drain, and melt in the reduced liquid. Cool slightly.

4   Fold in the apples.

5   The compote is ready to be used or served, or it may be covered and stored in the refrigerator for later use.

Blueberry compote

MAKES 1 LB 6 OZ/624 G

Blueberries (fresh or frozen)	1 lb	454 g
Sugar	5 oz	142 g
Rosemary	1 small sprig	1 small sprig
Lemon juice	1 fl oz	30 mL
Lemon zest, grated	2 tsp	6 g
Gelatin sheets (see step 3)		

1   Combine 8 oz/227 g of the blueberries with the sugar, rosemary, lemon juice, and zest in a sauce pot and cook, stirring occasionally, until the blueberries have just softened, 3 to 4 minutes.

2   Remove the rosemary sprig. Purée and strain. Add the remaining berries and weigh the mixture.

3   Multiply the weight of the berry mixture by 0.02 (2%) to determine the amount of gelatin needed. For example, 10 ounces gross weight will require 0.2 ounce of gelatin.

4   Bloom the gelatin in cold water and melt over low heat. Add to the berries.

5   The compote is ready to be used or served, or may it be covered and stored in the refrigerator for later use.

Cranberry sauce

MAKES 20 FL OZ/600 ML

Fresh cranberries	12 oz	340 g
Sugar	5 oz	142 g
Water	8 fl oz	240 mL
Vanilla beans	1 each	1 each

1   Combine the cranberries, sugar, and water in a saucepan. Split the vanilla bean, scrape the seeds into the pan, add the pod, and bring to a boil over medium heat, whisking to break up the cranberries. Boil until the sauce has reduced slightly and thickened, about 5 minutes. Remove from the heat, remove the vanilla bean pod, and cool completely.

2   The sauce is ready to be used or served, or it may be covered and stored in the refrigerator for later use.

Cider bourbon sauce

MAKES 32 FL OZ/960 ML

Apple cider	32 fl oz	960 mL
Bourbon	2 fl oz	60 mL
Arrowroot	1 oz	28 g

1   Combine 28 fl oz/840 mL of the cider with the bourbon in a saucepan and bring to a boil over medium heat.

2   Make a slurry with the arrowroot and the remaining 4 fl oz/120 mL cider. Gradually whisk the slurry into the cider mixture and bring back to a boil, whisking constantly until thickened. Immediately remove from the heat.

3   Strain the sauce through a fine-mesh sieve. Cool.

4   The sauce is ready to be used or served, or it may be covered and stored in the refrigerator for later use.

Fig butter

MAKES APPROXIMATELY 60 FL OZ/1.80 L

Black Mission figs	10 lb	4.54 kg
Sugar	7 lb	3.18 kg
Butter	1 lb	454 g
Vanilla beans, split and scraped	3 each	3 each

1   Trim the top and bottom off the figs.

2   Combine the figs and the remaining ingredients in a rondeau. Cook over medium heat until the figs completely break down, about 2 hours. Remove the vanilla bean pods.

3   Cool in an ice water bath and reserve in an airtight container under refrigeration.

Apple butter

MAKES 32 FL OZ/960 ML

Apples	7 lb	3.18 kg
Apple cider	24 fl oz	720 mL
Sugar	1 lb	454 g
Ground cardamom	1 tbsp	6 g
Ground cinnamon	2 tsp	4 g
Lemon zest, grated	1 tsp	3 g
Salt	¼ tsp	1.25 g

1   Peel, core, and slice the apples. Combine with the apple cider in a large heavy-bottomed saucepan, cover, and bring to a simmer. Simmer until the apples are a soft pulp, about 30 minutes.

2   Pass the apple pulp through a food mill and transfer to a saucepan.

3   Add the sugar, spices, zest, and salt and simmer, stirring frequently, until very thick, about 2 hours.

4   Cool completely.

5   The butter is ready to be used or served, or it may be covered and stored in the refrigerator for later use.

VARIATIONS   **MANGO BUTTER** Substitute mangoes for the apples and apple juice for the apple cider.

NECTARINE BUTTER Substitute nectarines for the apples and apple juice for the apple cider.

PEACH BUTTER Substitute peaches for the apples and peach juice or nectar for the apple cider.

PEAR BUTTER Substitute pears for the apples and pear juice or pear cider for the apple cider.

Pumpkin butter

MAKES ABOUT 30 FL OZ/900 ML

Pumpkins	6 lb	2.72 kg
Sugar	2 lb	907 g
Butter	1 lb	454 g
Vanilla beans, split and scraped	1 each	1 each
Ground cloves	pinch	pinch

1   Cut the pumpkins into quarters and scoop out the seeds.

2   Place the quartered pumpkins cut side up on a sheet pan. Bake at 325°F/163°C until the flesh is tender, about 25 minutes.

3   When cool enough to handle, peel off the skin with a paring knife.

4   Place the pumpkin flesh in a large pot with the sugar, butter, vanilla bean seeds and pod, and cloves. Cook over medium-low heat, stirring occasionally, until the volume has reduced by half, about 2 hours. The pumpkin will completely break down and turn into a smooth paste. Remove the vanilla bean pod.

5   Cool the pumpkin butter in an ice water bath and reserve in an airtight container under refrigeration.

Apple cumin butter

MAKES 1 LB 2 OZ/510 G

Cumin seeds	¼ tsp	1.25 mL
Superpomme	7 oz	198 g
Confectioners' sugar	6 oz	170 g
Apple cider	2½ fl oz	75 mL
Butter, ½-in/1-cm cubes	2 oz	57 g
Vanilla powder	1 tbsp	9 g
Calvados	1 tbsp	15 mL

1   Toast the cumin seeds in a small dry sauté pan until dark brown and their full flavor develops. Grind using a spice grinder.

2   Combine the cumin, Superpomme, sugar, cider, butter, and vanilla powder in a small sauce pot and bring to a gentle simmer.

3   Simmer for 2 minutes, stirring constantly.

4   Pour into a plastic container and cool to room temperature, stirring occasionally to prevent a skin from forming.

5   Add the Calvados and refrigerate until use.

Orange vanilla bean sauce

MAKES 16 FL OZ/480 ML

Orange juice	16 fl oz	480 mL
White wine	8 fl oz	240 mL
Sugar	4 oz	113 g
Cinnamon sticks	1 each	1 each
Vanilla beans	1 each	1 each
Tapioca starch	½ oz	14 g
Water	1 fl oz	30 mL
Orange liqueur	2 fl oz	60 mL

1   Combine the orange juice, wine, sugar, and cinnamon stick in a saucepan. Split the vanilla bean, scrape in the seeds, add the pod, and bring to a simmer. Stir to dissolve the sugar. Simmer for 15 minutes to reduce and blend the flavors.

2   Make a slurry with the tapioca starch and water. Gradually whisk the slurry into the sauce and cook, whisking, until the sauce thickens enough to coat the back of a spoon.

3   Remove from the heat, strain through a fine-mesh strainer, and add the orange liqueur. Cool and serve.

Classic caramel sauce

MAKES 32 FL OZ/960 ML

Heavy cream	24 fl oz	720 mL
Sugar	13 oz	369 g
Glucose syrup	10 oz	284 g
Butter, cubed, soft	2¼ oz	64 g

1   Place the cream in a saucepan and bring to a boil over medium heat. Keep warm over very low heat.

2   Prepare an ice water bath. Combine the sugar and glucose syrup in a heavy-bottomed saucepan and slowly cook over medium heat, stirring constantly, until all the sugar has dissolved. Stop stirring and continue to cook to a golden caramel. Remove from the heat and shock the saucepan in the ice bath to stop the cooking.

3 Remove from the ice bath and stir in the butter. Carefully stir in the hot cream, mixing until fully blended. Cool.

4 The sauce is ready to be used or served, or it may be covered and stored in the refrigerator for later use.

Espresso caramel sauce

MAKES 32 FL OZ/960 ML

Sugar	1 lb	454 g
Brewed coffee, warm	20 fl oz	600 mL
Espresso beans	1 oz	28 g
Cinnamon sticks	2 each	2 each
Vanilla beans	2 each	2 each
Heavy cream	10 fl oz	300 mL
Cornstarch	½ oz	14 g
Water	1 fl oz	30 mL
Butter	2 oz	57 g
Brandy	2 fl oz	60 mL

1 Add a small amount of the sugar to a medium-hot pan set over medium heat and allow it to melt, then add the remaining sugar in small increments, allowing each addition to melt fully before adding the next. Continue this process until all the sugar has been added to the pan. Cook to the desired color. Remove from the heat and shock in an ice water bath for 10 seconds to stop the cooking process.

2 Carefully add the coffee to the caramel and stir to combine. Tie the espresso beans and cinnamon sticks in a sachet and add. Split the vanilla beans, scrape the seeds into the mixture, and add the pods, and simmer until the caramel is infused with the flavoring ingredients, about 15 minutes. Add the cream. Remove the sachet and vanilla bean pods.

3 Make a slurry with the cornstarch and water. Gradually whisk the slurry into the sauce and bring to a boil. Remove the pan from the heat.

4 Stir in the butter and brandy and mix until fully blended.

5 The sauce is ready to be used or served, or it may be covered and stored in the refrigerator for later use.

Clear apple caramel sauce

MAKES 48 FL OZ/1.44 L

Sugar	1 lb	454 g
Apple juice, warm	28 fl oz	840 mL
Apple brandy, warm	4 fl oz	120 mL
Cinnamon sticks	1 each	1 each
Nutmeg, cracked	1 each	1 each
Butter	2 oz	57 g

1 To prepare the caramel, add a small amount of the sugar to a medium-hot pan set over medium heat and allow it to melt, then add the remaining sugar in small increments, allowing each addition to fully melt before adding the next. Continue this process until all the sugar has been added to the pan. Cook to the desired color.

2 Add the apple juice and apple brandy. Stir over medium heat to combine. Add the cinnamon stick and nutmeg and simmer for 20 minutes. Strain.

3 Stir in the butter.

4 The sauce is ready to be used or served, or it may be covered and stored in the refrigerator for later use.

NOTE Depending on desired consistency, the sauce can be thickened before the butter is added with a cornstarch slurry made with 1 tsp/3 g of cornstarch and 2 fl oz/60 mL of apple juice.

VARIATIONS **CLEAR ORANGE CARAMEL SAUCE** Omit the cinnamon and nutmeg. Split and scrape 1 vanilla bean, adding the seeds and pod to the caramel in step 2. Replace the apple juice with an equal amount of pulp-free orange juice, and the apple brandy with an equal amount of orange liqueur.

CLEAR PEAR CARAMEL SAUCE Replace the apple juice with an equal amount of pear cider and the apple brandy with an equal amount of pear liqueur.

Soft caramel filling

MAKES 1 LB 4 OZ/567 G

Heavy cream	6 fl oz	180 mL
Sugar	11 oz	312 g
Lemon juice	4 drops	4 drops
Butter	3 oz	85 g

1 Bring the cream to a boil; set aside but keep hot.

2 Combine the sugar and the lemon juice in a saucepan and cook over medium heat until the sugar is fully melted and has turned a deep amber color.

3 Slowly and carefully whisk in the hot cream. Whisk in the butter.

4 The filling is ready to be used or served, or it may be covered and stored in the refrigerator for later use.

Butterscotch sauce

MAKES 48 FL OZ/1.44 L

Light brown sugar	1 lb 7 oz	652 g
All-purpose flour	3½ oz	99 g
Salt	1 tsp	5 g
Milk	32 fl oz	960 mL
Egg yolks	2½ oz	71 g
Butter	2 oz	57 g
Vanilla extract	1 tbsp	15 mL

1 Combine the sugar, flour, and salt in a stainless-steel bowl over barely simmering water. Add the milk gradually, stirring with a whisk. Cook for 10 minutes.

2 Blend the egg yolks in a bowl and temper with a small amount of the brown sugar mixture, whisking constantly. Add the tempered egg yolks to the remaining brown sugar mixture and cook over barely simmering water, stirring constantly with a whisk, for 2 minutes.

3 Remove from the heat and stir in the butter and vanilla. Serve.

Milk chocolate caramel fudge sauce

MAKES 32 FL OZ/960 ML

Sugar	1 lb	454 g
Water	4 fl oz	120 mL
Light corn syrup	4 oz	113 g
Heavy cream, warm	20 fl oz	600 mL
Milk chocolate, finely chopped	7 oz	198 g

1   Combine the sugar, water, and corn syrup in a heavy-bottomed saucepan and bring to a boil over medium-high heat, stirring to dissolve the sugar. Cook without stirring to a rich golden amber.

2   Carefully blend the warm cream into the caramel. Remove the pan from the heat, add the chocolate, and stir until the chocolate is melted and thoroughly combined.

3   Adjust the consistency with more cream, if desired.

4   Serve warm or cold.

Ginger rum sauce

MAKES 24 FL OZ/720 ML

Pineapple juice	18 fl oz	540 mL
Sugar	8 oz	227 g
Vanilla beans	1 each	1 each
Ginger, ⅛-in/3-mm slices	1½ oz	43 g
Jamaican dark rum	3 fl oz	90 mL
Cornstarch	½ oz	14 g
Water	2 fl oz	60 mL
Butter	1½ oz	43 g

1   Bring the pineapple juice to a boil. Keep warm over very low heat.

2   To prepare the caramel, add a small amount of the sugar to a medium-hot pan set over medium heat and allow it to melt, then add the remaining sugar in small increments, allowing each addition to fully melt before adding the next. Continue this process until all the sugar has been added. Cook to the desired color.

3 Carefully add the pineapple juice to the caramel, stirring constantly. Split the vanilla bean, scrape in the seeds, and add the pod and the ginger. Simmer for 30 minutes to infuse the sauce.

4 Add the rum and bring the sauce back to a simmer.

5 Make a slurry with the cornstarch and water. Gradually add the slurry to the sauce, whisking constantly, and cook until the sauce comes back to a boil and coats the back of a spoon. Blend in the butter.

6 Serve warm or chilled.

Honey cardamom sauce

MAKES 20 FL OZ/600 ML

Apple juice	10 fl oz	300 mL
Pineapple juice	10 fl oz	300 mL
Sugar	12 oz	340 g
Honey	8 oz	227 g
Ground cardamom	½ tsp	1 g
Cornstarch	½ oz	14 g
Water	2 fl oz	60 ml
Butter	½ oz	14 g
Anise liqueur	1 tbsp	15 mL

1 Bring the apple juice and pineapple juice to a boil. Keep warm over very low heat.

2 Place the sugar in a heavy-bottomed saucepan and cook, stirring constantly, over medium heat to a rich golden brown, occasionally washing down the sides of the pan with a wet pastry brush.

3 Add the honey to the caramel and stir until incorporated. Carefully add the warm juice mixture, stirring constantly. Add the cardamom and simmer for 15 to 20 minutes to blend the flavors.

4 Make a slurry with the cornstarch and water. Gradually whisk the slurry into the sauce and cook, whisking constantly, until the sauce coats the back of a spoon.

5 Blend in the butter and anise liqueur.

6 Serve warm or cold.

Honey cognac sauce

MAKES 32 FL OZ/960 ML

Honey	1 lb 3 oz	539 g
Glucose syrup	9 oz	255 g
Cognac	4½ fl oz	135 mL
Ground cinnamon	2 tsp	4 g
Lemon juice	1 fl oz	30 mL

1   Combine the honey, glucose syrup, and cognac in a heavy-bottomed saucepan and bring to a boil over medium heat. Boil for 2 minutes.

2   Remove from the heat and add the cinnamon and lemon juice.

3   The sauce is ready to be used or served, or it may be covered and stored in the refrigerator for later use.

Vanilla Sauternes reduction

MAKES 20 FL OZ/600 ML

Sauternes	25 fl oz	750 mL
Vanilla beans, seeds only	4 each	4 each
Sugar	3 oz	85 g

1   Bring the Sauternes to a boil in a saucepan over medium heat, and reduce by one-quarter.

2   Add the vanilla bean seeds and sugar and heat, stirring, just until the sugar is dissolved, about 2 minutes. Strain through a fine-mesh sieve.

3   The reduction is ready to be used or served, or it may be covered and stored in the refrigerator for later use.

NOTE   Reducing the sauce too far will cause it to discolor.

Cherry sauce

MAKES 32 FL OZ/960 ML

Dried cherries	1 lb	454 g
Sugar	12 oz	340 g
Red wine	14 fl oz	420 mL
Cherry liqueur	1 fl oz	30 mL
Cinnamon sticks	2 each	2 each
Lemon juice	1 fl oz	30 mL

1   Combine the cherries, sugar, wine, cherry liqueur, and cinnamon sticks in a saucepan. Bring to a simmer over medium heat. Simmer until the cherries are tender, about 30 minutes.

2   Remove the cinnamon sticks, transfer the mixture to a food processor, and purée until smooth.

3   Strain the sauce through a fine-mesh strainer and stir in the lemon juice.

4   Serve warm or cold.

Pineapple honey beurre blanc

MAKES 1 LB/454 G

Pineapple juice	8 fl oz	240 mL
White wine	8 fl oz	240 mL
Honey	2 oz	57 g
Ginger, minced	½ oz	14 g
Allspice berries	8 each	8 each
Butter, ½-in/1-cm cubes	1 lb	454 g

1   Combine the pineapple juice, wine, honey, ginger, and allspice in a saucepan, bring to a boil, and boil until reduced to the consistency of a heavy syrup. Strain through a fine-mesh sieve.

2   Reduce the heat to low and whisk in the butter gradually to maintain the emulsion.

3   Keep warm in a bain-marie until ready to serve.

Champagne sauce

MAKES 32 FL OZ/960 ML

Champagne	16 fl oz	480 mL
Orange juice	4 fl oz	120 mL
Sugar	6 oz	170 g
White grapes, cut in half	4 oz	113 g
White wine	1½ fl oz	45 mL
Cornstarch	⅔ oz	19 g
Orange liqueur	1 tbsp	15 mL

1   Bring the Champagne and orange juice to a boil in a saucepan over medium heat. Add the sugar and grapes and simmer, stirring gently, until the grapes are tender, about 5 minutes.

2   Meanwhile, make a slurry with the white wine and cornstarch. Gradually whisk the slurry into the sauce and bring back to a boil, whisking constantly.

3   Strain through a fine-mesh sieve.

4   Stir in the orange liqueur. Cool completely.

5   The sauce is ready to be used or served, or it may be covered and stored in the refrigerator for later use.

VARIATION   **WHITE WINE SAUCE** Substitute white wine for the Champagne.

Orange hard sauce

MAKES 1 LB 9 OZ/709 G

Butter, soft	1 lb	454 g
Confectioners' sugar	9 oz	255 g
Orange zest, grated	½ oz	14 g
Orange juice	1 fl oz	30 mL

1   Cream together the butter and sugar on medium speed with the paddle attachment, scraping down the bowl periodically, until smooth and light in color, about 5 minutes.

2   Add the orange zest and juice and blend until fully incorporated.

3   Fill a pastry bag fitted with a #3 star tip with the mixture and pipe rosettes onto parchment paper. Chill well before serving.

Lemon hard sauce

MAKES 2 LB/907 G

Butter, soft	1 lb	454 g
Confectioners' sugar	9 oz	255 g
Dark rum	6½ fl oz	195 mL
Lemon juice	1 fl oz	30 mL

1   Cream together the butter and sugar on medium speed with the paddle attachment, scraping down the bowl periodically, until smooth and light in color, about 5 minutes.

2   Add the rum and lemon juice in several additions, blending well after each addition.

3   Fill a pastry bag fitted with a #3 star tip with the mixture and pipe rosettes onto parchment paper. Chill well before serving.

VARIATIONS   **HONEY HARD SAUCE** Substitute 2 tbsp/19 g honey for the confectioners' sugar.

ANISE HARD SAUCE Substitute 1 tbsp/15 mL anise extract for the rum.

Brown sugar butter rub

MAKES 1 LB 4 OZ/567 G

Butter	4 oz	113 g
Light brown sugar	1 lb	454 g

Melt the butter in a saucepan over low heat. Add the brown sugar and blend well. Allow the mixture to cool completely before applying to fruit.

Devil's fudge icing

MAKES 6 LB/2.72 KG

Cocoa powder, sifted	8 oz	227 g
Butter	8 oz	227 g
Light corn syrup	12 oz	340 g
Salt	½ oz	14 g
Vanilla extract	2 tsp	10 mL
Water, hot	8 oz	227 g
Confectioners' sugar	2 lb 8 oz	1.13 kg

1   Cream together the cocoa powder, butter, corn syrup, salt, and vanilla with the paddle attachment, starting on low speed and increasing to medium speed, until light and fluffy, about 5 minutes.

2   Add most of the water and mix well. Add the sugar and mix until smooth. Adjust the consistency with the remaining hot water as necessary.

3   Store at room temperature in a sealed container.

Chocolate whipped cream

MAKES 16½ OZ/468 G, ENOUGH FOR 2 HALF-SHEET ROULADES

Dark chocolate chips, 64%, melted, hot	4 oz	113 g
Vegetable oil	1 tbsp	15 mL
Heavy cream, whipped to soft peaks	12 oz	340 g

1   Combine the melted chocolate and oil in a bowl, mixing until well combined.

2   Add 3 oz/85 g of the whipped cream to the hot chocolate mixture and mix using a whisk until fully incorporated.

3   Add 4½ oz/128 g of the remaining whipped cream and stir, keeping a marble appearance in the mixture.

4   Add the remaining 4½ oz/128 g whipped cream and stir, keeping a marble appearance in the mixture. Use at once.

Vanilla and date milk dressing

MAKES 8 OZ/227 G

Milk	10 fl oz	300 mL
Sugar	6½ oz	184 g
Vanilla beans, split and scraped	1 each	1 each
Dates, finely chopped	2 each	2 each

1　Combine all the ingredients in a small sauce pot.

2　Bring to a boil over medium heat, then lower the heat to low and cook until the mixture turns a light beige caramel color, 30 minutes to 1 hour. Stir occasionally to prevent the milk from scalding.

3　Strain through a fine-mesh sieve, using a 1-oz/28-g ladle to help force the dates through the mesh. Let cool to room temperature and then refrigerate until needed.

4　Serve at room temperature.

Banana passion fruit broth

MAKES 6 LB/2.72 KG

Bottled spring water	44½ fl oz	1.34 L
Sugar	10¼ oz	291 g
Bananas, medium, very ripe	4 each	4 each
Passion fruit purée	1 oz	28 g
Orange juice	25 fl oz	750 mL

1　Combine the spring water and sugar in a large sauce pot. Slice the bananas horizontally into ¼-in/6-mm slices and add.

2　Bring to a gentle simmer (190° to 200°F/88° to 93°C) for 10 minutes.

3　Remove from the heat and cool to room temperature.

4　Stir in the passion fruit purée and orange juice. Strain through a fine-mesh sieve into a large plastic container. Cover and refrigerate overnight.

NOTE　For the Pear with Thai Jewels plated dessert (page 759), place the cooled poached pears in the broth. Make sure the pears are completely submerged; use a plate and parchment paper if necessary to weigh down the pears.

Spraying chocolate

MAKES 1 LB/454 G

Cocoa butter	8 oz	227 g
Couverture chocolate, roughly chopped	8 oz	227 g

1   Combine the cocoa butter and chocolate in a bowl and melt over barely simmering water. Place the chocolate mixture in a metal bain-marie and place it inside a larger bain-marie filled with hot water. Hold the chocolate mixture at 130°F/54°C.

2   Pour the chocolate mixture into an electric paint gun and spray onto frozen items immediately.

Guava jelly

MAKES 1 FRAME

Sugar	8¾ oz	248 g
Pectin, dry	½ oz	14 g
Guava purée	17¾ oz	503 g
Gelatin sheets	3 each	3 each

1   Combine the sugar, pectin, and guava purée in a saucepan and bring to a boil.

2   Bloom the gelatin in cold water. Drain and set aside.

3   Remove the pan from the heat, add the gelatin, and stir to combine.

4   Pour immediately into molds and freeze.

chapter fourteen

Frozen desserts

Sugar syrups, dairy and custard mixtures, and fruit purées may all be used as the base to make frozen desserts. Any of these bases may then be churn- or still-frozen. These two methods of production yield frozen desserts with vastly different textures. Understanding the principles of each type of frozen dessert will give the chef creative freedom to explore different possibilities of flavor, texture, and presentation.

Churned-frozen ice cream

The basic ingredients for ice cream are milk, cream, sugar, flavorings, and sometimes eggs. There are two basic types of ice cream. Custard ice cream, also known as French ice cream, is made with a base of a stirred egg custard (essentially a vanilla sauce). The techniques and precautions that are used in the production of a crème anglaise should be applied when producing this type of ice cream base. The use of pasteurized eggs is preferred to reduce the risk of spreading food-borne illness.

The second type of basic ice cream preparation does not use eggs. The base is made by simply heating cream with or without milk to incorporate sugar and other ingredients. An endless variety of ice cream can be produced with either method from these basic preparations by introducing different flavors and ingredients. (The same holds for the possibility of adjusting or substituting various milk products or sweeteners to produce an equally enjoyable dessert.)

Regardless of the type of base, it is good practice to age it under refrigeration (at approximately 40°F/4°C) for several hours before freezing. Aging allows the protein network to absorb more of the moisture present in the base, leaving less water available to form ice crystals, resulting in a smoother ice cream. Churn the chilled base only to "soft-serve" consistency and then extract from the machine, pack into containers, and place in a freezer for several hours to allow it to firm to a servable temperature and consistency.

How ingredients affect consistency and mouthfeel

All the ingredients add flavor to the ice cream, but each one also plays a part in determining consistency and mouthfeel. The eggs in custard ice cream make it richer and smoother than its eggless counterpart, both because of the fat and emulsifiers contributed by the egg yolks and because cooking the proteins present in the eggs binds or holds moisture, interfering with the formation of ice crystals, which results in smaller ice crystals, thus lending a smoother texture to the finished ice cream. (For more about emulsifiers and cooking proteins, see page 68).

The cream and eggs in ice cream allow for the incorporation of air during freezing. The air incorporated into ice cream, known as *overrun,* gives it a smoother mouthfeel and lighter body. Too much overrun, however, will diminish the flavor, make the ice cream too soft, and make it melt quickly. Overrun amounts, indicated in percentages, represent the amount of air contained in the ice cream. The legal limit for overrun imposed by the FDA is 100 percent, which would indicate the ice cream increasing in volume by half.

The solids present in milk and cream interfere with the formation of ice crystals, while their emulsifiers help to bind together the liquids and fats. Both of these actions affect mouthfeel, as they result in a finer, smoother texture.

Milk powder is often added to ice cream made without eggs. It helps to bind excess liquid in the mixture that would otherwise result in the formation of large ice crystals.

For best results, use a mixture of milk and cream to avoid having too much butterfat in the mix. The butterfat content of ice cream typically ranges from 10 to 14 percent. Butterfat is important, as it contributes both flavor and richness of mouthfeel.

However, too much fat will result in an undesirable grainy mouthfeel. For the same reason, use care in adding ingredients high in butterfat such as white chocolate, so as not to increase the fat content of the ice cream to an undesirable level.

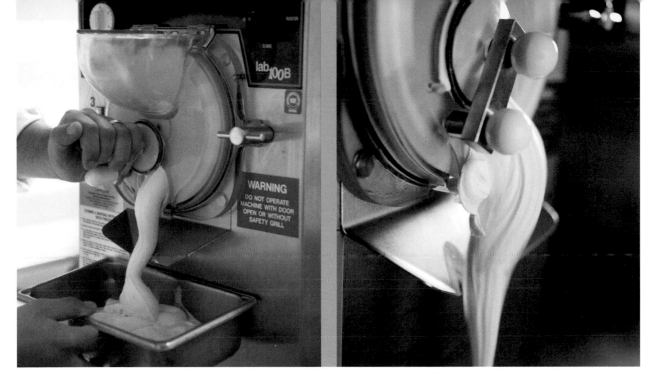

Testing churning ice cream for doneness   Extracting ice cream from the machine

Sugar both adds sweetness and lowers the freezing point of the base, keeping the ice cream from freezing too hard. Invert sugars such as corn syrup and glucose syrup improve texture and help prevent the formation of large ice crystals.

Adding flavorings

There are a number of methods for adding flavorings to ice cream. Flavorings such as vanilla bean, tea, coffee, and spices can be infused into the milk and cream as they are heating. Then the ice cream base is cooked as usual with the flavorings, which are strained out before freezing. Purées can be blended into the custard after it has cooled, or folded into still-soft, just-churned ice cream for a swirled effect. Melted chocolate can be added to the still-warm, just-cooked ice cream base, while nut pastes, such as peanut butter and praline paste, are added to the ice cream base after it is cooked. They may be added while the base is still warm or carefully blended into an aged, chilled base.

flavoring ice cream with extracts and compounds

Extracts or compounds such as praline paste and other concentrated, low-moisture flavorings can be added to an ice cream base without affecting the texture of the ice cream.

To use praline paste or other nut pastes (including peanut butter) or melted chocolate, make the ice cream base as directed. Add the desired flavoring and stir until evenly blended as soon as you remove the base from the heat, or add to a base that has been chilled and aged, blending carefully to ensure full incorporation.

adding fruits to ice cream

Fresh and puréed fruits are wonderful as garnishes or flavorings for ice creams and other frozen desserts. Depending on the fruit or product, they can be added whole or in chunks, folded in as a swirl, or used as a flavoring for the ice cream base. Whenever you use fresh fruit, taste it to see how sweet it is, then increase or decrease the amount of sweetener you are adding to the base as necessary.

To use fresh fruit as a garnish in ice cream, poach it in a sugar syrup to prevent it from freezing too hard. For soft fruits, bring the syrup to a boil, then remove from the heat, add the fruit, cover, and allow to stand until cool. Drain the fruit and chill. Fold the poached fruit into the soft ice cream just as it comes from the machine. For harder fruits,

use the same technique but leave the fruit in the syrup for approximately 15 minutes, making sure the temperature is maintained between 160° and 180°F/71° and 82°C.

To flavor an ice cream using a fruit purée such as raspberry, peach, mango, or banana, omit the milk when making the base. Age the ice cream as usual, then blend in the desired fruit purée in a quantity equal to the original amount of milk in the formula. Freeze as usual. For very strongly flavored fruits such as passion fruit, or fruit concentrates, replace only half of the milk in the formula with the fruit purée. When using a pulpy fruit purée to flavor an ice cream, homogenizing the mixture before freezing will create a better emulsion.

variegating ice creams

To make variegated (swirled) ice creams, fill a pastry bag fitted with a medium-size plain tip with a room-temperature garnish such as Hard Ganache (page 421), Marshmallows (page 814), nut paste, jam, preserves, or Soft Caramel Filling (page 455) and as the ice cream is extracted from the machine, stream in the garnish. Fold the ice cream mixture just enough to marbleize the ice cream with the ingredients. A good rule for the amount of an ingredient to use for variegation is approximately 20 percent of the total volume of the ice cream.

Ice cream is variegated as it is being extracted from the batch freezer.

Gelato

Opinions as to what makes a gelato unique will differ. If you ask an Italian pastry chef what *gelato* means, he will simply reply "ice cream," which is its literal translation. If you ask a pastry chef in the United States what it means, you will have many different opinions. Some will say that gelato should contain no heavy cream or egg yolks, some will say it should—and they would both be right. In Italy, they make gelato with milk alone, with milk and heavy cream, and with milk, heavy cream, and eggs. Despite the different opinions, there is one quality that makes it unique, and different from ice cream and custard-base ice cream, and that is its overrun (see "How Ingredients Affect Consistency and Mouthfeel," page 466). While most ice creams and custard-base ice creams have an overrun between 40 and 60 percent, the overrun for gelato is 20 percent, which makes it a denser, more compact product. If you incorporate any more air, it becomes ice cream or custard-base ice cream. The production of gelato is the same; it is the churning time that varies. With gelato, it is shorter, and therefore the finished product will have less air incorporated. The flavor the same but the texture is vastly different.

Sorbet and sherbet

Sorbet is a churned frozen dessert that is basically a mixture of sweetened fruit juice or purée and water. Unlike sherbet, sorbet never contains any dairy, but like sherbet, it may contain added emulsifiers to enhance softness and smoothness of flavor. Sorbet, in its simplest form, is a fairly concentrated sugar syrup with added flavoring or flavorings. These flavorings may range from a fresh fruit purée to a fruit juice such as lemon or even to a flavor infusion such as tea, sweet basil, mint, or thyme.

The sugar content of sorbet is approximately twice that of ice cream. If 10 percent of the sugar in a formula is added in the form of corn syrup, a smoother texture will result. Sorbets made with fruit juice as opposed to purée tend to separate. Juices lack the pulp contained in a purée, which helps to sustain the mixture of water, flavorings, and sugar. To help prevent separation when only fruit juice is used, add a commercial stabilizer or a measure of pasteurized egg whites. Similarly, a stabilizer should also be used when a formula calls for a high ratio of water.

A small amount of egg whites may be added to the sorbet base to give the final product a smoother texture; it is usually incorporated before the freezing process begins, or added toward the end of the process in the form of a frothy meringue. They add volume and make a creamier product with a lighter texture. They also act to help prevent the mixture from separating during long-term storage in the freezer. (For 64 fl oz/1.92 L sorbet base, add 1 oz/28 g pasteurized egg whites.) Purists, however, feel that the addition of egg white to a sorbet masks its clarity and freshness.

In a similar manner, chemical stabilizers such as xanthan gum extend suspension, promote air incorporation and even out air bubble distribution, and assure the cohesion of a finished product during storage.

1. Combine all ingredients and stir until evenly blended. Cover and chill thoroughly under refrigeration. Because sugar helps to control the freezing point of the mixture, it is important that the sugar content is in the proper percentage: If there is too much sugar, the mixture will not freeze; if there is too little sugar, the frozen mixture will be too hard.

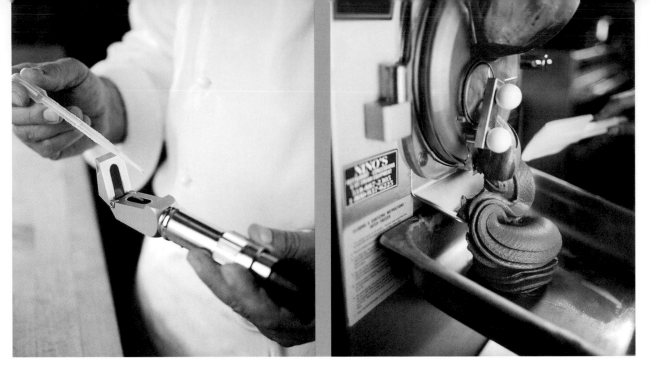

LEFT: Checking the sugar density of a sorbet with a refractometer

RIGHT: Compare the density of a sorbet as it comes out of the machine with that of ice cream (shown on page 467).

2. Process in an ice cream machine according to manufacturer's instructions. The constant churning that occurs during the freezing of a sorbet yields a smooth, creamy texture.

3. Pack into storage containers or molds and freeze for several hours, or overnight, before serving or using in plated desserts.

Sugar content

When making sorbets and sherbets, as well as granitas, it is essential that the sugar content (or density) of the syrup base be in the proper percentage. The density of a sugar solution is a measure of the amount of sugar dissolved in the liquid.

Baumé and Brix are the two most common scales used for measuring sugar density in the pastry shop. A saccharometer is used to measure Baumé (Be), which indicates the specific gravity of the solution. It registers the reading on a scale calibrated from 0° to 40° Be. A refractometer registers the percentage of sugar in a solution, expressed on the Brix scale. Most sorbets range in density from about 16° to 18° Be, or 30° Brix, depending on the ingredients and desired sweetness.

Sherbets, which are typically fruit flavored, contain more sugar but less dairy than ice cream. They may be made with milk (with or without cream), or with powdered, evaporated, or condensed milk. Emulsifiers such as pectin, gelatin, gums, egg whites, or meringue are often added for a smoother mouthfeel. Sherbets, like sorbets, are usually at approximately 30° Brix, with the dairy adding 1 to 2 percent butterfat, resulting in a richer mouthfeel.

When making sorbets or sherbets, remember that the sugar content of most fruits varies according to ripeness. Therefore, it may be necessary to adjust the consistency of the sorbet base by adding more liquid if it is too sweet or more sugar if it is too tart. Let taste be the most important factor.

Granita

Like sorbet, granita (also known as granité) is a light and refreshing frozen dessert based on sugar, water, and a flavored liquid such as a fruit juice or liqueur. However, the freezing process for granita, as well as its lower sugar content, make for a dessert with a very different texture. Unlike the creamy and smooth texture of sorbet, the texture of granita is similar to that of crushed ice. Also unlike sorbet, the freezing process of granita involves occasional stirring as opposed to constant agitation.

Granita can be made to taste sweet or savory. To make a savory granita, infuse the base with dried herbs such as thyme, sage, or rosemary. Granitas are often served as an intermezzo or as a component of a richer dessert.

1. Stir all the ingredients together until blended. It is important to make sure that the sugar content be in the proper percentage; if there is too much sugar, the base will not freeze (as sugar raises the freezing point of a solution), and if there is not enough sugar, the base will become too hard.

2. Pour into a prechilled hotel pan and place in the freezer. To freeze granita, use a conventional freezer and a container that allows for large surface area exposure.

3. Stir the mixture every 15 to 20 minutes with a fork until it resembles crushed ice. Stirring the mixture only occasionally encourages the formation of large ice crystals, whereas the relatively high sugar-to-liquid ratio and constant churning of sorbet yields a smooth, creamy texture.

    Granita may also be used to make shaved ice by freezing the mixture into a solid block, then shaving off portions using a metal spoon.

4. Cover tightly and freeze until needed.

Stirring a granita as it freezes

A finished granita

Molded frozen desserts

A wide array of molds and containers may be used to mold almost any type of frozen dessert into interesting shapes and forms. Something as simple as a bowl, cake ring, or charlotte mold or the most elaborate specialty pudding and bakeware molds can be used. You can use a single ice cream flavor in a mold lined with a layer of cake, or layer several different complementary flavors and colors in one mold. Add layers of cake or various garnish ingredients, such as chopped nuts or chocolate, or cake or cookie crumbs, to add both flavor and texture.

Regardless of the type of mold, the basic procedure for molding is the same.

1. Line molds with open bottoms, such as cake rings, with plastic wrap to prevent any leakage before the dessert is completely frozen. Lining the base and sides of this type of mold with a layer of cake is a common practice. If the sides of the mold are not lined with cake, the molded dessert is often iced before serving.

2. Whatever type of frozen product you are using, it must be soft enough to spread easily. If possible, use ice cream, frozen yogurt, sorbet, or sherbet directly from the ice cream machine, when it will be the perfect consistency. Working with soft ice cream or the like helps to ensure that no air pockets develop as the mold is filled. If the product you are using is frozen hard, let it stand at room temperature until it is soft and spreadable but not melting.

3. To fill a mold with one flavor of ice cream or other frozen dessert, fill the mold all at once, spreading the frozen dessert evenly. Periodically tap the mold gently on a counter to get rid of air pockets. Cover the filled mold tightly with plastic wrap and place it in the freezer until it is thoroughly frozen.

4. You can fold garnish ingredients, such as nuts or chopped chocolate, into the softened ice cream (or other frozen dessert) before layering it in the mold, or you can make layers of the garnishes, sprinkling them on top of each layer of ice cream after spreading it into the mold.

5. Molded frozen desserts must be frozen solid before they can be unmolded, so be sure to allow sufficient time for freezing.

6. To unmold the dessert, immerse the mold briefly in warm water and wipe dry before unmolding, or gently and quickly warm it over an open flame or using a blowtorch or blow-dryer. Invert the dessert onto the plate and gently lift the mold away, being careful not to touch the sides.

Still-frozen desserts

The air incorporated into the base of a frozen dessert gives it a light, smooth, spoonable texture. With still-frozen desserts, the air is incorporated before freezing rather than during, as it is for churned frozen desserts. Air is incorporated into these frozen desserts as is done for the preparation of a mousse. Aerated ingredients such as whipped cream, meringue, or beaten egg yolks are folded into a flavored base mixture just before it is deposited into containers and frozen.

There are three basic types of still-frozen desserts: frozen soufflés, parfaits, and bombes. Frozen soufflés (also known as *soufflés glacés*) contain whipped cream, meringue, and a flavoring such as a liqueur, juice, or chocolate. They are traditionally served in ramekins, as are hot soufflés. To mimic the look of a hot soufflé, the ramekins for frozen soufflés are prepared with a "collar," a piece of parchment paper or aluminum foil attached to the ramekin that extends an inch or two above its top. The soufflé mixture is then piped in and leveled off with the top of the collar. The parchment "collar" is removed before service, creating the look of a hot soufflé.

The air incorporated into the base of a frozen dessert gives it a light, smooth, spoonable texture. With still-frozen desserts, the air is incorporated before freezing rather than during, as it is for churned frozen desserts. Air is incorporated into these frozen desserts as is done for the preparation of a mousse. Aerated ingredients such as whipped cream, meringue, or beaten egg yolks are folded into a flavored base mixture just before it is deposited into containers and frozen.

Filling frozen soufflé molds

Unwrapping frozen soufflés after they've set

Parfaits are basically frozen mousse and may be made using almost any method by which a mousse is made. Classically these desserts are served in tall, narrow "parfait" glasses. The American version is layered with fruit and sauces. Bombes are always made using a pâte à bombe (egg yolks cooked over heat as they are beaten with sugar until they are light in color and texture). The pâte à bombe is then incorporated with meringue (with or without whipped cream) and a flavoring. The term *bombe,* however, has to do with the classic domed shape of this dessert.

Leveling parfait in a ring mold before freezing

Unmolding frozen bombes

Vanilla ice cream

MAKES 48 FL OZ/1.44 L

Milk	16 fl oz	480 mL
Heavy cream	16 fl oz	480 mL
Sugar	7 oz	198 g
Glucose syrup	1 oz	28 g
Salt	¼ tsp	1.25 g
Vanilla beans	1 each	1 each
Egg yolks	10 oz	284 g

1 Combine the milk, cream, 3½ oz/99 g of the sugar, the glucose syrup, and salt in a saucepan. Split the vanilla bean, scrape the seeds into the pan, add the pod, and bring the mixture just to a boil over medium heat. Immediately remove from the heat, cover the pan, and let steep for 5 minutes.

2 Remove the vanilla pod and return the mixture to a simmer.

3 Meanwhile, blend the egg yolks with the remaining 3½ oz/99 g sugar to make the liaison. Temper by gradually adding about one-third of the hot milk mixture, whisking constantly. Return the tempered egg mixture to the remaining hot milk in the saucepan and cook, stirring constantly, until the mixture thickens enough to coat the back of a spoon (180°F/82°C).

4 Strain the ice cream base into a metal container and cool in an ice water bath. Cool to below 40°F/4°C. Cover and refrigerate for a minimum of 12 hours, or overnight.

5 Process in an ice cream machine according to the manufacturer's instructions. Pack into storage containers or molds as desired and freeze for several hours before serving or using in plated desserts.

VARIATION **CINNAMON ICE CREAM** Replace the vanilla bean with ¼ tsp/1.25 g ground cinnamon in step 1.

Vanilla Ice Cream (page 475), Coffee
Ice Cream (page 478), and Chocolate
Ice Cream (opposite)

Chocolate ice cream

MAKES 48 FL OZ/1.44 L

Milk	16 fl oz	480 mL
Heavy cream	16 fl oz	480 mL
Sugar	7 oz	198 g
Glucose syrup	1 oz	28 g
Salt	¼ tsp	1.25 g
Vanilla beans, split and scraped	1 each	1 each
Egg yolks	10 oz	284 g
Bittersweet chocolate, melted	6 oz	170 g

1   Combine the milk, cream, 3½ oz/99 g of the sugar, the glucose syrup, salt, and vanilla pod and seeds in a saucepan and bring just to a boil over medium heat. Immediately remove from the heat, cover the pan, and let steep for 5 minutes.

2   Remove the vanilla pod and return the mixture to a simmer.

3   Blend the egg yolks with the remaining 3½ oz/99 g sugar to make the liaison. Temper by gradually adding about one-third of the hot milk mixture, whisking constantly. Return the tempered egg mixture to the remaining hot milk in the saucepan and cook, stirring constantly, until the mixture thickens enough to coat the back of a spoon (180°F/82°C).

4   Remove the pan from the heat and stir in the chocolate until smooth and fully combined. Strain into a metal container and cool in an ice water bath to below 40°F/4°C. Cover and refrigerate for a minimum of 12 hours, or overnight.

5   Process in an ice cream machine according to the manufacturer's instructions. Pack into storage containers and freeze for several hours before serving, molding, or using in plated desserts.

VARIATIONS   **MILK CHOCOLATE ICE CREAM** Reduce the sugar to 4 oz/113 g and replace the bittersweet chocolate with 8 oz/227 g milk chocolate.

WHITE CHOCOLATE ICE CREAM Reduce the sugar to 3 oz/85 g and replace the bittersweet chocolate with 8 oz/227 g white chocolate.

Coffee ice cream

MAKES 48 FL OZ/1.44 L

Milk	16 fl oz	480 mL
Heavy cream	16 fl oz	480 mL
Sugar	7 oz	198 g
Glucose syrup	1 oz	28 g
Coffee beans, coarsely ground	2 oz	57 g
Salt	¼ tsp	1.25 g
Egg yolks	10 oz	284 g

1   Combine the milk, cream, 3½ oz/99 g of the sugar, the glucose syrup, coffee beans, and salt in a saucepan and bring just to a boil over medium heat. Immediately remove from the heat, cover the pan, and let steep for 5 minutes.

2   Strain the mixture into a clean pan and return to a simmer.

3   Blend the egg yolks with the remaining 3½ oz/99 g sugar to make the liaison. Temper by gradually adding about one-third of the hot milk mixture, whisking constantly. Return the tempered egg mixture to the remaining hot milk in the saucepan and cook, stirring constantly, until the mixture thickens enough to coat the back of a spoon (180°F/82°C).

4   Strain the mixture into a metal container and cool in an ice water bath to below 40°F/4°C. Cover and refrigerate for a minimum of 12 hours, or overnight.

5   Process in an ice cream machine according to the manufacturer's instructions. Pack into storage containers and freeze for several hours before serving, molding, or using in plated desserts.

VARIATIONS **ALMOND ICE CREAM** Replace the coffee beans with 4 oz/113 g almond paste.

CARDAMOM ICE CREAM Replace the coffee beans with ½ oz/14 g chopped green cardamom pods.

GREEN TEA, EARL GREY, OR CHAI ICE CREAM Replace the coffee beans with ½ oz/14 g of green, Earl Grey, or spiced tea leaves.

PEANUT BUTTER ICE CREAM Replace the coffee beans with 4 oz/113 g peanut butter.

PISTACHIO ICE CREAM Replace the coffee beans with 4 oz/113 g pistachio paste.

PRALINE ICE CREAM Replace the coffee beans with 4 oz/113 g praline paste.

STAR ANISE ICE CREAM Replace the coffee beans with 1¼ oz/35 g toasted star anise. Do not strain the custard after cooking; leave the anise in the base during refrigeration, then strain before freezing.

TOASTED COCONUT ICE CREAM Replace the coffee beans with 6 oz/170 g lightly toasted unsweetened coconut.

Green Tea Ice
Cream

Armagnac vanilla ice cream

MAKES APPROXIMATELY 32 FL OZ/960 ML

Heavy cream	12½ fl oz	375 mL
Milk	16 fl oz	480 mL
Light corn syrup	2¾ oz	79 g
Vanilla extract	¼ tsp	1.25 mL
Nonfat milk powder	¾ oz	21 g
Sorbet stabilizer	¼ tsp	1.25 mL
Sugar	4⅓ oz	123 g
Glucose, powdered	½ oz	14 g
Salt	¼ tsp	1.25 g
Armagnac	1½ fl oz	45 mL

1   Combine the cream, milk, corn syrup, and vanilla in a sauce pot and heat to 180°F/82°C.

2   Meanwhile, combine the nonfat milk powder, sorbet stabilizer, sugar, glucose, and salt in a large bowl and mix together well. Pour the hot liquid over the dry ingredients. Mix well. Pour the mixture back into the sauce pot.

3   Return the pot to a boil, then maintain a simmer for at least 1 minute. Strain through a fine-mesh sieve into a metal container and cool in an ice water bath. When cool, stir in the Armagnac.

4   Refrigerate for at least 24 hours before churning.

5   Process in an ice cream machine according to the manufacturer's instructions. Pack into storage containers or molds and freeze for several hours before serving or using in plated desserts.

Raspberry ice cream

MAKES 48 FL OZ/1.44 L

Heavy cream	16 fl oz	480 mL
Sugar	7 oz	198 g
Glucose syrup	1 oz	28 g
Salt	¼ tsp	1.25 g
Egg yolks	10 oz	284 g
Raspberry purée	1 lb	454 g

1   Combine the cream, 3½ oz/99 g of the sugar, the glucose syrup, and salt in a saucepan and bring just to a simmer over medium heat.

2   Blend the egg yolks with the remaining 3½ oz/99 g sugar to make the liaison. Temper by gradually adding about one-third of the hot cream mixture, whisking constantly. Return the tempered egg mixture to the remaining hot milk in the saucepan and cook, stirring constantly, until the mixture thickens enough to coat the back of a spoon (180°F/82°C).

3   Strain the mixture into a metal container and cool in an ice water bath to below 40°F/4°C. Cover and refrigerate for a minimum of 12 hours, or overnight. Blend in the raspberry purée.

4   Process in an ice cream machine according to the manufacturer's instructions. Pack into storage containers or molds and freeze for several hours before serving or using in plated desserts.

VARIATIONS   **BANANA ICE CREAM** Replace the raspberry purée with an equal amount of banana purée.

MANGO ICE CREAM Replace the raspberry purée with an equal amount of mango purée.

PASSION FRUIT ICE CREAM Add 8 fl oz/240 mL of milk to the formula in step 1 with the cream. Replace the raspberry purée with 8 fl oz/240 mL of passion fruit concentrate.

PEACH ICE CREAM Replace the raspberry purée with an equal amount of peach purée.

Strawberry ice cream

MAKES 3 LB 7 OZ/1.56 KG›

Milk	6 fl oz	180 mL
Heavy cream	6 fl oz	180 mL
Trimoline	2 oz	57 g
Egg yolks	8 oz	227 g
Sugar	3 oz	85 g
Strawberry purée	1 lb 8 oz	680 g

1 Combine the milk, cream, and trimoline in a saucepan and bring just to a simmer over medium heat.

2 Blend the egg yolks with the sugar to make the liaison. Temper by gradually adding about one-third of the hot cream mixture, whisking constantly. Return the tempered egg mixture to the remaining hot milk in the saucepan and cook, stirring constantly, until the mixture thickens enough to coat the back of a spoon (180°F/82°C). Blend in the fruit purée and mix until smooth.

3 Strain the mixture into a metal container and cool in an ice water bath to below 40°F/4°C. Cover and refrigerate for a minimum of 12 hours, or overnight.

4 Process in an ice cream machine according to the manufacturer's instructions. Pack into storage containers or molds and freeze for several hours before serving or using in plated desserts.

Lemon verbena ice cream

MAKES 24 FL OZ/720 ML

Heavy cream	12.5 oz	354 g
Milk	16 oz	454 g
Light corn syrup	2.77 oz	79 g
Nonfat milk powder	0.75 oz	21 g
Sorbet stabilizer	¼ tsp	1.25 mL
Sugar	4¼ oz	120 g
Glucose, powdered	½ oz	14 g
Salt	¼ tsp	1.25 g
Lemon verbena, dried	1 tbsp	6 g

1 Combine the cream, milk, and corn syrup in a sauce pot and heat to 180°F/82°C.

2 Combine the nonfat milk powder, sorbet stabilizer, sugar, glucose, and salt in a medium stainless-steel bowl.

3 Pour the boiling liquids over the dry ingredients and mix to combine.

4 Return the liquid to the sauce pot and bring back to a boil.

5 Remove from the heat, add the verbena, and stir until homogenous. Cool to room temperature.

6 Strain through a fine-mesh sieve into a storage container. Cover and refrigerate for a minimum of 12 hours, or overnight.

7 Process in an ice cream machine according to the manufacturer's instructions. Pack into storage containers or molds as desired and freeze for several hours before serving or using in plated desserts.

Rum raisin ice cream

MAKES 3 LB 7 OZ/1.56 KG

Raisins	5 oz	142 g
Dark rum	4 fl oz	240 mL
Simple syrup (page 900)	4 fl oz	120 mL
Vanilla ice cream (page 475)	1 recipe	1 recipe

1 Combine the raisins, rum, and simple syrup. Let the raisins marinate for 24 hours at room temperature.

2 The same day you start the raisins, follow the vanilla ice cream recipe but substitute 1 tsp vanilla extract for the vanilla bean. Cover and refrigerate the base for a minimum of 12 hours, or overnight.

3 Process the ice cream in an ice cream machine according to the manufacturer's instructions.

4 Drain the raisins, pat dry, and mix with the ice cream after churning.

5 Pack into storage containers or molds as desired and freeze for several hours before serving or using in plated desserts.

Chocolate swirl ice cream

MAKES 48 FL OZ/1.44 L

Milk	16 fl oz	480 mL
Heavy cream	16 fl oz	480 mL
Sugar	7 oz	198 g
Glucose syrup	1 oz	28 g
Salt	¼ tsp	1.25 g
Vanilla beans, split and scraped	1 each	1 each
Egg yolks	10 oz	284 g
Hard ganache (page 421)	1 lb	454 g

1   Combine the milk, cream, 3½ oz/99 g of the sugar, the glucose syrup, salt, and vanilla pod and seeds in a saucepan and bring just to a boil over medium heat. Immediately remove from the heat, cover the pan, and let steep for 5 minutes.

2   Remove the vanilla pod and return the mixture to a simmer.

3   Blend the egg yolks with the remaining 3½ oz/99 g sugar to make the liaison. Temper by gradually adding about one-third of the hot milk mixture, whisking constantly. Return the tempered egg mixture to the remaining hot milk in the saucepan and cook, stirring constantly, until the mixture thickens enough to coat the back of a spoon (180°F/82°C).

4   Strain the mixture into a metal container and cool in an ice water bath to below 40°F/4°C. Cover and refrigerate for a minimum of 12 hours, or overnight.

5   Process in an ice cream machine according to the manufacturer's instructions.

6   Transfer to a bowl and fold in the ganache, leaving visible streaks for a marbleized effect.

7   Pack into storage containers and freeze for several hours before serving, molding, or using in plated desserts.

VARIATIONS   **CARAMEL SWIRL ICE CREAM** Substitute Soft Caramel Filling (page 455) for the ganache.

FRUIT SWIRL ICE CREAM Substitute highly reduced fruit purée for the ganache.

Soft caramel filling II

MAKES 1 LB 12 OZ/794 G

Sugar	1 lb	454 g
Lemon juice	½ tsp	2.50 mL
Heavy cream, warm	8 fl oz	240 mL
Butter	4 oz	113 g

1   Combine the sugar and lemon juice in a heavy-bottomed saucepan and bring to a boil over high heat, stirring constantly to dissolve the sugar. Cook without stirring to a rich golden brown.

2   Add the warm cream slowly. Whisk in the butter.

3   Remove from the heat, transfer to a container, and cool to room temperature. Cover and store at room temperature.

Buttermilk ice cream

MAKES 48 FL OZ/1.44 L

Milk	24 fl oz	720 mL
Heavy cream	8 fl oz	240 mL
Sugar	8 oz	227 g
Salt	¼ tsp	1.25 g
Egg yolks	10 oz	284 g
Vanilla extract	1 tbsp	15 mL
Buttermilk	8 fl oz	240 mL

1   Combine the milk, cream, 4 oz/113 g of the sugar, and the salt in a saucepan and bring just to a boil over medium heat.

2   Blend the egg yolks with the remaining 4 oz/113 g sugar to make the liaison. Temper by gradually adding about one-third of the hot milk mixture, whipping constantly. Return the tempered egg mixture to the remaining hot milk in the saucepan and cook, stirring constantly, until the mixture thickens enough to coat the back of a spoon (180°F/82°C).

3   Strain the mixture into a metal container and cool in an ice water bath to below 40°F/4°C. Blend in the vanilla extract and buttermilk. Cover and refrigerate for a minimum of 12 hours, or overnight.

4   Process in an ice cream machine according to the manufacturer's instructions. Pack into storage containers and freeze for several hours before serving, molding, or using in plated desserts.

Walnut praline ice cream

MAKES 48 FL OZ/1.44 L

ICE CREAM BASE		
Milk	16 fl oz	480 mL
Heavy cream	16 fl oz	480 mL
Sugar	7 oz	198 g
Glucose syrup	1 oz	28 g
Salt	¼ tsp	1.25 g
Walnut halves	14 oz	397 g
Vanilla beans, split and scraped	1 each	1 each
Egg yolks	10 oz	284 g
PRALINE		
Walnuts	14 oz	397 g
Granulated sugar	7 oz	198 g
Light brown sugar	2 oz	57 g
Ground cinnamon	1 tsp	2 g

1   To make the ice cream base, combine the milk, cream, 3½ oz/99 g of the sugar, the glucose syrup, salt, and walnuts in a saucepan. Add the vanilla pod and seeds, and bring the mixture just to a boil over medium heat. Immediately remove from the heat, cover the pan, and let steep for 5 minutes.

2   Remove the vanilla pod and return the mixture to a simmer.

3   Blend the egg yolks with the remaining 3½ oz/99 g sugar to make the liaison. Temper by gradually adding about one-third of the hot milk mixture, whisking constantly. Return the tempered egg mixture to the remaining hot milk in the saucepan and cook, stirring constantly, until the mixture thickens enough to coat the back of a spoon (180°F/82°C).

4   Strain the mixture into a metal container. Rinse and reserve the walnuts. Cool in an ice water bath to below 40°F/4°C. Cover and refrigerate for a minimum of 12 hours, or overnight.

5   To make the praline, lightly toast the walnuts in a 350°F/177°C oven, and chop them finely.

6   Add a small amount of the granulated sugar to a medium-hot pan set over medium heat and allow it to melt, then add the remaining sugar in small increments, allowing each addition to fully melt before adding the next. Continue this process until all the granulated sugar has been added to the pan, and cook to the desired color. Shock the pan in an ice water bath.

7   Sprinkle in the brown sugar and cinnamon, add the toasted chopped walnuts, and stir until mixed.

8 Pour the praline onto a tray that has been coated with nonstick baking spray. Allow the mixture to cool completely, then break it into pea-size pieces.

9 Process the ice cream base in an ice cream machine according to the manufacturer's instructions.

10 Fold in the walnut praline.

11 Pack into storage containers or molds as desired and freeze for several hours before serving or using in plated desserts.

Lemon frozen yogurt

MAKES 45 FL OZ/1.35 L

Plain yogurt (whole milk or low-fat)	32 fl oz	960 mL
Lemon juice	6 fl oz	180 mL
Sugar	6 oz	170 g
Glucose syrup	1½ oz	43 g

1   Combine all the ingredients, stirring until evenly blended.

2   Process in an ice cream machine according to the manufacturer's instructions. Pack into storage containers and freeze for several hours before serving, molding, or using in plated desserts.

Chocolate frozen yogurt

MAKES 45 FL OZ/1.35 L

Plain yogurt (whole milk or low-fat)	32 fl oz	960 mL
Sugar	4 oz	113 g
Glucose syrup	1 oz	28 g
Dark chocolate, melted	8 oz	227 g

1   Blend the yogurt, sugar, and glucose syrup, stirring until evenly blended. Temper the melted chocolate by gradually stirring in about one-third of the yogurt mixture. Then blend the chocolate and remaining yogurt mixture together. Cover and refrigerate for a minimum of 12 hours, or overnight.

2   Process in an ice cream machine according to the manufacturer's instructions. Pack into storage containers and freeze for several hours before serving, molding, or using in plated desserts.

Sorbet syrup (65° Brix)

MAKES 5 LB 8 OZ/2.49 KG

Sugar	3 lb	1.36 kg
Water	32 fl oz	960 mL
Glucose syrup	8 oz	227 g

1   Combine all the ingredients and bring to a boil, stirring occasionally.

2   Cool completely. Cover and store under refrigeration.

Strawberry frozen yogurt

MAKES 48 FL OZ/1.44 L

Plain yogurt (whole milk or low-fat)	32 fl oz	960 mL
Strawberry purée	12 oz	340 g
Sugar	8 oz	227 g
Glucose syrup	2 oz	57 g

1   Combine all the ingredients, stirring until evenly blended.

2   Process in an ice cream machine according to the manufacturer's instructions. Pack into storage containers and freeze for several hours before serving, molding, or using in plated desserts.

VARIATION   **RASPBERRY FROZEN YOGURT** Replace the strawberry purée with an equal amount of raspberry purée.

Lemon sorbet

MAKES 48 FL OZ/1.44 L

Sorbet syrup (opposite)	1 lb 4 oz	567 g
Lemon juice	15 fl oz	450 mL
Water	13 fl oz	390 mL

1   Combine all the ingredients and stir until evenly blended. Cover and chill thoroughly under refrigeration.

2   Process in an ice cream machine according to the manufacturer's instructions. Pack into storage containers and freeze for several hours before serving, molding, or using in plated desserts.

VARIATIONS   **KEY LIME SORBET** Replace the lemon juice with an equal amount of Key lime juice.

LIME SORBET Replace the lemon juice with an equal amount of lime juice.

Orange sorbet

MAKES 48 FL OZ/1.44 L

Sorbet syrup (page 488)	14 oz	397 g
Orange juice	15 fl oz	450 mL
Water	6 fl oz	180 mL

1   Combine all the ingredients and stir until evenly blended. Cover and chill thoroughly under refrigeration.

2   Process in an ice cream machine according to the manufacturer's instructions. Pack into storage containers and freeze for several hours before serving, molding, or using in plated desserts.

VARIATION   **BLOOD ORANGE SORBET** Replace the orange juice with an equal amount of blood orange juice.

Grapefruit sorbet

MAKES 48 FL OZ/1.44 L

Sorbet syrup (page 488)	12 oz	340 g
Grapefruit juice	15 fl oz	450 mL
Water	6 fl oz	180 mL

1   Combine all the ingredients and stir until evenly blended. Cover and chill thoroughly under refrigeration.

2   Process in an ice cream machine according to the manufacturer's instructions. Pack into storage containers or molds and freeze for several hours before serving or using in plated desserts.

Peach sorbet

MAKES 48 FL OZ/1.44 L

Sorbet syrup (page 488)	10 oz	284 g
Peach purée	15 oz	425 g
Water	6 fl oz	180 mL
Lemon juice	1 tbsp	15 mL

1   Combine all the ingredients and stir until evenly blended. Cover and chill thoroughly under refrigeration.

2   Process in an ice cream machine according to the manufacturer's instructions. Pack into storage containers or molds and freeze for several hours before serving or using in plated desserts.

VARIATIONS   **APRICOT SORBET** Replace the peach purée with an equal amount of apricot purée.

GUAVA SORBET Replace the peach purée with an equal amount of guava purée.

KIWI SORBET Replace the peach purée with an equal amount of kiwi purée.

MANGO SORBET Replace the peach purée with an equal amount of mango purée.

PEAR SORBET Replace the peach purée with an equal amount of pear purée.

PRICKLY PEAR SORBET Replace the peach purée with an equal amount of prickly pear purée.

RASPBERRY SORBET Replace the peach purée with an equal amount of raspberry purée.

Raspberry Sorbet

Granny Smith apple sorbet

MAKES 48 FL OZ/1.44 L

Sorbet syrup (page 488)	10 oz	284 g
Granny Smith apple purée	15 oz	425 g
Water	8 fl oz	240 mL
Lemon juice	1 tbsp	15 mL

1   Combine all the ingredients and stir until evenly blended. Cover and chill thoroughly under refrigeration.

2   Process in an ice cream machine according to the manufacturer's instructions. Pack into storage containers or molds and freeze for several hours before serving or using in plated desserts.

Granny Smith
Apple Sorbet

Banana sorbet

MAKES 48 FL OZ/1.44 L

Sorbet syrup (page 488)	10 oz	284 g
Banana purée	15 oz	425 g
Water	10½ fl oz	315 mL

1   Combine all the ingredients and stir until evenly blended. Cover and chill thoroughly under refrigeration.

2   Process in an ice cream machine according to the manufacturer's instructions. Pack into storage containers or molds and freeze for several hours before serving or using in plated desserts.

Black currant sorbet

MAKES 48 FL OZ/1.44 L

Sorbet syrup (page 488)	10 oz	284 g
Black currant purée	15 oz	425 g
Crème de cassis	3 fl oz	90 mL
Water	10 fl oz	300 mL

1   Combine all the ingredients and stir until evenly blended. Cover and chill thoroughly under refrigeration.

2   Process in an ice cream machine according to the manufacturer's instructions. Pack into storage containers or molds and freeze for several hours before serving or using in plated desserts.

Chocolate sorbet

MAKES 32 FL OZ/960 ML

Water	32 fl oz	960 mL
Sugar	4 oz	113 g
Cocoa powder	4 oz	113 g
Bittersweet chocolate, melted	9 oz	255 g

1   Combine the water, sugar, and cocoa powder in a saucepan and bring to a boil over medium heat. Remove the pan from the heat. Blend the mixture thoroughly into the melted chocolate.

2   Strain and refrigerate until chilled.

3   Process in an ice cream machine according to the manufacturer's instructions. Pack into storage containers and freeze for several hours before serving or using in plated desserts.

Coconut sorbet

MAKES 32 FL OZ/960 ML

Sorbet syrup (page 488)	8 oz	227 g
Coconut purée	1 lb 5½ oz	610 g
Water	2 fl oz	60 mL
Lime juice	1 fl oz	30 mL

1   Combine all the ingredients and stir until evenly blended. Cover and chill thoroughly under refrigeration.

2   Process in an ice cream machine according to the manufacturer's instructions. Pack into storage containers or molds and freeze for several hours before serving or using in plated desserts.

NOTE   Due to the high fat content of the coconut purée, the sorbet will have a smoother finished mouthfeel if it is blended in step 1 using a food processor or stick blender to fully emulsify.

Sangria sorbet

MAKES 32 FL OZ/960 ML

POACHED FRUIT		
Apples	1 each	1 each
Pears	1 each	1 each
Water	5 fl oz	150 mL
Sugar	2½ oz	71 g
Red wine	5 fl oz	150 mL
Orange juice	3¼ fl oz	98 mL
Cinnamon stick	1 each	1 each
Vanilla beans, split and scraped	1 each	1 each
Orange rind	1 each	1 each
Grapefruit juice	1 grapefruit	1 grapefruit
Grapefruit rind	1 each	1 each
SORBET		
Poaching liquid (above)	10 fl oz	300 mL
Sugar	1 oz	28 g
Grand Marnier	¾ fl oz	23 mL
Red wine	3¼ fl oz	98 mL
Apple cider	1 fl oz	15 mL

1   To make the poached fruit, peel and dice the apple and pear into medium dice ½ by ½ in/ 1 by 1 cm.

2   Combine the apple and pear with the remaining poaching ingredients in a medium sauce pot. Bring to a simmer and poach the apple and pear until very tender, about 15 minutes. Strain. Discard the cinnamon stick, vanilla bean pod, and rinds. Let the fruit cool; reserve the liquid separately.

3   Place the apple and pear in a food processor with 10 fl oz/300 mL of the poaching liquid and purée. Strain through a fine mesh-sieve using a ladle (1 fl oz/30 mL) to push the pulp through the mesh.

4   To make the sorbet, combine 10 fl oz/300 mL of the strained liquid, the sugar, Grand Marnier, red wine, and apple cider and stir until evenly blended. Cover and chill thoroughly under refrigeration.

5   Process in an ice cream machine according to the manufacturer's instructions. Pack into storage containers and freeze for several hours before serving, molding, or using in plated desserts.

Lychee sorbet

Lychee purée	16 oz	454 g
Sorbet syrup (page 488)	5½ oz	156 g
Lemon juice	2 tsp	10 mL
Sorbet stabilizer	¼ tsp	1.25 mL
Sugar	1 tsp	5 g

1   Combine the lychee purée, sorbet syrup, and lemon juice in a medium sauce pot and stir until evenly blended. Combine the stabilizer and sugar. Cook over medium-high heat to 104°F/40°C and add the stabilizer-sugar mixture. Continue to heat to 120°F/49°C. Bring to a boil and boil for 1 minute.

2   Transfer to a nonreactive metal container and cool in an ice water bath. Cover and refrigerate for a minimum of 12 hours, or overnight.

3   Process in an ice cream machine according to the manufacturer's instructions. Pack into storage containers and freeze for several hours before serving, molding, or using in plated desserts.

NOTE   For the Pear and Thai Jewels plated dessert (page 759), immediately after extraction place about 20 fl oz/600 mL of the sorbet into a pastry bag with a 1-in/3-cm opening. Pipe 12 small mounds of sorbet directly onto a frozen sheet pan. The mounds should be only as big as the space inside the cavity of the pear. Freeze until service.

Buttermilk sherbet

Buttermilk	21 fl oz	630 mL
Sugar	3½ oz	99 g
Honey	1¾ oz	50 g
Plain yogurt (whole milk or low-fat)	5 fl oz	150 mL
Vanilla beans, split and scraped	½ each	½ each

1   Combine all the ingredients in a saucepan. Heat over low heat, stirring to dissolve the sugar.

2   Transfer to a metal container and cool in an ice water bath. Cover and refrigerate until chilled.

3   Strain through a fine-mesh sieve.

4   Process in an ice cream machine according to the manufacturer's instructions. Pack into storage containers and freeze for several hours before serving, molding, or using in plated desserts.

Chocolate sherbet

MAKES 32 FL OZ/960 ML

Water	14 fl oz	420 mL
Milk	4 fl oz	120 mL
Sugar	5¼ oz	149 g
Glucose syrup	1½ oz	43 g
Cocoa powder	1 oz	28 g
Chocolate-flavored liqueur	4 fl oz	120 mL

1   Combine the water, milk, sugar, glucose syrup, and cocoa powder in a saucepan and bring to a boil over medium heat, stirring to dissolve the sugar. Boil for 3 minutes.

2   Remove from the heat and stir in the chocolate liqueur.

3   Strain through a fine-mesh sieve into a metal container and cool in an ice water bath. Cover and refrigerate for 6 hours or until fully chilled.

4   Process in an ice cream machine according to the manufacturer's instructions. Pack into storage containers and freeze for several hours before serving, molding, or using in plated desserts.

Vanilla bean sherbet

MAKES 24 FL OZ/720 ML

Milk	15 fl oz	450 mL
Heavy cream	6 fl oz	180 mL
Sugar	4½ oz	128 g
Water	3 fl oz	90 mL
Light corn syrup	2¼ oz	64 g
Vanilla extract	¼ tsp	1.25 mL
Vanilla beans, split and scraped	1 each	1 each

1   Combine all the ingredients in a saucepan. Bring to a boil, stirring to dissolve the sugar.

2   Strain through a fine-mesh sieve, transfer to a metal container, and cool in an ice water bath. Cover and refrigerate for a minimum of 12 hours, or overnight.

3   Process in an ice cream machine according to the manufacturer's instructions. Pack into storage containers and freeze for several hours before serving, molding, or using in plated desserts.

Mango granita

MAKES 32 FL OZ/960 ML

Water	22 fl oz	660 mL
Mango purée	8 oz	227 g
Sugar	4 oz	113 g
Dark rum	1½ fl oz	45 mL
Lemon juice	1½ fl oz	45 mL

1   Stir together all of the ingredients until blended and the sugar has dissolved.

2   Pour into a prechilled hotel pan and place in the freezer. Stir with a whisk every 15 to 20 minutes until it resembles crushed ice.

3   Cover tightly and freeze until needed.

Raspberry granita

MAKES 48 FL OZ/1.44 L

Raspberry purée	1 lb 8 oz	680 g
Water	24 fl oz	720 mL
Sugar	8 oz	227 g
Lemon juice	1 tbsp	15 mL

1   Stir together all of the ingredients until blended and the sugar has dissolved.

2   Pour into a prechilled hotel pan and place in the freezer. Stir with a whisk every 15 to 20 minutes until it resembles crushed ice.

3   Cover tightly and freeze until needed.

Fresh ginger granita

MAKES 40 FL OZ/1.20 L

Ginger, peeled	2 oz	57 g
Water	32 fl oz	960 mL
Sugar	4 oz	113 g
Lemon juice	2 tbsp	30 mL

1   Purée the ginger with 8 fl oz/240 mL of the water.

2   Combine the ginger purée, sugar, and the remaining 24 fl oz/720 mL water in a saucepan and cook over medium heat, stirring to melt the sugar, until it reaches 180°F/82°C.

3   Strain through a fine-mesh sieve and add the lemon juice.

4   Pour into a prechilled hotel pan and place in the freezer. Stir with a whisk every 15 to 20 minutes until it resembles crushed ice.

5   Cover tightly and freeze until needed.

Fresh Ginger Granita

Sour cherry granita

MAKES 28 FL OZ/840 ML

White wine	4 fl oz	120 mL
Honey	2 oz	57 g
Sugar	2 oz	57 g
Fresh sour cherries, pitted and puréed	1 lb	454 g

1   Stir together all of the ingredients until blended and the sugar has dissolved.

2   Pour into a prechilled hotel pan and place in the freezer. Stir with a whisk every 15 to 20 minutes until it resembles crushed ice.

3   Cover tightly and freeze until needed.

Green tea granita

MAKES 32 FL OZ/960 ML

Sugar	6 oz	170 g
Water	28 fl oz	840 mL
Green tea bags	4 each	4 each
Lemon juice	2 tbsp	30 mL

1   Combine the sugar and water and bring to a boil, stirring to dissolve the sugar. Add the tea bags, remove from the heat, and steep for 20 minutes.

2   Remove the tea bags and strain through a fine-mesh sieve if necessary. Add the lemon juice as needed.

3   Pour into a prechilled hotel pan and place in the freezer. Stir with a whisk every 15 to 20 minutes until it resembles crushed ice.

4   Cover tightly and freeze until needed.

Red wine and citrus granita

MAKES 48 FL OZ/1.44 L

Water	24 fl oz	720 mL
Red wine	14 fl oz	420 mL
Sugar	10 oz	284 g
Orange juice	6 fl oz	180 mL
Lemon juice	6 fl oz	180 mL
Vanilla beans, split and scraped	1 each	1 each

1 Combine all the ingredients in a saucepan. Bring to a boil. Reduce the heat and simmer for 4 to 5 minutes to blend the flavors.

2 Pour the mixture into a metal container and refrigerate until fully chilled, approximately 6 hours.

3 Strain into a prechilled hotel pan and place in the freezer. Stir with a whisk every 20 to 30 minutes until it resembles crushed ice.

4 Cover tightly and freeze until needed.

Red Wine and
Citrus Granita

501

Frozen chocolate bombe

MAKES 20 INDIVIDUAL DOMES (6 FL OZ/180 ML EACH)

Heavy cream	24 fl oz	720 mL
Bittersweet chocolate, finely chopped	9 oz	255 g
Egg yolks	9 oz	255 g
Sugar	6 oz	170 g
Vegetable oil	1 tbsp	15 mL
Vanilla sponge (page 268), 5 mm thick and 6 cm in diameter	20 disks	20 disks

1 Whip the cream to soft peaks, cover, and refrigerate.

2 Place the chocolate in a stainless-steel bowl over barely simmering water and melt to 140°F/60°C, stirring until smooth. Keep warm.

3 Make a pâte à bombe with the egg yolks and sugar.

4 Gently stir the oil into the hot chocolate. Fold the chocolate mixture into the pâte à bombe with a whisk until smooth.

5 Add the reserved whipped cream to the chocolate mixture and fold in rapidly but thoroughly with a whisk.

6 Fill the molds almost to the rim. Top each with a disk of vanilla sponge. Cover and freeze immediately.

VARIATIONS **FROZEN FRUIT BOMBE** Substitute 1 lb/454 g fruit purée for the chocolate.

FROZEN LEMON BOMBE Substitute 8 fl oz/240 mL lemon juice for the chocolate.

FROZEN MAPLE BOMBE Replace the sugar and water with 1 lb 9 oz/709 g maple syrup. Omit the chocolate.

FROZEN ORANGE, HAZELNUT, OR ALMOND LIQUEUR BOMBE Replace the chocolate with 16 fl oz/480 mL of the chosen liqueur, prepared as follows: Heat the liqueur and ignite it. When the flames die down, cool completely and add another 2 fl oz/60 mL of the same liqueur.

FROZEN PISTACHIO, ALMOND, OR PEANUT BUTTER BOMBE Substitute 8 oz/227 g pistachio paste, praline paste, or peanut butter for the chocolate.

Orange liqueur soufflé glacé

MAKES 12 SERVINGS (4½ FL OZ/135 ML EACH)

Eggs	8 oz	227 g
Egg yolks	6 oz	170 g
Sugar	4½ oz	128 g
Orange liqueur	4 fl oz	120 mL
Gelatin, granulated	¼ oz	7 g
Water	1½ fl oz	45 mL
Heavy cream, whipped to soft peaks	16 fl oz	480 mL

1   Cut 12 strips (2 by 11 in/5 by 28 cm) of parchment paper or aluminum foil. Wrap each one around a ramekin (4½ fl oz/135 mL) and fasten with tape. Place the ramekins on a sheet pan and place in the freezer until thoroughly chilled.

2   Combine the eggs, egg yolks, sugar, and orange liqueur in a mixer bowl and whisk constantly over simmering water until the mixture reaches 165°F/74°C.

3   Transfer the bowl to the mixer and whip the eggs on high speed with the whip attachment until three times their original volume and no longer increasing in volume.

4   Meanwhile, bloom the gelatin in the water and melt.

5   Fold the gelatin into the egg mixture. Fold in the whipped cream.

6   Pour the mixture into the prepared molds, level, and freeze.

Chocolate parfait

MAKES 4 LB/1.81 KG

Egg yolks	9 oz	255 g
Water	4⅓ fl oz	130 mL
Sugar	4½ oz	125 g
Bittersweet couverture chocolate, 70%	14 oz	397 g
Heavy cream, whipped to soft peaks	34 fl oz	1.02 L

1   Place the egg yolks in the mixer and beat on high speed with the whip attachment until light and fluffy, about 5 minutes.

2   Combine the water and sugar in a saucepan and bring to a boil over medium-high heat, stirring to dissolve the sugar. Continue to cook without stirring until the mixture reaches 260°F/127°C; brush down the sides of the saucepan occasionally with a dampened pastry brush.

3   Melt the chocolate to 135°F/57°C and set aside.

4   With the mixer on medium speed, carefully pour the cooked sugar syrup into the egg yolks in a fine stream, then beat until cooled to room temperature.

5   Gently fold the melted chocolate into the egg yolk mixture. Fold in the whipped cream.

6   Fill the prepared molds to the top and smooth the tops. Freeze until set.

Chocolate hazelnut parfait

MAKES 10 SERVINGS (4 FL OZ/120 ML EACH)

1-2-3 cookie dough (page 223)	1 lb	454 g
Gelatin, granulated	1 tsp	5 g
Water	2 fl oz	60 mL
Sugar	4½ oz	128 g
Eggs	1½ oz	43 g
Egg yolks	3¼ oz	92 g
Dark chocolate, melted	1¾ oz	50 g
Hazelnut paste	3¼ oz	92 g
Brandy	1 tbsp	15 mL
Vanilla extract	2 drops	2 drops
Nougatine, finely ground	¾ oz	21 g
Heavy cream, whipped to medium peaks	12 fl oz	360 mL
Brandied cherries	20 each	20 each

1   Roll the cookie dough to a thickness of ⅛ in/3 mm. Cut out 10 rounds using a 3-in/8-cm cutter. Transfer the cookies to a parchment-lined sheet pan. Bake at 350°F/177°C for 10 minutes or until golden brown. Cool completely on racks.

2   Place the 3-in/8-cm dome-shaped silicone-coated flexible fiberglass molds in the freezer until thoroughly chilled.

3   Bloom the gelatin in 1 fl oz/30 mL of the water and melt. Cool to 100°F/38°C. Reserve.

4   Combine the sugar and the remaining 1 fl oz/30 mL water in a small heavy-bottomed saucepan and cook over medium heat, stirring to dissolve the sugar. Continue to cook without stirring until the mixture reaches 248°F/120°C.

5   Meanwhile, beat the eggs and egg yolks in the mixer on high speed with the whip attachment until light in texture and color, about 5 minutes.

6   With the mixer on medium speed, carefully pour the cooked sugar syrup into the egg yolks in a fine stream, then beat until cooled to room temperature.

7   Blend the reserved gelatin into the egg yolk mixture. Blend in the melted chocolate, the hazelnut paste, brandy, vanilla extract, and nougatine. Fold in the whipped cream.

8   Using a pastry bag fitted with a #8 plain tip, pipe 3 oz/85 g of the parfait into each of the molds, filling them three-quarters full.

9   Place two cherries in the center of each parfait. Place a cookie on top of each parfait; the cookie should be flush with the top of the mold.

10 Cover the parfaits and freeze overnight.

Praline parfait

MAKES 15 SERVINGS (6 FL OZ/180 ML EACH)

Egg yolks	15 oz	425 g
Sugar	12 oz	340 g
Glucose syrup	1½ oz	43 g
Water	6 fl oz	180 mL
Praline paste	8 oz	227 g
Heavy cream, whipped until thickened	32 fl oz	960 mL

1   Place the egg yolks in the mixer and beat on high speed with the whip attachment until light and fluffy, about 5 minutes.

2   Combine the sugar, glucose syrup, and water in a saucepan and bring to a boil over medium-high heat, stirring to dissolve the sugar. Continue to cook without stirring until the mixture reaches 260°F/127°C; brush down the sides of the saucepan occasionally with a dampened pastry brush.

3   With the mixer on medium speed, carefully pour the cooked sugar syrup into the egg yolks in a fine stream, then beat until cooled to room temperature.

4   Gently fold the praline paste into the egg yolk mixture. Fold in the whipped cream.

5   Fill the molds to the top and smooth the tops. Freeze until set.

VARIATION   **MAPLE PARFAIT** Replace the sugar and water with 1 lb 9 oz/709 g maple syrup.

Frozen lemon savarin

MAKES 10 SERVINGS (4 FL OZ/120 ML EACH)

Gelatin, granulated	1 tsp	5 g
Water	1¾ fl oz	53 mL
Vanilla sponge (page 268), ⅛ in/3 mm thick, cut into 2½ in/6 cm disks	half sheet pan	half sheet pan
Light corn syrup	¾ oz	21 g
Sugar	4½ oz	128 g
Egg whites	2½ oz	71 g
Lemon juice	3 fl oz	90 mL
Lemon zest, grated	2 tsp	6 g
Plain yogurt (whole milk or low-fat)	2½ oz	71 g
Heavy cream, whipped to soft peaks	12 fl oz	340 g

1   Place 10 savarin molds on a sheet pan and place in the freezer until thoroughly chilled.

2   Bloom the gelatin in ¾ fl oz/23 mL of the water and melt.

3   Using a 3-in/8-cm round cutter, cut 10 disks of cake; reserve.

4   Combine the corn syrup, 3 oz/85 g of the sugar, and the remaining 1 fl oz/30 mL water in a saucepan and bring to a boil, stirring to dissolve the sugar. Continue to cook without stirring until the mixture reaches 240°F/116°C.

5   When the sugar syrup has reached approximately 230°F/110°C, begin to whip the egg whites on medium speed with the whip attachment until frothy. Gradually add the remaining 1½ oz/43 g sugar and whip to soft peaks.

6   When the sugar syrup reaches 240°F/116°C, add it to the meringue in a slow, steady stream while whipping on medium speed. Whip on high speed to stiff peaks, then whip on medium speed until cooled to room temperature.

7   Add the lemon juice and zest to the gelatin. Blend the mixture into the meringue. Fold in the yogurt, then the whipped cream.

8   Using a pastry bag fitted with a #4 plain tip, pipe 2¼ fl oz/68 mL of the parfait into each of the 10 chilled savarin molds, filling them nearly full.

9   Place a disk of vanilla sponge over each parfait; the disk should be flush with the top of the mold.

10   Cover the savarins and freeze overnight.

Frozen espresso and vanilla bombe

MAKES 48 INDIVIDUAL DOMES (6 FL OZ/18 ML EACH)

VANILLA MIX		
Heavy cream	32 fl oz	960 mL
Vanilla beans, seeds only	2 each	2 each
Egg yolks	12 oz	340 g
Sugar	8 oz	227 g
Water	2 fl oz	60 mL
Light corn syrup	1 tbsp	15 mL
ESPRESSO MIX		
Heavy cream	16 fl oz	480 mL
Egg yolks	7 oz	198 g
Sugar	4 oz	113 g
Water	1 fl oz	30 mL
Light corn syrup	1½ tsp	7.50 mL
Coffee extract	3 tbsp plus 1½ tsp	52.50 mL
Espresso powder	1 tbsp	15 mL
ASSEMBLY		
Caramelized nuts	as needed	as needed
Vanilla sponge (page 268), ⅛ in/3 mm thick, cut into 2½-in/6-cm disks	48 each	48 each

1   To prepare the vanilla mix, whip the cream to medium peaks, cover and refrigerate.

2   Add the vanilla bean seeds to the egg yolks, sugar, water, and corn syrup and make a pâte à bombe.

3   Fold in the reserved whipped cream. Transfer to a pitcher, cover, and reserve under refrigeration.

4   To prepare the espresso mix, whip the cream to medium peaks, cover, and refrigerate.

5   Make a pâte à bombe with the egg yolks, sugar, water, and light corn syrup. Beat in the coffee extract and espresso powder.

6   Gently fold in the reserved whipped cream using a rubber spatula. Do not overmix. Transfer to a pitcher, cover, and reserve under refrigeration.

7   Pour the two mixes into each mold at the same time. Fill each mold almost to the top, two-thirds full with the vanilla mix and one-third full with the espresso mix, to make a marbled effect. Drop a few caramelized nuts in each mold; they should sink. Cover each mold with a disk of vanilla sponge. Cover and freeze overnight.

part four

Assembling and finishing

Gallery of baked Strawberry Rhubarb Tart (page 530), Raspberry Mascarpone Tart (page 533), Zesty Lime Tart (page 537), and Apple Strudel (page 550)

chapter fifteen

Pies, tarts, and fruit desserts

*d*esserts and pastries such as pies, tarts, strudel, and cobblers give the pastry chef or baker the opportunity to showcase the natural, vibrant flavors of fruits and nuts as well as the sweetness and texture of cheeses and dairy products used to make creams and custards. When creating desserts of this type, think of what spices and preparation techniques will enhance and complement the textures, shapes, and flavors of these ingredients.

Rolling out dough and lining a pie or tart pan

1. Dust the work surface very lightly to ensure that very little additional flour or sugar is incorporated into the dough and to avoid clumps of flour that can become imbedded and baked into the dough, thus preserving its delicate texture and crumb. Lightly dust the dough as well to prevent it from sticking to the rolling pin. Make sure the dough is chilled before rolling, because if the butter or other fat in the crust becomes too soft, the dough will be difficult to handle. If necessary, massage the chilled dough or work it with the rolling pin until it is a malleable consistency. Usually the dough is rolled out directly on a work surface that has been dusted lightly with flour. Bread flour is the best choice for dusting. Because it is lower in starch and has a slightly more granular texture than other types of flour, bread flour dusts a surface more evenly with less clumping. Occasionally confectioners' sugar is used for dusting the work surface, typically for doughs with a higher sugar content.

2. Roll the dough from the center out. Lift and turn the dough as you roll so that you are rolling in all directions. This will keep the dough of even thickness and shape. Lifting and turning the dough will also help to keep it from sticking to the work surface and will reduce the amount of dusting necessary. To lift larger or more delicate pieces of dough, lay the dough over the rolling pin to keep it from tearing.

3. Work quickly and carefully. Dough for pies and tarts should be rolled to a thickness of ⅛ in/3 mm. Rolling the dough out slowly will allow the fat to become too soft and make it more likely to tear. Particularly delicate or tender doughs may have to be refrigerated intermittently during rolling to prevent that from occurring. This added step is often necessary when making a lattice top, which requires extra handling of the dough. If the

Rolling out dough into a round

Lining a pie pan with dough

dough tears while you are rolling it, simply patch the tear with a small scrap of dough and roll over it so that it becomes incorporated. If the dough is too thick, it may not bake through, and too much dough can overwhelm the flavors of the filling.

4. To transfer the rolled dough to the pie or tart pan, carefully roll it around the rolling pin, and then gently unroll over the pan. Gently press the dough into the pan, being careful not to tear or stretch the dough. Trim the edge of the dough so that it fits perfectly into the pan. Dock the bottom of the crust when necessary to prevent it from bubbling up. Docking is done by piercing the bottom of a crust in order to allow steam to escape during baking; the escape of steam through the holes in the crust helps to keep the dough flat and even.

Topping pies and tarts

The treatment of the top of a pie or tart makes it more interesting and appealing. Typically, toppings of dough or crumb for pies and tarts are used with fruit fillings. Topping a pie or tart helps to prevent the filling from drying during baking by keeping in moisture. Too much moisture, however, can be a bad thing. To prevent excessive moisture buildup and/or retention, cut steam vents into the top of a double-crust pie to allow steam to escape during baking. This will also allow the top crust to develop a crisp, flaky texture.

Crumb toppings create less of a moisture barrier, allowing for the release of steam during baking, and therefore do not require vents. Crumb toppings are quick and easy and add a different flavor and texture than crusts made of pastry dough. A pastry top may completely cover the pie or tart or may be cut into strips and woven to create a lattice pattern. Pastry doughs may also be rolled and cut into shapes used to adorn the top or edges of a pie or tart. Crimping the edges of a pie is another way to add a decorative element, and for double-crusted pies and tarts it also serves to seal in the filling and seal the top and bottom crusts together.

Finishing a tart or pie with crumb topping adds flavor as well as texture.

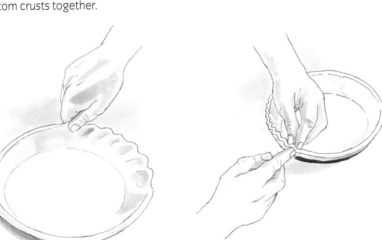

Crimping method one

Crimping method two

LEFT: Lay the top crust over the filled pie, allowing the crust to overhang the sides.

RIGHT: Cut holes in the top of the pie after the edges have been crimped.

Many bakers and pastry chefs apply a wash to the top and edges of their pies and tarts to promote the development of a golden brown crust. The wash may be anything from milk or cream to egg wash. For additional sweetness and texture, add a sprinkling of coarse sugar after applying the wash. If you choose to use a wash, use a pastry brush to apply it in a thin, even coat. Some like to apply two coats before baking to promote better shine and browning; apply the first coat of the wash, allow it to dry for 3 to 5 minutes, and then apply the final coat.

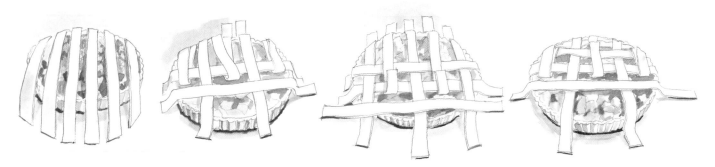

FROM LEFT TO RIGHT: To weave a lattice top, place strips over the tart in one direction, leaving the same amount of space between each one.

Turn back every other strip to place the crosswise strips. The first crosswise strip is placed in the center of the tart.

Place the last crosswise strip near the edge on one side of the tart.

Turn the tart 180 degrees to finish placing the crosswise strips.

Blind baking pie and tart shells

To blind bake means to bake an unfilled pie or tart shell partially or fully before adding the filling.

1. Line the dough with parchment paper and fill with pie weights, dry beans, or rice. The weights will prevent the bottom of the crust from bubbling up and the sides from collapsing or sliding down the sides of the pan during baking.

2. Place the pan in the preheated oven. The parchment and weights need only stay in the pan until the crust has baked long enough to set.

3. Once the crust has baked long enough so that it has set and will maintain its form (generally 10 to 12 minutes), remove the parchment and weights to allow for even browning.

4. Return the pan to the oven and bake the crust until the desired color is achieved. If the crust is to be baked again with a filling, bake it just until light golden brown. For a fully baked crust, bake to a deep golden brown, about 20 minutes. Pastry shells are partially prebaked when the time required to bake the filling will not be long enough to fully bake the crust. Shells are completely prebaked when they are to be filled with a filling that does not require further cooking or baking.

For blind baking, the shell is lined with parchment and weighted with dried beans or weights.

5. Brush prebaked pastry shells with a light coating of softened butter or melted chocolate and allow to set fully before filling. This will prevent moisture in the filling from seeping into the crust and making it soggy. Apply the thin coating to the shell using a pastry brush.

6. Place the shell in the refrigerator so that the butter or chocolate will harden, then fill the shell.

Working with puff pastry

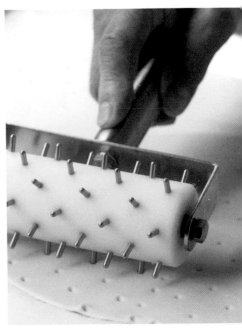

When working with puff pastry, keep it as cold as possible. Work in manageable batches, so that the dough won't sit at room temperature for too long. If the butter is allowed to soften, it will cause the layering to collapse and prevent the full rise of the dough.

Lightly dust the work surface with flour (preferably bread flour) to prevent the dough from sticking. Roll the dough from the center out in all directions, lifting and turning the dough as you work to prevent the gluten from being overworked in any one direction. Uneven rolling will cause the pastry to become misshapen during baking.

When using puff pastry to line a tart pan, it should be rolled very thin and docked well to inhibit excessive rising during baking. When blind baking puff pastry for items such as napoleons, it should be weighted down to prevent it from fully rising. If allowed to fully rise, it would be too flaky to cut into smaller portions or for building pastries.

Puff pastry is always baked at a relatively high temperature (400° to 425°F/204° to 218°C) to encourage the full rise. Lower temperatures would not create enough steam or set the structure of the pastry quickly enough, and it would either never rise or collapse.

Puff dough is docked before baking to prevent too high a rise.

Working with fresh fruit

For the most flavor, choose fruit that is in season. The best way to select fruit is to taste it. When tasting is not possible, select fruit with the desired color, aroma, and firmness (see "Selecting and Handling Fresh Produce" in Chapter 2, page 26, for more information on fruit). Combine fruits and berries to create different and more complex flavor profiles and textures, for example, strawberry and rhubarb, or pears and cranberries. Using different varieties of the same fruit can also have the same effect, for example, Granny Smith and Golden Delicious apples. High-moisture fruits such as peaches and cherries generally benefit from precooking with a starch before assembling into a pie, while lower-moisture fruits such as apples and pears can simply be tossed with sugar, starch, and flavorings and placed directly into a shell for baking.

Cutting and peeling fruit

Precise technique for cutting and peeling fruit is important for the uniformity and eye appeal of the final product.

Cutting Citrus Suprêmes

To cut citrus fruit into suprêmes (segments), slice off the top and bottom of the fruit, and slice the skin and white pith completely away. Then slice between the connective membranes on either side of each citrus segment to release it; twist the knife and use a scooping motion to cut out the suprême.

LEFT: Making citrus suprêmes

MIDDLE: Slicing a mango

RIGHT: Peeling a kiwi with a spoon

LEFT: Preparing melon balls

MIDDLE: Removing the core from pineapple slices with a cookie cutter

RIGHT: Coring a pear

Peeling and Slicing a Mango

Cut off the flesh from the broad sides of the pit in two large sections, cutting as close to the pit as possible. Then cut the flesh from the two narrow sides, following the curve of the pit. Remove the skin. Cube or slice the flesh as desired.

Peeling a Kiwi

To peel a kiwi, slice off one end of the fruit. Work the tip of a spoon down between the flesh and the skin and carefully slide it all the way around the fruit, then pop out the flesh. Cube or slice as desired.

Peeling and Seeding a Melon

To peel and seed a melon, use a chef's knife to peel off the skin, following the natural curve of the melon. Cut the melon in half and scoop out the seeds and strings with a spoon. Cube or slice the melon as desired.

Cutting Melon Balls

To use a melon baller or Parisian scoop to cut melon balls or ovals, halve the unpeeled melon and scoop out the seeds and strings. Scoop out the melon flesh, rotating the baller as you work to create spheres or ovals.

Peeling and Cutting a Pineapple

To peel and cut a pineapple, use a chef's knife to cut off the top and bottom of the fruit. Moving the blade of the knife with the contours of the fruit, cut away the skin, being careful to remove the "eyes" without removing too much of the edible flesh. To dice or cube the pineapple, slice the fruit from the core in four sections, make the slices the desired width, and then dice or cube. To cut the pineapple into rings, lay the peeled fruit on its side and cut into slices of the desired thickness. Remove the core from each slice using a small round cutter.

Pitting and Coring Fruit

To remove the pit from a stone fruit, cut around the circumference of the fruit, down to the pit, using the seam as a guide. Twist the two sections of the fruit in opposite directions to release the flesh from the seed.

To core apples and pears, either use a special coring tool or cut the fruit from the core in four segments. Then cube or slice as desired.

Peeled apples, pears, and other fruits that oxidize quickly when their flesh comes in contact with the air may be tossed in a small amount of lemon juice to prevent browning during preparation.

Strudel

As versatile as pie, strudel can be savory or sweet, provided the filling is low in moisture.

Vent the top of the strudel to allow excess moisture to escape to prevent the filling and dough from becoming too soft. Strudel dough is stretched to create a paper-thin sheet. The high-gluten content of bread flour and a resting time after mixing allows this dough to be stretched paper thin. During assembly, strudel dough is brushed with butter and rolled up to encase a filling. This creates a flaky pastry with many layers, just as are created by the lamination of puff pastry or by the layering of phyllo dough.

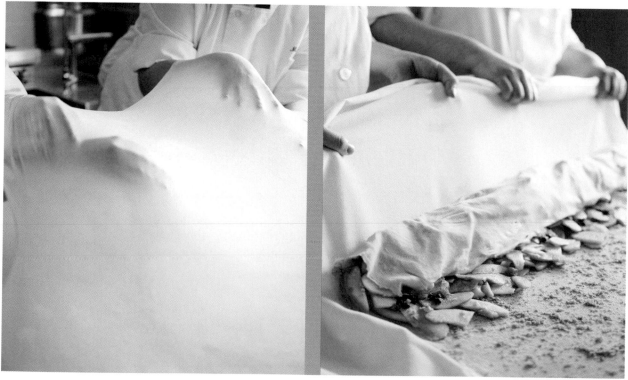

Stretching strudel dough

Rolling filling up in strudel dough

Clockwise from top right: Apple Pie (page 520), Blueberry Pie (page 522), Pecan Pie (page 529), and Pumpkin Pie (page 525)

Apple pie

MAKES 1 PIE (9 IN/23 CM)

Basic pie dough (page 222)	1 lb 4 oz	567 g
APPLE FILLING		
Sugar	5 oz	142 g
Tapioca starch	½ oz	14 g
Cornstarch or all-purpose flour	1 oz	28 g
Salt	½ tsp	2.50 g
Ground nutmeg	½ tsp	1 g
Ground cinnamon	½ tsp	1 g
Lemon juice	½ fl oz	15 mL
Butter, melted	1 oz	28 g
Golden Delicious apples, peeled, cored, and sliced ⅛ in/3 mm thick	1 lb 8 oz	680 g
Egg wash (page 892)	as needed	as needed

1   Divide the dough in half. Roll out one-half of the dough to ⅛ in/3 mm thick and line the pie pan. Reserve the other half, wrapped tightly, under refrigeration.

2   Combine the sugar, tapioca, cornstarch, salt, nutmeg, cinnamon, lemon juice, and melted butter and toss with the apples.

3   Fill the pie shell with the apple mixture. Brush the rim of the dough with egg wash.

4   Roll out the remaining dough to a thickness of ⅛ in/3 mm and place it over the filling. Crimp the edges to seal, then cut a few vents in the top of the pie.

5   Bake at 375°F/191°C until the filling is bubbling and the crust is a rich golden brown, about 45 minutes.

6   Serve warm, or cool to room temperature before serving.

VARIATION   Other fresh fruit, such as peaches or nectarines, can be substituted for the apples.

Cherry pie

MAKES 16 PIES (10 IN/25 CM EACH)

Basic pie dough (page 222)	20 lb	9.07 kg
CHERRY FILLING		
Cherry juice*	10 lb 8 oz	4.76 kg
Sugar	2 lb	907 g
Salt	½ oz	14 g
Clear gel starch	1 lb	454 g
Cherries,* thoroughly drained	18 lb	8.16 kg
Lemon juice	3 lemons	3 lemons
Butter	1 oz	28 g
Egg wash (page 892)	as needed	as needed

*Cherries and juice from #30 can, thawed and drained

1   Divide the dough into 32 equal parts. Roll out 16 portions ⅛ in/3 mm thick and line the pie pans. Reserve the remaining dough, wrapped tightly, under refrigeration.

2   Combine 9 lb/4.08 kg of the cherry juice with the sugar and salt in a sauce pot over medium heat and bring the mixture to a boil.

3   Dissolve the clear gel in the remaining cherry juice and slowly add to the boiling mixture, stirring continuously.

4   Bring the cherry juice mixture back up to a boil and cook for 5 minutes, until the mixture becomes transparent. Remove from the heat.

5   Using a wooden spoon, gently fold in the cherries, lemon juice, and butter. Cool.

6   Scale 2 lb/907 g of the filling for each pie and fill to the top of the prepared crusts.

7   Roll out the remaining dough ⅛ in/3 cm thick and place it over the filling. Crimp the edges to seal. Brush the top of the dough with egg wash. Cut vents in the top crust of the pies.

8   Bake the pies at 420°F/216°C until the crust browns, about 45 minutes. Cool on racks before serving.

NOTE   If the filling is not sweet enough, add more sugar.

Blueberry pie

MAKES 2 PIES (10 IN/25 CM EACH)

Basic pie dough (page 222)	2 lb 8 oz	1.13 kg
BLUEBERRY FILLING		
Blueberry juice, drained from frozen berries	28 fl oz	840 mL
Sugar	7 oz	198 g
Salt	½ tsp	2.50 g
Clear gel starch	2¾ oz	78 g
Blueberries, drained, frozen	3 lb	1.36 kg
Lemon juice	1 fl oz	30 mL
Egg wash (page 892)	as needed	as needed

1   Divide the dough into 4 equal parts. Roll out 2 portions ⅛ in/3 mm thick and line the pie pans. Reserve the remaining dough, wrapped tightly, under refrigeration.

2   Bring 24 fl oz/720 mL of the blueberry juice, the sugar, and salt to a boil in a sauce pot.

3   Combine the remaining 4 fl oz/120 mL blueberry juice with the clear gel starch and mix until smooth.

4   Add the starch mixture to the boiling juice, stirring constantly with a wooden spoon. Bring the mixture to a second boil. Boil for 1 minute.

5   Add the blueberries and lemon juice; stir and cook for 1 minute, until the mixture thickens.

6   Remove the mixture from the heat and cool completely.

7   Roll out the remaining 2 portions of dough ⅛ in/3 mm thick. Cut into strips ½ in/1 cm wide. Weave a lattice over the top of the pie, leaving a ½-in/1-cm space between each strip (see page 514 for instructions on weaving a lattice top). Brush the lattice crust with egg wash.

8   Bake the pies at 420°F/216°C until the crust browns, about 45 minutes.

NOTE   If there is not enough blueberry juice, make up the difference with water.

Blueberry pie with fresh berries

MAKES 1 PIE (10 IN/25 CM)

Basic pie dough (page 222)	1 lb 8 oz	680 g
BLUEBERRY FILLING		
Blueberries, fresh	1 lb 8 oz	680 g
Sugar	8 oz	227 g
Tapioca starch	1½ oz	43 g

1   Divide the dough into two equal pieces. Roll out one piece ⅛ in/3 mm thick and line the pie pan. Reserve the remaining dough, wrapped tightly, under refrigeration.

2   Combine the blueberries, sugar, and tapioca.

3   Roll out the remaining dough ⅛ in/3 mm thick. Place the berry mixture into the lined pie pan and place the remaining rolled dough on top. Trim and crimp together the edges to seal. Make a few vents on top.

4   Bake the pie at 420°F/216°C until golden brown, about 45 minutes.

Lemon meringue pie

MAKES 4 PIES (10 IN/25 CM EACH)

Basic pie dough (page 222)	2 lb 8 oz	1.13 kg
LEMON MERINGUE FILLING		
Water	64 fl oz	1.92 L
Sugar	2 lb	907 g
Salt	½ oz	14 g
Lemon juice	10 fl oz	300 mL
Lemon zest, grated	2 oz	57 g
Cornstarch	6 oz	170 g
Egg yolks	8 oz	227 g
Butter	4 oz	113 g
MERINGUE TOPPING		
Egg whites	14 oz	397 g
Granulated sugar	1 lb 12 oz	794 g
Confectioners' sugar	as needed	as needed

1   Divide the dough into 4 equal pieces, 10 oz/284 g each. Roll the dough out ⅛ in/3 mm thick and line the pie pans. Line the pie shells with parchment paper and fill with dry beans or pie weights. Bake the shells at 350°F/177°C until golden brown, about 30 minutes. Remove the weights. Cool completely.

2   Combine 48 fl oz/1.44 L water, 1 lb/454 g sugar, the salt, lemon juice, and zest in a sauce pot and bring to a boil.

3   Combine the remaining 1 lb/454 g of sugar and the cornstarch; thoroughly mix together.

4   Combine the egg yolks and the remaining 16 fl oz/480 mL of water. Add to the sugar-cornstarch mixture. Mix until thoroughly combined and reserve.

5   When the lemon juice mixture comes to a boil, temper the mixture into the egg yolk mixture. Put the combined mixtures back on the heat and return to a boil until the mixture thickens, about 2 minutes. Once thickened, remove from the heat immediately. Stir in the butter.

6   Scale 1 lb 10 oz/737 g of the pie filling into each of the 4 pie shells and let cool to room temperature.

7   To make the meringue topping, whip the egg whites in a clean bowl, gradually adding the sugar. Whip to stiff peaks.

8   Using a pastry bag with a #5 star tip or a palette knife, divide the meringue topping among the 4 pies and swirl into a decorative pattern. Dust with confectioners' sugar and bake at 425°F/218°C until the meringue is lightly browned, about 3 minutes. Serve.

Pumpkin pie

MAKES 8 PIES (10 IN/25 CM EACH)

Basic pie dough (page 222)	5 lb	2.27 g
PUMPKIN FILLING		
Water	106 fl oz	3.20 L
Pumpkin, canned	6 lb 10 oz	3 kg
Sugar	2 lb 9 oz	1.16 kg
Nonfat dry milk	14 oz	397 g
Bread flour	7 oz	198 g
Salt	1½ oz	43 g
Ground ginger	⅓ oz	9 g
Ground nutmeg	⅓ oz	9 g
Ground cinnamon	⅓ oz	9 g
Eggs	2 lb 3 oz	992 g

1   Divide the pie dough into 8 equal pieces. Roll out each piece ⅛ in/3 mm thick and line the pie pans.

2   Combine the water and pumpkin in the mixer and mix on low speed with the whip attachment until just combined.

3   Sift together the sugar, dry milk, flour, salt, and spices. Gradually add to the pumpkin mixture, mixing on medium speed until just combined.

4   Add the eggs in 3 additions, mixing until fully incorporated after each addition and scraping down the bowl as needed.

5   Scale 2 lb 7 oz/1.11 kg of the filling into each pie shell. Bake at 420°F/216°C until the filling sets and the crust browns, about 45 minutes. Serve or store in the refrigerator.

Vanilla cream pie

MAKES 1 PIE (9 IN/23 CM)

Basic pie dough (page 222)	10 oz	284 g
Milk	24 fl oz	720 mL
Sugar	6 oz	170 g
Vanilla beans, split and scraped	1 each	1 each
Cornstarch	2 oz	57 g
Eggs	3 oz	85 g
Egg yolks	2 oz	57 g
Butter	1 oz	28 g

1　Roll out the dough ⅛ in/3 mm thick and line the pie pan. Line the pie shell with parchment paper and fill with dry beans or pie weights. Bake the pie shell at 350°F/177°C until very light golden brown, about 15 minutes. Remove the beans and parchment and continue cooking to a golden brown, about 5 minutes. Cool completely.

2　Combine 18 fl oz/540 mL of the milk with 3 oz/85 g of the sugar in a saucepan. Add the vanilla bean seeds and pod. Bring the mixture to a boil, stirring to dissolve the sugar.

3　Meanwhile, combine the remaining 3 oz/85 g sugar with the cornstarch, stirring together with a whisk. Add the remaining 6 fl oz/180 mL milk, the eggs, and egg yolks and whisk to blend.

4　Temper the egg mixture by gradually adding one-third of the hot milk mixture, whisking constantly. Return the tempered egg mixture to the remaining milk mixture in the saucepan and cook, stirring constantly, just until it reaches a boil. Cook, stirring constantly, for an additional 2 minutes.

5　Remove the pan from the heat and whisk in the butter. Strain through a fine-mesh sieve.

6　Pour the hot filling into the prebaked pie shell. Cover the surface of the cream with plastic wrap placed directly against it to prevent a skin from forming. Cool to room temperature.

7　Chill before serving.

VARIATIONS　**BANANA CREAM PIE** Spread half of the filling into the pie shell. Cover with a layer of 8 oz/227 g sliced bananas, then top with the remaining filling.

CHOCOLATE CREAM PIE Add 3 oz/85 g melted bittersweet chocolate to the cream with the butter immediately after boiling.

COCONUT CREAM PIE Add 2 oz/57 g lightly toasted unsweetened coconut to the milk before heating it.

Sweet potato pie

MAKES 1 PIE (9 IN/23 CM)

Basic pie dough (page 222)	10 oz	284 g
Sweet potatoes	8 oz	227 g
Milk	8 fl oz	240 mL
Eggs, lightly beaten	4 oz	113 g
Sugar	3⅓ oz	94 g
Butter, melted	1 oz	28 g
Ground cinnamon	1 tsp	2 g
Ground allspice	¼ tsp	0.50 g
Ground mace	¼ tsp	0.50 g
Salt	¼ tsp	1.25 g

1 Roll out the dough ⅛ in/3 mm thick and line the pie pan. Line the pie shell with parchment paper and fill with dry beans or pie weights. Bake the pie shell at 350°F/177°C until very light golden brown, about 15 minutes. Cool completely.

2 Peel the sweet potatoes and prick with a fork. Lightly oil them and place on a rack in a baking pan.

3 Bake the potatoes at 350°F/177°C until very tender, about 35 minutes. Cool.

4 Mash the sweet potatoes until completely smooth. Combine with the remaining ingredients, blending well. Pour into the prebaked pie shell.

5 Bake at 350°F/177°C until the filling is set, about 35 minutes. Cool completely, and then refrigerate until the filling is completely set before serving.

Tarte tatin

MAKES 1 TART (9 IN/23 CM)

Granulated sugar	8 oz	227 g
Light brown sugar	4 oz	113 g
Ground cinnamon	½ tsp	1 g
Golden Delicious apples	6 each	6 each
Pâte brisée (page 222)	8 oz	227 g
Apple brandy	1 fl oz	30 mL

1 Butter a cake pan 9 in/23 cm in diameter and 2 in/5 cm deep.

2 Melt the granulated sugar in a heavy-bottomed pan, adding it in small increments and stirring after each addition until melted before adding more. Cook to a rich golden brown caramel.

3 Pour the caramel into the cake pan and cool completely.

4 Sprinkle the brown sugar on top of the caramel and dust with the cinnamon.

5 Peel, core, and halve the apples. Arrange them in a circular pattern, cut side down, to completely cover the bottom of the pan.

6 Roll out the pâte brisée ¼ in/6 mm thick and place it over the apples, slightly tucking it in around the edge of the pan.

7 Bake at 400°F/204°C until the crust is golden brown, about 45 minutes.

8 Invert the pan onto a rack set over a pan to drain the liquid.

9 Place the liquid in a pan and simmer over medium heat until it begins to thicken. Add the apple brandy and pour the mixture over the top of the tart just before serving.

Shingling apples atop caramel for a tarte tatin

Pecan pie

MAKES 1 PIE (9 IN/23 CM)

Basic pie dough (page 222)	10 oz	284 g
Sugar	½ oz	14 g
Bread flour	½ oz	14 g
Dark corn syrup	10½ oz	298 g
Eggs, beaten	3½ oz	99 g
Vanilla extract	1 tsp	5 mL
Salt	½ tsp	2.50 g
Butter, melted	1 oz	28 g
Pecan halves, toasted	4 oz	113 g

1   Roll out the dough ⅛ in/3 mm thick and line the pie pan.

2   Combine the sugar and flour in a bowl and whisk together. Add the corn syrup and blend thoroughly. Add the eggs, vanilla, and salt and mix until incorporated. Stir in the melted butter.

3   Spread the pecans evenly in the pie shell and pour the corn syrup mixture on top.

4   Bake at 450°F/232°C until the crust begins to brown, about 15 minutes. Reduce the oven temperature to 325°F/163°C and bake until the filling is set, about 25 minutes longer. Cool completely before serving.

VARIATIONS   **CHOCOLATE PECAN PIE** Add 6 oz/170 g chocolate chunks along with the pecans.

PECAN CRANBERRY PIE Add 5 oz/142 g fresh or frozen cranberries along with the pecans.

Puff pastry apple tart

MAKES 1 TART (9 IN/23 CM)

Butter puff pastry dough (page 231)	10 oz	284 g
Apricot jam	2 oz	57 g
Apples, peeled, cored, and finely chopped	1 each	1 each
Apples, peeled, cored, and sliced	4 each	4 each
Sugar	2 oz	57 g
Apricot glaze (page 426), warm	1 oz	28 g

1   Roll out the puff pastry ¼ in/6 mm thick. Cut a 10-in/25-cm circle from the dough.

2   Place the round of dough on a sheet pan lined with parchment paper. Spread a thin layer of apricot jam over the circle of dough, leaving a ½-in/1-cm border of dough around the entire tart. Spread the chopped apple over the jam. Arrange the sliced apples on top of the chopped apple in a fanned spiral, starting from the center and working out to the edges. Sprinkle the sugar on top of the apples.

3   Bake at 400°F/204°C until golden brown, about 20 minutes.

4   Using a pastry brush, glaze the tart with the apricot glaze. Serve warm or completely cooled.

Strawberry rhubarb tart

MAKES 1 TART (9 IN/23 CM)

Sugar	6 oz	170 g
Cornstarch	1¼ oz	35 g
Ground cinnamon	½ tsp	1 g
Ground cloves	pinch	pinch
Rhubarb (fresh or frozen), cut into 1 in/2-cm pieces	8 oz	227 g
Strawberries (fresh or frozen)	8 oz	227 g
Lemon juice	1 fl oz	30 mL
Pâte brisée (page 222)	1 lb 8 oz	680 g

1   Combine the sugar, cornstarch, cinnamon, and cloves. Toss together with the rhubarb, strawberries, and lemon juice.

2 Divide the pâte brisée in half. Roll out one piece ⅛ in/3 mm thick and line the tart pan. Spoon the filling into the tart shell.

3 Roll out the remaining dough ⅛ in/3 mm thick. Cut it into strips ½ in/1 cm wide. Weave a lattice over the top of the tart, leaving a ½-in/1-cm space between each strip (see page 514 for instructions on weaving a lattice top).

4 Bake at 450°F/232°C for 10 minutes. Reduce the temperature to 350°F/177°C and bake until the crust is golden brown, about 30 minutes more. Serve warm or completely cooled.

Rustic peach tart

MAKES 1 TART (9 IN/23 CM)

Blitz puff pastry (page 233)	10 oz	284 g
Peaches, peeled, pitted, and cut into ¼-in/6-mm slices	1 lb	454 g
Ground nutmeg	¼ tsp	0.50 g
Granulated sugar	2 oz	57 g
Egg wash (page 892)	as needed	as needed
Cake crumbs, fresh	1½ oz	43 g
Almonds, slivered (optional)	1½ oz	43 g
Coarse sugar	2 oz	57 g

1 Roll out the puff pastry ⅛ in/3 mm thick. Cut a 10-in/25-cm circle from the dough and place it on a parchment-lined sheet pan.

2 Toss the peaches with the nutmeg and sugar.

3 Brush the outside 1-in/3-cm perimeter of the puff pastry circle lightly with egg wash. Sprinkle the cake crumbs on top of the pastry, leaving a 2-in/5-cm border. Mound the peaches on top of the cake crumbs. Sprinkle the almonds on top of the fruit, if using.

4 Fold the edges of the puff pastry over the fruit, pleating the dough as necessary. Brush the pleated edge of the pastry lightly with egg wash and sprinkle with the coarse sugar.

5 Bake at 400°F/204°C until golden brown, about 1 hour. Cool on a wire rack. Serve warm or cold.

VARIATION Substitute apples, pears, or pitted sour cherries or apricots for the peaches.

Florida sunshine tart

MAKES 1 TART (9 IN/23 CM)

Butter puff pastry dough (page 231)	10 oz	284 g
Egg wash (page 892)	as needed	as needed
Classic caramel sauce (page 452)	4 oz	113 g
Pastry cream (page 370)	6 oz	170 g
Oranges, peeled	8 each	8 each
Apricot glaze (page 426), warm	2 oz	57 g

1   Roll out the puff pastry ¼ in/6 mm thick. Cut a 10-in/25-cm circle from the pastry. Cut a 9-in/23-cm circle from the center of the circle, creating a ring ½ in/1 cm wide.

2   Brush the puff pastry circle with egg wash. Cut the puff pastry ring to open it and place it on top of the circle to create a border around its edge. Cut off any excess so the ends of the border ring do not overlap. Brush the top of the ring with egg wash. Dock the bottom of the circle and place on a parchment-lined sheet pan.

3   Bake at 350°F/177°C until lightly browned, 15 to 20 minutes. Reduce the oven temperature to 300°F/149°C and bake until the shell is dry and golden brown, about 10 minutes longer.

4   Pour the caramel sauce into the shell while it is still warm and spread it evenly. Allow the caramel to cool completely and chill.

5   Using a pastry bag fitted with a #5 plain tip, pipe the pastry cream into the bottom of the shell in concentric circles.

6   Cut the oranges into suprêmes. Arrange the segments in a spiral in the shell, overlapping the segments and completely covering the pastry cream.

7   Brush the oranges with a thin layer of apricot glaze. Refrigerate until ready to serve.

Lemon fantasy tart

MAKES 1 TART (9 IN/23 CM)

1-2-3 cookie dough (page 223)	10 oz	284 g
Eggs	8 oz	227 g
Sugar	6¾ oz	191 g
Heavy cream	5 fl oz	150 mL
Lemon zest, grated	1 tsp	3 g
Lemon juice	4 fl oz	120 mL

1   Roll out the dough ⅛ in/3 mm thick and line the tart pan. Line the tart shell with parchment paper and fill with dry beans or pie weights. Bake the tart shell at 325°F/163°C until very light golden brown, 10 to 12 minutes. Cool completely.

2   Whisk together the eggs and sugar.

3   Whip the cream to soft peaks.

4   Add the lemon zest and juice to the egg mixture. Fold in the whipped cream.

5   Pour the filling into the tart shell. Bake at 350°F/177°C until just set, about 45 minutes.

6   Cool completely. Chill for several hours or until fully set.

Raspberry mascarpone tart

MAKES 1 TART (9 IN/23 CM)

1-2-3 cookie dough (page 223)	10 oz	284 g
Mascarpone	4 oz	113 g
Honey	2 oz	57 g
Vanilla extract	1 tsp	5 mL
Lemon juice	2 fl oz	60 mL
Heavy cream	6 fl oz	180 mL
Raspberries	8 oz	227 g
Apricot glaze (page 426), warm	2 oz	57 g

1   Roll out the dough ⅛ in/3 mm thick and line the tart pan. Line the tart shell with parchment paper and fill with dry beans or pie weights. Bake the tart shell at 350°F/177°C until very light golden brown, about 15 minutes. Remove the beans and parchment and continue cooking to a golden brown, about 5 minutes. Cool completely.

2   Mix the mascarpone, honey, vanilla, and lemon juice until well blended.

3   Whip the cream to soft peaks. Fold the whipped cream into the mascarpone mixture.

4   Pour the filling into the cooled tart shell and spread it evenly. Arrange the raspberries on top of the tart. Brush the berries with the warm glaze. Refrigerate until ready to serve.

Cheese tart

MAKES 1 TART (9 IN/23 CM)

1-2-3 cookie dough (page 223)	10 oz	284 g
Cream cheese	2 oz	57 g
Sugar	2⅔ oz	75 g
Eggs	6 oz	170 g
Heavy cream	4 fl oz	120 mL
Orange zest, grated	1 tbsp	9 g
Raspberries (fresh or frozen)	8 oz	227 g

1 Roll out the dough ⅛ in/3 mm thick and line the tart pan. Line the tart shell with parchment paper and fill with dried beans or pie weights. Bake at 350°F/177°C until very light golden brown, about 15 minutes. Cool completely.

2 Combine the cream cheese and sugar in the mixer and mix on medium speed with the paddle attachment until smooth. Gradually add the eggs, mixing until fully incorporated after each addition and scraping down the sides of the bowl periodically. Add the cream and orange zest and blend well.

3 Place the raspberries in the tart shell so they cover the bottom evenly. Pour the filling over the raspberries and spread it evenly.

4 Set the tart pan on a sheet pan and bake at 350°F/177°C until a knife blade inserted in the center comes out clean, 40 to 45 minutes. If the pastry begins to overbrown, cover the edges of the dough with strips of aluminum foil or pie shields. Remove the tart from the oven and cool on a wire rack. Let the tart rest at least 20 minutes before cutting into pieces. Serve hot, warm, or at room temperature.

Lemon mousse tart

MAKES 1 TART (9 IN/23 CM)

Rich short dough (page 224)	10 oz	284 g
Gelatin, granulated	2 tsp	10 g
Water	1 fl oz	30 mL
Heavy cream	8 fl oz	240 mL
Half-and-half	4 fl oz	120 mL
Sugar	3 oz	85 g
Egg yolks	2 oz	57 g
Vanilla extract	1 tsp	5 mL
Lemon juice	1 fl oz	30 mL

1   Roll out the dough ⅛ in/3 mm thick and line the tart pan. Line the tart shell with parchment paper and fill with dry beans or pie weights. Bake at 350°F/177°C until very light golden brown, about 15 minutes. Remove the beans and parchment and continue cooking to a golden brown, about 5 minutes. Cool completely.

2   Bloom the gelatin in the water.

3   Whip the cream to soft peaks. Cover and reserve under refrigeration.

4   Combine the half-and-half and 1½ oz/43 g of the sugar in a saucepan and bring to a simmer over medium heat, stirring to dissolve the sugar.

5   Blend the egg yolks with the remaining 1½ oz/43 g sugar to make the liaison. Temper by gradually adding about one-third of the hot half-and-half, whisking constantly. Return the tempered egg mixture to the hot half-and-half in the saucepan and cook, stirring gently, until the custard thickens enough to coat the back of a spoon. Strain.

6   Add the bloomed gelatin to the warm custard, blending well. Allow the mixture to cool slightly, then blend in the vanilla and lemon juice.

7   Gently blend one-third of the lemon custard mixture into the reserved whipped cream. Fold the cream into the remaining lemon mixture.

8   Pour into the prepared tart shell and spread evenly.

9   Refrigerate for 1 hour before serving.

Almond and pine nut tart

MAKES 1 TART (9 IN/23 CM)

1-2-3 cookie dough (page 223)	10 oz	284 g
Almond paste	6 oz	170 g
Sugar	2½ oz	71 g
Eggs	3 each	3 each
Vanilla extract	1 tsp	5 mL
All-purpose flour	1½ oz	43 g
Pine nuts	2 oz	57 g
Confectioners' sugar	as needed	as needed

1 Roll out the dough ⅛ in/3 mm thick and line the tart pan.

2 Combine the almond paste, sugar, and one-third of the eggs, blending until smooth. Add the remaining eggs one at a time, mixing until fully incorporated after each addition. Blend in the vanilla. Add the flour and mix until incorporated.

3 Pour the filling into the tart shell. Scatter the pine nuts over the top.

4 Bake at 350°F/177°C until the filling is set, about 35 minutes. Cool completely.

5 To serve, remove from the tart pan and dust with confectioners' sugar.

Caramel orange tart

MAKES 1 TART (9 IN/23 CM)

1-2-3 cookie dough (page 223)	10 oz	284 g
Heavy cream	10 fl oz	300 mL
Vanilla beans, seeds only	½ each	½ each
Orange juice	8 fl oz	240 mL
Sugar	3½ oz	99 g
Egg yolks, beaten	4 oz	113 g

1 Roll out the dough ⅛ in/3 mm thick and line the tart pan. Line the tart shell with parchment paper and fill with dry beans or pie weights. Bake the tart shell at 350°F/177°C until very light golden brown, about 15 minutes. Cool completely.

2 Pour the cream into a saucepan. Add the vanilla seeds and bring to a simmer. Remove from the heat, cover, and allow to steep for 15 minutes.

3 Combine the orange juice and sugar in a small saucepan over high heat and stir constantly until the mixture comes to a boil to ensure all the sugar is melted. Once it has come to a boil, stop stirring. Using a pastry brush, wash down the sides of the pan with cool water to prevent crystals from forming. Repeat as often as necessary to keep the sides of the pan clean until the sugar has reached a rich golden brown. Slowly add the cream, stirring until fully incorporated. Cool.

4 Blend the egg yolks into the caramel mixture.

5 Fill the tart shell with the caramel custard. Bake at 325°F/163°C until the filling is set, about 40 minutes.

6 Cool completely before serving.

Zesty lime tart

MAKES 1 TART (9 IN/23 CM)

1-2-3 cookie dough (page 223)	10 oz	284 g
Butter	5½ oz	156 g
Sugar	4½ oz	128 g
Lime zest, grated	¾ oz	21 g
Lime juice	4½ fl oz	135 mL
Egg yolks	2 oz	57 g
Candied lime peel (see Note, page 796)	2 oz	57 g

1 Roll out the dough ⅛ in/3 mm thick and line the tart pan. Line the tart shell with parchment paper and fill with dry beans or pie weights. Bake the tart shell at 350°F/177°C until very light golden brown, about 15 minutes. Remove the beans and parchment and continue cooking to a golden brown, about 5 minutes. Cool completely.

2 Combine the butter, 2¼ oz/64 g of the sugar, the lime zest, and juice in a saucepan and bring to a boil, stirring frequently to dissolve the sugar.

3 Blend the egg yolks with the remaining 2¼ oz/64 g sugar to make the liaison. Temper by gradually adding about one-third of the hot mixture, whisking constantly. Return to the saucepan and cook until thickened enough to evenly coat a spoon.

4 Strain the mixture into the tart shell. Chill thoroughly.

5 To serve, garnish with the candied lime peel.

Apple custard tart

MAKES 1 TART (9 IN/23 CM)

1-2-3 cookie dough (page 223)	10 oz	284 g
Apricot jam	2⅔ oz	75 g
Apples, peeled, cored, and cut into ¼-in/6-mm slices	3 each	3 each
Butter, melted	1 oz	28 g
Cinnamon sugar (page 897)	1 tsp	4 g
Eggs	6 oz	170 g
Sugar	4 oz	113 g
Sour cream	8 oz	227 g
Milk	6 fl oz	180 mL
Vanilla extract	½ tsp	2.50 mL
Apricot glaze (page 426), warm	5 oz	142 g
Sliced almonds, toasted and coarsely chopped	1 oz	28 g

1   Roll out the dough ⅛ in/3 mm thick and line the tart pan. Line the tart shell with parchment paper and fill with dry beans or pie weights. Bake the tart shell at 350°F/177°C until very light golden brown, about 15 minutes. Cool completely.

2   Spread the apricot jam over the bottom of the tart shell. Arrange the sliced apples in concentric circles on top of the jam. Using a pastry brush, brush the melted butter over the apples. Sprinkle with the cinnamon sugar.

3   Bake at 375°F/191°C until the apples are tender and the crust is golden brown, about 40 minutes.

4   Whisk together the eggs, sugar, sour cream, milk, and vanilla. Remove the tart from the oven and pour the sour cream mixture over the cooked apples, filling the tart shell to the top.

5   Reduce the oven temperature to 300°F/149°C and bake until the custard is set, about 35 minutes longer. Cool to room temperature.

6   Brush the top of the tart with the apricot glaze. Press the almonds around the edge of the tart.

Custard fruit tart

MAKES 1 TART (9 IN/23 CM)

Basic pie dough (page 222)	10 oz	284 g
Apricot jam	3 oz	85 g
Fresh fruit, sliced, peeled, and cored as necessary	1 lb	454 g
Egg yolks	7 oz	198 g
Sugar	4 oz	113 g
Heavy cream	16 fl oz	480 mL
Vanilla beans, seeds only	1 each	1 each
Lemon or orange zest	1 each	1 each
Apricot glaze (page 426), warm	as needed	as needed
Sliced almonds, finely chopped	1 oz	28 g

1   Roll the dough out ⅛ in/3 mm thick and line the tart pan. Line the tart shell with parchment paper and fill with dry beans or pie weights. Bake the tart shell at 350°F/177°C until very light and golden brown, about 15 minutes. Cool completely.

2   Spread the apricot jam over the bottom of the tart shell. Arrange the sliced fruit in concentric circles on top of the jam.

3   Bake at 375°F/191°C until the fruit is tender and the crust is golden brown, about 30 minutes.

4   Whisk together the egg yolks and 2 oz/57 g of the sugar to make the liason. In a saucepan, bring the cream, the remaining sugar, the vanilla seeds, and lemon zest to a boil. Temper by gradually adding about one-third of the hot cream mixture to the yolks, whisking constantly, and then add the remaining hot cream mixture. Strain.

5   Pour the custard base slowly over the fruit.

6   Bake at 325°F/163°C just until the custard is set, approximately 20 minutes. Cool completely before removing the tart pan.

7   Brush the surface and sides of the tart with the apricot glaze. Press the almonds around the edge of the tart.

Apple almond tart

MAKES 1 TART (9 IN/23 CM)

Pâte brisée (page 222)	10 oz	283 g
Frangipane for filling (page 896)	12 oz	340 g
Pastry cream (page 370)	8 oz	227 g
Apples, peeled, cored, and cut into ¼-in/6-mm slices	3 each	3 each
Cinnamon sugar (page 897)	2 oz	57 g
Apricot glaze (page 426), warm	3 oz	85 g
Sliced almonds, toasted and coarsely chopped	2 oz	57 g

1   Roll out the pâte brisée ⅛ in/3 mm thick and line the tart pan.

2   Combine the frangipane and pastry cream in the mixer and mix on medium speed with the paddle attachment, scraping down the bowl periodically, until well blended, about 3 minutes.

3   Pour the mixture into the tart shell and spread evenly.

4   Arrange the sliced apples on top of the pastry cream mixture in a fanned spiral, working from the center out. Sprinkle the apples with the cinnamon sugar.

5   Bake at 375°F/191°C until the filling is golden brown, about 40 minutes.

6   Using a pastry brush, brush the tart with the apricot glaze. Sprinkle the toasted almonds around the edge of the tart.

VARIATION   This tart can also be made with plums, peaches, apricots, nectarines, or other sliced fruit of choice.

Chocolate macadamia nut tart

MAKES 1 TART (9 IN/23 CM)

Chocolate short dough (page 224)	12 oz	340 g
Bittersweet chocolate, finely chopped	2 oz	57 g
Heavy cream	3 fl oz	90 mL
Instant espresso powder	1 tsp	3 g
Sugar	4 oz	113 g
Heavy cream, hot	4 fl oz	120 mL
Butter	1 oz	28 g
Macadamia nuts, lightly toasted	2 oz	57 g

1   Roll out the dough ⅛ in/3 mm thick and line the tart pan. Line the tart shell with parchment paper and fill with dry beans or pie weights. Bake the tart shell at 350°F/177°C until very light golden brown, about 15 minutes. Remove the beans and parchment and continue cooking to a golden brown, about 5 minutes. Cool completely.

2   Place the chocolate in a bowl. Bring the cream to a simmer, add the espresso, and stir until dissolved. Pour the cream over the chocolate, allow to stand for 5 minutes, and stir until melted and smooth. Cool.

3   Heat a heavy-bottomed pan. Add the sugar in small increments, stirring after each addition and making sure all the sugar is melted before adding more. Cook to a rich golden brown.

4   Remove the pan from the heat. Slowly stir in the hot cream, then stir in the butter. Cool slightly.

5   Pour approximately 2 oz/57 g of the caramel into the tart shell and spread it evenly over the bottom. Scatter half the macadamia nuts evenly over the caramel. Pour the ganache over the nuts and spread it evenly.

6   Freeze the tart for 1 hour.

7   Pour the remaining caramel onto the center of the tart and spread it evenly over the ganache. Arrange the remaining macadamia nuts on top of the tart. Refrigerate until fully chilled.

Belgian chocolate rice tart

MAKES 1 TART (9 IN/23 CM)

Pâte brisée (page 222)	10 oz	284 g
Basmati rice	3½ oz	99 g
Water	6 fl oz	180 mL
Milk	4 fl oz	120 mL
Butter	2 oz	57 g
Sugar	3½ oz	99 g
Dark chocolate, finely chopped	5⅔ oz	160 g
Egg yolks	5⅔ oz	160 g
Heavy cream	2⅔ fl oz	80 mL
Cocoa powder	as needed	as needed
Chantilly cream (page 420)	as needed	as needed

1   Roll out the pâte brisée ⅛ in/3 mm thick and line the tart pan. Line the tart shell with parchment paper and fill with dry beans or pie weights. Bake the shell at 350°F/177°C until very light golden brown, about 15 minutes. Cool completely.

2   Meanwhile, combine the rice and water in a saucepan and bring to a boil. Cover and simmer until the rice is tender, about 30 minutes. Remove from the heat.

3   Combine the milk, butter, and sugar in a saucepan and bring to a boil. Remove from the heat. Blend in the rice and chocolate and cool until just warm.

4   Add the egg yolks and cream to the rice mixture, blending well.

5   Pour the mixture into the tart shell and spread it evenly.

6   Bake at 375°F/191°C until the custard has set, about 15 minutes. Cool completely and then refrigerate until chilled.

7   Just before serving, dust the tart lightly with cocoa powder and garnish with Chantilly cream.

Walnut tart

MAKES 1 TART (9 IN/23 CM)

1-2-3 cookie dough (page 223)	10 oz	284 g
Walnuts	7 oz	198 g
Eggs	6 oz	170 g
Maple syrup	5 oz	142 g
Granulated sugar	4 oz	113 g
Butter, melted	1 oz	28 g
Brandy	1 fl oz	30 mL
Confectioners' sugar, for dusting	as needed	as needed

1   Roll out the dough ⅛ in/3 mm thick and line the tart pan. Line the tart shell with parchment paper and fill with dry beans or pie weights. Bake the tart shell at 350°F/177°C until very light golden brown, about 15 minutes. Cool completely.

2   Spread the walnuts evenly in the tart shell.

3   Combine the eggs, maple syrup, sugar, butter, and brandy, blending well. Pour into the tart shell.

4   Bake at 350°F/177°C until the filling is set, about 35 minutes. Cool completely.

5   Just before serving, dust lightly with confectioners' sugar.

Cranberry pecan tart

MAKES 1 TART (9 IN/23 CM)

1-2-3 cookie dough (page 223)	12 oz	340 g
Butter	4½ oz	128 g
Light corn syrup	10 oz	284 g
Light brown sugar	6 oz	170 g
Eggs	5 oz	142 g
Vanilla extract	1½ tsp	7.50 mL
Cranberries	2 oz	57 g
Pecans, chopped	4 oz	113 g
Pecan halves	10 oz	284 g

1   Roll out the dough ⅛ in/3 mm thick and line the tart pan. Line the tart shell with parchment paper and fill with dry beans or pie weights. Bake the tart shell at 350°F/177°C until very light golden brown, about 15 minutes. Cool completely.

2   Combine the butter, corn syrup, and sugar in a saucepan and heat, stirring, until the sugar has dissolved. Remove from the heat.

3   Whip the eggs in the mixer on medium speed with the whip attachment until pale in color and light in texture, about 5 minutes. Blend in the sugar mixture. Blend in the vanilla.

4   Spread the cranberries and chopped pecans evenly in the tart shell. Pour the filling evenly over them. Arrange the pecan halves on top of the filling in concentric circles.

5   Bake at 350°F/177°C until the filling is set, about 40 minutes. Cool completely and serve, or refrigerate until fully chilled and then serve.

Apricot clafoutis tart

MAKES 1 TART (9 IN/23 CM)

1-2-3 cookie dough (page 223)	10 oz	284 g
Apricots, halved	6 each	6 each
Cake flour	1¼ oz	35 g
Granulated sugar	1¾ oz	50 g
Butter, melted	1¾ oz	50 g
Milk	6 fl oz	180 mL
Heavy cream	6 fl oz	180 mL
Crème fraîche	½ oz	14 g
Egg yolks	1 each	1 each
Confectioners' sugar, for dusting	as needed	as needed

1   Roll out the dough ⅛ in/3 mm thick and line the tart pan. Line the tart shell with parchment paper and fill with dry beans or pie weights. Bake the tart shell at 350°F/177°C until very light golden brown, about 15 minutes. Cool completely.

2   Arrange the apricot halves in the tart shell in concentric circles with the cut sides down.

3   Whisk together the flour and sugar. Blend in the butter, milk, cream, and crème fraîche. Blend in the egg yolk.

4   Pour the filling over the apricots.

5   Bake at 350°F/177°C until the filling is set, about 45 minutes.

6   Lightly dust with confectioners' sugar. Serve warm.

Clafoutis

MAKES 10 SERVINGS (4 FL OZ/120 ML EACH)

Milk	12 fl oz	360 mL
Granulated sugar	4 oz	113 g
Salt	pinch	pinch
Vanilla beans, split and scraped	½ each	½ each
Eggs	3 each	3 each
All-purpose flour	1½ oz	43 g
Tart cherries, pitted	12 oz	340 g
Confectioners' sugar, for dusting	as needed	as needed

1   Coat 10 ramekins (4 fl oz/120 mL each) with a thin film of butter and dust them lightly with granulated sugar.

2   Combine the milk, 2 oz/57 g of the sugar, the salt, and the vanilla bean pod and seeds in a saucepan and bring to boil, stirring to dissolve the sugar.

3   Blend the eggs with the flour and the remaining 2 oz/57 g sugar to make the liaison. Temper by gradually adding about one-third of the hot milk, whisking constantly, and then add the remaining hot milk. Strain.

4   Divide the cherries equally among the prepared ramekins. Divide the custard mixture among the ramekins, pouring it over the cherries.

5   Bake in a hot water bath at 350°F/177°C until the custard is set, about 20 minutes.

6   Lightly dust with confectioners' sugar. Serve warm.

Spiced apple and dried fig cobblers

MAKES 20 COBBLERS (12 FL OZ/360 ML EACH)

Granny Smith apples	15 each	15 each
Light brown sugar	8 oz	227 g
Ground cinnamon	1¼ tsp	2.50 g
Ground nutmeg	½ tsp	1 g
Port, tawny	14 fl oz	420 mL
Red wine	14 fl oz	420 mL
Water	14 fl oz	420 mL
Granulated sugar	10 oz	284 g
Lemon juice	1 fl oz	30 mL
Oranges, cut into sixths (with peel)	2 each	2 each
Cinnamon sticks	2 each	2 each
Cloves	3 each	3 each
Black peppercorns, cracked	1 tbsp	8.50 g
Star anise, cracked	1 each	1 each
Dried figs, stem ends removed	1 lb 10 oz	737 g
Basic pie dough (page 222)	1 lb 6 oz	624 g
Egg wash (page 892)	as needed	as needed

1   Peel and core the apples. Cut into slices ¼ in/6 mm thick and toss with the brown sugar, cinnamon, and nutmeg.

2   Combine the port, red wine, water, granulated sugar, lemon juice, oranges, cinnamon sticks, cloves, peppercorns, and star anise in a pot and simmer gently for 20 minutes.

3   Strain the liquid into another pot. Add the figs and simmer until the figs are tender, about 20 minutes. Drain. (The liquid can be reserved for poaching other fruit.)

4   Cut the figs into quarters. Combine the figs with the apples.

5   Divide the filling evenly among 20 ramekins (12 fl oz/360 mL each).

6   Roll out the pie dough ¼ in/6 mm thick. Cut into 20 rounds big enough to cover the tops of the ramekins, approximately 4 in/10 cm in diameter.

7   Top the filled ramekins with the dough rounds. Lightly brush with egg wash.

8   Bake at 325°F/163°C until the tops are golden brown, about 20 minutes.

9   Serve warm.

Three-berry cobbler

MAKES 20 COBBLERS (12 FL OZ/360 ML EACH)

Strawberries, hulled and halved	2 lb	907 g
Raspberries	1 lb 10 oz	737 g
Blueberries	2 lb	907 g
Sugar	8 oz	227 g
Cornstarch	2½ oz	71 g
Basic pie dough (page 222)	1 lb 6 oz	624 g
Egg wash (page 892)	as needed	as needed

1 Combine all the berries in a bowl and toss with the sugar and cornstarch.

2 Divide the mixture evenly among 20 ramekins (12 oz/360 mL each).

3 Roll out the pie dough ¼ in/6 mm thick. Cut into 20 rounds big enough to cover the ramekins, approximately 4 in/10 cm in diameter.

4 Top the filled ramekins with the pie dough rounds. Lightly brush with egg wash.

5 Bake at 325°F/163°C until the tops are golden brown, about 20 minutes.

6 Serve warm.

Apple crisp

MAKES 20 SERVINGS (4 FL OZ/120 ML EACH)

CRISP TOPPING		
Quick-cooking oats	14 oz	397 g
Whole wheat flour	6⅓ oz	179 g
Dark brown sugar	1 lb	454 g
Sliced almonds, coarsely chopped	3⅓ oz	94 g
Ground cinnamon	1½ tbsp	9 g
Butter, cut into small cubes, chilled	12 oz	340 g
APPLE FILLING		
Golden Delicious apples, peeled, cored, and sliced ⅛ in/3 mm thick	36 each	36 each
Butter, cubed	8 oz	227 g
Light brown sugar	1 lb	454 g
Ground cinnamon	2 tsp	4 g
Dark raisins	4 oz	113 g
Golden raisins	4 oz	113 g
Salt	½ tsp	2.50 g
Lemon juice	as needed	as needed

1   To prepare the topping, combine the oats, flour, sugar, almonds, and cinnamon and toss together. Rub the butter into the mixture so that it resembles coarse meal.

2   Spread the topping mixture on a parchment-lined sheet pan and bake at 325°F/163°C until golden brown, 15 to 20 minutes. Cool.

3   To prepare the filling, sweat the apples in the butter in a large pan, stirring occasionally until they are just beginning to soften, about 5 minutes. Add the sugar and cinnamon, stirring to coat, and continue cooking until the apples are tender, about 5 minutes. Stir in the raisins and salt. Add lemon juice as necessary. Cool completely.

4   Divide the apple mixture evenly among 20 ramekins (4 fl oz/120 mL each). Top with the crisp topping.

5   Bake at 375°F/191°C until heated through, about 15 minutes.

6   Serve warm.

VARIATION   You can substitute other seasonal fruits for the apples.

Apple strudel

Granny Smith apples	5 lb	2.27 kg
Raisins	4 oz	113 g
Cinnamon sugar (page 897)	8 oz	227 g
Dried bread crumbs	6 oz	170 g
Butter, melted	8 oz	227 g
Strudel dough (page 230)	1 lb 12 oz	794 g

1   Peel and core the apples. Cut into slices ¼ in/6 mm thick and toss with the raisins and cinnamon sugar.

2   Toss the bread crumbs with 2 oz/57 g of the butter.

3   Cover a work surface with a large linen cloth and dust the cloth with bread flour. Divide the dough in half, set one portion aside, and cover. Roll the other portion into a rectangle 12 by 18 in/30 by 46 cm on the floured cloth and let the dough relax for 15 minutes, covered or buttered to prevent drying.

4   To stretch the dough, work with two people on opposite sides of the table. Place your hands under the dough and begin to lift and stretch it from the center out. Continue stretching until the dough is very thin and almost transparent.

5   Brush the dough with 4 oz/113 g of the remaining melted butter. Sprinkle half the bread crumbs evenly over the entire surface of the stretched dough and then place half of the sliced apples in a strip along one of the edges of the dough. Roll up the dough, starting by lifting up one edge of the linen, then continuing to use the linen to help you roll so that the pastry forms a tight log. Transfer the strudel to a sheet pan and repeat with the remaining dough and filling.

6   Brush the tops of the strudels with the rest of the melted butter. Vent the tops of the strudels by making a 1-in/3-cm cut in the dough at 2-in/5-cm intervals.

7   Bake at 350°F/177°C until light golden brown, about 25 minutes.

8   Serve immediately.

Warm apple charlottes

MAKES 12 CHARLOTTES (4½ FL OZ/135 ML EACH)

Butter	10 oz	284 g
Granny Smith apples, peeled, cored, and sliced ⅛ in/3 mm thick	2 lb	907 g
Vanilla beans, seeds only	1 each	1 each
Light brown sugar	4 oz	113 g
Ground ginger	1 tsp	2 g
Apricot jam	4 oz	113 g
Brandy	4 fl oz	120 mL
Lemon juice	1 fl oz	30 mL
Wheat Pullman loaves (page 125)	1 each	1 each

1   Place 2 oz/57 g of the butter in a sauté pan over medium-high heat and let it melt but not brown. Add the apples, vanilla bean seeds, sugar, and ginger and cook until the apples are just tender, about 5 minutes. Melt the remaining 8 oz/227 g of butter and reserve.

2   Add the apricot jam, brandy, and lemon juice, bring to a simmer, and cook over medium heat until nearly all the liquid has evaporated. Remove from the heat and let cool.

3   Remove the crust from the Pullman loaf and slice it into ¼-in/6-mm slices.

4   Brush each slice of bread with the melted butter. Quarter 20 slices.

5   Using 7 to 8 quarters of bread per mold, line the sides of 12 ramekins (4½ fl oz/135 mL each), slightly overlapping the pieces as necessary to completely cover the sides.

6   Using a 3-in/8-cm round cutter, cut 24 circles from the remaining Pullman slices. Place a round in the base of each ramekin.

7   Fill each ramekin with apple filling, pressing it down gently to pack it lightly. Top each filled ramekin with another Pullman round.

8   Bake at 375°F/191°C until golden brown, about 50 minutes. Unmold and serve warm with a sauce of choice and whipped cream if desired.

Cranberry pear strudel

MAKES 2 STRUDELS (24 IN/61 CM EACH), 24 SERVINGS

Dried cranberries	4 oz	113 g
White rum	4 fl oz	120 mL
Dried bread crumbs	4 oz	113 g
Butter	12 oz	340 g
Bartlett pears	5 lb	2.27 kg
Cinnamon sugar (page 897)	6 oz	170 g
Lemon juice	2 fl oz	60 mL
Strudel dough (page 230)	1 lb 12 oz	794 g

1   Soak the cranberries in the rum for 30 minutes, or until fully plumped; drain.

2   Sauté the bread crumbs in ½ oz/14 g of the butter until golden brown.

3   Peel and core the pears. Cut into slices ¼ in/6 mm thick and combine with the cranberries, cinnamon sugar, and lemon juice.

4   Cover a work surface with a large linen cloth and dust the cloth with flour. Divide the dough in half; set one portion aside and cover. Roll the remaining portion into a rectangle 12 by 18 in/30 by 46 cm on the floured cloth and allow the dough to relax for 15 minutes covered or buttered to prevent drying. Melt the remaining butter.

5   To stretch the dough, work with two people on opposite sides of the table. Place your hands under the dough and begin to lift and stretch the dough from the center out. Continue stretching until the dough is very thin and almost transparent.

6   Brush the dough with 4 oz/113 g of the remaining butter. Sprinkle half the bread crumbs evenly over the entire surface of the stretched dough and then place half of the sliced pears in a strip along one of the edges of the dough. Roll up the dough, starting by lifting one edge of the linen, then continuing to use the linen to help you roll so that the pastry forms a tight log. Transfer to a sheet pan and repeat with the remaining dough and filling.

7   Brush the tops of the strudels with the rest of the melted butter. Vent the tops of the strudels by making a 1-in/3-cm cut in the dough at 2-in/5-cm intervals.

8   Bake at 350°F/177°C until light golden brown. Brush the strudels again with butter and bake until golden brown, about 25 minutes.

9   Serve immediately.

Apple fritters

MAKES 20 FRITTERS (4 OZ/113 G EACH)

Berliner dough (page 146)	3 lb	1.36 kg
Pâte à choux (page 228)	8¾ oz	248 g
Golden Delicious apples, cut into brunoise	1 lb 2¾ oz	532 g
Cinnamon sugar (page 897)	¾ oz plus as needed	21 g plus as needed
Oil, for deep frying	as needed	as needed

1   Line sheet pans with parchment paper and grease lightly.

2   Roll the Berliner dough into a rectangle 12 by 16 in/30 by 41 cm; the dough should be ¼ in/6 mm thick.

3   With an offset spatula, spread the pâte à choux in an even layer (⅛ in/3 mm) over the Berliner dough, leaving a 1-in/3-cm strip of dough exposed along one long side.

4   Toss the apples with the cinnamon sugar and scatter evenly over the pâte à choux. Brush the exposed strip of dough lightly with water.

5   Starting with the side opposite the exposed strip, roll the dough up into a tight, even cylinder. Roll the cylinder gently back and forth to seal the seam.

6   Using a serrated knife, slice the cylinder into pieces ¾ in/2 cm wide. Lay the slices on the prepared sheet pans, leaving 1 in/3 cm between them to allow them to expand.

7   Proof, covered, until the dough springs back slowly to the touch but does not collapse, about 45 minutes.

8   Using a paring knife, cut the parchment paper around the fritters into individual squares.

9   Carefully flip each fritter into a deep fryer (350°F/177°C), quickly peel off the parchment, and fry until golden brown on the first side, 2 to 3 minutes. Turn and fry until the second side is golden and the fritter is cooked through, 2 to 3 minutes longer.

10   Lift the fritters from the hot oil with a spider or basket, allowing the oil to drain away over the fryer. Drain on paper towels briefly before rolling in cinnamon sugar.

chapter sixteen

Filled and assembled cacks and tortes

W hen selecting components to build a cake or torte, it is important to consider the combination of flavors and textures. Classic cakes and tortes are fine examples of flavor combinations and appealing designs and offer a foundation of inspiration for contemporary applications. Contemporary cakes and tortes explore new flavor combinations generated from the globalization of cuisine and culture.

Basics of cake assembly

Fillings for cakes may complement or contrast the flavor of the cake. For example, a chocolate cake could be filled with either a chocolate or a raspberry filling. The chocolate filling would make a richer cake, while the raspberry filling, with its fresh berry flavor, would cut the richness of the chocolate cake.

Texture is also important when selecting a filling for a cake. The general rule is that the texture of the filling should match that of the cake. Lighter aerated fillings should be used with lighter cakes, such as sponge or chiffon; a mousse filling should never be paired with a pound cake. Richer fillings such as paddled hard ganache or cream fillings are better choices for pairing with rich creamed cakes. When filling a cake with a rich, heavy filling, use less than you would if using a lighter, more delicate filling.

1. Cakes should be allowed to cool completely before cutting into layers. Cut the cakes into layers between ¼ and ½ in/6 mm and 1 cm thick. Typically, thinner layers will make a better cake than thicker layers. Fillings that are spread onto layers should generally be less than ½ in/1 cm thick and should not exceed the thickness of the cake layers. However, poured fillings such as Bavarian cream can be applied in layers thicker than the cake layers, as they are usually less rich and have a lighter texture than spread fillings.

2. Before slicing a cake into layers, trim any uneven areas from the sides and top. For the best results, use a cake-decorating turntable and a knife with a long, thin, serrated blade. Set the cake on a cardboard cake round and then on the turntable. First divide the cake by eye into the desired number of layers. Then insert the knife into the side

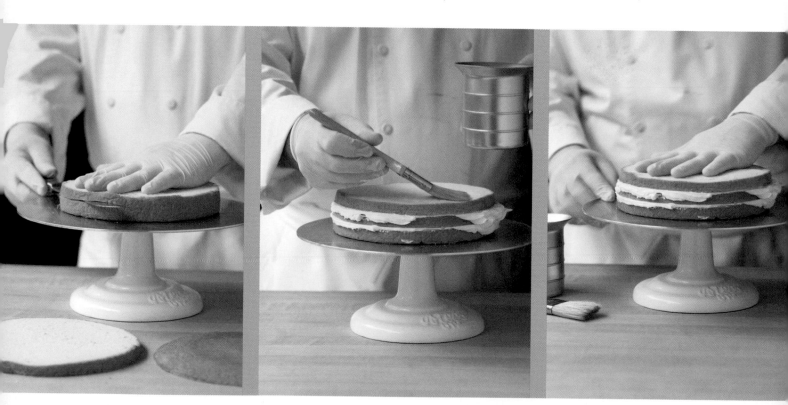

LEFT: Cutting even layers is important to the final portioned presentation of a cake.

MIDDLE: Soak the cut layers lightly with simple syrup.

RIGHT: Place the top layer onto a cake that has been filled with buttercream and press it gently into place.

of the cake at the appropriate level and, holding the knife steady and level and slowly rotating the turntable, move the blade of the knife into the cake to cut the layer. Remove the layer and set aside; repeat as necessary.

3. Brush loose crumbs from the cake layers. Brushing loose crumbs from the cake layers is done to prevent the crumbs from becoming incorporated into the final coat of icing or glaze.

4. Brush any of a variety of syrups, from plain simple syrup to one infused with spices or flavored with a liqueur, evenly over the cut surface of each layer as the cake is assembled. The syrup adds moisture to drier layers and adds flavor. The layers should be moistened but not drowned. In assembly, the cut surfaces of the cake should be moistened with simple syrup and should face the interior of the cake. For ease of application of any glaze or icing the cut surface should not be exposed—seal with ganache, buttercream, or jam if necessary. the bottom of a cake may be coated with thinned chocolate to seal it and to ease serving.

functions of garnish

The garnish for items in a bakery or pastry shop serves several important functions, one of which is adding visual appeal. Although a perfectly iced or glazed but otherwise unadorned cake can be a thing of beauty, it requires more interest and intricacy to entice most customers. Garnishing also gives bakers or pastry chefs a chance to display their skill. They can use their imagination, creativity, and knowledge to garnish cakes and pastries, using techniques and ingredients in unique combinations to make items look enticing and exciting.

Garnish can also be used to indicate the flavors and ingredients in the cake or pastry item. This serves the customers, helping them make a selection by informing them of the flavors used in the cake or pastry. For example, a Black Forest cake is a chocolate cake with a filling of cherries, and the typical garnish is chocolate shavings and whole preserved cherries.

Classic cakes, tortes, and pastries often have a specific, traditional way in which they have been garnished since their inception. The décor (garnish) of an item like this is always the same, serving both as a way to identify these items and as homage to the place or person responsible for the original cake or pastry.

In garnishing a cake or torte there are two basic approaches to the décor. The cake may be thought of as a whole, or it may be considered in terms of portions. Decorating a cake with portions in mind is an approach that developed in pastry shops where cakes are traditionally sold by the slice. Decorating cakes as a whole is the preferred approach where cakes are sold as a whole piece.

The final garnish on a cake can be used to illustrate the flavors contained within or to add a decorative element.

Molding cakes

Cakes assembled in a mold are those with delicate fillings that must set before they can be sliced and served. Examples of molded cake fillings include gelatin-based Bavarian cream, gelatin-based mousse, and softened ice cream.

1. Prepare the mold. A cake ring, also known as an entremet ring, may be used, in which case the ring should be set on a cardboard cake round on a flat sheet pan so the cake has a stable, movable, level base. Closed molds, such as bowls used to prepare charlottes or bombes, or cake pans, may also be used. If a closed mold is used, the cake will be inverted onto a serving plate, platter, or board when unmolded. Closed molds are often lined with plastic to ease unmolding.

2. Cut the cake layers to fit the mold. If the mold has graduated or tapered sides, the layers should have varying diameters to fit the mold. The layers may be cut so they will touch the sides of the mold, in which case their edges will be exposed when the cake is unmolded, making it necessary to finish or ice the sides of the cake. Or the layers may be cut so that a gap is left between the edge of the cake and the mold, and in this case the filling will surround the layers, serving as both icing and filling.

    In some instances, slices of cake may be used to line the sides of the mold as well. Used in this way, the cake adds an element of décor as well as flavor. Slices of roulade filled with jam are used to create the classic spiral finish for a charlotte royale. Layers of thin sponge cake tightly layered with jam may be sliced and used to create a basketweave or striped pattern. Other effects can be achieved using Joconde cake and stenciled, spread, or piped décor batter. Ladyfingers are the classic finish for charlotte russe.

3. Usually a cake layer is placed into the mold first. The exception is for molds such as bombes, which are inverted in unmolding so that the bottom becomes the top of the cake. In either case, cake and filling are added to the mold in alternating layers.

4. Each layer of cake should be moistened before it is placed in the mold.

5. Be sure to center the layers in the mold. The filling can be poured, spooned, or piped into the mold, but it is essential to add an equal amount each time to form layers of equal thickness.

6. You can add garnishes to the filling for additional flavor and textural interest. Fold the garnish ingredient into the filling to spread it evenly throughout the mixture, or sprinkle the garnish ingredients into the mold before adding the filling. The second technique is especially common with fresh fruit, to create a layer of garnish. Then the garnish is topped with filling (be sure the garnish remains evenly distributed and does not shift).

7. The top of a molded cake may be either filling or a cake layer. If a cake is to be iced with buttercream, the top layer must be cake. When the top of the cake will be glazed with a clear, marbleized, or lightly colored glaze, the top layer of the cake should be filling. Be sure to leave enough space at the top of the mold (approximately ⅛ in/3 mm) for the glaze.

8. Molded cakes are generally frozen or refrigerated in the mold so the filling and structure of the cake will be firm enough to withstand unmolding. To release the cake from the mold or ring, warm the sides by either dipping the mold in warm water or carefully running a lighted propane torch around the sides.

TOP LEFT: Placing décor sponge into ring

BOTTOM LEFT: Placing middle cake layer into ring

TOP RIGHT: Ladling mousse into ring

BOTTOM RIGHT: Smoothing top of Bavarian layer

Icing cakes

When icing a cake, you may wish to use a turntable. Some pastry chefs prefer to hold the cake (on its cardboard circle) on their fingertips and rotate it as they work. Either approach can yield excellent results, although holding the cake on your fingertips requires more control than using a turntable.

The best and most consistent way to achieve a clean coat of icing is to apply two coats. First apply a thin seal coat or crumb coat and allow it to set completely under refrigeration. This coat does not necessarily have to be the same icing as the final coat; it is intended to attach any loose crumbs to the cake and prevent them from becoming incorporated in the final coat. Choose something that is a complementary flavor; it can be a jam or jelly, a buttercream, or ganache—anything that will seal the cake and ease the application of the final coat. This first coat should be very thin to ensure that there will not be too much icing applied to the cake overall; it may even be thin enough so that the layers of cake are visible through the coating on the side. After the first coat has set, apply the thicker second layer.

1. Apply the icing generously to the top of the cake first, spreading it smoothly and evenly all the way out to the edges of the cake and slightly over them. The final coat of icing on a cake should be applied after a first coating, often referred to as a crumb coat; this first coating seals the cake and, once chilled, facilitates the application of the final icing.

2. Ice the sides of the cake: holding the spatula vertically so its tip points to the base of the cake, spread the icing onto the sides. Apply a generous amount of icing to the sides to ease smoothing and ensure a smooth finish. The size of the spatula depends on the size of the cake as well as what feels comfortable to you.

3. To smooth the sides of the cake, after applying the icing, hold the spatula vertically against the cake at a 45-degree angle, with the edge of the spatula touching the icing, and rotate the cake (by turning your hand or turning the turntable) against the spatula. (If you are holding the cake on your fingertips, hold the spatula with the handle below the cake; if you are working on a turntable, the tip of the spatula should just touch its surface.) This will not only smooth the icing but will also cause some of the excess icing from the sides to rise above the top of the cake, making a lip or ridge. Working from the edges toward the center and holding the spatula parallel to the top of the cake at a 45-degree angle, with its edge touching the surface, smooth the lip over and across the top to create a perfectly smooth top and a sharp angled edge.

4. At this point, the cake can be marked into portions if desired, using a straight-edged knife or long straight metal spatula. A variety of simple garnishes or décor can also be applied to the top of the cake. Garnishes and decorations can be added by piping the icing, filling, or glaze (such as a shell border or rosettes), with or without additional garnishes such as chocolate cutouts or cigarettes, tuiles, florentines, fresh berries or jam, and the like. The side of the cake can be finished using a spatula to a smooth surface, or using a cake comb or other tool to leave a texture or pattern. Garnishes such as toasted chopped nuts, cake crumbs, or chocolate shavings may be applied to the side of a cake by sprinkling or gently pressing to adhere. More intricate cakes are often adorned with piping or other fine décor work.

TOP LEFT: A crumb coat is applied to the sides of the cake.

BOTTOM LEFT: The top is smoothed last to create sharp, distinct edges.

TOP RIGHT: Icing is applied to the sides after it is applied to the top.

BOTTOM RIGHT: Combing the sides of a cake is only one of countless ways it may be finished.

Working with gelatin-based fillings

Gelatin-based fillings can be poured or piped to fill a wide variety of cakes and pastries. In either case, the fillings must be used immediately after they are made, before they set up.

Assemble all components, ingredients, and necessary equipment before beginning to make the filling. Be sure all advance preparation (e.g., whipping cream, slicing cake layers, cutting up fruit) is done. Then prepare the filling and assemble the cake or pastry.

Assembling a traditional layer cake

Traditional layer cakes call for different equipment and finishing techniques from molded cakes. The cake should be filled according to the type of cake (i.e., Black Forest, Boston cream, etc.) or flavor profile you desire. Filling options include jam, pudding, pastry cream, curd, buttercream, paddled ganache, whipped cream, mousse, and the like.

1. To assemble the cake, slice into layers. Cakes should be cooled completely before cutting into layers. Typically, thinner layers (¼ in to 1 cm thick) make for more uniform, even-flavored, and even-textured cakes. Divide the cake by eye into layers before cutting. Before beginning assembly, brush any loose crumbs from the layer surfaces.

2. Moisten with simple syrup if necessary. A simple syrup will add moisture to dryer layers (such as sponges). Simple syrup may also be flavored with liquor or infused with spice, thus lending additional flavor to a product. Syrup should be spread over the cut, interior-facing cake layers. The layers should be moistened, not soaked.

3. Place a dab of the filling or icing in the center of a cake round the same diameter as the cake and center the first cake layer on it. For ease of application of any glaze or icing, as well as for serving, the top and bottom layers of a cake should never be a cut surface.

4. Spread a layer of filling evenly over the layer. The amount of filling is determined by the type of filling used, its consistency (i.e., its lightness or density), and the intensity of its flavor. If the filling is the right consistency for piping, a good way to ensure an even layer is to use a pastry bag and pastry tip to fill the cake layers. Keep in mind that too much filling can cause the layers to slip as the cake is assembled and sliced. To keep certain types of fillings from oozing out between the layers as the cake is assembled or sliced, you can pipe a ring of buttercream or other icing around the edge of each layer before adding the filling.

5. As you assemble the cake, take time to straighten the layers if necessary.

6. Brush away any excess crumbs from the sides of the cake.

7. Once the cake is assembled, apply a thin layer of the icing, or, in some instances, the filling or a jam, to the top and sides of the cake for the seal or crumb coat. This coat adheres any remaining crumbs onto the cake, preventing them from becoming incorporated in the final coating of icing or glaze and marring its appearance.

The crumb coat does not have to be the same icing as the final coat. A complementary flavor may be chosen; anything that will seal the cake, thus facilitating the application of the final coat, is appropriate. The layer should be thin to ensure that there will not be too much icing applied to the cake.

8. The cake, with the crumb coat, is often refrigerated for an hour or so to allow the coating to set before applying the final coating of icing. This will ease the application of the final icing and ensure a smooth finished surface.

Glazing a cake

1. To glaze a traditional layer cake, apply a thin seal coat layer of something such as paddled ganache or jam to the cake. Refrigerate until the seal coat is set.

2. Prepare a glazing setup by placing a wire rack on a sheet pan. The rack will allow the glaze to run freely from the sides of the cake, while the sheet pan will catch the excess glaze, which, if it does not contain any crumbs, can be rewarmed and used on another item. Have ready a straight or offset long metal spatula for spreading the glaze. Before you glaze, if you desire, reserve some of the glaze for the décor.

3. Place the cake on the center of the wire rack. Check the consistency and temperature of the glaze. If it is too thick, rewarm it or, for glazes such as fondant, adjust the fluidity and temperature. The glaze should not be too warm, or it will not coat properly. It may run too much and could cause the seal coat to begin to melt, making it difficult to achieve the glossy look of a properly applied glaze. Be careful not to stir the glaze too much, as this will incorporate air and cause bubbles in the glaze on the surface of the cake.

Glazing a cake

4. Pour enough glaze onto the center of the cake to enrobe it. Working quickly, spread the glaze over the entire top of the cake with three swipes of a long metal icing spatula, working across the top of the cake in one direction (always pushing or drawing the glaze away from you) from one side to the other and then off the cake. Do not lift the spatula while it is on the cake, or it will pull up the seal coat and cause crumbs to become mixed with the glaze, destroying the finish; pulling or drawing the spatula toward you can have the same effect. In addition to covering the top of the cake, this technique will cause the glaze to run down over the sides, covering them as well. Once the top of the cake is covered, use the spatula to spread glaze over any small portions of the sides of the cake that were not covered.

5. Check the finish on the top of the cake. If any air bubbles have formed, they can be removed if you act quickly, using a sharp skewer, or by moving the flame of a propane torch over the surface.

Enrobing a cake in marzipan   Cutting a traditional Florentine garnish

Enrobing a cake in marzipan or other rolled icing

Marzipan is often used as a covering for cakes. It may be used as the final coating, or it may be used as an undercoating that is covered with an icing or glaze.

1. If it is to be covered, roll the marzipan very thin (approximately ¹⁄₁₆ in/1.5 mm). If it is to be the finished covering, roll it to approximately ¼ in/6 mm thick; this is thick enough to ensure a smooth finished surface. Marzipan can be rolled thin in order to be covered with an icing or a glaze. Another example of a rolled icing used to cover cakes is rolled fondant, a formable mixture of gelatin, water, corn syrup, glycerin, and confectioners' sugar.

2. Before applying the marzipan or other rolled icing, prepare the surface of the cake. Trim the sides so they are even, and apply a seal coat. The jam or buttercream coating should be thin so that the marzipan or icing will not slip or slide.

3. Apply the marzipan to the cake, using the palm of your hand in a circular motion to create a smooth, flat surface.

4. The cake is now ready to be finished.

Bavarian cream torte

MAKES 1 TORTE (8 IN/20 CM), 10 SERVINGS

Vanilla sponge (page 268)	1 each	1 each
Vanilla simple syrup (page 901)	5 fl oz	150 mL
Strawberry yogurt Bavarian (page 395)	1 lb	454 g
Heavy cream, whipped	16 fl oz	480 mL
Strawberries, halved	5 each	5 each
Dark chocolate shavings (see page 831)	1 oz	28 g

1   Place an 8-in/20-cm cake round on a sheet pan and place an 8-in/20-cm cake ring on top.

2   Slice the sponge cake into 3 even layers (between ¼ and ½ in/6 mm and 1 cm thick).

3   Place the layer cut from the bottom of the cake into the bottom of the cake ring with the cut side up and moisten it with simple syrup. Ladle 8 oz/227 g of the Bavarian cream on top of the sponge and spread it into an even layer. Top with a second sponge layer, cut from the center of the cake, and press down gently. Moisten the sponge with simple syrup. Ladle in the remaining 8 oz/227 g Bavarian cream and spread it evenly. Moisten the cut side of the remaining piece of cake with simple syrup, place it cut side down on top of the filling, and press down gently.

4   Cover the torte with plastic wrap and refrigerate or freeze until fully set.

5   To finish the torte, remove the plastic wrap. Warm the sides of the cake ring using a propane torch or a towel moistened with warm water and carefully remove the ring.

6   Coat the top and sides of the torte with whipped cream, reserving 6 oz/170 g for the finishing décor. Using a pastry bag fitted with a #5 plain tip, pipe 10 small domes of whipped cream around the outer edge of the top of the torte to mark portions. Place a strawberry half on each dome, resting it at a 45-degree angle pointing toward the center of the torte.

7   Garnish the bottom quarter edge of the side of the torte by gently pressing the chocolate shavings to adhere.

Charlotte royale

MAKES 1 CAKE (8 IN/20 CM), 10 SERVINGS

Frangipane cake sheet (page 330), 13½ by 17½ in/34 by 44 cm sheet	1 each	1 each
Raspberry jam	2 lb	907 g
Raspberry Bavarian cream (page 393)	2 lb	907 g
Vanilla sponge (page 268), 8 in/20 cm	1 each	1 each
Vanilla simple syrup (page 901)	3 fl oz	90 mL
Apricot glaze (page 426), warm	1 lb	454 g

1   Trim the edges of the frangipane and cut crosswise into 3 equal pieces. Spread a thin layer of jam on one strip and top with a second strip. Spread with jam and top with the final strip of frangipane. Cut the layered cake into 1-in/3-cm strips and cut each strip into slices ¼ in/6 mm thick.

2   Line a domed mold (48 fl oz/1.44 L) with plastic wrap, making sure some is hanging out of the mold. Line the mold with the frangipane slices to create a basketweave pattern.

3   Fill the mold with the raspberry Bavarian cream. Moisten the sponge with the simple syrup, place it top down on the filling, and press down gently. Cover with plastic wrap and refrigerate until completely set.

4   Unmold the bombe onto a cardboard round and place on an icing screen. Warm the apricot glaze and apply to the entire surface of the bombe. Allow to set and serve immediately or refrigerate.

Charlotte russe

MAKES 1 CAKE (8 IN/20 CM), 10 SERVINGS

Chocolate sponge (page 268), 8 in/20 cm	1 each	1 each
Vanilla simple syrup (page 901)	5 fl oz	150 mL
Ladyfingers (page 340)	20–25 each	20–25 each
Chocolate Bavarian cream (page 393)	8 oz	227 g
Bavarian cream (page 393)	8 oz	227 g
White chocolate shavings (see page 831)	2 oz	57 g
Dark chocolate shavings (see page 831)	2 oz	57 g

1   Place an 8-in/20-cm cake ring on an 8-in/20-cm cardboard cake round. Trim the sponge to a 7½-in/19-cm round. Slice the sponge into 3 even layers (between ¼ and ½ in/6 mm and 1 cm thick). Place one of the sponge layers in the bottom of the mold and moisten with simple syrup.

2   Line the inside of the ring with the ladyfingers, flat side facing in. Ladle the chocolate Bavarian cream on top of the sponge and spread it into an even layer. Top with the second layer of sponge and press down gently. Moisten the sponge layer with simple syrup. Ladle in the vanilla Bavarian cream and spread it evenly.

3   Cover with plastic wrap and refrigerate until the Bavarian cream has set completely.

4   Remove the plastic wrap and carefully lift away the cake ring.

5   Place a 4-in/10-cm ring in the center of the top of the cake and carefully fill it with the white chocolate shavings. Fill the space between the ring and the tops of the ladyfingers with the dark chocolate shavings. Remove the ring.

Chocolate sabayon torte

MAKES 1 TORTE (8 IN/20 CM), 10 SERVINGS

Chocolate sponge (page 268), 8 in/20 cm	1 each	1 each
Vanilla simple syrup (page 901)	4 fl oz	120 mL
Chocolate sabayon mousse (page 391)	1 lb 4 oz	567 g
Soft ganache (page 421), whipped to medium peaks	1 lb	454 g
Cake crumbs	as needed	as needed
Chocolate triangles (see page 827)	10 each	10 each
Chocolate shavings (see page 831)	1 oz	28 g

1 Slice 2 even layers from the sponge (between ¼ and ½ in/6 mm and 1 cm thick). Moisten the sponge layers with simple syrup. Place one layer in the bottom of an 8-in/20-cm cake ring. Add 10 oz/284 g of the sabayon and spread it evenly. Place another sponge layer in the mold and top with the remaining 10 oz/284 g sabayon. Place the final sponge layer on top.

2 Cover with plastic wrap and refrigerate until the sabayon has set completely.

3 To finish the cake, remove the plastic wrap. Warm the sides of the cake ring using a propane torch or a towel moistened with warm water and carefully remove the ring.

4 Ice the cake with whipped ganache, reserving 4 oz/113 g for décor. Trim the edge with cake crumbs. Using a pastry bag fitted with a #5 plain tip, pipe 10 small domes of whipped ganache around the outer edge of the top of the cake to mark portions.

5 Fan the chocolate triangles around the cake, placing the base end of each at the center of the cake and fixing the opposite end to a piped dome so each stands at a 45-degree angle. Garnish the bottom quarter edge of the side of the cake by gently pressing the chocolate shavings to adhere.

Wine cream torte

MAKES 1 TORTE (8 IN/20 CM), 10 SERVINGS

Large strawberries	13 each	13 each
Vanilla sponge (page 268), 8 in/20 cm	1 each	1 each
Simple syrup (page 900)	3 fl oz	90 mL
Wine Bavarian cream (page 393)	1 lb	454 g
Heavy cream, whipped to medium peaks	16 fl oz	480 mL
Dark chocolate shavings (see page 831)	as needed	as needed

1   Place an 8-in/20-cm cake ring on an 8-in/20-cm cardboard round and then on a sheet pan.

2   Halve 8 of the strawberries. Line the inside of the cake ring with the strawberry halves, with the cut sides facing out.

3   Slice 2 even layers from the sponge (between ¼ and ½ in/6 mm and 1 cm thick) and trim to 7-in/18-cm rounds. Place one layer in the bottom of the cake ring and moisten with simple syrup. Ladle 8 oz/227 g of wine Bavarian cream on top of the sponge and spread it into an even layer. Top with the second sponge layer and press down gently. Moisten the sponge with syrup. Ladle in the remaining 8 oz/227 g wine Bavarian cream and spread it evenly.

4   Cover with plastic wrap and refrigerate until completely set.

5   Remove the plastic wrap. Warm the sides of the cake ring using a propane torch or a towel moistened with warm water and carefully remove the ring.

6   Coat the top and sides of the cake with whipped cream, reserving 4 oz/113 g for garnish. Using a pastry bag fitted with a #5 plain tip, pipe 10 small domes of whipped cream around the outer edge of the top of the cake to mark portions. Slice the remaining strawberries in half and place a strawberry half on each dome.

7   Garnish the bottom quarter edge of the side of the cake by gently pressing the chocolate shavings to adhere.

Black Forest cake

MAKES 1 CAKE (8 IN/20 CM), 10 SERVINGS

Chocolate sponge (page 268), 8 in/20 cm	1 each	1 each
Kirsch-flavored simple syrup (page 900)	5 fl oz	150 mL
Soft ganache (page 421), whipped to medium peaks	1 lb	454 g
Cherry filling (page 521)	12 oz	340 g
Heavy cream, whipped	10 fl oz	300 mL
Brandied cherries	10 each	10 each
Chocolate shavings (see page 831)	2 oz	57 g

1 Slice 3 even layers from the sponge (between ¼ and ½ in/6 mm and 1 cm thick). Place one layer on an 8-in/20-cm cardboard cake round and moisten with simple syrup.

2 Using a pastry bag fitted with a #5 plain tip, pipe a ring of whipped ganache around the outer edge of the cake layer; then, leaving a gap of approximately 2 in/5 cm, pipe a circle of the ganache in the center of the layer. Fill the gap between the whipped ganache with cherry filling. Top with a second layer of sponge and pipe the remaining ganache evenly over it. Top with the last layer of sponge.

3 Finish the top and sides of the cake with whipped cream. Using a #5 plain tip, pipe 10 domes of whipped cream around the outer edge of the top of the cake to mark portions. Garnish each dome with a brandied cherry.

4 Pile some chocolate shavings in the center of the cake and garnish the bottom edge of the side of the cake by gently pressing the chocolate shavings to adhere.

CLOCKWISE FROM TOP CENTER: Hazelnut Torte (page 573), Bavarian Cream
Torte (page 565), Wine Cream Torte (page 569), Havana Torte (page 576),
Black Forest Cake (opposite)

Dobos torte

MAKES 1 TORTE (8 IN/20 CM), 10 SERVINGS

Dobos sponge layers (page 276), 8 in/20 cm	7 each	7 each
Brandy-flavored simple syrup (see page 900)	6 fl oz	180 mL
Mocha buttercream (page 418)	1 lb 8 oz	680 g
Sugar	6 oz	170 g
Lemon juice	¼ tsp	1.25 mL
Glucose syrup	1¼ oz	35 g
Butter, soft	1 oz	28 g
Chocolate, melted, tempered (see page 762)	8 oz	227 g

1   Trim the edges of 6 of the Dobos layers to make them 8 in/20 cm in diameter. Place one layer on an 8-in/20-cm cardboard cake round. Moisten with simple syrup and, reserving 8 oz/227 g of the buttercream for décor, apply a thin, even layer of buttercream. Top with a second Dobos layer, moisten with syrup, and spread with buttercream. Repeat the process with the remaining trimmed layers. Finish the top and sides of the cake with buttercream.

2   To prepare the caramel, combine the sugar, lemon juice, and glucose syrup in a heavy-bottomed saucepan set over medium heat and allow it to melt, stirring to dissolve. When all the sugar has dissolved, stop stirring and cook to the desired color. Remove from the heat and stir in the butter.

3   Spread the caramel in an even layer over the reserved Dobos layer. Cut into 10 even wedges and allow to cool completely. Dip the rounded edge of each wedge in the tempered chocolate. Allow to set completely.

4   Mark the torte into 10 portions. Using a pastry bag fitted with a #5 plain tip, pipe a small dome of buttercream on each portion. Fan the caramel-coated wedges around the torte, placing the pointed tip of each wedge at the center of the torte and fixing the opposite end in a buttercream dome to create a "pinwheel" effect.

Hazelnut torte

MAKES 1 TORTE (8 IN/20 CM), 10 SERVINGS

Hazelnut sponge (page 277), 8 in/20 cm	1 each	1 each
Brandy-flavored simple syrup (see page 900)	4 fl oz	120 mL
Raspberry jam	1½ oz	43 g
Hazelnut buttercream (page 418)	2 lb	907 g
Hazelnut Florentine (page 574), 8 in/20 cm	1 each	1 each
Hazelnuts, toasted and ground	2 oz	57 g

1   Slice 3 even layers from the sponge (between ¼ and ½ in/6 mm and 1 cm thick). Place one layer on an 8-in/20-cm cardboard round and moisten with simple syrup. Spread the jam in a thin, even layer on the first layer of sponge and then apply an even coating of buttercream. Top with a second sponge layer and press down gently. Moisten with syrup, apply an even coating of buttercream, and top with the remaining sponge layer.

2   Finish the top and sides of the torte with buttercream. Mark into 10 portions. Using a pastry bag fitted with a #5 plain tip, pipe a small dome of buttercream on each portion.

3   Cut the Florentine into 10 equal wedges. Fan the wedges around the torte, placing the pointed tip of each at the center of the torte and laying the opposite end on a dome to create a "pinwheel" effect.

4   Garnish the bottom quarter edge of the side of the torte by gently pressing the ground hazelnuts to adhere.

Hazelnut Florentine

MAKES 6 CIRCLES (8 IN/20 CM EACH)

Heavy cream	7 fl oz	210 mL
Sugar	8 oz	227 g
Butter	2 oz	57 g
Hazelnuts, finely ground	12 oz	340 g
Cake flour	½ oz	14 g

1   Trace six 8-in/20-cm circles on parchment paper. Line sheet pans with the parchment paper. Combine the cream, sugar, and butter in a saucepan and bring to a boil.

2   Blend in the hazelnuts and flour. Remove the pan from the heat.

3   Divide the mixture among the 6 circles; spread thinly and evenly.

4   Bake at 300°F/149°C until golden brown, about 20 minutes.

5   Allow the Florentines to rest on the sheet pans until they are set and no longer sticky, but are still warm.

6   Place an 8-in/20-cm cardboard cake round on top of each Florentine and trim the edges using a pastry wheel.

7   Immediately cut each round into 10 even wedges. Cool completely before applying to a cake.

VARIATIONS   **CHOCOLATE-DIPPED FLORENTINES** Dip ¼ in/6 mm of the end opposite the tip of each wedge in tempered chocolate.

CONFECTIONERS' SUGAR–DUSTED FLORENTINES Place a 7-in/18-cm cardboard cake round on top of the Florentine wedges while they are assembled in a circle and dust with confectioners' sugar.

Mocha torte

MAKES 1 TORTE (8 IN/20 CM), 10 SERVINGS

Vanilla sponge (page 268), 8 in/20 cm	1 each	1 each
Chocolate sponge (page 268), 8 in/20 cm	1 each	1 each
Coffee simple syrup (page 900)	8 fl oz	240 mL
Chocolate buttercream (page 418)	1 lb 6 oz	624 g
Marzipan coffee beans, for garnish	10 each	10 each
Hard ganache (page 421)	6 oz	170 g
Chocolate shavings (see page 831)	2 oz	57 g

1   Slice 2 even layers from each of the sponges (between ¼ and ½ in/6 mm and 1 cm thick).

2   Place a layer of the vanilla sponge on an 8-in/20-cm cardboard cake round and moisten with simple syrup. Apply an even coating of buttercream to the sponge layer, reserving 6 oz/170 g of the buttercream for décor. Top with a layer of chocolate sponge and press it down gently. Moisten with simple syrup and apply an even coating of buttercream. Top with the remaining vanilla sponge layer and apply an even coating of buttercream. Top with the remaining chocolate sponge layer.

3   Coat the top and sides of the torte with buttercream. Mark into 10 portions. Using a pastry bag fitted with a #5 plain tip, pipe a domed rosette of buttercream on each portion. Place a marzipan coffee bean in the center of each rosette. Using a parchment cone, pipe a small dome of ganache in the center of the torte. Then pipe a line of ganache on each marked portion, beginning at the center, looping around the rosette, and connecting again at the center to form a teardrop.

4   Garnish the bottom edge of the side of the torte with the chocolate shavings.

Chocolate almond torte

MAKES 1 TORTE (8 IN/20 CM), 10 SERVINGS

Chocolate almond cake (page 283), 8 in/20 cm	1 each	1 each
Apricot jam	9 oz	255 g
Hard ganache (page 421)	10 oz	284 g

1   Cut the cake into 2 even layers. Place one layer on an 8-in/20-cm cake round. Spread a thin layer of jam on the layer and top with the second layer.

2   Coat the top and sides of the cake with the remaining jam.

3   Glaze the torte with the ganache, reserving 4 oz/113 g for décor. Chill for 15 minutes.

4   Mark the torte into 10 portions. Rewarm the reserved ganache and, using a parchment cone, decorate each portion with a filigree of ganache.

Havana torte

MAKES 1 TORTE (8 IN/20 CM), 10 SERVINGS

Havana cake (page 280), 8 in/20 cm	1 each	1 each
Chocolate buttercream (page 418)	1 lb 8 oz	680 g
Hard ganache (page 421), warm	1 lb	454 g
Chocolate cigarettes (see page 829)	10 each	10 each

1   Place the cake on an 8-in/20-cm cardboard cake round. Reserve 4 oz/113 g of the buttercream for décor and coat the top and sides of the cake with the remainder. Refrigerate until the buttercream is firm.

2   Glaze the torte with the warm ganache. Allow to set.

3   Mark the torte into 10 portions. Using a pastry bag fitted with a #5 plain tip, pipe a small dome of buttercream on each portion. Place a chocolate cigarette on each portion so that it rests on the dome of buttercream.

Spanish vanilla torte

MAKES 1 TORTE (8 IN/20 CM), 10 SERVINGS

Spanish vanilla cake (page 282), 8 in/20 cm	1 each	1 each
Brandy-flavored simple syrup (see "Liquor-Flavored Simple Syrup," page 900)	8 fl oz	240 mL
Apricot jam	6 oz	170 g
Marzipan (page 852)	13 oz	369 g
Hard ganache (page 421)	1 lb	454 g
Marzipan flowers (see page 834), ¾ in/2 cm in diameter	10 each	10 each

1   Slice 3 even layers from the cake (between ¼ and ½ in/6 mm and 1 cm thick). Place one layer on an 8-in/20-cm cardboard cake round and moisten with simple syrup. Apply a thin coating of apricot jam to the layer. Top with a second layer and press down gently. Moisten with simple syrup, apply a thin coating of apricot jam, and top with the final layer of cake. Apply a thin coating of apricot jam to the top and sides of the cake, reserving 1 oz/28 g of the jam for décor.

2   On a work surface lightly dusted with sifted confectioners' sugar, roll out the marzipan to a circle about 15 in/38 cm in diameter and ⅛ in/3 mm thick. Carefully lift up the marzipan and drape it over the cake so that it completely covers it. Press the marzipan against the top and sides of the cake so that it adheres well. Using the palm of your hand in a rotating motion, smooth the marzipan as necessary. Using a sharp paring knife, trim the marzipan at the bottom edge of the cake.

3   Glaze the torte with the ganache, reserving 4 oz/113 g of the ganache for décor. Mark into 10 portions.

4   Place the remaining ganache in the mixer and beat on medium speed with the paddle attachment until light in color and texture. Mark the torte into 10 portions. Using a pastry bag fitted with a #3 plain tip, pipe a small dome of ganache on each portion. Place a marzipan flower on each dome. Using a parchment cone, pipe a small dot of apricot jam in the center of each flower.

Opera torte

MAKES 1 TORTE (8 IN/20 CM SQUARE)

Joconde sheet (page 284), 16½ by 24½ in/42 by 62 cm	1 each	1 each
Dark chocolate, melted	4 oz	113 g
Vegetable oil	½ oz	14 g
Coffee simple syrup (page 900)	8 fl oz	240 mL
Medium ganache (page 421), lightly whipped	6 oz	170 g
Coffee buttercream (page 418)	8 oz	227 g
Hard ganache (page 421), warmed to glaze	6 oz	170 g

1   Line a 10-in/25-cm cardboard cake round with a parchment circle of the same size. Cut the Joconde sheet into three 8½-in/22-cm squares.

2   Combine the chocolate and vegetable oil. Turn one Joconde layer upside down and thinly coat the top surface with the chocolate mixture. Place it chocolate side down on the parchment-lined cake round. Moisten the layer with simple syrup and spread with an even coating of medium ganache. Top with the next layer of cake, press it down gently, and coat evenly with 6 oz/170 g of the buttercream. Top with the final layer of cake, press down gently, and moisten with simple syrup.

3   Coat the top of the cake with the remaining buttercream. Refrigerate until the buttercream is firm.

4   Invert the cake carefully, peel the parchment circle off the bottom of the cake, and place the cake, buttercream-coated side up, on an 8-in/20-cm cardboard square. Glaze with the hard ganache, reserving 2 oz/57 g of the ganache for décor. Allow the glaze to set and trim the edges to make a perfect 8-in/20-cm square.

5   Using a parchment cone, pipe the word "opera" with cooled ganache across the top of the torte.

FROM LEFT TO RIGHT: Charlotte Royale (page 566), Opera Torte
(opposite), Gâteau St. Honoré (page 582)

Zebra torte

MAKES 1 TORTE (8 IN/20 CM), 10 SERVINGS

Vanilla sponge (page 268), 8 in/20 cm	1 each	1 each
Vanilla simple syrup (page 901)	5 fl oz	150 mL
Chocolate roulade sheet (page 274), 11½ by 16½ in/29 by 42 cm	1 each	1 each
Heavy cream	24 fl oz	720 mL
Confectioners' sugar, sifted	¾ oz	21 g
Rum	3 fl oz	90 mL
Dark chocolate round cutouts (see page 827), 1½ in/4 cm in diameter	10 each	10 each
Dark chocolate, melted, tempered	2 oz	57 g
Chocolate cake crumbs	3 oz	85 g

1   Place an 8-in/20-cm cardboard cake round on a sheet pan and place an 8-in/20-cm cake ring on top. Slice the vanilla sponge into 2 even layers (between ¼ and ½ in/6 mm and 1 cm thick), place one layer into the cake ring, and moisten with simple syrup.

2   Moisten the chocolate roulade sheet with the simple syrup. Combine 12 fl oz/360 mL of the heavy cream with the confectioners' sugar and 2 fl oz/60 mL of the rum and whip to medium peaks. Spread evenly over the moistened roulade and cut into strips 1½ in/4 cm wide.

3   Roll one of the strips into a spiral with the cream side in. Join the end of another strip to the end of the spiral and roll to continue the spiral. Repeat this process with the remaining strips to create a spiral approximately 8 in/20 cm in diameter. Carefully place the spiral into the cake ring. Moisten the remaining layer of the vanilla sponge with simple syrup and place on top of the spiral. Wrap the cake in the ring in plastic wrap and refrigerate for about 2 hours, or until the whipped cream layers have set.

4   Remove the plastic wrap and gently lift away the cake ring. Combine the remaining 12 fl oz/360 mL heavy cream with the remaining 1 fl oz/30 mL rum and whip to medium peaks. Finish the top and sides of the torte with the whipped cream, reserving 4 oz/113 g for décor.

5   Mark the torte into 10 portions. Using a pastry bag fitted with a #5 plain tip, pipe a small dome of the reserved whipped cream onto each portion. Place a chocolate cutout on each dome.

6   Mark the center of the torte with a 4-in/10-cm round cutter. Using a parchment cone, pipe a corneli design with the tempered chocolate into the marked circle. Garnish the bottom quarter edge of the side of the torte by gently pressing the chocolate cake crumbs to adhere.

Zuger kirsch torte

MAKES 1 TORTE (8 IN/20 CM)

Japonais meringue (page 898), 8-in/20-cm round, baked	2 each	2 each
Vanilla sponge (page 268), 8 in/20 cm	1 each	1 each
Kirsch buttercream (page 418)	14 oz	397 g
Kirsch-flavored simple syrup (see "Liqueur-Flavored Simple Syrup," page 901)	3 fl oz	90 mL
Sliced almonds, toasted	2 oz	57 g
Confectioners' sugar	1 oz	28 g
Candied cherries	10 each	10 each

1   Using a serrated knife, cut one of the japonais layers into 10 even wedges. Cut one layer from the sponge (between ¼ and ½ in/6 mm and 1 cm thick).

2   Place the remaining japonais layer on an 8-in/20-cm cake round and apply a thin layer of buttercream. Thoroughly moisten the sponge layer with simple syrup and place on top of the japonais layer. Apply a thin layer of buttercream. Arrange the cut japonais wedges on top, carefully fitting them together.

3   Coat the sides of the torte with the remaining buttercream. Press the toasted almonds onto the buttercream.

4   Dust the top of the torte heavily with the confectioners' sugar, then mark with a lattice pattern, using the back of a knife. Mark the portions with a candied cherry at the outer edge of each one.

Gâteau St. Honoré

MAKES 1 CAKE (8 IN/20 CM)

Butter puff pastry dough (page 231)	4 oz	113 g
Pâte à choux (page 228)	7½ oz	213 g
Kirsch-flavored pastry cream (see "Liqueur-Flavored Pastry Cream," page 370)	8 oz	227 g
Sugar	12 oz	340 g
Kirsch-flavored diplomat cream (page 394)	1 lb	454 g

1   Roll the puff pastry into an 8-in/20-cm circle, dock it, and place it on a parchment-lined sheet pan. Using a pastry bag fitted with a #8 plain tip, pipe a border of pâte à choux onto the puff pastry circle and a smaller ring in the center. Pipe approximately 12 small round cream puffs on a separate parchment-lined sheet pan.

2   Bake the puff pastry round and cream puffs at 375°F/191°C until golden brown, about 30 minutes. Cool.

3   Fill each of the cream puffs with some of the pastry cream.

4   To prepare the caramel, add a small amount of the sugar to a medium-hot pan set over medium heat and allow it to melt, then add the remaining sugar in small increments, allowing each addition to fully melt before adding the next. Continue this process until all the sugar has been added to the pan, and cook to the desired color. Dip the top of each cream puff into the caramel and place them caramel side down on a sheet pan that has been greased lightly. Once cool, dip the bottom of each puff into the caramel and stick it to the outside edge of the shell, spacing them evenly.

5   Fill the center of the gâteau with diplomat cream; it should come to within ½ in/1 cm of the tops of the cream puffs. Using a pastry bag fitted with a V-cut round tip or a large rose petal tip, pipe the diplomat cream in a Herringbone pattern on top of the gâteau.

Pithivier

MAKES 1 CAKE (8 IN/20 CM)

Butter, soft	8 oz	227 g
Sugar	8 oz	227 g
Ground almonds	3⅓ oz	94 g
Vanilla extract	1 tsp	5 mL
Eggs	4 oz	113 g
Butter puff pastry dough (page 231)	1 lb	454 g
Egg wash (page 892)	2 oz	57 g
Light corn syrup	1 oz	28 g

1 To prepare the filling, cream the butter and sugar on medium speed with the paddle attachment until light and fluffy, about 5 minutes.

2 Mix in the almonds and vanilla extract. Add the eggs one at a time, mixing until fully incorporated after each addition and scraping down the bowl as necessary.

3 Roll the puff pastry to a thickness of ⅛ in/3 mm. Chill until firm. Cut out two 8-in/20-cm circles from the pastry.

4 Place one of the circles on a parchment-lined sheet pan and spread or pipe the filling in the center of the circle, leaving a 1½-in/4-cm border all around. Brush the border lightly with egg wash. Place the remaining puff pastry circle on top, carefully lining up the edges of the 2 circles. Gently press the edges together. Cover with plastic wrap and chill for 20 minutes.

5 Using the back of a paring knife, scallop the edges of the pastry. Brush the pastry with egg wash and cut a spiral sunburst pattern in the top, working from the center out and being careful not to cut through to the filling.

6 Bake at 375°F/191°C until golden brown, 35 to 40 minutes. Brush the top of the pithivier with the corn syrup. Turn the oven up to 425°F/218°C and bake until the corn syrup has become a golden glaze, about 3 minutes longer.

7 Allow the pithivier to cool slightly before serving.

A pithivier is marked before baking.

Almond cake

MAKES 1 CAKE (8 IN/20 CM)

1-2-3 cookie dough (page 223)	8 oz	227 g
Italian buttercream (page 418)	1 lb 10 oz	737 g
Dark chocolate, melted	2 oz	57 g
Almond extract	½ tsp	2.50 mL
Brandy	2 fl oz	60 mL
Vanilla sponge (page 268), 8 in/20 cm	1 each	1 each
Raspberry jam	1 oz	28 g
Vanilla simple syrup (page 901)	4 fl oz	120 mL
Marzipan (page 852)	2 oz	57 g
Chocolate cigarettes (see page 829)	1 each	1 each

1   Roll out the dough ⅛ in/3 mm thick and cut out an 8-in/20-cm round. Transfer to a parchment-lined sheet pan. Chill at least 30 minutes.

2   Bake at 350°F/177°C until golden brown, 10 to 12 minutes. Cool completely.

3   Flavor 6 oz/170 g of the buttercream with the melted chocolate. Flavor the remaining buttercream with the almond extract and the brandy. Reserve 6 oz/170g of the brandy-flavored buttercream for décor.

4   Cut 3 even layers from the vanilla sponge (between ¼ and ½ in/6 mm and 1 cm thick).

5   Place the cookie round on a cardboard cake round and apply a thin coating of raspberry jam to the cookie round. Top with a sponge layer and moisten with simple syrup. Coat with the chocolate buttercream. Top with the second sponge layer, moisten with simple syrup, and coat with the almond brandy buttercream. Top with the third layer of sponge and moisten with simple syrup.

6   Finish the top and sides of the cake with the brandy-flavored buttercream.

7   Dust a work surface with confectioners' sugar and roll the marzipan to a thickness of ⅟₁₆ in/1.5 mm. With a 1-in/3-cm cutter, cut out 9 circles. Cut the circles in half. Press them against the base of the cake with the flat side down.

8   Using the reserved buttercream and a pastry bag fitted with a #3 plain tip, pipe a line of shells across the top of the cake, dividing the cake in half. Lay the chocolate cigarette at a 45-degree angle across the piped shell border.

Coffee chantilly torte

MAKES 1 TORTE (8 IN/20 CM)

1-2-3 cookie dough (page 223)	8 oz	227 g
Chiffon sponge (page 287), 8 in/20 cm	1 each	1 each
Soft ganache (page 421), whipped	6 oz	170 g
Kahlúa-flavored simple syrup (see "Liqueur-Flavored Simple Syrup," page 900)	4 fl oz	120 mL
Coffee Chantilly cream (page 420)	6 oz	170 g
Chantilly cream (page 420)	12 oz	340 g
Almonds, toasted and ground	4 oz	113 g
Striped chocolate triangles (see page 829)	5 each	5 each
Dark chocolate, melted, tempered	2 oz	57 g

1 Roll out the dough ⅛ in/3 mm thick and cut out an 8-in/20-cm round. Transfer to a sheet pan. Chill at least 30 minutes.

2 Bake at 350°F/177°C until golden brown, 10 to 12 minutes. Cool completely.

3 Slice two ¼-in/6-mm layers from the chiffon sponge.

4 Place the cookie round on an 8-in/20-cm cardboard cake round and coat with the whipped ganache. Top with a layer of chiffon sponge and moisten with simple syrup. Coat with the coffee Chantilly cream. Top with the second layer of chiffon sponge and moisten with simple syrup.

5 Finish the top and sides of the torte with the plain Chantilly cream, reserving 4 oz/113 g for décor. Press the ground almonds onto the base of the torte.

6 Using the reserved Chantilly cream and a pastry bag fitted with a #4 star tip, cover one-third of the top of the torte with rosettes. Place the chocolate triangles in the center of the torte. Using a parchment cone, pipe a continuous swirl of the tempered chocolate around the triangles.

Chestnut cake

MAKES 1 PAISLEY CAKE (8 IN/20 CM)

Chiffon sponge (page 287), 8 in/20 cm	1 each	1 each
Rum-flavored simple syrup (see "Liqueur-Flavored Simple Syrup," page 901)	5 fl oz	150 mL
Chestnut purée	10 oz	284 g
Italian meringue (page 416)	8 oz	227 g
Butter, soft	10 oz	284 g
Rum	2 fl oz	60 mL
Hard ganache (page 421)	6 oz	170 g
Candied chestnuts, for décor	3 each	3 each

1   Line the bottom of an 8-in/20-cm paisley mold (or an 8-in/20-cm ring mold) with a cardboard cake round, cutting it to fit. Line the sides of the paisley mold with a strip of acetate or plastic wrap, cutting it to fit.

2   Slice 3 even layers from the chiffon sponge (between ¼ and ½ in/6 mm and 1 cm thick). Moisten each layer with simple syrup.

3   Blend the chestnut purée into the Italian meringue. Add the butter and rum and blend until well combined.

4   Place one sponge layer in the mold and coat with a thin layer of the chestnut buttercream. Top with a second sponge layer and coat with a thin layer of buttercream. Top with the final sponge layer.

5   Crumb coat the cake.

6   Glaze the cake with the ganache. Place the candied chestnuts in the center of the cake.

Chocolate marquise torte

MAKES 1 HEXAGONAL TORTE (6 BY 10¼ IN/15 BY 26 CM)

Italian buttercream (page 418)	10 oz	284 g
Gianduja (page 807)	8 oz	227 g
Japonaise meringue (page 898), 6 by 10¼ in/15 by 26 cm, baked	1 each	1 each
Raspberry jam	2 oz	57 g
Chocolate chiffon sponge (page 288), 6 by 10¼ in/15 by 26 cm	3 each	3 each
Cointreau-flavored simple syrup (see "Liqueur-Flavored Simple Syrup," page 900)	7 fl oz	210 mL
Soft ganache, whipped (page 421)	5 oz	142 g
Marzipan (page 852)	12 oz	340 g
Hard ganache (page 421)	12 oz	340 g
White chocolate triangles (see page 827), 2½ by 2½ by 2 in/6 by 6 by 5 cm	7 each	7 each

1   Blend together the buttercream and gianduja.

2   Line the bottom of a hexagonal bottomless mold (6 by 10¼ in/15 by 26 cm) with cardboard, cutting it to fit. Trim the japonaise layer to fit inside the mold. Spread a thin coating of raspberry jam on the japonaise and place it in the bottom of the mold. Top with a layer of chiffon sponge and moisten with simple syrup. Coat with 5 oz/142 g of the gianduja buttercream. Top with a second layer of chiffon sponge, moisten with simple syrup, and coat with the soft ganache. Top with the last layer of chiffon sponge and moisten with simple syrup.

3   Coat the top of the torte with a thin layer of buttercream. Cover with plastic wrap and refrigerate until the buttercream is set.

4   Remove the plastic wrap. Warm the side of the cake ring using a propane torch or a towel moistened with warm water and carefully remove the ring. Coat the sides of the cake with the remaining buttercream, reserving 4 oz/113 g for décor.

5   Dust a work surface with confectioners' sugar and roll the marzipan to a rectangle ¹⁄₁₆ in/1.5 mm thick and large enough to cover the entire cake. Cover the torte with the marzipan. Smooth the top and sides and cut away the excess at the corners to create close, neat seams. Glaze the torte with the milk chocolate ganache. Refrigerate until firm.

6   Using a pastry bag fitted with a #4 plain tip, pipe a scrolled line of buttercream diagonally across the center of the torte. Place the white chocolate triangles in a line parallel to the left of the scrolled line, arranging them so that each triangle slightly overlaps the previous one.

Chocolate dacquoise torte

MAKES 1 TORTE (8 IN/20 CM)

Dacquoise (page 295), 8-in/20-cm rounds, baked	3 each	3 each
Soft ganache (page 421), whipped	26 oz	737 g
Dark chocolate rectangular cutouts (see page 827), 1½ by 3 in/4 by 8 cm	25 each	25 each
Hazelnuts, blanched and toasted	4 oz	113 g

1   Trim each dacquoise layer to a perfect 8-in/20-cm round.

2   Smear a dollop of the ganache in the center of an 8-in/20-cm cardboard cake round and place one of the dacquoise rounds on top. Coat the dacquoise with 6 oz/170 g of the ganache. Top with a second dacquoise round and coat it with 6 oz/170 g of the ganache. Top with the remaining dacquoise round.

3   Coat the top and sides of the torte with 5 oz/142 g of the ganache and refrigerate for about 1 hour to set firm. Finish the top and sides of the torte with the remaining ganache, reserving 4 oz/113 g for décor.

4   Reserve 3 chocolate rectangles. Press the remaining rectangles onto the sides of the torte, slightly overlapping them and completely covering the sides of the torte.

5   Using a pastry bag fitted with a #3 plain tip, pipe small domes of ganache around the top edge of the torte. At intervals of 2 in/5 cm to mark the portions, place a hazelnut on each dome. Place a cluster of the remaining hazelnuts slightly off center on the top of the torte. Break up the reserved chocolate rectangles and place next to the cluster of hazelnuts.

Chocolate mousse torte

MAKES 1 OVAL TORTE (5½ BY 11 IN/14 BY 28 CM)

Ladyfinger strip (page 340), 1½ by 24 in/4 by 61 cm, alternating vanilla and chocolate	1 each	1 each
Chocolate sponge sheet (page 268), 16½ by 24½ in/42 by 62 cm	1 each	1 each
Orange-flavored simple syrup	5 fl oz	150 mL
White chocolate mousse (page 382)	9 oz	255 g
Dark chocolate mousse (page 381)	9 oz	255 g
Hard ganache (page 421)	5 oz	142 g
White and dark chocolate ruffles (see page 832)	2 each	2 each

1   Line the bottom of an oval cake ring mold with cardboard, cutting it to fit. Line the sides of the mold with acetate. Line the inside of the mold with the ladyfinger strip with the flat side facing in.

2   Cut 2 ovals (5½ by 11 in/14 by 28 cm each) from the sheet of sponge. Place one in the mold and moisten with simple syrup. Spread the white chocolate mousse evenly over the layer. Top with the second layer of sponge, moisten, and spread evenly with the dark chocolate mousse.

3   Cover with plastic wrap and refrigerate until firm, at least 2 hours.

4   Glaze the top of the torte with a thin coating of ganache. Place the torte in the freezer for 30 minutes.

5   Warm the sides of the cake mold using a propane torch or a towel moistened with warm water and carefully remove the mold.

6   Garnish the top of the torte with the chocolate ruffles.

Chocolate ruffle cake

MAKES 1 CAKE (8 IN/20 CM)

High-ratio chocolate cake (page 265), 8 in/20 cm	1 each	1 each
Vanilla simple syrup (page 901)	5 fl oz	150 mL
Soft ganache, whipped (page 421)	16 oz	454 g
Dark chocolate, melted	1 lb 4 oz	567 g
Confectioners' sugar (optional)	3 oz	85 g

1   Slice 3 even layers from the cake (between ¼ and ½ in/6 mm and 1 cm thick). Place one of the cake layers on an 8-in/20-cm cardboard cake round. Moisten with simple syrup and coat with 4 oz/113 g of the ganache. Top with another layer of cake, moisten with simple syrup, and coat with 4 oz/113 g of the ganache. Top with the final layer of cake and moisten with simple syrup.

2   Coat the top and sides of the cake with 4 oz/113 g of the ganache.

3   Fill a pastry bag fitted with a medium-size plain tip with the remaining ganache. Pipe a border of nickel-size domes around the outer edge of the cake.

4   Warm 2 perfectly flat sheet pans in the oven until just warm to the touch (approximately 100°F/38°C). Ladle 10 oz/284 g of the melted chocolate onto the back of each sheet pan and spread evenly with an offset spatula.

5   Refrigerate the sheet pans for 15 minutes, then transfer to the freezer for 15 minutes.

6   Remove the pans from the freezer and let stand at room temperature until the chocolate becomes pliable, about 5 minutes.

7   Spread some of the chocolate on a piece of parchment approximately 3 in/8 cm wide, let it set lightly, and wrap around the cake.

8   With the same spatula, remove the chocolate from the pans, holding the tip of the spatula steady and rotating the handle end to create fans, or ruffles. Arrange the chocolate ruffles on the top of the cake in concentric circles, starting from the edge and working in, overlapping the circles to completely cover the top of the cake. Sprinkle lightly with confectioners' sugar, if desired.

NOTE   For this décor it is best to use a chocolate with a low cocoa butter content.

Gâteau praliné

MAKES 1 CAKE (8 IN/20 CM)

1-2-3 cookie dough (page 223)	8 oz	227 g
Hazelnut sponge cake (page 277), 8 in/20 cm	1 each	1 each
Praline paste	2 oz	57 g
French buttercream (page 419)	1 lb 12 oz	794 g
Nougatine, crushed	2 oz	57 g
Frangelico-flavored simple syrup (see "Liqueur-Flavored Simple Syrup," page 900)	6 fl oz	180 mL
Dark chocolate rectangular cutouts (see page 827), 1½ by 3 in/4 by 8 cm	25 each	25 each
Hazelnut dragées (page 793)	8 oz	227 g

1　Roll out the dough ⅛ in/3 mm thick and cut out an 8-in/20-cm round. Transfer to a sheet pan.

2　Bake at 350°F/177°C until golden brown, 10 to 12 minutes. Cool completely.

3　Slice 3 even layers from the sponge (between ¼ and ½ in/6 mm and 1 cm thick).

4　Blend the praline paste into the buttercream. Add the crushed nougatine to 10 oz/284 g of the praline buttercream and blend well. Reserve 6 oz/170 g of the buttercream for décor.

5　Place the cookie round on an 8-in/20-cm cardboard cake round and coat with 2 oz/57 g of the praline buttercream. Top with a layer of sponge, moisten with simple syrup, and coat with 5 oz/142 g of the nougatine buttercream. Top with a second layer of sponge, moisten with simple syrup, and coat with the remaining nougatine buttercream. Top with the remaining sponge layer.

6　Finish the top and sides of the cake with the praline buttercream. Press the chocolate rectangles onto the sides of the cake, overlapping them slightly and completely covering the sides of the cake.

7　Using a pastry bag fitted with a #3 star tip, pipe a shell border with the reserved buttercream around the top edge of the cake. Place the hazelnuts dragées on the border, spacing them evenly.

Gâteau Charlemagne

MAKES 1 CAKE (8 IN/20 CM)

Japonais meringue (page 898), 8-in/20-cm round, baked	2 each	2 each
Chocolate chiffon sponge (page 288), 8 in/20 cm	1 each	1 each
Hazelnut liqueur	2 fl oz	60 mL
Honey	1 oz	28 g
Diplomat cream (page 394)	10 oz	283 g
Frangelico-flavored simple syrup (see "Liqueur-Flavored Simple Syrup," page 900)	3 fl oz	90 mL
Chantilly cream (page 420)	8 oz	227 g
White chocolate round cutouts (see page 827), 3 in/8 cm	6 each	6 each
Cocoa powder, for dusting	as needed	as needed

1   Trim each japonais layer to a perfect 8-in/20-cm round. Slice one layer from the chiffon sponge (between ¼ and ½ in/6 mm and 1 cm thick).

2   Blend the hazelnut liqueur and honey into the diplomat cream.

3   Smear a dollop of the diplomat cream onto the center of an 8-in/20-cm cardboard cake round and place one of the japonais rounds on top. Coat with 5 oz/142 g of the diplomat cream. Top with the layer of chiffon sponge, moisten it with simple syrup, and coat with the remaining diplomat cream. Top with the remaining japonais round.

4   Coat the top and sides of the cake with the Chantilly cream.

5   Reserve 3 of the white chocolate rounds. Press the remaining chocolate rounds onto the sides of the cake, overlapping them slightly and covering the sides of the cake at evenly measured intervals.

6   Dust the top of the cake with cocoa powder, covering it completely.

7   Heat a small sharp knife and cut each of the reserved white chocolate circles in half. Place them around the top edge of the cake so they just touch one another, with the rounded side facing in.

Orange mousseline torte

MAKES 1 TORTE (8 IN/20 CM)

1-2-3 cookie dough (page 223)	8 oz	227 g
Orange chiffon sponge (page 287), 8 in/20 cm	1 each	1 each
Heavy cream, whipped to soft peaks	4 fl oz	120 mL
Orange curd (page 377)	8 oz	227 g
Orange marmalade	2 oz	57 g
Grand Marnier–flavored simple syrup (see "Liqueur-Flavored Simple Syrup," page 900)	6 fl oz	180 mL
Swiss meringue (page 416)	1 lb	454 g

1   Roll out the dough ⅛ in/3 mm thick and cut out an 8-in/20-cm round. Transfer to a sheet pan. Chill at least 30 minutes.

2   Bake at 350°F/177°C until golden brown, 10 to 12 minutes. Cool completely.

3   Cut the chiffon spong into 3 layers (between ¼ and ½ in/6 mm and 1 cm thick). Fold one-third of the whipped cream into the orange curd to lighten it, and then fold in the remaining whipped cream.

4   Place an 8-in/20-cm cardboard cake round on a sheet pan and place an 8-in/20-cm cake ring on top. Line the sides of the cake ring with an acetate strip or plastic wrap. Apply a thin coating of marmalade to the cookie round and place it in the cake ring. Top with a layer of chiffon sponge, moisten with simple syrup, and coat with 6 oz/170 g of the orange whipped cream. Top with a second layer of chiffon sponge, moisten with simple syrup, and coat with the remaining 6 oz/170 g orange whipped cream. Top with the final layer of chiffon sponge and moisten with simple syrup.

5   Coat the top and sides of the torte with meringue. Using a pastry bag fitted with a #5 star tip, pipe side-by-side columns of meringue all around the sides of the torte. Pipe swirls of meringue all over the top of the torte, then pipe a shell border around the base of the torte.

6   Using a propane torch, brown the meringue on the sides and top of the torte.

Parisian gâteau

MAKES 1 CAKE (8 IN/20 CM)

Swiss meringue (page 416)	1 lb	454 g
Soft ganache (page 421)	1 lb 4 oz	567 g
Dark chocolate, melted	2 oz	57 g
Coffee extract	½ fl oz	15 mL
Kahlúa	1 fl oz	30 mL
Chocolate shavings (see page 831)	4 oz	113 g
Confectioners' sugar	1 oz	28 g

1   Trace three 8-in/20-cm circles on a sheet of parchment paper and line a sheet pan with the parchment.

2   Using a pastry bag fitted with a #4 plain tip, pipe a spiral of meringue into each traced circle, starting in the middle and working outward to fill it completely.

3   Bake at 225°F/107°C until dry, about 40 minutes. Cool completely.

4   Combine the ganache, melted chocolate, coffee extract, and Kahlúa and blend well. Whip to firm peaks.

5   Place a meringue round on an 8-in/20-cm cake round and coat with 5 oz/142 g of the ganache. Top with a second layer of meringue and coat it with 5 oz/142 g of ganache. Top with the last layer of meringue, with the smooth side facing out.

6   Coat the top and sides of the gâteau with the remaining ganache. Press the chocolate shavings onto the top and sides of the gâteau to cover it completely. Dust the top lightly with the confectioners' sugar.

Orange torte

MAKES 1 TORTE (8 IN/20 CM)

Orange chiffon sponge (page 287), 8 in/20 cm	1 each	1 each
Ladyfinger strip (page 340), 2 by 24 in/5 by 61 cm, striped vanilla and chocolate	1 strip	1 strip
Orange-flavored simple syrup	3 fl oz	90 mL
Orange marmalade	1 oz	28 g
Orange diplomat cream (page 395)	1 lb 10 oz	737 g
Mirror glaze (page 424)	3 oz	85 g
Candied orange peel (page 796), julienne	3 oz	85 g

1   Place an 8-in/20-cm cardboard cake round on a sheet pan and place an 8-in/20-cm cake ring on it. Line the ring with plastic wrap.

2   Slice 2 layers from the chiffon sponge (between ¼ and ½ in/6 mm and 1 cm thick).

3   Line the inside of the cake ring with the ladyfinger strip so that the smooth side faces in. Place one layer of the chiffon sponge in the bottom of the ring and moisten with simple syrup. Coat with a thin layer of orange marmalade. Ladle 13 oz/369 g of the diplomat cream on top of the chiffon sponge layer and spread it into an even layer. Top with a second layer of chiffon sponge and press down gently. Moisten the chiffon sponge layer with simple syrup, coat with a thin layer of orange marmalade, and ladle in the remaining 13 oz/369 g diplomat cream.

4   Wrap tightly in plastic wrap and refrigerate overnight. (The torte can be frozen for up to 1 month.)

5   Glaze the top of the torte with the mirror glaze. Refrigerate until the glaze has fully set, about 20 minutes.

6   Warm the sides of the cake ring using a propane torch or a towel moistened with warm water and carefully remove the ring.

7   Garnish the top of the torte with the orange peel.

Passion fruit torte

MAKES 1 TORTE (8 IN/20 CM)

1-2-3 cookie dough (page 223)	8 oz	227 g
Chiffon sponge (page 287), 8 in/20 cm	1 each	1 each
Patterned Joconde strip (page 284), 2 by 24 in/5 by 61 cm	1 each	1 each
Raspberry jam	2 oz	57 g
Simple syrup (page 900)	3 fl oz	90 mL
Passion fruit mousse (page 379)	14 oz	397 g
Passion fruit mirror glaze (see Variation, page 427)	3 oz	85 g
Passion fruit	½ each	½ each
Kiwi, peeled and cut crosswise into slices ¼ in/6 mm thick	1 each	1 each
Mango, peeled and thinly sliced	1 each	1 each
Twisted dark chocolate ribbon (see page 831), ⅓ by 6 in/1 by 15 cm	1 each	1 each
Twisted white chocolate ribbon (see page 831), ⅓ by 6 in/1 by 15 cm	1 each	1 each

1   Roll out the dough ⅛ in/3 mm thick and cut out an 8-in/20-cm round. Transfer to a sheet pan.

2   Bake at 350°F/177°C until golden brown, 10 to 12 minutes. Cool completely.

3   Slice 2 layers from the chiffon sponge (between ¼ and ½ in/6 mm and 1 cm thick).

4   Place an 8-in/20-cm cardboard cake round on a sheet pan and place an 8-in/20-cm cake ring on top. Line the inside of the cake ring with an acetate strip or plastic wrap. Line the inside of the ring with the strip of Joconde. Coat the cookie round with raspberry jam and place in the bottom of the ring. Top with a layer of chiffon sponge and moisten with simple syrup. Ladle 7 oz/198 g of the passion fruit mousse on top of the chiffon sponge and spread it into an even layer. Top with the second layer of chiffon sponge, press down gently, and moisten with simple syrup. Ladle in the remaining 7 oz/198 g passion fruit mousse.

5   Wrap tightly in plastic wrap and refrigerate overnight. (The torte can be frozen for up to 1 month.)

6   Glaze the top of the torte with the mirror glaze.

7   Warm the sides of the cake ring using a propane torch or a towel moistened with warm water and carefully remove the ring.

8   Place the passion fruit half on top of the torte, slightly off center and seed side up. Place 2 kiwi slices next to the passion fruit half and fan the mango slices out from the kiwi slices. Place the chocolate ribbons to form an X over the fruit.

NOTE   Fresh fruit can be added to the filling. Any fruit purée can be used to change the flavor.

Strawberry yogurt Bavarian torte

MAKES 1 TORTE (8 IN/20 CM)

1-2-3 cookie dough (page 223)	8 oz	227 g
Chiffon sponge (page 287), 8 in/20 cm	1 each	1 each
Strawberry jam	1 oz	28 g
Kirsch-flavored simple syrup (page 900)	4 fl oz	120 mL
Strawberry yogurt Bavarian (page 395)	1 lb	454 g
Strawberries, thinly sliced	12 each	12 each
Chantilly cream (page 420)	8 oz	227 g
Marbled white and dark chocolate rectangular cutouts (see page 827), 1½ by 3 in/4 by 8 cm	25 each	25 each
Strawberries, quartered	2 each	2 each
Chocolate fan (see page 831)	1 each	1 each
Marbled chocolate cigarettes (see page 831)	1 each	1 each

1 Roll out the dough ⅛ in/3 mm thick and cut out an 8-in/20-cm round. Transfer to a baking sheet. Bake at 350°F/177°C until golden brown, 10 to 12 minutes. Cool completely.

2 Place an 8-in/20-cm cardboard cake round on a sheet pan and place an 8-in/20-cm cake ring on top. Line the ring with plastic wrap.

3 Slice 3 layers from the chiffon sponge (between ¼ and ½ in/6 mm and 1 cm thick).

4 Spread a thin coating of strawberry jam on the cookie round and place it in the bottom of the ring. Place a layer of chiffon sponge on the cookie base and moisten with simple syrup. Ladle 8 oz/227 g of the Bavarian cream on top of the chiffon sponge and spread it into an even layer. Arrange half of the sliced strawberries in concentric circles over the cream. Top with a second layer of chiffon sponge, press down gently, and moisten with simple syrup. Ladle in the remaining 8 oz/227 g Bavarian cream and cover in the same manner with the remaining sliced strawberries. Top with the last layer of chiffon sponge, press down gently, and moisten with simple syrup. Cover with plastic wrap and refrigerate until fully set.

5 Remove the plastic wrap. Warm the sides of the cake ring using a propane torch or a towel moistened with warm water and carefully remove the ring.

6 Coat the top and sides of the torte with the Chantilly cream. Press the chocolate rectangles onto the sides of the torte, overlapping them slightly and completely covering the sides of the torte. Arrange the quartered strawberries in the center of the torte. Place the chocolate fan in the center. Place the chocolate cigarette across the strawberries.

Peanut butter s'mores cake

MAKES 1 CAKE (6 IN/15 CM)

Marshmallows (page 814)	8 oz	227 g
Graham cracker crumbs	as needed	as needed
Graham cracker crust (page 228)	4 oz	113 g
Milk chocolate peanut butter gianduja (page 807)	3 oz	85 g
Flourless sponge (page 281), 5-in/13-cm rounds, ½ in/1 cm thick	1 each	1 each
Vanilla simple syrup (page 901)	3 fl oz	90 mL
Milk chocolate Bavarian cream (see page 393)	1 lb	454 g
Milk chocolate mirror glaze (see page 428)	1 lb	454 g
Toasted marshmallow	1 each	1 each
Chocolate cigarettes (see page 829)	1 each	1 each

1   Pipe the marshmallows into a 5½-in/14-cm circle onto oiled parchment. Sprinkle with graham cracker crumbs and freeze for 20 minutes, or until completely set.

2   Prepare the graham cracker crust and press into a 6-in/15-cm cake ring. Bake at 325°F/163°C in a convection oven for 6 minutes. Trim to a 5-in/13-cm round while still hot from the oven. Allow to cool completely before cake assembly.

3   Spread 3 oz/85 g of the gianduja on top of the graham cracker round and top with the round of flourless sponge, pressing gently to adhere. Soak the sponge with the simple syrup. Reserve.

4   Place a 6-in/15-cm cake ring mold on a sheet pan that has been lined with acetate.

5   Portion 8 oz of the Bavarian cream into the cake ring.

6   Lightly press the marshmallow round into the mousse so it comes up the sides of the marshmallow round.

7   Portion the remaining mousse into the ring and place the graham cracker–gianduja–flourless sponge layer on last with the graham cracker base facing up, pressing gently into place. Freeze the cake 6 hours, or overnight, until completely set.

8   Working with the cake still frozen, unmold by warming slightly with a torch. Glaze with the milk chocolate glaze and refrigerate until set. Garnish with a toasted marshmallow on a chocolate stick.

Caramel macadamia nut torte

MAKES 1 TORTE (6 IN/15 CM)

Macadamia cremeux (page 367)	7 oz	198 g
Japonais meringue (page 898)	1 recipe	1 recipe
Chocolate caramel ganache (page 423)	1½ oz	43 g
Toasted macadamia nuts	9½ oz	269 g
Caramel mousse (page 385)	1 lb	454 g
Chiffon sponge (page 287), 5-in/13-cm rounds, ½ in/1 cm thick	1 each	1 each
Caramel simple syrup (page 438)	3 oz	85 g
Caramel glaze (page 426)	1 lb	454 g
Milk chocolate fans (see page 831)	12–14 each	12–14 each
Chocolate mirror glaze (page 428)	4 oz	113 g
Marbleized chocolate plaques (see page 829)	1 each	1 each
Striped chocolate cigarettes (see page 830)	1 each	1 each

1 Freeze the macadamia cremeux in a 6-in/15-cm cake pan lined with plastic wrap. Freeze, for 6 hours, or overnight, until solid. Unmold from the pan and trim to a 5-in/13-cm circle. Keep frozen until needed.

2 Using a pastry bag fitted with a #4 plain pastry tip, pipe the japonais batter into a 5-in/13-cm round onto a parchment-lined sheet pan. Bake at 350°F/177°C until golden brown, 10 to 15 minutes. Cool completely before assembly.

3 Spread 1½ oz/43 g of tabled chocolate caramel ganache over the japonais meringue and top with 1½ oz/43 g of the toasted macadamia nuts. Keep at room temperature.

4 Reserve 5 oz/142 g of the caramel mousse and portion the rest into a 6-in/15-cm cake ring mold.

5 Place the macadamia cremeux on top of the mousse and press it gently into place so the mousse comes up the sides of the frozen cremeux.

6 Moisten chiffon sponge with the caramel simple syrup and place on top of the cremeux layer in the mold. Pour the reserved mousse on top of the chiffon sponge and lightly press the japonais layer into the mousse. Freeze the cake until set.

7 Spread the remaining mousse on top of the soaked chiffon sponge. Fill the cake mold with the remaining caramel mousse. Press the japonais layer on top, the ganache side down. Wrap the cake tightly in plastic wrap and freeze for 6 hours, or overnight, until set.

8 To finish the cake, warm the caramel glaze to 95°F/35°C and spread on top of the frozen cake while still in the ring. Refrigerate the cake for 15 minutes or until the glaze is completely set.

9 Unmold the cake and place on a 7-in/18-cm gold cake board.

10 Press the milk chocolate fans onto the sides of the torte, slightly overlapping them to completely cover the sides of the torte.

11 Garnish the torte, piping dots of chocolate mirror glaze on top. Arrange the remaining toasted macadamia nuts, the marble chocolate plaque, and the chocolate cigarette on the torte.

FROM LEFT TO RIGHT: Milk Chocolate Chai Latte Cake (page 603), Mochaccino Cake (page 602), Caramel Macadamia Nut Torte (opposite), and Peanut Butter S'mores Cake (page 599)

Mochaccino cake

MAKES 1 CAKE (6 IN/15 CM)

Italian cream (page 397)	7 oz	198 g
Coffee crispy base (page 349)	3 oz	85 g
Devil's food cake (page 266), 5-in/13-cm rounds ½ in/1 cm thick	2 each	2 each
Coffee mousse (page 383)	7 oz	198 g
Dark coffee mousse (page 384)	7 oz	198 g
Ultra-shiny chocolate glaze (page 424)	4 oz	113 g
Coffee macaroons (page 328)	8–10 each	8–10 each
Chocolate cigarettes (see page 829)	4 oz	113 g
Chocolate shavings (page 831)	4 oz	113 g

1   Freeze the Italian cream in a 6-in/15-cm cake pan that has been lined with plastic wrap. Remove from the pan and cut into a 5-in/13-cm round. Reserve in the freezer.

2   Spread the coffee crispy base on one layer of the devil's food cake, wrap tightly, and freeze until completely set.

3   Place the cake rings on a flat sheet pan lined with plastic wrap.

4   Portion 7 oz/198 g of the coffee mousse into a 6-in/15-cm cake ring.

5   Lightly press the frozen Italian cream into the mousse so the mousse comes up the sides of the Italian cream.

6   Place the plain devil's food cake round on top of the Italian cream. Place the cake in the freezer.

7   Portion 7 oz/198 g of the dark coffee mousse into the cake ring mold. Place the remaining dark coffee mousse in 2½-in/6-cm rings and freeze for garnish.

8   Place the reserved devil's food cake layer into the mousse with the crispy side down. Freeze.

9   Unmold the cake by warming the sides slightly with a torch. Glaze the top and sides with ultra-shinny chocolate glaze while still frozen.

10   Place on a clean cake board. Garnish the bottom quarter edge of the side of the cake by gently pressing the coffee macaroons to adhere. Spray the frozen mousse rings with chocolate and place in the center of the cake. Place the chocolate shavings on top and garnish with a dollop of whipped cream and chocolate coffee beans.

Milk chocolate chai latte cake

MAKES 1 CAKE (6 IN/15 CM)

Coffee crispy base (page 349)	6 oz	170 g
Flourless sponge (page 281), 5-in/13-cm rounds	2 each	2 each
Chai panna cotta (page 376)	6 oz	170 g
Chocolate chai mousse (page 380)	1 lb	454 g
Spraying chocolate (page 464)	as needed	as needed
Ultra-shiny chocolate glaze (page 424)	4 oz	113 g
Chocolate cinnamon stick décor	1 each	1 each
Star anise, for décor	1 each	1 each
Marbled plaques (see page 829)	12	12

1   Spread the coffee crispy base on one of the flourless sponge rounds and freeze until fully set, about 20 minutes.

2   Freeze the chai panna cotta in a 6-in/15-cm cake pan lined with plastic wrap. Remove from the pan and cut into a 5-in/13-cm round. Reserve in the freezer.

3   Place the cake ring on a sheet pan lined with plastic wrap.

4   Portion 8 oz/227 g of the milk chocolate chai mousse into a 6-in/15-cm cake ring.

5   Lightly press the plain flourless sponge into the mousse so it comes up the sides of the sponge.

6   Place the frozen panna cotta on top of the sponge and pour the remaining mousse on top, reserving 2 oz/57 g for garnish.

7   Place the sponge with the coffee crispy base on last, with the sponge facing up, pressing gently into place. Freeze the cake for 6 hours or until completely set.

8   Remove the cake from the ring by warming the sides slightly with a torch.

9   Place the reserved mousse in a pastry bag fitted with a #2 tip. Pipe a random pattern on the top left side of the cake. Freeze until firm.

10   Spray the entire cake with spraying chocolate and flood in the outlined pattern with shiny glaze.

11   Garnish the top with a chocolate cinnamon stick and star anise.

12   Place marbled plaques around the side of the cake, pressing gently to adhere.

Carrot cake

MAKES 1 CAKE (6 IN/15 CM)

Poached pear gelée (see page 813)	4 oz	113 g
Bavarian cheese mousse (page 388)	1 lb	454 g
Carrot cake (page 271), 5-in/13-cm rounds, ½ in/1 cm thick	2 each	2 each
Poached pear	½ each	½ each
Candied carrot chip	1 each	1 each

1   Place cake rings on a sheet pan lined with plastic wrap and place a textured sheet in the bottom of each ring.

2   Freeze the poached pear gelée in a 6-in/15-cm cake pan lined with plastic wrap. Remove the frozen gelée from the pan and cut into a 5-in/13-cm round. Reserve in the freezer.

3   Portion 8 oz/227 g of the Bavarian cheese mousse into a 6-in/15-cm cake ring.

4   Lightly press a round of carrot cake into the mousse so it comes up the sides of the cake.

5   Spread another 8 oz/227 g of the mousse on top of the carrot cake and lightly press the frozen round of gelée into the mousse so it comes up the sides of the gelée. Place the final layer of carrot cake on top and press into the mousse so it is level with the top of the cake ring. Freeze the cake for 6 hours, or overnight, until completely set.

6   Garnish with a half of a poached pear and a candied carrot chip.

Harvest apple cheesecake

MAKES 1 CAKE (6 IN/15 CM)

Linzer dough (page 227)	4 oz	113 g
Poached apple compote (page 447)	10 oz	284 g
Cinnamon ganache (page 422)	3 oz	85 g
Pumpkin cake (page 272), 5-in/13-cm rounds, ½ in/1 cm thick	1 each	1 each
Spiced cider simple syrup	2 oz	57 g
Pumpkin cheesecake mousse (page 390)	1 lb	454 g
Spiced mirror glaze (page 425)	4 oz	113 g

1 Roll out the linzer dough ¼ in/6 mm thick and refrigerate until firm. Cut the dough into a 5-in/13-cm round.

2 Bake at 350°F/177°C until golden brown, about 12 minutes. If the cookie spreads while baking, trim it while still warm. Cool completely.

3 Freeze the apple compote in two 6-in/15-cm cake pans lined with plastic wrap. Remove the frozen compote from the pans and cut one into a 5-in/13-cm round and the other with an apple-shaped cutter. Reserve in the freezer.

4 Spread 3 oz/85 g of the cinnamon ganache on the linzer cookie round. Place the pumpkin cake round on top and brush with the simple syrup.

5 Line a sheet pan with plastic wrap and place a 6-in/15-cm cake ring on top. Place the frozen apple-shaped compote in the center. Spread 8 oz/227 g of the cheesecake mousse into the prepared cake ring.

6 Lightly press the remaining frozen apple compote into the mousse so the mousse comes up the sides of the compote.

7 Fill the cake ring to ¾ in/2 cm from the top with the remaining cheesecake mousse. Press the linzer and pumpkin base into the mousse, making sure the linzer is level with the top of the ring. Freeze the cake for 6 hours, or overnight, until completely frozen.

8 Working with the cake still frozen and in the ring, ladle the mirror glaze flavored with apple cider reduction into the center of the cake. Spread with an offset spatula to cover the surface completely. Unmold the cake by warming the sides slightly with a torch. Garnish as desired and serve.

Lemon raspberry basil cake

MAKES 1 CAKE (6 IN/15 CM)

Candied lemon slices	8 each	8 each
Lemon cookie dough (page 223)	4 oz	113 g
Basil cremeux (page 366)	6 oz	170 g
Raspberry jam	2 oz	57 g
Citrus white chocolate sablés (page 318), 5-in/13-cm rounds	1 each	1 each
Lemon chiffon sponge (page 287), 5-in/13-cm rounds	2 each	2 each
Lemon mousse (page 386)	14 oz	397 g
Simple syrup (page 900)	3 fl oz	90 mL
Raspberry mirror glaze (see Variation, page 427)	4 oz	113 g
White chocolate ribbon (see page 831)	1 each	1 each
Fresh raspberries	3 each	3 each

1   Line a cake ring with candied lemon slices.

2   Roll out the cookie dough ¼ in/6 mm thick and cut into a 5-in/13-cm round.

3   Bake at 350°F/177°C until golden brown, about 12 minutes. If the cookie spreads while baking, trim it while still warm. Cool completely.

4   Freeze the basil cremeux in a 6-in/15-cm cake pan lined with plastic wrap. Remove the frozen cremeaux from the pan and cut into a 5-in/13-cm round. Reserve in the freezer.

5   Spread the raspberry jam on top of the sablé round and top with a round of chiffon sponge, pressing gently to adhere. Reserve.

6   Portion 6 oz/170 g of the lemon mousse into a 6-in/15-cm cake ring.

7   Lightly press the cremeux into the mousse so it comes up the sides of the cremeux.

8   Moisten the remaining chiffon sponge with the simple syrup and place on top of the cremeux.

9   Portion the remaining mousse into the ring and place the cookie sandwich on last with the cookie facing up, pressing gently into place. Freeze the cake for 6 hours, or overnight, until completely frozen.

10   Working with the cake still frozen and in the ring, ladle the mirror glaze into the center. Spread with an offset spatula to cover the surface completely. Refrigerate to set the glaze. Unmold the cake by warming the sides slightly with a torch. Garnish with the white chocolate ribbon and fresh raspberries.

TOP ROW, FROM LEFT: Lining a mold with candied lemon slices; assembling an entremet: adding a gelatin-based filling layer; adding the base to the entremet. The cake was built upside down to achieve a perfectly flat top.

BOTTOM ROW, FROM LEFT: Spreading an even layer of glaze on a frozen entremet; removing the ring from the cake while it is still frozen; finished Lemon Raspberry Basil Cake.

"Fig Newton" cake

MAKES 1 CAKE (6 IN/15 CM)

Patterned Joconde sponge (page 284)	1 sheet	1 sheet
Fresh figs	12 each	12 each
Fig Newton dough (page 236)	4 oz	113 g
Fig compote (page 447)	6 oz	170 g
Almond dacquoise (page 296), 5-in/13-cm rounds	2 each	2 each
Mascarpone mousse (page 389)	1 lb	454 g
Spray red-colored cocoa butter	as needed	as needed
Mirror glaze (page 424)	4 oz	113 g
Candied almonds	3 each	3 each
Candied orange peel	4 each	4 each

1　Lightly butter a 6-in/15-cm cake ring and line with the strip of Joconde that is cut 1 by 9 in/3 by 23 cm. Cut the fresh figs in half and place them cut side out, side by side around the interior of the cake ring just above the Joconde, trimming figs if necesssary so they don't come above the ring.

2　Roll out 4 oz/113 g of the Fig Newton dough ¼ in/6 mm thick and cut one 5-in/12-cm round. Bake in a preheated 325°F/163°C oven until golden brown, about 12 minutes. Cool completely. Trim with a 5-inch/13-cm cutter while still warm.

3　Spread 3 oz/85 g of the fig compote on top of the cookie round and top with a round of dacquoise. Press gently to adhere.

4　Spread 3 oz/85 g of the fig compote on top of the second dacquoise round and reserve.

5　Portion 8 oz/227 g of the mascarpone mousse in the cake ring.

6　Place the fig and dacquoise layer on top with the fig side into the mousse, and press gently into place so the mousse comes up the sides of the dacquoise.

7　Portion the remaining mousse into the cake ring and place the cookie sandwich on last with the cookie facing up, pressing gently into place. Freeze the cake for 6 hours, or overnight, until completely set.

8　Working with the cake still frozen and in the ring, spray a pattern on top of the cake with red-colored cocoa butter. Laddle the mirror glaze into the center of the cake. Spread with an offset spatula to cover the surface completely. Refrigerate to set the glaze. Unmold the cake by warming the sides slightly with a torch. Garnish with fresh figs, candied almonds, and candied orange peel.

Coconut pineapple passion fruit cake

MAKES 1 CAKE (6 IN/15 CM)

1-2-3 cookie dough (page 223)	3 oz	85 g
Décor biscuit (page 349)	1 sheet	1 sheet
Butter, softened	as needed	as needed
Braised pineapple (page 896)	1 each	1 each
White chocolate, melted	2 oz	57 g
Coconut dacquoise (page 296), 5-in/13-cm rounds	2 each	2 each
Coconut mousse (page 379)	8 oz	227 g
Passion fruit mousse (page 379)	8 oz	227 g
Candied pineapple	3 oz	85 g
Passion fruit glaze (see Variation, page 427)	4 oz	113 g
Passion fruit seeds	as needed	as needed
White chocolate spirals	as needed	as needed

1   Line a sheet pan with of plastic wrap and place a 6-in/15-cm cake ring on top.

2   Roll out the cookie dough ⅛ in/3 mm thick and cut into a 5-in/13-cm round.

3   Bake at 350°F/177°C until golden brown, about 12 minutes. If the cookie spreads while baking, trim it while still warm. Cool completely.

4   Cut the décor biscuit into a strip 1½ by 19 in/4 by 48 cm.

5   Brush the inside of the cake ring lightly with softened butter and line the interior with the décor biscuit strip.

6   Place three slices of the braised pineapple (⅛-in/3-mm thick) in the center of the ring, overlapping the slices so there is at least 1 in/3 cm of space between the ring and the edge of the pineapple.

7   Using a pastry brush, brush the white chocolate onto one of the dacquoise layers and sandwich with the cookie base.

8   Portion 8 oz/227 g of the coconut mousse on top of the pineapple in the cake ring.

9   Lightly press the dacquoise layer without the chocolate into the mousse so it comes up the sides of the dacquoise.

10   Portion 8 oz/227 g of the passion fruit mousse into the ring mold, bringing it ¾ in/2 cm from the top of the ring. Sprinkle with the candied pineapple.

11   Place the tart dough/dacquoise sandwich on last with the tart dough facing up, pressing gently into place. Freeze the cake overnight, or until completely frozen.

12 Working with the cake still frozen and in the ring, laddle the passion fruit glaze into the center of the cake. Spread with an offset spatula to cover the surface completely. Unmold the cake by warming the sides slightly with a torch and place on a platter or cake board. Garnish with passion fruit seeds and white chocolate spirals.

FROM FAR LEFT, CLOCKWISE: **Harvest Apple Cheesecake** (page 605), Coconut Pineapple Passion Fruit Cake (page 609), Lemon Raspberry Basil Cake (page 606), "Fig Newton" Cake (page 608), and Carrot Cake (page 604)

chapter seventeen

Breakfast pastries

for generations, Europeans have reveled in the pastries they enjoy each morning. In France, viennoiseries, or baked products that are sweeter and heavier than bread, are typically eaten at breakfast. Breakfast pastries include everything from flaky croissants to crisp, fruit-filled Danish to moist blueberry muffins.

CLOCKWISE FROM RIGHT:
Croissants (page 625), Bear
Claws (page 626), Schnecken
(page 631), and Cherry
Cheese Baskets
(page 629)

Croissant and Danish doughs

Croissant and Danish doughs have many similarities in ingredients and preparation method. They differ, however, in ratios of ingredients and application. Danish dough contains a higher percentage of fat and other enriching ingredients, which gives finished pastries using this dough flakier layers. Danish dough is commonly used to prepare individual as well as larger cake-style pastries, while croissant dough is used only to produce individually sized items.

1. Prepare croissant and Danish doughs as directed. Croissant and Danish doughs are laminated using the same principles that apply when making puff pastry; the only difference is that these two doughs have the additional leavening power of yeast. The addition of yeast to a laminated dough results in pastry that is tender and soft inside, rather than crisp as is puff pastry.

2. To work with croissant and Danish doughs after they are completely prepared, keep the dough chilled, taking out only the amount you can cut, fill, and shape in a relatively short amount of time. If the dough starts to warm as you work with it, you may lose some of the flaky, delicate texture that is the hallmark of a well-made Danish or croissant.

    Fully proofed croissants, ready to bake (TOP), and unproofed croissants just after shaping (BOTTOM)

    The delicate and flaky texture desired of this product is created by maintaining distinct layers of fat and dough throughout the process; warm dough may result in overly softened butter that oozes out of the layers during rolling.

3. Use a sharp knife when shaping or cutting the dough. Clean cuts will ensure that the baked item rises evenly. To keep cuts even and straight when cutting by hand, use a straightedge as a guideline. Pastry wheels are helpful when cutting large quantities of dough. Croissant dough may be cut using specialty cutters.

    As the pastry is cut, you may create scraps or trim. These scraps can be reserved and rerolled for use in pastries where high, straight rise is not critical. Scraps should be layered flat on top of each other, preserving the layers of fat and dough, and then rolled and stored under refrigeration or frozen.

4. After Danish or croissant doughs have been filled as desired and shaped, they are pan-proofed until nearly double in volume. Typically, they are lightly coated with egg wash. Depending upon the shaping and filling technique, Danish dough may be brushed with a clear fruit glaze or gel after baking for even greater moisture, flavor, and visual appeal.

    Using an egg wash creates a glossy, shiny crust.

CLOCKWISE FROM RIGHT: **Wreath Coffee Cake (page 633), Braided Coffee Cake (page 630), Chocolate and Pecan Babka (page 189)**

Coffee cakes

Coffee cakes are usually made with either sweet or Danish dough and are filled with a variety of items such as fruits, nuts, and smears. There are many ways to shape coffee cakes as well: Wreathed, braided, or twisted are common methods seen with these cakes.

Muffins

Muffins are a great addition to any breakfast plate. Typically the creaming method (see page 240) is used to make muffins, which results in rich baked goods with an exceptionally smooth, light, and even texture.

A variety of different fruits, flavors, nuts, and garnishes can be added to muffins to give them a special flare. Citrus zests can add a refreshing tang to your muffins; chocolate can give them a rich, decadent taste. The options are limitless when it comes to creating muffins.

Cranberry orange muffins

MAKES 1 DOZEN MUFFINS (3½ OZ/99 G EACH)

All-purpose flour	13 oz	369 g
Baking powder	2 tsp	6 g
Sugar	10½ oz	298 g
Butter, soft	2¾ oz	78 g
Salt	1½ tsp	7.50 g
Eggs	5 oz	142 g
Buttermilk	5 fl oz	150 mL
Vanilla extract	½ fl oz	15 mL
Vegetable oil	2¾ fl oz	83 mL
Cranberries (fresh or frozen)	11 oz	312 g
Orange zest, grated	1½ oz	43 g
Coarse sugar	2 oz	57 g

1   Coat the muffin tins with a light film of fat or use appropriate paper liners.

2   Sift together the flour and baking powder.

3   Cream together the sugar, butter, and salt on medium speed with the paddle attachment, scraping down the bowl periodically, until the mixture is smooth and light in color, about 5 minutes.

4   Whisk the eggs, buttermilk, vanilla, and oil together. Add to the butter-sugar mixture in 2 to 3 additions, mixing until fully incorporated after each addition and scraping down the bowl as needed.

5   Add the sifted dry ingredients and mix on low speed until evenly moistened. Fold in the cranberries and orange zest.

6   Scale 3½ oz/99 g batter into the prepared muffin tins, filling them three-quarters full.

7   Gently tap the filled tins to release any air bubbles and sprinkle with coarse sugar.

8   Bake at 375°F/191°C for 30 minutes, or until a skewer inserted near the center of a muffin comes out clean.

9   Cool the muffins in the tins for a few minutes, and then transfer to racks to cool completely.

NOTE   Replace the coarse sugar with Streusel Topping (page 901) for an alternative.

VARIATION   **BLUEBERRY MUFFINS** Omit the cranberries and orange zest and fold in 12 oz/340 g blueberries (fresh or frozen) in step 5 after adding the dry ingredients. Follow the remaining method as stated above.

Lemon poppy seed muffins

MAKES 4 DOZEN MUFFINS (4 OZ/113 G EACH)

Pastry flour	1 lb 8 oz	680 g
Bread flour	1 lb 8 oz	680 g
Baking powder	1¼ oz	35 g
Butter	2 lb	907 g
Sugar	2 lb 6½ oz	1.09 kg
Salt	1 tsp	5 mL
Crème fraîche or sour cream	1 lb 2 oz	510 g
Eggs	2 lb	907 g
Lemon juice	4½ oz	128 g
Lemon extract	1 tbsp	15 mL
Vegetable oil	8 oz	227 g
Lemon zest	1½ oz	43 g
Poppy seeds	4 oz	113 g
Coarse sugar	as needed	as needed

1   Coat the muffin tins with a light film of fat or use appropriate paper liners.

2   Sift together the flours and baking powder.

3   Cream together the butter, sugar, and salt on medium speed with the paddle attachment, scraping down the bowl periodically, until the mixture is smooth and light in color, about 5 minutes. Blend in the crème fraîche.

4   Whisk the eggs, lemon juice, lemon extract, and oil together. Add to the butter-sugar mixture in 2 to 3 additions, mixing until fully incorporated after each addition and scraping down the bowl as needed. Blend in the lemon zest and poppy seeds.

5   Add the sifted dry ingredients and mix on low speed until evenly moistened.

6   Scale 4 oz/113 g batter into the prepared muffin tins, filling them three-quarters full.

7   Gently tap the filled tins to release any air bubbles and sprinkle with coarse sugar.

8   Bake at 375°F/191°C for 30 minutes, or until a skewer inserted near the center of a muffin comes out clean.

9   Cool the muffins in the tins for a few minutes, then transfer to racks to cool completely.

Morning glory muffins

MAKES 1 DOZEN MUFFINS (4½ OZ/128 G EACH)

All-purpose flour	14 oz	397 g
Sugar	12¼ oz	347 g
Ground cinnamon	1 tsp	2 g
Baking soda	2¼ tsp	9 g
Salt	¼ tsp	1.25 g
Coconut, shredded	3½ oz	99 g
Raisins	5½ oz	156 g
Carrots, grated	5½ oz	156 g
Apples, grated	7 oz	198 g
Pineapple, crushed, drained	5½ oz	155 g
Walnuts, toasted and chopped	2¾ oz	78 g
Eggs	8 oz	227 g
Vegetable oil	7½ fl oz	225 g
Vanilla extract	1 tsp	5 mL
Rolled oats	as needed	as needed

1　Coat the muffin tins with a light film of fat or use appropriate paper liners.

2　Sift together the flour, sugar, cinnamon, baking soda, and salt. Blend the coconut, raisins, carrots, apples, pineapple, and walnuts into the sifted dry ingredients.

3　Combine the eggs, oil, and vanilla.

4　Blend the dry ingredient mixture into the egg mixture.

5　Scale 4½ oz/128 g batter into the prepared muffin tins, filling them three-quarters full. Gently tap the filled tins to release any air bubbles. Sprinkle rolled oats over the top of each muffin.

6　Bake at 375°F/191°C for 30 minutes, or until a skewer inserted near the center of a muffin comes out clean.

7　Cool the muffins in the tins for a few minutes, then transfer to racks to cool completely.

Bran muffins

MAKES 4 DOZEN MUFFINS (3½ OZ/99 G EACH)

Bread flour	1 lb 8 oz	680 g
Baking powder	1½ oz	43 g
Sugar	1 lb	454 g
Butter	8 oz	227 g
Salt	½ oz	14 g
Eggs	1 lb	454 g
Milk	1 lb	454 g
Honey	4 oz	113 g
Molasses	4 oz	113 g
Bran	8 oz	227 g

1. Coat the muffin tins with a light film of fat or use appropriate paper liners.

2. Sift together the flour and baking powder.

3. Cream together the sugar, butter, and salt on medium speed with the paddle attachment, scraping down the bowl periodically, until the mixture is smooth and light in color, about 5 minutes.

4. Combine the eggs and milk and add to the butter mixture in 3 additions, mixing until fully incorporated after each addition and scraping down the bowl as needed. Add the honey and molasses and blend until just incorporated.

5. Add the sifted dry ingredients and the bran and mix on low speed until evenly moistened.

6. Scale 3½ oz/99 g batter into the prepared muffin tins, filling them three-quarters full. Gently tap the filled tins to release any air bubbles.

7. Bake at 375°F/191°C for 30 minutes, or until a skewer inserted near the center of a muffin comes out clean.

8. Cool the muffins in the tins for a few minutes, then transfer to racks to cool completely.

Corn muffins

MAKES 4 DOZEN MUFFINS (3½ OZ/99 G EACH)

Bread flour	1 lb 2 oz	510 g
Pastry flour	1 lb 2 oz	510 g
Cornmeal	15 oz	425 g
Salt	1 oz	28 g
Baking powder	1½ oz	43 g
Eggs	12½ oz	354 g
Milk	30 fl oz	900 mL
Vegetable oil	1 lb 2 oz	510 g
Orange juice concentrate	1½ fl oz	45 mL
Sugar	1 lb 12 oz	794 g

1   Coat the muffin tins with a light film of fat or use appropriate paper liners.

2   Sift together the flours, cornmeal, salt, and baking powder.

3   Combine the eggs, milk, oil, orange juice, and sugar and mix on medium speed with the paddle attachment for 2 minutes.

4   Add the sifted dry ingredients and mix on low speed until fully incorporated.

5   Scale 4 oz/113 g batter into the prepared muffin tins, filling them three-quarters full. Gently tap the filled tins to release any air bubbles.

6   Bake at 400°F/204°C for 15 to 18 minutes, or until a skewer inserted near the center of a muffin comes out clean.

7   Cool the muffins in the tins for a few minutes, then transfer to racks to cool completely.

Crêpes suzette

MAKES 6 SERVINGS, 3 CRÊPES PER SERVING

Sugar	1½ oz	43 g
Butter, cubed	6 oz	170 g
Orange zest	1½ oz	43 g
Orange juice	12 fl oz	360 mL
Crêpes (page 229), 6 in/15 cm in diameter	18 each	18 each
Grand Marnier	3 fl oz	90 mL
Brandy or cognac	3 fl oz	90 mL

1   Preheat a crêpe pan over medium-low heat.

2   Sprinkle the sugar evenly across the bottom of the heated crêpe pan.

3   As the sugar begins to caramelize, add the butter to the outside edges of the pan and gently shake the pan, allowing the butter to evenly temper and blend with the sugar.

4   Add the orange zest and shake the pan gently to thoroughly blend all the ingredients until they become a light orange caramel color.

5   Pour the orange juice on the outside edges of the pan slowly, allowing it to temper and blend with the sugar. Shake the pan gently, incorporating all the ingredients and allowing the sauce to thicken.

6   Sandwich a crêpe between a fork and a spoon and place the crêpe into the sauce. Once one side of the crêpe is coated, flip it over to coat the other side of the crêpe. Repeat this process with the remaining crêpes (move quickly so the sauce does not become too thick).

7   Remove the pan from the heat, add the Grand Marnier, but do not flame, return to the heat, and shake gently.

8   Slide the pan back and forth over the front edge of the heat; allow the pan to get hot.

9   Remove the pan, add the brandy, tip the pan slightly to flame, and then shake the pan until the flame dies.

10   Plate 3 crêpes per portion; shingle one over the other and lightly coat with approximately 1 fl oz/30 mL of sauce.

Crêpes Normandy

MAKES 6 SERVINGS, 2 CRÊPES PER SERVING

Light brown sugar	6 oz	170 g
Butter, cubed	6 oz	170 g
Apples, peeled and sliced ¼ in/6 mm thick	3 each	3 each
Apple juice or cider	9 fl oz	270 mL
Crêpes (page 229), 6 in/15 cm in diameter	12 each	12 each
Calvados	3 fl oz	90 mL
Heavy cream, whipped	9 oz	255 g

1   Preheat a crêpe pan over medium-low heat.

2   Sprinkle the brown sugar evenly across the bottom of the heated crêpe pan.

3   As the sugar begins to caramelize, add the butter to the outside edges of the pan and gently shake the pan; this allows the butter to evenly temper and blend with the sugar.

4   Add the apples to the pan. Coat with the sauce and turn once.

5   Add the apple juice. Shake the pan gently to thoroughly blend all the ingredients until the sauce starts to thicken.

6   Sandwich a crêpe between a fork and spoon and place the crêpe into the sauce. Once one side is coated with sauce, flip the crêpe over and place several slices of apples in the crêpe. Fold the crêpe in half and move the crêpe to the edge of the pan.

7   Repeat this process with remaining crêpes (move quickly so the sauce does not become too thick).

8   Slide the pan back and forth over the front edge of the heat; allow the pan to get hot.

9   Remove the pan form the heat, add the Calvados, and tip the pan slightly to flame the Calvados. Shake the pan until the flame dies.

10   Plate 2 filled crêpes per portion, lightly coat with 1 fl oz/30 mL of sauce, and spoon a dollop of whipped cream over each crêpe.

Crêpes d'amour

Light brown sugar	1 oz	28 g
Butter, cubed	7 oz	198 g
Sliced almonds, blanched	3 oz	85 g
Orange juice	12 fl oz	360 mL
Strawberry liqueur	3 fl oz	90 mL
Strawberries, sliced ¼ in/6 mm thick	24 each	24 each
Crêpes (page 229), 6 in/15 cm in diameter	12 each	12 each
Vanilla ice cream, quenelle shaped	12 each	12 each
Brandy or cognac	3 fl oz	90 mL

1   Preheat a crêpe pan over medium-low heat.

2   Sprinkle brown sugar evenly across the bottom of the heated crêpe pan.

3   As the sugar begins to caramelize, add the butter to the outside edges of the pan and gently shake the pan; this allows the butter to evenly temper and blend with the sugar.

4   Shake the pan gently to thoroughly blend until all the ingredients become a light orange caramel color.

5   Add the sliced almonds and sauté until lightly colored.

6   Add the orange juice, strawberry liqueur, and strawberries, gently shake the pan to incorporate the ingredients, and allow the sauce to thicken.

7   Sandwich a crêpe between a fork and spoon and place the crêpe into the sauce. Once one side of the crêpe is coated in sauce, flip it over and place 2 oz/57 g of the sauce and strawberry mixture and 1 quenelle of ice cream in the crêpe.

8   Fold the crêpe in half and move it to the edge of the pan, and repeat the process with remaining crêpes (move quickly so the sauce does not become too thick).

9   Slide the pan back and forth over front edge of the heat; allow the pan to get hot.

10   Remove the pan from the heat, add the brandy, and tip the pan slightly to flame the brandy. Shake the pan until the flame dies.

11   Plate 2 crêpes per portion and lightly coat with 1 fl oz/30 mL of sauce, moving quickly so the ice cream does not melt.

Pain au chocolat

MAKES 12 PASTRIES

Croissant dough (page 234)	1 lb 14 oz	851 g
Egg wash (page 892)	as needed	as needed
Chocolate batons, 3 in/8 cm long	24 each	24 each

1   Roll the croissant dough into a rectangle 5 by 36 in/13 by 91 cm. Trim the edges so they are even.

2   With a long edge of the rolled dough facing you, brush the bottom half of the rectangle with egg wash. Place the chocolate batons in pairs the entire length of the dough, starting one-third of the way from the top of the rectangle. Fold the top of the dough over the batons, leaving 1½ in/4 cm of dough at the bottom. Fold the folded dough containing the chocolate over again, so that the seam is centered on the bottom of the dough.

3   Brush the dough with egg wash. Cut into 12 segments 3 in/8 cm long, so that each pair of chocolate batons is contained within one pastry. Place on a parchment-lined sheet pan, making 4 rows of 3 pastries each.

4   Proof at 85°F/29°C for 1 hour, or until doubled in size.

5   Brush the pastries with egg wash. Bake at 375°F/191°C until well browned, about 15 minutes.

Rolling pain au chocolate

Properly baked croissant. Note the internal structure. (Pain au Chocolate, page 623, is shown in the background.)

Croissants

MAKES 11 CROISSANTS

Croissant dough (page 234)	2 lb 4 oz	1.02 kg
Egg wash (page 892)	as needed	as needed

1. Roll the dough into a rectangle 9 by 24 in/23 by 61 cm.

2. Cut 11 isosceles triangles, 9 in/23 cm high and 4 in/10 cm at the base, from the dough.

3. Make a ¾-in/2-cm slit in the center of the base of each triangle. Working with one triangle at a time, gently stretch each of the 3 points of the triangle to elongate them. Place the triangle on an unfloured table with the narrow point directly away from you. Roll the triangle up from the base, exerting gentle pressure with your fingertips. Place seam side down on a parchment-lined sheet pan, making 4 rows. Shape the croissants into crescents, so that the ends curve inward at the front.

4. Brush the croissants with egg wash. Proof at 85°F/29°C for 1 hour, or until doubled in size.

5. Brush the croissants with egg wash again. Bake at 375°F/191°C until well browned, about 15 minutes.

VARIATION **ALMOND CROISSANTS** Before rolling up the croissants, using a pastry bag fitted with a #4 plain tip, pipe ½ oz/14 g Almond Filling (page 894) onto the base of each triangle. Leave the rolled croissants straight rather than making crescent shapes. After the second egg wash, sprinkle un-toasted sliced almonds onto the croissants.

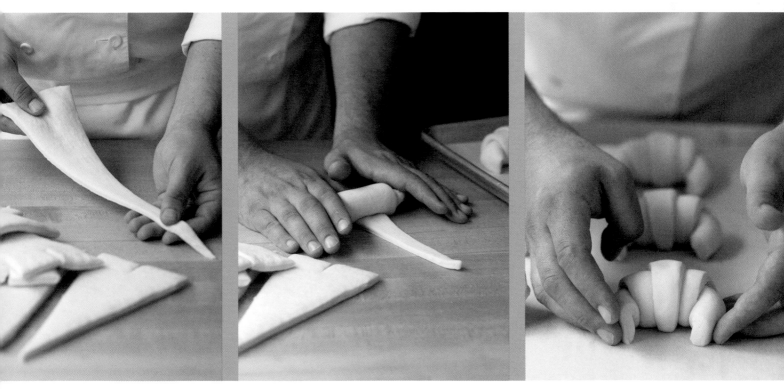

LEFT: Stretching the triangle of croissant dough   MIDDLE: Rolling into a cylinder   RIGHT: Shaping into a crescent

Bear claws

MAKES 12 PASTRIES

Danish dough (page 235)	2 lb	907 g
Egg wash (page 892)	as needed	as needed
Almond filling (page 894)	1 lb 2 oz	510 g
Sliced almonds	4 oz	113 g
Apricot glaze (page 426), warm	as needed	as needed

1   Roll the dough into a rectangle 5 by 48 in/13 by 122 cm.

2   Brush the dough lightly with egg wash. Using a pastry bag fitted with a #9 plain tip, pipe a cylinder of filling lengthwise down the center of the dough. Fold the dough over the filling, lining up the edges carefully. Press the edges together to seal them.

3   Cut the dough crosswise into strips 4 in/10 cm wide.

4   Using a bench scraper, make 4 cuts in the seamed edge of each pastry. Curve the pastry back to open the cuts. Place the pastries on a parchment-lined sheet pan, making 4 rows of 3 pastries each.

5   Brush the pastries lightly with egg wash. Proof at 85°F/29°C for 1 hour, or until doubled in size.

6   Brush the pastries lightly with egg wash again. Sprinkle with the sliced almonds.

7   Bake at 375°F/191°C until golden brown, about 17 minutes.

8   Brush the pastries with the warm glaze while they are still hot. Cool completely before serving.

Cheese pockets

MAKES 12 POCKETS

Danish dough (page 235)	1 lb 8 oz	680 g
Egg wash (page 892)	as needed	as needed
Cheese Danish filling (page 895)	12 oz	340 g
Sliced almonds	4 oz	113 g
Apricot glaze (page 426), warm	as needed	as needed

1   Roll the dough into a rectangle 12 by 16 in/30 by 41 cm. Cut the dough into twelve 4-in/10-cm squares.

2   Brush each square lightly with egg wash. Using a pastry bag fitted with a #5 plain tip, pipe 1 oz/28 g of the cheese filling onto the center of each square. One at a time, fold the corners of the dough over the filling into the center, so that each corner overlaps the previous one. Seal the pocket by pressing gently on the overlapped corners. Pierce the center of the pocket with the almonds to ensure they stay closed.

3   Brush the pockets lightly with egg wash. Proof at 85°F/29°C for 1 hour, or until doubled in size.

4   Brush the pockets lightly with egg wash again. Bake at 350°F/177°C until golden brown, about 17 minutes.

5   Brush the pastries with the warm glaze while they are still hot.

Filling the squares of Danish dough with cheese filling   Brushing the baked pastries with apricot glaze

Cherry half-pockets

MAKES 12 PASTRIES

Danish dough (page 235)	1 lb 8 oz	680 g
Egg wash (page 892)	as needed	as needed
Cherry filling (page 521)	12 oz	340 g
Apricot glaze (page 426), warm	as needed	as needed

1   Roll the dough into a rectangle 12 by 16 in/30 by 41 cm. Cut the dough into twelve 4-in/10-cm squares.

2   Brush each square lightly with egg wash. Place 1 oz/28 g of the cherry filling at the center of each square. Fold one corner of the dough over just so it covers the filling, and press to seal. Stretch the opposite corner of dough over the first folded corner and around to go under the finished pocket. Pinch lightly to seal.

3   Brush the pockets lightly with egg wash. Proof at 85°F/29°C for 1 hour, or until doubled in size.

4   Brush the pockets lightly with egg wash again. Bake at 375°F/191°C until golden brown, about 17 minutes.

5   Brush the pockets with the warm glaze while they are still hot.

Cherry cheese baskets

MAKES 12 PASTRIES

Danish dough (page 235)	1 lb 8 oz	680 g
Egg wash (page 892)	as needed	as needed
Cheese Danish filling (page 895)	8 oz	227 g
Cherry filling (page 521)	8 oz	227 g
Apricot glaze (page 426), warm	as needed	as needed

1   Roll the dough into a rectangle 12 by 16 in/30 by 41 cm. Cut the dough into twelve 4-in/10-cm squares.

2   Fold each square diagonally in half. Position a folded square so that the corner opposite the fold is pointing away from you. Insert the tip of the knife about ¼ in/6 mm from the corner and ½ in/1 cm from the edge of the dough and cut down through the dough, parallel to the edge, going through the folded side. Repeat on the opposite side, being careful not to cut through the corner.

3   Open out the square and brush lightly with egg wash. Fold over one of the cut corners so that its outside edge aligns with the newly cut inside edge on the opposite side. Repeat with the opposite side. Place on a parchment-lined sheet pan, and repeat with the remaining squares of dough.

4   Brush the pastries lightly with egg wash. Proof at 85°F/29°C for 1 hour.

5   Dock the centers of the pastries. Using a pastry bag fitted with a #6 plain tip, pipe ½ oz/14 g of the cheese filling onto the center of each pastry. Then, using a #8 plain tip, pipe ½ oz/14 g of the cherry filling on top of the cheese on each pastry.

6   Brush the dough lightly with egg wash again. Bake at 350°F/177°C until golden brown, about 17 minutes.

7   Brush the pastries with the warm glaze while they are still hot.

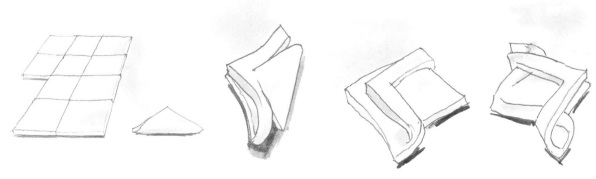

FROM LEFT TO RIGHT: Cutting the dough into 4-inch squares
Cutting through the dough parallel to the edge of the dough
Folding the first cut corner
Folding the second cut corner

Braided coffee cake

MAKES 1 CAKE (12 IN/30 CM LONG), 8 SLICES (1½ IN/4 CM EACH)

Danish dough (page 235)	1 lb	454 g
Egg wash (page 892)	as needed	as needed
Apple filling (page 549)	12 oz	340 g
Coarse sugar, for sprinkling	as needed	as needed
Apricot glaze (page 426), warm	as needed	as needed

1 Roll the dough into a rectangle 9 by 12 in/23 by 30 cm. Make a fringe down each long side of the dough by making cuts 3 in/8 cm long at intervals of 1 in/3 cm, leaving an uncut portion of dough in the center 3 in/8 cm wide.

2 Brush the dough lightly with egg wash. Place the filling in the middle of the uncut center portion of dough. One strip of dough at a time, fold the fringes over the filling at a 45-degree angle, alternating the sides and overlapping them.

3 Place on a parchment-lined sheet pan. Proof at 85°F/29°C for 1½ hours.

4 Brush the pastry lightly with egg wash again. Sprinkle with coarse sugar. Bake at 350°F/177°C until golden brown, about 40 minutes.

5 Brush the pastry with the warm glaze while it is still hot.

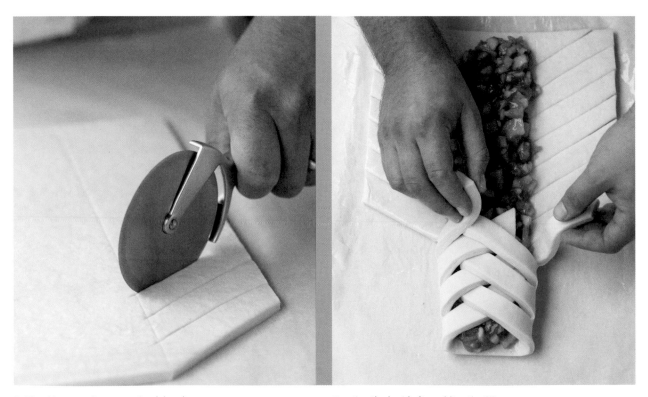

Cutting fringes in the rectangle of dough   Creating the braid after adding the filling

Rolling the filling inside the dough

Slicing the schnecken roulade into portions

Schnecken

MAKES 12 PASTRIES

Danish dough (page 235)	1 lb 4 oz	567 g
Pastry cream (page 370)	5 oz	142 g
Cinnamon sugar (page 897)	½ oz	14 g
Pecans, toasted and chopped	3 oz	85 g
Dried currants	3 oz	85 g
Egg wash (page 892)	as needed	as needed
Apricot glaze (page 426), warm	as needed	as needed

1   Roll the dough into a rectangle 8 by 16 in/20 by 41 cm.

2   Spread the pastry cream over the dough, leaving a bare strip of dough 1 in/3 cm wide along one of the long sides. Sprinkle the cinnamon sugar onto the pastry cream. Sprinkle the pecans and currants evenly over the cream. Roll lightly over the top with a rolling pin to press the nuts and currants into the cream.

3   Starting from the long side with the filling, roll up the dough into a roulade 16 in/41 cm long and press gently to seal.

4   Cut the roulade into 12 equal pieces. Place the pieces cut side down on a parchment-lined sheet pan, making 4 rows of 3 pastries each.

5   Brush the pastries lightly with egg wash. Proof at 85°F/29°C for 1 hour.

6   Lightly brush the pastries with egg wash again. Bake in a 375°F/191°C convection oven until golden brown, about 17 minutes.

7   Brush the pastries with the warm glaze while they are still hot.

Twist coffee cake

MAKES 1 CAKE (14 IN/36 CM LONG), 9 SLICES (1½ IN/4 CM EACH)

Danish dough (page 235)	1 lb 8 oz	680 g
Raspberry jam	8 oz	227 g
Egg wash (page 892)	as needed	as needed
Apricot glaze (page 426), warm	as needed	as needed

1   Roll the dough into a rectangle 8 by 14 in/20 by 36 cm.

2   Spread the jam over the dough, leaving bare a strip of dough 1 in/3 cm wide along one of the long sides.

3   Starting from the long side with the filling, roll up the dough into a roulade 14 in/36 cm long and press gently to seal. Using a sharp paring knife, cut 3 parallel lines down the length of the roulade to within 1 in/3 cm of each end of the roulade.

4   Holding the roulade at each end, gently twist it, and then shape it loosely into a spiral and place on a parchment-lined sheet pan.

5   Brush the spiral lightly with egg wash. Proof at 85°F/29°C for 1½ hours.

6   Brush with egg wash again. Bake at 350°F/177°C until golden brown, about 45 minutes.

7   Brush the spiral with the warm glaze while it is still hot. Cool completely before serving.

Danish twists

MAKES 12 PASTRIES

Danish dough (page 235)	2 lb 2 oz	964 g
Butter, melted	1 oz	28 g
Cinnamon sugar (page 897)	1 oz	28 g
Egg wash (page 892)	as needed	as needed
Raspberry jam	8 oz	227 g
Apricot glaze (page 426), warm	as needed	as needed

1   Roll the dough into a rectangle 12 by 24 in/30 by 61 cm.

2   Brush the dough with the melted butter. Sprinkle the cinnamon sugar over the dough. Roll over the dough lightly with a rolling pin so the sugar adheres to it. Fold the dough crosswise in half to make a 12-in/30-cm square. Roll the dough to seal and slightly stretch it.

3   Cut the dough into 12 even strips. One at a time, hold each strip and both ends and twist it, then shape it loosely into a spiral and place on a parchment-lined sheet pan, leaving a 2-in/5-cm space between pastries.

4   Brush the spirals lightly with egg wash. Proof at 85°F/29°C for 1 hour, or until doubled in size.

5   Brush the spirals lightly with egg wash again, stipple the centers, and using a pastry bag fitted with a #3 plain tip, pipe jam into the center of each Danish twist.

6   Bake in a 375°F/191°C convection oven until golden brown, about 17 minutes.

7   Brush the Danish twists with the warm glaze while they are still hot.

Wreath coffee cake

MAKES 1 CAKE, 9 SLICES (1½ IN/4 CM EACH)

Danish dough (page 235)	1 lb 8 oz	680 g
Hazelnut filling (page 895)	12 oz	340 g
Egg wash (page 892)	as needed	as needed
Sliced almonds	4 oz	113 g
Apricot glaze (page 426), warm	as needed	as needed

1   Roll the dough into a rectangle 8 by 14 in/20 by 36 cm.

2   Spread the filling over the dough. Starting from a long side, roll the dough up into a roulade 14 in/36 cm long and transfer to a parchment-lined sheet pan, placing the roulade seam side down.

3   Using a bench scraper, cut almost all the way through one side of the roulade at intervals of 1 in/3 cm, and join the ends to form a wreath. Twist each sliced portion outward to expose the interior.

4   Brush the wreath lightly with egg wash. Proof at 85°F/29°C for 1½ hours.

5   Brush the wreath lightly with egg wash again, and sprinkle with the almonds. Bake at 350°F/177°C until golden brown, about 45 minutes.

6   Brush the wreath with the warm glaze while it is still hot.

LEFT: Cutting slits almost through the dough

RIGHT: Forming the log into a wreath, twisting each section outward

Pineapple twists

MAKES 40 PASTRIES

Danish dough (page 235)	8 lb	3.63 kg
Braised pineapple (page 896)	4 lb	1.81 kg
Egg wash (page 892)	3 oz	85 g
Apricot glaze (page 426), warm	3 oz	85 g

1   Roll the dough into a rectangle 80 by 160 in/203 by 406 cm and ¼ in/6 mm thick.

2   Let the dough relax in the freezer for 30 minutes, covered in plastic wrap, until firm to the touch.

3   Meanwhile, slice the braised pineapple quarters into ⅛-in/3-mm triangles.

4   Cut the dough into rectangles 2 by 4 in/5 by 10 cm to obtain approximately 40 rectangles.

5   Using a wheel cutter, cut an incision inside each rectangle about 3 in/8 cm long.

6   Take one end of the rectangle and twist it through the incision; do the same with the other end of the rectangle in the opposite direction.

7   Brush the twists with egg wash. Place 5 pineapple triangles on top of each piece of dough, shingling the slices.

8   Proof at 82°F/28°C until doubled in size, about 2 hours.

9   Bake at 365°F/185°C until golden brown, 7 to 8 minutes. While the pastry is still hot, brush with the warm glaze to coat the surface.

VARIATION   Braise other fruits such as apples, pears, bananas, or stone fruit and use in the place of pineapple.

LEFT: **Cutting a slit in the dough**   MIDDLE: **Twisting the dough**   RIGHT: **Adding the pineapple topping**

Pain au raisin

MAKES 40 PASTRIES

Croissant dough (page 234)	8 lb	3.63 kg
Pastry cream (page 370)	2 lb	907 g
Poached raisins (page 899), drained	1 lb	454 g
Egg wash (page 892)	3 oz	85 g
Apricot glaze (page 426), warm	3 oz	85 g

1   Roll out all dough into a rectangle 18 by 20 in/46 by 51 cm and ¼ in /6 mm thick. Let the dough relax in the refrigerator for 30 minutes, covered in plastic wrap, until firm to the touch.

2   Spread the pastry cream evenly on the surface of the dough.

3   Sprinkle the poached raisins on top of the pastry cream, distributing them evenly. Place both of your hands on either side of the dough and evenly roll the dough away from you and into the shape of a roulade.

4   With the end of the roll at the bottom of the rolled dough, cut 1-in/3-cm pieces and place on a parchment-lined sheet pan; place no more than 12 pieces per sheet pan.

5   Brush the pastries with egg wash. Proof at 82°F/28°C until doubled in size, about 2 hours.

6   Bake at 365°F/185°C until golden brown, 7 to 8 minutes. While the pastry is still hot, brush with the warm glaze to coat the surface.

VARIATION   Substitute poached and drained currants or cranberries or chopped pecans or walnuts for the raisins.

Apricot pillows

MAKES 40 PASTRIES

Danish dough (page 235)	8 lb	3.63 kg
Egg wash (page 892)	3 oz	85 g
Almond filling (page 894)	2 lb	907 g
Canned apricot halves, drained	40 each	40 each
Apricot glaze (page 426), warm	3 oz	85 g
Pistachios, toasted and chopped	6 oz	170 g

1   Sheet out the Danish dough to ¼ in/6 mm thick. Let the dough relax in the freezer for 30 minutes, covered in plastic wrap, until firm to the touch.

2   Cut out disks using a 3-in/8-cm ring cutter; mark the inside center of the disks with a 2-in/5-cm ring cutter, being careful to cut only halfway through the dough.

3   Brush the disks with egg wash. Pipe ¾ oz/21 g of the almond filling inside the score, about ¼ in/6 mm high, and place an apricot half, skin side up, on top of the filling.

4   Brush the dough with the egg wash. Proof at 82°F/28°C until doubled in size, about 2 hours.

5   Bake at 365°F/185°C until golden brown, 7 to 8 minutes. While the pastry is still hot, brush with the warm glaze to coat the surface. Sprinkle the toasted pistachios on top.

VARIATION   Use other poached stone fruit such as peaches, plums, or cherries instead of apricots.

Pumpkin fontaines

MAKES 40 PASTRIES

Danish dough (page 235)	8 lb	3.63 kg
Egg wash (page 892)	3 oz	85 g
Cream cheese filling (page 895)	2 lb	907 g
Pumpkin butter (page 450)	2 lb	907 g
Apricot glaze (page 426), warm	3 oz	85 g
Walnuts, toasted and chopped	8 oz	227 g

1   Sheet out the Danish dough to ¼ in/6 mm thick. Let the dough relax in the freezer for 30 minutes, covered in plastic wrap, until the dough is firm to the touch.

2   Using a wheel cutter and ruler (or a 4-in/10-cm stencil), cut out 4-in/10-cm squares to obtain 40 pieces, about 3 oz/85 g each.

3   Using a 2-in/5-cm half-circle cutter, with the curve to the outside, cut completely through the dough on the left half of the square.

4   Brush the square with egg wash. Fold the left side of the square onto the right side, leaving the cut half circle lying flat on the pan.

5   Pipe a ring of a little less than ½ oz/14 g cream cheese filling onto the outside edge of each half circle. Then pipe a little less than ½ oz/14 g of the pumpkin butter into the center of the half circle. Brush the squares with egg wash.

6   Proof at 82°F/28°C until doubled in size, about 2 hours. Brush with egg wash again.

7   Bake at 365°F/185°C until golden brown, 7 to 8 minutes. While the pastry is still hot, brush with the warm glaze to coat completely. Sprinkle with the walnuts.

VARIATION   Substitute Fig Butter (page 449) and roasted figs for the pumpkin butter. Pipe the fig butter on top of the cream cheese and place one or two roasted figs on top of the fig butter before baking.

chapter eighteen

Individual pastries

*i*ndividual pastries, created from pastry doughs or batters with fillings, may be constructed as single portions or as a larger item, such as a cake, which is individually garnished and portioned. Individual pastries encompass a wide variety of baked goods, from very refined to rustic. Depending on the type of pastry, it may be appropriate for sale in a retail bakeshop, for service during breakfast or brunch, with coffee or tea, at receptions, or on a dessert menu.

637

Tartlets

By scaling down the formulas for various pies and tarts, the pastry chef can prepare a number of individual pastries. Most of the tartlet formulas in this chapter were developed using a 3-in/8-cm ring mold or tartlet pan (with the exception of those that are "free-form"), but the formulas can be easily adapted to suit molds of other sizes or shapes. The same basic principles used for preparing large pies and tarts apply to tartlets. They can be baked in a mold or free-form (as with a galette). They may be made using short dough or puff pastry dough. Depending on the type of filling, the shells may be partially or completely prebaked. They may be filled with fresh or poached fruits, nuts, chocolate ganache, or custard. Fillings may be precooked and poured into a baked shell or baked with the crust. Many types of fillings contain components that combine techniques; for example, one component of a filling could be a frangipane filling, which would be baked with the crust, then jam could be added in a thin, even layer, and the tart finished by topping it with fresh berries or other fruit. Combining elements in this way gives the pastry chef freedom to explore different flavor and textural profiles to create unique desserts.

Prebaked tartlet shells should be left in the ring molds while they are filled, to support them during assembly and until the filling sets.

Lining a ring mold with tart dough

Poached fruits

Poached fruits may be featured as a main component of a plated dessert, in fillings or toppings, or as garnish. Usually, fruits to be poached should be firm enough to hold their shape during cooking. Very tender fruits such as berries and bananas are generally not cooked using this technique. The greater the amount of sugar added to the poaching liquid, the more firm the end result will be. Using wine as part or all of the poaching liquid will have a similar effect. Poaching liquids that include some wine may be reduced and served as a sauce with the poached fruit or plated dessert.

Prepare the fruit as necessary. In some cases, it may be desirable to remove the peel, core, and seeds or pits before poaching the fruit. Combine the fruit with the poaching liquid, often a mixture of simple syrup, spices, and occasionally wine, and bring to a bare simmer. Reduce the heat and gently poach the fruit until it is tender. Test the fruit by piercing it with a sharp knife. There should be little to no resistance. Allow the fruit to cool in the poaching liquid, if possible. Poached fruits may be stored overnight or served immediately.

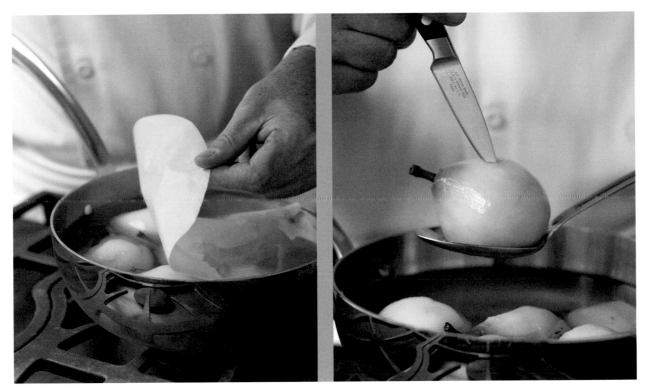

LEFT: Placing a piece of parchment paper over the poaching fruits to submerge them into the poaching liquid

RIGHT: Piercing the fruit with a paring knife to test for doneness

Layered pastries and roulades

Layered individual pastries can be composed of various types of cake or pastry that are baked as sheets so they can be layered or rolled with a complementary filling. Properly assembled, the evenly filled, level layers make a dramatic and visually appealing pastry when sliced. A variety of icings, such as ganache, buttercream, whipped cream, fondant, or a clear glaze, may be applied to the assembled pastry. These large layered pastries can be cut into a variety of shapes, such as triangles or rectangles, to make individual portions. Assembling pastries in this manner results in very little loss or trim, making them an economical choice for production. Many traditional, classic, and contemporary cakes can be adapted with only minor modifications to suit this style of assembly.

Roulades are made from a sheet of cake or other cake that is flexible enough to be rolled without splitting. The sheet of cake is spread with an even layer of filling and then rolled, chilled, iced, and decorated. The roulade is then sliced into individual portions for service. Roulades are easy to prepare and can be made ahead and finished as needed.

Pastries formed in molds

You can use a variety of small portion-size molds to shape such pastry components as mousse, Bavarian cream, and other stable creams. In most cases, gelatin is added to the cream to give it enough structure to hold its shape after it is unmolded.

There are several styles and materials to choose from. One option is flexible molds made of silicone, produced in hemisphere, pyramid, and other shapes. Cups, bowls, and other small containers also work well.

Combine components in a variety of colors, flavors, and textures, as we have done here. To add texture, consider small cookies, ladyfingers, sponge, or fresh fruit. To add color, include a garnish of a contrasting color.

Containers

Pastry chefs are often on the lookout for unusual and attractive containers for presenting and serving special pastries and other desserts. Glass containers have several appealing qualities. Clear glass gives a pastry an immediate visual impact. Stemmed coupe glasses, hurricane glasses, and oversized martini glasses automatically give the pastry height.

Natural and edible containers, including hollowed-out citrus fruits and containers such as puff pastry cases (known as *vol-au-vents* or *bouchées*), pâte à choux puffs, and tuile cups, are all part of the classic pastry repertoire and can be other attractive choices.

Phyllo dough

Phyllo dough is made only of flour and water (and occasionally a small amount of oil). The dough is stretched and rolled until it is extremely thin, then cut into sheets. Much like a laminated dough such as puff pastry, the sheets are layered to create many flaky layers of pastry that encase or hold a filling, which may be anything from fruit to a mousse or cream. But instead of being rolled into the dough as it is for laminated doughs, the butter is melted and brushed onto the dough sheets before they are baked, as is done with strudel.

Many bakeshops purchase frozen phyllo dough sheets. This dough must thaw and come to room temperature before it can be worked with. Phyllo dough can dry out quickly and become brittle enough to shatter, so after it is removed from its wrapping, it is important to cover it with dampened towels and plastic wrap. Use a pastry brush to apply the butter in an even coat and then, if desired, sprinkle with cake or bread crumbs to keep the layers separate as they bake.

Brushing layers of phyllo dough with butter

Piped pastries

A variety of individual pastries can be made using meringue or pâte à choux. Both of these elements are shaped by piping, then baked and filled. Meringues can be piped into containers, filled, and served, or piped into disks and assembled like a sandwich. The fillings paired with meringue are usually high in fat to contrast with the lean flavor and crisp mouthfeel of the meringue.

Pâte à choux can be piped into oblongs for éclairs, into rings for Paris-Brest, into domes for cream puffs, or into more intricate shapes to create the classic swan. After baking, a filling is piped into the pâte à choux either by slicing it open or by using a small pastry tip to puncture the shell and inject the filling. Pastries of this type are typically glazed or dusted with confectioners' sugar to finish. It is important when preparing either type of shell (meringue or pâte à choux) that it be baked until dry and crisp and allowed to cool completely before filling.

Piping éclairs onto a sheet pan

Apple galettes

MAKES 12 GALETTES

Currants	3 oz	85 g
Brandy	3 fl oz	90 mL
Blitz puff pastry (page 233)	1 lb 8 oz	680 g
Apples	2 lb 8 oz	1.13 kg
Butter, melted	2 oz	57 g
Sugar	1 oz	28 g
Apricot glaze (page 426), warm	as needed	as needed

1   Combine the currants and brandy in a small bowl and let stand until the currants are fully plumped (see "Dried Fruits," page 243).

2   Roll out the puff pastry ⅛ in/3 mm thick. Transfer to a parchment-lined sheet pan, cover, and let rest for 30 minutes under refrigeration.

3   Using a 4¼-in/11-cm cutter, cut 12 rounds from the puff pastry. Dock the pastry rounds.

4   Peel, halve, and core the apples. Cut into slices ¹⁄₁₆ in/1.5 mm thick.

5   Arrange the apple slices in concentric rings on the puff pastry round, working from the outside in and overlapping the slices slightly; they should stack up in the center to a height of approximately 1 in/3 cm. Drizzle the melted butter over the galettes and sprinkle with the sugar.

6   Bake at 375°F/191°C until the pastry is golden brown and dry on the bottom, about 50 minutes.

7   Transfer the galettes to a 425°F/218°C convection oven and bake until the edges of the apples are golden brown, about 2 minutes. Cool to room temperature.

8   Brush the tops of the galettes with the apricot glaze. Drain the currants and scatter over the galettes before the glaze sets.

Fresh Fruit Tartlets (opposite), Victorias (page 653),
and other assorted pastries

Tartlet shells

MAKES 12 TARTLET SHELLS

1-2-3 cookie dough (page 223)	1 lb 4 oz	567 g
Egg wash (page 892)	as needed	as needed

1 Roll out the dough ⅛ in/3 mm thick. Using a 4-in/10-cm cutter, cut 12 rounds.

2 Assemble on a parchment-lined sheet pan if using rings. Fit the rounds into 3-in/8-cm tartlet rings or pans, pressing the dough into place against the sides of the rings or tartlet pans. Smooth and trim the top edges.

3 Place the shells under refrigeration or in the freezer until very firm. Line the frozen shells with foil or parchment and fill with pie weights or dry beans.

4 Bake at 375°F/191°C until the shells have just begun to brown, about 20 minutes (for more information on blind baking (see page 515).

5 Remove the foil or parchment and weights. Lightly brush the pastry with egg wash. Bake until golden brown, about 10 minutes longer.

Fresh fruit tartlets

MAKES 12 TARTLETS

1-2-3 cookie dough (page 223)	1 lb 4 oz	567 g
Almond filling (page 894)	9 oz	255 g
Orange-flavored simple syrup	2 fl oz	60 mL
Pastry cream (page 370)	3 oz	85 g
Fresh fruit, peeled and cored as necessary, sliced	1 lb 8 oz	680 g
Apricot glaze (page 426), warm	as needed	as needed

1 Roll out the dough ⅛ in/3 mm thick. Using a 4-in/10-cm cutter, cut 12 rounds. Place the rounds in 3-in/8-cm tart rings.

2 Dock the bottoms of the tartlet shells. Using a pastry bag fitted with a #5 plain tip, pipe the almond filling into the shells, filling them halfway.

3 Brush the almond filling with the simple syrup. Spread a thin coating of pastry cream in each tartlet shell. Arrange the fruit in the shells. Brush the fruit with the warm glaze.

4 Bake at 375°F/191°C until the shells and filling are golden brown, about 30 minutes. Cool to room temperature.

Bittersweet chocolate orange tartlets

MAKES 12 TARTLETS

Heavy cream	6 fl oz	180 mL
Sugar	2 oz	57 g
Orange zest, grated	1 tbsp	9 g
Egg yolks	6 oz	170 g
Dark chocolate, melted	3½ oz	99 g
Orange-flavored liqueur	1 fl oz	30 mL
Tartlet shells (page 643), prebaked	12 each	12 each
Apricot glaze (page 426), warm	as needed	as needed
Candied orange peel (page 796)	2 oz	57 g

1   Combine the cream, 1 oz /28 g of the sugar, and the grated orange zest in a saucepan and bring to a boil. Remove from the heat, cover, and steep for 5 minutes.

2   Blend the egg yolks with the remaining 1 oz /28 g sugar to make the liaison. Temper by gradually adding about one-third of the hot cream mixture, whisking constantly. Add the remaining hot cream.

3   Add the melted chocolate and liqueur to the custard mixture, blending well. Strain the custard.

4   Divide the filling evenly among the tartlet shells, filling them to within ⅛ in/3 mm of the top.

5   Bake at 325°F/163°C just until the custard sets, about 15 minutes. Cool to room temperature.

6   Brush the tops of the tartlets with the warm glaze. Garnish each tartlet with a few strips of candied orange peel.

Citrus tartlets

MAKES 12 TARTLETS

Heavy cream	4 fl oz	120 mL
Lemon juice	2 fl oz	60 mL
Orange juice	1 fl oz	30 mL
Lemon zest, grated	1 tsp	3 g
Sugar	4 oz	113 g
Eggs	4 oz	113 g
Egg yolks	2 oz	57 g
Tartlet shells (page 643), prebaked	12 each	12 each
Sugar, for sprinkling	as needed	as needed
Chantilly cream (page 420)	3 oz	85 g
Candied lemon peel (see Note, page 796)	1 oz	28 g

1   Combine the heavy cream, lemon juice, orange juice, lemon zest, and 3 oz/85g of the sugar in a saucepan and heat, stirring to dissolve the sugar, until the mixture reaches 180°F/82°C.

2   Blend the eggs and egg yolks with the remaining 1 oz/28 g sugar to make the liaison. Temper by gradually adding about one-third of the hot cream, whisking constantly. Add the remaining hot cream, and strain.

3   Divide the filling evenly among the tartlet shells, filling them to within ⅛ in/3 mm of the top.

4   Bake at 300°F/149°C until the custard is just set, about 20 minutes. Cool to room temperature. Chill the tartlets until fully set.

5   Sprinkle a thin layer of sugar evenly on top of each tartlet. Caramelize the sugar using a blowtorch. Cool completely.

6   Using a pastry bag fitted with a #5 star tip, pipe a rosette of Chantilly cream onto each tartlet. Place several strips of candied lemon peel on each rosette.

Pear custard tartlets

MAKES 12 TARTLETS

Pears, fresh, peeled, halved, and cored	6 each	6 each
Tartlet shells (page 643), prebaked (see Note)	12 each	12 each
Crème brûlée mixture (page 361)	12 oz	340 g
Apricot glaze (page 426), warm	as needed	as needed

1   Slice each pear half lengthwise into ¼-in/6-mm slices, keeping the pear half intact. Place a sliced pear half in each of the tartlet shells and fan it slightly. Pour the custard mixture evenly over the fruit.

2   Bake at 325°F/163°C until the custard is set, about 20 minutes. Cool completely.

3   Unmold the tartlets and brush with the warm glaze.

NOTE   It is important to brush these shells particularly well with egg wash before prebaking.

Lemon curd tartlets

MAKES 12 TARTLETS

Lemon curd (page 377), freshly prepared	1 lb 2 oz	510 g
Tartlet shells (page 643), prebaked	12 each	12 each
Swiss meringue (page 416)	10 oz	284 g

1   Divide the warm lemon curd evenly among the tartlet shells. Chill for 1 hour, or until the curd sets.

2   Divide the meringue among the tartlets, mounding it on top of each one. Smooth the meringue using a palette knife, then create a pattern of parallel lines across the tartlet.

3   Brown the meringue using a torch or under a salamander.

NOTE   The lemon curd can be cooled before filling the shells, but it will fill the tartlet more easily and create a smoother top if it is used while still warm.

Raspberry curd tartlets

MAKES 10 TARTLETS

Gelatin, granulated	1½ tsp	7 g
Water	2 fl oz	60 mL
Red food coloring	2 drops	2 drops
Orange-flavored liqueur	½ fl oz	15 mL
Raspberry purée	14 fl oz	420 mL
Eggs	5¼ oz	149 g
Egg yolks	4½ oz	128 g
Sugar	3½ oz	99 g
Butter, cut into ½-in/1-cm cubes	5¼ oz	149 g
Tartlet shells (page 643), 6 in/15 cm in diameter, prebaked	10 each	10 each

1   Bloom the gelatin in the water and melt. Stir the food coloring into the liqueur.

2   Combine the raspberry purée, eggs, egg yolks, and sugar in a heavy-bottomed saucepan and bring to a boil, stirring frequently to dissolve the sugar.

3   Remove from the heat and whisk in the melted gelatin and butter. Add the liqueur. Strain the curd through a fine-mesh strainer.

4   Carefully pour 2½ oz/71 g of the curd into each of the tartlet shells; the curd should come to the top of the shells.

5   Place the tartlets in the freezer for 2 hours.

6   Wrap the tartlets in plastic wrap and freeze until needed.

Margarita chiffon tartlets

MAKES 10 TARTLETS

Water	7 fl oz	210 mL
Cornstarch	¾ oz	21 g
Granulated sugar	8 oz	227 g
Egg yolks	3 oz	85 g
Lime juice	2 fl oz	60 mL
Orange juice concentrate	1 oz	28 g
Tequila	3 fl oz	90 mL
Gelatin, granulated	1½ tsp	7 g
Egg whites	4 oz	113 g
Tartlet shells (page 643), prebaked	10 each	10 each
Simple syrup (page 900)	4 fl oz	120 mL
Coarse sugar	10 oz	284 g

1   In a bowl, combine 3 fl oz/90 mL of the water with the cornstarch to make a slurry. Add 2 oz/57 g of the sugar and the egg yolks and whisk together thoroughly.

2   Combine 2 oz/57 g of the sugar with the remaining 4 fl oz/120 mL water in a saucepan and bring to a boil, stirring to dissolve the sugar and creating a hot syrup.

3   Temper the egg yolk mixture by gradually adding about one-third of the hot syrup, whisking constantly. Return the tempered egg yolk mixture to the hot syrup in the saucepan and continue cooking until the mixture comes to a boil, whisking constantly.

4   Combine the lime juice, orange juice concentrate, and tequila.

5   Bloom and melt the gelatin using 2 fl oz/60 mL of the juice mixture.

6   Whisk the melted gelatin and the remaining juice into the warm egg mixture. Strain through a fine-mesh strainer.

7   Place the egg whites and remaining 4 oz/113 g of sugar in a mixer bowl and whisk until thoroughly combined.

8   Place the bowl over a pot of barely simmering water and slowly whisk the mixture until it reaches 165°F/74°C.

9   Transfer the bowl to the mixer and whip on high speed with the whip attachment until stiff peaks form.

10   Gently fold one-third of the meringue into the citrus mixture, then fold in the remaining meringue.

11 Brush the rim of each tartlet shell lightly with simple syrup, and dip each rim in coarse sugar. Using a pastry bag fitted with a #6 plain tip, pipe 2 oz/57 g of the filling into each tartlet shell. Refrigerate the tartlets until fully chilled and set.

Pecan cranberry tartlets

MAKES 12 TARTLETS

Dark corn syrup	8 oz	227 g
Eggs	6 oz	170 g
Light brown sugar	4 oz	113 g
Butter	1¼ oz	35 g
All-purpose flour	½ oz	14 g
Pecan halves, toasted	6 oz	170 g
Cranberries, fresh or frozen	3 oz	85 g
Tartlet shells (page 643), prebaked	12 each	12 each
Apricot glaze (page 426), warm	as needed	as needed
Heavy cream, whipped	3 oz	85 g

1 Combine the corn syrup, eggs, sugar, and butter in a saucepan over medium heat. Warm the mixture until the sugar and butter are melted and all the ingredients are fully combined. Remove the pan from the heat. Stir in the flour and strain the mixture through a fine-mesh strainer.

2 Divide the pecans and cranberries among the tartlet shells, spreading them in an even layer.

3 Pour the corn syrup mixture over the nuts and cranberries, filling the shells to within ⅛ in/3 mm of the top.

4 Bake at 325°F/163°C just until the filling is set, about 25 minutes. Cool to room temperature.

5 Brush the tops of the tarts with the warm glaze. Using a pastry bag fitted with a #5 star tip, pipe a rosette of whipped cream onto each tartlet.

Pear frangipane tartlets

MAKES 12 TARTLETS

1-2-3 cookie dough (page 223)	1 lb 4 oz	567 g
Frangipane for filling (page 896)	9 oz	255 g
Small pears, poached (page 899) and halved	12 each	12 each
Apricot glaze (page 426), warm	as needed	as needed
Sliced almonds, toasted and chopped	3 oz	85 g

1   Roll out the dough ⅛ in/3 mm thick. Using a 4-in/10-cm cutter, cut 12 rounds. Place the rounds in 3-in/8-cm tartlet rings. Dock the bottoms of the tartlet shells.

3   Using a pastry bag fitted with a #5 plain tip, pipe the frangipane into the shells, filling them halfway. Slice the pears and fan them on top of the frangipane.

4   Bake at 375°F/191°C until the shells and filling are golden brown, about 45 minutes. Cool to room temperature.

5   Brush the tops of the tartlets with the warm glaze. Arrange a thin border of almonds around the edge of each tartlet.

Pineapple tartes tatin

MAKES 10 TARTLETS

Sugar	1 lb 6 oz	624 g
Light corn syrup	4 oz	113 g
Butter	8 oz	227 g
Water	2 fl oz	60 mL
Pineapple	2 each	2 each
Pâte brisée (page 222)	1 lb 11 oz	765 g

1   Combine the sugar and corn syrup in a heavy-bottomed saucepan and bring to a boil over high heat, stirring to dissolve the sugar. Cook covered for 1 minute.

2   Remove the cover, reduce the heat to medium, and cook the caramel to a rich golden brown. Add the butter and water and stir until fully incorporated.

3   Divide the caramel evenly among ten 4¾-in/12-cm tartlet pans.

4   Peel and core the pineapple (see page 517). Cut into ½-in/1-cm cubes. Place 3 oz/85 g diced pineapple on top of the caramel in each tartlet pan.

5   Roll the pâte brisée out ¹⁄₁₆ in/1.5 mm thick. Using a 4¾-in/12-cm fluted cutter, cut 10 rounds.

6   Place a round of pâte brisée on top of each tartlet. The pâte brisée should be flush with the edges of the tartlet pan.

7   Bake at 375°F/191°C until the pastry is golden brown, about 15 minutes. Cool slightly in the pans. Invert on a serving plate to unmold.

Strip tartlets

MAKES 12 PASTRIES

Butter puff pastry dough (page 231)	6 oz	170 g
Egg wash (page 892)	as needed	as needed
Pastry cream (page 370)	6 oz	170 g
Assorted fruit, peeled, trimmed, and cut, as necessary	8 oz	227 g
Apricot glaze (page 426), warm	as needed	as needed

1   Roll the puff pastry dough into a rectangle 4 by 16 in/10 by 41 cm. Transfer to a parchment-lined sheet pan, cover, and let rest under refrigeration for 30 minutes or more.

2   Remove the dough from the sheet pan and cut it lengthwise into one strip 3 in/8 cm wide and two strips ½ in/1 cm wide.

3   Place the 3-in/8-cm-wide strip on a parchment-lined sheet pan, dock, and brush with egg wash. Lay the ½-in/1-cm-wide strips on top of the edges of the larger strip and brush them with egg wash.

4   Bake at 375°F/191°C until the pastry has risen and begun to brown, about 30 minutes. Turn the oven down to 325°F/163°C and bake until golden brown, about 20 minutes more. Cool to room temperature.

5   Cut most of the pastry out of the center of the strip, if necessary, leaving only a thin bottom layer. Using a pastry bag fitted with a medium-sized plain tip, pipe the pastry cream evenly over the center of the strip. Arrange the fruit on top of the pastry cream. Brush the fruit with the warm glaze and allow to set.

6   Using a serrated knife, cut the strip into 12 even portions.

Pecan passions

MAKES 12 TARTLETS

Chocolate short dough (page 224)	12 oz	340 g
Soft caramel filling (page 455)	12 oz	340 g
Pecans, toasted and chopped	6 oz	170 g
Soft ganache (page 421)	8 oz	227 g
Heavy cream	10 fl oz	300 mL

1   Roll out the dough into a rectangle 10 by 14 in/25 by 36 cm.

2   Lay the rectangle of dough carefully over twelve 3-in/8-cm tartlet pans that have been arranged closely together. Gently press the dough into the molds. Run a rolling pin across the molds to cut away the excess.

3   Blind bake the shells at 375°F/191°C until fully baked, about 15 minutes (for instructions on blind baking, see page 515). Cool completely.

4   Divide half of the caramel filling evenly among the tartlet shells. Scatter half of the pecans over the caramel. Cool completely.

5   Whip the ganache with 4 fl oz/120 mL of the cream on high speed with te whip attachment to a mousse-like consistency. Using a palette knife, spread a layer of whipped ganache into each shell. Freeze the tartlets until the filling is firm.

6   Divide the remaining caramel filling among the tartlets, spreading it over the ganache in a thin layer. Scatter the remaining pecans over the top. Whip the remaining cream. Using a pastry bag fitted with a #5 star tip, pipe a rosette of whipped cream on top of each tartlet.

Victorias

MAKES 36 PASTRIES

Butter puff pastry dough (page 231)	2 lb	907 g
Egg wash (page 892)	as needed	as needed
Pâte à choux (page 228)	2 lb 8 oz	1.13 kg
Sliced almonds	4 oz	113 g
Rum	as needed	as needed
Heavy cream, whipped	48 fl oz	1.44 L
Pastry cream (page 370)	2 lb 4 oz	1.02 kg
Strawberries	1 lb 4 oz	567 g
Confectioners' sugar, for dusting	as needed	as needed

1   Roll out the puff pastry ⅟₁₆ in/1.5 mm thick. Transfer to a parchment-lined sheet pan, cover, and allow to rest under refrigeration for 1 hour.

2   Dock the pastry. Using a 4-in/10-cm cutter, cut 36 rounds. Fit them into individual brioche molds. Trim the excess dough from the tops of the molds.

3   Brush the inside of the shells lightly with egg wash. Using a pastry bag fitted with a #5 plain tip, pipe the pâte à choux into each shell, filling them one-third full. Using a small palette knife, spread the pâte à choux so it reaches up the sides to the top of the molds, making the surface concave. Toss the almonds with just enough rum to moisten and sprinkle over the pâte à choux.

4   Bake at 375°F/191°C until the puff pastry is dry and the pâte à choux is golden brown, about 50 minutes. Cool completely.

5   Unmold the pastries. Using a serrated knife, slice the tops from the finished shells; reserve the tops.

6   Fold half of the whipped cream into the pastry cream. Fill the shells two-thirds full with the pastry cream. Arrange the berries on the cream.

7   Using a pastry bag fitted with a #5 star tip, pipe the remaining whipped cream on top of the berries. Place the reserved pastry tops on the whipped cream and dust with confectioners' sugar.

Classic napoleons

MAKES 16 NAPOLEONS (2 BY 3¼ BY 1½ IN/5 BY 8 BY 4 CM EACH)

Butter puff pastry dough (page 231)	1 lb 5½ oz	610 g
Diplomat cream (page 394)	2 lb 2¼ oz	971 g
Apricot glaze (page 426), warm	as needed	as needed
Rolled fondant (page 859)	8 oz	227 g
Simple syrup (page 900)	2 fl oz	60 mL
Bittersweet chocolate, melted	2 oz	57 g

1   Roll the puff pastry to a rectangle 16½ by 24½ in/42 by 62 cm and ⅛ in/3 mm thick. Place the puff pastry on a parchment-lined sheet pan and allow it to rest under refrigeration for at least 1 hour.

2   Dock the puff pastry generously. Place a piece of parchment paper on top of the puff pastry dough. Place a sheet pan on top of the parchment paper to control the rise of the pastry.

3   Bake at 375°F/191°C for 20 minutes. Rotate the pan and continue to bake for 7 to 10 minutes, or until golden brown and dry throughout. If necessary, remove the sheet pan and parchment from the top of the puff pastry during the final 10 minutes of baking to allow the puff pastry to brown. Cool the puff pastry to room temperature.

4   Trim the edges of the puff pastry using a long, flat, serrated knife. Cut the puff pastry into three strips 6½ by 16 in/17 by 41 cm.

5   Spread half of the diplomat cream with a medium offset spatula in a smooth, even layer on one of the puff pastry strips.

6   Gently place the second puff pastry strip on top of the diplomat cream. Spread the remaining diplomat cream on top of the puff pastry sheet in a smooth, even layer. Place the final puff pastry sheet upside down on top of the diplomat cream. Smooth the sides of the napoleon with an offset spatula to remove any excess diplomat cream.

7   Wrap the napoleon and freeze overnight.

8   To finish, allow the napoleon to thaw for 10 to 15 minutes. Brush the apricot glaze in a thin, even layer on top.

9   Gently warm the fondant over barely simmering water to 100°F/38°C. Thin the fondant with the simple syrup until it is fluid and only slightly viscous. Pour on top of the napoleon in the center of the puff pastry and spread in a thin, even layer over the entire surface.

10   Pour the melted chocolate into a parchment paper cone with a very thin tip. Pipe thin lines of chocolate lengthwise along the fondant ¼ in/6 mm apart.

11   Drag the tip of a paring knife horizontally across the chocolate lines in alternating directions ¼ in/6 mm apart. The chocolate lines may be piped closer together to create a more finely marbled look. Allow the fondant to set completely before slicing.

12 Fill a large bain-marie with hot water. Using a long, serrated knife warmed in the hot water, trim the edges of the napoleon.

13 Slice the napoleon in half lengthwise. Using a warm, serrated knife, slice each napoleon strip into 8 pieces. Clean the knife in between each cut.

LEFT: Puff pastry for napoleons and other pastries must be weighted during baking to ensure flat, even layers.

MIDDLE: Layering puff pastry sheets and diplomat cream to make classic napoleons

RIGHT: Dragging the tip of a paring knife across the chocolate lines in alternating directions to create the décor for napoleons

Strawberry napoleons

MAKES 16 NAPOLEONS (2 BY 3¼ IN/5 BY 8 CM EACH)

Butter puff pastry dough (page 231)	1 lb 5½ oz	610 g
Apricot glaze (page 426), warm	4 fl oz	120 mL
Fondant	1 lb	454 g
Simple syrup (page 900)	5 fl oz	150 mL
Pink food coloring	as needed	as needed
Strawberries, whole (roughly the same size)	50 each	50 each
Grand Marnier diplomat cream (page 394)	2 lb 4 oz	1.02 kg
Vanilla sponge crumbs (page 268), for garnish	as needed	as needed
Chocolate cigarettes (see page 829)	16 each	16 each

1   Roll the puff pastry to a rectangle 16½ by 24½ in/42 by 62 cm and ⅛ in/3 mm thick. Place the puff pastry on a parchment-lined sheet pan and allow it to rest under refrigeration for at least 1 hour.

2   Cut off one-third (8 by 16 in/20 by 41 cm) of the puff pastry dough and place it on a separate sheet pan. Reserve the remaining puff pastry dough in the refrigerator.

3   Score the smaller piece of dough with a lattice wheel and gently pull the puff pastry apart to create the lattice pattern. Place a piece of parchment paper on top of the puff pastry dough. Place a sheet pan on top of the parchment paper to control the rise of the pastry.

4   Bake at 375°F/191°C until golden brown, 10 to 15 minutes. Cool to room temperature before trimming.

5   Using a long, serrated knife, trim the lattice into 16 rectangles, 2 by 3¼ in/5 by 8 cm each. Brush a thin layer of apricot glaze over the top of the lattice puff pastry.

6   Gently warm the fondant over a water bath to 100°F/38°C. Thin the fondant with the simple syrup until it is very fluid and only slightly viscous. Add the food coloring.

7   Place the lattice puff pastry on a rack. Slowly pour the fondant over the puff pastry. Remove the lattice puff pastry from the rack so that the fondant does not glue it to the rack. Reserve.

8   To assemble the napoleon, dock the remaining puff pastry generously using a dough docker. Place a piece of parchment paper on top of the puff pastry dough. Place a sheet pan on top of the parchment paper to control the rise of the pastry.

9   Bake at 375°F/191°C until golden brown, 20 to 25 minutes. If necessary, remove the sheet pans from the top of the puff pastry during the final 10 minutes of baking to allow the puff pastry to brown. Cool to room temperature.

10   Using a long, serrated knife, trim the edges of the puff pastry. Cut the puff pastry into 2 strips 6½ by 16 in/17 by 41 cm. Brush a thin layer of apricot glaze onto one of the puff pastry strips to help the strawberries adhere better.

11 Cut off the tops of the strawberries. Place 36 whole strawberries point up in 3 equally spaced rows of 12 on the glazed strip. Cut 6 strawberries in half and place the strawberries, cut side facing out, along each long edge of the strip. Make sure that the cut strawberries come right up to the edge.

12 Using a pastry bag fitted with a #8 plain tip, pipe approximately half of the diplomat cream on top of the strawberries, making sure to fill in the crevices in between the strawberries. The diplomat cream should come ½ in/1 cm above the layer of strawberries.

13 Place the second plain strip of puff pastry on top of the diplomat cream. Spread the remaining diplomat cream on top of the puff pastry in a smooth, even layer. Be sure to come right up to the edge of the puff pastry without going over the edge. Gently smooth the sides of the napoleon, using an offset spatula.

14 Refrigerate the napoleon for 1 hour to allow the diplomat cream to set.

15 Fill a large bain-marie with hot water. Using a long, serrated knife warmed in the hot water, trim the edges of the napoleon.

16 Using a warm long, serrated knife, slice the napoleon in half lengthwise. Gently press cake crumbs into the longer sides of the napoleon (the sides without strawberries).

17 Cut each strip of napoleon into 8 pieces. Be sure to clean the knife in between each slice. Using a long, straight spatula, gently place one lattice top on each of the napoleon slices. Halve the remaining strawberries and garnish each slice with a strawberry half and a chocolate cigarette.

Mocha mousse slices

MAKES 45 SLICES (1¼ BY 3 IN/3 BY 8 CM EACH)

1-2-3 cookie dough (page 223)	1 lb 4 oz	567 g
Mocha mousse (page 391)	5 lb 5 oz	2.41 kg
Chocolate sponge sheet (page 268), 11½ by 16½ in/29 by 42 cm	1 each	1 each
Coffee simple syrup (page 900)	4 fl oz	120 mL
Ultra-shiny chocolate glaze (page 424)	16 fl oz	480 mL
Heavy cream, whipped	12 fl oz	360 mL
Marzipan coffee beans or chocolate-covered espresso beans	45 each	45 each

1   Roll out the dough to a rectangle 13 by 17 in/33 by 43 cm. Trim to precisely 12 by 16 in/30 by 41 cm. Dock the dough.

2   Bake at 375°F/191°C until light golden brown, about 25 minutes.

3   Place a rectangular frame or mold 12 by 16 in/30 by 41 cm with sides 2 in/5 cm high around the baked cookie. Ladle half of the mousse onto the baked cookie dough and spread it evenly. Place the sponge on the mousse and press down lightly. Brush the sponge generously with the syrup. Ladle the remaining mousse over the sponge, filling the mold to the top, and spread it evenly.

4   Freeze the assembled mold until the mousse is firm enough to cut.

5   Pour the chocolate glaze evenly over the top of the frozen mousse. Allow the glaze to set.

6   Remove the frame and trim the edges of the assembled slab. Slice it crosswise into strips 3 in/8 cm wide and then cut each strip into pieces 1¼ in/3 cm wide.

7   Using a pastry bag fitted with a #5 plain tip, pipe a small dome of whipped cream on one end of the top of each slice. Place a coffee bean on each dome. Refrigerate until ready to serve.

Chocolate roulade slices

MAKES 24 SLICES

Soft ganache (page 421)	10 oz	284 g
Heavy cream	6 fl oz	180 mL
Roulade (page 273),16½ by 24½ in/42 by 62 cm)	1 each	1 each
Confectioners' sugar, for dusting	as needed	as needed

1   Combine the ganache and cream and whip on high speed with the whip attachment until medium-stiff peaks form.

2   Spread the ganache mixture evenly over the roulade sheet.

3   Cut the sheet in half to create a rectangle 12 by 16 in/30 by 41 cm. Roll up each roulade tightly, creating two logs 12 in/30 cm long.

4   Chill the roulades for 30 minutes, or until the ganache is set.

5   Lay a strip of parchment paper ¾ in/2 cm wide over the middle of the length of each roulade and dust it with confectioners' sugar. Remove the strip.

6   Slice each roulade into 12 portions.

Using parchment paper to roll the roulade

Frangipane triangle slices

MAKES 12 SLICES

Frangipane cake (page 330)	1 half sheet pan	1 half sheet pan
Bittersweet chocolate, melted	3 oz	85 g
Italian buttercream (page 418)	1 lb	454 g
Hard ganache (page 421), melted	12 oz	340 g

1   Trim the edges from the frangipane cake and cut lengthwise into 3 strips 3 by 16 in/8 by 41 cm each.

2   Blend the melted chocolate into the buttercream. Spread 3 oz/85 g of the buttercream onto one strip of frangipane. Place a second strip on top of the buttercream and spread with 3 oz/85 g buttercream. Place the third strip of frangipane on top.

3   Refrigerate the strip until the buttercream is firm, at least 1 hour.

4   Cut the assembled strip lengthwise in half on the diagonal to create 2 triangular strips. Spread 4 oz/113 g of the buttercream onto the solid frangipane side of one of the triangular strips, and place the solid frangipane side of the other strip against the buttercream, pressing to adhere, creating a triangular, vertically layered cake.

5   Chill the assembled strip until the buttercream has set.

6   Seal the outside of the strip with the remaining buttercream. Chill until set, about 1 hour.

7   Place the strip on a wire rack set in a sheet pan. Glaze the strip with the ganache, spreading it along the sides to completely cover as you ladle the glaze. Chill until set, about 1 hour.

8   Slice the strip into 12 portions.

Mango raspberry slices

MAKES 12 SLICES

Vanilla sponge sheet (page 268), 11½ by 16½ in/29 by 42 cm	1 each	1 each
Raspberry jam	4 oz	113 g
Patterned Joconde sponge rectangle (page 284), 9 by 16 in/23 by 41 cm	1 each	1 each
Mango mousse (page 379)	3 lb	1.36 kg
Patterned Joconde sponge strip (page 284), 4¼ by 16 in/11 by 41 cm	1 each	1 each

1   Cut the vanilla sponge crosswise into 3 strips. Spread the jam evenly over one strip and roll up, starting from a long side.

2   Line a 12-in/30-cm triangular terrine mold with plastic wrap.

3   Place the larger rectangle of Joconde sponge in the mold so that the sides are flush with the edges of the mold. Pour half of the mousse into the mold.

4   Lay the roulade in the center of the mousse. Pour the remaining mousse into the mold to within ¼ in/6 mm of the top.

5   Lay the strip of Joconde sponge on the mousse, lining it up so that the edges are flush with the edges of the other sponge.

6   Cover and refrigerate overnight.

7   Unmold and slice into 12 portions.

Praline slices

MAKES 12 SLICES

Hazelnut sponge sheet (page 277), 11½ by 16½ in/29 by 42 cm	1 each	1 each
Italian buttercream (page 418)	1 lb 4 oz	567 g
Praline paste	2 oz	57 g
Rum-flavored simple syrup (see Liquor-Flavored Simple Syrup, page 900)	3 fl oz	90 mL
Hazelnuts, toasted and finely ground	3 oz	85 g
Hazelnuts dragées (page 793)	12 each	12 each

1   Trim the hazelnut sponge and slice lengthwise into 3 strips, 3 by 16 in/8 by 41 cm each.

2   Combine the buttercream with the praline paste and mix until smooth.

3   Moisten one of the sponge strips with one-third of the syrup, and spread 4 oz/113 g of the buttercream over it. Place a second strip on top of the buttercream, moisten with another one-third of the syrup, and spread 4 oz/113 g of the buttercream over it. Top with the final strip of sponge and moisten with the remaining syrup.

4   Chill the assembled strip until the buttercream is set, about 1 hour.

5   Trim the sides of the assembled strip. Coat the top and sides with the remaining buttercream, reserving 4 oz/113 g for décor. Mark into 12 portions. Using a pastry bag fitted with a #3 star tip, pipe a rosette of buttercream off center on each slice.

6   Press the ground hazelnuts onto the frosted sides of each slice to completely cover the bottom half of each side. Garnish each slice by placing a hazelnut dragée on the buttercream rosette.

Raspberry marzipan slices

MAKES 12 SLICES

Vanilla sponge sheet (page 268), 11½ by 16½ in/29 by 42 cm	1 each	1 each
Framboise-flavored simple syrup (see Liqueur-Flavored Simple Syrup, page 900)	3 fl oz	90 mL
Raspberry jam	1 oz	28 g
Italian buttercream (page 418)	12 oz	340 g
Marzipan (page 852), colored pale pink	1 lb	454 g
Tempered chocolate (see page 762), for garnish	as needed	as needed

1   Trim the vanilla sponge and slice lengthwise into 3 strips, 3 by 16 in/8 by 41 cm each.

2   Moisten one of the sponge strips with one-third of the syrup. Spread with a thin coat of jam and then with 3 oz/85 g of the buttercream. Place a second strip on top of the buttercream. Moisten with one-thrid of the syrup and spread with a thin coat of jam and then with 3 oz/85 g of the buttercream. Top with the final strip of sponge and moisten with the remaining syrup. Wrap the strip in plastic wrap.

3   Place the assembled strip on a parchment-lined sheet pan and place another piece of parchment paper on top of the strip. Weight by placing a second sheet pan on top of the strip and a heavy pan or two 1-lb/454-g weights on top, and refrigerate overnight.

4   Coat the top and sides of the strip with the remaining buttercream.

5   Roll the marzipan into a rectangle ¹⁄₁₆ in/1.5 mm thick. Texture the rolled marzipan with a textured rolling pin.

6   Drape the marzipan over the strip and gently press the marzipan to remove all wrinkles and to attach it to the strip. Trim the excess from the bottom edges.

7   Mark the strip into 12 portions. Garnish each piece with tempered chocolate by piping a stylish *R* or filigree using a parchment cone.

8   Chill until firm enough to slice, about 1 hour.

Raspberry wine cream slices

MAKES 45 SLICES (1¼ BY 3 IN/3 BY 8 CM EACH)

1-2-3 cookie dough (page 223)	1 lb 4 oz	567 g
Raspberry jam	4 oz	113 g
Vanilla sponge sheet (page 268), 12 by 16 in/30 by 41 cm	1 each	1 each
Raspberry-flavored simple syrup	4 fl oz	120 mL
Wine Bavarian cream (page 393)	4 lb 14 oz	2.21 kg
Raspberry mirror glaze (see Variation, page 427)	1 lb	454 g
Heavy cream, whipped	12 oz	340 g
Chocolate cigarettes (see page 829)	45 each	45 each

1   Roll the cookie dough into a rectangle 13 by 17 in/33 by 43 cm. Trim to precisely 12 by 16 in/30 by 41 cm. Dock the dough.

2   Bake at 375°F/191°C until light golden brown, about 25 minutes. Cool completely.

3   Spread the raspberry jam onto the baked cookie. Place a frame (12 by 16 by 1¾ in/30 by 41 by 4.5 cm) around it. Place the vanilla sponge on the jam and press down gently. Moisten the sponge with the syrup. Pour the wine cream into the frame, filling it to the top, and spread it evenly. Freeze the assembled frame until the wine cream is set.

4   Pour the glaze over the frozen wine cream to coat it. Allow the glaze to set.

5   Remove the frame and trim the edges of the assembled strip. Slice into 45 portions. Using a pastry bag fitted with a #5 star tip, pipe a domed rosette of whipped cream slightly off center on top of each slice. Place a chocolate cigarette on each slice, resting one end on the whipped cream rosette. Refrigerate until ready to serve.

Chocolate caramel bombes

MAKES 24 BOMBES

Chocolate sponge sheet (page 268)	1 each	1 each
Chocolate mousse (page 380)	2 lb 8 oz	1.13 kg
Soft caramel filling II (page 485)	12 oz	340 g
Simple syrup (page 900)	4 fl oz	120 mL
Ultra-shiny chocolate glaze (page 424)	36 fl oz	1.08 L
1-2-3 cookie dough (page 223) fluted round 3¼-in/8-cm cutouts, baked	24 each	24 each
Striped chocolate cigarettes (page 830)	24 each	24 each

1 Using a 2-in/5-cm cutter, cut 24 rounds from the chocolate sponge.

2 Using a pastry bag fitted with a #5 plain tip, pipe the chocolate mousse into twenty-four 3-in/8-cm hemispherical flexible silicone molds, filling them two-thirds full.

3 Using a pastry bag fitted with a #5 plain tip, pipe ½ oz/14 g of the caramel filling into the center of each chocolate bombe. Be careful not to pipe the caramel filling too far down into the mousse, or it may leach through the mousse and show when unmolded.

4 Place a sponge round on top of each mousse and gently press to bring the cake flush with the top of the mold. Brush each sponge lightly with the syrup.

5 Freeze the bombes until they are solid.

6 Unmold the bombes and place them dome side up on a wire rack set over a sheet pan. Ladle the chocolate glaze over each bombe to coat completely. Let stand until the glaze sets.

7 Place each bombe on a fluted cookie. Garnish each with a chocolate cigarette.

Chocolate mousse bombes

MAKES 24 BOMBES

Vanilla sauce (page 428)	8 fl oz	240 mL
Hard ganache (page 421), melted	8 oz	227 g
Gelatin, granulated	½ oz	14 g
Water	4 fl oz	120 mL
Egg whites, pasteurized	2 oz	57 g
Sugar	2 oz	57 g
Heavy cream, whipped to very soft peaks	16 fl oz	480 mL
Ultra-shiny chocolate glaze (page 424)	36 fl oz	1.08 L
1-2-3 cookie dough (page 223) fluted round 3¼-in/8-cm cutouts, baked	24 each	24 each
Dark chocolate fans (see page 831)	24 each	24 each

1   Combine the vanilla sauce with the melted ganache.

2   Bloom and melt the gelatin in the water. Blend the gelatin into the vanilla sauce mixture. Set aside.

3   Beat the egg whites until frothy. Slowly add the sugar and whip to a stiff-peak meringue.

4   Stir the vanilla sauce mixture over an ice water bath just until it begins to thicken. Fold in the meringue. Fold in the whipped cream.

5   Using a pastry bag fitted with a #5 plain tip, immediately pipe the mixture into twenty-four 3-in/8-cm hemispherical flexible silicone molds.

6   Freeze the bombes until solid.

7   Unmold the bombes and place them, dome side up, on a wire rack set over a sheet pan. Warm the glaze to a pourable consistency and ladle over each bombe to coat completely. Let stand until the glaze sets.

8   Place each bombe on a fluted cookie. Gently press a chocolate fan to the side of each bombe to adhere.

Chocolate peanut butter bombes

MAKES 10 BOMBES

Devil's food cake sheet (page 266), 11½ by 16½ in/29 by 42 cm	1 each	1 each
Peanut butter	10 oz	284 g
Milk chocolate Bavarian cream (page 393)	2 lb 8 oz	1.13 kg
Chocolate short dough (page 224)	1 lb	454 g
Ultra-shiny chocolate glaze (page 424)	20 fl oz	600 mL

1 Using a 2-in/5-cm cutter, cut 10 rounds from the devil's food cake.

2 Using a pastry bag fitted with a #6 plain tip, pipe 1 oz/28 g of peanut butter onto each round of cake.

3 Using a #5 plain tip, pipe 4 oz/113 g of the cream into each of ten 3-in/8-cm hemispherical flexible silicone molds, filling them to within ½ in/1 cm of the top. Flip a cake round upside down onto each mold and push the peanut butter into the mousse; push down until the cake is flush with the top of the mold.

4 Level the top of each bombe by scraping off any excess cream. Freeze the bombes for 8 hours, or until firm.

5 Roll out the short dough ⅛ in/3 mm thick. Using a 3¼-in/8-cm fluted cutter, cut 10 rounds from the dough.

6 Bake the rounds in a 350°F/177°C deck oven until golden brown, 8 to 10 minutes. Cool.

7 Warm the glaze to 120°F/49°C.

8 Unmold the bombes and flip them upside down onto a wire rack set over a parchment-lined sheet pan. Enrobe each bombe with 2 fl oz/60 mL of the glaze.

9 Place each bombe on a cookie base. Place the bombes in the refrigerator to set the glaze.

Lemon bombes with macerated raspberries

MAKES 24 BOMBES

Raspberries (fresh or frozen)	6 oz	170 g
Orange-flavored liqueur	4 fl oz	120 mL
Vanilla sponge cake sheet (page 268)	1 each	1 each
Lemon mousse (page 386)	2 lb 4 oz	1.02 kg
Apricot glaze (page 426), warm	72 fl oz	2.16 L
1-2-3 cookie dough (page 223) fluted round 3¼-in/8-cm cutouts, baked	24 each	24 each
Chocolate fans (see page 831)	24 each	24 each

1   Combine the raspberries with the liqueur and allow to macerate for 1 hour or longer.

2   Using a 2-in/5-cm cutter, cut 24 rounds from the vanilla sponge.

3   Using a pastry bag fitted with a #5 plain tip, pipe the lemon mousse into 3-in/8-cm hemi-spherical flexible silicone molds, filling them two-thirds full.

4   Remove the raspberries from the liqueur, reserving the liqueur, and dry them on a towel. Place 3 or 4 berries in each mold, pressing them lightly into the mousse. Be careful not to press them in too far, or they will show when the bombes are unmolded.

5   Place a sponge round on top of each bombe and press gently into the mousse to bring the level of the mousse up to the top of the molds. Brush each sponge lightly with the reserved liqueur.

6   Freeze the bombes until firm.

7   Unmold the bombes and place them, dome side up, on a wire rack set over a sheet pan. Glaze with the apricot glaze, using a fondant dropper or ladle. Let the glaze set.

8   Place each bombe on a fluted cookie. Garnish each with a chocolate fan.

Melon sherry cream

MAKES 12 PASTRIES

Patterned Joconde sponge (page 284)	1 each	1 each
Tiramisù cream (page 396)	9 fl oz	270 mL
Melon balls, ¼ in/6 mm in diameter	12 oz	340 g
Gelatin, granulated	1 oz	28 g
Water	17 fl oz	510 mL
Cream sherry	16 fl oz	480 mL
Sorbet syrup (page 488)	1 lb 4 oz	567 g
Lime juice	½ fl oz	15 mL
Sliced almonds, blanched, toasted, and chopped	4 oz	113 g

1   Lightly brush the inside of 12 ring molds, 2¾ in/7 cm in diameter and at least 1½ in/4 cm high, with vegetable oil. Coat the inside with sugar and place on a parchment-lined sheet pan.

2   Using a 2¾-in/7-cm cutter, cut 12 rounds from the Joconde sponge. Place each round on a prepared mold.

3   Using a pastry bag fitted with a #5 plain tip, pipe the tiramisù cream into the molds, filling them to ½ in/1 cm from the top. Put a single layer of melon balls in each mold.

4   Bloom and melt the gelatin in 8 fl oz/240 mL of the water.

5   Combine the sherry, sorbet syrup, lime juice, and the remaining 9 fl oz/270 mL water in a stainless-steel bowl. Blend in the gelatin. Stir gently over an ice water bath, using a rubber spatula so as not to create air bubbles, until the mixture begins to thicken.

6   Immediately pour the gelatin mixture over the melon balls, covering them completely and filling the molds to the top.

7   Refrigerate or freeze until thoroughly set, at least 2 hours.

8   Remove from the molds. Gently press the chopped almonds onto the side of each dessert to adhere.

Summer pudding

MAKES 10 SERVINGS

Butter, soft	4 oz	113 g
Brioche loaf dough (page 186)	2 lb	907 g
Egg wash (page 892)	2 oz	57 g
Strawberries	12 oz	340 g
Crème de cassis	6 fl oz	180 mL
Lemon juice	1 fl oz	30 mL
Sugar	8 oz	227 g
Raspberries	11 oz	312 g
Blueberries	11 oz	312 g
Blackberries	11 oz	312 g

1 Brush each of 2 cylindrical molds, 6¾ in/17 cm in diameter and 8 in/20 cm tall, with 2 oz/57 g of the softened butter.

2 Divide the brioche dough into two 1-lb/454-g pieces. Round each into a ball and place in one of the prepared molds.

3 Allow the dough to proof, covered, until it springs back lightly to the touch, 45 minutes to 1 hour; there should be a small indentation left in the dough, but it should not collapse. Brush the dough lightly with egg wash.

4 Bake in a 325°F/163°C deck oven until the brioche is dark golden brown on top and golden brown in the center cracks, about 45 minutes. Toward the end of baking, if the brioche is a deep brown but requires a little additional baking time, it may be necessary to remove the brioche from the molds and dry it out slightly in the oven. Cool to room temperature.

5 Unmold the brioche and slice crosswise into rounds 3/8-in/1-cm thick. Using a 2½-in/6-cm round cutter, cut 30 disks out of the brioche slices.

6 Cut the strawberries in halves or quarters, depending on size, for uniform pieces.

7 Combine the crème de cassis, lemon juice, and sugar in a large pot and bring to a boil. Reduce the heat to a low simmer, add the strawberries, and poach just until they begin to release their juices. Add the remaining fruit and poach until it is tender. (This will only take a few minutes, depending on the ripeness of the berries.) Remove from the heat.

8 Place 1 brioche disk in the bottom of each of ten soufflé cups (4 fl oz/120 mL each). Place 1 oz/28 g of fruit on each brioche disk and top with another brioche disk. Place another 1 oz/28 g of fruit on each one, and place the remaining brioche disks on top.

9 Cover the puddings with a sheet of parchment paper and place a sheet pan on top. Weight down the sheet pan with a heavy pan or two 1-lb/454-g weights. Refrigerate overnight.

10 Carefully unmold the puddings. Serve chilled.

White and dark chocolate mousse in glasses

MAKES 12 SERVINGS (5 FL OZ/140 ML EACH)

Hard ganache (page 421), melted	6 oz	170 g
White chocolate mousse (page 382)	1 lb 8 oz	680 g
Dark chocolate mousse (page 381)	1 lb 8 oz	680 g
Heavy cream, whipped	3 oz	85 g
Striped chocolate cigarettes (see page 830)	12 each	12 each

1   One at a time, pour ½ oz/14 g of the ganache in the bottom of each of twelve martini glasses (5 fl oz/150 mL each) and rapidly tip each glass in 4 directions to create 4 arcs of ganache on the inside of the glass.

2   Using a pastry bag fitted with a #5 plain tip, pipe the white chocolate mousse into the glasses, filling each halfway and making the top of the mousse as even and level as possible. Using a #5 plain tip, pipe the dark chocolate mousse on top of the white chocolate mousse, filling each glass to the top. Using a palette knife, smooth the top of the mousse level with the top of the glasses.

3   Using a #3 star tip, pipe a small rosette of whipped cream on top of each mousse-filled glass. Lean a chocolate cigarette on each rosette of whipped cream.

4   Refrigerate until ready to serve.

Raspberry mousse in glasses

MAKES 12 SERVINGS

Raspberry sauce (page 435)	6 fl oz	180 mL
Raspberry mousse (page 379)	1 lb 8 oz	680 g
Heavy cream, whipped	3 oz	85 g
White chocolate fans (see page 381)	12 each	12 each
Raspberries	36 each	36 each

1   Put 1 tbsp/15 mL of the raspberry sauce into each of twelve cordial glasses (4 fl oz/120 mL each). Using a pastry bag fitted with a #5 plain tip, pipe the mousse into the glasses, filling them to the top. Using a palette knife, smooth the mousse level with the tops of the glasses.

2   Using a #3 plain tip, pipe a small dome of whipped cream onto the center of each mousse. Lean a chocolate fan against each dome and stack 3 raspberries at the base of each fan. Refrigerate until ready to serve.

Tiramisù in glasses

MAKES 12 SERVINGS

Ladyfingers (page 340), 3 in/8 cm	36 each	36 each
Coffee simple syrup (page 900)	4 fl oz	120 mL
Tiramisù cream (page 396)	1 lb 5 oz	595 g
Chocolate shavings (see page 831)	3 oz	85 g
Confectioners' sugar	as needed	as needed
Ground cinnamon	as needed	as needed

1   Brush the backs of the ladyfingers with the syrup. Stand 3 ladyfingers in each of twelve cordial glasses (4 fl oz/120 mL each) so that the domed side of the ladyfingers is pressed against the side of the glasses.

2   Using a pastry bag fitted with a #5 plain tip, pipe the tiramisù cream into the glasses, filling them to within ½ in/1 cm of the tops of the ladyfingers. Scatter the chocolate shavings over the filling, covering it completely. Dust with confectioners' sugar and cinnamon. Refrigerate until ready to serve.

Trifles

MAKES 12 TRIFLES

Currant jelly	8 oz	227 g
Rum-flavored simple syrup (see Liquor-Flavored Simple Syrup, page 900)	6 fl oz	180 mL
Dry sherry	3 fl oz	90 mL
Vanilla sponge (page 268), cut into ½-in/1-cm cubes	9 oz	255 g
Fresh fruit, cut into ½-in/1-cm cubes	1 lb 2 oz	510 g
Diplomat cream (page 394), made without gelatin	3 lb	1.36 kg
Heavy cream, whipped	6 oz	170 g
Chocolate cigarettes (see page 829)	12 each	12 each

1   Divide the jelly evenly among twelve stemmed glasses (9 fl oz/270 mL each).

2   Combine the syrup and sherry.

3   Place the vanilla sponge cubes in a bowl, add the syrup mixture, and toss to moisten evenly. Divide half of the sponge cubes evenly among the glasses. Top with half of the fruit, dividing it evenly.

4   Using a pastry bag fitted with a #5 plain tip, pipe a layer of diplomat cream on top of the fruit. Divide the remaining sponge cubes among the glasses, and then divide the remaining fruit among them. Pipe the remaining diplomat cream on top; the glasses should be filled to within ¼ in/6 mm of the top.

5   Using a #4 star tip, pipe a rosette of whipped cream on top of each trifle. Garnish each with a chocolate cigarette. Refrigerate until ready to serve.

Phyllo cups

MAKES 12 CUPS

Phyllo dough sheets, 4 in/10 cm square	48 each	48 each
Butter, melted	as needed	as needed

1 Lay out 12 phyllo squares on the work surface. Brush each with melted butter, and top with a second phyllo square. Repeat this process 2 more times, rotating the square of phyllo slightly each time so that the corners do not align.

2 Place each stack of phyllo in 12 ramekins (6 fl oz/180 mL each) or other ovenproof containers, pressing them to the bottom and sides.

3 Bake at 375°F/191°C until golden brown, about 10 minutes.

4 To serve, fill the cups as desired with a mousse, cream, or poached pear.

Meringue swans

MAKES 20 SWAN HALVES

Egg whites	6 oz	170 g
Salt	pinch	pinch
Vanilla extract	½ tsp	2.50 mL
Sugar	12 oz	340 g

1 Place the egg whites, salt, and vanilla in a bowl and whisk until frothy.

2 Gradually add the sugar while continuing to whisk, and then whisk to stiff peaks.

3 Trace 20 swans on a piece of parchment paper, making 10 left halves and 10 right halves. Flip the parchment paper over and place on a sheet pan, so that the side with the tracing is against the pan.

4 Using a pastry bag fitted with a #3 plain tip, pipe meringue into the traced body of each swan, using the same motion that you would use to pipe a shell border; start at the tip of the wing and end at the bottom, making sure that the bottom edge is smooth. Fill in the head of each stencil with meringue.

5 Cut the parchment paper into rectangles so that there are 2 swan halves, one on top of another, on each. Drape the swan halves over a dowel 3 in/8 cm in diameter, so they will have a slight curve when dry.

6 Place the swans in a turned-off oven with a pilot light. Allow the swans to dry overnight. Alternatively, bake the meringue at 200°F/93°C for several hours, until dry. Cool to room temperature and peel off the parchment paper. Store in an airtight container until ready to assemble.

Vacherins

MAKES 12 VACHERINS

Swiss meringue (page 416)	10 oz	284 g

1 Trace 12 ovals, 1½ by 3½ in/4 by 9 cm each, on a full sheet of parchment paper, leaving 3 in/8 cm between them.

2 Flip the parchment paper over and place on a sheet pan, so that the side with the tracing is against the pan.

3 Using a pastry bag fitted with a #3 plain tip, pipe meringue into each traced oval in a spiral motion, beginning at the center and moving out toward the edge, keeping the tip just above the parchment paper while piping. Once each disk is complete, pipe a second layer of meringue all around the outer edge and a third layer if necessary or desired, building a "wall" for the container. The finished vacherins should be 1¼ in/3 cm tall. You may build the "wall" by piping spikes, as shown, or by piping rosettes, one long tube, or any boarder that will create a container.

4 Place the sheet pan in a turned-off oven with a pilot light. Allow the vacherins to dry out overnight.

NOTES To finish vacherins, fill them with a sorbet, mousse, or cream and garnish with anything from chocolate shavings to fresh or poached fruit.

Vacherins should be filled à la minute to prevent them from absorbing too much moisture from the filling and losing their crisp texture. If vacherins must be filled in advance, brush the inside and top rim with tempered white or dark chocolate.

Piping meringue rounds to prepare vacherins

Chocolate éclairs

MAKES 12 ÉCLAIRS

Pâte à choux (page 228)	1 lb	454 g
Egg wash (page 892)	as needed	as needed
Diplomat cream (page 394; see Note)	1 lb	454 g
Fondant	8 oz	227 g
Dark chocolate, melted	3 oz	85 g
Light corn syrup	as needed	as needed

1 Pipe the pâte à choux into cylinders 4 in/10 cm long on parchment-lined sheet pans using a #8 plain pastry tip and lightly brush with egg wash.

2 Bake at 360°F/182°C until the cracks formed in the pastries are no longer yellow, about 50 minutes. Cool to room temperature.

3 Pierce each end of the éclairs using a skewer or similar instrument.

4 Fill the éclairs with the diplomat cream from each end using a #1 plain piping tip.

5 Warm the fondant over a hot water bath, add the melted chocolate, and thin to the proper viscosity with corn syrup.

6 Top the filled éclairs with the chocolate fondant either by dipping or by enrobing using the back of a spoon.

NOTE Gelatin is optional in the diplomat cream for this application.

Praline éclairs

MAKES 12 ÉCLAIRS

Pâte à choux (page 228)	1 lb	454 g
Egg wash (page 892)	as needed	as needed
Sliced almonds	48 slices	48 slices
Sugar	8 oz	227 g
Water	3 fl oz	90 mL
Light corn syrup	1¾ oz	50 g
Pastry cream (page 370)	12 oz	340 g
Praline paste	2 oz	57 g
Chantilly cream (page 420)	9 oz	255 g

1 Pipe the pâte à choux into cylinders 4 in/10 cm long using a #5 plain pastry tip.

2 Brush with egg wash and bake at 360°F/182°C until the cracks are no longer yellow, about 50 minutes. Cool to room temperature.

3 Stretch plastic wrap tightly over the back of a sheet pan.

4 For each éclair, place 4 almond slices on the sheet pan in a row the length of the éclairs.

5 To make the topping, cook the sugar, water, and corn syrup until it turns light golden brown. Shock the pan in a bowl of cool water.

6 Dip the top quarter of each éclair into the caramel. Place each éclair caramel side down onto a line of almonds and press down lightly. Cool until the caramel hardens.

7 Remove the éclairs from the sheet pan, and slice off the caramel-coated tops.

8 Combine the pastry cream with the praline paste and mix until well combined.

9 Fill the bottoms of the éclairs with the praline pastry cream.

10 Using a #5 star pastry tip, pipe a spiral of Chantilly cream onto each éclair base.

11 Place the caramel-coated tops on the cream at an angle to expose the cream.

Cream puffs

MAKES 12 CREAM PUFFS

Pâte à choux (page 228)	1 lb	454 g
Egg wash (page 892)	as needed	as needed
Sliced almonds	2 oz	57 g
Granulated sugar	1 oz	28 g
Pastry cream (page 370)	12 oz	340 g
Chantilly cream (page 420)	9 oz	255 g
Confectioners' sugar	as needed	as needed

1   Pipe the pâte à choux into bulbs 1½ in/4 cm in diameter onto parchment-lined sheet pans using a #5 plain pastry tip and brush lightly with egg wash.

2   Stick several almond slices into the top of each bulb so that they protrude from the top. Sprinkle each lightly with the granulated sugar.

3   Bake at 360°F/182°C until the cracks formed in the pastries are no longer yellow, about 50 minutes. Cool to room temperature. Slice the top off each of the baked pastries.

4   Pipe the pastry cream into the bases using a #5 plain pastry tip, being careful not to overfill them.

5   Pipe a double rosette of Chantilly cream on top of the pastry cream using a #5 star tip.

6   Place the tops of the pastries on the Chantilly cream and lightly dust with confectioners' sugar.

VARIATION   Place strawberries or other fruit on top of the pastry cream and pipe the Chantilly cream onto the fruit.

Filling the baked puffs with pastry cream

Chocolate teardrops

MAKES 40 PASTRIES

Chocolate, melted, tempered (see page 762)	1 lb	454 g
Chocolate sponge sheet (page 268), 11½ by 16½ in/29 by 42 cm	2 each	2 each
Raspberry Bavarian cream (page 393; optional)	14 oz	408 g
Fruit gelées (page 813; optional)	40 each	40 each
Chocolate mousse (page 380)	3 lb 4 oz	1.47 kg
Cocoa powder	as needed	as needed

1   Using an offset spatula, spread a thin layer of tempered chocolate (dark, milk, white, or a mix) onto a 1¼ by 8-in/3 by 20-cm piece of acetate.

2   Bring the two end pieces of the acetate together with the chocolate on the inside to form a teardrop shape. Clamp the two ends together with a clip. Let the chocolate set well by leaving the teardrops at room temperature for 1 to 2 hours.

3   Using a 2½-inch round cutter, cut the chocolate sponge into 40 circles. Place a chocolate sponge round in the bottom of the teardrop. If desired, place an insert such as a raspberry Bavarian cream dome or fruit gelée in the center, on top of the sponge. Fill the chocolate teardrop to the top of the mold with chocolate mousse. Smooth with a spatula.

4   Place the filled teardrops in the freezer overnight.

5   Lightly dust with cocoa powder. Carefully remove the clip and acetate from the chocolate teardrop shape. Garnish as desired.

NOTE   Other flavors of Bavarian cream can be used.

Forming chocolate teardrop containers with strips of acetate

Pistachio and chocolate pyramids

MAKES 48 PYRAMIDS (3½ BY 3½ IN/9 BY 9 CM)

Pistachio cream (page 371)	1 lb 1½ oz	496 g
Pâte à glacier, dark	as needed	as needed
Pistachio sponge sheets (page 278), 11½ by 16½ in/29 by 42 cm	2 each	2 each
Simple syrup (page 900)	32 fl oz	960 mL
Kirsch	16 fl oz	480 mL
Chocolate mousse (page 380)	8 lb 14 oz	4.03 kg
Dark spraying chocolate (page 464)	as needed	as needed
Caramelized pistachios	48 each	48 each
Chocolate plaques (see page 829), 3½ in/9 cm	48 each	48 each

1   One day in advance, make the pistachio cream and pipe it into pyramid molds (1 by 1 in/3 by 3 cm each). Freeze the molds overnight.

2   Using a pastry brush, apply a thin layer of pâte à glacier on top of the sponge and let it set. Once set, flip the sponge over and soak it with simple syrup and kirsch.

3   Slice the cake into squares slightly larger than 3½ by 3½ in/9 by 9 cm.

Filling the pyramids with a pistachio pyramid-shaped cake

Spraying the pyramids with chocolate

4   Pipe or ladle the chocolate mousse into 3½ by 3½-in/9 by 9-cm pyramid molds, filling the molds two-thirds of the way to the top.

5   Unmold the frozen pistachio cream pyramids and push one gently into the center of each mousse-filled mold.

6   Top the pyramids with a pistachio sponge square, with the pâte à glacier–coated side facing away from the mousse.

7   Freeze the molds overnight

8   Unmold the pyramids while still frozen. Using a paint gun, spray a light coating of dark spraying chocolate at 130°F/54°C to give the pyramids a velvety look.

9   Trim the excess sponge from the bottom of the pyramids.

10   Garnish with a pistachio and a chocolate square on top of each pyramid.

Monte Alban

MAKES 1 SHEET PAN–SIZE FRAME (11½ BY 16½ IN/29 BY 42 CM)

Soft hazelnut dacquoise (page 297)	3 lb 14 oz	1.76 kg
Rustle (page 350)	2 lb 2 oz	964 g
Chocolate parfait (page 504)	4 lb 8 oz	2.04 kg
Pâte à glacier	as needed	as needed
Red-tinted spraying chocolate (page 464)	as needed	as needed

1   Do not take off the parchment paper on which the dacquoise was baked. Trim the dacquoise to 11½ by 16½ in/29 by 42 cm and reserve.

2   Spread the rustle batter evenly onto a silicone mat. Place a piece of parchment paper over the batter and roll out with a rolling pin. Place an 11½ by 16½-in/29 by 42-cm frame on top of the batter and gently press down to mark the size of the frame on the batter. Remove the frame and place the rustle in the freezer.

3   Place a decorative pastry mat on a sheet pan and place the frame on top of the mat. Fill the frame to three-quarters of its depth with the parfait, spreading the parfait evenly with an offset spatula. Reserve the remaining parfait. Place the pan in the freezer for 30 to 40 minutes.

4   Take the rustle out of freezer, remove the parchment paper, and trim to the size of the frame. Let the rustle come back to room temperature, 5 to 10 minutes.

5   Place the rustle, silicone mat up, on top of the parfait in the frame and freeze for 5 minutes. Once hardened, peel back the silicone mat.

6 Using an offset spatula, spread the remaining parfait on top of the rustle. Place the dacquoise on top of the parfait. Carefully remove the parchment. Using a pastry brush, coat the dacquoise with a thin layer of pâte à glacier.

7 Flip the assemblage over so that the mat is facing upward. Lay a pastry board on top of the assembled frame to bind the layers together. Place in the freezer until frozen, 10 to 12 hours or overnight.

8 Gently peel back the decorative mat, then remove the frame. Using a spray gun, spray redtinted spraying chocolate on the pastry to bring out the shaded relief pattern and give a velvety appearance. Trim the pastry and slice to the desired size.

Spreading the parfait on the decorative mat

Peeling back the decorative mat

Happiness

MAKES 1 HALF SHEET PAN–SIZE FRAME (17¾ BY 12⅞ IN/45 BY 33 CM)

1-2-3 cookie dough (page 223)	3 lb	1.36 kg
Guava jelly (page 464)	1 lb 11 oz	756 g
Coconut Joconde dough (page 286)	2 lb 2½ oz	1.03 kg
Passion fruit mousse (see Variation, page 379)	3 lb 5 oz	1.50 kg
Mango mirror glaze (see Variation, page 427)	2 lb 4 oz	1.02 kg
White chocolate triangle cutouts (see page 827) painted with yellow, orange, and green cocoa butter	as needed	as needed

1   Roll out the cookie dough ⅛ in/3 mm thick to the size of a half sheet pan. Dock the dough and chill it for 20 minutes.

2   Place a frame on top of the cookie dough and bake at 350°F/177°C until light golden, 7 to 10 minutes. While baking, the frame will drop into the dough, marking the outline of the frame.

3   Melt the jelly and pour it onto the baked cookie dough inside the frame while the cookie dough is still hot. Spread the jelly evenly with an offset spatula. Let the jelly set.

4   Evenly spread the Joconde dough on a parchment-lined sheet pan and bake at 375°F/191°C until golden brown, 10 to 12 minutes. When cool enough to handle, cut the Joconde to the size of the frame (17¾ by 12⅞ in/45 by 33 cm). Do not peel off the parchment paper. Cool completely.

5   Flip the Joconde over and place it on top of the jelly; peel off the parchment paper.

6   Pour the mousse on top of the Joconde, filling the frame all the way to the top. Smooth out the mousse with an offset spatula. Freeze overnight.

7   With a ruler and a warm clean knife, mark a grid on top of the cake while it is still frozen, to the desired size of the pastry. Put the cake back into the freezer for 20 minutes.

8   Remove the cake from the freezer and apply a thin layer of the mango mirror glaze on top, spreading evenly with an offset spatula. Clean off any excess glaze on the sides the frame and allow to set. Warm the sides of the frame with a torch and remove it.

9   Using a warm, clean knife, cut each slice to finish and garnish the pastry with white chocolate triangle cutouts. Put the rest of the cake back on a parchment-lined sheet pan and back into the freezer while working on each slice.

Glazing the pastry with mango mirror glaze

Coconut frangipane

MAKES 48 OVAL CAKES

Coconut frangipane cake (page 329), baked but still warm	4 lb 8 oz	2.04 kg
Simple syrup (page 900)	24 fl oz	720 mL
Rum	16 fl oz	480 mL
Swiss meringue (page 416)	2 lb	907 g

1   While still warm, use a pastry brush to soak the coconut frangipane cakes with simple syrup and rum.

2   Once the cakes are cooled, remove them from the oval molds and set on a parchment-lined sheet pan. Using a flat pastry tip, pipe the Swiss meringue in a snake-like motion on top of the cake.

3   Brûlée the meringue with a torch, just enough to get a nice golden brown appearance.

Russian

MAKES 14 SANDWICH CAKES

Biscuit russe dough (page 300)	14 oz	397 g
Confectioners' sugar	as needed	as needed
Pistachio mousseline (page 392)	1 lb 7 oz	652 g
Caramelized pistachios	42 each	42 each

1   Before baking the biscuits, dust confectioners' sugar over them and wait for 10 minutes. Dust once more. Bake at 325°F/163°C until a light golden color, 10 to 12 minutes.

2   Reserve the best 14 biscuits for the top. On the other biscuits, pipe ½-in/1-cm pearls of mousseline using a #4 plain piping tip: Pipe 5 pearls around the outside of the biscuit first, then fill the center. Chill until the mousseline sets completely, 20 to 30 minutes.

3   Place the reserved biscuits on top of the chilled mousseline and sprinkle with confectioners' sugar. Garnish the top of the biscuits with 3 caramelized pistachios each.

Piped
desserts.
FROM LEFT TO
RIGHT: Russian
(opposite),
Coconut
Frangipane
(opposite),
Cream Puffs
(page 676),
and Hazelnut
Dacquoise
(page 684)

Hazelnut dacquoise

MAKES 14 SANDWICH CAKES

Dacquoise meringue (page 298)	1 lb 6 oz	624 g
Praline mousseline (page 392)	1 lb 7 oz	652 g
Confectioners' sugar	as needed	as needed
Hazelnut dragée (page 793)	14 each	14 each

1   Reserve the best 14 meringues for the top.

2   On the other meringues, pipe ½-in/1-cm pearls of mousseline using a #4 plain pastry tip: Pipe 5 pearls around the outside of the meringue first, then fill the center. Chill until the mousseline sets completely, 20 to 30 minutes.

3   Place the reserved meringues on top of the mousseline and sprinkle with confectioners' sugar. Garnish the top with 1 hazelnuts dragée each.

Molded desserts.
FROM LEFT TO RIGHT: Happiness (page 681), Chocolate Caramel Mousse Dessert (page 686), Chocolate Teardrops (page 677), Paulina (opposite), and Monte Alban (page 679)

Paulina

MAKES 50 ROUNDS (2¾ IN/7 CM EACH)

Yellow, orange, and green decorating batter, for patterned Joconde sponge	1 lb 3 oz each	539 g each
Patterned Joconde sponge batter (page 284) for sheets 17¾ by 12⅞ in/45 by 33 cm	2 each	2 each
1-2-3 cookie dough (page 223)	2 lb	907 g
Pâte à glacier, white	as needed	as needed
Lime or lemon curd (page 377), cooled	3 lb 3 oz	737 kg
Cream cheese mousse (page 387)	1 lb 10 oz	1.65 kg
Mirror glaze (page 424), cold	3 oz	85 g

1 Using a small paintbrush, apply a thin layer of yellow, orange, and green decorating batter to 2 entire silicone mats by blotting the bristles onto the mat in a sponge-like manner. Freeze the painted mats for 30 minutes.

2 Divide the sponge batter evenly between the painted mats, spreading it quickly (before the decorating batter melts) but gently (to avoid losing volume).

3 Bake at 400°F/204°C until the sponges are not sticky and are a light golden brown color, about 7 minutes.

4 Line each ring mold with 8¼-in/21-cm strips of acetate. Cut the Joconde into strips 8⅛ by 1⅛ in/21 by 3 cm for the inside of the molds. The strips of Joconde should not be as high as the walls of the mold; leave about ½ in/1 cm between the top of the Joconde and the top of the ring mold.

5 Using a 2½-in/6-cm cutter, cut the remaining Joconde into circles; reserve.

6 Roll out the cookie dough ⅛-in/3-mm thick. Using a 2½-in/6 cm cutter, cut 50 rounds from the dough. Place the rounds on a parchment-lined sheet pan and bake in a 375°F/191°C oven until golden, 7 to 10 minutes.

7 Once cool, brush the cookies with a thin layer of pâte à glacier and place at the bottom of each ring mold. On top of the cookie, pipe the curd ½ in/1 cm thick into the molds. Top the curd with the remaining Joconde rounds.

8 Fill the molds to the top with the cream cheese mousse. Wipe the molds clean, and even off the top with an offset spatula. Freeze overnight. (Reminder: Reserve any extra mousse in case it settles in the mold overnight and is no longer even with the top.)

9 If necessary, slightly reheat the mousse, whip by hand, and add to the tops of the molds, making sure the tops are flat and even.

10 Remove the rings from the dessert, but do not remove the acetate.

11 Using an offset spatula, evenly spread the cold glaze over the dessert. Remove the acetate from the desserts while they are still frozen. Decorate the pastry as desired.

Chocolate caramel mousse dessert

MAKES 22 ROUNDS (2¾ IN/7 CM EACH)

1-2-3 cookie dough (page 223)	2 lb	907 g
Vanilla sponge sheet (page 268), 11½ by 16½ in/29 by 42 cm	1 each	1 each
Simple syrup (page 900)	as needed	as needed
Chocolate caramel mousse (page 386)	4 lb 2 oz	1.87 kg
Poached apple or pear (page 898), small dice	5 each	5 each
Spraying chocolate (page 464)	as needed	as needed
Hard ganache (page 421)	1 lb	454 g
Chocolate disks (see "Tempered Chocolate Stencils and Cutouts," page 827), for garnish	22 each	22 each
Meringue sticks	44 each	44 each

1 Roll out the cookie dough ⅛ in/3 mm thick. Using a 2½-in/6-cm cutter, cut 22 rounds. Place the rounds on a parchment-lined sheet pan and bake at 375°F/191°C until golden, 7 to 10 minutes. Cool completely.

2 Using a 2½-in/6-cm cutter, cut the sponge into 22 rounds. Soak the sponge with the simple syrup.

3 Place the 2¾-in/7-cm ring molds on a sheet pan and line the inside of each mold with acetate.

4 Place a cookie round in the bottom of each ring mold. Place a sponge round on top of each cookie.

5 Using a pastry bag fitted with a #4 piping tip, pipe the mousse into the mold, working from the outside in, filling the mold two-thirds of the way up the side and leaving an empty circle in the center. Make sure there are no air bubbles in the piped mousse.

6 Fill a new pastry bag with the fruit and cut a hole in the bottom of the bag big enough to pipe the fruit through it. Pipe the fruit into the empty circle on top of the sponge.

7 Pipe the remaining mousse to the top of the mold. Smooth the top with a small offset spatula.

8 Freeze the molds for 10 to 12 hours or overnight.

9 To finish the pastries, remove the rings and place the pastries at least 1 in/3 cm apart on top of an upside-down sheet pan covered with parchment paper. Remove the acetate from the pastries.

10 Heat the spraying chocolate to 95°F/35°C and splatter the pastries with the spraying chocolate, making random lines of chocolate on the tops and sides.

11 Pipe 3 dots of ganache on top of each pastry, forming a triangle, and place the chocolate disk on top of the ganache. Before service, place 2 meringue sticks onto the disk.

chapter nineteen

Savory baking

Savory baking enables the pastry chef to deepen the professional repertoire. Execution of these products will broaden the understanding of how savory baked goods can provide an opportunity for lighter dining, creative amuse plates, and nourishing accompaniment to an informal gathering, cocktail reception, or large-scale catering event.

The importance of savory for a pastry chef or baker

The essential elements of savory baking include an understanding of the varied global influences on savory baking technique and the ability to adapt already-developed traditional baking and pastry skills to the novel and nontraditional aspects of savory baking. For example, layered pastry dishes from the Mediterranean, the Middle East, and Asia are often served as a nourishing and affordable option to a more formal meal.

Current trends include numerous influences on flavor profile, texture, and ingredients that may have been unfamiliar or wholly exotic only a generation ago. For example, the inclusion of spices, spice mixtures, vegetables, seasoned meat fillings, and nuts or seeds engage the palate and stimulate the imagination in a way the strict adherence to traditional baking techniques may not.

An important additional consideration is the ability of savory baking to marry techniques with which the baking or pastry student may be familiar with a variety of foods and cooking techniques that may be unfamiliar. Preparing a savory meat-and-vegetable-filled pastry, for example, can allow hands-on experience with meat cuts, grinding, knife skills, filleting, sautéing, braising, and simmering.

Flavor profiles and food trends

Popular influences on flavors are evident in the crossover between the preparation of traditional pastry and savory pastry flavored with aromatics and herbs. These ingredients allow for a fusion of flavors and textures not traditionally found in a strictly segregated baking or pastry kitchen. Chefs with the proper training and exposure are then able to identify, assess, and prepare a range of savory dishes.

Some savory baking or pastry items are intended to be served as an accompaniment to a hot broth, while others, such as savory scones, are intended to be served warm or cold, as a complement to a light meal or stand-alone bakery take-away item. The essential techniques used for making sweet or dessert items are wholly recognizable. It is the varied and diverse combination of novel or nontraditional ingredients that is of interest.

Seasonality is an important consideration when preparing a menu including savory baking and pastry items. Fresh herbs, seasonal produce, and high-quality supplemental ingredients are of concern to the professional chef seeking to expand the items available on the menu while respecting that the overall quality of the end product.

For this reason, the professional chef may consider the quality of products used in savory baking and the origin of these ingredients, including farming techniques, organic certification, and the distance from the crop or livestock source to eventual delivery for kitchen preparation. It is not always financially practical nor possible given intended use, but as with the current trend toward a broader and more inclusive array of ingredients, the source of such ingredients and the distance traveled is an important consideration for the modern chef and his or her customers.

Finally, savory baking and pastry items allow the professional chef to expand market appeal and to diversify both the niche and the menu for his or her cookery. The audience for savory baking and pastry includes restaurant patrons served an amuse or other small and flavorful side and café customers for whom smaller portions and premise cooking limitations place a premium on maximizing space, plating options, and storage. Brunches allow novel combinations of ingredients that are still wholly usable and value-added as nutritious additions to baked goods, pastries, and batter-based products. Puff pastries, hors d'oeuvres, and bite-size portions of ingredients complementary to a later meal service, such as canapés filled with a variation on the entrée, are another way in which baked goods and pastries with savory ingredients can enhance the overall enjoyment of food in a variety of professional cooking venues.

Cutting vegetables and fresh herbs

There are several basic knife cuts with which you should be familiar.

Chopping and mincing

Coarse chopping is generally used for mirepoix or similar flavoring ingredients that are to be strained out of the dish and discarded. It is also appropriate when cutting vegetables that will be puréed. Trim the root and stem ends and peel the vegetables if necessary.

Slice or cut through the vegetables at nearly regular intervals until the cuts are relatively uniform. This need not be a perfectly neat cut, but all the pieces should be roughly the same size.

Mincing is a very fine cut, suitable for many vegetables and herbs. Onions, garlic, and shallots are often minced.

1. Rinse and dry herbs well. Strip the leaves from the stems.

2. Gather the herbs into a tight ball before slicing them, which produces a very coarse chop. Use your guiding hand to hold them in place.

3. Position the knife so that it can slice through the pile and chop coarsely.

4. Once the herbs are coarsely chopped, use the fingertips of your guiding hand to hold the tip of the chef's knife in contact with the cutting board. Keeping the tip of the blade against the cutting board, lower the knife firmly and rapidly, repeatedly cutting through the herbs.

5. Continue to cut the herbs until the desired fineness is attained.

6. Green onions and chives are minced differently. Rather than cutting repeatedly, slice them very finely.

Chiffonade

The chiffonade cut is used for leafy vegetables and herbs. The result is a fine shred, often used as a garnish or bed. Use a chef's knife to make very fine, parallel cuts to produce fine shreds. For Belgian endive, remove the leaves from the core and stack them. Make parallel lengthwise cuts to produce a shred. For greens with large leaves, such as romaine, roll individual leaves into cylinders before cutting crosswise. Stack smaller leaves, such as basil, one on top of the other, then roll them into cylinders and cut crosswise.

LEFT: Slicing garlic   MIDDLE: Mincing herbs   RIGHT: Chiffonading basil

OTHER KNIFE CUTS

STANDARD VEGETABLE CUTS

Fine julienne	1⁄16 by 1⁄16 by 1–2 in	2 by 2 by 25–50 mm
Julienne/allumette	1⁄8 by 1⁄8 by 1–2 in	4 by 4 by 25–50 mm
Bâtonnet	1⁄4 by 1⁄4 by 2–2½ in	6 by 6 by 50–60 mm
Fine brunoise	1⁄16 by 1⁄16 by 1⁄16 in	2 by 2 by 2 mm
Brunoise	1⁄8 by 1⁄8 by 1⁄8 in	4 by 4 by 4 mm
Small dice	1⁄8 by 1⁄8 by 1⁄8 in	6 by 6 by 6 mm
Medium dice	½ by ½ by ½ in	12 by 12 by 12 mm
Large dice	¾ by ¾ by ¾ in	20 by 20 by 20 mm

ADDITIONAL VEGETABLE CUTS

Paysanne	½ by ½ by 1⁄8 in	12 by 12 by 4 mm
Fermière	1⁄8–½ in, as desired	4–12 mm
Lozenge	½ by ½ by 1⁄8 in, diamond cut	12 by 12 by 4 mm
Rondelle	1⁄8–½ in, as desired round cut	4–12 mm
Tourné	7-sided oblong cut, approximately 2 in	50 mm

Dicing

TOP LEFT: Square off the vegetable.

BOTTOM LEFT: Cut bâtonnet from slices.

TOP RIGHT: Slice parallel cuts of equal thickness.

BOTTOM RIGHT: Cut dice from bâtonnet.

Chopping onion

Slicing horizontally after scoring vertically

Chopping

Cooking methods

The ability to properly execute any cooking method is imperative to the successful outcome of any formula. Consider the instructions in each individual technique. What is the basic final result? How many steps are there? What is the mise en place for each step?

Sautéing

Sautéing is a technique that cooks food rapidly in a little fat over relatively high heat. Certain menu items, listed as seared/pan-seared, charred/pan-charred, or pan-broiled, are essentially sautéed. Those terms on a menu have come to suggest that even less oil is used than for a traditional sauté. Sautéed dishes typically include a sauce made with the drippings, or *fond*, left in the pan.

Searing may be a first step for some roasted, braised, or stewed foods. They are cooked quickly in a small amount of oil over direct heat. The difference between searing and sautéing is not how the technique is performed, but that these foods are not cooked completely as a result of being seared. Searing is used as an effective way to develop flavor and color for the longer, slower cooking methods.

Stir-frying, associated with Asian cooking and successfully adapted by innovative Western chefs, shares many similarities with sautéing. Foods are customarily cut into small pieces—usually strips, dice, or shreds—and cooked rapidly in a little oil. They are added to the pan in sequence; those requiring the longest cooking times are added first, those that cook quickly only at the last moment. The sauce for a stir-fry, like that of a sauté, is made or finished in the pan to capture the dish's entire flavor.

Choose the most tender cuts for sautéing, from the rib or loin, as well as portions of the leg, of beef, veal, lamb, pork, or large game animals. Poultry and game bird breasts are often preferred for sautéing. Firm or moderately textured fish are easier to sauté than very delicate fish. Shellfish, in and out of the shell, also sauté well. Select the cooking fat according to the flavor you want to create, food cost, availability, and smoke point.

The base for a pan sauce in sautéing may vary to suit the flavor of the main item. Brown sauces such as demi-glace or jus lié, veloutés, reduced stocks (thickened with a slurry if necessary), vegetable coulis, or tomato sauce may be used. Consult specific recipes.

A sauté pan has short, sloped sides and is wider than it is tall to encourage rapid moisture evaporation. It is made of a metal that responds quickly to rapid heat changes. Woks are used to prepare stir-fries. Pan-seared and pan-broiled items are often prepared in heavy-gauge pans that retain heat, such as cast-iron pans. Have tongs or spatulas available to turn foods and remove them from the pan, holding pans to reserve foods while a sauce is prepared or finished, and all appropriate service items (heated plates, garnishes, and accompaniments).

Placing arugula in a sauté pan

Sautéed arugula

Sweating

Sweating is cooking an item, usually vegetables, in a covered pan in a small amount of fat until it softens and releases moisture but does not brown. In some instances, items are begun cooking by sweating and later finished in an item like a quiche or savory tart. It is important not to allow browning when initially cooking the vegetables, as they may burn when cooked further.

Sweating diced onions and red peppers in a sauté pan

Steaming

Cooked surrounded by water vapor in a closed cooking vessel, steamed foods have clean, clear flavors. Steam circulating around the food provides an even, moist environment. Steaming is an efficient and highly effective way to prepare naturally tender fish and poultry. Properly steamed foods are plump, moist, and tender; they generally do not lose much of their original volume. They often retain more intrinsic flavor than foods cooked by other methods because the cooking medium does not generally impart much flavor of its own. Colors also stay true.

The best foods for steaming are naturally tender and of a size and shape that allow them to cook in a short amount of time. Cut food into the appropriate size, if necessary. Fish is generally cooked as fillets, although there are some typical presentations of whole fish. Similarly, boneless, skinless poultry breasts, or suprêmes, steam well. Shellfish can be left in the shell, unless otherwise indicated; for example, scallops are customarily removed from the shell. Shrimp may also be peeled before steaming.

LEFT: Steaming broccoli: Place raw broccoli over boiling water.

RIGHT: The finished broccoli should be tender and bright green.

Many different liquids are used for steaming. Water is common, but a flavorful broth or stock, court bouillon, wine, or beer can also be used, especially if the steaming liquid is served along with the food. Adding such aromatic ingredients as herbs and spices, citrus zest, lemongrass, ginger, garlic, and mushrooms to the liquid boosts its flavor as well as that of the food being steamed. Sometimes food is steamed on a bed of vegetables in a closed vessel; the vegetables' natural moisture becomes part of the steam bath cooking the food. Fillings, marinades, and wrappers can all be used in preparing steamed foods. Fish is sometimes wrapped to keep it exceptionally moist.

Small amounts of food can be steamed using a small insert. Larger quantities, or foods that require different cooking times, are better prepared in a tiered steamer. Remember that it is important to allow enough room for steam to circulate completely around foods as they cook to encourage even, rapid cooking.

Pressure steamers—which reach higher temperatures than tiered steamers—and convection steamers are good choices for steaming large quantities. The chef can then prepare appropriately sized batches throughout a meal period or handle the more intense demands of a banquet or institutional meal situation.

Grilling and broiling

Grilling and broiling are quick cooking techniques that are used for naturally tender, serving-size or smaller pieces of meat, poultry, or fish. By contrast, roasting and baking require a longer cooking time and are frequently used with larger cuts of meat, whole birds, and dressed fish.

Grilling cooks food with radiant heat from a source located below it. Some of the juices are actually reduced directly on the food while the rest drip away. Grilled foods have a slightly charred flavor, resulting from the juices and fats that are rendered as the food cooks, as well as from direct contact with the rods of the grill rack.

Broiling is similar to grilling but uses a heat source located above the food rather than below. Frequently, delicate foods like lean white fish are brushed with butter or oil, put on a heated, oiled sizzler platter, and then placed on the rack below the heat source instead of directly on the rods.

Tender portion-size cuts of poultry, cuts of meat from the loin, rib, or top round areas, and fillets of such fatty fish as tuna and salmon are suited to grilling and broiling. Lean fish may also be grilled or broiled if they are coated with oil or an oil-based marinade. Some less tender cuts of meat such as hanger or flank steak may also be used if they are cut very thin.

Grilling vegetables

All meat and fish should be cut to an even thickness. When preparing meat for grilling or broiling, pound meats and fish lightly if necessary to even their thickness. Meat should be trimmed of excess fat and all silverskin and gristle. Some foods are cut into strips, chunks, or cubes and then threaded onto skewers. The food itself should be seasoned and in some cases lightly oiled.

Different parts of the grill are hotter than others. Divide the grill into zones of varying heat intensity, including a very hot section for quickly searing foods and an area of moderate to low heat for slow cooking and holding foods. (if the grill is wood- or charcoal-fired, set aside an area for igniting the fuel, which may be too hot and smoky to cook foods over directly.) Zones may also be allocated for different types of foods, in order to prevent an undesirable transfer of flavors. Developing a system for placing foods on the grill or broiler, whether by food type or by range of doneness, helps speed up work on the line.

Woods such as mesquite, hickory, or apple are frequently used to impart special flavors. Hardwood chips, herb stems, grapevine trimmings, and other aromatics can be soaked in cold water and then thrown on the grill fire to create aromatic smoke. The sauce that accompanies a grilled item is prepared separately.

Roasting

Roasting, whether by pan roasting, baking, smoke-roasting, or poêléing, is a way of cooking by indirect heat in an oven. Spit-roasting is more like grilling or broiling. Either way, the result is a crusty exterior and tender interior. The term "baking" is often used interchangeably with roasting; however, it is most typically used in relation to breads, cakes, pastries, and the like.

Rotisserie cooking involves placing the food on a rod that is turned either manually or by a motor. The radiant heat given off by a fire or gas jet cooks the food while constant turning creates a basting effect and ensures that the food cooks evenly.

Roasting, as it is most often practiced today, is more similar to baking than it is to spit-roasting or rotisserie cooking. In an oven, roasted foods are cooked through contact with dry heated air held in a closed environment. As the outer layers become heated, the food's natural juices turn to steam and penetrate the food more deeply. The rendered juices, also called pan drippings or fond, are the foundation for sauces prepared while the roast rests. Roasting commonly refers to large, multiportion meat cuts, whole birds, and dressed fish.

Smoke-roasting is an adaptation of roasting that allows foods to take on a rich, smoky flavor. The food cooks in a tightly closed environment or in a smoker setup. This can be done over an open flame or in the oven.

Roasted vegetables

Tender meats from the rib, loin, and leg give the best results. Young, tender birds may be roasted whole, as may dressed fish. Trim away any excess fat and silverskin. A layer of fat or poultry skin helps to baste foods naturally as they roast. Season meats, poultry, and fish before roasting to fully develop their flavor. For additional flavor during roasting, herbs or aromatic vegetables may be used to stuff the cavity or to insert under the skin.

Foods such as whole birds, chicken breasts, and chops may be stuffed before roasting. Season the stuffing and chill it to below 40°F/4°C before combining it with raw meat, fish, or poultry. Allow enough time for the seasonings to interact with the food before starting to roast. Place fresh herbs in the cavity of a bird before trussing, rub seasonings on the skin, or slip them under the skin.

A good roasting pan has a flat bottom with relatively low sides to encourage hot air to circulate freely around the roasting food. Select a pan that holds the food comfortably but is not so large that the pan juices will scorch. Food to be roasted may be set on a roasting rack, which permits the hot air to contact all of the food's surfaces, but good results are also possible when foods are set in very shallow roasting or baking pans elevated by aromatics, such as mirepoix. The pan should remain uncovered.

You may need butcher's twine or skewers, as well as an instant-read thermometer and a kitchen fork. Have an additional pan to hold the roasted food while a sauce is made from the pan drippings. Strainers and skimmers or ladles are needed to prepare the sauce. Have a carving board and an extremely sharp carving knife nearby for final service.

Best results are achieved when the oven is at the correct roasting temperature before the roasting pan is put into it. If searing foods in a very hot oven, heat the oven to 425° to 450°F/218° to 232°C. Roast large cuts such as prime rib or turkey at a low to moderate temperature throughout roasting; a deeply browned exterior is the result of the extended roasting time. Start smaller or more delicate foods at a low to moderate temperature (300° to 325°F/149° to 163°C) and then brown them at the very end of roasting by increasing the temperature of the oven from 350° to 375°F/177° to 191°C.

Barding and Larding

Two traditional preparation techniques for roasted foods that are naturally lean are barding (tying thin sheets of fatback, bacon, or caul fat around a food) and larding (inserting small strips of fatback into a food). The extra fat provides additional flavor and also helps keep the meat tender and juicy. Venison, wild boar, game birds, and certain cuts of beef or lamb may be candidates for barding or larding. Variations using different products are also employed to give different flavors to roasted foods. For example, a roast, rather than being larded with fatback, may be studded with slivers of garlic. The garlic will not have the same tenderizing effect as the fatback, but it will add plenty of flavor.

Today, with increased concern over the amount of fat in diets, every trace of visible fat or skin is often removed in an effort to reduce fat in the final dish, even though the amount of fat released from skin or fat layers as foods roast does not penetrate far into the meat. Fat and skin provide some protection from the drying effects of an oven without dramatically changing the amount of fat in the meat, and foods stripped of their natural protection of fat or skin can become dry and lose flavor.

Frying

Pan Frying

Pan-fried foods have a richly textured crust and a moist, flavorful interior, producing a dish of intriguing contrasts in texture and flavor. When a carefully selected sauce is paired with a dish, the effects can range from home-style to haute cuisine. Pan-fried food is almost always coated—dredged in flour, coated with batter, or breaded. Food is fried in enough oil to come halfway or two-thirds up its side; it is often cooked over less intense heat than in sautéing. The product is cooked by the oil's heat rather than by direct contact with the pan. In pan frying, the hot oil seals the food's coated surface, thereby locking in the natural juices. Because no juices are released, and a larger amount of oil is involved, sauces accompanying pan-fried foods are usually made separately.

Pan-fried food is usually portion-size or smaller. Select cuts that are naturally tender, as you would for a sauté. Rib or loin cuts, top round, or poultry breasts are all good choices. Lean fish such as sole or flounder are also well suited to pan frying. Trim away any fat, silverskin, and gristle. Remove the skin and bones of poultry and fish fillets if necessary or desired. You may want to pound cutlets for an even thickness and to shorten cooking time. This means that the exterior will brown without overcooking in the same time that the meat cooks through.

Ingredients for breading include flour, milk or beaten eggs, and bread crumbs or cornmeal.

The fat for pan frying must be able to reach high temperatures without breaking down or smoking. Vegetable oils, olive oil, and shortenings may all be used for pan frying. Lard, goose fat, and other rendered animal fats have a place in certain regional and ethnic dishes. The choice of fat makes a difference in the flavor of the finished dish.

The pan used for pan frying must be large enough to hold foods in a single layer without touching. If the food is crowded, the temperature of the fat will drop quickly and a good crust will not form. Pans should be made of heavy-gauge metal and should be able to transmit heat evenly. The sides should be higher than those appropriate for sautés to avoid splashing hot oil out of the pan as foods are added to the oil or turned during cooking. Have on hand a pan lined with paper towels to blot away surface fat from fried foods. Tongs or slotted spatulas are typically used to turn foods. Select shallow, wide containers to hold coatings, breading, or batters.

Deep-Frying

Deep-fried foods have many of the same characteristics as pan-fried foods, including a crisp, browned exterior and a moist, flavorful interior. Deep-fried foods, however, are cooked in enough fat or oil to completely submerge them. In deep-frying, significantly more fat is used than for either sautéing or pan frying. The food is almost always coated with a standard breading, a batter such as a tempura or beer batter, or a simple flour coating. The coating acts as a barrier between the fat and the food, and also contributes flavor and texture.

To cook rapidly and evenly, foods must be trimmed and cut into a uniform size and shape. Select cuts that are naturally tender; some typical choices include poultry, seafood, and vegetables. Remove the skin and bones of poultry and fish fillets if necessary or desired. Be certain to season the food before adding a coating. Deep-frying is also suitable for croquettes and similar dishes made from a mixture of cooked, diced meats, fish, or poultry, bound with a heavy béchamel and breaded.

Breadings and coatings are common for deep-fried foods. Standard breading can be done three to four hours ahead and items refrigerated before frying, but ideally breading should be done as close to service as possible. A batter or plain flour coating is applied immediately before cooking.

Electric or gas deep fryers with baskets are typically used for deep-frying, although it is also feasible to fry foods using a large pot. The sides should be high enough to prevent fat from foaming over or splashing, and the pot wide enough to allow the chef to add and remove foods easily. Use a deep-fat frying thermometer to check the fat's temperature, regardless of whether you use an electric or gas fryer or a pot on a stovetop. Become familiar with the fryer's recovery time (the time needed for the fat to regain the proper temperature). After foods are added, the fat will lose temperature for a brief time. The more food added, the more the temperature will drop and the longer it will take to come back to the proper level.

Kitchens that must fry many kinds of food often have several different fryers to help prevent flavor transfer. Have a pan lined with paper towels to blot fried foods before they are served. Tongs, spiders, and baskets help add foods to the fryer and remove them when properly cooked.

Savory baking and pastry products

Quiche

Quiche is a savory custard baked in a pie shell and may include a variety of savory, aromatic, and other ingredients. Of French origin, this savory pie is often accompanied by herbs incorporated into the custard, or enhanced with cheese or other appropriate products. Quiche is often served as a brunch or buffet item, and can be readily portion-cut and served with complementary meat or vegetable items.

Tarts

Tarts are made from shallow, straight-sided pastry crust that is either fluted or plain, filled with a savory or sweet mixture. They may be either filled with fresh ingredients and served or cooked and then served either warm or cooled.

Mousse

Mousses are foams made with beaten egg whites with or without whipped cream folded into a flavored base. These items may be either sweet or savory.

Pizzas and sandwiches

These are bread-based items to which any number of toppings or fillers are added, most often a meat, fish, or poultry item with complementary vegetables, herbs, and sauce. Cheese often accompanies both the hot open-faced pizza and the sandwich, open-faced or closed, grilled or cold.

Brie en croûte

MAKES 50 PIECES

Butter puff pastry dough (page 231)	3 lb 8 oz	1.59 kg
Brie, small cubes	8 to 12 oz	227 to 340 g
Egg wash (page 892)	as needed	as needed

1   Divide the puff pastry dough in half and roll the 2 pieces to approximately ⅛ in/3 mm thick.

2   Using a 1½-in/4-cm round cutter, mark on one sheet of dough where the cheese will be placed. Mark the circles about 1 in/3 cm apart.

3   Meanwhile, put the other sheet of puff pastry dough in the freezer to keep it cold.

4   Place a piece of the cheese inside each marked circle. Brush egg wash around the cheese.

5   Take the second sheet of dough from the freezer and cover the first piece and the cheese with it.

6   Using a slightly smaller round cutter, gently press around the cheese to seal the 2 pieces of dough together. Place in the freezer for 20 minutes before cutting.

7   Cut each piece of dough using a fluted cutter 2¼ in/5 cm in diameter.

8   Brush the tops of the dough rounds with egg wash and refrigerate overnight.

9   Place the dough rounds on a wire rack over a sheet pan and bake at 375°F/191°C until the exterior is a deep golden brown, about 40 minutes. Serve.

NOTE   You can also add sautéed garlic or other flavoring to the cheese before sealing it in the puff pastry dough. The cheese alone has very little flavor.

Spinach feta quiche

MAKES 1 QUICHE (9 IN/23 CM)

Pâte brisée (page 222)	10 oz	284 g
Onion, chopped	2 oz	57 g
Butter	1 oz	28 g
Spinach, chopped, steamed, and drained	4 oz	113 g
Milk	6 fl oz	180 mL
Heavy cream	6 fl oz	180 mL
Eggs	4 oz	113 g
Egg yolks	2 oz	57 g
Salt	½ tsp	2.50 g
Ground black pepper	½ tsp	1 g
Feta, small cubes	3 oz	85 g

1   Roll out the pâte brisée ⅛ in/3 mm thick and line a tart pan. Line the tart shell with parchment paper and fill with dried beans or pie weights. Bake at 350°F/177°C until very light golden brown, about 15 minutes. Cool completely.

2   Sauté the onion in the butter until translucent. Add the spinach and cook until wilted. Drain.

3   Combine the milk and cream in a saucepan and bring to a simmer.

4   Combine the eggs, egg yolks, salt, and pepper in a bowl, stirring with a whisk. Add about one-third of the hot milk mixture to the eggs while whisking constantly. Add the remaining hot milk mixture, stirring to incorporate.

5   Spread the spinach mixture in the tart shell and sprinkle the cheese on top. Pour the custard mixture over the top.

6   Bake at 350°F/177°C just until the custard is set, about 45 minutes. Serve warm, at room temperature, or chilled.

VARIATIONS   **QUICHE LORRAINE** Omit the spinach, onion, and feta. Use 1 lb/454 g grated Gruyère and 1 lb/454 g bacon, diced, rendered, and drained. Make the custard as directed above, fill the tart shell, and bake as directed.

THREE-CHEESE QUICHE Omit the spinach, onion, and feta. Use 8 oz/227 g grated Gruyère, 1 lb/454 g ricotta, and 6 oz/170 g grated Parmesan. Make the custard as directed above, fill the tart shell, and bake as directed.

Spinach and goat cheese quiche

MAKES 1 QUICHE (9 IN/23 CM)

Basic pie dough (page 222)	1 lb 4 oz	567 g
Vegetable oil	1 oz	28 g
Onion, minced	2¼ oz	64 g
Spinach leaves, blanched, squeezed dry, and chopped	8 oz	227 g
Salt	½ tsp	2.50 g
Ground black pepper	¼ tsp	0.5 g
Heavy cream	6 fl oz	180 mL
Eggs	2 each	2 each
Fresh goat cheese, crumbled	1½ oz	43 g
Grated Parmesan	¾ oz	21 g
Sun-dried tomatoes, chopped	1 oz	28 g

1   Roll out the pie dough ⅛ in/3 mm thick and line a pie pan. Line the crust with parchment paper and fill with dried beans or pie weights. Bake at 350°F/177°C until very light golden brown, about 15 minutes. Cool completely.

2   Heat the oil in a large sauté pan over medium heat. Add the onion and sauté, stirring frequently, until translucent, 3 to 4 minutes. Add the spinach and sauté until very hot, about 4 minutes. Remove from the heat. Season with ¼ tsp/1.25 g of the salt and a pinch of the pepper.

3   Transfer to a colander and let the spinach drain and cool while preparing the custard.

4   Whisk together the cream and eggs. Stir in the goat cheese, Parmesan, sun-dried tomatoes, and spinach. Season with the remaining salt and pepper. Spread the mixture evenly over the crust.

5   Place the quiche pan on a baking sheet and bake at 350°F/177°C until a knife blade inserted in the center comes out clean, 40 to 45 minutes. If the crust begins to overbrown, cover the edges of the crust with strips of aluminum foil or a pie shield.

6   Remove the quiche from the oven and cool on a rack. Let the quiche rest for at least 20 minutes before cutting in pieces. Serve hot, warm, or at room temperature.

Caramelized onion quiche

MAKES 1 QUICHE (9 IN/23 CM)

Basic pie dough (page 222)	1 lb 4 oz	567 g
Extra-virgin olive oil	1 oz	28 g
Yellow onions, thinly sliced	7½ oz	213 g
Heavy cream	6 oz	170 g
Milk	6½ oz	184 g
Eggs	6 oz	170 g
Salt	½ tsp	2.50 g
Ground black pepper	¼ tsp	0.5 g
Grated provolone	12 oz	340 g

1   Roll out the pie dough ⅛ in/3 mm thick and line the pie pan. Line the crust with parchment paper and fill with dried beans or pie weights. Bake at 350°F/177°C until very light golden brown, about 15 minutes. Cool completely.

2   Heat the olive oil in a sauté pan over medium heat. Add the onions and sauté, stirring frequently, until golden and very soft (caramelized), about 15 minutes. Remove and reserve.

3   Whisk together the cream, milk, eggs, salt, and pepper in a medium bowl. Stir in the onions and 8 oz/227 g of the cheese. Pour the egg mixture evenly into the crust. Sprinkle the remaining cheese evenly over the top of the quiche.

4   Place the quiche pan on a baking sheet and bake at 350°F/177°C until a knife blade inserted in the center comes out clean, 40 to 45 minutes. If the crust begins to overbrown, cover the edges of the crust with strips of aluminum foil or pie shields.

5   Remove the quiche from the oven and cool on a rack. Let the quiche rest for at least 20 minutes before cutting in pieces. Serve hot, warm, or at room temperature.

Cheddar cheese wafers

MAKES 120 WAFERS

All-purpose flour	1 lb 2 oz	510 g
Cayenne	½ tsp	1 g
Salt	1 tsp	5 g
Ground black pepper	½ tsp	1 g
Butter, room temperature	1 lb	454 g
Cheddar, shredded	1 lb	454 g
Eggs	2 oz	57 g
Sesame seeds, for garnish	as needed	as needed

1   Sift together the flour, cayenne, salt, and pepper.

2   Mix the butter on medium speed with the paddle attachment until soft, 2 to 3 minutes.

3   Add the Cheddar and mix slightly until thoroughly incorporated, about 1 minute.

4   Add the eggs and mix on low speed until fully combined.

5   Add the sifted flour mixture and mix on low speed until just combined. Scrape down the bowl as necessary.

6   Turn out the dough onto a parchment-lined sheet pan and spread it so that it is no higher than the edge of the pan. Wrap tightly in plastic wrap.

7   Place the dough in the refrigerator overnight or in the freezer until thoroughly chilled, at least 30 minutes.

8   Turn out the dough onto a lightly floured work surface. Slice the dough into 3-in/8-cm strips.

9   Cut the strips to make ¼-in/6-mm wafers.

10   Press the sesame seeds gently into the dough.

11   Place the wafers onto a parchment-lined sheet pan.

12   Bake at 350°F/177°C until light brown, 25 to 30 minutes. Cool completely on racks. Store in an airtight container until ready to serve.

Ham and cheese crescents

MAKES 70 CRESCENTS

Butter puff pastry dough (page 231)	3 lb	1.36 kg
Prepared mustard	as needed	as needed
Swiss cheese	12 oz	340 g
Ham	12 oz	340 g
Egg wash (page 892)	as needed	as needed

1   Roll out the puff pastry to ⅛ in/3 mm thick. Using a pizza wheel, cut into 3¾-in/10-cm squares. Cut the squares in half on the diagonal to make even triangles.

2   Using a small paper cone, pipe a pea-size dot of mustard onto each triangle.

3   Cut the cheese and ham into 3½-in/9-cm batons. Place the cheese and ham batons on the triangles. Brush the tips of the triangles with egg wash.

4   Roll up the triangle in the same shape as a croissant, starting at the long side opposite the tip first, rolling up so that the tip ends up on the underside of the roll. Brush the crescents with egg wash.

5   Bake at 375°F/191°C until the bottoms are a dark golden brown, 12 to 15 minutes. Cool on the baking pans. Serve.

VARIATION   You can also use chopped blanched broccoli florets and cheese to fill the crescents.

Leek and mushroom tart

MAKES 2 TARTS (12 IN/30 CM EACH)

Butter puff pastry dough (page 231)	1 lb 4 oz	567 g
Leeks, white and light green parts only	2 lb	907 g
Olive oil	as needed	as needed
Shallots, finely chopped	3 oz	85 g
White mushrooms, sliced	8 oz	227 g
Crème frâiche	8 oz	227 g
Salt	as needed	as needed
Ground black pepper	as needed	as needed

1 Divide the dough into 2 parts, roll out ⅛ in/3 mm thick, and line 2 tart pans. Line the tart shells with parchment paper and fill with dried beans or pie weights. Bake at 350°F/177°C until very light golden brown, about 15 minutes. Cool completely.

2 Slice the leeks ¹⁄₁₆ in/1.5 mm thick. Wash and drain the leeks well.

3 In a medium sauté pan, heat the olive oil. Sweat the leeks and shallots until wilted and translucent, about 15 minutes. Do not let them brown.

4 Sauté the mushrooms separately in olive oil.

5 Combine the sweated leeks and shallots with the crème frâiche and mix until well combined. Place half of the mixture in each tart shell, leaving a ½-in/1-cm space from the top of the tart shell.

6 Top with the sautéed mushrooms.

7 Sprinkle salt and pepper on top of the mushrooms.

8 Place the tart pans on a baking sheet and bake at 375°F/191°C until a knife blade inserted in the center comes out clean, 40 to 45 minutes. If the pastry begins to overbrown, cover the edges with strips of aluminum foil or pie shields.

9 Remove the tarts from the oven and cool on racks. Let the tarts rest for at least 20 minutes before cutting. Serve hot, warm, or at room temperature.

Leek and Mushroom Tart (opposite),
Onion Tart (page 708)

Onion tart

MAKES 2 TARTS (9 IN/23 CM EACH)

Basic pie dough (page 222)	1 lb 8 oz	680 g
Onions	3 lb	1.36 kg
Olive oil	1 oz	28 g
Eggs	4 oz	113 g
Heavy cream	8 oz	227 g
Salt	as needed	as needed
Ground black pepper	as needed	as needed

1   Divide the dough into 2 parts, roll out ⅛ in/3 mm thick, and line 2 tart pans. Line the tart shells with parchment paper and fill with dried beans or pie weights. Bake at 350°F/177°C until very light golden brown, about 15 minutes. Cool completely.

2   Peel and slice the onions ⅛ in/3 mm thick. In a sauté pan, heat the olive oil and sweat the onions until translucent and limp, about 10 minutes. Do not let the onions brown. Cool.

3   Combine the eggs and cream in a bowl and whisk them together. Add the cooled onions. Add salt and pepper as needed.

4   Divide the mixture evenly between the tart shells.

5   Place the tart pans on a baking sheet and bake at 375°F/191°C until a knife blade inserted in the center comes out clean, 40 to 45 minutes. If the pastry begins to overbrown, cover the edges with strips of aluminum foil or pie shields.

6   Remove the tarts from the oven and cool on racks. Let the tarts rest for at least 20 minutes before cutting. Serve hot, warm, or at room temperature.

VARIATION   Other ingredients such as raw salmon or spiced ham may be diced and added along with the onions.

Potato tart

MAKES 3 TARTS (10 IN/25 CM EACH)

Butter puff pastry dough (page 231)	1 lb 8 oz	680 g
Potatoes, such as Yukon gold	1 lb	454 g
Asparagus	4 oz	113 g
Bacon	8 oz	227 g
Butter, melted	2 oz	57 g
Salt	as needed	as needed
Ground black pepper	as needed	as needed

1   Divide the dough into 3 parts, roll out ⅛ in/3 mm thick, and line 3 tart pans. Line the tart shells with parchment paper and fill with dried beans or pie weights. Bake at 350°F/177°C until very light golden brown, about 15 minutes. Cool completely.

2   Peel the potatoes, place in a large pot filled with cold salted water, and bring to a boil. Boil the potatoes until easily pierced with a fork, about 20 minutes. Take the pot off the heat and let the potatoes cool; slice into disks approximately ⅛ in/3 mm thick.

3   Bring another pot of salted water to a boil. Trim the ends and peel the asparagus. Boil the asparagus until tender, about 5 minutes. Place in an ice water bath to stop the cooking and to cool. If the asparagus spears are thick, slice in half lengthwise after cooling.

4   Dice the bacon and cook in a sauté pan until crisp. Drain the fat well.

5   Fan the potato slices around the tart shells, overlapping them toward the center. Evenly divide the bacon and asparagus and sprinkle over the potatoes. Brush the melted butter over the entire tarts.

6   Cover and refrigerate overnight.

7   Lightly sprinkle salt and pepper over the top of the tart. Place the tart pans on a baking sheet and bake at 375°F/191°C until a knife blade inserted in the center comes out clean, 40 to 45 minutes. If the pastry begins to overbrown, cover the edges with strips of aluminum foil or pie shields.

8   Remove the tarts from the oven and cool on racks. Let the tarts rest for at least 20 minutes before cutting. Serve hot, warm, or at room temperature.

Tomato tart

MAKES 2 TARTS (10 IN/25 CM EACH)

Butter puff pastry dough (page 231)	1 lb	454 g
Tomatoes	1 lb 8 oz	680 g
Basil, chiffonade	as needed	as needed
Salt	as needed	as needed
Ground black pepper	as needed	as needed
Mozzarella, shredded	as needed	as needed

1   Divide the dough into 2 parts, roll out ⅛ in/3 mm thick, and line 2 tart pans. Line the tart shells with parchment paper and fill with dried beans or pie weights. Bake at 350°F/177°C until very light golden brown, about 15 minutes. Cool completely.

2   Slice the tomatoes into ¼-in/6-mm rounds.

3   Arrange the tomatoes on the tart shells, fanning them toward the center, and leaving ½ in/1 cm around the edge of the tart shell.

4   Scatter the basil over the tomatoes. Sprinkle with salt and pepper. Top with the mozzarella.

5   Place the tart pans on a baking sheet and bake at 375°F/191°C until a knife blade inserted in the center comes out clean, 40 to 45 minutes. If the pastry begins to overbrown, cover the edges with strips of aluminum foil or pie shields.

6   Remove the tarts from the oven and cool on racks. Let the tarts rest for at least 20 minutes before cutting in pieces. Serve hot, warm, or at room temperature.

Blue cheese tart

MAKES 5 TARTS (4 IN/10 CM EACH)

Pâte brisée (page 222)	1 lb	454 g
Cream cheese	8 oz	227 g
Blue cheese	8 oz	227 g
Eggs	4 oz	113 g
Sour cream	3 fl oz	90 mL
Heavy cream	4 fl oz	120 mL
Minced chives	1 tbsp	3 g
Minced flat-leaf parsley	1 tbsp	3 g
Minced thyme	2 tsp	2 g
Sautéed minced shallots	1 tsp	3 g
Salt	½ tsp	2.50 g
Ground white pepper	¼ tsp	0.50 g

1   Divide the dough into 5 parts, roll out ⅛ in/3 mm thick, and line 5 tart pans. Line the tart shells with parchment paper and fill with dried beans or pie weights. Bake at 350°F/177°C until very light golden brown, about 15 minutes. Cool completely.

2   Cream the cheeses on medium speed with the paddle attachment until smooth. Gradually add the eggs, mixing until fully incorporated after each addition and scraping down the sides of the bowl periodically. Add the sour cream, cream, chives, parsley, thyme, shallots, salt, and pepper and blend well.

3   Pour the mixture into the prepared crusts and bake at 300°F/149°C until a knife blade inserted in the center comes out clean, about 20 minutes.

4   Remove from the oven and let the tarts rest for at least 10 to 15 minutes. Serve warm or at room temperature.

Sun-dried tomato and goat cheese tartlets

MAKES 30 PIECES

Blitz puff pastry (page 233)	1 lb	454 g
Minced garlic	1 tbsp	9 g
Ground white pepper	1 tsp	2 g
Chopped basil	3 tbsp	9 g
Whole milk	6 fl oz	180 mL
Dry sherry	2 fl oz	60 mL
Eggs	3 each	3 each
All-purpose flour	¼ oz	7 g
Fresh goat cheese, crumbled	4 oz	113 g
Green onions, minced	1 oz	28 g
Sun-dried tomatoes, minced	3½ oz	99 g

1   Roll out the dough ⅛ in/3 mm thick. Dock the dough.

2   Cut 30 rounds from the dough using a cutter 2 in/5 cm in diameter. Press gently into 1¾-in/4-cm tart molds.

3   Cover the dough in the molds with a small piece of foil and fill with dried beans or pastry weights. Bake at 425°F/218°C for 5 minutes. Cool completely. Remove the foil and weights.

4   Combine the garlic, pepper, basil, milk, and sherry in a food processor. Add the eggs and flour and process until just blended.

5   Toss together the goat cheese, green onions, and tomatoes. Place 2½ tsp/22.50 mL of the mixture into each tartlet. Fill each tartlet two-thirds full with the egg mixture.

6   Bake at 350°F/177°C until set, about 15 minutes. Remove from the oven and let the tartlets rest for at least 10 minutes. Serve warm or at room temperature.

Creamed wild mushroom tartlets

MAKES 30 PIECES

Pâte brisée (page 222)	1 lb	454 g
Dry jack cheese, finely grated	2 oz	57 g
Flat-leaf parsley, chopped	1 oz	28 g
Ground black pepper	2 tsp	4 g
Assorted wild mushrooms (shiitake, porcini, oyster, etc.), small dice	1 lb	454 g
Shallots, minced	2 each	2 each
Butter	2 oz	57 g
Brandy	1 tbsp	15 mL
Sherry	1 tbsp	15 mL
Heavy cream	2 fl oz	60 mL

1   Roll out the dough ⅛ in/3 mm thick. Cut 30 rounds from the dough using a cutter 2 in/5 cm in diameter and press gently into 1¾-in/4-cm tart molds.

2   Cover the dough in the molds with a small piece of foil and fill with dried beans or pastry weights. Bake at 425°F/218°C for 5 minutes. Remove the foil and weights.

3   Combine the cheese, parsley, and pepper and reserve.

4   Sauté the mushrooms and shallots in the butter. Add the brandy, sherry, and cream.

5   Fill each tartlet with ½ oz/14 g of the mushroom mixture while still warm and top with a sprinkle of the cheese mixture.

6   Serve warm.

Petit bouche duxelles

MAKES 40 PIECES

Butter puff pastry dough (page 231)	3 lb	1.36 kg
Egg wash (page 892)	as needed	as needed
Mushrooms, finely chopped	1 lb 8 oz	680 g
Shallots, minced	2 oz	57 g
Butter	as needed	as needed
Brandy	1 tbsp	15 mL
Salt	as needed	as needed
Ground white pepper	as needed	as needed

1   Roll out the dough ½ in/1 cm thick. Cut 40 rounds from the dough using a fluted cutter 2 in/ 5 cm in diameter.

2   Brush the dough rounds with egg wash. Place back in the freezer if the rounds get too soft.

3   Using a 1-in/3-cm round cutter, cut three-quarters of the way through the puff rounds. Make sure you do not cut all the way through.

4   Bake the dough rounds at 375°F/191°C, placing a wire rack on top of them on the sheet pan to help keep a uniform height. Bake until the rounds are golden brown, about 10 minutes. Once the rounds have cooled slightly, remove the cut tops with a sharp knife and reserve.

5   Sauté the mushrooms and shallots in the butter. Just before the liquid has all evaporated, deglaze the pan with the brandy.

6   Season with salt and pepper as needed.

7   Fill each pastry round with ½ oz/14 g of the mushroom mixture. Replace the reserved top as a cap. Serve warm.

Wild mushroom pizza

MAKES 25 PIZZA ROUNDS (12 IN/30 CM EACH)

Butter	4 oz	113 g
All-purpose flour	2½ oz	71 g
Milk	48 fl oz	1.44 L
Extra-virgin olive oil	10 oz	284 g
Oyster mushrooms, stemmed	2 lb 8 oz	1.13 kg
White mushrooms, sliced	1 lb 4 oz	567 g
Shiitake mushrooms, stemmed	1 lb 4 oz	567 g
Dried morels, rehydrated	1¼ oz	35 g
Dried porcini, rehydrated and chopped	1¼ oz	35 g
Shallots, minced	1¼ oz	35 g
Garlic, chopped	1 oz	28 g
Port wine	24 fl oz	720 mL
Parsley, chopped	1¼ oz	35 g
Chopped thyme	1¼ tsp	1.25 g
Chopped tarragon	1¼ tsp	1.25 g
Ground nutmeg	1 tsp	2 g
Salt	1 tbsp	15 g
Ground black pepper	1 tbsp	6 g
Mascarpone	6½ oz	184 g
Duram pizza dough (page 144)	25 rounds	25 rounds
Aged Monterey jack, grated	2 lb 6 oz	1.08 kg
Parmesan, grated	1 lb 3 oz	539 g
Chives, minced	1 oz	28 g

1   Melt ½ oz/14 g of the butter in a sauce pot. Add the flour, stirring to incorporate, and cook over medium heat, stirring constantly, for 5 minutes. Do not let the roux develop any color.

2   Gradually add the milk, whisking constantly. Cook, stirring constantly, until the sauce coats the back of a spoon. Remove from the heat.

3   Melt the remaining 3½ oz/99 g butter with the olive oil in a saucepan over medium heat. Add all the mushrooms and sauté until lightly browned, approximately 10 minutes.

4   Add the shallots and garlic and sauté until aromatic. Deglaze the pan with the port and reduce for several minutes, until most of the liquid has evaporated. Add the parsley, thyme, tarragon, nutmeg, salt, and pepper.

5   For each pizza, place a dough round on an oven peel or sheet pan that has been dusted with semolina flour. Spread 5 oz/142 g of the mushroom sauce on the dough. Top with 1½ oz/ 43 g of the Jack cheese, ¾ oz/21 g of the Parmesan, and about 1 tsp/1 g of the chives.

6   Bake in a 500°F/260°C deck oven until golden brown around the edges, 3 to 4 minutes. Serve at once.

Margherita pizza

MAKES 25 PIZZA ROUNDS (12 IN/30 CM EACH)

Garlic, minced	2½ oz	71 g
Extra-virgin olive oil	1 lb 4 oz	567 g
Tomatoes (canned crushed), drained	3 lb 12 oz	1.70 kg
Salt	2 tsp	10 g
Ground black pepper	2 tsp	4 g
Chopped rosemary	2 tbsp	6 g
Duram pizza dough (page 144)	25 rounds	25 rounds
Semolina flour	as needed	as needed
Mozzarella, grated	3 lb 2 oz	1.42 kg
Parmesan, grated	12½ oz	354 g
Basil, chiffonade	1½ oz	43 g

1   Sweat the garlic in the olive oil over low heat until translucent, about 6 minutes.

2   Add the tomatoes, salt, and pepper. Cook covered over medium heat until the sauce has thickened slightly and has a good aroma, about 30 minutes.

3   Add the rosemary and cook for 15 minutes.

4   For each pizza, place a dough round on an oven peel or sheet pan dusted with semolina flour. Cover the dough with 3 oz/85 g of the sauce, leaving a ½-in/1-cm border. Top with 2 oz/ 57 g of the mozzarella, ½ oz/14 g of the Parmesan, and 1½ tsp/1.50 g of the basil.

5   Bake in a 500°F/260°C deck oven until golden brown around the edges, 3 to 4 minutes. Serve at once.

Spanakopita

MAKES 80 PIECES

Butter, solid	3 oz	85 g
Shallots, minced	2 oz	57 g
Garlic, minced	4 cloves	4 cloves
Spinach, stemmed	3 lb	1.36 kg
Feta, crumbled	1 lb	454 g
Pine nuts, toasted	3 oz	85 g
Salt	as needed	as needed
Ground black pepper	as needed	as needed
Phyllo dough	1 lb	454 g
Butter, melted	as needed	as needed

1 Melt the solid butter in a sauté pan over moderate heat until it starts to bubble. Add the shallots and garlic and sweat until translucent.

2 Add the spinach and sauté gently until the spinach is wilted, 1 to 2 minutes. Transfer the spinach mixture to a stainless-steel bowl and cool to room temperature. Add the cheese and nuts and season with salt and pepper. Refrigerate until needed.

3 Lay 1 sheet of phyllo dough on a cutting board. Brush lightly with melted butter. Place another sheet of phyllo dough directly on the buttered sheet and brush it lightly with butter. Repeat with a third sheet of phyllo. Keep the remainder of the phyllo dough covered until needed, to prevent drying out.

4 Cut the phyllo dough lengthwise into 6 even strips. Place 1 oz/28 g of spinach filling on the bottom right corner of each strip. Fold the bottom right corner of the strip diagonally to the left side of the strip to create a triangle of dough encasing the filling. Fold the bottom left point of the dough up along the left side of the dough to make a triangle and seal in the filling.

5 Fold the bottom left corner of the dough diagonally to the right side of the dough to form a triangle. Fold the bottom right point up along the right edge of the dough. Repeat until the end of the dough is reached and you have a triangle of layered phyllo dough with the filling wrapped inside. Place the phyllo triangle on a parchment-lined sheet pan and brush with melted butter.

6 Repeat with each strip. Bake at 375°F/191°C until golden brown, about 15 minutes. Serve.

Place the filling on the bottom right corner of each strip. Fold to make a triangle and seal in the filling.

Smoked salmon mousse

MAKES 3 LB 9 OZ/1.62 KG

Smoked salmon, diced	1 lb 8 oz	680 g
Fish velouté (page 893), cold	8 fl oz	240 mL
Gelatin, granulated	1 oz	28 g
Fish stock (page 892) or water, cold	8 fl oz	240 mL
Salt	as needed	as needed
Ground black pepper	as needed	as needed
Heavy cream, whipped to soft peaks	16 fl oz	480 mL

1 Combine the smoked salmon and velouté in a food processor and process to a smooth consistency. Push through a sieve and transfer to a bowl.

2 Bloom the gelatin in the cold stock. Melt over simmering water until the mixture reaches 90° to 110°F/32° to 43°C.

3 Blend the gelatin into the salmon mixture. Season with salt and pepper.

4 Fold in the whipped cream. Shape the mousse as desired. Refrigerate for at least 2 hours to firm the mousse.

savory mousse tartlets

Prebaked tartlet and barquette shells filled with cold savory mousse are a good choice for hors d'oeuvres. Brush the interior of the shells with a thin coat of softened butter and allow it to set firm. The butter will let the shell remain crisp after it is filled with the mousse. Using a pastry bag fitted with a star or plain pastry tip, pipe the mousse in a corkscrew spiral or a simple, but perfectly executed, rosette and decoratively garnish with some fresh herbs or brunoise of red pepper—something that reflects the flavor of the mousse is always appropriate.

Red pepper mousse in endive

MAKES 30 PIECES

Onions, minced	3 oz	85 g
Finely minced garlic	1 tsp	4 g
Vegetable oil	1 fl oz	30 mL
Red peppers, small dice	1 lb 4 oz	567 g
Chicken stock	8 fl oz	240 mL
Saffron threads, crushed	pinch	pinch
Tomato paste	1 oz	28 g
Salt	as needed	as needed
Ground white pepper	as needed	as needed
Gelatin, granulated	1 tbsp	9 g
White wine	2 fl oz	60 mL
Heavy cream, whipped	6 fl oz	180 mL
Endive spears	30 each	30 each
Red pepper, slivered	2 peppers	2 peppers

1 Sauté the onions and garlic in the oil until golden. Add the diced peppers, stock, saffron, tomato paste, salt, and pepper. Simmer until all the ingredients are tender and the liquid is reduced by half.

2 Bloom the gelatin in the wine.

3 Purée the red pepper mixture in a blender. Add the bloomed gelatin while the red pepper mixture is still hot and blend to combine all ingredients well.

4 Cool the mixture over an ice water bath until it mounds when dropped from a spoon. Fold in the whipped cream.

5 Pipe the mousse into the endive spears and garnish each with a sliver of red pepper.

Blue cheese mousse

MAKES 2 LB/907 G

Blue cheese	1 lb 4 oz	567 g
Cream cheese	12 oz	340 g
Kosher salt	1 tbsp	15 g
Ground black pepper	½ tsp	1 g
Heavy cream, whipped to soft peaks	4 fl oz	120 mL

1   Purée the blue and cream cheeses until very smooth. Add the salt and pepper. Fold the whipped cream into the mousse until well blended. There should be no lumps.

2   The mousse is ready to use to prepare canapés or as a filling or dip.

VARIATION   **GOAT'S MILK CHEESE MOUSSE** Substitute fresh goat's milk cheese for the blue cheese.

Smoked salmon mousse barquettes

MAKES 30 BARQUETTES

Smoked salmon, diced	5 oz	142 g
Fish velouté (page 893)	6 fl oz	180 mL
Aspic gelée (page 892), warm	1 fl oz	30 mL
Heavy cream	4 fl oz	120 mL
Tabasco sauce	¼ tsp	1.25 mL
Salt	⅓ oz	9 g
Ground black pepper	as needed	as needed
Barquettes made from pâte brisée (page 222), prebaked	30 each	30 each
Salmon roe	2 oz	57 g
Dill sprigs	30 each	30 each

1   Purée the smoked salmon and velouté in a food processor until very smooth. Add the warm aspic gelée while the processor is running. Transfer to a bowl.

2   Whip the cream to soft peaks and fold gently but thoroughly into the salmon mixture. Season with the Tabasco, salt, and pepper.

3   Pipe about ½ oz/14 g salmon mousse into each barquette, garnish with a little salmon roe and a dill sprig, and chill until firm. The barquettes are ready to serve, or they can be refrigerated for up to 1 hour.

Gougères

MAKES 120 PIECES

Milk	12 fl oz	360 mL
Water	12 fl oz	360 mL
Butter	12 oz	340 g
Salt	pinch	pinch
Sugar	pinch	pinch
Bread flour	12 oz	340 g
Eggs	12 oz	340 g
Cayenne	pinch	pinch
Red peppers, cut into brunoise	½ oz	14 g
Swiss cheese, grated	12 oz	340 g
Egg wash (page 892)	as needed	as needed
Parmesan, grated, for garnish	as needed	as needed

1 Bring the milk, water, butter, salt, and sugar to a boil over medium heat, stirring constantly.

2 Add the flour all at once, stirring vigorously to combine.

3 Cook the mixture over medium heat, stirring constantly until the mixture pulls away from the sides and a thin coating is formed on the bottom.

4 Transfer the mixture to the mixer. Beat briefly on medium speed with the paddle attachment to cool the dough slightly. Add the eggs, a small amount at a time, and beat until fully incorporated.

5 Add the cayenne, peppers, and Swiss cheese and mix until fully incorporated.

6 Using a pastry bag fitted with a #6 plain tip, pipe the dough into 1½-in/4-cm rounds onto a parchment-lined sheet pan. Brush with egg wash. Sprinkle the Parmesan on top.

7 Bake at 375°F/191°C until golden brown, 10 to 12 minutes.

VARIATIONS **HERB-TOMATO GOUGÈRES** Substitute olive oil for the butter. Increase the salt to 1 tbsp/15 g and omit the cayenne, red peppers, Swiss cheese, and Parmesan. Add to the dough in step 5: ½ tsp/1 g ground black pepper, 2 oz/57 g finely chopped oil-packed sun-dried tomatoes, 3 tbsp/9 g finely chopped basil, and 4 tsp/4 g finely chopped thyme. Pipe into domes approximately ¾ in/2 cm in diameter. Bake at 350°F/177°C for about 35 minutes.

MINIATURE GOUGÈRES Omit the red pepper and Parmesan and substitute Gruyère for the Swiss cheese. Pipe into domes approximately ¾ in/2 cm in diameter. Bake at 350°F/177°C for about 35 minutes.

Crabmeat and avocado profiteroles

MAKES 30 PIECES

Pâte à choux dough (page 228)	1 recipe	1 recipe
Egg wash (page 892)	as needed	as needed
Crabmeat, cleaned	4 oz	113 g
Avocado, ripe, small dice	½ each	½ each
Lime juice	2 fl oz	60 mL
Buttermilk	1 tbsp	15 mL
Minced chives	1 tsp	1 g
Minced cilantro	1 tsp	1 g
Salt	as needed	as needed
Cayenne	as needed	as needed

1   Using a pastry bag fitted with a #5 plain tip, pipe the pâte à choux into 30 bulbs 1½ in/4 cm in diameter onto parchment-lined sheet pans. Brush lightly with egg wash.

2   Bake at 360°F/182°C until the cracks formed in the pastries are no longer yellow, about 50 minutes. Cool to room temperature. Slice the top off each of the baked pastries.

3   Combine the crabmeat, avocado, lime juice, and buttermilk. Fold in the chives and cilantro and season with salt and cayenne.

4   Split the puffs and fill with the crabmeat mixture. Serve immediately.

Southwest chicken salad in profiteroles

MAKES 30 PIECES

Pâte à choux dough (page 228)	1 recipe	1 recipe
Egg wash (page 892)	as needed	as needed
Chicken, dark meat, cooked, small dice	1 lb	454 g
Tomato concassé	2 oz	57 g
Lime, cut into suprêmes, then diced small	1 each	1 each
Roasted pepper, small dice	½ oz	14 g
Minced jalapeño	1 tsp	5 g
Shallots, minced	1 oz	28 g
Finely minced garlic	1 tsp	4 g
Minced cilantro	2 tbsp	6 g
Chopped marjoram	2 tsp	2 g
Minced chives	2 tsp	2 g
Salt	as needed	as needed
Ground black pepper	as needed	as needed

1 Using a pastry bag fitted with a #5 plain tip, pipe the pâte à choux into 30 bulbs 1½ in/4 cm in diameter onto parchment-lined sheet pans. Brush lightly with egg wash.

2 Bake at 360°F/182°C until the cracks formed in the pastries are no longer yellow, about 50 minutes. Cool to room temperature. Slice the top off each of the baked pastries.

3 Combine the chicken, tomato, lime, roasted pepper, jalapeño, shallots, garlic, and herbs. Season with salt and pepper. Marinate for 2 hours under refrigeration.

4 Split the puffs and fill with the chicken mixture. Serve immediately.

Palmiers with prosciutto

MAKES 35 TO 40 PIECES

Blitz puff pastry (page 233)	8 oz	227 g
Tomato paste	2½ oz	71 g
Prosciutto, 12 thin slices	5 oz	142 g
Parmesan, finely grated	¾ oz	21 g

1 Roll the pastry dough into a 10-in/25-cm square. Brush one-half of the pastry with the tomato paste. Lay the prosciutto over the tomato paste, then dust with some of the cheese.

2 Fold the 2 outer quarters of the dough toward each other to meet in the middle, leaving a ½-in/1-cm gap. Sprinkle the remaining cheese on top of the length of the dough. Complete the book fold (see page 220). Cover the dough and refrigerate until firm, about 1 hour.

3 Slice the dough ¼ in/6 mm thick and lay flat on parchment-lined baking sheets. Place a sheet of parchment paper on top to help keep the palmiers a uniform height. Bake at 400°F/204°C until golden brown, about 10 minutes. Remove the top paper for the last few minutes of baking to allow for browning. Transfer to racks to cool. Store in airtight containers.

Mushroom bruschetta

MAKES 20 BRUSCHETTA

Oyster mushrooms	1 lb	454 g
Olive oil	3½ fl oz	105 mL
Minced garlic	2 tsp	5 g
Chopped thyme	1¼ tsp	1.25 g
Minced oregano	1¼ tsp	1.25 g
Chopped marjoram	1¼ tsp	1.25 g
Salt	as needed	as needed
Ground black pepper	as needed	as needed
Baguette (page 154)	5 in	13 cm

1 Trim the mushrooms and gently rub off any dirt with paper towels.

2 Heat 2 fl oz/60 mL of the oil over low heat. Sauté the mushrooms in the oil until lightly caramelized. Add the garlic and continue sautéing until fragrant.

3 Add the thyme, oregano, and marjoram. Remove the pan from the heat. Season well with salt and pepper.

4 Cut the baguette into slices about ¼ in/6 mm thick, brush with the remaining oil, and toast in a 375°F/191°C oven until lightly golden along the edges, about 10 minutes.

5 Top each toast with about ¾ oz/21 g sautéed mushrooms. Serve warm or at room temperature.

VARIATION Grated cheese may be sprinkled on top and the bruschetta and finished under a broiler or in a hot oven.

Croque monsieur

MAKES 10 SANDWICHES

Pullman bread	20 slices	20 slices
Dijon mustard	10 oz	284 g
Gruyère, 10 thin slices	8 oz	227 g
Boiled ham, 10 slices	1 lb 4 oz	567 g
Muenster, 10 thin slices	8 oz	227 g
Butter, soft	4 oz	113 g

1 Spread the bread slices with the mustard. On 10 of the bread slices, layer 1 slice each of Gruyère, ham, and Muenster over the mustard. Top the sandwiches with the remaining bread slices.

2 Griddle both sides of the sandwiches on a lightly buttered 325°F/163°C griddle until the bread is golden, the cheese is melted, and the sandwich is heated through.

3 Cut the sandwiches on the diagonal and serve immediately.

VARIATIONS **CROQUE MADAME** Some recipes simply add a fried egg to the croque monsieur. In the United States and England, the ham is usually replaced with sliced chicken breast. Use Emmentaler instead of Gruyère. Griddle as directed.

MONTE CRISTO Dip any version in beaten egg and griddle as you would French toast.

Black bean empanadas

MAKES 24 EMPANADAS

EMPANADA FILLING		
Olive oil	½ oz	14 g
Onion, small dice	1 oz	28 g
Minced garlic	¾ tsp	2 g
Ground cumin	¼ tsp	0.50 g
Dried Mexican oregano	¼ tsp	0.50 g
Black beans (cooked or canned), drained and rinsed	12 oz	340 g
Salt	1 tsp	5 g
Ground black pepper	¼ tsp	0.50 g
Water	1½ fl oz	45 mL
Queso blanco, crumbled, or Cheddar, grated	1 oz	28 g
EMPANADA DOUGH		
All-purpose flour	3½ oz	99 g
Masa harina	2 oz	57 g
Baking powder	1½ tsp	4.50 g
Salt	¾ tsp	3.75 g
Canola oil or lard, melted and cooled	1 tbsp	15 mL
Eggs	2 each	2 each
Water	1 fl oz	30 mL
Egg wash (page 892)	as needed	as needed
Canola oil, for frying (or as needed)	1 lb 7 oz	652 g
Kosher salt, for garnish	as needed	as needed

1   To make the filling, heat the olive oil in a medium sauté pan over medium-high heat. Add the onion and garlic and sauté, stirring frequently, until tender, 3 to 4 minutes.

2   Stir in the cumin and oregano and cook for 30 seconds more. Add the beans and season with salt and pepper.

3   Purée the bean mixture with the water. If the beans are too stiff to purée easily, add additional water as needed.

4   Transfer the beans to a bowl and stir in the cheese. The filling is ready to use immediately, or it can be stored in a covered container in the refrigerator for up to 2 days.

5   To prepare the dough, combine the flour, masa harina, baking powder, and salt in a bowl. Add the oil and mix by hand with a wooden spoon until evenly distributed.

6   In a small bowl, stir together the eggs and water. Add gradually to the flour mixture, stirring as you add.

7   Knead the dough until it is pliable, about 3 minutes. Adjust the consistency of the dough with more flour or water if needed.

8   To assemble the empanadas, roll out the dough 1⁄16 in/1.5 mm thick.

9   Using a 3-in/8-cm round cutter, cut the dough into 24 circles.

10   Place 2½ tsp/12.50 mL of the filling on each circle. Brush the edges of the dough with the egg wash, fold in half, and seal the edges by crimping with the tines of a fork.

11   Place the empanadas on parchment-lined baking sheets, cover, and refrigerate until ready to use. They may be held for up to 24 hours or frozen for up to 3 weeks. Thaw completely in the refrigerator before frying.

12   Heat the oil in a deep fryer or deep skillet to 350°F/177°C. Add the empanadas to the hot oil a few at a time and fry until golden brown and crisp, turning if necessary to brown both sides evenly, 3 to 4 minutes.

13   Drain briefly on paper towels. Sprinkle with a little kosher salt and serve very hot.

Potato crêpes with crème fraîche and caviar

MAKES 30 PIECES

Puréed cooked potatoes	12 oz	340 g
All-purpose flour	1 oz	28 g
Eggs	4 oz	113 g
Egg whites	3 oz	85 g
Heavy cream (or as needed)	2 fl oz	60 mL
Salt	as needed	as needed
Ground white pepper	as needed	as needed
Grated nutmeg	pinch	pinch
Vegetable oil	as needed	as needed
Crème fraîche	4 fl oz	120 mL
Caviar	1 oz	28 g
Dill sprigs	as needed	as needed
Smoked salmon slices (optional)	6 oz	170 g

1   Combine the potatoes and flour on low speed with the paddle attachment. Add the eggs one at a time, then the whites. Adjust the consistency with the cream to that of a pancake batter; season with salt, pepper, and nutmeg.

2   Coat a nonstick griddle or sauté pan lightly with oil. Pour the batter as for pancakes into silver dollar–size portions. Cook until golden brown on the bottom; turn and finish on the second side, about 2 minutes total cooking time.

3   Serve the crêpes warm with small dollops of crème fraîche and caviar, a small dill sprig, and a smoked salmon slice, if desired.

VARIATION   **DILL CRÊPES** Chop some of the dill, add to the heavy cream, and heat slightly. Cool before preparing the crêpe batter.

chapter twenty

Plated desserts

When designing a plated dessert, the pastry chef must consider the composition, exploring the possibilities of contrasting and complementing flavors and textures as well as color and style. Equally important to consider are the customer base, specific event or menu needs, and the environment for preparation and service.

Trends in plated desserts

When designing a dessert menu, it is essential to consider current trends to keep your menu fresh and interesting. Among current trends is the use of "architectural style" in constructing plated desserts. Sophisticated customers will likely expect to see such cutting-edge desserts on the menu.

Current trends also include a return to more rustic-style desserts such as galettes and "comfort food" like pies and cobblers. The appeal of these desserts lies in their simplicity of flavor, style, and presentation.

It's also important to look at classic desserts with a contemporary eye and perhaps introduce ingredients that are not typical for the particular preparation to give them new life.

Contrast: flavor, taste, texture, temperature, and eye appeal

The pastry contrast table that follows is a visual guide to understanding the basic characteristics that can be used by the pastry chef in the creation of a plated dessert. When conceptualizing desserts, think about incorporating a number of contrasting characteristics into the dessert by using different components, but never add components just to have another contrasting element. The number of components should make sense for the dessert.

Keep the idea of contrast in mind when adding new desserts to a current menu or designing a new menu. A balanced menu should contain warm and cold, sweet and tart, and rich and lean desserts.

Combining contrasting elements on one dessert plate will keep the palate interested and excited. The classic apple pie à la mode is a perfect example. Think of how it relates to the contrast table: An exceptional apple pie will have a crisp, flaky crust and perhaps a filling that still retains a little tartness from the apples, while the ice cream will lend its creamy, soft nature. The pie should be served warm to bring out its flavors and aromas, as well as to provide temperature contrast with the cold ice cream.

Contrasting elements in a plated dessert are divided among flavor and aroma, taste, texture, temperature, and eye appeal. When using the following chart, keep a generic understanding of culture and regional availability of ingredients to ensure the most successful combinations. Seasonality will ensure the best possible flavor in any dessert, as well as keep price and costs down. Flavor and taste combinations are the most interrelated components on this chart. Depending on your selection of ingredients, one will naturally follow the other. Also keep in mind that sweetness will vary only in intensity, but will be a component of all desserts to some degree.

The object of the textural component is to have a balance of mouthfeel—too much crunch is not necessarily a good thing. It is also important to be aware of the temperature of the components on any plate or menu. While each plate does not necessarily need contracting elements of temperature, a menu should certainly present the spectrum.

Presentation does not mean the plate needs to be intricately presented. Today, one of the biggest trends is toward minimalism: presenting authentic, natural flavors in as fresh and simple a manner as possible.

CONTRAST TABLE

SEASONALITY	FLAVOR AND AROMA	TASTE	TEXTURE	TEMPERATURE	PRESENTATION
Fall	Chocolate	Sweet	Crunchy	Frozen	Shape
Spring	Vanilla	Salty	Crisp	Chilled	Volume
Summer	Fruit	Bitter	Brittle	Cool	Color
Winter	Spice	Acidic	Chewy	Room temperature	Visual texture
	Nut	Umami	Creamy	Warm	
			Liquid	Hot	
			Icy		
			Tender		
			Cakey		

Restaurant desserts

Use the contrast table to help create a restaurant menu. It will help keep every plate fresh, different, and original. Remember that some desserts will not be practical because of a particular kitchen setup.

A restaurant menu should change with every season; however, you will always have a few items that will remain constant, with only the garnish changing. Maintaining seasonality with your menu will keep better costs as well as better flavors. It will also make marketing easier, as the freshest items will have the best flavors and will appeal more to the customers. Use specials to highlight ingredients at their seasonal peak. A good barometer for the success of a dessert is how well it sells, but also keep in mind that items that don't sell well may have a poor placement or wording on the menu; if corrected, an item that used to be problematic could become one of the best sellers.

A key ingredient to the success of any dessert menu is the preservice meeting. You have to make the waiters aware of your food. They should hear about it and taste it to become excited about it. Often items that sell well are favorites of the wait staff.

Dessert station mise en place

When setting up a dessert station, whether for a large banquet kitchen or a small restaurant, there are several important considerations. The size and configuration of the work area, as well as its location in relation to the ovens, refrigerators, and freezers, determine how certain jobs are accomplished. For example, if you are preparing a hot soufflé, the location of the oven is an important factor in determining how and where the soufflé will be plated. In the same vein, if you are plating frozen desserts, the location of and access to freezer space must be considered. Keep often-used items within easy reach, and easy to see. Keep efficient workflow in mind too—plates should move in a single direction.

The station must typically be able to accommodate a variety of service pieces. Some pieces may need to be kept hot or cold for service. During service, you will also need to have a variety of nonfood items at hand: paper and side towels, skewers or toothpicks, latex gloves, and equipment such as palette knives and pastry bags. Returning items to their rightful position each time you use them will help you become more efficient and avoid lost time spent searching for missing items.

To keep the station clean and sanitary, have a container of sanitizing solution available, as well as clean cloths or paper towels and hot water to wipe plates before they leave the station.

Plating frozen desserts

Frozen desserts are an important component of any dessert menu. While frozen desserts are commonly used as complementary components of various plated desserts, they can also serve as the main component. They can be produced in many and varied flavors, are suitable for use with different types of containers, such as tuile cookies or molded chocolate cups, and can be molded in any variety of forms. They work well in an endless number of combinations. Of course, successful plated frozen desserts rely on conveniently located freezer space for storage and service.

Plated desserts at banquets

In most cases, any dessert that can be prepared and served for ten can also be served for a hundred. However, for larger-volume plating, equipment, storage, timing of service, and labor must all be considered.

When planning a dessert for a banquet menu, consider the general concept of the dessert. Certain restrictions may immediately become apparent. Lack of equipment (not enough of a particular mold, for example) might force you to change the shape or look of a dessert. Timing can sometimes be a restrictive element for preparations such as hot soufflés, and in some cases you may want to reformulate the dessert to increase its shelf life.

Keep sauces that are to be used in plastic squeeze bottles or a funnel dropper. These give you more control over the amount and location of the sauce on the plate or dessert and make it easy to store the sauces at the station.

Apple crêpes with cranberries, caramel sauce, and ice cream

MAKES 10 DESSERTS

Golden Delicious apples	13 each	13 each
Sugar	6 oz	170 g
Butter	3 oz	85 g
Crêpes (page 229), 6 in/15 cm in diameter	20 each	20 each
Clear apple caramel sauce (page 454)	20 fl oz	600 mL
Poached cranberries (page 899)	80 each	80 each
Vanilla ice cream (page 475)	20 fl oz	600 mL

1   Peel, quarter, core, and tourné the apples. Toss the apples with the sugar.

2   Melt 1 oz/28 g of the butter in a 10-in/25-cm sauté pan over medium-high heat. Add one-third of the apples and sauté until golden brown on all sides. Transfer to a hotel pan. Sauté the remaining apples in 2 batches, using 1 oz/28 g butter each time.

3   Fold the crêpes into quarters.

4   Ladle 2 fl oz/60 mL sauce onto each warm 10-in/25-cm plate. Place 2 folded crêpes in the center of each plate, overlapping them slightly and pointing them toward the top of the plate.

5   Place 5 apple pieces on the bottom half of each plate, arranging them in an arc around the crêpes, pointing out and evenly spaced. Scatter 8 cranberries around the apples and crêpes.

6   Using a #16 scoop, place 2 fl oz/60 mL of ice cream onto the center of the crêpes on each plate.

Banana-peanut-chocolate dome

MAKES 10 DESSERTS

Chocolate chiffon sponge (page 288)	1 lb 10 oz	737 g
Peanut crispy base (page 348)	5 oz	142 g
Banana syrup (page 438)	10 oz	284 g
Dark chocolate mousse (page 381)	1 lb 5½ oz	610 g
Banana cremeux (page 365), frozen, 1-in disks	3 lb 12½ oz	1.72 kg
Chocolate mirror glaze (page 428)	1 lb 1¼ oz	602 g
Banana tuiles (page 346)	15¾ oz	447 g
Peanut butter sauce (page 429)	8¾ oz	248 g
Peanuts, roasted and salted	20 each	20 each

1   Cut the chocolate chiffon sponge and peanut crispy base into 4-in/10-cm rounds. Brush the sponge with the banana syrup to moisten. Press together 1 sponge round and 1 crispy base so they stick.

2   Place dome-shaped flexible silicone molds face down on a sheet pan. Using a pastry bag with a 1-in/3-cm opening, pipe the chocolate mousse three-quarters of the way up the mold.

3   Unmold the banana cremeux disks. Press the frozen disks into the mousse in the center of the dome mold, pressing down gently until the cremeux is level with the top of the mousse. Place a sponge–crispy base round on top of each mold, sponge side down, and gently press into the mold, completely filling it. Freeze until completely frozen, about 2 hours.

4   Unmold the domes and place on a wire rack over a sheet pan. Bring the chocolate mirror glaze to 90°F/32°C over barely simmering water and, using a 2-fl-oz/60-mL ladle, pour the glaze evenly over the frozen domes, making sure the entire dome is covered.

5   Allow the domes to thaw for 3 hours under refrigeration before plating.

6   Place a glazed dome slightly off center on each plate. Spike a tuile into the dome as in the photo. Using a small spoon, spoon ½ oz/14 g of the peanut butter sauce onto each plate in a teardrop shape. Sprinkle some coarsely chopped salted peanuts on the sauce and serve.

Optional Fresh
Banana Slices

Banana Tuile

Chocolate Mousse
Chocolate Glaze

Banana Cremeaux

Chocolate Chiffon Sponge

Peanut Crispy Base

Peanut Butter Sauce

New York cheesecake

MAKES 10 DESSERTS

Cheesecake (page 291), sliced	10 each	10 each
Pear compote	5 oz	142 g
Light corn syrup	as needed	as needed
White pear and huckleberry sauce (page 440)	5 oz	142 g
Sangria sorbet (page 495)	20 oz	567 g

1 Slice the cheesecake into rectangles 2 by 3½ in/5 by 9 cm. Using a small spoon, place ½ oz/14 g of the pear compote on top of each portioned cheesecake.

2 Place a pea-size dot of corn syrup on the plate in the spot where the cheesecake is going to be. Place another pea-size dot of corn syrup in the spot on the plate where the sorbet will sit, approximately 3 in/8 cm away from the cheesecake.

3 Place the cheesecake on the corn syrup. Spoon ½ oz/14 g of pear sauce between the cheesecake and the other drop of corn syrup. Make sure there are whole huckleberries on each plate.

4 Using a #16 scoop, place 2 fl oz/60 mL of the sorbet on top of the remaining corn syrup on each plate.

Pear Compote

Cheesecake

Graham Crust

Sangria Sorbet

White Pear and Huckleberry Sauce

Pumpkin crème brûlée

MAKES 10 DESSERTS

Jack Be Little pumpkins, scrubbed	10 each	10 each
Pumpkin crème brûlée base (page 363)	60 fl oz	1.80 L
Brûlée sugar blend (page 896)	10 oz	284 g
Spice mix (page 902)	1 lb 4 oz	567 g
Honey tuiles (page 346), scarecrow templates (see page 903)	10 each	10 each
Cinnamon sticks	50 each	50 each
Cloves	120 each	120 each
Star anise	30 each	30 each

1 Cut the top ½ in/1 cm off each pumpkin; reserve these lids. Scoop the seeds and membranes out of each pumpkin. If necessary, shave a very thin layer off the bottom of the pumpkins so they stand perfectly upright. (Be careful to shave off as little flesh as possible; if there are any holes in the bottom of the pumpkin, the base will leak out.)

2 Fill each pumpkin with 6 fl oz/180 mL of crème brûlée base. Place the pumpkins in a hotel pan. Add water to come halfway up the side of the pumpkins.

3 Bake in a 300°F/149°C deck oven until the custard is set, about 40 minutes. Remove the pumpkins from the water bath and allow to cool to room temperature.

4 Cover the pumpkins and refrigerate them overnight.

5 Sprinkle ½ oz/14 g brûlée sugar over each crème brûlée. Caramelize the sugar evenly with a torch (be careful not to burn the edges of the pumpkins).

6 Sprinkle 2 oz/57 g of the spice mix in the center of each chilled 10-in/25-cm plate. Place the pumpkins on top of the spice mix (the spice mix will anchor the pumpkins in place).

7 Place a scarecrow body in each crème brûlée, toward the back of the pumpkin. Place a scarecrow leg in front of each body, draping it over the side of the pumpkin. Lean the reserved lid against the pumpkin, opposite the scarecrow leg.

8 Place 5 cinnamon sticks, 12 cloves, and 3 star anise around the pumpkin on each plate in a decorative fashion.

Tropical fruit vacherin with passion fruit sauce

MAKES 10 DESSERTS

Kiwis	5 each	5 each
Pomegranates	3 each	3 each
Pineapple	1 each	1 each
Papayas	3 each	3 each
Vacherins (page 674), 1½ by 3½ by 1¼ in/4 by 9 by 3 cm	10 each	10 each
Dark chocolate, melted, tempered (see page 762)	10 oz	284 g
Mango sorbet (page 491)	15 fl oz	450 mL
Passion fruit sauce (page 435)	10 fl oz	300 mL

1 Peel the kiwis and cut each into 6 wedges. Cut the pomegranates in half. Gently scoop out all of the seeds. Cut 1 in/3 cm off the top and bottom of the pineapple. Carefully cut off the peel and remove the eyes. Core the pineapple. Cut it into planks 1 by 2 in/3 by 5 cm and ¼ in/6 mm thick. Peel the papayas, cut them in half, and remove the seeds. Cut the papayas into 1-in/3-cm cubes. Wrap all the fruit in plastic wrap and refrigerate until ready to assemble.

2 Brush the inside of each vacherin with 1 oz/28 g chocolate. Allow the chocolate to set completely.

3 Using a #20 scoop, place 1½ fl oz/45 mL of the sorbet in the left side of each vacherin. Arrange about 1½ oz/43 g pineapple, 1½ oz/43 g papaya, 1 oz/28 g pomegranate seeds, and 4 kiwi wedges next to the mango sorbet.

4 Ladle 2 fl oz/60 mL passion fruit sauce into the center of each chilled 10-in/25-cm plate. Place a vacherin slightly above the center of each plate.

Dates and pistachios in kataifi with lemon sorbet and cardamom sauce

MAKES 10 DESSERTS

Dates, pitted and coarsely chopped	10 oz	284 g
Pistachios, coarsely chopped	6¼ oz	177 g
Almond filling (page 894)	1 lb 4 oz	567 g
Pernod	1½ fl oz	45 mL
Kataifi	1 lb 4 oz	567 g
Butter, melted	5 oz	142 g
Honey cardamom sauce (page 457)	20 fl oz	600 mL
Lemon sorbet (page 489)	20 fl oz	600 mL
1-2-3 cookies (page 223), 2 in/5 cm in diameter, ⅛ in/3 mm thick, baked	10 each	10 each

1   Mix together 8½ oz/241 g of the dates, 5 oz/142 g of the pistachios, the almond filling, and the Pernod until thoroughly combined.

2   Lay out 2 pieces of plastic wrap, each 24 in/61 cm long. On one piece, use 12 oz/340 g of the kataifi to make a rectangle 6 by 18 in/15 by 46 cm. On the other piece, use the remaining 8 oz/227 g kataifi to make a rectangle 6 by 12 in/15 by 30 cm. Brush the longer rectangle with 3 oz/85 g of the melted butter. Brush the shorter rectangle with the remaining 2 oz/57 g melted butter.

3   Using a pastry bag fitted with a #5 plain tip, pipe 1 lb 4 oz/567 g of the pistachio-date filling along the long edge of the longer rectangle closest to you, about 1 in/3 cm from the edge. Pipe the remaining 13 oz/369 g filling along the long edge of the shorter rectangle. Use the plastic wrap to help roll the kataifi around the filling, like a roulade. Carefully transfer both rolls onto a parchment-lined sheet pan.

4   Bake at 400°F/204°C until golden brown, about 30 minutes. Allow to cool slightly, but make sure they are warm for serving. Cut the rolls into 3-in/8-cm slices.

5   Ladle 2 fl oz/60 mL sauce onto each warm 10-in/25-cm plate. (The sauce should come out to the rim of the plate.) Cut each of the slices in half and place one-half of a kataifi slice toward the top of each plate, angling it slightly so that it is pointing toward the left side of the plate. Lean another half of a slice of kataifi across the first, pointing toward the right side of the plate.

6   Using a #16 scoop, place 2 fl oz/60 mL of the sorbet below the kataifi slices on each plate. Sprinkle a pinch of the remaining pistachios on top of the sorbet, sprinkle a pinch of the remaining dates on the sauce, and lean a cookie against the sorbet.

Gratin of lemon-lime chibouste

MAKES 10 DESSERTS

Roulade (page 273), 11½ by 16½ in/29 by 42 cm	1 each	1 each
Simple syrup (page 900)	6 fl oz	180 mL
Lemon-lime chibouste (page 398)	1 lb 14 oz	851 g
Raspberries	1 lb	454 g
Brûlée sugar blend (page 896)	5 oz	142 g
Swiss meringue (page 416)	10 fl oz	300 mL
Lemon chips (page 898)	20 each	20 each
Papaya sauce (page 435)	20 fl oz	600 mL

1   Using a 3-in/8-cm cutter, cut 10 disks out of the roulade. Place a disk in the bottom of each of 10 rings, 3 in/8 cm in diameter and 1½ in/4 cm tall.

2   Brush each roulade disk with ½ fl oz/15 mL lemon syrup. Using a pastry bag fitted with a #6 plain tip, pipe 1½ oz/43 g chibouste in an even layer on top of each roulade disk.

3   Arrange 8 raspberries in a ring on top of the chibouste in each mold, placing them ½ in/1 cm from the outer edge of the chibouste. Press them down slightly. Pipe 1½ oz/43 g chibouste on top of the raspberries in each mold. Using a small offset spatula, level off the top of the chibouste so that it is flush with the top of the ring.

4   Freeze the chibouste overnight.

5   Remove the rings from the chibouste. Sprinkle ½ oz/14 g brûlée sugar blend evenly on top of each chibouste. Caramelize the brûlée sugar evenly using a torch. Allow the molten sugar to cool.

6   Using a pastry bag fitted with a #6 plain tip, pipe 3 mounds of Swiss meringue onto the center of each chibouste. Toast the meringue lightly with a torch.

7   Stand 1 lemon chip in the center of the toasted meringues so that they are at an angle to each other.

8   Ladle 2 fl oz/60 mL of the papaya sauce onto each chilled plate. Using a small offset spatula, place a chibouste in the center of each plate. Place 8 raspberries around each chibouste.

Summer pudding with honey tuile and frozen yogurt

MAKES 10 DESSERTS

Summer pudding (page 669)	10 each	10 each
Heavy cream, lightly whipped	10 fl oz	300 mL
Linzer cookies (page 227), 1¼ in/3 cm diameter, fluted	10 each	10 each
Raspberry frozen yogurt (page 489)	10 fl oz	300 mL
Honey tuile baskets (page 346)	10 each	10 each
Blueberries	5 oz	142 g
Raspberries	5 oz	142 g
Blackberries	5 oz	142 g

1 Place a summer pudding toward the top of each chilled plate. Spoon 1 fl oz/30 mL whipped cream over the lower half of each pudding, so it cascades off the sides of the pudding.

2 Place a linzer cookie 3 in/8 cm from the lower right of each summer pudding. Using a #30 scoop, place 1 fl oz/30 mL of frozen yogurt on each cookie.

3 Place a honey tuile basket 4 in/10 cm from the lower left of each pudding. Place ½ oz/14 g of each berry in each basket.

Walnut cheesecake with dried cherry sauce and vanilla bean sherbet

MAKES 10 DESSERTS

Walnut cheesecake (page 293), frozen	1 each	1 each
Nougatine tuile triangles (page 347), 1½ by 3 in/4 by 8 cm at the base	10 each	10 each
Dried cherry sauce (page 445)	5 fl oz	150 mL
Lace nut tuiles (page 344), 2 in/5 cm	10 each	10 each
Vanilla bean sherbet (page 497)	10 fl oz	300 mL
Striped chocolate cigarettes (see page 830)	10 each	10 each

1 While the cheesecake is semifrozen, cut it into 12 portions. Place a nougatine tuile triangle on each of 10 portions.

2 Drizzle ½ fl oz/15 mL sauce over each chilled 10-in/25-cm plate. Place a slice of cheesecake on the right section of each plate, pointing down.

3 Place a lace nut tuile 1 in/3 cm to the left of each slice of cheesecake. Using a #30 scoop, place 1 fl oz/30 mL of the sherbet in the center of each tuile. Place a chocolate cigarette on top of each scoop of sherbet.

Funnel cake with maple syrup and summer fruit sauces

MAKES 10 DESSERTS

Milk, room temperature	24 fl oz	720 mL
Instant dry yeast	⅔ oz	19 g
All-purpose flour	1 lb 5 oz	595 g
Salt	pinch	pinch
Egg yolks	1½ oz	43 g
Vegetable oil, for deep-frying	as needed	as needed
Confectioners' sugar	3 oz	85 g
Maple syrup	10 fl oz	300 mL
Raspberry sauce (page 435)	10 fl oz	300 mL
Kiwi coulis (page 432)	10 fl oz	300 mL
Mango coulis (page 432)	10 fl oz	300 mL
Star anise ice cream (page 479)	20 fl oz	600 mL

1   To make the funnel cakes, combine the milk and yeast with 10 oz/284 g of the flour. Cover and allow to ferment for 45 minutes.

2   Add the remaining flour, the salt, and egg yolks, and mix. Allow to ferment 45 minutes, or until double in size.

3   Stir the batter. Using a pastry bag with a #3 plain tip, pipe the batter into oil at 360°F/182°C to form 10 small individual cakes. Fry until golden, turning once. Remove from the hot oil and drain on paper towels.

4   Dust the funnel cakes liberally with confectioners' sugar.

5   Using a plastic squeeze bottle, drizzle 1 fl oz/30 mL maple syrup in a spiral pattern over the center of each warm plate. Using a squeeze bottle, place 12 drops of raspberry sauce around the inner rim of the plate. (Do not use more than 1 fl oz/30 mL of each fruit sauce per plate.) Using a squeeze bottle, place a drop of kiwi coulis to the left of each raspberry sauce drop, leaving space for the mango coulis. Using a squeeze bottle, place a drop of mango coulis to the left of each kiwi coulis drop. The sauces should run together slightly.

6   Place a funnel cake in the center of each plate. Using a #16 scoop, place a 2 fl oz/60 mL of the ice cream on the center of each funnel cake.

Caramelized pineapple with ginger rum sauce and coconut sorbet

MAKES 10 DESSERTS

Pineapple	2 each	2 each
Sugar	10 oz	284 g
Butter	4 oz	113 g
Ginger rum sauce (page 456)	20 fl oz	600 mL
Honey tuile cups (page 346)	10 each	10 each
Coconut sorbet (page 494)	20 fl oz	600 mL
Coconut, lightly toasted	2½ oz	71 g

1 Cut the top and bottom of the pineapples, carefully cut off the peel, and cut out the eyes. Remove the core and cut 10 slices ⅜ in/9 mm thick.

2 Lightly coat both sides of each slice of pineapple with sugar.

3 Melt 1 oz/28 g of the butter in a large sauté pan over medium-high heat. Add a single layer of pineapple slices and sauté until golden brown on the first side. Flip the pineapple slices over gently and sauté until golden brown on the other side. Transfer to a hotel pan. Repeat this process with the remaining pineapple slices, cooking them in 3 batches and using 1 oz/28 g butter for each batch.

4 Ladle 2 fl oz/60 mL rum sauce onto each warm 10-in/25-cm plate. Place a pineapple slice in the center of each plate, and place a honey tuile cup in the center of the pineapple slice.

5 Using a #16 scoop, place 2 fl oz/60 mL of the sorbet in the center of each honey tuile cup. Sprinkle toasted coconut around the edges of the sauce on each plate.

Almond apple financier with date dressing

MAKES 10 DESSERTS

Almond apple financiers (page 290), frozen	10 each	10 each
Apple cumin butter (page 451)	7½ oz	213 g
Phyllo dough décor (page 350)	10 each	10 each
Vanilla and date milk dressing (page 463)	10 oz	284 g
Armagnac vanilla ice cream (page 480)	20 oz	567 g

1   Unmold the apple-almond financier while still frozen. Let it sit and temper to room temperature. Once tempered, place financier on a diagonal in the center of the plate.

2   Using a small spoon, place a ¾-oz/21-g dollop of the apple butter in the center of the cake. Place 1 phyllo dough décor on top of the apple butter and gently press down to securely adhere the décor to the butter. Spoon out the date dressing in one corner of the plate in a swooping motion to form a half moon shape. Using 2 soup spoons, shape a quenelle out of the ice cream, and place on top of the phyllo.

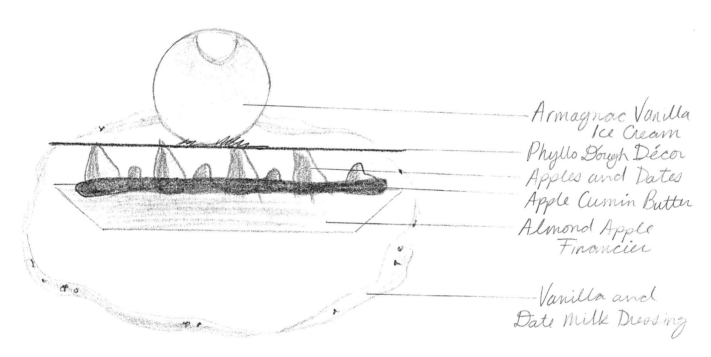

Armagnac Vanilla
Ice Cream
Phyllo Dough Décor
Apples and Dates
Apple Cumin Butter
Almond Apple
Financier

Vanilla and
Date Milk Dressing

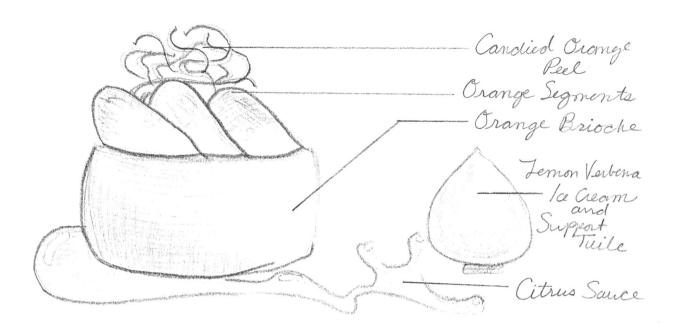

Candied Orange
Peel
Orange Segments
Orange Brioche

Lemon Verbena
Ice Cream
and
Support
Tuile

Citrus Sauce

Pain perdu

MAKES 10 DESSERTS

Butter, soft, or cooking spray	as needed	as needed
Orange brioche dough (page 186)	1 lb 4 oz	567 g
Crème caramel with Grand Marnier (page 368), hot	11¾ oz	333 g
Clarified butter or oil	as needed	as needed
Light corn syrup	as needed	as needed
Tuiles*	1 lb 10 oz	737 g
Citrus sauce (page 436)	7½ oz	213 g
Candied orange peel strips (page 796)	30 each	30 each
Lemon verbena ice cream (page 482)	1 lb 4 oz	567 g

*The choice of tuile is up to the pastry cook. Any tuile will work well.

1 Butter 10 rings 2½ in/6 cm in diameter and 1½ in/4 cm high, or spray lightly with cooking spray and place on a sheet pan lined with parchment paper. Scale the brioche dough into 10 pieces, 2 oz/57 g each, and roll into balls. Place each ball into a ring and proof at 80° to 85°F/27°to 29°C until doubled in size, 1½ to 2 hours.

2 Bake in a 375°F/191°C convection oven until golden brown, 15 to 20 minutes.

3 Remove the rings and place the brioches on a cooling rack. Using a serrated knife, trim the top and bottom of the brioches to leave each slice of brioche 1¼ in/3 cm thick.

4 Strain the crème caramel into a half hotel pan. Soak the brioche rounds on one side until half of the liquid is absorbed, 2 to 3 minutes. Flip and soak the other side until there is no crème caramel left.

5 Heat a large nonstick sauté pan over low heat for 1 minute. Grease with clarified butter or oil. Place the soaked brioches in the pan and cook until golden brown, 1½ minutes on each side. Remove from the pan and place on a cooling rack; cover with plastic wrap while still warm and cool to room temperature.

6 To plate, place each brioche on a lightly greased sizzle platter and heat in a 350°F/177°C oven for 3 to 4 minutes.

7 Place a pea-size drop of corn syrup about 3 in/8 cm from where the brioche will lie. Place a tuile on top of the corn syrup. Place the brioche on the plate. Fan 3 orange suprêmes from the citrus sauce on top of the brioche. Pour ¾ oz/21 g of the citrus sauce over the orange segments and onto the plate as in the photo. Place 3 strips of candied orange peel on top of the orange segments.

8 Using a #16 scoop, place 2 fl oz/60 mL of the ice cream on top of the tuile.

Praline parfait dessert

MAKES 10 DESSERTS

Swiss meringue (page 416)	9 oz	255 g
Praline parfaits (page 506), frozen	10 each	10 each
Spraying chocolate (page 464)	16 oz	454 g
Chocolate sauce (page 432)	10 oz	284 g
Dacquoise*	10 each	10 each

*The choice of dacquoise is up to the pastry cook. Any dacquoise will work well.

1   Place the Swiss meringue in a piping bag with a sultan tip. Place the tip of the piping tip ¼ in/6 mm above a parchment-lined sheet pan and squeeze the bag firmly until the meringue touches the parchment and spreads out to form a hollow round. Bake at 200°F/93°C for 2 hours with the oven door cracked. Let the meringue cool on the sheet pan. Gently remove the meringue from the parchment and place in an airtight container until needed.

2   Remove the parfaits from the freezer and unmold. Scatter them on a half sheet pan lined with parchment paper, at least 3 in/8 cm apart. Bring the spraying chocolate to 120°F/49°C in a bowl over barely simmering water and place into the container of the paint gun. From 14 in/36 cm away, spray in a fluid motion, coating the parfaits. Reserve the parfaits.

3   Using a #30 ladle, place 1 fl oz/30 mL of the chocolate sauce in the center of each plate. Using the back of the ladle, spread out the sauce in a circular motion until it has a 3½-in/9-cm diameter around the plate. Place the dacquoise off center of the chocolate sauce. Place the parfait in the center of the dacquoise. Place the Swiss meringue on top of the parfait.

NOTE   A little more sauce can be added in the center of the meringue if desired.

Optional Chocolate Cigarette

Optional Chocolate-coated Raisins

Swiss Meringue

Praline Parfait

Optional Chocolate-coated Pecans

Dacquoise

Chocolate Sauce

Strawberries three ways

MAKES 10 DESSERTS

Angel food cake batter (page 267)	1 lb 8 oz	680 g
Crème brûlée (page 361), unbaked	1 lb 6¼ oz	629 g
Strawberry terrine (page 402)	8½ oz	241 g
Chantilly cream (page 420)	8 oz	227 g
Tarragon sprigs, extra small	10 each	10 each
Strawberry tarragon sauce (page 439)	9½ oz	269 g

1   Bake the angel food cake in savarin molds in a 350°F/177°C convection oven until golden brown, 8 to 10 minutes. Cool, then unmold.

2   Place the crème brûlée mixture into 3-in/8-cm molds and freeze for at least 2 hours. Once frozen, unmold the crème brûlée and place in the cavity of the angel food cakes.

3   Unmold the strawberry terrines directly on top of the angel food cakes. Allow the terrine to thaw for 2 hours, refrigerated.

4   Place the cake and terrine in the center of each plate. Place a quenelle of Chantilly cream on top of the terrine. Spike the Chantilly with a tarragon sprig.

5   Drizzle ¾ oz/21 g of the strawberry tarragon sauce around each cake-terrine.

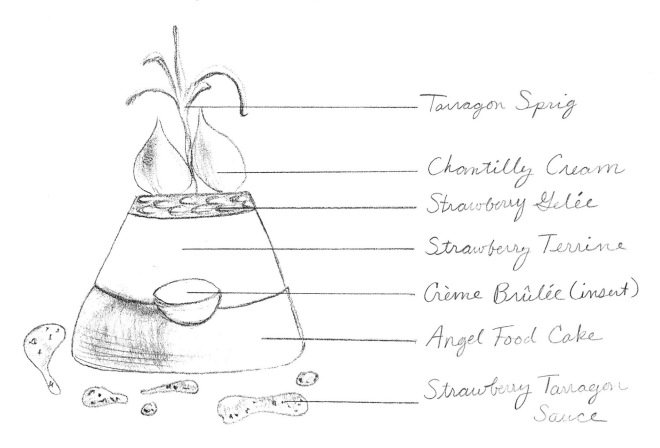

Tarragon Sprig

Chantilly Cream

Strawberry Gelée

Strawberry Terrine

Crème Brûlée (insert)

Angel Food Cake

Strawberry Tarragon Sauce

Tropical savarin Madagascar

MAKES 10 DESSERTS

Savarins (page 299)	10 each	10 each
Savarin syrup (page 437), hot	40 fl oz	1.20 L
Rum (optional)	as needed	as needed
Mirror glaze (page 424)	4 fl oz	120 mL
Chantilly cream (page 420)	8 oz	227 g
Braised pineapple and sauce (page 896), sliced into triangles	1 lb 6 oz	624 g
Pineapple chips (page 893)	10 each	10 each

1   Dip the savarins one by one into the hot syrup, porous side down first, until the savarin sinks halfway into the syrup, about 1 minute. Using a large slotted spoon, gently flip over the savarin to soak until it sinks three-quarters of the way down, 45 seconds to 1 minute, making sure that the savarin does not fall apart. Carefully scoop out the savarin with the slotted spoon and gently place on a wire rack over a sheet pan. Cool the savarins and syrup to room temperature. Squirt rum on top of the savarins while cooling, if desired. Refrigerate for 1 hour.

2   Make a glaze by combining 2 oz/57 g of the mirror glaze with 1½ to 2 fl oz/45 to 60 mL of the savarin syrup. Dip the tops of each savarin into the glaze. Place the savarins, glazed side up, onto a parchment-lined sheet pan.

3   Using a pastry bag fitted with a #6 star tip, pipe a double rosette of Chantilly cream into the center of each glazed savarin. Refrigerate until needed.

4   In a sauce pot over medium heat, warm the pineapple in its braising liquid until hot.

5   To plate, place the savarin on one side of the plate. Place the pineapple pieces tapering away from the savarin on the opposite side of the plate. Pour 1 tablespoon of the hot braising liquid on top of the pineapple pieces to coat. Place the pineapple chip at a 45-degree angle onto the Chantilly cream rosette.

Pineapple Chip

Chantilly Cream

Braised Pineapple

Savarin

Pineapple Braising Liquid

Pear and Thai jewels

MAKES 10 DESSERTS

Chocolate leaf-shaped tuiles (page 345)	10 each	10 each
Lychee sorbet (page 496), extracted but not aged	20 fl oz	600 mL
Poached pears (page 899), drained and blotted dry	10 each	10 each
Seasonal fruit, cubed ¼ by ¼ in/6 by 6 mm as necessary	10 oz	284 g
Lychees, fresh, peeled and halved	10 each	10 each
Banana passion fruit broth (page 463)	20 fl oz	600 mL

1 Fill a half sheet pan ¼ in/6 mm high with cold water and place another half sheet pan on top. Place a piece of foil on the top sheet pan and place in the freezer. Make a hole about ⅛ in/3 mm in diameter in the top of each tuile so it can be placed over a pear stem. Reserve.

2 Place the sorbet in a pastry bag with an opening 1 in/3 cm wide. Pipe 12 small mounds of sorbet directly onto the foil on the sheet pan. (Pipe mounds only as big as the space inside the cavity of the pears.) Freeze until needed for service. Place the sorbet insert into the cavity of each pear and place the pears, standing upright, in the center of soup bowls.

3 Arrange the diced fruit and 2 lychee halves around each pear. Pour over about 2 fl oz/60 mL banana passion fruit broth, so the fruit is halfway submerged in the broth. Place a chocolate leaf tuile over the pear stem. Serve immediately.

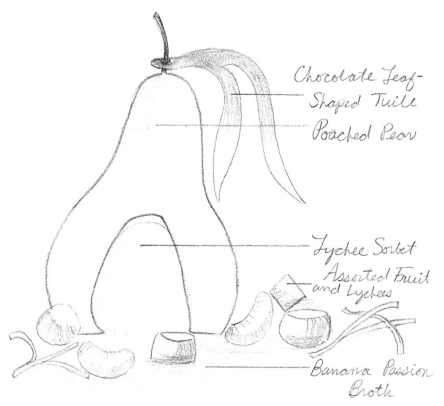

Chocolate Leaf-Shaped Tuile

Poached Pear

Lychee Sorbet

Assorted Fruit and Lychees

Banana Passion Broth

Granité dessert sampler

MAKES 10 DESSERTS

Honey	3 oz	85 g
Framboise	3 oz	85 g
Raspberries	40 each	40 each
Bananas	3 each	3 each
Sugar	2 oz	57 g
Nougatine tuiles (page 347), 2½ in/6 cm in diameter	30 each	30 each
Mango granita (page 498)	15 fl oz	450 mL
Fresh ginger granita (page 499)	15 fl oz	450 mL
Raspberry granita (page 498)	15 fl oz	450 mL
Fruit salsa (page 443)	5 oz	142 g
Spun sugar balls (page 855)	10 each	10 each

1   Gently warm the honey and framboise together. Pour over the raspberries and allow them to macerate for 1 hour.

2   Cut the bananas into ¼-in/6-mm slices and lay out on a sheet pan. Sprinkle a pinch of sugar on top of each banana slice. Caramelize the sugar evenly with a torch. Reserve the banana slices.

3   Place 3 tuiles equidistant from each other in a circular fashion on each chilled 10-in/25-cm plate, so that the ends point in to the center and out to the edge of the plate.

4   Using an oval scoop, scoop 1½ fl oz/45 mL mango granita into the top tuile on each plate. Scoop 1½ fl oz/45 mL ginger granita into the right tuile. Scoop 1½ fl oz/45 mL raspberry granita into the left tuile.

5   Place 3 caramelized banana slices between the tuiles in the top left section of the plate. Place ½ oz/14 g fruit salsa between the tuiles in the top right section of the plate. Place 4 macerated raspberries between the tuiles in the bottom section of the plate.

6   Place a spun sugar ball where the tuiles meet in the center of each plate.

chapter twenty-one

Chocolates and confections

*t*his chapter introduces principles and techniques involved with working with chocolate and sugar. These techniques are used to make ganaches, gianduja, caramels, candied fruit, fondant, marzipan, and gelées, as well as aerated, molded, and deposited candies, chocolates, and other confections.

Melting chocolate

1. Chocolate that is to be melted should be finely chopped. The smaller the pieces, the more surface area is exposed, and the quicker the chocolate melts, helping to prevent overheating. This is an important consideration, as overheating chocolate will render it unusable. A heavy chef's knife is generally best for chopping chocolate, but some pastry chefs prefer to use a long serrated knife because the serrated blade breaks the chocolate into fine shards ideal for melting.

2. A hot water bath is usually used for melting chocolate, but it is important that moisture (steam, water, or condensation) never comes in contact with the chocolate. Moisture causes chocolate to "seize," or to become thick and grainy, rendering it unfit for tempering and most other uses. For this reason, it is important that the bowl (or the top of a double boiler) is completely dry and that the bowl (or top) fits snugly over the pan of water, forming a tight seal.

3. The water should be steaming hot but not simmering.

4. Gently stir the chocolate occasionally as it melts. Gently stirring the chocolate ensures even heating and melting.

5. Remove the chocolate from the heat promptly once it is fully melted. Removing the chocolate promptly will keep the chocolate from becoming overheated.

A microwave may also be used to melt chocolate. Some pastry chefs consider it the best choice because the chocolate does not come near water. The chocolate must be chopped or broken into small pieces about the same size. Use medium power rather than high and heat the chocolate for 30-second intervals, removing and stirring it after each to ensure even heating and melting.

Working with couverture

Couverture is chocolate that contains a minimum of 32 percent cocoa butter. This means it is thinner when melted than other chocolates and can easily form a thin coating, making it ideal for dipping and enrobing confections.

The temperature of the workspace and the temperature of the items to be coated are important factors in ensuring that tempered chocolate retains its smooth, glossy appearance when set. When coating or dipping items in couverture, recrystallization must take place within a specific period of time. The ambient temperature should be between 65° and 70°F/18° and 21°C. The item to be dipped or enrobed should also be at room temperature. Confections that are too warm could cause the chocolate to bloom or to have a matte finish, while items that are too cold could "shock" the couverture, resulting in a dull finish.

Tempering chocolate

Chocolate is purchased in temper, but in order to work with it, it must be melted and then tempered again, so that as it cools and sets it will return to the same state as when purchased. Tempered chocolate has the snap and gloss associated with good chocolate, and will store better and for a longer period of time. Dipping or coating confections in tempered chocolate adds flavor, improves appearance, and helps to preserve them, as the tempered chocolate prevents moisture migration and keeps the filling from coming in contact with the air, which can cause spoilage.

Tempering is accomplished through a specific process of cooling and agitation. There are several different methods of tempering chocolate, but all are based on the same general principles. Chocolate contains different types of fat crystals. When tempering chocolate, the object is to get the right type of crystals to form. Otherwise, when the chocolate sets, it will lack hardness, snap, and shine, and will bloom. First, the chocolate must be heated to the following temperatures to ensure that all the different types of fat crystals melt: 110° to 120°F/43° to 49°C for dark chocolate, 105° to 110°F/41° to 43°C for milk chocolate and white chocolate. A portion of chocolate that is already in temper is then added to "seed" the untempered chocolate and begin the formation of the beta crystals (the desirable stable fat crystals). Then the chocolate must be cooled to about 80°F/27°C while being constantly agitated. It is gradually brought back up to the appropriate working temperature. When tempering chocolate, it is best to melt more than you will need, as it is easier to keep larger amounts of chocolate in temper.

WORKING TEMPERATURES FOR TEMPERED CHOCOLATE

Dark chocolate	86° to 90°F/30° to 32°C
Milk chocolate	84° to 87°F/29° to 31°C
White chocolate	84° to 87°F/29° to 31°C

The temperatures given above are ranges because different brands of chocolate vary in terms of tempering. Each chocolate manufacturer, in fact, has specific recommended working temperatures for the couvertures it produces.

Seed method

1. Chopped tempered chocolate—approximately 25 percent of the weight of the melted chocolate to be tempered—is added to the warm (110°F/43°C) melted chocolate and gently stirred to melt and incorporate it. The stable crystals in the chopped chocolate help stimulate the formation of stable beta crystals in the untempered chocolate.

2. The whole mass is then brought to the appropriate working temperature.

Block method

1. With the block method of chocolate tempering, a single block of tempered chocolate is added to warm melted chocolate and gently stirred until the desired temperature is reached. The block of chocolate not only reduces the temperature of the melted chocolate, but also provides the seed crystals necessary for tempering.

2. After the chocolate is brought into temper, the seed, or block of chocolate, is removed. The block can be used again. This method is simple and effective, but slightly more time-consuming than other methods of tempering.

Seeding chocolate to bring it to temper

Tabling method

1. Approximately one-third of the melted chocolate (at 110°F/43°C) is poured onto a marble surface and spread back and forth with a spatula and scraper until it begins to thicken. A marble surface is used because it has a high thermal mass and so is most efficient in pulling heat from product it is in contact with.

2. As the tabled chocolate begins to set, the beta crystals form and it becomes dull and takes on a pastelike consistency. This resulting mass is then added to the remaining melted chocolate and gently stirred to seed the chocolate to be tempered with the stable beta crystals.

3. The whole mass is then gradually brought to the appropriate working temperature.

Tabling chocolate to bring it to temper

For any method of tempering chocolate, it is wise when finished to test the chocolate, making sure that it is in full temper. To do this, dip a tool such as a small spatula into the chocolate and set it aside. Continuing to gently stir the tempered chocolate, examine how the chocolate cools on the spatula. Properly tempered chocolate should set within 3 to 5 minutes at room temperature, and should be streak-free with a satiny shine. Chocolate not in full temper may be streaky, speckled, and dull, and will set more slowly; if this occurs the chocolate needs to be seeded further until full temper is achieved.

LEFT TO RIGHT: Chocolate that is in temper, untempered that has set with spots, and untempered still wet with streaks

Tempered chocolate sets quickly. Working with relatively large amounts helps to keep it from cooling and setting too rapidly. If tempered chocolate begins to set and thicken as you work, act quickly so the chocolate will not have to be melted and retempered: Stirring constantly, hold the bowl of chocolate directly over a burner for 2 to 3 seconds; remove the chocolate from the heat while continuing to stir. Repeat the process, checking the temperature of the chocolate each time after removing the bowl from the heat so the chocolate does not overheat and come out of temper, until the chocolate is again at the optimal working temperature and consistency. Be careful not to return the bowl to the heat until the bottom of the bowl feels cooler than body temperature.

thinning tempered chocolate

To thin the tempered chocolate for dipping, use 10 percent cocoa butter per weight of chocolate; blend in and temper before dipping.

Cream ganache

Cream ganache has a wide range of uses, from filling centers for confections to glazing and filling cakes and pastries. In confectionery work, cream ganache is most commonly used as the center for truffles, but other confections are made with ganache as well.

The consistency of ganache may be hard, soft, or any variation in between, depending on the ratio of chocolate to cream. Soft ganache and medium ganache are not firm enough, nor do they have an adequate shelf life, to be used in confectionery work. As a rule, hard ganache is required for piped and rolled truffle centers.

Chocolate and cream are the basic ingredients for making ganache, but other ingredients may be added for flavoring and to provide a smoother texture. The addition of butter and/or corn syrup or glucose syrup can yield a superior finished product in both flavor and texture. Butter is added to the ganache to increase fat content when some of the cream in the formula is replaced with liqueur. Typically, the amount of butter to be added is half the weight of the liqueur. The butter is usually added to the ganache after the chocolate is fully melted. (For more information, see "Butter Ganache," page 767.)

Light corn syrup or glucose syrup may be added to ganache to help prevent recrystallization of the sugar and maintain a smooth texture. The weight of the added corn syrup generally should not exceed 10 percent of the total weight of the ganache. Light corn syrup is typically added to the cream before it is boiled.

1. Chop the chocolate into small pieces of uniform size so the pieces will melt quickly and at the same rate. Dark, milk, or white chocolate may be used to make cream ganache. Milk and white chocolate contain less cocoa solids and less cocoa butter than a dark variety and so require a higher recipe ratio of chocolate to cream. Percentages of cocoa solids or butter may also vary based on the chocolate manufacturer, so ratios should be adjusted as needed.

2. Bring heavy cream to a boil in a heavy-bottomed saucepan.

3. Pour the hot cream over the chocolate. Let the mixture stand undisturbed for a few minutes to allow the hot cream to begin melting the chocolate. When combining the chocolate and cream, some pastry chefs add the chocolate directly to the pan of hot cream; however, this practice risks scorching the chocolate on the bottom of the hot pan.

4. Stir the mixture gently to blend and melt the chocolate completely without incorporating air. If the chocolate is not fully melted at this point, warm the ganache over simmering water, stirring gently. When making ganache to be tabled, it is advisable to allow the boiled cream to cool to 170°F/77°C in order not to melt all the stable cocoa butter crystals.

LEFT: **Tabling the ganache**
MIDDLE: **Ganache at the proper consistency for piping**
RIGHT: **Piping truffles from the prepared ganache**

Flavoring ganache for truffles

Infusion is an effective method of flavoring cream ganache.

1. Bring the cream to a boil, add the flavoring, and remove the pan from the heat. Examples of common flavorings to be infused into ganache include vanilla, coffee, teas, and spices.

2. Cover and allow to stand until the flavor has been infused into the cream, 5 to 10 minutes.

3. After steeping, aromatics such as teas, herbs, and spices are strained out of the cream.

4. After straining, water or milk should be added as necessary to bring the liquid to its original weight so the finished ganache will be the proper consistency.

5. Before the infused cream is added to the chocolate, it should be rewarmed so it is hot enough to melt the chocolate.

A liqueur or other spirit may be added for flavoring. Pastes and compounds may also be used. Because these are strongly flavored, they are usually added to taste to the finished ganache.

Butter ganache

The sweetener used for butter ganache must be smooth—that is, its texture must not be discernible on the palate, because the mixture does not contain enough moisture to melt the sweetener. Examples of sweeteners well suited for making butter ganache are jam, corn syrup, glucose syrup, and fondant. The amount of sweetener used may equal as much as half the weight of the butter. The basic ratios for butter ganache are 2:1 or 2½:1 chocolate to butter.

Spirits and liqueurs added for flavoring should be added last. When adding spirits, be careful to maintain the 2:1 or 2½:1 ratio of chocolate to butter. The spirit is calculated as part of the butter. To maintain the ratio, you can reduce the amount of butter or recalculate the quantity of chocolate based on the new value of butter plus spirit.

Butter ganache may be either piped or spread into a slab and cut to form confections. The butter is treated differently depending on which of the two techniques is used. If the ganache is to be piped, the butter is creamed with the sweetener until light and aerated. If the ganache is to be spread out into a slab to harden and be cut, the butter is blended with the sweetener, incorporating as little air as possible; if too much air is incorporated into the butter, the ganache is likely to crack when cut.

Butter ganache must be worked with quickly and in small batches. Once it has set, it is very difficult to bring butter ganache back to a working consistency, as softening would require heat and that would ruin the structure by melting the butter.

1. Mix a sweetener with softened butter.

2. Add tempered chocolate and flavoring. Tempered chocolate must be used for making butter ganache. The chocolate must be in temper when it is added to the butter or the butter ganache will not set properly.

Egg ganache

This ganache is made much the same way as is cream ganache: melting chocolate by blending it with a hot liquid. The distinguishing difference is the type of hot liquid; for egg ganache, cream is heated with butter and then blended with egg yolks before it is added to the chocolate. Egg ganache, like cream ganache, may also be flavored by infusion.

making stencils

The stencil (also known as a cutout or base) is a component of many different types of confections. A stencil provides a base for piped fillings.

To form stencils, spread a thin, even layer of tempered chocolate onto a sheet of parchment paper laid out on a wooden work surface or countertop (a marble, metal, or other cold surface would cause the chocolate to set too quickly). Allow the chocolate to set until it begins to firm, then cut disks, typically with a ¾-inch/2-cm round cutter. Allow the chocolate to set completely on the parchment paper.

Forming truffles and other ganache confections

Piping

Ganache that is to be used as a center for a confection must be agitated (through stirring or tabling) so that it is firm enough to be piped or shaped. When the ganache has the proper consistency, it is piped, then rolled into perfect spheres, which will be coated with tempered chocolate or otherwise finished.

1. Ganache that will be portioned by piping should not be refrigerated because it will become too firm. Instead, agitate the ganache by stirring it in a bowl or working it on a marble surface (tabling) to bring it to piping consistency. Care must be taken not to overwork the ganache, or it will separate, resulting in a grainy texture.

2. For piping truffles, a #3 or #4 plain tip is most commonly used. Sometimes the ganache is piped onto tempered chocolate disks to form a teardrop or peak shape; in this case the confection is allowed to set until firm and then dipped. For truffles, pipe the ganache into even rows of small round domes onto parchment-lined sheet pans.

3. After it has been portioned, allow the ganache to set at room temperature until firm. At this point, depending on the desired shape, they should be rolled by hand to create a perfect sphere. Centers should never be dipped when cold, as the chocolate coating will be thick and will not have the desired shine.

Scooping

Scooping may be the easiest method for portioning ganache for truffles, but it has certain disadvantages. The moisture added to the ganache by dipping the scoop in hot water changes the texture and flavor. In addition, although scooping requires less skill, it is much more time-consuming than piping.

1. Chill the ganache until it has firmly set.

2. Using a very small ice cream scoop or a Parisian scoop, dip the scoop in hot water, scoop the ganache, and then release the truffle onto a parchment-lined sheet pan. Allow to set until firm.

3. Roll the portioned ganache into perfect spheres. Finish as desired.

Alternative method

An alternative method for portioning ganache is to pour it into a frame made by metal caramel rulers, spread it evenly if necessary, and allow it to set until firm. After the ganache has set, the bars are removed and the ganache is spread with a thin coat of tempered chocolate. Once the chocolate has set, the slab of ganache is inverted onto a guitar cutter. The cut pieces are dipped in tempered chocolate and finished. Ganache that is slabbed may also be cut by hand using a sharp knife or small cutters.

LEFT: Rolling truffles after the ganache has been portioned and has set firm enough to handle

RIGHT: Precoating truffles

Coating truffles in tempered chocolate

One of the distinguishing characteristics of a high-quality truffle is a thin outer coating of tempered couverture. Two coats of chocolate should always be applied, a precoat and a final coat. As the outer shell of tempered chocolate coating hardens, it contracts and tightens around the ganache center, sometimes developing small cracks that allow the ganache or sugar within to seep out of the shell. Precoating truffles can prevent this from happening; it also makes the centers easier to handle and prolongs the shelf life of the final product.

1. To precoat a truffle, smear a small amount of tempered chocolate over the palm of your hand and gently roll the ganache center in the chocolate. It is important, with each coat, to use only enough chocolate for a thin coating; this reduces the chance of the truffles developing feet (chocolate that pools around the base). Set the coated truffle on a parchment-lined sheet pan and repeat the process with the remaining truffles. Allow the precoat to set completely before applying the second, final coating.

2. Apply the final coat of chocolate in the same manner as the precoat, but make a thicker coat by using more chocolate.

Dipping confections

1. To dip a center, place it in the tempered chocolate, slip the dipping fork under the confection in the chocolate, and, with a scooping motion, pick it up so that it is sitting right side up on the fork. When dipping confections, make sure to use a bowl of chocolate large enough to immerse them easily.

2. Gently raise and lower the confection on the fork a few times, allowing the base to just touch the surface of the melted chocolate. This removes excess chocolate from the dipped confection, so a foot does not form. (A foot occurs when excess chocolate pools around the base of the confection.)

3. Remove the confection from the bowl, gently scraping it on the edge of the bowl to remove any remaining excess chocolate from the base and to slide the confection so that one edge is hanging over the end of the fork. Sliding the confection until one edge is hanging over the end of the fork is done to facilitate a clean and easy transfer of the product from the fork to the sheet pan.

4. Carefully lower that edge of the confection onto the clean parchment-lined sheet pan and gently pull the fork out from under the confection.

Purchased premade chocolate shells can also be used to make truffles (see page 772).

Finishing truffles and confections

Décor is important in confectionery not only for eye and taste appeal, but also as a means of differentiating one filling from another. A dusting of cocoa powder is the classic finishing technique for truffles, but they can also be dusted with confectioners' sugar. Truffles and other round confections can also be rolled in a garnish, such as chocolate shavings or curls, chopped nuts, or toasted flaked coconut. Rolling a just-dipped truffle on a wire screen is another option that creates an erratic but aesthetically pleasing spiked surface. When spiking truffles, be sure to remove them from the screen before the chocolate sets completely.

Decorated transfer sheets can be applied to the top of any smooth, flat confection. After the confection has been dipped, immediately lay the transfer sheet on its surface. After the coating is completely set, remove the sheet.

Another common décor for flat confections is made with a dipping fork. After the confection has been dipped, allow it to set for a moment, and then touch the fork to its surface, lifting the chocolate up to create small waves.

TOP LEFT: Proper workflow for dipping chocolates

BOTTOM LEFT: Creating a decoration with the dipping instrument

TOP RIGHT: Spiking chocolate truffles

BOTTOM RIGHT: Finishing techniques, from top: nuts, transfer sheets, filigree, fruit confit, dried fruit powder, waves created with a dipping instrument

Premade chocolate shells

Premade shells guarantee consistent shape and size, are time efficient, and make packaging easier due to their uniformity. Of course, the cost and quality of the shells must be taken into consideration.

Typically, premade shells are used for fillings too soft to be formed by piping or rolling. The shells must be filled carefully and completely because any small air pockets will allow mold to grow. Additionally, although hollow shells permit the use of soft fillings, you must be mindful of the water content of fillings and their potential for spoilage.

After the shells are filled, they are capped with chocolate. The cap should extend over the edges of the hole in the shell so that as it hardens and contracts it will remain attached to the shell.

Molding chocolates

Couverture is always used for molding, as its high percentage of cocoa butter makes for a more fluid chocolate. The tempered chocolate used to fill the molds should be as warm as possible within the ideal working temperature range.

1. Clean and temper the molds to room temperature. Chocolate molds should be completely clean and at room temperature before use. They should always be polished with a clean soft cloth to remove any debris or water spots, which would give the surface of the unmolded chocolate a blotchy or dull appearance. The temperature of the mold is also important. If a mold is cold, the chocolate will set too quickly; if the mold is warm, it may bring the chocolate out of temper.

2. When using molds that have an intricate design, first brush some of the chocolate into the mold. Brushing forces chocolate into the crevices of the design, ensuring that the detail of the mold will show clearly when the chocolate is unmolded.

3. Pour the tempered chocolate into the mold, completely filling it.

4. Working quickly, tap or vibrate the mold to release any air pockets and to ensure that the chocolate fills all the crevices.

5. Immediately invert the mold, pouring the excess chocolate back into the container of tempered chocolate, leaving only a thin coating in the mold. Do not reinvert the mold, or chocolate may pool, creating a layer of chocolate that is too thick. Instead, suspend the mold upside down by balancing the edges on two containers or bars over a sheet of clean parchment paper and let stand until the chocolate in the mold reaches a semisolid consistency.

6. To clean the surface of the mold, hold the mold at a 45-degree angle, bracing one edge against a flat surface; starting halfway up the mold, push a bench scraper down the mold, removing any chocolate on or above the surface of the mold. The edges of the chocolate must be flush with the surface of the mold so that the chocolate can be properly sealed after filling. If the chocolates are not properly sealed, they will have a shorter shelf life. Turn the mold around and remove excess chocolate from the other half.

7. Fill the mold 80 to 90 percent full with the desired filling, which must be liquid enough so that there is no possibility of creating air pockets.

8. Once it is filled, tap or vibrate the mold to release any air bubbles and settle the filling. To ensure that the mold is not overfilled, hold the mold up at eye level and look across the surface; there should be no filling visible above the surface. Any excess filling should be removed before the seal coat of chocolate is applied, or the filling will become mixed into the chocolate, which will not harden or effectively seal the confection.

9. Coat and seal the molded confections by drizzling on a thin layer of tempered chocolate, then gently spreading the chocolate out to cover and completely seal.

10. Let stand until the chocolate is in a semisolid state (it should be wet and tacky but not fluid), then clean the surface of the mold using a bench scraper as described above.

11. Chill molded chocolates under refrigeration for 5 to 10 minutes; do not freeze. To test whether the chocolates are ready to be unmolded, give the tray a slight twist; you should hear a crackle. With clear plastic molds, you can check the underside to see if the chocolates are releasing.

12. To unmold, turn the mold upside down and, holding it at a 45-degree angle, gently but firmly tap it once. Molded chocolates must be handled carefully at every step of the process. Even when finished, the chocolates can be damaged easily; picking up fingerprints, smudges, scratches, and the like will render a delicious product visually unappealing.

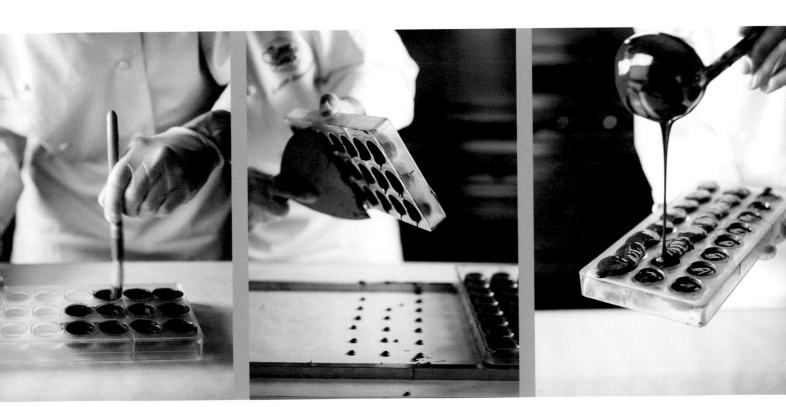

LEFT: Brushing chocolate into the molds

MIDDLE: Suspending a mold upside down and scraping its surface

RIGHT: Drizzling a chocolate seal over a filled mold

LEFT: Incorporating the nut-fruit mixture with the thinned chocolate
RIGHT: Depositing the prepared rochers onto a sheet pan

Rochers

The ideal rocher is shaped like a haystack. The individual shapes of the nuts or candied fruit should be clearly visible through the chocolate. Tossing the nuts or fruit with melted cocoa butter before adding the chocolate will act to thin the chocolate and give more definition to the shape of the nuts or fruits.

Work quickly and in small batches when making rochers. If the chocolate is too firm when it is deposited, the confections will not hold together and will have a dull finish.

Knackerli

For knackerli, as with rochers, it is important to work in small, manageable batches to ensure the chocolate disks do not set too much or completely before the garnish is added.

Gianduja

Gianduja may be made with any variety of chocolate—dark, milk, or white. It is traditionally made with either hazelnuts or almonds, but other nuts may be substituted in part or in whole. The nuts can be roasted to any degree desired.

The final variable in the production of gianduja is the ratio of nuts to sugar to chocolate. For a firmer gianduja, use more chocolate. For a softer gianduja, use less. The basic ratio for a medium-consistency gianduja that is suitable for candy centers is 1 part nuts to 1 part sugar to 1 part dark chocolate (or 1¼ parts milk or white chocolate). If possible, gianduja should be

ground in a mélangeur for the smoothest texture, but a food processor will make an acceptable gianduja. When using a food processor, always use confectioners' sugar, not granulated.

Because of its low moisture content, gianduja is not prone to spoilage and has a long shelf life.

Dragées

To ensure the desirable thin coating of caramel, only a relatively small amount of sugar is used when making dragées. The larger the nut, the less sugar you should use. Typical proportions by weight vary from 3 parts nuts to 1 part sugar for small nuts to 6 parts nuts to 1 part sugar for large nuts.

The nuts used for dragées should not be toasted, as they will roast as the sugar caramelizes.

TOP LEFT: The sugar syrup crystallized on the nuts.

BOTTOM LEFT: Adding the chocolate and stirring to coat the dragée nuts

TOP RIGHT: Pulling the nuts apart on a marble after the sugar casing has caramelized

BOTTOM RIGHT: A variety of dragées

Cooking sugar to different stages

When cooking sugar, all your equipment must be clean and free of any grease. The sugar must also be free of impurities, such as flour or other ingredients. Sugar has a very high caramelization point and any impurities in the sugar are likely to burn at a much lower temperature, before the sugar begins to caramelize. A copper or other heavy-bottomed saucepan should be used to ensure constant, even heat. Sugar may be cooked by one of two methods: *wet* or *dry*.

When cooking or caramelizing sugar by any method, a small amount of an acid (typically lemon juice at approximately ¼ tsp/1.25 mL for 8 oz/227 g of sugar) can be added to help prevent crystallization from occurring during cooking. (For more information on crystallization, see page 762.)

Regardless of the cooking method, when caramelizing sugar, it is important to stop the cooking process by shocking the pan in an ice water bath just as, or just before, it reaches the desired color. Sugar retains heat and can easily become too dark or burn if the cooking process is not arrested.

It is also important to heat any liquids to be added to the caramel and to add them carefully. Caramelized sugar is very hot and will splatter when a colder ingredient is introduced.

Wet method

The wet method is best used when sugar must be cooked to a specific stage or temperature.

1. Combine the sugar in a saucepan with 30 percent or more of its weight in water. The sugar is intended to dissolve in the added water; if not enough water is added the result may be undissolved sugar crystals in the syrup that in turn could cause recrystallization.

2. Place the pan over high heat and stir constantly until the mixture comes to a boil to ensure all the sugar is melted. As the dissolved sugar is heated, the water evaporates, acting to increase the concentration of sugar; as the temperature increases, water continues to evaporate, leaving behind a supersaturated noncrystalline sugar solution. Stirring constantly is important as agitation will prevent the collision of particles in the solution that leads to crystallization.

3. Once it has come to a boil, stop stirring and skim off any impurities.

4. Using a pastry brush, wash down the sides of the pan with cool water to prevent crystals from forming. Crystallization of the cooking sugar occurs readily on the side of the pan where crystals are deposited from evaporating liquid. These crystals, in turn, can easily act to "seed" the rest of the sugar in the pan, causing it to begin to crystallize, becoming lumpy and granular. Repeat as often as necessary to keep the sides of the pan clean until the sugar has reached the desired temperature, consistency, and color.

   A "seed" in this context is anything that will act as a surface hosting the growth of sugar crystals. Examples of seeds are whole sugar crystals, air bubbles, or skewers (as sometimes used in making candy). Brushing the sides of the pan with cool water prevents crystals from forming by adding moisture lost in evaporation during cooking.

Dry method

The dry method is used exclusively for caramelizing. The characteristically nutty and roasted flavor of caramel is best achieved through the use of this method.

1. Add a small amount of the sugar to a preheated medium-hot pan set over medium heat and allow it to melt.

2. Add the remaining sugar in small increments, allowing each addition of sugar to fully melt before adding the next. Continue this process until all the sugar has been added to the pan. Cook to the desired color. Using this method, sugar crystals are melted through the application of heat, resulting in sugar that caramelizes almost as soon as it melts. Because it cooks so quickly, it is important to monitor the sugar constantly.

Caramelize part of the sugar and add the remainder in parts for an even, smooth caramel.

Of the two techniques for cooking sugar—wet and dry—only the wet method allows the sugar to be cooked to and used at the various stages that are vital for countless preparations. The dry method of sugar cooking melts the sugar crystals by the application of heat, resulting in sugar that caramelizes almost as soon as it melts.

The wet method of sugar cooking, however, dissolves the sugar in water; then as the solution cooks, the water evaporates, acting to increase the concentration of sugar and resulting in a supersaturated, noncrystalline sugar solution. The concentration of the sugar solution increases as the solution is cooked, the temperature increases, and more of the water evaporates.

1. To cook sugar by the wet method, use a heavy-bottomed pot to ensure even heat conduction. The water should equal approximately 30 percent of the weight of the sugar. If too little water is used, there may be undissolved sugar crystals in the syrup, which may cause recrystallization.

2. Bring the mixture to a boil, stirring constantly. Stirring constantly is important, as agitation will prevent the collision of particles in the solution that lead to crystallization.

3. When the mixture comes to a boil, stop stirring.

4. Skim the impurities that rise to the surface.

5. Brush down the sides of the pan using a pastry brush moistened with cool water. Brushing the sides of the pan with cool water prevents crystals from forming by adding moisture lost in evaporation during cooking.

6. Add the acid ingredient (cream of tartar, lemon juice, etc.), if using. Adding a small amount of an acid can help prevent crystallization during cooking; when boiled with a dilute acid, sugar will result in an invert sugar that interferes with the crystallization process.

SUGAR STAGES AND TEMPERATURES

STAGE	DEGREES FAHRENHEIT	DEGREES CELSIUS
Thread	215–230	102–110
Soft ball	240	116
Firm ball	245	118
Hard ball	250–260	121–127
Soft crack	265–270	129–132
Hard crack	295–310	146–154
Caramel	320	160

Soft caramels

If the mixture for caramels is undercooked, they will be too soft and will not have the proper caramel flavor. If it is overcooked, they will be too firm. Although a thermometer is helpful in making caramels, the final assessment of whether the caramel is ready should be determined by testing the batch using ice water and a spoon. If the caramel is too firm, more liquid can be added to adjust the consistency.

Soft caramels may be flavored in any number of ways. Strong flavorings such as coffee beans, hazelnut paste, or spices can be added to the cream at the beginning of the cooking process. To make fruit caramels, replace up to half of the liquid in the recipe with a fruit purée. When using a fruit purée, it is advisable to cut the amount of glucose syrup by half, and it is likely that you will have to cook the caramels to a higher temperature to achieve the same consistency, due to the acidity of the fruit and the reduced amount of milk solids in the formula.

Pouring soft caramels between bars   Cutting the caramel once it is properly set

Peanut brittle

Some caution is necessary when making peanut brittle. Temperature and color must be carefully monitored to achieve the characteristic flavor and texture. If your peanut brittle is pale or milky white and granular, it probably was either not cooked to a high enough temperature or was stirred too much and/or too rapidly during cooking. Peanut brittle demands a slow, steady stir, especially after the peanuts have been added. As a general rule, if the mixture has reached the proper temperature but the color is not fully developed, continue cooking to the desired color.

Stretching peanut brittle

Hard candies

Oils, extracts, and concentrated synthetic or natural flavors are the most common flavorings used for hard candies. These flavorings are added at the end of the cooking process because they are often not heat-stable and because any acid they contain will prevent the finished product from becoming completely hard. Hard candies can be poured onto a slab, partially cooled, and then pulled and cut, or they can be cast in starch molds or other types of molds.

Classic truffles

MAKES 50 TRUFFLES

Heavy cream	8 fl oz	240 mL
Light corn syrup	1 oz	28 g
Dark chocolate, finely chopped	1 lb	454 g
Butter, soft	1 oz	28 g
Dark chocolate, melted, tempered, for coating	as needed	as needed

1   Bring the cream and corn syrup to a boil.

2   Pour the hot cream over the chocolate and allow to sit, without stirring, for 2 minutes. Gently stir the mixture using a wooden spoon or rubber spatula until fully blended and smooth. If necessary, heat over a hot water bath to melt all of the chocolate. Add the butter and stir until melted and smooth. Allow to set until the ganache reaches room temperature. To table the ganache, work it with a metal spatula on a clean marble work surface until it is piping consistency.

3   Fill a pastry bag fitted with a #4 plain tip and pipe out truffles onto parchment-lined sheet pans. Allow the truffles to set until firm.

4 Roll the truffles by hand until perfectly round. Place on a clean parchment-lined sheet pan. Cover and allow to set until firm. Depending on the ambient temperature and the consistency of the ganache, it may be necessary to refrigerate the truffles at this point just until they are firm enough to coat.

5 To finish the truffles, spread a small amount of the tempered chocolate in the palm of your hand and gently roll each truffle in the chocolate to coat. Place the coated truffles on a clean parchment-lined sheet pan. Allow the chocolate to set completely, then repeat the process.

Tea truffles

MAKES 52 TRUFFLES

Heavy cream	4 fl oz	120 mL
Milk	4 fl oz	120 mL
Earl Grey tea	½ oz	14 g
Dark chocolate, finely chopped	8 oz	227 g
Milk chocolate, finely chopped	8 oz	227 g
Butter, soft	2 oz	57 g
Dark chocolate, melted, tempered, for coating	as needed	as needed

1 Bring the cream and milk to a boil. Remove from the heat, add the tea, cover, and allow to steep for 10 minutes.

2 Strain the mixture through dampened cheesecloth and wring out thoroughly. Add water if necessary to return the liquid to 8 fl oz/240 mL.

3 Bring the liquid back to a boil and pour it over the chopped chocolates. Allow to sit for 3 minutes, then stir until well blended and smooth. If necessary, heat over a hot water bath to melt all of the chocolate.

4 Gently stir in the butter until melted and smooth. Allow to set until the ganache reaches room temperature. To table the ganache, work it with a metal spatula on a clean marble work surface until it is piping consistency.

5 Fill a pastry bag fitted with a #3 or #4 plain tip and pipe out truffles onto parchment-lined sheet pans. Allow the truffles to set until firm.

6 Roll the truffles by hand until perfectly round. Place on a clean parchment-lined sheet pan. Allow to set until firm. Depending on the ambient temperature and the consistency of the ganache, it may be necessary to refrigerate the truffles at this point just until they are firm enough to coat.

7 To finish the truffles, spread a small amount of tempered chocolate in the palm of your hand and gently roll each truffle in the chocolate to coat. Place the coated truffles on a clean parchment-lined sheet pan. Allow the chocolate to set completely, then repeat the process.

Coconut lime truffles

MAKES 160 TRUFFLES

Heavy cream	7 oz	198 g
Glucose syrup	2 oz	57 g
Cream of coconut	4 oz	113 g
Lime zest, finely grated	2 limes	2 limes
White chocolate, chopped	1 lb 12 oz	794 g
Lime juice	3 limes	3 limes
White chocolate, melted, tempered, for dipping	as needed	as needed
Lime zest, finely grated, for garnish	as needed	as needed

1   Combine the cream, glucose syrup, cream of coconut, and lime zest in a saucepan and bring to a boil.

2   Pour over the chopped chocolate. Stir gently until the chocolate melts entirely. If the chocolate does not completely melt, gently warm over barely simmering water until it melts and the ganache is smooth.

3   Stir in the lime juice.

4   Pour into a half hotel pan and cover. Allow the ganache to set until it reaches room temperature. To table the ganache, work it with a metal spatula on a clean marble work surface until it is piping consistency.

5   Fill a pastry bag fitted with a #4 round tip and pipe out ¼ oz/7 g balls onto parchment-lined sheet pans. Allow the truffles to set until firm.

6   Roll the truffles by hand until perfectly round. Dip in tempered white chocolate. Garnish with lime zest before the chocolate sets.

Sesame ginger truffles

MAKES 130 TRUFFLES

Ginger, thinly sliced	1½ oz	43 g
Heavy cream	9 oz	255 g
Glucose syrup	2½ oz	71 g
Tahini paste	1½ oz	43 g
Bittersweet chocolate, finely chopped	1 lb 2 oz	510 g
Toasted sesame oil	1 tbsp	15 mL
Dark chocolate, melted, tempered, for dipping	as needed	as needed
Sesame seeds, toasted	as needed	as needed

1   Combine the ginger and cream in a sauce pot. Bring to a boil. Remove from the heat and cover. Allow to steep for 5 minutes.

2   Strain out the ginger using dampened cheesecloth. Wring the cheesecloth well. Add water if necessary to bring the cream back to 9 oz/255 g.

3   Combine the infused cream, glucose syrup, and tahini and bring to a boil. Pour over the chopped chocolate. Stir gently until the chocolate melts entirely. If the chocolate does not completely melt, gently warm over barely simmering water until it melts and the ganache is smooth.

4   Stir in the sesame oil.

5   Pour into a half hotel pan and cover. Allow the ganache to set until it reaches room temperature. To table the ganache, work it with a metal spatula on a clean marble work surface until it is piping consistency.

6   Fill a pastry bag fitted with a #4 round tip and pipe out ¼ oz/7 g balls onto parchment-lined sheet pans. Allow the truffles to set until firm.

7   Roll the truffles by hand until perfectly round. Dip in tempered chocolate and garnish with toasted sesame seeds before the chocolate sets.

Honey lavender truffles

MAKES 130 TRUFFLES

Lavender flowers, dried	1 tbsp	15 mL
Heavy cream	9 oz	255 g
Honey	3 oz	85 g
Milk chocolate, chopped	1 lb 7 oz	652 g
Milk chocolate, melted, tempered, for dipping	as needed	as needed
Lavender flowers, dried, for garnish	as needed	as needed

1   Combine 1 tbsp/15 mL of the lavender flowers and the cream in a small saucepan. Heat just to a simmer. Remove from the heat, cover, and allow to steep for 5 minutes.

2   Strain out the lavender using dampened cheesecloth. Wring the cheesecloth well. Add water if necessary to bring the cream back to 9 oz/255 g.

3   Combine the infused cream and the honey and bring to a boil. Pour over the chopped chocolate. Stir gently until the chocolate melts entirely. If the chocolate does not completely melt, gently warm the ganache over barely simmering water until it melts and the ganache is smooth.

4   Pour into a half hotel pan and cover. Allow the ganache to set until it reaches room temperature. To table the ganache, work it with a metal spatula on a clean marble work surface until it is piping consistency.

5   Fill a pastry bag fitted with a #4 round tip and pipe out ¼ oz/7 g balls onto parchment-lined sheet pans. Allow the truffles to set until firm.

6   Roll the truffles by hand until perfectly round. Dip in the tempered chocolate. Garnish with a few dried lavender flowers before the chocolate sets.

Milk chocolate truffles

MAKES 120 TRUFFLES

Vanilla beans	1 each	1 each
Heavy cream	8 fl oz	240 mL
Milk chocolate, finely chopped	1 lb 5 oz	595 g
Butter, soft	2½ oz	71 g
Milk chocolate, melted, tempered, for coating	as needed	as needed

1   Split the vanilla bean and scrape the seeds into the cream. Add the pod to the cream and bring to a boil. Allow to steep for 10 minutes.

2   Strain the cream through dampened cheesecloth. Wring the cheesecloth well. Add water if necessary to return the liquid to 8 fl oz/240 mL.

3   Bring the liquid back to a boil and pour over the chopped chocolate. Allow to sit for 3 minutes, then stir gently with a wooden spoon or rubber spatula until well blended and smooth. If necessary, heat over a hot water bath to melt all of the chocolate. Gently stir the butter into the ganache until melted and smooth.

4   Pour into a half hotel pan and cover. Allow the ganache to set until it reaches room temperature. To table the ganache, work it with a metal spatula on a clean marble work surface until it is piping consistency.

5   Fill a pastry bag fitted with a #3 or #4 plain tip and pipe out truffles onto parchment-lined sheet pans. Allow the truffles to set until firm.

6   Roll the truffles by hand until perfectly round. Place on a clean parchment-lined sheet pan. Allow the truffles to set until firm. Depending on the ambient temperature and the consistency of the ganache, it may be necessary to refrigerate the truffles at this point just until they are firm enough to coat.

7   To finish the truffles, spread a small amount of tempered milk chocolate in the palm of your hand and gently roll each truffle in the chocolate to coat. Place the coated truffles on a clean parchment-lined sheet pan. Allow the chocolate to set completely, then repeat the process.

Rum truffles

MAKES 85 TRUFFLES

Heavy cream	5 fl oz	150 mL
Milk chocolate, finely chopped	11 oz	312 g
Butter, soft	½ oz	14 g
Rum	1¼ fl oz	38 mL
Milk chocolate truffle shells	85 each	85 each
Milk chocolate, melted, tempered, for coating	as needed	as needed

1   Bring the cream to a boil. Pour over the chopped chocolate. Allow to sit for 3 minutes, then stir with a wooden spoon or rubber spatula until well blended and smooth. If necessary, heat over a hot water bath to melt all of the chocolate.

2   Gently stir in the butter until melted and smooth. Stir in the rum.

3   Pour the ganache into a half hotel pan. Cover, placing plastic wrap directly on the surface, and cool to 85°F/29°C.

4   Pipe into the truffle shells. Seal and dip in the tempered milk chocolate. After dipping, place the confections on a wire screen and roll them to create a spiked finish. Place on a parchment-lined sheet pan.

Orange truffles

MAKES 120 TRUFFLES

Heavy cream	8 fl oz	240 mL
Corn syrup	1 oz	28 g
White chocolate, finely chopped	1 lb 12 oz	794 g
Butter, soft	1 oz	28 g
Cointreau	2 fl oz	60 mL
Candied orange peel (page 796), finely minced	4 oz	113 g
Milk chocolate, melted, tempered, for coating	as needed	as needed

1   Bring the cream to a boil. Add the corn syrup and stir until incorporated.

2   Pour the hot cream over the chopped chocolate. Allow to sit for 3 minutes, then stir gently with a wooden spoon or rubber spatula until fully blended and smooth. If necessary, heat over a hot water bath to melt all of the chocolate.

3   Gently stir in the butter and liqueur until smooth and completely blended. Add the orange peel and blend thoroughly.

4   Pour the ganache into a half hotel pan and cover, placing plastic wrap directly on the surface. Allow the ganache to cool completely.

5   Table the ganache by working it with a metal spatula on a clean marble work surface until it is piping consistency.

6   Fill a pastry bag fitted with a #3 or #4 plain tip and pipe out truffles onto parchment-lined sheet pans. Allow the truffles to set until firm.

7   Roll the truffles by hand until perfectly round. Place on a clean parchment-lined sheet pan. Allow the truffles to set until firm. Depending on the ambient temperature and the consistency of the ganache, it may be necessary to refrigerate the truffles at this point just until they are firm enough to coat.

8   To finish the truffles, spread a small amount of tempered chocolate in the palm of your hand and gently roll each truffle in the chocolate to coat. Allow the chocolate to set completely, then repeat the process.

Pistachio ganache confections

MAKES 120 PIECES

Marzipan, for base	as needed	as needed
Dark chocolate, melted, tempered, for coating and dipping	as needed	as needed
Heavy cream	8 fl oz	240 mL
Dark chocolate, finely chopped	1 lb	454 g
Pistachio paste	2½ oz	71 g
Dark rum	1 fl oz	30 mL
Pistachios, blanched and finely chopped	as needed	as needed

1   Roll out the marzipan 4 by 6 in/10 by 15 cm and ⅛ in/3 mm thick. Brush with a thin layer of tempered dark chocolate. Allow the chocolate to set completely.

2   Cut the marzipan lengthwise into strips ⅜ in/9 mm wide.

3   Bring the cream to a boil. Pour over the chopped chocolate. Allow to sit for 3 minutes, then stir gently with a wooden spoon or rubber spatula until fully blended and smooth. If necessary, heat over a hot water bath to melt all of the chocolate. Stir in the pistachio paste and rum until fully blended. Cool to room temperature.

4   To table the ganache, work it with a metal spatula on a clean marble work surface until it is piping consistency.

5   Fill a pastry bag fitted with a #2 plain tip with the ganache and pipe in a spiral onto the marzipan strips. Allow the ganache to set completely.

6   Cut the marzipan strips into 1 in/3 cm lengths. Dip in tempered dark chocolate. Sprinkle with chopped pistachios before the chocolate sets.

Butter ganache confections

MAKES 100 PIECES

Dark chocolate, melted, tempered	as needed	as needed
Butter, soft	4½ oz	128 g
Glucose syrup	1¼ oz	35 g
White chocolate, melted, tempered	8 oz, plus as needed for dipping	227 g, plus as needed for dipping
Cocoa butter, melted and cooled to 86°F/30°C	½ oz	14 g
Dark rum	2¾ fl oz	83 mL
Coarse sugar	as needed	as needed

1   Spread a thin layer of tempered dark chocolate on a sheet of parchment paper and allow to set until firm but still malleable. Using a ¾-in/2-cm round cutter, cut out 100 disks, leaving them attached to the parchment paper. Allow the chocolate to set completely.

2   Cream together the butter and glucose syrup on medium speed with the paddle attachment, scraping down the bowl periodically, until smooth, fluffy, and lighter in color, about 5 minutes. Using a handheld whisk, vigorously blend in 8 oz/227 g tempered white chocolate and the cocoa butter until fully combined and creamy. Blend in the rum.

3   Allow the mixture to cool until it is firm enough to hold its shape when piped, about 3 minutes.

4   Fill a pastry bag fitted with a #6 plain tip with the ganache and pipe a teardrop shape onto each chocolate disk. Allow the ganache to set completely.

5   Dip each confection in tempered white chocolate and place on a parchment-lined sheet pan. Decorate the tip of each chocolate with a sprinkling of coarse sugar.

Honey passion fruit butter ganache pralines

MAKES 120 PIECES

Passion fruit concentrate	6 oz	170 g
Butter, soft	5 oz	142 g
Honey	4 oz	113 g
Milk chocolate, melted, tempered	1 lb 6 oz, plus as needed for dipping	624 g, plus as needed for dipping

1   Boil the passion fruit concentrate until reduced by half its volume.

2   Mix together the butter and honey. Blend in 1 lb 6 oz/624 g chocolate and then the passion fruit concentrate. Pour into a frame (6 by 12 by ½ in/15 by 30 by 1 cm), cover, and allow to set overnight.

3   Brush a thin coating of tempered milk chocolate on one side of the slab. Allow the chocolate to set completely.

4   Remove the frame. Cut the slab into rectangles ½ by 1¼ in/1 by 3 cm and dip in tempered milk chocolate. Allow the chocolate to set completely, about 30 minutes.

Raspberry creams

MAKES 100 PIECES

Butter, soft	4 oz	113 g
Seedless raspberry jam	6 oz	170 g
Milk chocolate, melted	4 oz	113 g
Semisweet chocolate, melted	3½ oz	99 g
Cocoa butter, melted and cooled to 86°F/30°C	1 oz	28 g
Raspberry liqueur	1 fl oz	30 mL
Milk chocolate, melted, tempered, for dipping	as needed	as needed
Dark chocolate, melted, tempered, for dipping	as needed	as needed

1   Place a metal frame (9 by 12 by ½ in/23 by 30 by 1 cm) on parchment paper or a silicone baking mat.

2   Mix together the butter and jam by hand, scraping down the bowl periodically, just until homogeneous.

3 Blend together the milk and semisweet chocolates with the cocoa butter. Temper the chocolate mixture. (See page 762 for tempering instructions.)

4 Gently fold the chocolate mixture into the butter mixture. Blend in the liqueur. Spread the mixture evenly in the prepared frame. Allow to set until firm.

5 Brush the raspberry cream with a thin layer of tempered dark or milk chocolate and allow the chocolate to set completely.

6 Remove the frame and cut the slab into strips ½ in/1 cm wide. Cut the strips into ¾-in/2-cm diamonds. Dip in tempered dark or milk chocolate. Allow the chocolate to set completely, about 30 minutes.

Fujiyamas

MAKES 100 PIECES

Dark chocolate, melted, tempered	as needed	as needed
Butter, soft	4½ oz	128 g
Corn syrup	½ oz	14 g
Cocoa butter, melted and cooled to 86°F/30°C	1 oz	28 g
White chocolate, melted	9 oz	255 g
Crème de cassis	3½ oz	99 g
White chocolate, melted, tempered, for garnish	as needed	as needed

1 Spread a thin layer of tempered dark chocolate onto a sheet of parchment paper and allow to set until firm but still malleable. Using a ¾-in/2-cm round cutter, cut out 100 disks, leaving them attached to the parchment paper. Allow the chocolate to set completely.

2 Cream together the butter and corn syrup on medium speed with the paddle attachment, scraping down the bowl periodically, until smooth, fluffy, and lighter in color, about 5 minutes.

3 Blend together the cocoa butter and white chocolate and temper.

4 Using a handheld whisk, vigorously blend the chocolate–cocoa butter mixture into the butter mixture until fully combined and creamy. Blend in the liqueur.

5 Allow the mixture to cool until it is firm enough to hold its shape when piped, about 3 minutes.

6 Fill a pastry bag fitted with a #5 plain tip with the ganache and pipe a peak shape onto each chocolate disk. Allow to set until firm.

7 Dip in tempered dark chocolate and allow the chocolate to set completely.

8 Decorate each piece with a "snowcap" of white chocolate by piping tempered white chocolate on the tip.

Apricot pralines

MAKES 100 PIECES

Dark chocolate, melted, tempered	as needed	as needed
Butter, soft	4½ oz	128 g
Apricot jam	3 oz, plus as needed for piping	85 g, plus as needed for piping
Glucose syrup	1¼ oz	35 g
Milk chocolate, melted, tempered	8 oz, plus as needed for dipping	227 g, plus as needed for dipping
Cocoa butter, melted and cooled to 86°F/30°C	½ oz	14 g
Apricot brandy	2¾ fl oz	83 mL
Coarse sugar, for garnish	as needed	as needed

1   Spread a thin layer of tempered dark chocolate onto a sheet of parchment paper and allow to set until firm but still malleable. Using a ¾-in/2-cm round cutter, cut out 100 disks, leaving them attached to the parchment paper. Allow the chocolate to set completely.

2   Cream together the butter, 3 oz/85 g of the apricot jam, and the glucose syrup on medium speed with the paddle attachment, scraping down the bowl periodically, until smooth, fluffy, and lighter in color, about 5 minutes. Vigorously blend in the 8 oz/227 g milk chocolate and the cocoa butter until fully combined and creamy. Blend in the apricot brandy.

3   Allow the ganache to cool until it is firm enough to hold its shape when piped, about 3 minutes.

4   Fill a small parchment piping cone with apricot jam and pipe a small dot onto the center of each chocolate disk.

5   Fill a pastry bag fitted with a #2 plain tip with the ganache and pipe a teardrop shape over each jam dot. Allow the ganache to set completely.

6   Dip each disk in tempered milk chocolate. Allow the chocolate to set until tacky, then sprinkle with coarse sugar. Allow the chocolate to set completely.

Almond dragées

MAKES 110 PIECES

Sugar	5 oz	142 g
Water	1½ fl oz	45 mL
Almonds, whole, blanched	1 lb	454 g
Butter	½ oz	14 g
Dark chocolate, melted, tempered	12 oz	340 g
Cocoa powder	½ oz	14 g

1   Combine the sugar and water in a heavy-bottomed saucepan and stir to ensure that all the sugar is moistened. Bring to a boil over high heat, stirring constantly. When the syrup comes to a boil, stop stirring and skim the surface to remove any scum. Continue to cook without stirring until the syrup reaches the thread stage (215° to 230°F/102° to 110°C). Remove from the heat.

2   Immediately add the nuts and stir until the sugar crystallizes. Return to the heat and stir constantly until the sugar melts and caramelizes on the nuts.

3   Stir in the butter. Pour the mixture onto a marble slab and immediately separate the clusters of nuts. Allow to cool completely on the slab, then place in a bowl and chill for 3 minutes under refrigeration.

4   Add 4 oz/113 g of the tempered chocolate and stir (so the nuts don't stick together) until the chocolate sets. Repeat with another 4 oz/113 g chocolate. Add the remaining 4 oz/113 g chocolate and stir until it is almost set. Add the cocoa powder and stir to coat. Toss the nuts in a strainer to sift off the excess cocoa powder.

VARIATIONS   **HAZELNUT DRAGÉES** Substitute whole blanched hazelnuts for the almonds.

WALNUT DRAGÉES Substitute whole walnuts for the almonds

Rochers

MAKES 100 PIECES

Almonds, blanched, sliced or slivered	1 lb	454 g
Liqueur or spirits of choice	3 fl oz	90 mL
Sugar	3 oz	85 g
Milk chocolate, melted, tempered	12 oz	340 g

1 Toss the almonds together with the liqueur and sugar.

2 Spread on a sheet pan. Toast in a 350°F/177°C oven, turning the mixture several times to ensure even color, until golden brown, about 10 minutes. Cool completely.

3 Combine one-third of the chocolate with one-third of the nut mixture, toss together to coat the nuts evenly, and spoon out into high little mounds on a parchment-lined sheet pan. Repeat with the remaining chocolate and nuts in 2 more batches. Allow the chocolate to set completely.

NOTE Any variety of nuts may be used. Any type of chocolate may be used in place of milk chocolate. Chopped dried fruit may be used with the nuts.

Knackerli

MAKES 50 PIECES

Dark chocolate, melted, tempered	8 oz	227 g
Pistachios, blanched	50 each	50 each
Dried cranberries	50 each	50 each
Dried apricots, coarsely chopped	10 each	10 each

1 Fill a parchment cone with the tempered chocolate and pipe onto a parchment-lined sheet pan in 1-in/3-cm disks.

2 When the chocolate has begun to set, place 1 pistachio, 1 cranberry, and 1 piece of apricot onto each disk.

3 Allow the chocolate to fully set before removing the disks from the parchment paper.

NOTES Tempered milk or white chocolate may be substituted for the dark chocolate.

The chocolate may be piped in larger or smaller disks if desired.

Any type of nuts or dried fruit may be substituted for the pistachios, cranberries, and apricots. It is important to remember when making knackerli that the size of the nuts and fruits should correspond to the size of the chocolate disk and that the colors and flavors should complement each other.

Praline-filled chocolate cups

MAKES 120 CONFECTIONS

Dark chocolate, melted, tempered	as needed	as needed
Butter, soft	8 oz	227 g
Fondant	8 oz	227 g
Praline paste	8 oz	227 g

1   Coat the inside of 120 foil cups, ⅞ in/2 cm in diameter by ⅝ in/1.5 cm high, with tempered dark chocolate. Allow the chocolate to set completely.

2   Cream the butter, fondant, and praline paste on medium speed with the paddle attachment, scraping down the bowl periodically, until smooth and light in color, about 5 minutes.

3   Fill a pastry bag fitted with a #2 plain tip with the praline mixture and pipe into the cups, filling them 80 percent full. Allow to set until firm.

4   Fill a parchment cone with tempered dark chocolate and pipe onto the top of each filled cup in a spiral motion, creating a seal. Tap each cup to smooth the top.

5   Allow the chocolate to set.

Candied orange peel

MAKES 9½ OZ/269 G

Orange peel, cut into strips ¼ by 2 in/6 mm by 5 cm	8 oz	227 g
Water	as needed	as needed
Light corn syrup	4 oz	113 g
Sugar	1 lb	454 g

1   Place the orange peels in a pan of cold water to cover and bring to a boil; drain. Repeat this process 3 times, using fresh cold water each time, to remove some of the bitterness from the pith.

2   Combine 12 oz/360 mL water, the corn syrup, and sugar in a heavy-bottomed saucepan and bring to a boil, stirring to dissolve the sugar. Reduce to a very low simmer, add the peels, and poach until translucent, about 1 hour.

3   Store the peels in the syrup in a tightly covered container under refrigeration. If the peels are not to be dipped in chocolate, toss them in granulated sugar before drying on wire racks.

4   To dry the peels, drain them and spread on a wire rack set over a parchment-lined sheet pan. Allow to dry and crystallize overnight at room temperature. Alternatively, place the peels on a parchment-lined sheet pan in a 280°F/138°C convection oven for 1½ hours.

NOTE   Lemon, lime, or grapefruit peels may be used in place of the orange peels.

Peel is opaque before cooked and translucent afterward.

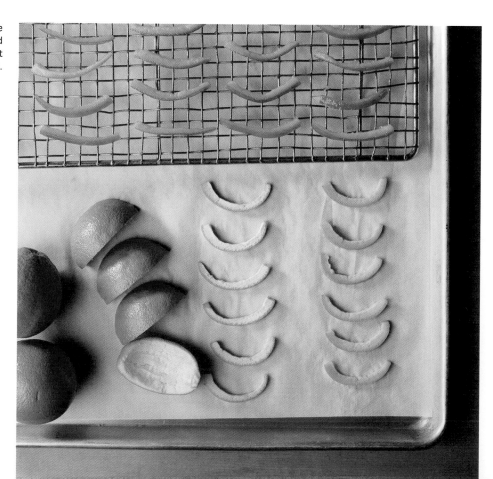

Soft caramels

MAKES 126 PIECES

Evaporated milk	14 fl oz	420 mL
Sugar	14 oz	397 g
Vanilla beans, split and scraped	¾ each	¾ each
Orange zest, grated	½ oz	14 g
Glucose syrup	4 oz	113 g
Butter	½ oz	14 g
Dark chocolate, melted, tempered, for coating and dipping	as needed	as needed

1   On a piece of lightly oiled parchment paper, set up a frame (6 by 12 in/15 by 30 cm) of caramel rulers.

2   Combine the evaporated milk, sugar, vanilla bean seeds and pod, and orange zest in a heavy-bottomed saucepan and bring to a boil, stirring constantly. Add the glucose syrup while continuing to stir. Continue cooking, stirring, to 245°F/118°C (the consistency should resemble the firm ball stage). Stir in the butter.

3   Immediately pour the mixture into the prepared frame. Remove the vanilla bean pod and cool completely.

4   Brush the caramel with a thin layer of tempered dark chocolate and allow the chocolate to set completely.

5   Using caramel cutters, cut the slab into ⅞-in/2-cm squares. Dip in tempered dark chocolate and allow to set.

Toffee

MAKES 400 PIECES

Heavy cream	13 fl oz	390 mL
Sugar	1 lb 6 oz	624 g
Glucose syrup	4 oz	113 g
Vanilla beans, scraped seeds only	¾ each	¾ each

1 Combine all the ingredients in a heavy-bottomed saucepan and cook over medium heat, stirring constantly and occasionally washing down the sides of the pan with a wet pastry brush, until the mixture reaches 293°F/145°C.

2 Pour the toffee onto a silicone baking mat (12 by 16 in/30 by 41 cm); it should be about ⅛ in/3 mm thick. Cool slightly until the toffee begins to set, but not so much that it is brittle.

3 Using caramel cutters, score the toffee into ⅞-in/2-cm squares. Cool completely.

4 Break the toffee apart at the scored marks. If the plain toffee is to be stored, it should be immediately wrapped tightly in plastic wrap or placed in an airtight container.

Raspberry caramels

MAKES 160 PIECES

Evaporated milk	9 fl oz	270 mL
Seedless raspberry purée	6 fl oz	180 mL
Sugar	14 oz	397 g
Lemon zest, grated	1 tbsp	9 g
Glucose syrup	4 oz	113 g
Butter	⅔ oz	19 g
Dark chocolate, melted, tempered, for dipping	as needed	as needed

1 On a silicone baking mat, set up a frame (6½ by 12 in/17 by 30 cm) of caramel rulers.

2 Combine the evaporated milk, raspberry purée, sugar, and lemon zest in a heavy-bottomed saucepan and bring to a boil, stirring constantly. Add the glucose syrup while continuing to stir. Cook, stirring, to 230°F/110°C.

3 Add the butter and continue cooking to 245°F/118°C, or firm ball stage. Immediately pour the caramel into the prepared frame and cool.

4 Brush the cooled caramel with a thin layer of tempered dark chocolate and allow the chocolate to set completely.

5 Using caramel cutters, cut into ⅞-in/2-cm squares. Dip in tempered dark chocolate and allow to set.

Peanut brittle

MAKES 6 LB/2.72 KG

Sugar	1 lb 12 oz	794 g
Water	12 fl oz	360 mL
Glucose syrup	1 lb 4 oz	567 g
Peanuts, blanched	2 lb	907 g
Salt	½ oz	14 g
Butter	2 oz	57 g
Vanilla extract	½ fl oz	15 mL
Baking soda	2 tsp	8 g

1 Combine the sugar, water, and glucose syrup in a heavy-bottomed saucepan and stir to ensure all the sugar is moistened. Bring to a boil over high heat, stirring constantly.

2 When the syrup comes to a boil, stop stirring and skim the surface to remove any impurities. Continue to cook without stirring to 264°F/129°C, occasionally washing down the sides of the pan using a wet pastry brush.

3 Add the peanuts and salt. Continue cooking, stirring gently with a wooden spoon, until the mixture reaches 318°F/159°C.

4 Remove from the heat and stir in the butter and vanilla until incorporated. Stir in the baking soda. Pour the mixture onto a lightly oiled marble work surface. Cool slightly, to a plastic texture.

5 Wearing latex gloves to protect your hands, pull the brittle, working from the edges and breaking off pieces as they harden. (This must be done quickly, before the brittle hardens, so it's best to have two people work on it.) The pieces will be different shapes and sizes.

Pecan butter crunch

MAKES 4 LB 11 OZ/2.13 KG

Butter	1 lb	454 g
Sugar	1 lb	454 g
Water	3 fl oz	90 mL
Salt	⅔ oz	19 g
Pecans, lightly toasted and coarsely chopped	12 oz	340 g
Dark chocolate, melted, tempered	14 oz	397 g

1   Melt the butter in a heavy-bottomed saucepan. Add the sugar, water, and 1 tsp/5 g of the salt. Bring to a rolling boil over high heat. Cook, stirring constantly with a wooden spoon, until the mixture reaches 295°F/146°C and is light golden brown.

2   Pour the mixture onto a full-size silicone baking mat and spread evenly over the mat with an offset metal spatula; the mixture should be about ⅛ in/3 mm thick. Cool completely.

3   Toss the pecans with the remaining salt.

4   Spread the cooled toffee with a thin layer of the tempered chocolate. While the chocolate is still fluid, scatter half of the pecans over the top. Allow the chocolate to set completely.

5   Turn the slab of toffee over and brush with a thin layer of tempered chocolate. While the chocolate is still fluid, scatter the remaining pecans over the top. Allow to set completely, then break into pieces.

Leaf croquant

MAKES 70 PIECES

Almonds, blanched and lightly toasted	1 lb	454 g
Confectioners' sugar	2 oz	57 g
Sugar	1 lb	454 g
Glucose syrup	2 oz	57 g
Dark chocolate, melted, tempered, for dipping	as needed	as needed

1   Grind the almonds and confectioners' sugar to a thick paste in a food processor.

2   Place the sugar in a heavy-bottomed saucepan and cook over medium heat, stirring constantly, to a rich golden brown. Blend in the glucose syrup.

3 Immediately pour the caramel into a rectangle on a sheet pan lined with a silicone baking mat, spreading it evenly over the mat. Cool just enough to be able to handle: it should still be very warm; if it cools too much, it will crack.

4 Spread the almond paste over two-thirds of the caramel. Warm the slab if necessary to make it malleable. Make a three-fold (see page 220), folding the third with no almond paste over first.

5 Warm the slab if necessary and roll it into a rectangle. Make another three-fold, and roll the slab out again. Repeat for a total of five three-folds.

6 Cut the croquant into ⅞-in/2-cm squares. If it has cooled too much to cut, rewarm it.

7 Cool the pieces completely. Dip them in tempered dark chocolate and allow to set.

Hard candies

MAKES 120 PIECES

Water	10 fl oz	300 mL
Sugar	1 lb 11 oz	765 g
Glucose syrup	5½ oz	156 g
Cream of tartar	¼ tsp	1 g
Coloring	as desired	as desired
Flavoring	as desired	as desired

1 Lightly oil a frame (8 by 12 by ½ in/20 by 30 by 1 cm).

2 Combine the water and sugar in a heavy-bottomed saucepan and bring to a boil, stirring constantly. Stir in the glucose syrup and cream of tartar and, if using, add powdered or liquid coloring as desired. Return the syrup to a boil.

3 Continue to cook without stirring, occasionally washing down the sides of the pan using a wet pastry brush, until the mixture reaches 293°F/145°C.

4 Immediately pour into the prepared frame. Cool for 3 minutes, then add paste coloring, if using, and the desired flavoring, and fold it into the sugar.

5 While still hot and pliable, pull out and twist the sugar until satiny in appearance (twisting multiple colors is also possible). Snip into small candies with sharp scissors. Cool.

6 Store in an airtight container.

NOTE Add the flavoring according to the manufacturer's instructions.

Mint fondant

MAKES 100 PIECES

Mint leaves	35 each	35 each
Fondant	1 lb 13 oz	822 g
Brandy	as needed	as needed
Peppermint oil	1 drop	1 drop
Dark chocolate, melted, tempered, for dipping	as needed	as needed

1 Grind the mint leaves with 8 oz/227 g of the fondant in a food processor until smooth.

2 Transfer the mint mixture to a bowl, stir in the remaining 1 lb 5 oz/595 g fondant, and heat over a water bath until the mixture reaches 175°F/79°C. Adjust the consistency with brandy; the fondant should be thin enough to be deposited with the fondant funnel but should not be runny. Blend in the peppermint oil.

3 Dispense with a fondant funnel into molds on a parchment-lined sheet tray. The finished fondant should be ¾ in/2 cm in diameter and ¼ in/6 mm thick. Allow to set until firm, about 10 minutes.

4 Dip the fondants into tempered dark chocolate, transfer to parchment-lined sheet pans, and, when the chocolate has begun to set, use a three-pronged dipping fork to make 3 lines across the surface of each confection.

Fudge

MAKES 4 LB 4 OZ/1.93 KG

Milk	8 fl oz	240 mL
Heavy cream	12 fl oz	360 mL
Sugar	2 lb	907 g
Light corn syrup	6 oz	170 g
Butter	1 oz	28 g
Salt	½ tsp	2.50 g
Unsweetened chocolate, finely chopped	8 oz	227 g
Vanilla extract	1 tbsp	15 mL
Walnut halves	5 oz	142 g

1 Line the bottom and sides of a half sheet pan with aluminum foil.

2 Combine the milk and cream. Pour 8 fl oz/240 mL of the mixture into a heavy-bottomed saucepan, add the sugar and corn syrup, and bring to a boil, stirring constantly to dissolve. Continue to cook and stir until the mixture reaches 230°F/110°C.

3 Add the butter and salt and stir to blend. Slowly add the remaining milk-cream mixture and continue to cook to 236°F/113°C. Add the chocolate and vanilla. Stir twice and pour onto a clean marble surface. Do not stir again. Allow to cool to 120°F/49°C.

4 Agitate the mixture by working it with a metal spatula on the marble surface until it begins to thicken. Quickly add the nuts before the fudge becomes too thick, and pour onto the prepared sheet pan. Allow to set completely before cutting into 1-in/3-cm squares.

VARIATIONS Substitute any of the following for the unsweetened chocolate: white or dark chocolate, peanut butter, or pistachio or praline paste.

You can also omit the walnuts and add 1 oz/28 g of garnish for every 8 oz/227 g fudge. For example, for white chocolate and dried cherry fudge, substitute white chocolate for the unsweetened chocolate and add 8½ oz/241 g dried cherries.

Maple Fudge

MAKES 132 PIECES

Maple syrup	3 lb 1 oz	1.39 kg
Invert sugar	6 oz	170 g
Heavy cream	12 oz	340 g
Glucose syrup	5 oz	142 g
Fondant	6 oz	170 g
Vanilla extract	1 oz	28 g
Walnuts, toasted, chopped	9 oz	255 g

1 Combine the maple syrup, sugar, cream, and glucose syrup in a heavy-bottomed saucepan. Cook the mixture to 245°F/118°C, stirring constantly.

2 Pour onto a marble slab and place the fondant, vanilla extract, and toasted walnuts on top of the cooked syrup.

3 Let the mixture cool to 122°F/50°C. Agitate using a scraper until the mixture turns creamy and opaque, about 8 minutes.

4 Place the fudge into a frame (12 by 12 by ½ in/30 by 30 by 1 cm) set on lightly oiled parchment paper.

5 Place a sheet of oiled parchment paper on top of the fudge and use a rolling pin to flatten the top. Allow the fudge to crystalize before removing the parchment.

6 Cut the fudge into 1-in/3-cm squares.

Frappe chocolate fudge

MAKES 1 HALF SHEET PAN (12⅞ BY 17¾ IN/ 33 BY 45 CM)

FRAPPE		
Gelatin, granulated	2 tsp	7 g
Water, cold	3 fl oz	90 mL
Vanilla extract	1 tsp	5 mL
Sugar	14 oz	397 g
Glucose syrup	8 oz	227 g
Molasses, unsulfured	1½ oz	43 g
FUDGE		
Semisweet chocolate, finely chopped	2 lb	907 g
Unsweetened chocolate, chopped	4 oz	113 g
Vanilla extract	¾ fl oz	23 mL
Frappe (above)	1 lb 10½ oz	751 g
Evaporated milk	18 fl oz	540 mL
Sugar	3 lb 12 oz	1.70 kg
Butter, cut into ¼-in/6-mm slices	12 oz	340 g
Walnuts, chopped	12 oz	340 g

1   To prepare the frappe, bloom the gelatin in 1½ fl oz/45 mL of the cold water with the vanilla extract. Melt over hot water.

2   Cook the sugar, glucose syrup, molasses, and remaining 1½ fl oz/45 mL water to 241°F/116°C, stirring constantly. Let the mixture cool to 208°F/98°C and stir in the gelatin solution.

3   Whip the mixture on high speed with the whip attachment until medium peaks form.

4   To prepare the fudge, line a half sheet pan with aluminum foil. Place the chopped chocolates, vanilla extract, and frappe in a large bowl.

5   Warm the evaporated milk, stir in the sugar, and cook, stirring constantly, to 235°F/113°C. Turn off the heat, add the butter, and stir for 10 seconds to incorporate. Melt the chocolates together.

6   Pour the hot milk-sugar mixture onto a marble slab; add the frappe and chocolate. Agitate the mixture until blended and smooth.

7   Fold in the chopped nuts.

8   Pour immediately into the prepared sheet pan and allow to set to room temperature. Chill before removing from the pan and cutting into 1-in/3-cm squares.

LEFT: Cooked syrup is poured onto the marble and frappe and chocolate are added.

RIGHT: The mixture is agitated until blended and smooth.

VARIETIES OF
FINISHED FUDGE FROM
BACK TO FRONT:
Peanut Butter
Fudge (page 802),
Fudge (page 802),
Maple Fudge
(page 803), Frappe
Chocolate Fudge
(page 804)

Nuss bonbon

MAKES 85 PIECES

Fondant	8 oz	227 g
Almond paste	10 oz	284 g
Sugar	5 oz	142 g
Heavy cream, hot	8 fl oz	240 mL
Walnuts, finely chopped	10 oz	284 g
Dark chocolate, melted, tempered, for coating and dipping	as needed	as needed
Walnut halves	85 each	85 each
Dark chocolate, melted, tempered	as needed	as needed
Cocoa butter	as needed	as needed

1   Grind together the fondant and almond paste in a food processor until smooth.

2   Place the sugar in a heavy-bottomed saucepan and cook over medium heat, stirring constantly, to a rich golden brown, occasionally washing down the sides of the pan using a wet pastry brush.

3   Add the hot cream to the caramel, stirring until blended. Add the almond paste mixture and the chopped walnuts. Cook, stirring constantly, until the mixture reaches 248°F/120°C; it will pull away from the sides of the saucepan.

4   Immediately pour onto a lightly oiled sheet of parchment paper. Place another lightly oiled parchment sheet on top and roll into a slab ½ in/1 cm thick.

5   Brush the slab with a thin layer of tempered dark chocolate and allow the chocolate to set completely.

6   Cut into pieces using a 1-in/3-cm oval praline cutter. Top each bonbon with a walnut half and dip in tempered dark chocolate thinned with cocoa butter.

Gianduja

MAKES 1 LB 8 OZ/680 G

Hazelnuts, blanched and toasted	8 oz	227 g
Confectioners' sugar	8 oz	227 g
Dark chocolate, coarsely chopped	8 oz	227 g

1   Process the nuts and 2 oz/57 g of the sugar together in a food processor to an oily paste. Add the chocolate and remaining sugar and process for 1 to 2 more minutes, until as smooth as possible.

2   Table the gianduja until it begins to thicken.

3   Cool completely. Wrap tightly in plastic wrap and store in a cool, dry place.

VARIATIONS   **MILK CHOCOLATE GIANDUJA** Substitute milk chocolate for the dark chocolate and very lightly toasted blanched almonds for the hazelnuts. Reduce the sugar to 6 oz/170 g.

WHITE CHOCOLATE GIANDUJA Substitute white chocolate for the dark chocolate and very lightly toasted blanched almonds for the hazelnuts. Reduce the sugar to 6 oz/170 g.

Milk chocolate peanut butter gianduja

MAKES 12 OZ/340 G

Milk chocolate, coarsely chopped	4¼ oz	120 g
Creamy peanut butter	7 oz	198 g
Trimoline	1 oz	28 g

1   Melt the chocolate in a bowl over barely simmering water until smooth.

2   Warm the peanut butter separately over barely simmering water. Combine the chocolate and peanut butter and stir until well combined. Stir in the trimoline.

3   Cool completely. Wrap tightly in plastic wrap and store in a cool, dry place.

Branchli Branches

MAKES 55 PIECES

Gianduja (page 807), melted	8 oz	227 g
Praline paste	4 oz	113 g
Confectioners' sugar	4 oz	113 g
Dark chocolate, melted	5 oz	142 g
Coconut oil, melted and cooled to 92°F/33°C	2½ oz	71 g
Nougatine couverture, tempered, for dipping	as needed	as needed

1   Combine the gianduja, praline paste, sugar, chocolate, and coconut oil in a bowl and blend thoroughly. Allow to set.

2   Table the mixture until it reaches a piping consistency.

3   Fill a pastry bag fitted with a #5 plain tip with the mixture and pipe into strips 16 in/41 cm long and ¼ in/6 mm thick onto parchment paper. Allow to set until firm.

4   Cut into pieces 2 in/5 cm long. Dip into tempered nougatine couverture and allow to set completely.

Three brothers

MAKES 100 PIECES

Gianduja (page 807)	1 lb	454 g
Hazelnut dragées (page 793)	1 lb	454 g
Dark chocolate, melted, thinned with cocoa butter, and tempered, for dipping	as needed	as needed

1   Table the gianduja until it reaches a piping consistency.

2   Fill a pastry bag fitted with a #3 straight tip with the gianduja and pipe into ¾-in/2-cm bulbs on a parchment-lined sheet pan.

3   Place 3 dragée hazelnuts together on each bulb of gianduja. Allow to set.

4   Dip in thinned tempered dark chocolate and allow the chocolate to set completely.

Tremors

MAKES 120 PIECES

Dried cherries, chopped	3 oz		85 g
Sliced almonds, blanched, toasted, and coarsely chopped	5 oz		142 g
Gianduja (page 807), melted	1 lb		454 g
Milk chocolate, melted, tempered	1 lb		454 g

1   Line 4 triangle molds with plastic wrap.

2   Combine the cherries and almonds with the gianduja, folding them in with a rubber spatula.

3   Table the mixture until it is very cool to the touch.

4   Spread the mixture into the prepared molds. Allow to set at room temperature. Refrigerate for 10 minutes to allow the mixture to release from the mold.

5   Remove the triangular strips from the molds. Brush with a thin layer of the tempered milk chocolate and allow it to set completely.

6   Enrobe one strip in tempered milk chocolate. (Enrobe and slice only one strip at a time; if the chocolate sets too hard, it will crack when cut.) Immediately remove the strip from the rack. When the chocolate is just set, place on a parchment-lined sheet pan and slice into ½-in/1-cm pieces. Repeat with the remaining strips.

Pistachio marzipan

MAKES 1 LB 9 OZ/709 G

Almonds, blanched	4½ oz	128 g
Pistachios, blanched	4½ oz	128 g
Sugar	1 lb	454 g
Water	5 fl oz	150 mL
Glucose syrup	2 oz	57 g
Kirsch, rum, or other spirit	as needed	as needed

1   Lightly oil a clean marble slab or silicone baking mat.

2   Combine the almonds and pistachios in a food processor and pulse just until coarsely ground. Set aside.

3   Combine the sugar, water, and glucose syrup in a heavy-bottomed saucepan and stir to ensure all the sugar is moistened. Bring to a boil over high heat, stirring to dissolve the sugar. When the syrup reaches a boil, stop stirring and skim the surface to remove any impurities. Continue to cook without stirring, occasionally washing down the sides of the pan using a wet pastry brush, to 250°F/121°C, or hard ball stage.

4   Add the ground nuts to the syrup, stir only twice, and immediately pour the mixture onto the prepared surface. Allow to cool to room temperature.

5   Grind the mixture to a paste in a food processor, adding only as much of the spirit as necessary for processing. Add a little spirit if the marzipan starts to separate.

6   If storing the marzipan, wrap tightly in plastic wrap and store in a cool, dry place.

Walnut marzipan

MAKES 1 LB 9 OZ/709 G

Almonds, blanched	4½ oz	128 g
Walnuts	4½ oz	128 g
Sugar	1 lb	454 g
Water	5 fl oz	150 mL
Glucose syrup	2 oz	57 g
Kirsch, rum, or other spirit	as needed	as needed

1   Lightly oil a clean marble slab or silicone baking mat.

2   Combine the almonds and walnuts in a food processor and pulse just until coarsely ground. Set aside.

3   Combine the sugar, water, and glucose syrup in a heavy-bottomed saucepan and stir to ensure all the sugar is moistened. Bring to a boil over high heat, stirring to dissolve the sugar. When the syrup reaches a boil, stop stirring and skim the surface to remove any impurities. Continue to cook without stirring, occasionally washing down the sides of the pan using a wet pastry brush, to 250°F/127°C, or hard ball stage.

4   Add the ground nuts to the syrup, stir only twice, and immediately pour the mixture onto the prepared surface. Allow to cool to room temperature.

5   Grind the mixture to a paste in a food processor, adding only as much of the spirit as necessary for processing. Add a little more spirit if the marzipan starts to separate.

6   If storing the marzipan, wrap tightly in plastic wrap and store in a cool, dry place.

NOTE   Alternatively, to finish, roll the marzipan out ⅜ in/9 mm thick. Cut into 1-in/3-cm diamonds. Dip in tempered dark chocolate. When the chocolate is almost set but still tacky, place a toasted walnut half on top of each diamond.

Tree trunks

MAKES 118 PIECES

Gianduja (page 807), melted	1 lb	454 g
Pistachio marzipan	1 lb	454 g
Cocoa butter, melted	as needed	as needed
Dark chocolate, melted, tempered, for coating	as needed	as needed

1 Table the gianduja until it is firm enough to hold its shape when piped.

2 Fill a pastry bag fitted with a #5 or #6 straight tip with the gianduja and pipe cylinders 16 in/41 cm long onto a parchment-lined sheet pan. Allow to set until firm, 10 to 15 minutes.

3 Roll the marzipan out on a clean marble slab into a rectangle 16 in/41 cm long and ¼ in/6 mm thick. Brush with a thin layer of cocoa butter.

4 Place one cylinder of gianduja on the marzipan and roll up the marzipan to encase the gianduja, overlapping the seam slightly; cut the marzipan at that point. Smooth the seam, then roll until as smooth as possible.

5 Brush the log with tempered chocolate to coat. Continue to brush until the chocolate starts to set, creating a bark-like pattern. Slice ½ in/1 cm thick on a slight bias. Do not let the chocolate set completely before cutting.

Fruit gelées

MAKES 125 PIECES

Applesauce	11 oz	312 g
Fruit purée of choice	1 lb	454 g
Glucose syrup	3 oz	85 g
Pectin powder	1 oz	28 g
Sugar	3 lb 3½ oz, plus as needed for coating	1.46 kg, plus as needed for coating
Lemon juice	1 fl oz	30 mL

1 Spread the applesauce in a hotel pan and place in a 200°F/93°C oven for 30 minutes to remove moisture.

2 Line a half sheet pan with parchment paper.

3 Combine the applesauce, fruit purée, and glucose syrup in a heavy-bottomed saucepan. Blend the pectin with 3½ oz/99 g of the sugar and, off the heat, whisk into the fruit purée mixture. Bring to a rolling boil over medium heat, stirring constantly.

4 Add 1 lb 8 oz/680 g of the sugar and return to a rolling boil. Add the remaining 1 lb 8 oz/680 g sugar, return to a rolling boil, and boil for 2½ minutes.

5 Stir in the lemon juice. Pour onto the prepared half sheet pan and allow to set overnight.

6 Sprinkle the fruit slab with sugar. Using a guitar, cut into 1¼-in/3-cm squares. Toss the gelées in sugar to coat.

Gelées on a guitar to be cut into bite-size portions

Marshmallows

MAKES 1 HALF SHEET PAN (12⅞ BY 17¾ IN/ 33 BY 45 CM)

Gelatin, granulated	1¼ oz	35 g
Water, cold	16 fl oz	480 mL
Granulated sugar	1 lb 8 oz	680 g
Glucose syrup	12 oz	340 g
Honey	12 oz	340 g
Vanilla extract	1 tbsp	15 mL
Confectioners' sugar, for cutting	as needed	as needed

1   Line a half sheet pan with parchment paper.

2   Bloom the gelatin in 8 fl oz/240 mL of the cold water.

3   Combine the granulated sugar, glucose syrup, honey, and the remaining 8 fl oz/240 mL water in a heavy-bottomed saucepan and stir to ensure all the sugar is moistened. Bring to a boil over high heat, stirring to dissolve the sugar. When the syrup reaches a boil, stop stirring and skim the surface to remove any impurities. Continue to cook without stirring, occasionally washing down the sides of the pan using a wet pastry brush, to 252°F/122°C. Remove from the heat and cool to approximately 210°F/99°C.

LEFT: The marshmallow mixture is spread into a sheet pan.

RIGHT: Cutting the marshmallows requires a fair amount of confectioners' sugar.

4 While the syrup is cooling, melt the gelatin over simmering water. Remove from the heat and stir in the vanilla.

5 Stir the gelatin mixture into the syrup. Whip the mixture on high speed with the whip attachment until medium peaks form.

6 Spread the mixture evenly in the prepared sheet pan. The easiest way to do this is to place the mixture in the pan, place a sheet of oiled parchment paper on top, and roll out the marshmallow into the pan. Allow to set completely before unmolding and cutting.

7 Remove the slab from the pan, inverting onto a work surface, and peel off the paper. Cut the marshmallows into 1-in/3-cm squares, dusting with confectioners' sugar as necessary.

VARIATION   **CINNAMON MARSHMALLOWS** Add 1 tbsp/6 g ground cinnamon in step 5 after the gelatin is added.

Seafoam

MAKES 125 PIECES

Sugar	3 lb	1.36 kg
Glucose syrup	1 lb 10 oz	737 g
Water	14 fl oz	420 mL
Honey	1½ oz	43 g
Gelatin solution (page 898)	¼ oz	7 g
Baking soda	1½ oz	43 g

1 Butter and lightly flour 2 disposable aluminum half hotel pans.

2 Cook the sugar, glucose syrup, and water to 280°F/138°C, stirring constantly just until the sugar has dissolved. Stop stirring once the mixture comes to a boil.

3 Add the honey and continue to cook to 302°F/150°C.

4 Remove the pan from the heat and allow to cool for 5 minutes.

5 Blend in the gelatin solution. Blend in the baking soda and allow the mixture to rise to the top of the pan.

6 Pour into the prepared pans. Cool overnight.

7 Remove the slab from the pan, inverting onto a work surface, and peel off the paper. Cut into 1-in/3-cm pieces.

NOTE   This confection may be dipped in tempered dark chocolate after cutting.

Nougat montélimar

MAKES 100 PIECES

Sugar	11½ oz	326 g
Water	3½ fl oz	105 mL
Glucose syrup	2 oz	57 g
Honey, boiling	8 oz	227 g
Egg whites	2 oz	57 g
Vanilla beans, scraped seeds only	½ each	½ each
Almonds, blanched and toasted	7 oz	198 g
Hazelnuts, blanched and toasted	2½ oz	71 g
Pistachios, blanched	2½ oz	71 g
Assorted dried fruit	5 oz	142 g
Sliced almonds, blanched and toasted	2½ oz	71 g
Cocoa butter, melted	3½ oz	99 g
Dark chocolate, melted, tempered, for dipping	as needed	as needed

1   Combine 11 oz/312 g of the sugar, the water, and glucose syrup in a heavy-bottomed saucepan and stir to ensure all the sugar is moistened. Bring to a boil over high heat, stirring to dissolve the sugar. When the syrup reaches a boil, stop stirring and skim the surface to remove any impurities. Continue to cook without stirring, occasionally washing down the sides of the pan using a wet pastry brush, to 310°F/154°C.

2   Add the honey and bring once more to 310°F/154°C.

3   Meanwhile, whip the egg whites and the remaining ½ oz/14 g sugaon medium speed with the whip attachment until soft peaks form.

4   With the mixer on medium speed, pour the hot syrup into the egg whites in a fine stream, beating until fully incorporated. Continue to whip until lighter in color, about 4 minutes; the meringue should still be warm.

5   Warm the vanilla bean seeds, blanched almonds, hazelnuts, pistachios, dried fruit, and sliced almonds in a low oven. Fold into the meringue.

6 Transfer the nougat onto an oiled sheet of parchment paper and roll out to ¼ in/6 mm thick. Cool completely.

7 Cut the slab into strips ¾ in/2 cm wide. Cut the strips into 1-in/3-cm pieces. Stand the pieces of nougat on end (that is, on one short end). Brush the top edge of each one with melted cocoa butter to seal it. Dip only to the upper edge in tempered dark chocolate, so that the top surface is uncoated nougat.

VARIATION For a different finish, the slab of nougat can be coated on both sides with tempered dark chocolate and then cut into pieces.

Rolling out the nougat   Cutting the nougat

Soft chocolate nougat

MAKES 100 PIECES

Granulated sugar	1 lb 6 oz	624 g
Water	6 fl oz	180 mL
Glucose syrup	1 lb 9 oz	709 g
Egg whites	2 oz	57 g
Vanilla extract	1 tbsp	15 mL
Nonfat dry milk	4½ oz	128 g
Confectioners' sugar	1½ oz	43 g
Dark chocolate, melted	4 oz	113 g
Cocoa butter, melted	1½ oz	43 g
Dark chocolate, melted, tempered, for dipping	as needed	as needed

1   Combine the granulated sugar, water, and 1 lb 7 oz/652 g of the glucose syrup in a heavy-bottomed saucepan and stir to ensure all the sugar is moistened. Bring to a boil over high heat, stirring to dissolve the sugar. When the syrup reaches a boil, stop stirring and skim the surface to remove any impurities. Continue to cook without stirring, occasionally washing down the sides of the pan using a wet pastry brush, to 252°F/122°C.

2   When the mixture reaches 230°F/110°C, in a mixer on medium speed, with the whip attachment, begin to whip the egg whites and the remaining 2 oz/57 g glucose syrup until the whites form medium peaks. Add the vanilla extract.

3   When the syrup reaches 252°F/122°C, pour it into the egg whites in a fine stream, whipping until fully incorporated. Let cool slightly.

4   Sift together the dry milk and confectioners' sugar. Slowly fold the mixture into the meringue until fully incorporated. Cool until just warm to the touch.

5   Blend together the melted dark chocolate and cocoa butter. Add to the meringue and fold to combine.

6   Pour the mixture onto a sheet of oiled parchment paper. Place another sheet of oiled parchment paper on top and roll the mixture to ⅜ in/9 mm thick. Allow to cool completely.

7   Brush the nougat with a thin layer of tempered dark chocolate and allow the chocolate to set completely.

8   Cut the nougat into 1-in/3-cm squares with a hot knife, wiping the knife clean after each cut. Dip in tempered dark chocolate and let set completely.

NOTE   The texture of this nougat improves as it crystallizes after dipping.

(OPPOSITE PAGE) FINISHED VARIETIES OF NOUGATS FROM TOP TO BOTTOM: Nougat Montélimar (page 816), Soft Chocolate Nougat (above), variation of Nougat Montélimar with dried cherries, dried apricots, almonds, pistachios, and hazelnuts (page 816)

Chocolate nut clusters

MAKES 5½ OZ/156 G

Pecans, coarsely chopped	2 oz	57 g
Sugar	1½ oz	43 g
Water	½ oz	14 g
Dark chocolate, 64%, chopped	1½ oz	43 g

1   Combine the pecans, sugar, and water and cook, stirring constantly, to a light caramel color.

2   Spread the mixture on a parchment-lined half sheet pan. Freeze for 1 hour.

3   Melt the chocolate in a medium bowl and bring into temper.

4   Break apart the nuts into small clusters and drop into the chocolate. Stir until the clusters are well coated. Separate the clusters on a sheet of parchment paper.

5   Let the clusters set completely. Store in an airtight container.

NOTE   The mixture may be used as the base for individual pastries or desserts by placing at the bottom of a mold.

chapter twenty-two

Décor

décor is the finishing touch given to any pastry or cake. The pastry chef employs a variety of techniques and materials to craft a look that not only displays creativity and skill but also sets his or her pastries, cakes, and other desserts apart.

Tools for décor

Using a pastry bag and coupler

Buttercream or icing décor work requires many different and specialized pastry tips. When working with many different tips or colors of buttercream or icing, it is most efficient to use a coupler with the pastry bag. A coupler is a two-piece attachment that allows piping tips to be easily interchanged without having to empty the bag.

Making a parchment piping cone

Preparing and using a parchment piping cone is an important part of décor work. To make a parchment cone, it is easiest to use a precut sheet of parchment paper (16 by 24 in/41 by 61 cm). Otherwise, cut a sheet this size from a roll of parchment paper. Place the parchment sheet on a flat surface with the length running parallel to the edge of the work surface. Take the lower left-hand corner and bring it up so that the point of the corner is adjacent to and level with the upper right-hand corner; it should look like two peaks of identical height. Firmly crease the fold. Insert a long, sharp knife (preferably not a serrated slicer) into the folded paper with the edge of the blade toward the creased edge and carefully cut the paper in half at the crease, using a single smooth stroke. The cut edge of each sheet will form the point of each piping cone, so it must be sharp and exact. A clean cut, not possible when tearing the paper or cutting it with scissors, enables piped icings or glazes to fall in a clean, straight line. The cone will also last longer because the clean edge will not absorb moisture as quickly as a ragged one would.

A small piping cone permits closer and tighter control, necessary for the fine work of piping letters, borders, and individual piped designs. Cut the parchment paper into quarters and use the four rectangles (8 by 12 in/20 by 30 cm) to make smaller cones as desired.

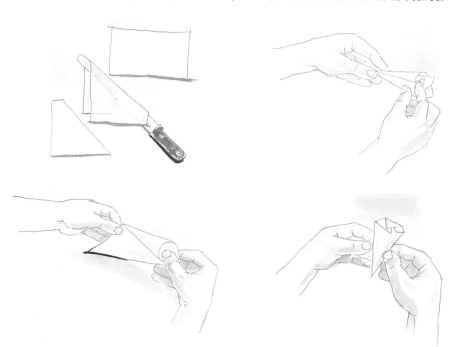

TOP LEFT: Folding the parchment paper on the diagonal and cutting with a knife

BOTTOM LEFT: Making a pivot point along the longest edge opposite the 90-degree angle

TOP RIGHT: Rolling into a funnel shape, making a fine point and folding over the paper to fix the cone in place from the sugar

BOTTOM RIGHT: Sealing the filled cone by crimping and folding over the top

Piping buttercream borders and flowers

The technique for piping buttercream is similar to that for piping spritz cookies. The pastry bag is placed in the starting position, pressure is applied to pipe out the buttercream, and then the pressure is released just before the bag is lifted away, leaving the finished décor. By combining different tips and different motions—for example, by moving the tip in an up-and-down, circular, or back-and-forth motion—you can create many different patterns and effects.

Piping a shell border

1. Fit a pastry bag with a star tip. Holding the piping bag at a 45-degree angle, place the tip close to the surface of the cake.

2. Squeeze the bag, allowing the icing to fan forward in a rounded shape while lifting the tip slightly.

3. Lower the tip back to the surface while slowly relaxing the pressure on the bag.

4. Stop squeezing the bag and pull the tip away from the rounded head of the shell, keeping the tip on the surface of the cake to form the "tail" of the shell.

5. To form the next shell, place the star tip at the end of the first shell and repeat.

Piping a buttercream leaf

1. Fit a piping bag with a leaf tip.

2. Place the tip close to the surface and pipe out icing to form a base for the leaf.

3. Relaxing the pressure on the piping bag, pull the tip up and away from the leaf base to form the rest of the leaf. Stop exerting pressure on the bag as you pull the tip away to form the tip of the leaf.

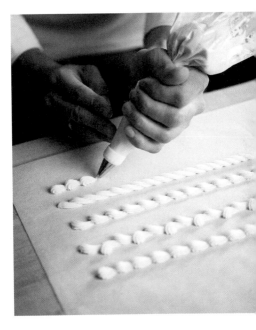

Piping a shell border

Piping a buttercream rose

1. Fit a piping bag with a rose tip. Attach a small square of parchment paper to the top of a rose nail with a small dot of icing to make it easier to remove the rose once the icing has set. Hold the piping bag in your dominant hand and the rose nail in the other. Hold the bag so that the opening in the piping tip is vertical and the wider end is at the bottom.

2. The rose will be built on a cone of icing. To make the cone, place the wide end of the piping tip on the surface of the nail, with the narrower end angled slightly inward. Squeeze the bag while turning the nail clockwise, keeping the piping bag and tip in the same position.

3. To form the first inner petal of the rose, place the wide end of the tip on the cone of icing, with the narrower end angled slightly inward. Squeeze the piping bag while pulling it away from the cone, creating a ribbon of icing; at the same time, turn the rose nail counterclockwise, wrapping the ribbon of icing up and around the inner cone, ending by overlapping the point at which you began piping.

4. To form the first row of three petals, place the wide end of the piping tip near the base of the inner petal, with the narrow end pointing straight up. Position the first petal over the opening of the inner petal: Pipe a ribbon of icing around and down, turning the nail counterclockwise one-third of a turn at the same time. Form the next two petals following the same procedure, beginning each petal near the center of the previous one.

5. For a larger rose, keep adding rows of petals in the same manner, increasing the number in each row and always adding an odd number of petals to keep the rose from looking square or boxy.

6. Once the icing is set, remove the rose from the nail. Use a small metal spatula to remove the rose from the paper and place it as desired.

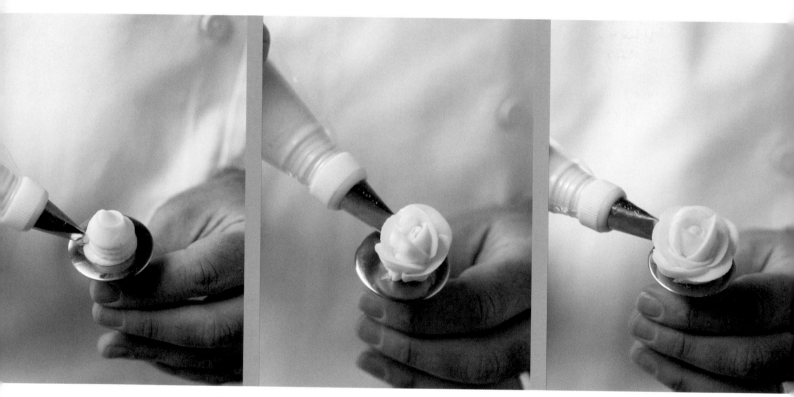

LEFT: **Creating the inner cone of icing** MIDDLE: **Piping the first petals** RIGHT: **Adding petals**

Working with royal icing

Royal icing décor is typically piped on parchment or plastic sheets, allowed to dry, and stored in airtight containers for later use. Royal icing is easily colored using food coloring or by airbrushing it. Generally, royal icing is not intended to be consumed, at least in any measurable quantity, as it has no flavor and is only sweet.

Care must be used in handling royal icing. When exposed to air, the icing dries quickly, becoming hard and brittle. If any of the dried icing gets incorporated into the icing being used for décor work, the hardened particles will block the piping tip. For this reason, it is always good practice to keep the sides of the container holding the icing clean. Remove any dried particles of icing from the sides of the container promptly with a clean damp cloth before they can fall back into the icing. While you work, keep a clean, damp paper towel directly on the surface of the icing in the container to prevent a crust form forming.

Store royal icing under refrigeration with a piece of plastic wrap or a dampened paper towel placed directly on the surface. Cover the bowl or container tightly with plastic wrap to keep it airtight.

For piping royal icing, a small parchment cone may be used, but for intricate work, a very fine round writing pastry tip is usually best. The tip facilitates the production of a perfectly formed bead of icing, which in turn will enhance the quality of the décor.

Royal icing is often used to execute elaborate designs that are then dried and fitted or otherwise secured onto cakes and décor pieces. Usually a template or pattern is used to make this type of décor. Place the template or pattern under a piece of acetate or other food-safe plastic and secure it with tape or paper clips so it does not slip as you pipe the figure by tracing the template. Using a template ensures consistent results, and the technique is especially useful when the same pattern is to be repeated on a cake or décor piece.

Filling an outlined shape with royal icing

When making large or very intricate patterns, it is usually necessary to pipe more than one layer of royal icing. Pay close attention to any connecting points or joints to ensure the finished piece will be strong enough to be lifted from the plastic and secured to the finished cake or other object. As you are planning the pattern of loops, keep in mind that loops that cross, intersect, or lie on top of one another result in greater stability of the sugar work.

Another technique often used with royal icing is called flood work. To do flood work or to make a run-out, an outline of a pattern or motif is piped onto acetate and allowed to dry until firm. Then thinned royal icing is used to fill in the interior of the pattern. This icing should be thin enough to fill in the design easily, with little extra manipulation or spreading necessary, minimizing the chance that any lines or imprints will be left in the finished piece. A good way to test the consistency of royal icing for flood work is to have the icing in a container, spoon some out, and allow it to drip back into the container. The drips going back into the container should disappear without a trace at the count of ten.

Flood work and run-outs with royal icing

1. Outline each shape with a thin line of piped royal icing. Allow the icing to dry.

2. Thin the remaining royal icing with water until a small amount dropped back into the bowl from the tip of a spoon flattens back into the surface in 10 seconds. Color the icing as desired.

3. Fit a piping bag with a #2 plain tip. Fill the bag halfway with the royal icing. To fill the outlines with icing, begin at the edges of each one and work toward the center. At the edge of the shape, hold the tip a short distance away from the piped outline and allow the icing to flow toward the outline, creating a rounded edge. Continue piping, allowing each successive pass of icing to flow into the previous one, creating a smooth surface.

4. Place the shapes under a heat lamp or other heat source to dry. The more quickly the icing dries, the shinier the finish.

String work with royal icing

1. Thin the royal icing to a medium-thick consistency. Strain it through a double layer of cheesecloth.

2. Fit a pastry bag with a #0 or #00 plain tip. Fill the bag halfway with the royal icing. Test the consistency of the icing by piping a string. If the icing is too soft, it will sag and break under its weight; if the icing is too stiff, it will not fall into a smooth string. Adjust the consistency of the icing if necessary with confectioners' sugar, water, or additional egg whites.

3. Touch the tip of the pastry tip to the first attachment point, then pull the bag away while applying even pressure to it, allowing the string of icing to fall away from the tip. Do not move the tip downward; simply allow the icing to fall in a smooth curve. When the loop of icing is the desired length, touch the tip of the pastry tip to the next point to attach the string.

4. Repeat the process, using care to produce loops of the same length each time. As you are planning the pattern of loops, keep in mind that loops that cross, intersect, or lie on top of one another result in greater stability of the sugar work.

Creating a string with royal icing

Overpiping

The overpiping technique is mostly seen in England and is their most used piping discipline. When a cake is displayed with the overpiping technique, it gives a shadowing effect and gives the piping height because it is stacked. This is an elegant approach for most cakes. Because the piping has eye appeal, it's striking for merchandising displays.

There are many borders that can be overpiped. Whatever border you identify, be sure to make the first layer of piping as straight as possible. Once you have established a solid first line, the rest of the lines that you will be stacking should be straight.

When overpiping using royal icing, as demonstrated, you should identify a series of round tips suitable for the application. In most cases a #3 tip for the base line is good to start with. When you start to stack the lines, identify the next smaller tip in the series of tips, in this case a #2. Follow this method of tip selection until you reach the desired finish to your stack. There are tips that are as fine as #00.

Do not overfill the parchment bag with icing. When piping with a small tip, a half-ounce of icing per bag should cover one surface of the cake. Each time you fill a small parchment bag with icing it should be worked to a smooth consistency.

Overpiping technique

Tempered chocolate décor

Using tempered chocolate (which will harden) rather than melted chocolate for piping enables the confectioner or pastry chef to pipe designs onto parchment paper, allow them to set firm, and then remove them from the paper and place them as desired on finished products for ornamentation and garnish. Because the piped details will become rigid once set, they can be made ahead and stored for later use. In addition, tempered chocolate designs can be used for numerous décor effects, as they do not have to lie flat. When piping tempered chocolate, use a small parchment cone, because the chocolate can easily harden in the cone if the environment is cool.

Piping chocolate filigrees and writing

1. Make a parchment cone and fill it no more than halfway with piping chocolate. Fold over the top and cut a tiny hole in the tip of the cone.

2. Touch the tip of the cone to the surface on which you are piping and, exerting even pressure, pull the cone up and away from the surface to create a string of chocolate. Keeping the piped string of chocolate constant and even, move the parchment cone slowly and evenly to control the way in which the string falls onto the surface. To create small loops in the filigree or writing, for example, pause at the top of the piped element and allow the string to fall in a small loop.

3. To end a motif or word, touch the tip of the parchment cone back to the surface.

Tempered chocolate stencils and cutouts

Stencils and cutouts have many applications. They can be used as a garnish for a pastry, cake, or plated dessert, as the base for piped confections, or, in décor work, as either the focal point or a component of a larger display piece.

Stencils and cutouts may be made of white, milk, or dark chocolate. Generally, the chocolate should be spread thin, but the exact thinness will depend on the intended use.

Making chocolate triangles (spread-and-cut method)

1. Pour tempered chocolate onto a sheet of parchment paper. With an offset spatula, spread the chocolate into a thin, even layer. Allow the chocolate to set slightly.

2. Run a cake comb lengthwise through the chocolate in a wave pattern, slightly overlapping each pass so that there are no uncombed areas of chocolate. Try to keep the thickness of the chocolate even throughout.

3. Allow the chocolate to set until it becomes fudgy. It should be soft enough that you can draw a knife point through it without cracking but set enough so that the cut does not refill with chocolate.

4. Using a ruler and the point of a paring knife, cut the chocolate into triangles with 1¾-in/4-cm sides and a 4-in/10-cm base: First cut the sheet of chocolate lengthwise into strips 4 in/10 cm wide. Then mark the edges of each strip at intervals of 1¾ in/4 cm. Using the ruler, connect the marks on the diagonal to make triangles.

5. Slide the sheet of chocolate onto the back of a sheet pan. Place another sheet of parchment paper on top of the chocolate. Place a second sheet pan, bottom side down, on top of the parchment paper. Grasp both sheet pans firmly and flip the sheet pan sandwich over. Remove what is now the top sheet pan. The parchment paper on which you spread the chocolate is now facing up. Carefully peel this parchment paper away from the chocolate triangles, starting at one corner. Removing the parchment paper at this point allows the chocolate to set completely without curling.

NOTES For a very shiny finished surface, spread the chocolate onto a sheet of acetate rather than parchment paper. When cutting the partially set chocolate into triangles, cut completely through the acetate. Leave the chocolate triangles on the acetate until time for service so that the surface does not become marred. Do not touch the shiny surface of the chocolate, as it will pick up fingerprints readily.

Any shapes can be cut out of spread chocolate, with or without combing it first. You can use ring cutters to make disks, or templates made out of stiff plastic or paper.

If desired, stripe the chocolate in the same manner as for striped chocolate cigarettes (page 830).

Combing the chocolate

Cutting out triangles when the chocolate is almost set

Making striped chocolate triangles

1. Cut two strips of acetate 6 by 18 in/15 by 46 cm.

2. Spread white chocolate 1⁄16 in/1.5 mm thick over one of the strips. Using the smallest side of a square-toothed cake comb, comb through the white chocolate to create a zigzag pattern. Allow the chocolate to set slightly.

3. Spread dark chocolate thinly and evenly over the white chocolate. Transfer the acetate strip to a cutting board and allow the chocolate to set for 10 seconds.

4. Place the other acetate strip on top of the dark chocolate. Cut the strip lengthwise in half to make two strips 3 in/8 cm wide. Cut triangles with a base 1 in/3 cm wide out of each strip.

5. Place another cutting board on top of the triangles to keep them flat. Allow the triangles to set for a minimum of 3 hours. Remove the acetate from the triangles when you are ready to use them.

Making marbleized chocolate plaques

1. Drizzle tempered white chocolate, milk chocolate, and dark chocolate onto a sheet of acetate, overlapping the different colors of chocolate. With a long offset spatula, spread the chocolates into thin, even layers, allowing them to merge and flow together. Do not mix the chocolates too vigorously, or the finished plaques will look muddy instead of attractively marbled.

2. Allow the chocolate to set until it becomes fudgy. It should be soft enough that you can draw a knife point through it without cracking but set enough so that the cut does not refill with chocolate.

3. Using a ruler and the point of a paring knife, cut the chocolate into rectangles 2 by 2¾ in/5 by 7 cm: First cut the sheet of chocolate lengthwise into strips 2¾ in/7 cm wide. Then mark the edges of the strips at intervals of 2 in/5 cm. Using the ruler, connect the marks from top to bottom.

4. Slide the sheet of chocolate onto the back of a sheet pan. Place another sheet of parchment paper on top of the chocolate. Place a second sheet pan, bottom side down, on top of the parchment paper. Grasp both sheet pans firmly and flip the sheet pan sandwich over. Leave the sheet pans stacked until the chocolate is completely set. Leave the chocolate rectangles on the acetate until you are ready to use them.

Making chocolate cigarettes

1. Drizzle a thin line of tempered chocolate onto a marble surface, parallel to the edge of the marble. Using an offset spatula, spread the chocolate in a thin, even layer. Let the chocolate set slightly.

2. When the chocolate is somewhat set, place a Plexiglas strip the width of the desired finished length of the cigarettes on top of the chocolate and evenly trim the edges of the chocolate strip with a bench scraper or putty knife.

3. With the bench scraper or putty knife, begin scraping cigarettes from one short end of the chocolate strip with a quick, abrupt motion; it should feel as though you are trying to scrape off a thin layer of marble. If the chocolate is not set enough, the cigarettes will not curl properly; and if the chocolate has set too much, the cigarettes will crack and break. Chocolate that is just slightly too cool can be warmed with the palm of your hand.

4. To trim the cigarettes, warm a sharp knife. Place the blade at the desired point and allow the heat of the knife to melt the chocolate.

Forming dark chocolate cigarettes

Making mini-cigarettes

1. Spread tempered chocolate on a marble surface no wider than the width of the tool you will be using to form the cigarettes, or, when the chocolate is somewhat set, use the tip of a paring knife to score the chocolate into narrow strips. Let the chocolate set briefly.

2. Using the same motion as described above, scrape the chocolate into mini-cigarettes. It is important to scrape the chocolate with a motion directly parallel to the length of the strip; otherwise, the mini-cigarettes will curl into each other and be difficult to separate.

Making striped chocolate cigarettes

1. Drizzle a small amount of tempered white chocolate onto a marble surface. With an offset spatula, spread the chocolate in a strip parallel to the edge of the marble. Allow the chocolate to set until thick in consistency.

2. Draw a square-toothed cake comb firmly through the chocolate, scraping all the way down to the marble to make thin lines of chocolate. Try to keep the lines of chocolate straight and parallel to the edge of the marble.

3. Working quickly, drizzle dark chocolate over the white chocolate and spread it thinly and evenly with an offset spatula. The dark chocolate should fill the channels left in the white chocolate by the comb; spread it thin enough so that the white chocolate shows through the dark chocolate.

Backing the striped white chocolate with dark chocolate

4. When the chocolate is no longer tacky but still pliable and somewhat soft, place a Plexiglas strip the width of the desired finished length of the cigarettes on top of the chocolate and evenly trim the edges of the chocolate strip with a bench scraper or putty knife.

5. With the bench scraper or putty knife, begin scraping cigarettes from one short end of the chocolate strip with a quick, scraping motion; it should feel as though you are trying to scrape off a thin layer of marble. If the chocolate is too warm, the cigarettes will not curl properly; and if the chocolate is too cool, the cigarettes will crack and break. Chocolate that is just slightly too cool can be warmed with the palm of your hand.

6. To trim the cigarettes, warm a sharp knife. Place the blade at the desired point and allow the heat of the knife to melt the chocolate.

VARIATION **MARBLED CIGARETTES** Marble the chocolate as for marbleized chocolate plaques, then shape as for chocolate cigarettes.

Making chocolate fans

1. Fill a parchment piping cone with tempered chocolate. Pipe four or five quarter-size rounds of chocolate onto a parchment-lined sheet pan, spacing the rounds about 4 in/10 cm apart.

2. With the back of a spoon, spread chocolate across the parchment paper in an arc away from one round of chocolate. Repeat the motion four more times, beginning each arc at approximately the same point and making each arc shorter than the one before it, slightly overlapping the arcs. This motion creates a "fan" of chocolate with two ridges in it. Do not make the chocolate too thin or the fan will break. The base of the fan should be thicker than the top edges. Repeat with the remaining rounds of chocolate. Allow the chocolate to set completely.

3. The fans can be used as they are, or the top edges can be neatened with a warmed round metal cutter.

Making chocolate bands

1. Place a strip of acetate the desired width of the chocolate band on a marble surface or piece of parchment paper. Drizzle tempered chocolate onto the acetate. With an offset spatula, spread the chocolate thinly and evenly over the entire surface of the acetate; some of the chocolate should go over the long sides of the acetate.

2. Allow the chocolate to set slightly, so that the acetate can be picked up without the chocolate running. The chocolate should still be fluid enough to adhere to the surface or item where it is applied.

3. Pull up a corner of the acetate, then carefully lift up the acetate strip and apply the chocolate band to the desired surface. Place the band carefully, starting with one end; once it touches the surface, it cannot be moved without damaging the chocolate.

4. Peel away ½ in/1 cm of the acetate from the end you first attached, and overlap the other end of the band so that the chocolate adheres to itself. While the chocolate is still slightly tacky, use scissors to trim the acetate and the chocolate where it overlaps.

5. To preserve its shiny finish, leave the acetate on the chocolate until time for service.

Making chocolate shavings

1. Brace a large block of tempered chocolate against the near edge of a parchment-lined sheet pan.

2. Hold a sharp chef's knife so that the flat of the blade is straight up and down and the tip of the blade is pointing to your left. Using a smooth scraping motion, pull the blade across the surface of the chocolate, without digging the blade into the chocolate. To create small shavings, use a short scraping motion; for larger shavings, use a longer motion.

3. Use an offset spatula to move the shavings. Do not pick up the shavings with your hands or they will melt.

Making chocolate ruffles

1. Place a sheet pan in a low-temperature oven until it is just warm. Have ready a bowl of melted but not tempered chocolate that is also warm (just above body temperature). The chocolate and the sheet pan should be approximately the same temperature.

2. Pour the chocolate onto the back of the sheet pan and spread it thinly and evenly with an offset spatula, covering the back of the pan completely.

3. Place the sheet pan in the freezer until the chocolate is set but still malleable. (If the chocolate becomes too hard, remove the pan from the freezer and allow it to sit at room temperature until the chocolate is malleable.)

4. Brace the sheet pan against a wall or the backsplash of a counter. Using a bench scraper or putty knife, begin scraping the chocolate off the sheet pan in long strips. As you scrape, use your other hand to gather one of the long edges of the chocolate strip to create a ruffle.

5. Store the ruffles in a cool, dry place.

Working with modeling chocolate

Modeling a chocolate rose

1. Each rose will need approximately 4 oz/33 g of modeling chocolate. Knead the modeling chocolate until it is pliable.

2. Shape about one-quarter of the modeling chocolate into the center of the rose by shaping it into a cone and then rolling the tip of the cone on the work surface so it is thin. Flatten the bottom of the center so that it stands up on its own.

3. Roll out the remaining modeling chocolate on the baking mat until it is 1⁄16 in/1.5 mm thick.

4. Cut out 10 circles with the 1¼-in/3-cm cutter. Remove the excess modeling chocolate and wrap it tightly in plastic warp. Cover the circles with plastic wrap.

5. Two of the rounds will be used to make the bud. Attach the first petal by connecting it to the tip of the base and then wrapping it around. Smooth the base of the petal into the center of the flower. Repeat this process with the other petal. For a more realistic appearance, tuck each petal inside the previous one so they overlap slightly.

6. The next row needs three petals that are attached to the bud and slightly overlap. Curl back the edge of one side of each petal and attach the petals so the uncurled side is tucked into the previous petal.

7. You can repeat this process with another row of five petals.

NOTE These same techniques can be applied to making roses out of marzipan and gum paste, as shown in the illustration on page 835.

Modeling chocolate leaves

1. Knead a small amount of modeling chocolate until it is pliable.

2. Roll out the modeling chocolate on a silicone baking mat until it is ⅛ in/3 mm thick. Cut out the leaves with the leaf cutter. Gather the excess modeling chocolate and wrap it tightly in plastic wrap so it does not dry out. Cover the leaf cutouts with a piece of plastic wrap.

3. Dust the leaf veiner with cocoa powder if you are using dark or milk modeling chocolate, or cornstarch if you are using white modeling chocolate.

4. Vein each leaf and store on a parchment-lined sheet pan.

5. Once they are dry, brush off any excess cornstarch or cocoa powder.

NOTES If you do not have a leaf veiner, shape the leaves by draping them over an egg carton. This will bend and shape them to make them look more realistic.

This method may be used for gum paste as well.

Working with marzipan

Marzipan is a paste made of ground almonds and sugar. The best-quality marzipan, made with fresh nuts and the proper proportion of sugar, has a fresh, natural flavor. Marzipan can be used as a center (to be enrobed in chocolate) or as a confection by itself.

There are a number of methods for making marzipan, but for the small-scale confectioner, the classic French method is the most practical. The nuts are coarsely ground, and a syrup of sugar, water, and glucose is boiled to the appropriate temperature. The cooked syrup is poured over the nuts and they are spread on a lightly oiled marble surface to cool. Once cooled, the sugar-coated nuts are ground to a paste consistency.

The ratio of almonds to sugar varies depending on the intended use of the finished product, as does the temperature to which the syrup is cooked—the hotter the syrup, the firmer the marzipan. For confectionery work, the syrup is usually cooked to 257°F/125°C to make a firm marzipan. The syrup for a pâtisserie marzipan, which is used for fine décor work, is cooked only to 246°F/119°C, resulting in a softer marzipan. Marzipan should be ground in a mélangeur, a special machine with adjustable marble rollers. The mélangeur produces the smoothest possible finished product. However, if a mélangeur is unavailable, a food processor is acceptable.

When marzipan is ground without sufficient moisture, it will separate and appear oily. If this occurs, add a small amount of liquid, either a spirit or syrup, to the marzipan to return it to the proper consistency. The liquid enables the marzipan to reabsorb the oil that has separated out. It may also be necessary to add a small amount of confectioners' sugar.

Marzipan should be firm but not dry or brittle. To fix marzipan that is too hard or dry, massage in a few drops of liquor or glucose. To fix marzipan that is too brittle, for each 2 lb 4 oz/1.02 kg of marzipan, massage in a piece of fondant approximately the size of a walnut. If the marzipan is so soft that it sticks to your hands or the work surface, massage in confectioners' sugar or a mixture of equal parts powdered milk and cornstarch. You can replace from 25 to 50 percent of the almonds in marzipan with other nuts such as hazelnuts or pistachios.

Marzipan flower cutouts

1. On a surface dusted with confectioners' sugar, roll a piece of marzipan with a small rolling pin to between ¹⁄₁₆ and ⅛ in/1.5 and 3 mm thick.

2. With a small flower cutter, cut out flower shapes from the marzipan. With the small end of a marzipan ball tool, press the center of each flower into a piece of urethane foam to create an indentation in the center of the flower.

3. To make centers for the flowers, shape small pieces of marzipan into tiny balls and place one in the indentation in each flower. Position the centers while the marzipan is still soft so that they will stay in place.

4. To create layered flowers, cut flower shapes with different sizes of cutters and different colors of marzipan. Stack the shapes and press them into the foam at the same time.

Making a marzipan rose

1. Form a small piece of marzipan into a cylinder about 1½ in/4 cm long and ½ in/1 cm in diameter. Make an indentation in the cylinder approximately two-thirds of the way down the cylinder. Taper the cylinder to a point. Stand this cone on your work surface, pressing gently so that the bottom adheres to the surface.

2. Form a piece of marzipan into a rope approximately ½ in/1 cm in diameter. Cut it into four pieces and roll them into small balls about ½ in/1 cm in diameter.

3. Place the balls on a marble surface, about 2 in/5 cm away from the front edge of the marble. Using a plastic bowl scraper, flatten the front edge of each ball with three short strokes. Use a smooth motion, pushing down on the marzipan and pulling the scraper toward you in one motion. The front edge of the marzipan petals should be very thin but the back edge should remain quite thick. (The difference in thickness will allow you to form a delicate-looking rose that will still support its own weight.)

4. Holding the blade of a clean, sharp slicer flat against the marble, cut each petal off the marble. Make a small cut in the center of the thick edge of each petal, then overlap the resulting two sections and press them together to form a cupped shape.

5. To form the first inner petal of the flower, place one petal on the prepared marzipan cone, with the thin edge at the top and the thick edge at the indentation in the cone. Hold the petal tightly against the cone and wrap it all the way around the cone so that the edges overlap. The highest point of the petal should be just above the tip of the cone. There should be a tiny hole at the top of the wrapped petal, but the cone should no longer be visible. Use your fingers to gently turn back a small section of the top edge of the petal. Gently squeeze the bottom of the petal into the indentation in the cone.

TOP ROW: Form a cone and press to adhere to the work surface. Using a plastic bowl scraper, flatten and shape balls to make petals.

To form the first inner petal of the flower, place one petal on the prepared marzipan cone, with the thin edge at the top and the thick edge at the indentation in the cone.

Wrap the petal tightly all the way around the cone so that the edges overlap. Use your fingers to gently turn back a small section of the top edge of the petal.

Make a small cut in the center of the thick edge of each petal, then overlap the resulting two sections and press them together to form a cupped shape.

BOTTOM ROW: Use your fingers to gently turn back a small section of the top edge of the petal.

Position the formed petals around the cone, or center of the rose.

Gently squeeze the bottom of the rose to create a rounded base. Cut the extra marzipan away from the base.

Allow the rose to dry at room temperature.

6. Use the remaining three petals to form the first layer of rose petals. Place one of these petals on the rose, with its center in line with the edge of the first petal. The top of this petal and the subsequent ones should be even with or just slightly above the top of the inner petal. Press the bottom left side of the petal into the rose, leaving the right side open.

7. Position the other two petals in the same fashion, so that their centers line up with the previous petal's left edge, and gently curl the thin right edge of each petal back with your finger. The third petal's left edge should nestle inside the first petal's open right

side. Gently press all the petals' bottom edges together and squeeze the bottom of the rose into the indentation in the cone, forming a rounded bottom to the rose.

8. Make another slightly thicker snake out of marzipan and cut it into five pieces. Form these into balls and then petals in the same fashion as above.

9. Use these five petals to form the second layer of rose petals. Place them on the rose in the same fashion, but with each petal overlapping the previous one by only about one-third. The tops of these petals should also be even with or just slightly above those of the previous petals. Gently curl each side of these five petals back and create a crease or point in the middle of the petal.

10. If desired, add another layer of seven petals to the rose.

11. Gently squeeze the bottom of the rose to create a rounded base. Cut the extra marzipan away from the base. Allow the rose to dry at room temperature.

Marzipan plaques

1. Dust a work surface with confectioners' sugar. Roll a piece of marzipan to ¹⁄₁₆ in/1.5 mm thick using a small rolling pin.

2. Using a cutter or a template and sharp paring knife, cut a circle, oval, or other desired shape out of the marzipan.

3. Lay the plaque on a flat surface and, using your fingers and the palm of your hand, buff and smooth the cut edges and the top surface of the plaque, being careful not to crack or break the marzipan.

4. Place the plaque on a parchment-lined sheet pan and allow to dry at room temperature until it is completely hard. Use an emery board or very fine sandpaper to smooth any rough edges. Pipe lettering on the plaque or decorate as desired.

NOTE This method may be used for pastillage as well.

Sugar work

Making blown sugar strawberries

1. Warm a piece of red sugar in the microwave until it is hot and pliable but not so hot that it is fluid; check it frequently to ensure that it does not become too hot in one place while it is still hard in another.

2. Place the sugar under a heat lamp. Knead a small amount of crystal sugar into it to create the look of strawberry seeds.

3. Make a "foot" of sugar on the pipe by wrapping a small piece of sugar around the tip of the pipe, so the sugar strawberry will adhere to the pipe. Knead and pull the remaining sugar with your hands until it is a consistent texture and temperature. With your open right hand, grasp the piece of sugar and then close your hand, forcing a round ball of sugar out through your closed thumb and forefinger. Cut this ball away from the main piece of sugar.

4. Push your finger down into the center of the ball of sugar, creating an indentation. Make sure the thickness of the sugar is the same all the way around the indentation; if it varies in thickness, the sugar is more likely to blow out in a thin spot.

5. Heat the foot of sugar on the sugar pump over a Sterno flame, then place the ball of sugar on the tip of the pipe, being sure to leave enough space inside the indentation above the end of the pipe so that air will be able to come out of the pipe. Squeeze and press the base of the sugar ball around the end of the pipe, attaching it to the sugar foot.

6. Hold the ball of sugar in one hand and squeeze the pump with the other until the ball of sugar expands. Stop pumping and shape the sugar into a strawberry with your hands; at the same time, mold a thick stem at the base of the strawberry that protrudes above the end of the pipe. Continue to alternately pump air into the strawberry and shape it until it is the shape and thickness desired. The thinner the walls of the strawberry, the shinier the sugar will be when it cools.

7. Cool the strawberry under a blow-dryer. To cut the strawberry away from the pump, heat just the thick stem over the Sterno flame. Place the open blades of a pair of scissors around the stem and slowly and gently close them until the sugar cracks.

Shape the strawberry with your fingers.

Gently cut the strawberry off the pipe.

Making straw sugar

1. Warm a piece of sugar in the microwave until it is hot and pliable but not so hot that it is fluid; check it frequently to ensure that it does not become too hot in one place while it is still hard in another.

2. Place the sugar under a heat lamp. Cut a piece approximately 1½ by 6 in/4 by 15 cm from the piece of sugar. Pull it into a long cylinder. Fold the cylinder in half and bring the ends together, allowing the two halves to touch along their long sides and adhere to each other. Repeat two or three times.

3. Holding the piece of sugar at either end, fold it into a tube, allowing the long sides to adhere. From this point on, it is important to handle the sugar gently and touch the center of the piece as little as possible to retain the long tubes of air that you are building into the sugar. Fold the tube in half, as in step 2, and allow the long sides to adhere to each other. Repeat two or three times.

4. Repeat step 3 two more times, handling the sugar by the ends as much as possible.

5. Pull the sugar into a long cylinder and bend and shape it as desired. If the sugar is still warm enough, you can cut the ends with scissors. If it is too cool, warm the section to be cut over a Sterno flame and then cut carefully with scissors. Cool the sugar with a blow-dryer.

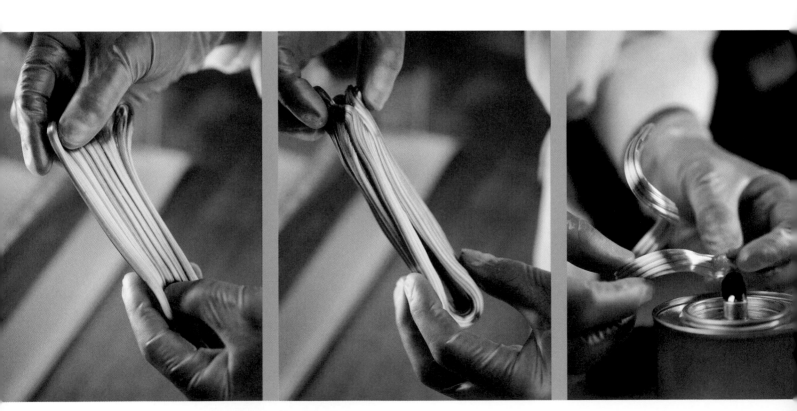

LEFT: Joining the long sides of the sugar

MIDDLE: Forming the sugar into a tube

RIGHT: Heating a small lump of sugar in order to attach a flower to the straw sugar

Making a pulled sugar blossom

1. Warm a piece of white sugar in the microwave until it is hot and pliable but not so hot that it is fluid; check frequently to ensure that it does not become too hot in one place while it is still hard in another.

2. Place the sugar under a heat lamp. With both hands, grasp the sugar firmly at the opposite ends of the piece and pull your hands apart, pulling the sugar to form a thin edge. This thin edge is important because it is the thinness of the petals' edges that will give the flowers a delicate appearance.

3. Place the piece of sugar on the edge of a sugar workbox with the thin pulled edge protruding over the edge. With the index finger and thumb of your right hand, grasp the thin edge of sugar and pull it down. With the index finger and thumb of your left hand, pin the sugar directly above your right thumb. With a short, sharp movement, pull your right hand away while pinning hard with your left. This will create a tapered, rounded petal. Repeat the process until you have five matching petals.

4. To assemble the flower, heat the tapered end of one petal over a flame. Place it next to another petal, overlapping the edges. Repeat with the remaining petals, overlapping them evenly. Heat the last petal until it is pliable enough that its edge can be slipped under the edge of the first petal. Cool the flower with a blow-dryer.

5. To make the stamen for the flower, warm a piece of light yellow or gold sugar in the microwave. Cut off a small piece of the sugar with scissors. Pull the piece of sugar into a very thin strand. Working quickly, bring the ends of the strand together to create a large loop. Loop the strands twice more, and pin them together about ½ to ¾ in/1 to 2 cm below the tops of the loops. The sugar should still be warm enough so that the strands adhere to one another. Cut the loops open with scissors.

6. Place the blades of the scissors at the point where the strands are pinned together and use the scissors to gently break the sugar. Heat this pinned end in the Sterno flame and attach it to the center of the flower.

TOP LEFT: Pulling the sugar into a thin edge

BOTTOM LEFT: Placing the petals on the flower

TOP RIGHT: Pulling the thin edge down and away from the sugar

BOTTOM RIGHT: Pulling the flower stamen

Making pulled sugar leaves

1. Warm a piece of light green sugar in the microwave until it is hot and pliable but not so hot that it is fluid; check frequently to ensure that it does not become too hot in one place while it is still hard in another.

2. Place the sugar under a heat lamp. With both hands, grasp the sugar firmly at the opposite ends of the piece and pull your hands apart, pulling the sugar to form a thin edge. This thin edge is important because it is the thinness of the leaves' edge that will give them a delicate appearance.

3. Place the piece of sugar on the edge of a sugar workbox with the thin pulled edge protruding over the edge. With the index finger and thumb of your left hand, grasp the thin edge of sugar and pull it down and away. Cut the sugar strip at an angle with scissors to create a leaf shape.

4. Immediately place the sugar piece into the bottom half of a silicone leaf mold and press down on it firmly with the top of the mold. Then remove the leaf from the mold and, while it is still warm, pin the thicker end of the leaf slightly. Curve the leaf slightly to make it look more realistic. Cool under a blow-dryer. Repeat to make more leaves as needed.

5. To attach the leaves, heat the thicker end of each leaf over a flame. Press the heated end of the leaf to a base stem or petal and cool the joint with a blow-dryer.

LEFT: Cutting the pulled sugar at an angle
MIDDLE: Removing the leaf from the mold
RIGHT: Attaching the leaf to the sugar piece

Making a pulled sugar ribbon

1. Warm one piece of white sugar and one piece of red sugar in the microwave until they are hot and pliable but not so hot that they are fluid; check frequently to ensure that the sugar does not become too hot in one place while it is still hard in another.

2. Place both pieces of sugar under a heat lamp. Cut off five pieces of white sugar, each approximately ¾ by 3 in/2 by 8 cm. Cut off two pieces of red sugar of approximately the same size. Lay the pieces of sugar in a row in this order: white, red, white, white, white, red, white; place the pieces close together so that they adhere to one another.

3. Pull the sugar band lengthwise until it is long enough to double back on itself. Bring the two ends of the sugar together and allow the long sides of the sugar to adhere to each other. Flatten the piece of sugar into a wide, thick ribbon.

4. Grasping one end of the ribbon in your left hand, begin pulling the ribbon out with your right hand. Apply pressure evenly, using your right hand to smooth out the length of the ribbon until you have created a very thin, delicate ribbon.

5. When the ribbon is the desired length and thickness, trim the ends at an angle with scissors. If necessary, warm the ribbon slightly under the heat lamp to shape and curve it as desired.

NOTE For ribbons of three or more colors, simply add more colors of sugar in the same manner. The colors can be arranged in any sequence, but ribbons tend to look prettier if the different colors are separated by white sugar.

LEFT: Beginning to pull the ribbon

MIDDLE: Lengthening the ribbon

RIGHT: Shaping the ribbon

Working with sugar pastes

Pastillage is a pure white sugar paste. It is not sensitive to ambient humidity, making it possible to assemble pieces well in advance and hold them at room temperature. Pastillage should not be refrigerated. Sugar paste décor may be made in advance and stored almost indefinitely in controlled conditions of temperature and humidity. Gum paste and pastillage are essentially the same medium; however, gum paste is more elastic and may be rolled thinner and manipulated more easily without cracking. Most gum paste and pastillage décor elements should be dried overnight before use. When working with sugar pastes, the work surface and all tools must be kept clean and free of any debris, as the white paste accentuates any impurities. Keep sugar paste covered with plastic wrap as much as possible as it is being worked with because it dries out quickly. Rolled fondant is used for covering cakes as well as creating décor elements. However, it does not dry to a brittle state as easily and therefore cannot be used for the same applications as pastillage or gum paste. It will develop a dry outer crust, so care should be taken to keep it covered when working.

Making a pastillage link twist

1. Roll out the pastillage ¹⁄₁₆ in/1.5 mm or thinner on a nonstick surface.

2. Cut teardrop shapes from the pastillage.

3. Carefully cut a slit down the center of each cut piece, leaving ¼ in/6 mm uncut at each end. Lift up one piece and flip the flat end in through the slit.

LEFT: Cutting a slit in the middle of the pastillage piece
MIDDLE: Twisting the base of the pastillage piece through the cut
RIGHT: Letting the pastillage dry in the final shape

4. Insert a pin into a piece of foam. Lean the flat end of the pastillage piece against the pin so that it is propped perpendicular to the rest of the piece, which should be lying flat on the foam. Repeat with the remaining cut pieces.

5. Allow to dry until stiff.

Making a gum paste rose

1. Roll a piece of gum paste with a small rolling pin to ¹⁄₁₆ in/1.5 mm or thinner. Keep the gum paste covered with a piece of plastic wrap when you are not working with it. Have ready a prepared cotton cone with a piece of wire attached to the flat end for the center of the flower.

2. Cut a set of petals out of the gum paste with a five-petal cutter. Cut the petals apart into one group of two petals and one of three petals. Roll the large end of a gum paste ball tool over the edges of the two-petal group to thin them. With a toothpick or a thin knitting needle, roll up one side of each petal. Roll the toothpick firmly across the surface of the petal to draw up and curl the edge of the petal.

3. Turn the petals over and brush the base with Gum Glue (page 860). Without separating the petals, wrap the first petal around the cotton inner cone: The uncurled side of the petal should be wrapped around the cone and the curled side of the petal should be slightly open. Fit the uncurled side of the second petal into the open side of the first petal and wrap the second petal around the first. Press gently to attach the petals to each other and to the cotton cone; the top of the petals should form a tight spiral. (For a rosebud, follow the procedure to this point, but do not add any more petals.)

4. Thin the edges, curl, and brush glue on the three-petal group in the same fashion. Wrap these petals around the first two, overlapping the petals and fitting the third petal inside the uncurled edge of the first. Press gently to attach the petals to one another.

5. For a larger rose, cut another group of five petals. Separate them again into one group of two petals and one of three petals. Thin the edges of the two-petal group as above and curl back both edges of each petal. Turn the petals over and brush the base with gum glue. Wrap the petals around the rose as before, overlapping them slightly.

6. Thin the edges, curl, and brush glue on the three-petal group in the same fashion. Wrap these petals around the rose, overlapping them; the last petal should overlap the first one of the two-petal group. Press gently to attach the petals to one another.

7. Form a hook out of the end of the wire attached to the inner cotton cone and hang the rose upside down to dry.

TOP LEFT: Thinning the edges of the petals with a ball tool

TOP RIGHT: Curling the edges of the petals

BOTTOM LEFT: Wrapping the first layer of petals

BOTTOM RIGHT: Adding another layer of petals

Making a gum paste magnolia

1. Massage together equal parts of gum paste and pastillage.

2. Roll approximately 1 tsp/5 mL of the mixture into a ball, then roll half of the ball into a point. Attach the rounded base of the pointed ball to a piece of floral wire. Attach twisted paper strands to the wire at the base of the ball.

3. Using sharp, pointed scissors, cut V-shaped snips into the sides of the pointed ball.

4. Roll out the remaining gum paste mixture 1⁄16 in/1.5 mm thick.

5. Using the templates in Appendix B (page 905), cut three large and three small petals from the paste.

6. Attach the small petals to the wire so that the pointed ball rests in the center (for detailed instructions, see "Making a Marzipan Rose," page 834). Attach the large petals so that each fills a space between two of the smaller petals.

Molding a gum paste–pastillage mixture

1. Massage together equal parts of gum paste and pastillage. Roll out 1⁄4 in/6 mm thick.

2. Place the desired mold over the rolled sugar paste and cut to the shape with a sharp paring knife using the mold as a template.

3. Place the cut shape in the mold and press it down firmly with the top of the mold. Carefully peel the molded shape away from the mold and drape it over a curved object, such as a rolling pin, or a flat work surface. Allow to dry for approximately 1 hour.

4. Shift the shape slightly to ensure that it does not stick to the rolling pin or other surface. Allow to dry completely.

Unmolding a pastillage marzipan leaf for the magnolia cake

Making a fondant swag

1. Roll a strip of fondant 6 by 3 in/15 by 20 cm and 1⁄8 in/3 mm thick on a lightly greased surface.

2. Lay the fondant over 3 1⁄4-in/8.5-cm dowels, and coax the fondant down and over each dowel. The edges of the fondant should be downward facing.

3. Remove the dowels and draw up the ends to create a swag.

4. Pinch the ends together and trim if necessary.

5. Dampen the ends with water to make them tacky and gently press them on to a fondant-iced cake.

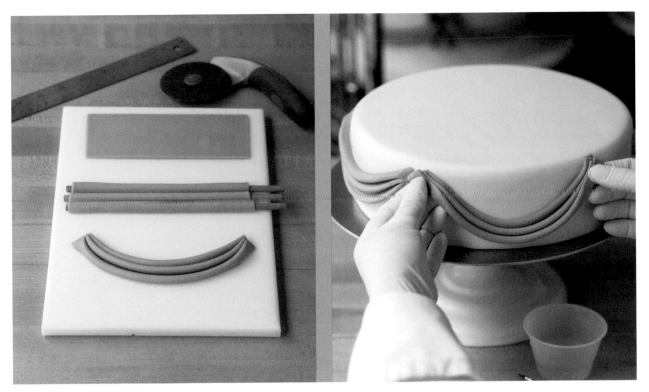

LEFT: Roll the fondant into a rectangle of the desired size. Lay the fondant over 3¼-in/8.5-cm dowels, and coax the fondant down and over each dowel; the edges of the fondant should be face down. Remove the dowels and draw up the ends to create a swag. Pinch the ends together and trim if necessary.

RIGHT: Dampen the ends with water to make them tacky and gently press them on to a fondant-iced cake.

Making a fondant bow

1. Dust the work surface with cornstarch or confectioners' sugar. Roll out a portion of the fondant or gum paste to ⅛ in/3 mm thick. Using a ruler, measure a rectangle ¾ by 5 in/ 2 by 13 cm. Cut out the rectangle with a pizza cutter or a knife, ensuring the edges are straight.

2. Dab a small amount of water at each end of the strip. Place a piece of floral wire at the base of one end of the strip. Fold the strip in half, using your fingers to create a large loop. Press down gently to secure the two ends together.

3. Dust the inside of the loop with a cornstarch pouch. Fill the loop with a wad of cotton balls and place on the parchment-lined sheet tray. Repeat this process to make the second loop for the bow.

4. Make six to seven loops for a large bow and five for a smaller bow.

5. Allow the loops to dry for a minimum of 24 hours. Once dry, remove the cotton balls supporting the loop. If some of the cotton strands are stuck to the bow, remove them with a pair of tweezers.

6. To make the ribbons, roll out a piece of fondant or gum paste to ⅛ in/3 mm thick. Cut the piece of fondant into one rectangle 3 by 8 in/ 2 by 20 cm. Using a knife or the cutter, cut out a triangle from both ends of the strip, making V shapes. Dip the

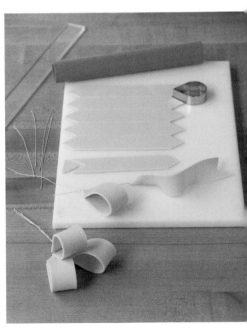

Bow technique

end of a piece of wire into some water and insert the wire into the base of the ribbon. Use the egg carton to shape the ribbon and let it dry for 24 hours. Repeat this process to make as many ribbons as you would like.

7. Once the components are dry, use floral tape to secure the loops and the ribbons together. Do not shape any of the pieces by pulling on the fondant because they might break. Adjust the wire and this will automatically move the loop or ribbon.

8. Cut off any excess wire and insert the wire into the cake.

NOTE This method may be used with pastillage as well.

Making dogwood flowers

1. Roll out just enough fondant or gum paste to make small batches of flowers at a time. Dust the surface with cornstarch or confectioners' sugar and roll out a piece of gum paste or fondant to ⅛ in/3 mm thick. Keep the piece of sugar paste covered with plastic wrap.

2. Use the dogwood cutter to cut out a flower from the sugar paste. Dust the dogwood mold with cornstarch or confectioners' sugar. Place the dogwood in the base of the mold and place the other half on top. Press down lightly and remove the flower.

3. Use the egg carton that has been dusted with cornstarch or confectioners' sugar to shape the flower. Repeat this process with the other flowers and let them dry for 24 hours.

4. Once the flowers are dry, pipe several small dots with the pale yellow royal icing in the center of each flower.

5. To make the flowers appear more realistic, use pale green powdered food coloring to dust around the centers of each flower. Next, accent the edges of the four petals of each flower with pink or red powdered food coloring.

Making dogwood flowers

NOTE The dogwood cutters can be exchanged for other types of flowers, such as daisies and hydrangeas, but the techniques remain the same.

Making a hydrangea flower

1. Roll a small piece of fondant into a seamless ball about ½ in/1 cm in diameter.

2. Taper one end so it becomes cone-shaped.

3. With an auger tool, poke a hole in the center of the wide end. Snip four petals with a scissor. Pinch each petal between your fingers to flatten.

4. Place the flower upside down on the matte and thin petals with a ball tool.

5. Turn the flower right side up and put in one of the holes. Using gentle pressure, draw a knitting needle across each petal from end to center, creating a crease and curling the petal slightly.

6. Make a loop in the end of a #000 g. wire, dip it in gum glue, and insert it through the flower until it is no longer visible.

Making a fondant ribbon rose

1. Roll out a strip of fondant 2 by 6 in/5 by 15 cm and ⅛ in/3 mm thick on a lightly greased surface.

2. Fold in half, forming a strip 1 by 6 in/3 by 12 cm.

3. Twist one end of the strip down to form the bud.

4. Begin wrapping the fondant strip around the bud.

5. Continue wrapping and gently squeeze the bottom to open and shape the flower.

Embellishing

1. Set up a coloring station on parchment paper to include powdered food color, various brushes, and coloring tools.

2. Pick up a bit of color on a soft dry brush and tap out excess onto the parchment.

3. Gently brush color onto the flowers, being careful to add color a little at a time.

LEFT: Progression of steps and tools for making hydrangea flowers
MIDDLE: Ribbon rose technique
RIGHT: Embellishing a finished hydrangea flower with luster dust

Buttercream for décor

MAKES 10 LB/4.54 KG

High-ratio shortening	2 lb 8 oz	1.13 kg
Confectioners' sugar, 6x, sifted	2 lb 8 oz	1.13 kg
Swiss meringue buttercream (page 417), whipped	5 lb	2.27 kg

Cream the shortening and sugar to full volume. Add the buttercream and bring back to full volume. Store in the refrigerator until needed.

Chocolate dome

MAKES 1 DOME

Bittersweet chocolate, melted, tempered	as needed	as needed

1   Pour the chocolate into a 2¾-in/7-cm polycarbonate dome mold. Allow the chocolate to set for approximately 30 seconds, just until some of the chocolate begins to set.

2   Invert the mold over the bowl of chocolate to allow most of the chocolate to spill out, leaving a hollow shell dome.

3   Allow the chocolate to set completely, and gently unmold.

4   Store in an airtight container. Use as desired.

Chocolate piping gel

MAKES 11 LB/4.99 KG

Dark chocolate, 64%, finely chopped	1 lb	454 g
Gel	10 lb	4.54 kg

Warm the chocolate to 130°F/54°C and add one-third of the gel. Stir gently using a whisk until totally blended. Add the rest of the gel and stir thoroughly. Strain through cheesecloth and keep in airtight containers.

Royal icing

MAKES 1 LB 3 OZ/539 G

Egg whites	2½–3 oz	71–85 g
Cream of tartar	¼ tsp	1.25 mL
Confectioners' sugar	1 lb	454 g

1   Place the egg whites in a clean, grease-free mixer bowl. Mix on low speed with the whip attachment just until the whites begin to break up.

2   Add the cream of tartar and continue mixing on low speed until the whites become frothy.

3   Gradually add the sugar and continue to mix until the icing holds a peak and is dull in appearance.

4   Transfer to a glass container and press a moist towel directly on the surface of the icing. Store under refrigeration, covered tightly with plastic wrap.

NOTES   If the icing becomes runny, it can be rewhipped each day before use.

Sugar or egg whites can be added to adjust the consistency as necessary.

Dark modeling chocolate

MAKES 1 LB 6 OZ/624 G

Dark chocolate, 64%, chopped	1 lb	454 g
Light corn syrup	6¼ oz	177 g
Cocoa powder	as needed	as needed

1   Melt the chocolate to 90°F/32°C. Warm the corn syrup to the same temperature and blend into the chocolate until incorporated. Avoid overmixing.

2   Spread onto a parchment-lined sheet pan, cover, and refrigerate for 1 hour.

3   Store at room temperature overnight.

4   Form into logs and wrap with plastic wrap. Refrigerate until needed.

5   To soften, cut into 2-in/5-cm strips. Slice into ⅛-in/3-mm pieces. Knead on a clean work surface until workable, dusting with cocoa powder if necessary.

NOTES   Use a clean rolling pin and cocoa powder to roll out dark modeling chocolate.

Modeling chocolate is used for stems like flowers and fruit. It is edible and can be used for dessert containers. However, use it sparingly. Its main use is to create parts of a centerpiece that would be difficult to carve or shape out of couverture such as hands, faces, and the like.

White modeling chocolate

MAKES 5 LB 8 OZ/2.5 KG

White chocolate	4 lb	1.81 kg
Light corn syrup	1 lb 8 oz	680 g
Confectioners' sugar	as needed	as needed

Mixing white modeling chocolate

1   Melt the chocolate to between 85° and 90°F/29 to 32°C. Bring the corn syrup to approximately the same temperature, 90°F/32°C.

2   Add the corn syrup to the chocolate. Blend just until incorporated. Avoid overmixing.

3   Spread the chocolate in a parchment-lined sheet pan. Cover with plastic wrap and chill for several hours under refrigeration.

4   Store in dry storage overnight.

5   Portion into 1-lb/454-g pieces, form into rolls, and wrap each piece individually until needed.

6   To soften, cut the piece into 2-in/5-cm strips. Cut into ⅛-in/3-mm slices and knead on a clean surface, dusting with sifted confectioners' sugar as needed.

NOTES   This mixture is good for flowers, ribbons, bows, and cake coverings. The same recipe can be used for milk chocolate; however, if it is too soft, add a bit of water.

This modeling chocolate can also be colored if desired. Use paste colors, kneading the colors into the chocolate.

White modeling chocolate is a great substitute for rolled fondant and works well for enrobing cakes.

Marzipan for modeling and cake covering

MAKES 17 LB 2 OZ/7.77 KG

Almond paste	7 lb	3.18 kg
Confectioners' sugar	7 lb	3.18 kg
Fondant	2 lb	907 g
Glucose syrup	1 lb	454 g
Brandy	2 fl oz	60 mL

Blend together the almond paste and confectioners' sugar on low speed with the paddle attachment, about 2 minutes. Add the fondant, glucose syrup, and brandy and mix just until the mixture is smooth. Store in an airtight container under refrigeration.

NOTES   You will need approximately 1 lb 4 oz/567 g marzipan to cover a 10-in/25-cm cake.

The consistency of marzipan can be adjusted as necessary. Molded marzipan fruits and similar items require a firmer consistency so they hold their shape. Knead additional confectioners' sugar into the marzipan by hand until the desired consistency is achieved.

Overworked marzipan becomes excessively oily and loses its characteristic smooth, claylike texture. If this happens, knead in a small measure of simple syrup. This will rebind the oils and solids. Additional confectioners' sugar may be added to achieve the original consistency again as well.

Poured sugar

MAKES 32 LB 6 OZ/14.69 KG

Sugar	20 lb	9.07 kg
Water	8 lb	3.63 kg
Glucose syrup	4 lb 6 oz	1.98 kg

1   Place the sugar and water in a large copper or heavy-gauge sauce pot. Bring to a boil, stirring constantly with a wooden spoon or a wire whisk. Using a clean, wet pastry brush, wash the sides of the pot. Remove any crystals that may adhere to the sides of the pot with a small tea sieve or ladle.

2   After the mixture comes to a boil, stop stirring and add the glucose. Continue to wash the sides of the pot until the mixture comes to the proper temperature (see Notes).

3   Shock the pot in a cold water bath. Allow the surface bubbles to dissipate and pour it into a prepared frame or mold.

NOTES   To control crystallization, add 1 drop of acid at 266°F/130°C for every 2 lb/907 g of sugar syrup being cooked, along with any color or whitening.

Final cooking temperature will range from 310° to 320°F/154° to 160°C depending on the size of the piece as well as the color desired.

For a pure white-colored sugar, add whitening and cook sugar syrup only to 295°F/146°C.

Various marbleized effects can be achieved by swirling a small amount of food coloring into the sugar before pouring it into forms or frames.

The actual volume amount needed will vary depending on the size of the piece being produced.

Rock sugar

MAKES 3 LB/1.36 KG

Sugar	2 lb	907 g
Water	1 lb	454 g
Royal icing (page 851), stiff	2 tbsp (heaping)	37 mL

1   Line a mold with aluminum foil. Lightly brush the foil with oil.

2   Bring the sugar and water to a boil, washing the sides of the pot with a wet pastry brush so that crystals do not form. Boil to 295°F/146°C.

3   Remove from the heat and whisk in the royal icing. The mixture will rise and collapse.

4   Return to the heat and bring to a boil again. Pour into the prepared mold. Cool completely, break into pieces, and store in an airtight container.

NOTE   Rock sugar can be colored if desired. Add the color at 266°F/130°C. It can also be left white and color can be applied with an airbrush.

Spun sugar

MAKES 1 LB 3 OZ/539 G

Sugar	1 lb	454 g
Water	5 fl oz	150 mL
Light corn syrup	3½ oz	99 g

1   Combine the sugar and water in a heavy-bottomed saucepan and stir to ensure all the sugar is moistened. Bring to a boil over high heat, stirring frequently to dissolve the sugar. Wash down the sides of the pan with a wet pastry brush to remove any sugar crystals. When the mixture comes to a boil, stop stirring and skim the surface to remove any scum.

2   Add the corn syrup and cook, occasionally washing down the sides of the pan with a wet pastry brush, until the syrup reaches 293°F/145°C.

3   Shock the pan in an ice water bath for 10 seconds. Allow the sugar to cool undisturbed at room temperature until it reaches the consistency of honey.

4   Lightly oil a foil-covered template and set it on a small container so that it is raised above the surface of the table, over a silicone baking mat.

5 With a fork, gently drizzle the sugar back and forth over the template, allowing the sugar to fall over the sides of the template. Drizzle more sugar back and forth across the first strands, creating a grid of sugar strands.

6 With scissors, cut away the excess sugar that has fallen over the sides of the template. Remove the spun sugar from the template and warm it briefly under a heat lamp until it is pliable enough to bend or curve as desired.

NOTES Isomalt may be substituted for the corn syrup to ensure that the sugar syrup remains clear.

For caramel-colored spun sugar, cook the sugar until it reaches a light golden brown.

VARIATION **SPUN SUGAR BALL** Follow the directions through step 3. Set up 2 metal bars 8 in/20 cm apart, resting on containers, so they are above the work surface. Use a fork to drizzle the sugar quickly back and forth over the metal bars until a netting of sugar is formed. Gather the sugar into a ball.

Drizzling the sugar over the template

Cutting away the excess sugar

Pulled sugar

MAKES 5 LB 4 OZ/2.38 KG

Sugar	2 lb	907 g
Water	6½ fl oz	195 mL
Light corn syrup	32 fl oz	906 mL
Glucose syrup	7 oz	198 g
Tartaric acid (opposite)	4 drops*	4 drops*
Color	as needed	as needed

*The number of drops of acid can be adjusted for humidity or environmental conditions as well as for the skill level of the person pulling the sugar.

1   In a copper or heavy-gauge sauce pot, bring the sugar and water to a boil, stirring constantly. Wash the sides of the pot with a wet pastry brush to remove any crystals that may adhere.

2   When the mixture comes to a boil, stop stirring and add the corn syrup and glucose. Bring back to a boil. Cover and store at room temperature.

3   For final cooking for pulling, bring back to boil. Continue to wash the sides of the pot throughout the boiling of the sugar. Add acid as necessary, and color if using, at 266°F/137°C. Cook to a final temperature of 315°F/156°C. Pour onto a lightly oiled marble slab.

NOTE   Final cooking temperature as well as the amount of acid used can be adjusted according to one's skill level as well as weather conditions such as high humidity and warm weather.

Tartaric acid

MAKES 8 FL OZ/227 G

Water	4 fl oz	120 mL
Tartaric acid, granulated	4 oz	113 g

Bring the water to a boil. Add the acid and stir to dissolve. To store, put into a medicine bottle with a dropper.

Pastillage

MAKES 1 LB 4 OZ/567 G

Confectioners' sugar, sifted	1 lb	454 g
Cream of tartar	⅛ tsp	0.60 mL
Gum tragacanth	4 tsp	20 mL
Water, hot	2 fl oz	60 mL
Shortening	as needed	as needed

1   Put 8 oz/227 g of the sugar, the cream of tartar, and the gum tragacanth in the mixer. Add 1 oz/30 mL of the water and mix on medium speed with the paddle attachment to a paste.

2   Add more of the sugar and water alternately until the mixture forms a kneadable dough. (You may not need all the sugar or all the water.)

3   Remove from the mixer bowl and knead on the work surface until smooth. Form into a log, coat the log with a little shortening, and wrap with plastic wrap. Wrap again with a wet towel and then once more with plastic wrap or put into a plastic bag.

Gum paste

MAKES 1 LB 8 OZ/680 G

Gelatin, granulated	½ oz	14 g
Water	4 fl oz	120 mL
Glucose syrup	3⅓ oz	94 g
Shortening	¾ oz	21 g
Confectioners' sugar, sifted	2 lb	907 g
Gum tragacanth	1¾ oz	50 g

1   Bloom the gelatin in the water for 5 to 10 minutes. Melt over a hot water bath.

2   Add the glucose and shortening. Warm until all the shortening melts. (The mixture should be hot.)

3   In a 5-quart bowl, sift together the sugar and the gum tragacanth. Add the gelatin mixture all at once and mix until it comes together.

4   Blend in a mixer on medium speed with the paddle attachment for 5 minutes. (The right consistency should be soft but not wet.)

5   Remove from the mixer and quickly knead together on a work surface rubbed with a small amount of shortening. Wrap tightly in 2 layers of plastic wrap.

Rolled fondant

MAKES APPROXIMATELY 2 LB/907 KG

Water	1½ oz	43 g
Gelatin, granulated	2¼ tsp	11.25 mL
Light corn syrup	4⅓ oz	123 g
Glycerin (optional)	1½ tbsp	22.50 mL
Confectioners' sugar, sifted	1 lb 8 oz	680 g

1   Combine the water and gelatin and heat gently to dissolve only, about 90°F/32°C. Remove from the heat and stir in the corn syrup and glycerin, if using.

2   Add the sugar and mix until smooth and well combined. Form into a log.

3   Lightly coat with shortening. Wrap with plastic wrap, sealing tightly.

NOTE   It is not necessary to refrigerate the fondant. Best results are achieved if the fondant is used the same day it is made, as it will tighten up overnight.

Covering a cake with rolled fondant

Gunge

Water	as needed	as needed
Old gum paste (page 858)	as needed	as needed

Take 2 parts water and 1 part old gum paste, put in a pot, and boil until it is the consistency of glue.

Gum glue

MAKES 8 FL OZ/240 ML

Gum arabic	1 tbsp (heaping)	6 g
Water	8 fl oz	240 mL

Combine the gum arabic and water in a small bowl. Cover with a damp cloth and let stand until the gum arabic has completely dissolved. Store covered under refrigeration.

NOTES   Brush onto finished gum paste items to give them a shiny surface.

This is used as an adhesive for sugar paste work.

chapter twenty-three

Wedding and specialty cakes

Wedding and specialty cakes are a culmination of the talent, skills, and knowledge of the pastry chef or baker. To make a beautiful and flavorful cake, the pastry chef or baker must hone his or her skills in almost all aspects of the baking and pastry arts. Creation and development of cakes such as the ones in this chapter are limited only by the creativity of the individual.

Traditional wedding cakes

Traditional British-style wedding cakes are perhaps the quintessential wedding cakes, from which most other wedding cake styles are derived. These are, in general, unfilled dark fruit-cakes. The richness of the cake reflects a time when refrigeration was unavailable. Dried fruit, sugar, suet, and thick layers of coatings and icings helped the cakes stay fresh for one year, as the top layer would be saved and eaten on the couple's first anniversary. The cakes are traditionally coated with a layer of jam, then with marzipan, and finally with several coats of royal icing. The jam and marzipan keep the white icing from absorbing oils or moisture from the cake, while protecting the cake itself from moisture loss and staling.

Traditional British-style cakes consist of three tiers supported by pillars, generally pastillage, and both the icing and the decoration, which consists of royal icing piping and pastillage, are pure white. To some traditionalists, the British cake remains the only true wedding cake. Because the cake does not require refrigeration, which would damage sugar décor work, very detailed decorations, often baroque or gothic in style, can be applied. However, the labor-intensive nature of this style of cake is a drawback for most pastry chefs and bakers today—nor are these cakes to everyone's taste. In addition, the royal icing used for décor is very hard and brittle, making it difficult to cut such a cake cleanly or easily.

The British cultural influence is reflected in the styles of wedding cakes that evolved in countries colonized by Britain. The Australian and South African styles are shining examples of this influence. Decoration consists of minute royal icing piping and gum paste flowers. Colors, if used at all, are the softest of pastels. Although these cakes may be quite ornate, their overall appearance is very soft and delicate. The tiers may simply be stacked, may be supported on pillars, or, often, may be displayed on offset asymmetrical cake stands.

In the Australian-style wedding cake, as with the British, it is not uncommon for tiers to be octagons, squares, or horseshoe shapes. The primary appeal of Australian cakes is their ornate yet delicate appearance. Beautiful realistic flowers are created from gum paste, and royal icing embroidery, string work, flood work, and ornaments are used to create stunning and intricate effects. The very detailed style of decoration, however, can be a disadvantage to the pastry chef or baker, in that it is labor-intensive and therefore expensive to produce.

The South African–style cake is very similar, but it can be distinguished from the Australian style by the large yet delicate wings made of royal icing filigree and flood work that extend over the cake.

The British cake also spawned American-style cakes. American wedding cakes are most clearly defined by the use of buttercream icing, buttercream piping décor, and buttercream roses, often colored. There is no single cake type of choice in American cakes, but pound cakes, high-ratio cakes, génoise, and carrot cakes are most common. Regardless of the style of cake, good judgment and craftsmanship are required for the production of a cake that is cost-effective and attractive. Highly decorated cakes such as these should always be made with high-quality ingredients so that the finished cake can be both a delicious dessert and an impressive showpiece.

The modern wedding cake

Clean, straight lines and simple decorations in the form of cutouts of chocolate, pastillage, marzipan, or nougatine define contemporary wedding cakes. Fresh flowers or fresh fruits are frequently used. The cake itself may be almost any variety, from cheesecake to mousse cake to sponge with fruit, or even a charlotte. Almost any type of icing may be used, with whipped cream and good-quality buttercream most common. Offset cake stands are the rule for modern cakes, since they are too light and fragile to be stacked.

The advantages of modern-style cakes are efficiency in production, and visual and taste appeal. Simple elegance and a light, fresh appearance are the objectives, in contrast to the baroque ornamentation of more traditional styles. Cutouts can be made in advance, then placed on the cake relatively quickly for decoration. Fresh fruit and flowers are beautiful in their own right and require little assistance from the pâtissier.

The taste of the finished product is an important factor in favor of the modern-style wedding cake, with virtually no restrictions on the type of cake or fillings. Generally, as with modern cuisine, fresh and seasonal products are employed to their best advantage. If a customer loves fresh strawberry charlotte, there is no reason the pâtissier cannot create a festive, attractive wedding cake composed of charlottes. Many people seek out the unusual, and a modern-style wedding cake can be tailored to their liking.

Specialty cakes

Specialty cakes employ many of the same techniques as do wedding cakes. There are two elements that distinguish wedding cakes from specialty cakes: Specialty cakes are typically not tiered or stacked as are wedding cakes, and they are most often less ornately decorated. In some respects, however, the creation of a specialty cake presents fewer restrictions for the pastry chef or baker's creativity. Specialty cakes are less limited by shape, color, and type of décor. Types of décor for these cakes will be restricted only by ambient temperature and humidity.

Building a properly supported cake

Adequate support for a tiered cake is, of course, an important consideration in the construction of the cake. If the tiers are to be stacked without pillars, they will generally require added support (possible exceptions are British- and Australian-style cakes, which are often solid enough not to require additional support). This added support can be supplied by wooden dowels or pipes cut to length and inserted into each tier prior to placing the next tier on top. Thus, the weight of the tiers above is supported by the dowels rather than by the cake below. If pillars or columns are used, each type has its own system for providing strength and support to the layers above.

Scheduling the production of a wedding or specialty cake

The timetable for cake production varies widely depending on the style of cake being produced. A sample schedule is given below.

PRIOR TO DAY 1: Design and produce decorations; prepare hardware.

DAY 1: Bake cake layers.

DAY 2: Fill cake layers and seal-coat the cake.

DAY 3: Ice and decorate cake.

DAY 4: Transport cake and set it up.

This schedule is designed for lighter, freshly made cakes. Rich, dense British- or Australian-style cakes are often allowed to mature and ripen for weeks, meaning that the cake can be baked well ahead of time. For any cake, most of the time-consuming decorations can be made well in advance as long as there are adequate dry storage facilities. Creating the décor for the cake generally must begin several days prior to assembling and serving both because of the time involved in the decoration and the time required for royal icing string work to dry. Do not refrigerate this type of cake; the sugar decorations will melt.

Sketching the design on paper

Transporting the cake

Cakes to be transported to job sites require special packaging to ensure their safe arrival. In general, the farther the cake must travel, the less finished it should be prior to arrival at the site. For tiered cakes, each tier can be assembled as much as possible. However, stacking the cake on site will make the cake easier to maneuver. Once stacked, a cake becomes very heavy and cumbersome. To transport, place each tier in a box on a nonskid carpet pad and then place each box on the floor of the vehicle to be used for transportation, again on a nonskid carpet pad. Fragile gum paste or pulled sugar flowers and ornaments are best placed on the cake after it reaches its destination.

Costing wedding cakes

Wedding cakes are generally priced by the portion. There are many factors influencing the price, including:

LABOR COST. This is by far the highest expense, especially for fancy cakes. An Australian-style cake will cost more per portion than an American-style cake, as it requires many more hours of skilled labor to produce. It is also a more unusual product.

MARKET SEGMENT AND LOCATION. Price will be dictated in part by who the customer is, what the ticket for a wedding averages in a given locale, and whether the wedding cake is sold retail (private) or wholesale (caterer).

FOOD COST. Originally a relatively small expense, this is becoming more crucial for modern cakes with fresh and high-quality ingredients.

UNIQUE FEATURES. If you are selling to an affluent market segment, you will be able to charge more for something as important as a wedding cake. Customers are willing to pay extra for a product they cannot get elsewhere.

Heart-shaped wedding cake

MAKES 60 SERVINGS

Carrot cake (page 271), 6-, 8-, and 10-in/15-, 20-, and 25-cm heart shapes	1 each	1 each
Cake board, 10-in/25-cm heart, covered in white fondant with a white ribbon around outer edge	1 each	1 each
Cream cheese icing (page 420)	4 lb 8 oz	2.04 kg
Rolled fondant (page 859), colored peach	5 lb	2.27 kg
Buttercream for décor (page 850)	10 oz	284 g
Gum paste roses (see page 844), full	9 each	9 each
Gum paste roses (see page 844), half open	12 each	12 each
Gum paste rosebuds (see page 844)	14 each	14 each
Gum paste leaves (see Note, page 833)	34 each	34 each
Royal icing (page 851)	8 oz	227 g

1   Place the 10-in/25-cm cake layer on the cake board. Slice the cake into 3 even layers and fill with cream cheese icing. Crumb-coat the cake with icing. Insert 6 dowels in the cake: 1 in the center, 2 at the top, 1 at each side, and 1 at the base and trim so they are flush with the surface of the cake. Roll out the fondant ⅛ in/3 mm thick. Carefully cover the cake with the fondant and smooth the top and sides. Trim the fondant from the bottom edge of the cake.

2   Repeat the slicing, filling, crumb-coating, and covering process with the 8-in/20-cm cake and the 6-in/15-cm cake, inserting 4 dowels in the 8-in/20-cm cake and none in the 6-in/15-cm cake.

3   Place the 8-in/20-cm cake on top of the bottom tier, with the right side and right rear corner aligned with the 10-in/25-cm cake so that the assembled cake is offset. Place the 6-in/15-cm cake on top of the second tier, aligning the right sides and right rear corners.

4   Using a pastry bag fitted with a #3 star tip, pipe a shell border of buttercream around the base each tier.

5   Arrange a spray of roses and leaves in the center of the top tier of the cake, using 5 full roses, 5 half-open roses, 7 rosebuds, and 8 leaves, attaching each with a small dab of royal icing.

6   Arrange a spray on the left side of the middle and bottom tiers and one on the cake board, placing each spray slightly in front of the previous one to create a cascading effect: use 2 full roses, 2 half-open roses, 3 rosebuds, and 10 leaves for the spray on the 8-in/20-cm tier. Use 1 full rose, 3 half-open roses, 3 rosebuds, and 10 leaves for the spray on the 10-in/25-cm tier. Use the remaining 1 full rose, 2 half-open roses, 1 rosebud, and 6 leaves for the spray on the cake board.

White buttercream magnolia wedding cake

MAKES 80 SERVINGS

Chiffon sponge (page 287), 4-, 8-, and 12-in/10-, 20-, and 30-cm rounds	1 each	1 each
Cake board, 4-in/10-cm round, 9-in/23-cm round, and 16-in/41-cm hexagonal, covered in white fondant with a white ribbon around outer edge	1 each	1 each
Strawberry mousse (page 379)	3 lb 8 oz	1.59 kg
Buttercream for décor (page 850)	3 lb	1.36 kg
Pastillage/marzipan leaves (see page 833), ½ by 2 in/1 by 5 cm	16 each	16 each
Pastillage/marzipan leaves (see page 833), 1 by 2½ in/3 by 6 cm	16 each	16 each
Gum paste magnolias (see page 846)	7 each	7 each

1   Slice each of the cakes into three 1-in/3-cm layers. Place one of the 4-in/10-cm layers on a cardboard cake round of the same size. Apply an even coating of mousse, using 6 oz/170 g. Top with a second layer, apply the same amount of mousse, and top with the third layer. Coat the top and sides of the cake with buttercream. Refrigerate until the filling has set, at least 2 hours.

2   Repeat the process with the two remaining cakes, using 10 oz/284 g mousse for each of the layers of the 8-in/20-cm cake and 12 oz/340 g mousse for each of the layers of the 12-in/30-cm cake.

3   Place the largest cake on the 16-in/41-cm hexagonal cake board. Insert 9 dowels in the cake: 1 directly in the center and the other 8 around the center to form a circle 5 in/13 cm in diameter. Trim the dowels so they are flush with the surface of the cake.

4   Coat a circular drum separator (3 by 6 in/8 by 15 cm) with buttercream. Place it in the center of the cake, directly over the dowels. Place the 8-in/20-cm cake on the 9-in/23-cm cake board and place it on top of the drum separator. Insert 4 dowels in the 8-in/20-cm cake: 1 directly in the center and the remaining three 1½ in/4 cm from the center to form a triangle around the center dowel. Place the smallest cake on top, in the center of the middle tier. Trim each of the dowels so they are flush with the surface of the cake.

5   Using a pastry bag fitted with a #4 shell tip, pipe a shell border of buttercream around the base of each tier and the drum separator. Using a #2 plain tip, pipe buttercream scrollwork on each of the bottom two tiers: 6 scrolls on the 12-in/30-cm cake and 6 scrolls on the 8-in/20-cm cake, spacing them evenly.

6   Attach the small lace leaves to the sides of the top tier by gently pressing the ends into the buttercream, with the tips pointing directly up. Attach the large lace leaves to the sides of the drum separator by gently pressing the ends into the buttercream, with the tips pointing directly up.

7 Place one of the magnolias in the center of the top tier. Place the remaining magnolias around the sides of the bottom tier, centering them between the piped scrollwork designs.

Anniversary cake

MAKES 12 SERVINGS

Chiffon sponge (page 287), 10-in/25-cm round	1 each	1 each
Cake board, 10-in/25-cm round, covered in white fondant with a white ribbon around outer edge	1 each	1 each
Strawberry jam	1 lb 8 oz	680 g
Apricot jam	1 lb	454 g
Marzipan (page 852)	1 lb 4 oz	567 g
Fondant, warm	3 lb	1.36 kg
Straw sugar base (see page 838)	1 each	1 each
White poured sugar base, 4-in/10-cm round	1 each	1 each
Blown sugar strawberries (see page 836)	3 each	3 each
Pulled sugar blossoms (see page 839)	3 each	3 each
Pulled sugar leaves (see page 841)	10 each	10 each
Pulled sugar ribbon, (see page 842), red and white	1 each	1 each
Spun sugar triangle (page 854)	1 each	1 each
Dark chocolate, melted, tempered, for writing	as needed	as needed
Oval pastillage plaque (see page 836), 1 by 1½ in/3 by 4 cm	1 each	1 each

1   Slice the cake into three 1-in/3-cm layers. Place one layer on the cake board. Spread evenly with 12 oz/340 g of the strawberry jam. Top with a second cake layer and spread evenly with the remaining strawberry jam. Top with the last layer of cake.

2   Coat the top and sides of the cake with the apricot jam.

3   Roll out the marzipan ⅛ in/3 mm thick. Carefully cover the cake with the marzipan and smooth the top and sides.

4   Thin the warm fondant to the proper glazing consistency. Place the cake on a wire rack set over a sheet pan. Glaze the cake with the fondant.

5   Attach a white satin ribbon ½ in/1 cm wide to the base of the cake, gently pressing it onto the fondant while it is still slightly tacky to create a finished border.

6   Attach the straw sugar base to the poured sugar base by melting small nails of sugar for pulling or blowing and using them as glue. (See pages 836 to 842 for more information on working with pulled and blown sugar.)

7 Attach the sugar strawberries, blossoms, leaves, and sugar ribbon to the base in the same manner to form an attractive spray. Attach the spun sugar triangle to the back of this centerpiece.

8 Place the sugar centerpiece slightly off center on top of the cake.

9 Using a parchment cone filled with tempered dark chocolate, write "Happy Anniversary" on the pastillage plaque and place it on top of the cake next to the sugar centerpiece.

Congratulations cake

MAKES 12 SERVINGS

Royal icing (page 851)	10 oz	284 g
Dobos sponge (page 276), 7 by 10-in/18 by 25-cm ovals	7 each	7 each
Simple syrup (page 900)	8 fl oz	240 mL
Chocolate buttercream (page 418)	2 lb 8 oz	1.13 kg
Rolled fondant (page 859), colored pistachio green	5 lb	2.27 kg
Pastillage décor link twists (see page 843)	20 each	20 each
Poured sugar (page 853)	as needed	as needed

1   Using royal icing, pipe and flood the C for the "Congratulations," using the template in Appendix B (page 905). Let set for several hours, until completely dry. (See page 825 for more information on flood work.)

2   Place a Dobos layer on a cardboard cake board of the same size. Moisten with simple syrup, apply a thin coating of buttercream, and top with another layer of sponge. Repeat the process with the remaining layers.

3   Coat the top and side of the cake with the remaining buttercream.

4   Roll out the fondant ¼ in/6 mm thick. Carefully cover the cake with the fondant and smooth the top and sides. Trim the fondant from the bottom edge of the cake. Cover the sides of an oval drum 4 by 7 in/10 by 18 cm with rolled fondant. Smooth and trim.

5   Roll out the remaining fondant ¼ in/6 mm thick and cover an oval cake board of the same dimensions as the cake with the rolled fondant and cover its edges with ribbon. Place the drum on the cake board, then place the cake on the drum, being sure to center it perfectly.

6   Color a small portion of the royal icing the same green as the fondant. Using a pastry bag fitted with a #4 shell tip, pipe a small shell border around the base of the drum and the edges of the cake board.

7   Using small dabs of royal icing, attach the pastillage links to the sides of the cake, positioning them so that the untwisted ends hang from the bottom of the cake and the sides of the links just touch one another. Using a #1 plain pastry tip or a parchment cone, pipe royal icing strings to connect the pastillage links.

8   Place the royal icing C on the top left side of the cake. Color a small portion of royal icing gold. Using a parchment cone, pipe the rest of the word "Congratulations," then pipe some small accents on the C. Using a parchment cone, pipe spirals of plain royal icing on top of the cake.

9   Pour some liquid poured sugar into small silicone jewel molds. Allow them to cool completely and solidify. Using small dabs of royal icing, attach the sugar jewels to the C in the "Congratulations."

Mother's Day butterfly cake

MAKES 30 SERVINGS

Pastillage (page 857)	2 lb	907 g
Royal icing (page 851)	1 lb 8 oz	680 g
White modeling chocolate (page 852)	2 lb	907 g
Lemon chiffon sponge (page 287), 12-in/30-cm round	1 each	1 each
Simple syrup (page 900)	as needed	as needed
White chocolate buttercream (page 418)	3 lb	1.36 kg
Rolled fondant (page 859)	2 lb	907 g

1   Roll out the pastillage ¼ in/6 mm thick. Using the template in Appendix B (page 903), cut 2 butterfly wings from the pastillage. Flip one over to have left and right wings. Allow to dry completely.

2   Using a pastry bag fitted with a #1 plain tip, pipe and flood the design on top of the pastillage wings with royal icing, according to the diagram in Appendix B. (Have a straight pin handy to pop any air bubbles that form while piping.) Immediately place the wings under a heat lamp and allow to harden completely. (The faster a crust forms, the higher the shine of the finished décor.)

3   Using the modeling chocolate, form the body of the butterfly; it should be 8 in/20 cm long and ¾ in/2 cm wide. Use food coloring markers to make markings on the body using the photo opposite as a guide. Attach two wires 2 in/5 cm long to the head for antennae.

4   Using the butterfly wing template, cut 6 layers of lemon chiffon cake. Place one of the layers on a cake board cut to the same dimensions. Moisten it with simple syrup, coat it lightly with buttercream, and top with a second layer. Moisten the second layer with simple syrup, coat lightly with buttercream, and top with a third layer. Repeat the process with the remaining 3 layers in mirror image, so that you have a left wing and a right wing. Coat the top and sides of each wing with buttercream.

5   Roll out the fondant ¼ in/6 mm thick. Carefully cover each of the wings with fondant and smooth the top and sides. Trim the fondant from the base of the cake.

6   Cover a cake board cut into a butterfly shape 2 in/5 cm larger than the cake with rolled fondant. Place the wings side by side on the board.

7   Place a pastillage wing on each half of the cake, securing them with royal icing. Using royal icing, attach the butterfly body between the 2 wings.

8   Using a pastry bag fitted with a #4 star tip, pipe a shell border of buttercream around the edges of the wings and around the base of the cake.

Hydrangea cake

MAKES 190 SERVINGS

Chiffon sponge (page 287), 4 in/10 cm high, 4-, 8-, 12-, and 16-in/10-, 20- 30-, and 41-cm squares, filled and seal-coated	1 each	1 each
Cake board, 20-in/51-cm square, covered in blue fondant with a pink ribbon around outer edge	1 each	1 each
Royal icing (page 851)	8 oz	227 g
Rolled fondant (page 859), colored blue	10 lb	4.54 kg
Dowels	25 each	25 each
Rolled fondant (page 859), colored yellow	2 lb	907 g
Styrofoam rounds, 2, 6, and 8 in/5, 15 and 20 cm	1 each	1 each
Gum paste roses (see page 844), full	9 each	9 each
Gum paste roses (see page 844), half open	6 each	6 each
Gum paste leaves (see page 833)	8 each	8 each
Gum paste hydrangeas (see page 848), punch flowers	240 each	240 each

1 Attach the 16-in/41-cm cake to the cake board with a touch of royal icing.

2 Carefully cover the cake with the blue fondant and smooth the top and sides. Trim the fondant from the bottom edge of the cake. Place 2 dowels in the center of the cake. Then form an oval pattern with 10 more, placing 3 at the top, 2 on either side, and 3 at the bottom, making sure that each dowel is approximately 3 in/8 cm from the outer edge of the cake.

3 Repeat the covering and doweling process with the 3 other cakes, inserting 9 dowels in the 12-in/30-cm cake, 4 in the 8-in/20-cm cake, and none in the 4-in/10-cm cake.

4 Roll out the yellow fondant to ⅛ in/3 mm thick. Cut into four 1½-in/4-cm wide strips, each strip long enough to wrap around the outside base of one of the cakes. You will need strips approximately 16 in/41 cm, 32 in/81 cm, 48 in/122 cm, and 64 in/163 cm long. Wrap the strips around the base of each cake, adhering with royal icing.

5 Cut each of the Styrofoam rounds in half on an angle to make wedges. Attach each wedge and each cake with a touch of royal icing as you progress: Place the largest wedge in the center of the largest cake and place the 12-in/30-cm cake on top. Place the mid-size wedge in the center of the 12-in/30-cm cake in the opposite direction and place the 8-in/20-cm cake

on top. Place the smallest wedge in the center of the 8-in/20-cm cake and place the 4-in/10-cm cake on the very top.

6   Arrange a spray of roses, leaves, and hydrangeas in the gap between each of the tiers of the cake, attaching each with a small dab of royal icing.

Dogwood flowers cake

MAKES 200 SERVINGS

Chiffon sponge (page 287), 4 in/10 cm high, 6-, 8-, 10-, 12-, and 14-in/15-, 20- 25-, 30-, and 36-cm rounds, filled and seal-coated	1 each	1 each
Cake board, 20-in/51-cm round, covered in green fondant with a brown ribbon around outer edge	1 each	1 each
Royal icing (page 851)	1 lb	454 g
Rolled fondant (page 859), colored green	15 lb	6.80 kg
Dowels	31 each	31 each
Dark modeling chocolate (page 851), for branches	2 lb	907 g
Dark chocolate, melted, tempered	1 lb	454 g
Gum paste dogwood flowers (see page 848), large	20–25 each	20–25 each
Gum paste dogwood flowers (see page 848), small	20–25 each	20–25 each
Modeling chocolate leaves (see page 833)	16 each	16 each

1   Attach the 14-in/36-cm cake to the cake board with a touch of royal icing. Carefully cover the cake with the green fondant and smooth the top and sides. Trim the fondant from the bottom edge of the cake. Place 2 dowels in the center of the cake. Then form an oval pattern with 10 more, placing 3 at the top, 2 on either side, and 3 at the bottom, making sure that each dowel is approximately 3 in/8 cm from the outer edge of the cake.

2   Repeat the covering and doweling process with the 4 other cakes, inserting 9 dowels in the 12-in/30-cm cake, 6 in the 10-in/25-cm cake, 4 in the 8-in/20-cm cake, and none in the 6-in/15-cm cake. Stack the cakes in descending size order, attaching each with a touch of royal icing and making sure to center each cake on its base.

3   Roll the remaining green fondant into a rope ¼ in/6 mm thick. Twist 2 ropes together and attach a twisted rope border around the bottom of each tier.

4   Roll tapered ropes of the modeling chocolate for branches in lengths from 2 to 8 in/5 to 20 cm. Each rope should come to a point. Fasten these ropes to the sides of the cake using tempered chocolate. Attach the flowers and leaves to the branches with tempered chocolate.

5   Place a centerpiece of modeling chocolate branches and gum paste dogwood flowers in the center of the top tier of the cake.

Overpiped cake

MAKES 12 SERVINGS

Chiffon sponge (page 287), 10-in/25-cm round	1 each	1 each
Cake board, 10-in/25-cm round, covered in white fondant with a white ribbon around outer edge	1 each	1 each
Buttercream for décor (page 850)	10 oz	284 g
Rolled fondant (page 859), white	2 lb	907 g
Green food coloring	as needed	as needed
Gum paste roses (see page 844)	7 each	7 each
Gum paste rosebuds (see page 844)	as needed	as needed
Gum paste leaves (see page 833)	8 each	8 each
Royal icing (page 851), colored yellow	2 oz	57 g
Royal icing (page 851), white	1 lb 3 oz	539 g
Royal icing (page 851), colored purple	1 lb	454 g
Royal icing (page 851), colored green	4 oz	113 g

1   Place the cake on the cake board. Slice into 3 even 1-in/3-cm-thick layers. Cover the bottom layer with ½ in/1 cm of buttercream. Place the second cake layer and cover with ½ in/1 cm of buttercream. Place the remaining cake layer on top and crumb-coat the top and sides with the remaining buttercream icing.

2   Roll out the fondant ⅛ in/3 mm thick. Carefully cover the cake with the fondant and smooth the top and sides. Trim the fondant from the bottom edge of the cake.

3   Massage a bit of green food coloring into the remaining white fondant and roll tapered ropes for branches in lengths from 2 to 4 in/5 to 10 cm. Each rope should come to a point to create vines. Create a cluster of gum paste roses, rosebuds, leaves, and vines in the center of the top of the cake and pipe small pearls of yellow royal icing around the flowers. When assembling the roses and buds, you will need to identify the amount of flowers that are needed to cover the space available. In most cases 2 large roses, 1 medium rose, and 4 buds should be enough for the bunch to be effective. As shown, some clusters are effective fillers for the display.

4   Using white royal icing, pipe a pearl border around the bottom edge of the cake (see Note). With a very fine piping tip and more white royal icing, pipe strings of filigree around the outer edge of the cake. Using the same tip, pipe swags around the outside of the cake and around the pearl border at the base of the cake. Allow each of these embellishments to dry, then pipe over the existing lines. Repeat this process five to eight times to create the "overpiped" elements.

5   Using the purple royal icing, pipe bunches of small violets around the outside of the cake where each of the swags meet and single violets around the base of the cake. Use a fine piping tip and the yellow royal icing to pipe small dots at the center of each violet. With a small leaf tip and the green royal icing, pipe small leaves in the violets.

6   Use the small rose tip and a nail to pipe the flower. Push the icing out of the bag into five petals onto a small square of parchment paper. Let set for 1 hour and pipe the yellow dot. Let set overnight. Peel the flowers off the parchment and apply onto the cluster. Attach each flower with soft royal icing.

NOTE   When piping the pearl border, use a round tip. The icing should be smooth but not too soft. Squeeze the icing out of the bag, making sure your tip is just touching the surface. The action is to push out the icing, then stop and move on to the next pearl.

Tiffany box cake

MAKES 24 SERVINGS

Chiffon sponge (page 287), 8 by 8 by 4-in/20 by 20 by 10-cm square, filled and seal-coated	1 each	1 each
Cake board, 8-in/20-cm square, covered with white fondant	1 each	1 each
Royal icing (page 851)	1 lb	454 g
Rolled fondant (page 859), colored bright blue	3 lb	1.36 kg
Rolled fondant (page 859), colored pale blue	2 lb	907 g
Edible pearl or luster dust	as needed	as needed
Rolled fondant strips (see page 859), white, 1¼ by 9 in/3 by 23 cm, ⅛ in/3 mm thick	4 each	4 each
Pastillage loops (see page 847), white, 1¼ in/3 cm wide	18 each	18 each
Pastillage ribbon ends (see page 847), white, 1¼ in/3 cm wide	2 each	2 each

1   Attach the 14-in/36-cm cake to the cake board with a touch of royal icing.

2   Roll out the bright blue fondant ⅛ in/3 mm thick. Carefully cover the cake with the fondant and smooth the top and sides. Trim the fondant from the bottom edge of the cake.

3   Roll out the pale blue fondant to ⅛ in/3 mm thick. Carefully cover the top and 1 in/3 cm down the sides of the cake; trim the fondant to an even edge. Roll thin ropes of the bright blue fondant and attach with royal icing to outline the top and bottom edges and the corners of the pale blue fondant "box top."

4   Pipe small pearls of royal icing around the base of the cake using a #7 plain tip. After the icing border has completely dried, brush it with pearl dust.

5   To wrap the "ribbon" around the box, place the each of the fondant strips in the center of a side of the cake, meeting in the top center of the cake. Trim the ends at the top so they so not overlap. Adhere the strips with a touch of royal icing. Brush the strips with pearl dust.

6   Create a bow by attaching the pastillage loops together with royal icing. Prop up the loops with pieces of balled-up plastic wrap until the bow has completely dried. Brush the two bow ends and the fully dried bow with pearl dust. Fasten the bow ends to the center of the cake with a touch of royal icing. Fasten the bow on top of the ends with more royal icing.

Chocolate tiered cake

MAKES 165 SERVINGS

Chocolate chiffon sponge (page 288), 4 in/10 cm high, 8-, 12-, and 16-in/20-, 30-, and 41-cm rounds, filled and seal-coated	1 each	1 each
Cake board, 20-in/51-cm round, covered in chocolate fondant, with a brown ribbon around outer edge	1 each	1 each
Royal icing (page 851)	1 lb	454 g
Chocolate fondant	10 lb	4.54 kg
Dowels	15 each	15 each
Dark modeling chocolate (page 851)	2 lb	907 g
Edible gold powder	as needed	as needed
Clear alcohol	as needed	as needed
Dark modeling chocolate roses (see page 832), large	15–20 each	15–20 each
Dark modeling chocolate roses (see page 832), small	4–5 each	4–5 each
Dark modeling chocolate leaves (see page 833)	12 each	12 each
Dark modeling chocolate buds (see page 832)	4–5 each	4–5 each
Dark chocolate, melted, tempered	as needed	as needed

1   Attach the 16-in/41-cm cake to the cake board with a touch of royal icing.

2   Roll out the chocolate fondant ⅛ in/3 mm thick. Carefully cover the cake with the fondant and smooth the top and sides. Trim the fondant from the bottom edge of the cake.

3   Place 1 dowel in the center of the cake. Form an oval pattern with another 8 dowels, placing 2 at the top, 2 on either side, and 2 at the bottom, making sure that each dowel is approximately 3 in/8 cm from the outer edge of the cake.

4   Repeat the covering, trimming, and doweling process with the other two cakes, using 6 dowels for the 12-in/30-cm cake and none for the 8-in/20-cm cake. Stack the cakes in descending size order, attaching each with a touch of royal icing and making sure to center each cake on its base.

5   Roll the dark modeling chocolate into a log. Flatten the log with a rolling pin to 2 in/5 cm thick. Roll the band to ⅛ in/3 mm thick. Using a line-textured rolling pin, apply the texture to the band. Cut the band into 1-in/3-cm-wide strips. Wrap a dark chocolate band around the base of each cake, smoothing the seams. Retexture the seam areas as necessary. Embellish the top edge of each band with a thin line of gold dust applied with clear alcohol.

6   Create a large spray of roses and leaves for the top of the cake and secure with tempered chocolate. Create smaller sprays of roses and leaves placed randomly at the base of each tier.

Link twist cake

MAKES 150 SERVINGS

Chiffon sponge (page 287), 4 in/10 cm high, 7-, 11-, and 15-in/18-, 28-, and 38-cm rounds, filled and seal-coated	1 each	1 each
Cake board, 20-in/51-cm round covered in pale pink fondant, with a white ribbon around outer edge	1 each	1 each
Royal icing (page 851)	2 lb	907 g
Rolled fondant (page 859), colored pink	5 lb	2.27 kg
Dowels	21 each	21 each
Gum paste roses (see page 844), colored dark red, large	5 each	5 each
Gum paste rosebuds (see page 844), colored dark red	3 each	3 each
Gum paste leaves (see page 833), colored green	8 each	8 each
Poured sugar vase	1 each	1 each
Pastillage link twists (see page 843), colored pink	45 each	45 each
Silver dragées	45 each	45 each

1. Place the 15-in/38-cm cake on the cake board and attach with a touch of royal icing.

2. Roll out the fondant ⅛ in/3 mm thick. Carefully cover the cake with the fondant and smooth the top and sides. Trim the fondant from the bottom edge of the cake. Place 2 dowels in the center of the cake. Then form an oval pattern with 10 more dowels, placing 3 at the top, 2 on either side, and 3 at the bottom, making sure that each dowel is approximately 3 in/8 cm from the outer edge of the cake.

3. Repeat the covering and doweling process with the other 2 cakes, using 9 dowels for the 11-in/28-cm cake, and none for the 7-in/18-cm cake. Stack the cakes in descending size order, attaching each with a touch of royal icing and making sure to center each cake on its base.

4. Create a spray of gum paste roses, buds, and leaves for the sugar vase, place in the center of the top tier, and secure with a touch of royal icing.

5. Pipe a pearl border of royal icing around the base of each tier, using a #7 plain tip. About 1 in/3 cm down from the top of each tier, adhere the link twists 2½ in/6 cm apart using royal icing.

6. Using a #1 plain tip, pipe swags of royal icing between the tops of the link twists.

7. Pipe strings of royal icing to create swags around the side of each cake, connecting at the base of the link twists. Repeat two times so that there are 3 strings connecting each link twist, each draping slightly lower that the previous. Using royal icing, secure a silver dragée to the tip of each link twist where these swags meet.

Drapes and swags cake

MAKES 208 SERVINGS

Chiffon sponge (page 287), 4 in/10 cm high, 6-, 8-, 10-, 12-, and 14-in/15-, 20-, 25-, 30-, and 36-cm rounds, filled and seal-coated	1 each	1 each
Cake board, 16-in/41-cm round, covered in white fondant, with a white ribbon around outer edge	1 each	1 each
Royal icing (page 851)	2 lb	907 g
Rolled fondant (page 859)	15 lb	6.80 kg
Dowels	31 each	31 each
Fondant swags (see page 846), colored purple, 4 in/10 cm	5 each	5 each
Fondant swags (see page 846), colored purple, 4½ in/11 cm	7 each	7 each
Fondant swags (see page 846), colored purple, 6½ in/17 cm	8 each	8 each
Gum paste bows (see page 847), colored purple	20 each	20 each
White modeling chocolate roses (see page 832), colored purple, large	10 each	10 each
White modeling chocolate roses (see page 832), colored purple, small	7 each	7 each
Chocolate dome (page 850)	1 each	1 each

1   Attach the 14-in/36-cm cake to the cake board with a touch of royal icing.

2   Roll out the fondant ⅛ in/3 mm thick. Carefully cover the cake with the fondant and smooth the top and sides. Trim the fondant from the bottom edge of the cake. Place 2 dowels in the center of the cake. Then form an oval pattern with 10 more dowels, placing 3 at the top, 2 on either side, and 3 at the bottom, making sure that each dowel is approximately 3 in/8 cm from the outer edge of the cake.

3   Repeat the covering and doweling process with the other 4 cakes, using 9 dowels for the 12-in/30-cm cake, 6 for the 10-in/25-cm cake, 4 for the 8-in/20-cm cake, and none for the 6-in/15-cm cake. Stack the cakes in descending size order, attaching each with a touch of royal icing and making sure to center each cake on its base.

4   Using water to make the ends tacky, attach the swags to the center of the sides of the 14-in/36-cm, 10-in/25-cm, and 6-in/15-cm tiers.

5   Attach the gum paste bows between the swags with royal icing. Pipe a pearl border around each tier at the bottom, using royal icing with a #7 piping tip.

6   Using royal icing with a #7 piping tip, pipe a Swiss dot (pearls) design 1½ in/4 cm apart on the 12-in/30-cm and 8-in/20-cm tiers.

7 Create a centerpiece for the top tier by attaching the roses to the dome with royal icing. Attach the centerpiece on top with a touch of royal icing.

Painted rose cake

MAKES 38 SERVINGS

Chiffon sponge (page 287), 4 in/10 cm high, 10-in/25-cm round, filled and seal-coated	1 each	1 each
Cake board, 12-in/30-cm round, covered in white fondant with a white ribbon around outer edge	1 each	1 each
Rolled fondant (page 859)	3 lb	1.36 kg
Fondant ribbon roses (see page 849), colored pale pink	8 each	8 each
Fondant ribbon roses (see page 849), colored deep pink	8 each	8 each
Fondant leaves (see page 833), colored green	10 each	10 each
Royal icing (page 851)	as needed	as needed
Clear alcohol	2 oz	57 g
Powdered food color: pink, magenta, leaf green, sage green, and brown	as needed	as needed
Rolled fondant (page 859), colored green	14 oz	397 g
Rolled fondant (page 859), colored brown	8 oz	227 g

1   Attach the cake to the cake board with a touch of royal icing.

2   Roll out the fondant ⅛ in/3 mm thick. Carefully cover the cake with the fondant and smooth the top and sides. Trim the fondant from the bottom edge of the cake.

3   Create a spray of ribbon roses and leaves for the center of the cake and attach with royal icing.

4   Using clear alcohol, liquefy the food colors and paint vines, leaves, and thorns on the sides of the cake. Paint circles of pink for the rose bases and indicate petals with magenta.

5   Roll a rope of green fondant ½ by 45 in/1 by 114 cm and lay it in a zigzag design for the border on top, attaching with water.

6   For the bottom border, roll a rope of brown fondant ½ in/1 cm and attach to the base of the cake with water. Roll a rope of green fondant ½ in/1 cm and lay around the brown. Crimp the two together by hand-forming a scalloped edge.

Elemental recipes

Aspic gelée

MAKES 32 FL OZ/960 ML

CLARIFICATION		
Onion, roughly chopped	2 oz	57 g
Carrots, roughly chopped	1 oz	28 g
Celery, roughly chopped	1 oz	28 g
Ground beef	12 oz	340 g
Egg whites, beaten	3 each	3 each
Tomato concassé	3 oz	85 g
STOCK		
Stock (see Note)	32 fl oz	960 mL
Sachet d'épices (page 894)	1 each	1 each
Kosher salt	¼ tsp	1.25 g
Ground white pepper	as needed	as needed
Gelatin, granulated (see page 902)	as needed	as needed

1   Mix all the ingredients for the clarification. Blend with the stock. Mix well.

2   Bring the mixture to a slow simmer, stirring frequently until a raft forms.

3   Add the sachet d'épices and simmer for 45 minutes, or until the appropriate flavor and clarity are achieved. Baste the raft occasionally.

4   Strain the consommé. Adjust the seasoning with salt and pepper as needed.

5   Cool the consommé in an ice water bath.

6   Soften the gelatin in cold water, then melt over simmering water. Add to the consommé.

7   Refrigerate until needed. Warm as necessary for use.

NOTE Choose an appropriate stock depending upon the intended use. For example, if the aspic is to be used to coat a seafood item, prepare a lobster stock and use ground fish in place of the beef for the clarification.

Egg wash

MAKES 16 FL OZ/480 ML

Eggs	8 oz	227 g
Milk	8 fl oz	240 mL
Salt	pinch	pinch

Combine the eggs, milk, and salt using a wire whip.

NOTES   There are infinite variations possible from this basic egg wash to best suit different uses and tastes. For example, water or cream can be substituted for some or all of the milk.

Egg yolks can be substituted for all or a portion of the whole eggs.

Sugar can also be added.

Fish stock

MAKES 128 FL OZ/3.84 L

Bones and trim from lean white-fleshed fish	10 lb	4.54 kg
Vegetable oil	2 fl oz	60 mL
Onions, roughly chopped	8 oz	227 g
Parsnips, roughly chopped	4 oz	113 g
Celery, roughly chopped	4 oz	113 g
Cold water	160 fl oz	4.80 L
White wine	8 fl oz	240 mL

1   Sauté the fish bones and trim in the oil until the bones become white.

2   Add the mirepoix and continue to sauté for another 10 to 15 minutes.

3   Add the water and wine and simmer for 30 minutes.

4   Strain the stock. Cool over an ice bath. Store under refrigeration.

Fish velouté

MAKES 64 FL OZ/1.92 L

Fish stock (opposite)	80 fl oz	2.40 L
Blond roux, as needed	4 to 8 oz	113 to 227 g
Salt	½ tsp	2.50 g
Ground black pepper	¼ tsp	0.50 g

1 Bring the stock to a boil.

2 Whip the roux into the stock. Work out all the lumps.

3 Simmer for 30 to 40 minutes, skimming the surface as necessary.

4 Season with salt and pepper as needed.

5 Strain the sauce. Cool over an ice water bath and store covered in the refrigerator until needed.

Pan grease

MAKES 3 LB/1.36 KG

Shortening	1 lb	454 g
Bread flour	1 lb	454 g
Vegetable oil	1 lb	454 g

Blend the shortening and flour on low speed with the paddle attachment until a smooth paste forms. Gradually add the oil and blend until smooth.

NOTE Coat the inside of cake and loaf pans with the mixture to create a nonstick surface.

Pesto

MAKES 18 OZ/510 G

Pine nuts	2½ oz	71 g
Garlic	½ oz	14 g
Basil leaves	6 oz	170 g
Parmesan, grated	3½ oz	99 g
Ground black pepper	1 tsp	2 g
Salt	2 tsp	10 g
Olive oil	6 fl oz	180 mL

1 Combine the pine nuts, garlic, basil, Parmesan, pepper, and salt in a food processor fitted with a metal chopping blade. Process to blend.

2 Add the olive oil with the processor running and process until smooth.

Pineapple chips

MAKES APPROXIMATELY 180 CHIPS

Pineapple, peeled, trimmed, and cut into ¹⁄₁₆-in/1.5-mm slices	2 each	2 each
Simple syrup (page 900)	16 fl oz	480 mL

1 Place the pineapple slices on silicone baking mats and brush with the simple syrup.

2 Bake at 180°F/82°C until crisp and dry, about 3 hours. Store in an airtight container.

Tomato sauce

MAKES 2 LB 5 OZ/1.05 KG

Olive oil	2 oz	57 g
Yellow onions, small dice	4 oz	113 g
Garlic, minced	1¼ oz	35 g
Tomato concassée	1 lb 12 oz	794 g
Sugar	½ oz	14 g
Dried basil	1 tbsp plus ½ tsp	7 g
Dried rosemary, crushed	1 tbsp plus ½ tsp	7 g
Dried oregano	1 tbsp plus ½ tsp	7 g
Dried tarragon	1 tbsp plus ½ tsp	7 g
Salt	as needed	as needed
Ground black pepper	as needed	as needed

1   Heat the oil in a sauteuse over medium heat. Sauté the onions until translucent and tender. Add the garlic and sauté for 2 minutes.

2   Add the remaining ingredients and simmer for 25 minutes.

3   Cool the tomato sauce over an ice water bath. Store covered under refrigeration.

Sachet d'épices

MAKES 1 SACHET

Parsley stems	4 each	4 each
Thyme leaves	½ tsp	2.50 mL
Bay leaf	1 each	1 each
Peppercorns, cracked	½ tsp	2.50 mL
Garlic clove, crushed	1 each	1 each

Place all the ingredients on a piece of cheesecloth approximately 4 in/10 cm square. Gather up the edges and tie with butcher's twine, leaving a long tail of string to tie to the pot handle.

Almond filling

MAKES 3 LB 8 OZ/1.59 KG

Almond paste	1 lb	454 g
Butter	1 lb	454 g
Eggs	1 lb	454 g
Cake flour	8 oz	227 g

1   Cream together the almond paste and butter on medium speed fitted with the paddle attachment until smooth, about 5 minutes.

2   On low speed, add the eggs, one at a time, scraping down the bowl after each addition. Once the egg is fully incorporated, add another until all eggs are added.

3   Add the cake flour and mix on low speed until fully incorporated.

4   Store in an airtight container under refrigeration.

Almond-cassis filling

MAKES 1 LB 5¼ OZ/602 G, ENOUGH FILLING FOR 1 COFFEE CAKE

Almond paste	10½ oz	298 g
Baker's sugar	5¼ oz	149 g
Egg yolks	2 oz	57 g
Cassis (black currant) purée	3½ oz	99 g

Combine all the ingredients and mix on medium speed with the paddle attachment until a uniform paste is obtained, about 5 minutes. Store in an airtight container under refrigeration.

Cheese Danish filling

MAKES 4 LB 10 OZ/2.10 KG

Cream cheese	3 lb	1.36 kg
Sugar	12 oz	340 g
Cornstarch	6 oz	170 g
Lemon zest, grated	1 tsp	3 g
Orange zest, grated	1 tsp	3 g
Vanilla extract	1 tbsp	15 mL
Eggs	8 oz	227 g

1   Cream together the cream cheese, sugar, cornstarch, lemon and orange zests, and vanilla on medium speed with the paddle attachment until light and smooth.

2   Add the eggs gradually, one at a time, scraping down the bowl periodically, until fully blended. Store under refrigeration if not using immediately.

3   Fill pastries as desired and bake.

Chocolate filling

MAKES 2 LB/907 G

Butter, melted	11¾ oz	332 g
Light brown sugar	11¼ oz	318 g
All-purpose flour	1½ oz	43 g
Cocoa powder	1½ oz	43 g
Honey	2 tbsp	37 g
Eggs	5 oz	142 g
Vanilla extract	2 tsp	10 ml

Make the filling the day before needed. In a mixer with a paddle attachment mix the butter and sugar on medium speed for 2 minutes or until completely combined. Add the flour, cocoa powder, and honey and mix on medium speed until completely combined, scraping the bowl occasionally. Blend in the eggs and vanilla extract. Refrigerate in a covered container until needed.

Cream cheese filling

MAKES 1 LB 4 OZ/567 G

Cream cheese	1 lb	454 g
Confectioners' sugar	4 oz	113 g
Vanilla extract	1 fl oz	30 mL
Lemon zest, grated	1 tsp	3 g

1   Cream together the cream cheese, confectioners' sugar, vanilla extract, and lemon zest on medium speed with the paddle attachment, scraping down the bowl periodically, until smooth in texture and light in color, about 5 minutes. Store under refrigeration if not using immediately.

2   Pipe or otherwise deposit to fill pastries before baking.

Hazelnut filling

MAKES 6 LB/2.72 KG

Almond paste	1 lb	454 g
Sugar	1 lb	454 g
Butter	1 lb	454 g
Hazelnuts, lightly toasted and finely ground	3 lb	1.36 kg
Ground cinnamon	½ oz	14 g

1   Blend the almond paste with the sugar on medium speed with the paddle attachment until light and smooth. Add the butter and blend on medium speed until smooth. Add the hazelnuts and cinnamon and blend until fully combined. Store under refrigeration if not using immediately.

2   Fill pastries as desired and bake.

Frangipane for filling

MAKES 2 LB 5½ OZ/1.06 KG

Almond paste	1 lb	454 g
Sugar	2½ oz	71 g
Eggs	8 oz	227 g
Butter	8 oz	227 g
Cake flour	3 oz	85 g

1 Cream together the almond paste and sugar; add a small amount of egg to be sure there are no lumps. Add the butter and cream well. Gradually add the remaining eggs. Add the flour and mix until just combined. Store under refrigeration if not using immediately.

2 Use only as a filling for tart shells or pithiviers.

Braised pineapple

MAKES ENOUGH FOR APPROXIMATELY 40 DANISH

Pineapple	1 each	1 each
Orange juice	128 fl oz	3.84 L
Sugar	1 lb	454 g

1 Cut both ends off the pineapple and cut off the skin. Cut the pineapple in quarters lengthwise. Cut along the pointed edge to cut out the core. Discard the skin and core (if not using for Savarin Syrup, page 437).

2 Place the pineapple in a hotel pan. Pour over the orange juice and sprinkle the sugar on top of the pineapple. Cover the hotel pan with foil. Braise in a 325°F/163°C convection oven until the pineapple is tender, about 45 minutes.

3 Let cool. Remove the pineapple from the pan and reserve separately under refrigeration.

Brûlée sugar blend

MAKES 1 LB/454 G

Granulated sugar	8 oz	227 g
Light brown sugar	8 oz	227 g

Combine the two sugars and spread out on a sheet pan. Allow to air-dry overnight. Process the sugar mixture in a food processor until very fine. Sift through a fine-mesh strainer. Store tightly covered in a cool, dry place.

Candied rose petals

MAKES 20 PETALS

Rose petals, untreated	20 each	20 each
Pasteurized egg whites	2 oz	57 g
Superfine sugar	as needed	as needed

1 Lightly brush both sides of the petals with the egg whites.

2 Make an even layer of sugar approximately ¼ in/6 mm deep in a half sheet pan. Arrange the petals in the sugar, making sure they do not touch. Sprinkle additional sugar over the petals to cover completely.

3 Remove the petals from the sugar and place them on a clean parchment-lined sheet pan. Allow to air-dry, then use or store in an airtight container.

NOTE Mint leaves or other edible untreated flowers may be processed in the same way.

Cinnamon smear

MAKES APPROXIMATELY 4 LB/1.81 KG

Butter, melted	1 lb 7 oz	652 g
Dark brown sugar	1 lb 6 oz	624 g
Light corn syrup	2½ oz	71 g
Pastry flour	3 oz	85 g
Cinnamon	3 oz	85 g
Eggs	9 oz	255 g
Vanilla extract	1½ tsp	7.50 mL

1 Combine the butter, brown sugar, and corn syrup and mix on medium speed with the paddle attachment until smooth, about 5 minutes.

2 Add the flour and cinnamon and mix on low speed until smooth, about 5 minutes. Add the eggs and vanilla a little at a time, scraping down the sides of the bowl regularly to ensure an even texture. Continue to mix until all of the wet ingredients are fully incorporated, about 2 minutes more.

3 Place the smear in a storage container and refrigerate if it is not to be used right away. The batter must be softened by paddling before using after refrigeration.

VARIATION Replace the corn syrup with 2½ oz/71 g honey.

Cinnamon sugar
MAKES 9 OZ/255 G

Sugar	8 oz	227 g
Ground cinnamon	1 oz	28 g

Blend the sugar and cinnamon until fully combined. Store in an airtight container at room temperature.

VARIATION CINNAMON SUGAR (STRONG) Reduce the sugar to 5 oz/142 g.

Citrus-flavored syrup
MAKES 192 FL OZ/5.76 L

Water	128 fl oz	3.84 L
Sugar	4 lb	1.81 kg
Orange, halved	1 each	1 each
Lemon, halved	1 each	1 each
Vanilla bean, split and scraped	1 each	1 each

Combine all the ingredients in a saucepan and stir to ensure all the sugar is moistened. Bring to a boil. Simmer over medium heat for 15 minutes. Remove from the heat and cool completely. Strain the syrup. Store, tightly covered, under refrigeration.

VARIATION SPICED FLAVORED SYRUP FOR CAKES Add 1 nutmeg (cracked), 1 cinnamon stick, and 1 tbsp/15 mL black peppercorns to the mixture along with the vanilla bean.

Coconut shavings
MAKES 1 LB 4 OZ/567 G

Coconuts, halved	2 each	2 each
Simple syrup (page 900)	8 fl oz	240 mL

1 Place the coconut halves on a sheet pan. Bake at 350°F/177°C until the flesh just begins to pull away from the shells, 5 to 7 minutes. Cool completely.

2 Remove the coconut flesh from the shells and remove the brown skin. Using a vegetable peeler, shave strips 2 in/5 cm long from the flesh.

3 Toss the coconut shavings with the simple syrup, then drain any excess syrup.

4 Spread the coconut shavings on a parchment-lined sheet pan. Bake in a 350°F/177°C deck oven until lightly toasted, 8 to 10 minutes.

5 Allow the coconut shavings to cool to room temperature. Store in an airtight container at room temperature.

Coffee concentrate
MAKES 64 FL OZ/1.92 L

Dark-roast coffee beans, coarsely ground	1 lb	454 g
Water	64 fl oz, plus more as needed	1.92 L, plus more as needed
Sugar	2 lb	907 g

1 Combine the coffee and water in a saucepan, bring to a boil, and boil for 10 minutes.

2 Strain through a sieve set over a bowl, then return the volume of the liquid to 64 fl oz/1.92 L by pouring additional hot water through the coffee grounds.

3 Combine the sugar and 16 fl oz/480 mL of the coffee mixture in a saucepan and bring to a boil, stirring to dissolve the sugar. Continue cooking until the sugar caramelizes.

4 Gradually add the remaining coffee mixture to the caramel. Continue cooking the mixture until it reaches 325°F/163°C. Cool completely. Store in an airtight container at room temperature.

NOTE Use the concentrate sparingly to flavor buttercreams, syrups, and mousses.

Danish glaze

MAKES 25½ FL OZ/765 ML

Apricot jam	9 oz	255 g
Water	6 fl oz	180 mL
Light corn syrup	9 oz	255 g
Liquor (such as rum)	1½ fl oz	45 mL

Combine all the ingredients in a saucepan and stir. Bring to a boil, stirring to incorporate.

NOTE Use the glaze while it is still warm, applying it to the items with a pastry brush.

Gelatin solution

MAKES 7 OZ/198 G

Water, cold	6 fl oz	180 mL
Gelatin, granulated	1 oz	28 g

Bloom the gelatin in the water for 5 minutes. Heat the bloomed gelatin over a warm water bath until fully dissolved. Store, tightly covered, under refrigeration. Warm to melt and add to formula as desired.

NOTE Use this solution to stabilize whipped cream used for filling or icing cakes and pastries.

Japonais meringue

MAKES 4 LB/1.81 KG

Hazelnuts, finely ground	1 lb	454 g
Confectioners' sugar	1 lb	454 g
Egg whites	1 lb	454 g
Granulated sugar	1 lb	454 g

1   Combine the hazelnuts and confectioners' sugar; rub together well.

2   Place the egg whites in a bowl and whisk until frothy. Gradually add the granulated sugar while continuing to whip, then whip to stiff peaks.

3   Fold the hazelnut mixture into the meringue.

4   Pipe into the desired shapes and bake at 150° to 200°F/66° to 93°C until the meringue has hardened.

VARIATION: JAPONAIS ROUNDS

Makes 40 rounds (2 in/5 cm each)

1   Before preparing the japonais, line a sheet pan with parchment paper. Trace forty 2-in/5-cm rounds on the paper and turn the paper over to avoid contact between the pen or marker and the batter.

2   Fill a piping bag fitted with a #2 tip with the mixture. Pipe dime-size mounds around the traced rounds, pulling up at the end of each dot to make a tail of batter. Continue piping around to fill in the entire 2-in/5-cm round. Bake as directed above.

Lemon chips

MAKES APPROXIMATELY 20 CHIPS

Simple syrup (page 900)	16 fl oz	480 mL
Lemons, ends removed, cut into ¹⁄₁₆-in/1.5-mm slices	2 each	2 each

1   Bring the simple syrup to a boil. Poach the lemon slices for 1 minute, or until limp.

2   Place the slices on a silicone baking mat. Bake in a 180°F/82°C oven for 3 hours, or until crisp and dry. Store in an airtight container.

Poaching liquid for fruit

MAKES 34 FL OZ/1.02 L

Wine	20 fl oz	600 mL
Water	10 fl oz	300 mL
Sugar (optional; use with tart fruit)	4 oz	113 g
Cinnamon stick	1 each	1 each
Cloves	6 each	6 each

1   Combine all the ingredients and bring to a simmer.

2   Peel fruit and shape, if necessary. Cook the fruit in the poaching liquid until tender. Cool the fruit in the liquid. Store under refrigeration in the poaching liquid.

NOTES To vary the flavor of the poaching liquid, try different types of wine (red or white), or add fruit purée or juice to the poaching liquid.

You can also use different types of spices: nutmeg, peppercorns, or allspice, for example.

Add saffron to light-colored poaching liquids to impart flavor and a golden yellow color to the fruit.

Port poaching liquid

MAKES 52 FL OZ/1.56 L

Port	32 fl oz	960 mL
Sugar	1 lb 4 oz	567 g
Cinnamon stick	½ each	½ each
Vanilla bean, split	1 each	1 each
Orange zest, grated	⅔ oz	19 g

1   Combine all the ingredients in a saucepan and bring to a simmer, stirring to dissolve the sugar.

2   Add peeled and prepped fruit to the simmering liquid and poach until slightly underdone. Cool the fruit in the liquid. Store under refrigeration in the poaching liquid.

Poached cranberries

MAKES 1 LB 8 OZ/680 G

Simple syrup (page 900)	48 fl oz	1.44 L
Cranberries	1 lb	454 g

Heat the simple syrup to a simmer. Add the cranberries and continue to simmer for 10 minutes. Remove from the heat and cool completely. Store the cranberries in the syrup under refrigeration until ready to use.

Poached pears

MAKES 12 POACHED PEARS

Water	75 fl oz	2.25 L
Sugar	15 oz	425 g
Lemon juice	7 each	7 each
Pears, d'Anjou	12 each	12 each

1   Combine the water, sugar, and lemon juice in a pot large enough to hold 12 pears. Bring the liquid to a boil over high heat. Boil for 1 minute. Reduce the heat to medium.

2   Meanwhile, trim the bottom of each pear to make it flat, core out the bottom with a melon baller, and peel with a sharp paring knife; leave the stem attached. Once a pear is prepped, submerge it immediately into ice water acidified with lemon juice.

3   Once all of the pears are prepped, place them into the poaching liquid and simmer for 30 to 60 minutes at 190° to 200°F/88° to 93°C. Make sure the pears are completely submerged; use a plate and parchment paper if necessary to weigh them down. Once the pears have become slightly tender, remove the pot from the heat and let the pears sit in the poaching liquid until tender, about 1 hour and 30 minutes.

4   Cool pears to room temperature. Reserve, covered, under refrigeration.

NOTE For the Pear with Thai Jewels (page 759) plated dessert, soak the pears in the Banana Passion Fruit Broth (page 463) overnight. Make sure they are completely submerged.

Poached raisins

MAKES 4 LB 8 OZ/2.04 KG, ENOUGH FOR 80 PAINS AU RAISIN

Dark raisins	8 oz	227 g
Golden raisins	8 oz	227 g
Sugar	2 lb	907 g
Water	32 fl oz	960 mL
Orange, skin	2 each	2 each
Cinnamon sticks	3 each	3 each

1   Combine all the ingredients in an 8-quart pot. Bring to a boil over high heat.

2   Once boiling, take the pot off the heat and cover with plastic wrap. Let sit for 1 hour.

3   Transfer the liquid and raisins to an airtight container and refrigerate.

4   When ready to use, strain the needed amount of raisins out of the liquid and pat dry with paper towels.

Roasted Black Mission figs

MAKES APPROXIMATELY 2 LB 3 OZ/992 G

Black Mission figs, very ripe	1 lb 1½ oz	489 g
Sugar	14 oz	397 g
Dry port	3½ oz	99 g
Cinnamon sticks (optional)	3 sticks	3 sticks
Cloves (optional)	1 tsp	5 mL
Vanilla beans, split and scraped (optional)	1 each	1 each
Orange zest, grated (optional)	1 each	1 each

1   Trim the stem end and bottom of the figs. Cut an X in the top and bottom of each fig.

2   Place each fig in a standing position in a hotel pan. Sprinkle the sugar on top. Pour the port on top of the figs. Add the spices and other flavors, if using. Roast in a 325°F/163°C convection oven until the figs are just tender, about 20 minutes.

3   Let the figs cool in the pan.

4   Reserve the figs and roasting liquid, covered, under refrigeration.

Saffron poaching liquid

MAKES 32 FL OZ/960 ML

White wine	36 fl oz	1.08 L
Lemon juice	1½ fl oz	45 mL
Cinnamon stick	1 each	1 each
Cloves	6 each	6 each
Sugar	5 oz	142 g
Saffron threads	pinch	pinch

1   Combine all the ingredients in a saucepan and bring to a simmer, stirring to dissolve the sugar.

2   Add peeled and prepped fruit to the simmering liquid and poach until slightly underdone. Cool the fruit in the liquid. Store under refrigeration in the poaching liquid.

Simple syrup

MAKES 32 FL OZ/960 ML

Sugar	1 lb	454 g
Water	16 fl oz	480 mL

Combine the sugar and water in a saucepan and stir to ensure all the sugar is moistened. Bring to a boil, stirring to dissolve the sugar. Store covered in the refrigerator until needed.

NOTE Simple syrup may be made with varying ratios of sugar to water depending on the desired use and the sweetness and flavor of the cake or pastry to which it is to be applied.

VARIATIONS

COFFEE SIMPLE SYRUP After the sugar and water come to a boil, add 1 oz/28 g ground coffee. Remove the pan from the heat, cover, and allow to steep for 20 minutes. Strain to remove the grounds.

LIQUEUR-FLAVORED SIMPLE SYRUP To flavor simple syrup with a liqueur such as framboise, kirsch, or Kahlúa, add 4 fl oz/120 mL of the desired liqueur to the syrup after it has cooled completely.

LIQUOR-FLAVORED SIMPLE SYRUP To flavor simple syrup with a liquor such as brandy or rum, add 2 fl oz/60 mL of the desired liquor to the syrup after it has cooled completely.

VANILLA SIMPLE SYRUP After the sugar and water comes to a boil, add 1 vanilla bean, split and scraped. Remove the pan from the heat, cover, and allow to steep for 20 minutes. Strain to remove the pod.

Stabilized solution for whipped cream

MAKES 32 FL OZ/960 ML

Gelatin, granulated	1 oz	28 g
Cold water	16 fl oz	480 mL
Hot water	16 fl oz	480 mL

1   Bloom the gelatin in the cold water.

2   Add the hot water and stir to dissolve the gelatin.

3   Cover tightly and store under refrigeration.

4   To use, melt 3 oz/85 g of the gelatin mixture and add to 16 fl oz/480 mL of heavy cream. Whip to desired peaks.

Streusel topping

MAKES 4 LB/1.81 KG

Butter	1 lb	454 g
Sugar	1 lb	454 g
Bread flour	2 lb	907 g
Ground cinnamon	1 tbsp	6 g

Cream the butter and sugar together until light and fluffy on medium speed with the paddle attachment. Add the flour and cinnamon and mix to a rough crumb. Store under refrigeration.

Vanilla sugar

MAKES 1 LB/454 G

Vanilla bean, split	1 each	1 each
Sugar	1 lb	454 g

Place the vanilla bean and sugar in a lidded jar, cover tightly, and shake well. Let stand for at least 1 week before using.

NOTES Vanilla sugar can also be made using confectioners' sugar.

Vanilla beans used to infuse custards, sauces, and other liquids can be used to make vanilla sugar if first rinsed and allowed to thoroughly air-dry.

Walnut praline paste

MAKES 4 LB/1.81 KG

Walnuts, lightly toasted and roughly chopped	2 lb	907 g
Sugar	2 lb	907 g

1   Spread the walnuts on a marble surface.

2   Place the sugar in a heavy-bottomed saucepan and cook over medium heat, stirring constantly, to a rich golden brown.

3   Pour the caramel over the walnuts. Cool to room temperature.

4   Break up the praline and grind to a soft paste in a food processor. Store in an airtight container at room temperature.

Bieber spice

MAKES 2 LB 6 OZ/1.08 KG

Ground cinnamon	12 oz	340 g
Ground coriander	12 oz	340 g
Ground nutmeg	3 oz	85 g
Ground anise	6 oz	170 g
Ground cloves	4 oz	113 g
Ground ginger	1 oz	28 g

Combine all the spices. Store in an airtight container at room temperature.

Lebkuchen spice
Gingerbread spice

MAKES 2 OZ/57 G

Ground cinnamon	1½ tbsp	9 g
Ground cloves	1 tbsp plus ½ tsp	7 g
Ground nutmeg	2 tsp	4 g
Ground anise	1½ tbsp	9 g
Ground ginger	1 tbsp plus ½ tsp	7 g
Ground fennel	1½ tbsp	9 g
Ground coriander	1½ tbsp	9 g

Combine all the spices. Store in an airtight container at room temperature.

Spice mix for pumpkin crème brûlée

MAKES 1 LB 2 OZ/510 G

Brûlée sugar blend (page 896)	8 oz	227 g
Light brown sugar	8 oz	227 g
Ground cinnamon	1 oz	28 g
Ground cloves	1 oz	28 g

Thoroughly combine all of the ingredients. Store in an airtight container.

RATIOS FOR GRANULATED GELATIN PER QUANTITY OF LIQUID

PER GALLON/3.84 LITERS	PER PINT/480 ML	GEL STRENGTH
2 oz/57 g	¼ oz/7 g	Delicate gel
4 oz/113 g	½ oz/14 g	Coating gel
6–8 oz/170–227 g	1 oz/28 g	Sliceable gel
10–12 oz/284–340 g	1¼–1½ oz/35–43 g	Firm gel
16 oz/454 g	2 oz/57 g	Mousse strength

Décor Templates

Butterfly cake template

Scarecrow template

Filigree templates

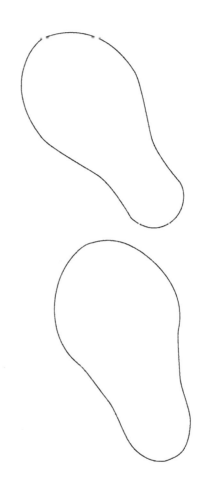

Congratulations "C" template

Magnolia petals template

Conversions, Equivalents, and Calculations

WEIGHT MEASURE CONVERSIONS

To calculate weight conversions into metric, multiply the number of ounces by 28.35.

¼ oz	7 g
½ oz	14 g
1 oz	28 g
4 oz (¼ lb)	113 g
8 oz (½ lb)	227 g
16 oz (1 lb)	454 g
24 oz (1 lb 8 oz)	680 g
32 oz (2 lb)	907 g
40 oz (2 lb 8 oz)	1.13 kg
48 oz (3 lb)	1.36 kg

Metric values have been rounded.

VOLUME MEASURE CONVERSIONS

To calculate volume conversions into metric, multiply the number of ounces by 30.

1 tsp	5 mL
½ fl oz (1 tbsp)	15 mL
1 fl oz (2 tbsp)	30 mL
8 fl oz (1 c)	240 mL
16 fl oz (1 pt)	480 mL
32 fl oz (1 qt)	960 mL
128 fl oz (1 gal)	3.84 L
Dash (liquid) = less than ⅛ tsp	0.63 mL
Pinch (dry) = less than ⅛ tsp	0.63 mL

Metric values have been rounded.

LENGTH MEASURE CONVERSIONS

To calculate length conversions into metric, multiply the number of inches by 2.54.

¼ in	6 mm
½ in	1 cm
1 in	3 cm
2 in	5 cm
4 in	10 cm
6 in	15 cm
7 in	18 cm
8 in	20 cm
9 in	23 cm
10 in	25 cm
12 in (1 ft)	30 cm

Metric values have been rounded.

TEMPERATURE CONVERSIONS

To convert Fahrenheit to Celsius: $(°F - 32) \times \frac{5}{9} = °C$

DEGREES FAHRENHEIT (°F)	DEGREES CELSIUS (°C)
32	0
40	4
140	60
150	66
160	71
170	77
212	100
275	135
300	149
325	163
350	177
375	191
400	204
425	218
450	232
475	246
500	260

Readings and Resources

Books

Baking and Pastry Arts

The Baker's Manual, 5th ed. Joseph Amendola and Nicole Rees. John Wiley & Sons, 2003.

The Baker's Trade. Zachary Y. Schat. Acton Circle Publishing Company, 1998.

Baking with Julia: Based on the PBS Series Hosted by Julia Child. Julia Child and Dorie Greenspan. William Morrow & Co., 1996.

The Bread Bible: Beth Hensperger's 300 Favorite Recipes. Beth Hensperger. Chronicle, 1999.

The Bread Builders: Hearth Loaves and Masonry Ovens. Daniel Wing and Alan Scott. Chelsea Green Pub Co., 1999.

Buffets Sucrés: Sweet Buffets. Lenôtre School. C.H.I.P.S., 1997.

The Cake Bible, 8th ed. Rose Levy Beranbaum. William Morrow & Co., 1988.

The Chocolate Bible. Christian Teubner et al. Chartwell Books, 2004.

Chocolate Desserts by Pierre Hermé. Pierre Hermé and Dorie Greenspan. Little, Brown & Company, 2001.

The Classic and Contemporary Recipes of Yves Thuriès, French Pastry. Yves Thuriès. Rhona Poritzky Lauvand, trans. John Wiley & Sons, 1997.

The Classic and Contemporary Recipes of Yves Thuriès, Modern French Pastry. Yves Thuriès. Rhona Poritzky Lauvand, trans. John Wiley & Sons, 1997.

The Classic and Contemporary Recipes of Yves Thuriès, Restaurant Pastries and Desserts. Yves Thuriès. Rhona Poritzky Lauvand, trans. John Wiley & Sons, 1997.

Desserts by Pierre Hermé. Pierre Hermé, Dorie Greenspan, and Hartmut Kiefer. Little, Brown & Company, 1998.

English Bread and Yeast Cookery. Elizabeth David and Wendy Jones. National Book Network, 1995.

Flatbreads and Flavors: A Culinary Atlas. Jeffrey Alford and Naomi Duguid. Morrow/Avon, 1995.

Four-Star Desserts. Emily Luchetti. HarperCollins, 1996.

French Professional Pastry Series: Creams, Confections, and Finished Desserts. Roland Bilheux and Alain Escoffier. John Wiley & Sons, 1998.

French Professional Pastry Series: Decorations, Borders and Letters, Marzipan, Modern Desserts. Roland Bilheux and Alain Escoffier. John Wiley & Sons, 1998.

French Professional Pastry Series: Doughs, Batters, and Meringues. Roland Bilheux and Alain Escoffier. John Wiley & Sons, 1998.

French Professional Pastry Series: Petits Fours, Chocolate, Frozen Desserts, and Sugar Work. Roland Bilheux and Alain Escoffier. John Wiley & Sons, 1997.

French Professional Pastry Series: Special and Decorative Breads. Roland Bilheux, Alain Escoffier, Daniel Hervé, and Jean-Marie Pouradier. John Wiley & Sons, 1997.

Grand Finales: A Neoclassic View of Plated Desserts. Tish Boyle and Timothy Moriarty. John Wiley & Sons, 2000.

Grand Finales: The Art of the Plated Dessert. Tish Boyle and Timothy Moriarty. John Wiley & Sons, 1996.

The Making of a Pastry Chef. Andrew MacLauchlan. John Wiley & Sons, 1999.

A Modernist View of Plated Desserts (Grand Finales). Tish Boyle and Timothy Moriarty. John Wiley & Sons, 1997.

Nancy Silverton's Breads from the La Brea Bakery: Recipes for the Connoisseur. Nancy Silverton with Laurie Ochoa. Random House, 1996.

The New International Confectioner, 5th ed. Wilfred J. France. Virtue, 1987.

Les Pains et Viennoiseries: Bread, Viennese Breads, and Pastry. Lenôtre School. C.H.I.P.S., 1995.

La Pasticceria: Pastries, Cakes and Desserts. Stefano Laghi and Rossano Boscolo. C.H.I.P.S., 1996.

Patisserie: An Encyclopedia of Cakes, Pastries, Cookies, Biscuits, Chocolate, Confectionery and Desserts. Aaron Maree. HarperCollins, 1994.

The Pie and Pastry Bible. Rose Levy Beranbaum. Simon & Schuster, 1998.

Practical Baking. William J. Sultan. John Wiley & Sons, 1996.

The Professional Pastry Chef, 4th ed. Bo Friberg. John Wiley & Sons, 2002.

Les Recettes Fruitées: Recipes for Fruit. Lenôtre School. C.H.I.P.S., 1998.

Les Recettes Glacées: Ice Cream and Iced Desserts. Lenôtre School. C.H.I.P.S., 1995.

Simply Sensational Desserts: 140 Classic Desserts for the Home Baker From New York's Famous Patisserie and Bistro. Francois Payard et al. Broadway Books, 1999.

Special and Decorative Breads: Traditional, Regional and Special Breads, Fancy Breads—Viennese Pastries—Croissants, Brioches—Decorative Breads—Presentation Pieces. Alain Couet, Éric Kayser, et al. John Wiley & Sons, 1997.

Understanding Baking, 3rd ed. Joseph Amendola and Nicole Rees. John Wiley & Sons, 2002.

The Village Baker. Joe Ortiz. Ten Speed Press, 1993.

Food History

Culture and Cuisine: A Journey Through the History of Food. Jean-François Revel. Helen R. Lane, trans. Da Capo, 1984.

Food and Drink Through the Ages, 2,500 B.C. to 1937 A.D. Barbara Feret. Maggs Brothers, 1937.

Food in History. Reay Tannahill. Random House, 1995.

Sanitation and Safety

Applied Foodservice Sanitation Textbook, 4th ed. Educational Foundation of The National Restaurant Association, 1993.

Basic Food Sanitation. The Culinary Institute of America, 1993.

HAACP: Reference Book. Educational Foundation of The National Restaurant Association, 1993.

Food Science

CookWise: The Secrets of Cooking Revealed. Shirley Corriher. Morrow/Avon, 1997.

Food Science, 3rd ed. Helen Charley. Macmillan, 1994.

On Food and Cooking: The Science and Lore of the Kitchen. Harold McGee. Simon & Schuster, 1997.

The Curious Cook. Harold McGee. Hungry Minds, 1992.

Equipment

Food Equipment Facts: A Handbook for the Foodservice Industry, revised and updated ed. Carl Scriven and James Stevens. Van Nostrand Reinhold, 1989.

The New Cook's Catalogue: The Definitive Guide to Cooking Equipment. Emily Aronson, Florence Fabricant, and Burt Wolf. Knopf, 2000.

The Professional Chef's Knife Kit, 2nd ed. The Culinary Institute of America. John Wiley & Sons, 1999.

General Product Identification and Mise en Place

A Concise Encyclopedia of Gastronomy. André Louis Simon. Overlook, 1983.

Cheese Primer. Steven Jenkins. Workman Publishers, 1996.

Cheeses of the World. U.S. Department of Agriculture. Peter Smith, 1986.

Larousse Gastronomique. Jenifer Harvey Lang, ed. Crown, 1988.

Spices, Salt and Aromatics in the English Kitchen. Elizabeth David. Penguin, 1972.

The Book of Coffee and Tea, 2nd ed. Joel Schapira, David Schapira, and Karl Schapira. St. Martin's, 1996.

The Chef's Book of Formulas, Yields and Sizes, 3rd ed. Arno Schmidt. John Wiley & Sons, 2003.

The Chef's Companion: A Concise Dictionary of Culinary Terms, 2nd ed. Elizabeth Riely. John Wiley & Sons, 1996.

The Complete Book of Spices: A Practical Guide to Spices and Aromatic Seeds. Jill Norman. Viking, 1995.

The Cook's Ingredients. Philip Dowell and Adrian Bailey. Reader's Digest Association, 1990.

The Master Dictionary of Food and Wine, 2nd ed. Joyce Rubash. John Wiley & Sons, 1996.

The New Food Lover's Companion, 4th ed. Sharon Tyler Herbst and Ron Herbst. Barron's, 2007.

The Oxford Companion to Food. Alan Davidson. Oxford University Press, 1999.

The World Encyclopedia of Food. Patrick L. Coyle. Facts on File, 1982.

Uncommon Fruits & Vegetables: A Commonsense Guide. Elizabeth Schneider. William Morrow & Co., 1998.

Vegetables from Amaranth to Zucchini. Elizabeth Schneider. William Morrow & Co., 2001.

General Cookery

Escoffier Cook Book. Auguste Escoffier. Crown, 1941.

Escoffier: The Complete Guide to the Art of Modern Cookery. Auguste Escoffier. John Wiley & Sons, 1995.

Ma Gastronomie. Ferdinand Point. Frank Kulla and Patricia S. Kulla, trans. Lyceum, 1974.

The Professional Chef, 8th ed. The Culinary Institute of America. John Wiley & Sons, 2006.

Le Répertoire de la Cuisine. Louis Saulnier. Barron's, 1977.

Periodicals

AMERICAN CAKE DECORATING
4215 White Bear Parkway, Suite 100
St. Paul, MN 55110-7635
Telephone: 651-293-1544
Fax: 651-653-4308
www.americancakedecorating.com

ART CULINAIRE
40 Mills Street
Morristown, NJ 07960
Telephone: 800-SO-TASTY
Fax: 973-993-8779
www.getartc.com

BAKERS JOURNAL
222 Argyle Avenue
Delhi, Ontario, N4B2Y2
Canada
Telephone: 519-582-2513
Fax: 519-582-4040

THE BAKING SHEET
King Arthur Flour Company
PO Box 1010
Norwich, VT 05055
Telephone: 800-827-6836
www.kingarthurflour.com

BAKING AND SNACK
4800 Main Street, Suite 100
Kansas City, MO 64112
Telephone: 816-756-1000
Fax: 816-756-0494
www.bakingbusiness.com

BON APPÉTIT
6300 Wilshire Boulevard
Los Angeles, CA 90048
Telephone: 800-765-9419
www.bonappetit.com

CAKE: CRAFT AND DECORATION
Cake Magazine Subscription Dept.
Tower House, Sovereign Park
Market Harborough LE169EF
United Kingdom
Telephone: 01858 439605
www.cake-craft.com

CAKES AND SUGARCRAFT
Squires Kitchen Magazine Publishing
  Ltd.
Alfred House, Hones Business Park
Farnham, Surrey GU9 8BB
United Kingdom
Telephone: 01252 727572
Fax: 01252 714714
www.squires-group.co.uk

CHEF MAGAZINE
20 West Kinzie, 12th Floor
Chicago, IL 60610
Telephone: 888-545-3676 Ext. 10
www.chefmagazine.com

CHEF EDUCATOR TODAY
20 West Kinzie, 12th Floor
Chicago, IL 60610
Telephone: 888-545-3676 Ext.10
Fax: 800-444-9745
www.chefedtoday.com

CHOCOLATIER
P.O. Box 333
Mt. Morris, IL 61054
Telephone: 815-734-5816

CONFECTIONER MAGAZINE
155 Pfingsten Road, Suite 205
Deerfield, IL 60015
Telephone: 847-205-5660
Fax: 847-205-5680

COOK'S ILLUSTRATED
17 Station Street
Brookline, MA 02445
Telephone: 617-232-1000
Fax: 617-232-1572

**FANCY FOOD AND CULINARY
PRODUCTS**
20 North Wacker Drive, Suite 1865
Chicago, IL 60606
Telephone: 312-849-2220 Ext. 48
Fax: 312-849-2174

FINE COOKING
The Taunton Press, Inc.
63 S. Main Street
Newtown, CT 06470-5506
Telephone: 203-426-8171
www.finecooking.com

FOOD ARTS
387 Park Avenue South
New York, NY 10016
Telephone: 212-684-4224
Fax: 212-779-3334

FOOD & WINE
1120 Avenue of the Americas
New York, NY 10036
Telephone: 800-333-6569
www.foodandwine.com

GOURMET
4 Times Square
New York, NY 10036-6563
Telephone: 800-365-2454
www.gourmet.com

MODERN BAKING
P.O. Box 9400
Collingswood, NJ 08108-0940
www.bakery-net.com

NATION'S RESTAURANT NEWS
Telephone: 800-944-4676
Fax: 212-756-5215
www.nrn.com

PASTRY ART & DESIGN
P.O. Box 333
Mt. Morris, IL 61054
Telephone: 815-734-5816

SAVEUR
P.O. Box 420235
Palm Coast, FL 32142-0235
www.saveur.com

TEA AND COFFEE
26 Broadway, Floor 9m
New York, NY 10004
Telephone: 212-391-2060
Fax: 212-827-0945
www.teaandcoffee.net

WINE AND SPIRITS
2 West 32nd Street, Suite 601
New York, NY 10001
Telephone: 212-695-4660

WINE SPECTATOR
P.O. Box 37367
Boone, IA 50037-0367
Telephone: 800-752-7799

Organizations

**AMERICAN CULINARY
FEDERATION (ACF)**
P.O. Box 3466
St. Augustine, FL 32085
Telephone: 904-824-4468

**AMERICAN INSTITUTE OF
BAKING**
1213 Bakers Way
Manhattan, KS 66502
Telephone: 785-537-4750
www.aibonline.org

**BREAD BAKERS GUILD OF
AMERICA**
3203 Maryland Avenue
North Versailles, PA 15137
Telephone: 412-322-8275
www.bbga.org

CHEFS COLLABORATIVE 2000
282 Moody Street, Suite 207
Waltham, MA 02453
Telephone: 781-736-0635
www.chefscollaborative.org

**INTERNATIONAL COUNCIL ON
HOTEL/RESTAURANT AND INSTITU-
TIONAL EDUCATION (CHRIE)**
3205 Skipwith Road
Richmond, VA 23294
Telephone: 804-747-4971
www.chrie.org

**INTERNATIONAL ASSOCIATION OF
CULINARY PROFESSIONALS (IACP)**
455 South Fourth Street, Suite 650
Louisville, KY 40202
Telephone: 800-928-4227
Fax: 502-589-3602
www.iacp.com

THE JAMES BEARD FOUNDATION
167 West 12th Street
New York, NY 10011
Telephone: 212-675-4984
www.jamesbeard.org

LES DAMES D'ESCOFFIER (LDEI)
c/o AEC Management Resources
P.O. Box 4961
Louisville, KY 40204
Telephone: 502-456-1851
Fax: 502-456-1821
www.ldei.org

**THE MID-ATLANTIC BAKERS
ASSOCIATION**
P.O. Box 4141
Harrisburg, PA 17111-4141
Telephone: 717-561-4155
www.midatlanticbakers.org

**NATIONAL RESTAURANT
ASSOCIATION (NRA)**
1200 17th Street, NW
Washington, DC 20036
Telephone: 202-331-5900
www.restaurant.org

**RETAILER'S BAKERY
ASSOCIATION**
14239 Park Center Drive
Laurel, MD 20707-5261
Telephone: 800-638-0924
www.rbanet.com

**WOMEN CHEFS AND
RESTAURATEURS (WCR)**
455 South Fourth Street, Suite 650
Louisville, KY 40202
Telephone: 502-581-0300
www.womenchefs.org

WOMEN'S FOODSERVICE FORUM
1650 West 82nd Street, Suite 650
Bloomington, MN 55431
Telephone: 866-368-8003
Fax: 952-358-2119
www.womensfoodserviceforum.com

Glossary

ACID: A substance having a sour or sharp flavor. Foods generally referred to as acids include citrus juice, vinegar, and wine. A substance's degree of acidity is measured on the pH scale; acids have a pH of less than 7.

ACTIVE DRY YEAST: A dehydrated form of yeast that needs to be hydrated in warm water (105°F/41°C) before use. It contains about one-tenth the moisture of compressed yeast.

ADULTERATED FOOD: Food that has been contaminated to the point that it is considered unfit for human consumption.

AERATION: Incorporation of air by beating or whipping the ingredients together.

AEROBIC BACTERIA: Bacteria that require the presence of oxygen to function.

AGAR-AGAR: A gelling agent derived from certain sea vegetables. It is eight times stronger than gelatin.

AGITATE: To stir.

ALBUMIN: A water-soluble protein found in egg whites.

ALKALI: A substance that tests at higher than 7 on the pH scale. Baking soda is an example of an alkaline ingredient.

ALMOND PASTE: A mass of ground almonds and sugar.

ALPHA CRYSTALS: Large crystals in untempered chocolate. They are not uniform or stable, and must be melted at 83°F/28°C to properly temper chocolate.

AMYLOPECTIN: A component of starch composed of irregularly branched molecules. With a high presence of amylopectin, a starch will act to increase viscosity to a greater extent without causing a gel to form.

AMYLOSE: A component of starch composed of long, linear molecules. The higher the presence of amylose, the more the substance is prone to gel.

ANAEROBIC BACTERIA: Bacteria that do not require oxygen to function.

ASH CONTENT: The mineral content in flour.

AUTOLYSE: A resting period for dough after mixing the flour and water. This rest allows the dough to fully hydrate and to relax the gluten.

BACTERIA: Microscopic organisms. Some have beneficial properties; others can cause food-borne illnesses when foods they contaminate are ingested.

BAKING POWDER: A chemical leavening agent composed of sodium bicarbonate, an acid, and a moisture absorber such as cornstarch. When moistened and exposed to heat, it releases carbon dioxide to leaven a batter or dough.

BAKING SODA: A chemical leavening agent. Sodium bicarbonate is an alkali that when combined with an acid breaks down and releases carbon dioxide. This reaction causes the product to leaven as it is baked.

BATTER: A pourable mixture of combined ingredients, high in liquefiers.

BAUMÉ (BÉ): The scale for expressing the specific gravity of a liquid or the method for measuring the density of sugar syrups. It is expressed in degrees.

BENCH REST: In yeast dough production, the stage that allows the gluten in preshaped dough to relax before the final shaping. Also known as secondary fermentation.

BETA CRYSTALS: The small, stable fat crystals that give chocolate its shine and snap.

BIGA: Italian for an aged dough. A type of pre-ferment containing 50 to 60 percent water and ⅓ to ½ percent instant yeast.

BITTERSWEET CHOCOLATE: Chocolate containing a minimum of 35 percent chocolate liquor with varying amounts of sweeteners and cocoa butter.

BLANCH: To remove the skins from nuts by scalding.

BLEND: To fold or mix ingredients together.

BLIND BAKE: To partially or completely bake an unfilled pastry crust.

BLOCK METHOD: A method for tempering chocolate in which a block of tempered chocolate is added to melted chocolate and agitated until the proper temperature is reached, at which time the block is removed.

BLOOMING: (1) The process of allowing gelatin to soften in cold water (gelatin sheets) or soak up cold water (granulated gelatin). (2) For chocolate, see Fat Bloom and Sugar Bloom.

BOULANGER: French for "baker."

BRAN: The tough outer layer of a grain kernel and the part highest in fiber.

BRIX SCALE: A scale of measurement (decimal system) used to determine the density and concentration of sugar in a solution. It is expressed in degrees.

CARAMELIZATION: The process of cooking sugar in the presence of heat. The temperature range in which sugar caramelizes is approximately 320° to 360°F/160° to 182°C. The browning of sugar enhances the flavor and appearance of food.

CHEMICAL LEAVENER: An ingredient such as baking soda or baking powder used in a chemical action to produce carbon dioxide gas to leaven baked goods.

CHOCOLATE LIQUOR: The product made by grinding cocoa beans without adding sugar or cocoa butter.

COATING CHOCOLATE: Chocolate made with fats other than cocoa butter, which does not require tempering to use.

COCOA BUTTER: The fat extracted from the cacao bean.

COMMON MERINGUE: A mixture of egg whites and sugar, beaten until it reaches soft, medium, or stiff peaks. Also called French meringue.

COMPOUND CHOCOLATE: See Coating Chocolate.

COMPRESSED FRESH YEAST: Moist yeast is that must be refrigerated because it is extremely perishable.

COUVERTURE: A type of chocolate specifically designed for coating or incorporation with other ingredients. Extra cocoa butter is added to increase its smoothness, flexibility, and gloss after tempering. The cocoa butter content of couverture should be at least 32 percent.

CREAMING: Blending fats and sugar together to incorporate air.

CROSS CONTAMINATION: The transference of disease-causing elements from one source to another through physical contact.

CRUMB: The interior texture of baked goods.

CRYSTALLIZATION: A process that occurs when sugar is deposited from a solution.

DENATURE: To alter the original form of a substance. In proteins, exposure to heat or acid will denature or "cook" the protein.

DEXTROSE: A simple sugar made by the action of acids or enzymes on starch. Also known as corn sugar.

DISACCHARIDE: A double or complex sugar. When fructose and dextrose are bonded together, this is called sucrose, or table sugar. Maltose is another example of a disaccharide.

DISSOLVING: Heating bloomed gelatin until it is transparent and liquid.

DOCK: To pierce dough lightly with a fork or dough docker (resembles a spiked paint roller) to allow steam to escape during baking. This helps the dough to remain flat and even.

DOCTOR: A substance that is added to a sugar solution to help prevent crystallization. Common doctors are acids and glucose.

DOUGH: A mixture of ingredients high in stabilizers and often stiff enough to cut into shapes.

DUTCH-PROCESS COCOA: Cocoa made by adding alkali to nibs or to cocoa powder to develop certain flavors, reduce acidity, and make it more soluble.

EMULSION: The suspension of two ingredients that do not usually mix. Butter is an emulsion of water in fat.

ENDOSPERM: The inside portion of a grain, usually the largest portion, composed primarily of starch and protein.

ENRICHED DOUGH: Dough that is enriched includes ingredients that add fat or vitamins. Examples of these ingredients are sugar, eggs, milk, and fats.

FACULTATIVE BACTERIA: Bacteria that can survive both with and without oxygen.

FAT BLOOM: The white cast and soft texture of chocolate that is the result of poor tempering or exposure of the chocolate to high temperatures. Although fat bloom is visually and texturally unappealing, the chocolate is safe to eat.

FERMENTATION: A process that happens in any dough containing yeast. As the yeast eats the sugars present in the dough, carbon dioxide is released, which causes the dough to expand. It begins as soon as the ingredients are mixed together and continues until the dough reaches an internal temperature of 138°F/59°C during baking. Fermentation alters the flavor and appearance of the final product.

FOAMING: The process of beating eggs (whole eggs, yolks, or whites) to incorporate air until they form a light, fluffy substance with many small air bubbles.

FOLDING: (1) Incorporating a lighter mixture into a heavier one. (2) The process of bending a dough over itself during the bulk fermentation stage to redistribute the available food supply for the yeast, equalize the temperature of the dough, expel gases, and further develop the gluten in the dough.

FONDANT: Sugar, cooked with corn syrup, that is induced to crystallize by constant agitation, in order to produce the finest possible crystalline structure. Fondant is used as centers in chocolate production, and as a glaze in pastries.

FOOD-BORNE ILLNESS: An illness in humans caused by the consumption of an adulterated food product. In order for a food-borne illness to be considered official, it must involve two or more people who have eaten the same food, and it must be confirmed by health officials.

FORMULA: A recipe in which measurements for each ingredient are given as percentages of the weight for the main ingredient.

FRUCTOSE: A monosaccharide that occurs naturally in fruits and honey. Also known as fruit sugar or levulose.

GANACHE: An emulsion of chocolate and cream. Ganache may also be made with butter or other liquids in place of the cream.

GÂTEAU: French for "cake."

GEL: (Noun) A colloidal dispersion of solids that trap water. (Verb) To set to a firm or semifirm state by a colloidal dispersion of solids that trap water.

GELATIN: A protein derived from the skins and tendons of animals. Gelatin is used as a binder and stabilizer. It is available in granulated and sheet forms.

GELATINIZATION: The process in which heated starch granules that are suspended in liquid begin to absorb liquid and swell in size.

GERM: The embryo of a cereal grain that is usually separated from the endosperm during milling because it contains oils that accelerate the spoilage of flours and meals.

GLIADIN: A protein found in wheat flour. The part of gluten that gives it extensibility and viscosity.

GLUCOSE: (1) A monosaccharide that occurs naturally in fruits, some vegetables, and honey. Also known as dextrose. (2) A food additive used in confections.

GLUTEN: The protein component in wheat flour that builds structure and strength in baked goods. It is developed when the proteins glutenin and gliadin are moistened and agitated (kneaded). It provides the characteristic elasticity and extensibility of dough.

GLUTENIN: A protein found in wheat flour. The part of gluten that gives it strength and elasticity.

GRAIN: (Verb) To crystallize. Fondant is agitated until it grains. (Noun) A seed or fruit of a cereal grass.

GUM ARABIC: A water-soluble vegetable substance obtained from the stems and branches of various species of acacia trees. It is used to thicken, emulsify, and stabilize foods such as candy and ice cream.

GUM PASTE: A white modeling substance made from gum tragacanth or gelatin, water, glucose, and sugar.

GUM TRAGACANTH: A substance obtained from the Asian shrub *Astragalus gummifier* that is used to thicken, emulsify, and stabilize foods.

HOMOGENIZE: To mix ingredients together so their particles are reduced to a uniform size and are distributed evenly throughout the mixture.

HUMECTANT: A type of food additive used to promote moisture retention.

HYDRATE: To combine ingredients with water.

HYDRATION PERCENTAGE: The amount of liquid absorbed in a formula.

HYDROGENATION: The process in which hydrogen atoms are added to an unsaturated fat molecule, making it partially or completely saturated at room temperature. Vegetable oils are hydrogenated to create shortening.

HYDROLYZE: To chemically split one compound into other compounds by taking up the elements of water. Cornstarch is hydrolyzed to produce corn syrup.

HYGROSCOPIC: Absorbing moisture from the air. Sugar and salt are both hygroscopic ingredients.

INFECTION: Contamination by disease-causing agents, such as bacteria, consumed via foods.

INFUSE: To flavor by allowing an aromatic to steep in the substance to be flavored. Infusions may be made either hot or cold.

INTOXICATION: Poisoning. A state of being tainted with toxins, particularly those produced by microorganisms that have infected food.

INVERT SUGAR: Sucrose that has been broken down (inverted) into a mix of dextrose (glucose) and levulose (fructose). It is sweeter and more soluble than sucrose, and does not crystallize as easily.

ITALIAN MERINGUE: A mixture of whipped egg whites and hot sugar syrup (140°F/60°C), whipped further until shiny, fluffy, and cool.

KUCHEN: German for "cake" or "pastry."

LACTIC ACID: An acid produced when lactose is fermented. It occurs naturally when milk is soured.

LACTOSE: The simple sugar found in milk.

LAMINATION: The technique of creating alternating layers of fat and dough through a process of repeated rolling and folding.

LEAN DOUGH: A yeast dough that does not contain fats or sugar.

LEAVENING: Raising or lightening by air, steam, or gas (carbon dioxide). In baking, leavening occurs with yeast (organic), baking powder or baking soda (chemical), and steam (physical/mechanical).

LECITHIN: A naturally occurring emulsifier found in egg yolks and legumes.

LEVULOSE: A simple sugar found in honey and fruits. It is also known as fructose or fruit sugar.

LIQUEFIER: An ingredient that helps to loosen a dough or batter and make it more fluid. Sugar, fats, and water or milk are examples of liquefiers in baking.

MAILLARD REACTION: A complex browning reaction that results in the particular flavor and color of foods that do not contain much sugar, such as bread. The reaction, which involves carbohydrates and amino acids, is named after the French scientist who first discovered it.

MARZIPAN: A pliable dough of almonds and sugar. Marzipan may also be flavored by the addition of nuts other than almonds.

MASKING: Covering a cake with icing, frosting, or glaze.

MERINGUE: A white, frothy mass of beaten egg whites and sugar. Versions are common (or French) meringue, Italian meringue, and Swiss meringue.

MIGNARDISES: An assortment of small, two-bite-size pastries.

MILK CHOCOLATE: Sweet chocolate to which whole or skim milk powder has been added. It must contain at least 10 percent chocolate liquor by weight, although premium brands contain more.

MILLE-FEUILLE: French for "thousand leaves." This pastry, made from puff pastry dough, is known in America as a napoleon.

MISE EN PLACE: French for "put in place." The preparation and assembly of ingredients, pans, utensils, and plates or serving pieces needed for a particular dish or service period.

MIXING: The combination of ingredients.

MONOSACCHARIDE: A single or simple sugar and the basic building block of sugars and starches. Fructose, glucose, levulose, and dextrose are examples of monosaccharides.

NAPPÉ: The consistency of a liquid that will coat or cover the back of a spoon.

ORGANIC LEAVENER: Yeast. A living organism operates by fermenting sugar to produce carbon dioxide gas, causing the batter or dough to rise.

OVEN SPRING: The rapid initial rise of yeast doughs when placed in a hot oven. Heat accelerates the growth of the yeast, which produces more carbon dioxide gas, and also causes this gas to expand. This continues until the dough reaches a temperature of 140°F/60°C.

OVERRUN: The increase in volume of ice cream caused by the incorporation of air during the freezing process.

PAIN: French for "bread."

PAR-BAKE: To start and then interrupt the baking process to finish it at a later time.

PASTILLAGE: See Gum Paste.

PÂTE À GLACIER, BLOND: Coating chocolate that is light in color.

PATHOGEN: A disease-causing microorganism.

PATISSIER: French for "pastry chef."

PECTIN: A gelling agent or thickener found in fruits, particularly in apples, quince, and the skins of citrus fruits.

PETIT FOUR: A small bite-size cake, pastry, cookie, or confection. The term is French for "small oven."

PH SCALE: A scale with values from 0 to 14 representing degrees of acidity. A measurement of 7 is neutral, 0 is most acidic, and 14 is most alkaline. Chemically, pH measures the concentration and activity of the element hydrogen.

PHYSICAL LEAVENING: A process that occurs when air and/or moisture that is trapped during the mixing process expands as it is heated. This can occur through foaming, creaming, or lamination. Also known as mechanical leavening.

POLYSACCHARIDE: A complex carbohydrate such as a starch that consists of long chains of saccharides, amylose, and amylopectin.

POOLISH: A semiliquid starter dough with equal parts (by weight) of flour and water blended with yeast and allowed to ferment for 3 to 15 hours.

PRE-FERMENT: A piece of dough saved from the previous day's production to be used in the following day's dough.

PRESHAPING: The gentle first shaping of dough. Also known as rounding.

PROOF: To allow yeast dough to rise.

PROTEASES: Enzymes that break down the collagen in gelatin and do not allow it to set or gel. This destructive enzyme is found in kiwi, pineapple, papaya, and other fruits.

RATIOS: A general formula of ingredients that can be varied.

RECIPE: A specific formula of ingredients and amounts.

RETROGRADATION: The process in which starches high in amylose revert back to their insoluble form after they are gelatinized and then undergo freezing, refrigeration, or aging. This reaction causes changes in texture and appearance.

SACCHARIDE: A sugar molecule.

SANITATION: The preparation and distribution of food in a clean environment by healthy food workers.

SANITIZE: To kill pathogenic organisms chemically or by moist heat.

SCALE: (1) To measure ingredients by weight. (2) To multiply or divide the quantities in a formula to change the yield. (3) To portion batter or dough according to weight or size.

SCORE: To make incisions into dough that allow steam to escape and the crust to expand. Also known as slashing or docking.

SECONDARY FERMENTATION: See Bench Rest.

SEED: (1) In chocolate tempering, a portion of tempered chocolate added to melted chocolate to begin the formation of beta crystals. (2) Anything that acts as a surface to which sugar will adhere and crystallize.

SEED METHOD: A method of tempering chocolate. Chopped tempered chocolate (seeds) are added to the melted chocolate and agitated until the desired temperature is reached.

SEMISWEET CHOCOLATE: Chocolate that contains between 15 and 35 percent chocolate liquor. In addition to chocolate liquor, it contains added cocoa butter, sugar, vanilla or vanillin, and often lecithin.

SHORTENING AGENTS: Fats and oils. This term is derived from fat's ability to split the long, elastic gluten strands that can toughen dough and batters. This tenderizing effect renders the strands more susceptible to breaking or "shortening," resulting in a more tender and less dense crumb.

STABILIZER: An ingredient that helps to develop the solid structure or "framework" of a finished product. Flour and eggs act as stabilizers in baking.

STARTER: A mixture of flour, liquid, and commercial or wild yeast that is allowed to ferment. The starter must be "fed" with flour and water to keep it alive and active.

STEEP: To allow to infuse.

SUCROSE: Table sugar. A disaccharide extracted from sugarcane or sugar beets; consists of glucose and fructose joined together in the molecule.

SUGAR BLOOM: The result of damp storage conditions for milk or dark chocolate. When the moisture evaporates, a white crust of sugar crystals is left behind. Like fat bloom, it is visually and texturally unappealing, but the chocolate is still safe to eat.

SWISS MERINGUE: A mixture of egg whites and sugar heated over simmering water until it reaches 140°F/60°C; it is then whipped until it reaches the desired peak and is cool.

TABLING METHOD: A method of tempering chocolate. A percentage of the chocolate is poured onto a marble slab and agitated until it begins to set. It is then added back to the remaining melted chocolate and stirred until it reaches the proper working temperature.

TART: A shallow, usually open-faced pastry shell with filling.

TARTLET: A small, single-serving tart.

TEMPER: (1) To melt, agitate, and cool chocolate to ensure that it retains its smooth gloss, crisp "snap" feel, and creamy texture. (2) To heat gently and gradually, as in the process of incorporating hot liquid into a liaison to gradually raise its temperature.

TEXTURE: The interior grain or structure of a baked product as shown by a cut surface; the feeling of a substance under the fingers.

TORTE: German for "cake." It can be multilayered or a single, dense layer.

TOXIN: A naturally occurring poison, particularly those produced by the metabolic activity of living organisms such as bacteria.

TRUFFLE: A ganache center that is usually coated with chocolate. Truffles are round and are named after the fungus that they resemble.

UNSWEETENED CHOCOLATE: Chocolate liquor without added sugar or flavorings.

VIRUS: A type of pathogenic microorganism that can be transmitted in food. Viruses cause such illnesses as measles, chicken pox, infectious hepatitis, and colds.

VISCOSITY: The quantity that describes a fluid's resistance to flow.

WHIP: To beat an item, such as cream or egg whites, to incorporate air.

WHITE CHOCOLATE: True white chocolate, such as that found in Europe, is made from cocoa butter, milk, sugar, and flavorings, and it contains no chocolate liquor. In the United States, white confectionery coating, made with vegetable fat instead of cocoa butter, is more readily available.

Index